DAILY
YOUTH BIBLE

Scripture
union

Authentic

DAILY YOUTH BIBLE
Copyright © 2004 Authentic Media
The Holy Bible, New Century Version
Copyright © 1987, 1988, 1991 by Thomas Nelson, Inc.
This anglicised edition copyright © 1993 by Authentic Media.

09 08 07 06 05 04   7 6 5 4 3 2 1

Devotional materials commissioned and compiled by Scripture Union. All rights reserved. The majority of the notes contained in this New Testament have been adapted from Scripture Union's *One Up* Bible reading guides. The notes were written by the following people: Jenny Baker, Tony Bower, Steve Bullock, Elaine Carr, Andrew Cupples, Judith Forster, Dave Gatward, Ems Hancock, Rosanne Hawke, Darren Hill, Steve Holloway, Gill Hutchinson, Howard Ingham, Christina Lacey, Mike Law, David Lawrence, Peter Lee, Sylvia Lester, Ben Mizen, Lucy Moore, Philip Mounstephen, Hugh Morrison, Claire Pedrick, Andy Saunders, Smeeee, John Stephenson, Mark Tomlinson, Meg Thomson, Steve Tilley, Phil Wason and Julia Wilthew.

One Up is edited by 'Tricia Williams.

The right of Scripture Union to be identified as the author of the devotional material in this publication has been asserted by them under the Copyright, Designs and Patents act 1988. © 2004 Scripture Union.

Blue Hardback   ISBN: 1-86024-433-5 Blue Paperback   ISBN: 1-86024-454-8

Purple/Yellow Hardback ISBN: 1-86024-434-3 Purple/Yellow Paperback ISBN: 1-86024-456-4

Published by Authentic Media,
9 Holdom Avenue, Bletchley, Milton Keynes, Bucks, MK1 1QR, UK.
Cover design by David Lund Design & Advertising.

Text design and book production by Bookprint Creative Services,
P.O. Box 827, BN21 3YJ, England.
Printed in Great Britain.

Introduction

This New Testament is here to help you meet with God, to engage with his Word, and to help you become more like him. It is a guide to change your life.

An encounter with someone has an impact on us: it could be big or small. Meeting with God, however, can provide the biggest impact in anyone's life.

In the past when God met with people big things happened, and these things are recorded in the Bible. God is still in the business of meeting people, and through the work of Jesus and by the power of the Holy Spirit we can meet with God.

God will change our lives; our changed lives will affect our close friends and people we meet; and then as a bigger community (churches etc.) we can affect the lives of those in the world, making it a better place to be.

How to use the notes

There are enough notes in this New Testament for you to read one six days a week for a year. If you can do this, then great. However, if you find that you can't manage a reading that often don't worry. The important thing is to hear God's Word in your life and respond appropriately.

To enable this, you may find the following points helpful.

- **Pray**
  Start by asking God to help you understand and learn what you read.

- **Read**

  Read the verses of the Bible that are given for the day's reading.

- **Think**

  Think about what you have read in the Bible and then look at the comments made in the file. What have you read about God, Jesus or the Holy Spirit? Is there a promise from God which you can now believe? What do you need to avoid? Is there something you now need to do? What have you learnt? You may find it helpful to record your thoughts in a notepad or journal.

- **Act**

  Ask God to help you act on what you have learnt.

In short, each time you read, ask yourself:
- What is God saying to me?
- What must I do about it?

Publisher's note

As you read the Bible passages you will, at times, come across verse numbers with no verse to go with them. This is because these verses are present in some early Greek manuscripts but not others, and the New Century Version of the Bible has chosen to omit them.

Some well-known Bible stories and verses from the New Testament

Jesus' birth	Matthew 1:18–25
	Luke 2:1–7
The wise men	Matthew 2:1–12
The shepherds	Luke 2:8–20
The devil tempts Jesus	Matthew 4:1–11
	Mark 1:12,13
	Luke 4:1–13
Jesus walks on the water	Matthew 14:22–36
	Mark 6:45–52
	John 6:16–21
The good Samaritan	Luke 10:25–37
The son who was lost	Luke 15:11–32
The feeding of 5,000	Matthew 14:13–21
	Mark 6:30–44
	Luke 9:10–17
	John 6:1–15
The raising of Lazarus	John 11:1–44
The first Palm Sunday	Matthew 21:1–11
	Luke 19:28–44
	John 12:12–16
The last supper	Matthew 26:17–30
	Mark 14:12–26
	Luke 22:7–30
	John 13:1–30

The crucifixion	Matthew 27:32–56
	Mark 15:21–41
	Luke 23:26–49
	John 19:16–37
God's love	John 3:16
The resurrection	Matthew 28:1–15
	Mark 16:1–18
	Luke 24:1–12
	John 20:1–18
The ascension	Mark 16:19,20
	Luke 24:50–53
	Acts 1:6–11
The Holy Spirit comes	Acts 2:1–13
Saul's conversion	Acts 9:1–19
God's plan	Romans 8:28
The fruit of the Spirit	Galatians 5:22,23
Jesus' humility	Philippians 2:5–11
Be a young example	1 Timothy 4:12

DAILY
YOUTH BIBLE

A family affair

How far back can you trace your family tree? It is quite easy to go one or two generations but what about further? Do you know of anyone famous, or infamous in your genealogy?

 Matthew 1:1–25

The Family History of Jesus

1 This is the family history of Jesus Christ. He came from the family of David, and David came from the family of Abraham.

²Abraham was the father of Isaac.
Isaac was the father of Jacob.
Jacob was the father of Judah and his brothers.

³Judah was the father of Perez and Zerah.
(Their mother was Tamar.)
Perez was the father of Hezron.
Hezron was the father of Ram.

⁴Ram was the father of Amminadab.
Amminadab was the father of Nahshon.
Nahshon was the father of Salmon.

⁵Salmon was the father of Boaz.
(Boaz's mother was Rahab.)
Boaz was the father of Obed.
(Obed's mother was Ruth.)
Obed was the father of Jesse.

⁶Jesse was the father of King David.
David was the father of Solomon.
(Solomon's mother had been Uriah's wife.)

⁷Solomon was the father of Rehoboam.
Rehoboam was the father of Abijah.
Abijah was the father of Asa.

⁸Asa was the father of Jehoshaphat.
Jehoshaphat was the father of Jehoram.
Jehoram was the father of Uzziah.

⁹Uzziah was the father of Jotham.
Jotham was the father of Ahaz.
Ahaz was the father of Hezekiah.

¹⁰Hezekiah was the father of Manasseh.
Manasseh was the father of Amon.
Amon was the father of Josiah.

¹¹Josiah was the grandfather of Jehoiachin and his brothers.
(This was at the time that the people were taken to Babylon.)

¹²After they were taken to Babylon:
Jehoiachin was the father of Shealtiel.
Shealtiel was the grandfather of Zerubbabel.

¹³Zerubbabel was the father of Abiud.
Abiud was the father of Eliakim.
Eliakim was the father of Azor.

¹⁴Azor was the father of Zadok.
Zadok was the father of Akim.
Akim was the father of Eliud.

¹⁵Eliud was the father of Eleazar.
Eleazar was the father of Matthan.
Matthan was the father of Jacob.

¹⁶Jacob was the father of Joseph.
Joseph was the husband of Mary,
and Mary was the mother of Jesus.
Jesus is called the Christ.

¹⁷So there were fourteen generations from Abraham to David. And there were fourteen generations from David until the people were taken to Babylon. And there were fourteen generations from the time when the people were taken to Babylon until Christ was born.

The Birth of Jesus Christ

¹⁸This is how the birth of Jesus Christ came about. His mother Mary was engaged to marry Joseph, but before they married, she learned she was pregnant by the power of the Holy Spirit. ¹⁹Because Mary's husband, Joseph, was a good man, he did not want to disgrace her in public,

so he planned to divorce her secretly.

20While Joseph thought about these things, an angel of the Lord came to him in a dream. The angel said, "Joseph, descendant of David, don't be afraid to take Mary as your wife, because the baby in her is from the Holy Spirit. 21She will give birth to a son, and you will name him Jesus, because he will save his people from their sins."

22All this happened to bring about what the Lord had said through the prophet: 23"The virgin will be pregnant. She will have a son, and they will name him Immanuel," which means "God is with us".

24When Joseph woke up, he did what the Lord's angel had told him to do. Joseph took Mary as his wife, 25but he did not have sexual relations with her until she gave birth to the son. And Joseph named him Jesus.

This is Jesus' family tree (probably with some generations missing). Matthew was showing Jewish readers that Jesus was the Messiah, God's chosen Servant King. It was important for Matthew and the readers of his gospel that Jesus' family line showed that he was descended from David and Abraham.

Recognise some names here? Jesus' ancestors included a prostitute, an adulterer and at least one murderer! Yet God used them to do amazing things.

Think

Do you sometimes think you're not good enough for God to use?

Pray

Lord, use me to touch the lives of others.

Extra

Spend some time looking through the Old Testament and reading the stories of the people who were Jesus' ancestors. Why not start with Rahab in Joshua 2.

Bouncy castles?

Going on a long journey to somewhere you haven't been before can be very exciting, especially if it is for a well-earned holiday. Today we can travel hundreds, even thousands, of miles by jumping on a plane. However, it wasn't always that easy.

 Matthew 2:1–23

Wise Men Come to Visit Jesus

2 Jesus was born in the town of Bethlehem in Judea during the time when Herod was king. When Jesus was born, some wise men from the east came to Jerusalem. ²They asked, "Where is the baby who was born to be the king of the Jews? We saw his star in the east and have come to worship him."

³When King Herod heard this, he was troubled, as well as all the people in Jerusalem. ⁴Herod called a meeting of all the leading priests and teachers of the law and asked them where the Christ would be born. ⁵They answered, "In the town of Bethlehem in Judea. The prophet wrote about this in the Scriptures:

⁶'But you, Bethlehem, in the land of Judah,
   are important among the tribes of Judah.
 A ruler will come from you
  who will be like a shepherd for my people Israel.'"   *Micah 5:2*

⁷Then Herod had a secret meeting with the wise men and learned from them the exact time they first saw the star. ⁸He sent the wise men to Bethlehem, saying, "Look carefully for the child. When you find him, come and tell me so I can worship him too."

⁹After the wise men heard the king, they left. The star that they had seen in the east went before them until it stopped above the place where the child was. ¹⁰When the wise men saw the star, they were filled with joy. ¹¹They came to the house where the child was and saw him with his mother, Mary, and they bowed down and worshipped him. They opened their gifts and gave him treasures of gold, frankincense and myrrh. ¹²But God warned the wise men in a dream not to go back to Herod, so they returned to their own country by a different way.

Jesus' Parents Take Him to Egypt

¹³After they left, an angel of the Lord came to Joseph in a dream and said, "Get up! Take the child and his mother and escape to Egypt, because Herod is starting to look for the child so he can kill him. Stay in Egypt until I tell you to return."

¹⁴So Joseph got up and left for Egypt during the night with the child and his mother. ¹⁵And Joseph stayed in Egypt until Herod died. This happened to bring about what the Lord had said through the prophet: "I called my son out of Egypt."

Herod Kills the Baby Boys

¹⁶When Herod saw that the wise men had tricked him, he was furious. So he gave an order to kill all the baby boys in Bethlehem and in the surrounding area who were two years old or younger. This was in keeping with the time he learnt from the wise men. ¹⁷So what God had said through the prophet Jeremiah came true:

18"A voice was heard in Ramah
of painful crying and deep sadness:
Rachel crying for her children.
She refused to be comforted,
because her children are dead."

Jeremiah 31:15

Joseph and Mary Return

19After Herod died, an angel of the Lord spoke to Joseph in a dream while he was in Egypt. 20The angel said, "Get up! Take the child and his mother and go to the land of Israel, because the people who were trying to kill the child are now dead."

21So Joseph took the child and his mother and went to Israel. 22But he heard that Archelaus was now king in Judea since his father Herod had died. So Joseph was afraid to go there. After being warned in a dream, he went to the area of Galilee, 23to a town called Nazareth, and lived there. And so what God had said through the prophets came true: "He will be called a Nazarene."

How do you think you would have felt after riding hundreds of kilometres on a bouncy castle (sorry, camel!)? These guys – perhaps from the region we now know as Iraq – were excited. They knew something important was happening and they wanted to be in on it. What had they seen (v 2)?

King Herod *wasn't* pleased. Why?

Think

When you think about God do you feel ...

- excited?
- afraid?
- something else?

What is it that makes you feel like that?

Pray

Lord I feel . . . . when I think about following you. Show me one way that I can be a better follower today.

Ready when you are

How do you get ready for these?

- Cooking a meal
- Taking an exam
- Going to a party

To get the best out of any event, preparation is one key to success.

 Matthew 3:1–4:11

The Work of John the Baptist

3 About that time John the Baptist began preaching in the desert area of Judea. ²John said, "Change your hearts and lives because the kingdom of heaven is near." ³John the Baptist is the one Isaiah the prophet was talking about when he said:

"This is a voice of one
who calls out in the desert:
'Prepare the way for the Lord.
Make the road straight for him.'"

Isaiah 40:3

⁴John's clothes were made from camel's hair, and he wore a leather belt around his waist. For food, he ate locusts and wild honey. ⁵Many people came from Jerusalem and Judea and all the area around the Jordan River to hear John. ⁶They confessed their sins, and he baptised them in the Jordan River.

⁷Many of the Pharisees and Sadducees came to the place where John was baptising people. When John saw them, he said, "You are all snakes! Who warned you to run away from God's coming punishment? ⁸Do the things that show you really have changed your hearts and lives. ⁹And don't think you can say to yourselves, 'Abraham is our father.' I tell you that God could make children for Abraham from these

rocks. ¹⁰The axe is now ready to cut down the trees, and every tree that does not produce good fruit will be cut down and thrown into the fire.

¹¹"I baptise you with water to show that your hearts and lives have changed. But there is one coming after me who is greater than I am, whose sandals I am not good enough to carry. He will baptise you with the Holy Spirit and fire. ¹²He will come ready to clean the grain, separating the good grain from the chaff. He will put the good part of the grain into his barn, but he will burn the chaff with a fire that cannot be put out."

Jesus is Baptised by John

¹³At that time Jesus came from Galilee to the Jordan River and wanted John to baptise him. ¹⁴But John tried to stop him, saying, "Why do you come to me to be baptised? I need to be baptised by you!"

¹⁵Jesus answered, "Let it be this way for now. We should do all things that are God's will." So John agreed to baptise Jesus.

¹⁶As soon as Jesus was baptised, he came up out of the water. Then heaven opened, and he saw God's Spirit coming down on him like a dove. ¹⁷And a voice from heaven said, "This is my Son, whom I love, and I am very pleased with him."

The Temptation of Jesus

4 Then the Spirit led Jesus into the desert to be tempted by the devil. [2]Jesus ate nothing for 40 days and nights. After this, he was very hungry. [3]The devil came to Jesus to tempt him, saying, "If you are the Son of God, tell these rocks to become bread."

[4]Jesus answered, "It is written in the Scriptures, 'A person does not live by eating only bread, but by everything God says.'"

[5]Then the devil led Jesus to the holy city of Jerusalem and put him on a high place of the Temple. [6]The devil said, "If you are the Son of God, jump down, because it is written in the Scriptures:

'He has put his angels in charge of you.
They will catch you in their hands
so that you will not hit your foot on a rock.'"
                                        Psalm 91:11–12

[7]Jesus answered him, "It also says in the Scriptures, 'Do not test the Lord your God.'"

[8]Then the devil led Jesus to the top of a very high mountain and showed him all the kingdoms of the world and all their splendour. [9]The devil said, "If you will bow down and worship me, I will give you all these things."

[10]Jesus said to the devil, "Go away from me, Satan! It is written in the Scriptures, 'You must worship the Lord your God and serve only him.'"

[11]So the devil left Jesus, and angels came and took care of him.

John knew that people needed to get ready for Jesus (3:3). He didn't ask them to prepare by putting on their best clothes or doing the housework. John urged them to change their hearts and lives.

Think

If you knew you were going to meet Jesus today, what one thing would you want to change about yourself? Why?

Pray

Ask God to help you change that one thing.

Follow the leader

What would make you leave everything for a complete stranger?

- Their fashion sense
- Their money
- Their looks

It still happens today. People meet someone who completely changes their lives. Sometimes falling in love can cause it, whilst at other times it is down to realising that the other person is offering something unique that they would like to have.

 Matthew 4:12–5:12

Jesus Begins Work in Galilee

¹²When Jesus heard that John had been put in prison, he went back to Galilee. ¹³He left Nazareth and went to live in Capernaum, a town near Lake Galilee, in the area near Zebulun and Naphtali. ¹⁴Jesus did this to bring about what the prophet Isaiah had said:

¹⁵"Land of Zebulun and land of Naphtali
along the sea,
beyond the Jordan River.
This is Galilee where the non-Jewish
people live.
¹⁶These people who live in darkness
will see a great light.
They live in a place covered with the
shadows of death,
but a light will shine on them."

Isaiah 9:1–2

Jesus Chooses Some Followers

¹⁷From that time Jesus began to preach, saying, "Change your hearts and lives, because the kingdom of heaven is near."

¹⁸As Jesus was walking by Lake Galilee, he saw two brothers, Simon (called Peter) and his brother Andrew. They were throw-ing a net into the lake because they were fishermen. ¹⁹Jesus said, "Come follow me, and I will make you fish for people." ²⁰So Simon and Andrew immediately left their nets and followed him.

²¹As Jesus continued walking by Lake Galilee, he saw two other brothers, James and John, the sons of Zebedee. They were in a boat with their father Zebedee, mending their nets. Jesus told them to come with him. ²²Immediately they left the boat and their father, and they followed Jesus.

Jesus Teaches and Heals People

²³Jesus went everywhere in Galilee, teaching in the synagogues, preaching the Good News about the kingdom of heaven, and healing all the people's diseases and sicknesses. ²⁴The news about Jesus spread all over Syria, and people brought all the sick to him. They were suffering from different kinds of diseases. Some were in great pain, some had demons, some were epileptics and some were paralysed. Jesus healed all of them. ²⁵Many people from Galilee, the Ten Towns, Jerusalem, Judea and the land across the Jordan River followed him.

Jesus Teaches the People

5 When Jesus saw the crowds, he went up on a hill and sat down. His followers came to him, ²and he began to teach them, saying:

³"Those people who know they have
  great spiritual needs are happy,
  because the kingdom of heaven belongs
  to them.

⁴Those who are sad now are happy,
  because God will comfort them.

⁵Those who are humble are happy,
  because the earth will belong to them.

⁶Those who want to do right more than
  anything else are happy,
  because God will fully satisfy them.

⁷Those who show mercy to others are
  happy,
  because God will show mercy to them.

⁸Those who are pure in their thinking are
  happy,
  because they will be with God.

⁹Those who work to bring peace are
  happy,
  because God will call them his
  children.

¹⁰Those who are treated badly for doing
  good are happy,
  because the kingdom of heaven belongs
  to them.

¹¹"People will insult you and hurt you. They will lie and say all kinds of evil things about you because you follow me. But when they do, you will be happy. ¹²Rejoice and be glad, because you have a great reward waiting for you in heaven. People did the same evil things to the prophets who lived before you.

How many people left everything to follow Jesus (v 18–22)?

What was their work (v 18,21)?

Did they take ages to make up their minds (v 20,22)?

Think

If you had been one of those people on the beach who Jesus called, what would you have done?

Pray

Ask God for the strength to put him before everything else this year.

Extra

You might find it helpful to list the things that stop you from putting Jesus first in your life. Once you have the list look through it and make a conscious effort to put Jesus ahead of those things.

Nothing but the truth

Are you more likely to do something if you've just *said* you will or if you've *promised* you'll do it?

 Matthew 5:13–37

You are like Salt and Light

13"You are the salt of the earth. But if the salt loses its salty taste, it cannot be made salty again. It is good for nothing, except to be thrown out and walked on.

14"You are the light that gives light to the world. A city that is built on a hill cannot be hidden. 15And people don't hide a light under a bowl. They put it on a lampstand so the light shines for all the people in the house. 16In the same way, you should be a light for other people. Live so that they will see the good things you do and will praise your Father in heaven.

The Importance of the Law

17"Don't think that I have come to destroy the law of Moses or the teaching of the prophets. I have not come to destroy them but to bring about what they said. 18I tell you the truth, nothing will disappear from the law until heaven and earth are gone. Not even the smallest letter or the smallest part of a letter will be lost until everything has happened. 19Whoever refuses to obey any command and teaches other people not to obey that command will be the least important in the kingdom of heaven. But whoever obeys the commands and teaches other people to obey them will be great in the kingdom of heaven. 20I tell you that if you are no more obedient than the teachers of the law and the Pharisees, you will never enter the kingdom of heaven.

Jesus Teaches About Anger

21"You have heard that it was said to our people long ago, 'You must not

murder anyone. Anyone who murders another will be judged.' 22But I tell you, if you are angry with a brother or sister, you will be judged. If you say bad things to a brother or sister, you will be judged by the council. And if you call someone a fool, you will be in danger of the fire of hell.

23"So when you offer your gift to God at the altar, and you remember that your brother or sister has something against you, 24leave your gift there at the altar. Go and make peace with that person, and then come and offer your gift.

25"If your enemy is taking you to court, become friends quickly, before you go to court. Otherwise, your enemy might turn you over to the judge, and the judge might give you to a guard to put you in jail. 26I tell you the truth, you will not leave there until you have paid everything you owe.

Jesus Teaches About Sexual Sin

27"You have heard that it was said, 'You must not be guilty of adultery.' 28But I tell you that if anyone looks at a woman and wants to sin sexually with her, in his mind he has already done that sin with the woman. 29If your right eye causes you to sin, take it out and throw it away. It is better to lose one part of your body than to have your whole body thrown into hell. 30If your right hand causes you to sin, cut it off and throw it away. It is better to lose one part of your body than for your whole body to go into hell.

Jesus Teaches About Divorce

31"It was also said, 'Anyone who divorces his wife must give her a written divorce paper.' 32But I tell you that anyone who divorces his wife forces her to be guilty of adultery. The only reason for a man to divorce his wife is if she has sexual relations with another man. And anyone who marries that divorced woman is guilty of adultery.

Make Promises Carefully

33"You have heard that it was said to our people long ago, 'Don't break your promises, but keep the promises you make to the Lord.' 34But I tell you, never swear an oath. Don't swear an oath using the name of heaven, because heaven is God's throne. 35Don't swear an oath using the name of the earth, because the earth belongs to God. Don't swear an oath using the name of Jerusalem, because that is the city of the great King. 36Don't even swear by your own head, because you cannot make one hair on your head become white or black. 37Say only yes if you mean yes, and no if you mean no. If you say more than yes or no, it is from the Evil One.

What difference would it make if we simply told the truth? Which of these might happen?

☐ Get into trouble

☐ Make people trust you

☐ Allow other people to be honest too

☐ Build up society

☐ Be embarrassing

☐ You'd be respected

Think

Can you tell nothing-but-the-truth today?

Pray

Lord, let my "yes" mean "yes" and my "no" mean "no".

Out to impress?

When you do something good what is your motivation? Are you trying to impress someone?

 Matthew 5:38–6:15

Don't Fight Back

38"You have heard that it was said, 'An eye for an eye, and a tooth for a tooth.' 39But I tell you, don't stand up against an evil person. If someone slaps you on the right cheek, turn to him the other cheek as well. 40If someone wants to sue you in court and take your shirt, let him have your coat as well. 41If someone forces you to go with him a kilometre, go with him 2 kilometres. 42If a person asks you for something, give it to him. Don't refuse to give to someone who wants to borrow from you.

Love All People

43"You have heard that it was said, 'Love your neighbour and hate your enemies.' 44But I say to you, love your enemies. Pray for those who hurt you. 45If you do this, you will be true children of your Father in heaven. He causes the sun to rise on good people and on evil people, and he sends rain to those who do right and to those who do wrong. 46If you love only the people who love you, you will get no reward. Even the tax collectors do that. 47And if you are nice only to your friends, you are no better than other people. Even those who don't know God are nice to their friends. 48So you must be perfect, just as your Father in heaven is perfect.

Jesus Teaches About Giving

6 "Be careful! When you do good things, don't do them in front of people to be seen by them. If you do that, you will have no reward from your Father in heaven.

2"When you give to the poor, don't be like the hypocrites. They blow trumpets in the synagogues and on the streets so that people will see them and honour them. I tell you the truth, those hypocrites already have their full reward. 3So when you give to the poor, don't let anyone know what you are doing. 4Your giving should be done in secret. Your Father can see what is done in secret, and he will reward you.

Jesus Teaches About Prayer

5"When you pray, don't be like the hypocrites. They love to stand in the synagogues and on the street corners and pray so people will see them. I tell you the truth, they already have their full reward. 6When you pray, you should go into your room and close the door and pray to your Father who cannot be seen. Your Father can see what is done in secret, and he will reward you.

7"And when you pray, don't be like those people who don't know God. They continue saying things that mean nothing, thinking that God will hear them because of their many words. 8Don't be like them, because your Father knows the things you need before you ask him. 9So when you pray, you should pray like this:

'Our Father in heaven,
may your name always be kept holy.
10May your kingdom come
and what you want be done,
here on earth as it is in heaven.
11Give us the food we need for each day.

12Forgive us for our sins,
    just as we have forgiven those who
        sinned against us.
13And do not cause us to be tempted,
    but save us from the Evil One.'

14Yes, if you forgive others for their sins, your Father in heaven will also forgive you for your sins. 15But if you don't forgive others, your Father in heaven will not forgive your sins.

Some of the religious leaders in Jesus' day wanted everyone to know how good they were. They made sure everyone knew all about their "good" deeds.

What is Jesus warning against (6:1)? Why?

What should your attitude be (6:3,4)?

Who sees when you do the right thing (6:4)?

Think

Have you ever felt fed up because no one has noticed you've done something good?

Are you ever guilty of trying to appear super-spiritual just to impress people (e.g. at church)? It's a good feeling when other people praise us, but who does Jesus say we should be out to impress (6:3,4)?

Pray

Lord, help me to do what you want, whether or not other people notice. Help me to want, more than anything else, to please you.

Don't worry, be happy

Going to college, managing your finances, buying a house, saving for a pension … Aargh! Hey, maybe it's better being a teenager. You don't have to worry about these things … yet!

Matthew 6:16–7:6

Jesus Teaches About Worship

16"When you give up eating, don't put on a sad face like the hypocrites. They make their faces look sad to show people they are giving up eating. I tell you the truth, those hypocrites already have their full reward. 17So when you give up eating, comb your hair and wash your face. 18Then people will not know that you are giving up eating, but your Father, whom you cannot see, will see you. Your Father sees what is done in secret, and he will reward you.

God is More Important than Money

19"Don't store treasures for yourselves here on earth where moths and rust will destroy them and thieves can break in and steal them. 20But store your treasures in heaven where they cannot be destroyed by moths or rust and where thieves cannot break in and steal them. 21Your heart will be where your treasure is.

22"The eye is a light for the body. If your eyes are good, your whole body will be full of light. 23But if your eyes are evil, your whole body will be full of darkness. And if the only light you have is really darkness, then you have the worst darkness.

24"No one can serve two masters. The person will hate one master and love the other, or will follow one master and refuse to follow the other. You cannot serve both God and worldly riches.

Don't Worry

25"So I tell you, don't worry about the food or drink you need to live, or about the clothes you need for your body. Life is more than food, and the body is more than clothes. 26Look at the birds in the air. They don't plant or harvest or store food in barns, but your heavenly Father feeds them. And you know that you are worth much more than the birds. 27You cannot add any time to your life by worrying about it.

28"And why do you worry about clothes? Look at how the lilies in the field grow. They don't work or make clothes for themselves. 29But I tell you that even Solomon with his riches was not dressed as beautifully as one of these flowers. 30God clothes the grass in the field, which is alive today but tomorrow is thrown into the fire. So you can be even more sure that God will clothe you. Don't have so little faith! 31Don't worry and say, 'What will we eat?' or 'What will we drink?' or 'What will we wear?' 32The people who don't know God keep trying to get these things, and your Father in heaven knows you need them. 33The thing you should want most is God's kingdom and doing what God wants. Then all these other things you need will be given to you. 34So don't worry about tomorrow, because tomorrow will have its own worries. Each day has enough trouble of its own.

Be Careful About Judging Others

7 "Don't judge other people, or you will be judged. ²You will be judged in the same way that you judge others, and the amount you give to others will be given to you.

³"Why do you notice the little piece of dust in your friend's eye, but you don't notice the big piece of wood in your own eye? ⁴How can you say to your friend, 'Let me take that little piece of dust out of your eye'? Look at yourself! You still have that big piece of wood in your own eye. ⁵You hypocrite! First, take the wood out of your own eye. Then you will see clearly to take the dust out of your friend's eye.

⁶"Don't give holy things to dogs, and don't throw your pearls before pigs. Pigs will only trample on them, and dogs will turn to attack you.

Jesus said, don't worry about money (or possessions) *ever* (6:34)! God, your Heavenly Father, knows what you need (6:32). That doesn't mean being careless about what you have. But it does mean getting your priorities right.

What should be more important than anything (6:33)?

Think

What are some of the things that you worry about, both now and for the future? Write them down on a sheet of paper. Read 6:31–33 aloud and then tear up the paper.

Pray

Lord, I give to you all my worries about money. Thank you that you will provide for me. Help me to trust you.

Ask God

Imagine it's your birthday soon. Do you give hints or ask for what you want?

Matthew 7:7–8:4

Ask God for What You Need

7"Ask, and God will give to you. Search, and you will find. Knock, and the door will open for you. 8Yes, everyone who asks will receive. Everyone who searches will find. And everyone who knocks will have the door opened.

9"If your children ask for bread, which of you would give them a stone? 10Or if your children ask for a fish, would you give them a snake? 11Even though you are bad, you know how to give good gifts to your children. How much more will your heavenly Father give good things to those who ask him!

12"Do to others what you want them to do to you. This is the meaning of the law of Moses and the teaching of the prophets.

The Way to Heaven is Hard

13"Enter through the narrow gate. The gate is wide and the road is wide that leads to hell, and many people enter through that gate. 14But the gate is small and the road is narrow that leads to true life. Only a few people find that road.

People Know You by Your Actions

15"Be careful of false prophets. They come to you looking gentle like sheep, but they are really dangerous like wolves. 16You will know these people by what they do. Grapes don't come from thornbushes, and figs don't come from thorny weeds. 17In the same way, every good tree produces good fruit, but a bad tree produces bad fruit. 18A good tree cannot produce bad fruit, and a bad tree cannot produce good fruit. 19Every tree that does not produce good fruit is cut down and thrown into the fire. 20In the same way, you will know these false prophets by what they do.

21"Not all those who say that I am their Lord will enter the kingdom of heaven. The only people who will enter the kingdom of heaven are those who do what my Father in heaven wants. 22On the last day many people will say to me, 'Lord, Lord, we spoke for you, and through you we forced out demons and did many miracles.' 23Then I will tell them clearly, 'Get away from me, you who do evil. I never knew you.'

Two Kinds of People

24"Everyone who hears my words and obeys them is like a wise man who built his house on rock. 25It rained hard, the floods came and the winds blew and hit that house. But it did not fall, because it was built on rock. 26Everyone who hears my words and does not obey them is like a foolish man who built his house on sand. 27It rained hard, the floods came and the winds blew and hit that house, and it fell with a big crash."

28When Jesus finished saying these things, the people were amazed at his teaching, 29because he did not teach like their teachers of the law. He taught like a person who had authority.

Jesus Heals a Sick Man

8 When Jesus came down from the hill, great crowds followed him. 2Then a

man with a skin disease came to Jesus. The man bowed down before him and said, "Lord, you can heal me if you will."

³Jesus reached out his hand and touched the man and said, "I will. Be healed!" And immediately the man was healed of his disease. ⁴Then Jesus said to him, "Don't tell anyone about this. But go and show yourself to the priest and offer the gift Moses commanded for people who are made well. This will show the people what I have done."

If your parents or guardians give you good things, how much more is God going to give you things that are good for you (7:9–11)?

Do Jesus' words make it sound as though it will always be easy getting an answer from God (7:7,8)?

What kind of things should we ask God for (7:11)?

Think

When you spend time with God in prayer, what is the balance between asking for yourself and asking for others?

What are you asking God to give or do for other people (7:12)?

Pray

What would God like you to ask him for yourself and for one or two others?

Galilee, stormy, sorted

Have you ever been scared? I don't mean the temporary fear, or thrill, of riding a white knuckle ride. What I mean is the fear of actually losing your life.

Matthew 8:5–27

Jesus Heals a Soldier's Servant

⁵When Jesus entered the city of Capernaum, an army officer came to him, begging for help. ⁶The officer said, "Lord, my servant is at home in bed. He can't move his body and is in much pain."

⁷Jesus said to the officer, "I will go and heal him."

⁸The officer answered, "Lord, I am not worthy for you to come into my house. You only need to command it, and my servant will be healed. ⁹I, too, am a man under the authority of others, and I have soldiers under my command. I tell one soldier, 'Go,' and he goes. I tell another soldier, 'Come,' and he comes. I say to my servant, 'Do this,' and my servant does it."

¹⁰When Jesus heard this, he was amazed. He said to those who were following him, "I tell you the truth, this is the greatest faith I have found, even in Israel. ¹¹Many people will come from the east and from the west and will sit and eat with Abraham, Isaac and Jacob in the kingdom of heaven. ¹²But those people who should be in the kingdom will be thrown outside into the darkness, where people will cry and grind their teeth with pain."

¹³Then Jesus said to the officer, "Go home. Your servant will be healed just as you believed he would." And his servant was healed that same hour.

Jesus Heals Many People

¹⁴When Jesus went to Peter's house, he saw that Peter's mother-in-law was sick in bed with a fever. ¹⁵Jesus touched her hand, and the fever left her. Then she stood up and began to serve Jesus.

¹⁶That evening people brought to Jesus many who had demons. Jesus spoke and the demons left them, and he healed all the sick. ¹⁷He did these things to bring about what Isaiah the prophet had said:

"He took our suffering on him
 and carried our diseases."   *Isaiah 53:4*

People Want to Follow Jesus

¹⁸When Jesus saw the crowd around him, he told his followers to go to the other side of the lake. ¹⁹Then a teacher of the law came to Jesus and said, "Teacher, I will follow you wherever you go."

²⁰Jesus said to him, "The foxes have holes to live in, and the birds have nests, but the Son of Man has no place to rest his head."

²¹Another man, one of Jesus' followers, said to him, "Lord, first let me go and bury my father."

²²But Jesus told him, "Follow me, and let the people who are dead bury their own dead."

Jesus Calms a Storm

²³Jesus got into a boat, and his followers went with him. ²⁴A great storm arose on

the lake so that waves covered the boat, but Jesus was sleeping. 25His followers went to him and woke him, saying, "Lord, save us! We will drown!"

26Jesus answered, "Why are you afraid? You don't have enough faith." Then Jesus got up and gave a command to the wind and the waves, and it became completely calm.

27The men were amazed and said, "What kind of man is this? Even the wind and the waves obey him!"

The disciples are told off for being afraid, although when faced with drowning I wonder what our response would be?

What does Jesus link their fear to (v 26)?

When Jesus calms the storm he shows the disciples that they shouldn't be afraid. How would you answer the question in verse 27?

Think

What storms do we have in our lives that we are afraid of? How often do we lose our faith in God to help us face the problems that we have?

Pray

Dear Lord, be with me when I am scared. Help me to realise that you are with me through all that I do.

Reactions

Just because you're doing good stuff, it doesn't mean that people are always going to be grateful. Sometimes people react in the opposite way to how you'd expect them to act.

Matthew 8:28–9:17

Jesus Heals Two Men with Demons

28When Jesus arrived at the other side of the lake in the area of the Gadarene people, two men who had demons in them met him. These men lived in the burial caves and were so dangerous that people could not use the road by those caves. 29They shouted, "What do you want with us, Son of God? Did you come here to torture us before the right time?"

30Near that place there was a large herd of pigs feeding. 31The demons begged Jesus, "If you make us leave these men, please send us into that herd of pigs."

32Jesus said to them, "Go!" So the demons left the men and went into the pigs. Then the whole herd rushed down the hill into the lake and were drowned. 33The herdsmen ran away and went into the town, where they told about all of this and what had happened to the men who had demons. 34Then the whole town went out to see Jesus. When they saw him, they begged him to leave their area.

Jesus Heals a Paralysed Man

9 Jesus got into a boat and went back across the lake to his own town. 2Some people brought to Jesus a man who was paralysed and lying on a mat. When Jesus saw the faith of these people, he said to the paralysed man, "Be encouraged, young man. Your sins are forgiven."

3Some of the teachers of the law said to themselves, "This man speaks as if he were God. That is blasphemy!"

4Knowing their thoughts, Jesus said, "Why are you thinking evil thoughts? 5Which is easier: to say, 'Your sins are forgiven,' or to tell him, 'Stand up and walk'? 6But I will prove to you that the Son of Man has authority on earth to forgive sins." Then Jesus said to the paralysed man, "Stand up, take your mat and go home." 7And the man stood up and went home. 8When the people saw this, they were amazed and praised God for giving power like this to human beings.

Jesus Chooses Matthew

9When Jesus was leaving, he saw a man named Matthew sitting in the tax collector's booth. Jesus said to him, "Follow me," and he stood up and followed Jesus.

10As Jesus was having dinner at Matthew's house, many tax collectors and "sinners" came and ate with Jesus and his followers. 11When the Pharisees saw this, they asked Jesus' followers, "Why does your teacher eat with tax collectors and sinners?"

12When Jesus heard them, he said, "It is not the healthy people who need a doctor, but the sick. 13Go and learn what this means: 'I want kindness more than I want animal sacrifices.' I did not come to invite good people but to invite sinners."

Jesus' Followers are Criticised

14Then the followers of John came to Jesus and said, "Why do we and the Pharisees often give up eating for a certain time, but your followers don't?"

¹⁵Jesus answered, "The friends of the bridegroom are not sad while he is with them. But the time will come when the bridegroom will be taken from them, and then they will give up eating.

¹⁶"No one sews a patch of unshrunken cloth over a hole in an old coat. If he does, the patch will shrink and pull away from the coat, making the hole worse. ¹⁷Also, people never pour new wine into old leather bags. Otherwise, the bags will break, the wine will spill and the wine bags will be ruined. But people always pour new wine into new wine bags. Then both will continue to be good."

How did people react to the different things Jesus did?

- Some were grateful (9:8)

- Some asked questions (9:11)

- Some got scared and told him to go away (8:34)

- Some dropped everything and followed him (9:9)

Think

If you were there, what would you have done? How would you have reacted to Jesus? How will you react to Jesus today?

Pray

Ask God to help you to respond in the right way to what Jesus says and does.

Motley crew

Some of the biggest stories from history involve some of the most unlikely people. Clark Gable was one of the biggest Hollywood heart-throbs of the twentieth century and yet he allegedly had bad breath and big ears. Einstein, possibly science's greatest mind, failed one of his first major exams.

Matthew 9:18–10:10

Jesus Gives Life to a Dead Girl and Heals a Sick Woman

18While Jesus was saying these things, a leader of the synagogue came to him. He bowed down before Jesus and said, "My daughter has just died. But if you come and lay your hand on her, she will live again." 19So Jesus and his followers stood up and went with the leader.

20Then a woman who had been bleeding for twelve years came behind Jesus and touched the edge of his coat. 21She was thinking, "If I can just touch his clothes, I will be healed."

22Jesus turned and saw the woman and said, "Be encouraged, dear woman. You are made well because you believed." And the woman was healed from that moment on.

23Jesus continued along with the leader and went into his house. There he saw the funeral musicians and many people crying. 24Jesus said, "Go away. The girl is not dead, only asleep." But the people laughed at him. 25After the crowd had been thrown out of the house, Jesus went into the girl's room and took hold of her hand, and she stood up. 26The news about this spread all around the area.

Jesus Heals More People

27When Jesus was leaving there, two blind men followed him. They cried out, "Have mercy on us, Son of David!"

28After Jesus went inside, the blind men went with him. He asked the men, "Do you believe that I can make you see again?"

They answered, "Yes, Lord."

29Then Jesus touched their eyes and said, "Because you believe I can make you see again, it will happen." 30Then the men were able to see. But Jesus warned them strongly, saying, "Don't tell anyone about this." 31But the blind men left and spread the news about Jesus all around that area.

32When the two men were leaving, some people brought another man to Jesus. This man could not talk because he had a demon in him. 33After Jesus forced the demon to leave the man, he was able to speak. The crowd was amazed and said, "We have never seen anything like this in Israel."

34But the Pharisees said, "The prince of demons is the one that gives him power to force demons out."

35Jesus travelled through all the towns and villages, teaching in their synagogues, preaching the Good News about the kingdom and healing all kinds of diseases and sicknesses. 36When he saw the crowds, he felt sorry for them because they were hurting and helpless, like sheep without a shepherd. 37Jesus said to his followers, "There are many people to harvest but only a few workers to help harvest them.

22

³⁸Pray to the Lord, who owns the harvest, that he will send more workers to gather his harvest."

Jesus Sends Out His Apostles

10 Jesus called his twelve followers together and gave them authority to drive out evil spirits and to heal every kind of disease and sickness. ²These are the names of the twelve apostles: Simon (also called Peter) and his brother Andrew; James son of Zebedee, and his brother John; ³Philip and Bartholomew; Thomas and Matthew, the tax collector; James son of Alphaeus, and Thaddaeus; ⁴Simon the Zealot and Judas Iscariot, who turned against Jesus.

⁵Jesus sent out these twelve men with the following order: "Don't go to the non-Jewish people or to any town where the Samaritans live. ⁶But go to the people of Israel, who are like lost sheep. ⁷When you go, preach this: 'The kingdom of heaven is near.' ⁸Heal the sick, raise the dead to life again, heal those who have skin diseases and force demons out of people. I give you these powers freely, so help other people freely. ⁹Don't carry any money with you— gold or silver or copper. ¹⁰Don't carry a bag or extra clothes or sandals or a walking stick. Workers should be given what they need.

Take a look at the list of disciples. They include Peter, who denied Jesus, Thomas, who doubted Jesus, and Judas, who betrayed Jesus. There is Matthew, who, as a tax collector, was one of the most despised people in Judea. And Simon the Zealot, who was a political fanatic, a revolutionary in waiting.

And yet Jesus chose them as his disciples.

Think

What powers does Jesus give to this unlikely collection of disciples (10:1)?

What would Jesus want you to do?

Pray

Dear Lord, I'm certainly not perfect. My faults are . . . .
. . . . (add your own list). But you have chosen me to do your work. Thank you, and give me the strength to do what you ask me to.

Hard times

There are lots of ways in which you can be different to other people:

- the way you look
- the way you talk
- the way you act

People who are different often get given a hard time – and that's mostly just because they *are* different.

Matthew 10:11–40

¹¹"When you enter a city or town, find some worthy person there and stay in that home until you leave. ¹²When you enter that home, say, 'Peace be with you.' ¹³If the people there welcome you, let your peace stay there. But if they don't welcome you, take back the peace you wished for them. ¹⁴And if a home or town refuses to welcome you or listen to you, leave that place and shake its dust off your feet. ¹⁵I tell you the truth, on the Judgement Day it will be better for the towns of Sodom and Gomorrah than for the people of that town.

Jesus Warns His Apostles

¹⁶"Listen, I am sending you out like sheep among wolves. So be as clever as snakes and as innocent as doves. ¹⁷Be careful of people, because they will arrest you and take you to court and whip you in their synagogues. ¹⁸Because of me you will be taken to stand before governors and kings, and you will tell them and the non-Jewish people about me. ¹⁹When you are arrested, don't worry about what to say or how to say it. At that time you will be given the things to say. ²⁰It will not really be you speaking but the Spirit of your Father

speaking through you.

²¹"Brothers will give their own brothers to be killed, and fathers will give their own children to be killed. Children will fight against their own parents and have them put to death. ²²All people will hate you because you follow me, but those people who keep their faith until the end will be saved. ²³When you are treated badly in one city, run to another city. I tell you the truth, you will not finish going through all the cities of Israel before the Son of Man comes.

²⁴"A student is not better than his teacher, and a servant is not better than his master. ²⁵A student should be satisfied to become like his teacher; a servant should be satisfied to become like his master. If the head of the family is called Beelzebul, then the other members of the family will be called worse names!

Fear God, Not People

²⁶"So don't be afraid of those people, because everything that is hidden will be shown. Everything that is secret will be made known. ²⁷I tell you these things in the dark, but I want you to tell them in the light. What you hear whispered in your ear

you should shout from the house-tops. 28Don't be afraid of people, who can kill the body but cannot kill the soul. The only one you should fear is the one who can destroy the soul and the body in hell. 29Two sparrows cost only a penny, but not even one of them can die without your Father's knowing it. 30God even knows how many hairs are on your head. 31So don't be afraid. You are worth much more than many sparrows.

Tell People About Your Faith

32"All those who stand before others and say they believe in me, I will say before my Father in heaven that they belong to me. 33But all who stand before others and say they do not believe in me, I will say before my Father in heaven that they do not belong to me.

34"Don't think that I came to bring peace to the earth. I did not come to bring peace, but a sword. 35I have come so that

'a son will be against his father,
    a daughter will be against her mother,
a daughter-in-law will be against her
    mother-in-law.

36   A person's enemies will be members of
    his own family.'   *Micah 7:6*

37"Those who love their father or mother more than they love me are not worthy to be my followers. Those who love their son or daughter more than they love me are not worthy to be my followers. 38Whoever is not willing to carry the cross and follow me is not worthy of me. 39Those who try to hold on to their lives will give up true life. Those who give up their lives for me will hold on to true life. 40Whoever accepts you also accepts me, and whoever accepts me also accepts the One who sent me.

Following Jesus can be very hard, and a lot of people who follow Jesus find that their friends and their families aren't happy with it – sometimes they even turn against them. But Jesus says that through all this, you don't have to be afraid, because he'll always stand by you. He's always looking out for you.

Think

Imagine: God knows how many hairs there are on your head. God's looking after every one of them. How is that scary? How is that comforting?

Pray

Ask God to give you courage when people give you a hard time for being a Christian.

25

How you'll know

Sometimes you're going to meet with new ways of doing things.
How do you know if they're right or wrong?

 Matthew 10:41–11:24

⁴¹"Whoever meets a prophet and accepts him will receive the reward of a prophet. And whoever accepts a good person because that person is good will receive the reward of a good person. ⁴²Those who give one of these little ones a cup of cold water because they are my followers will truly get their reward."

Jesus and John the Baptist

11 After Jesus finished telling these things to his twelve followers, he left there and went to the towns in Galilee to teach and preach.

²John the Baptist was in prison, but he heard about what Christ was doing. So John sent some of his followers to Jesus. ³They asked him, "Are you the One who is to come, or should we wait for someone else?"

⁴Jesus answered them, "Go and tell John what you hear and see: ⁵the blind can see, the crippled can walk and people with skin diseases are healed. The deaf can hear, the dead are raised to life and the Good News is preached to the poor. ⁶Those who do not stumble in their faith because of me are blessed."

⁷As John's followers were leaving, Jesus began talking to the people about John. Jesus said, "What did you go out into the desert to see? A reed blown by the wind? ⁸What did you go out to see? A man dressed in fine clothes? No, those who wear fine clothes live in kings' palaces. ⁹So why did you go out? To see a prophet? Yes, and I tell you, John is more than a prophet. ¹⁰This was written about him:

'I will send my messenger ahead of you,
who will prepare the way for you.'
Malachi 3:1

¹¹I tell you the truth, John the Baptist is greater than any other person ever born, but even the least important person in the kingdom of heaven is greater than John. ¹²Since the time John the Baptist came until now, the kingdom of heaven has been going forwards in strength, and people have been trying to take it by force. ¹³All the prophets and the law of Moses told about what would happen until the time John came. ¹⁴And if you will believe what they said, you will believe that John is Elijah, whom they said would come. ¹⁵You people who can hear me, listen!

¹⁶"What can I say about the people of this time? What are they like? They are like children sitting in the market place, who call out to each other,

¹⁷'We played music for you, but you did not
dance;
we sang a sad song, but you did not
cry.'

¹⁸John came and did not eat or drink like other people. So people say, 'He has a demon.' ¹⁹The Son of Man came, eating and drinking, and people say, 'Look at him! He eats too much and drinks too much wine, and he is a friend of tax collectors and sinners.' But wisdom is proved to be right by what it does."

Jesus Warns Unbelievers

²⁰Then Jesus criticised the cities where he did most of his miracles, because the people did not change their lives and stop

sinning. 21He said, "How terrible for you, Korazin! How terrible for you, Bethsaida! If the same miracles I did in you had happened in Tyre and Sidon, those people would have changed their lives a long time ago. They would have worn rough cloth and put ashes on themselves to show they had changed. 22But I tell you, on the Judgement Day it will be better for Tyre and Sidon than for you. 23And you, Capernaum, will you be lifted up to heaven? No, you will be thrown down to the depths. If the miracles I did in you had happened in Sodom, its people would have stopped sinning, and it would still be a city today. 24But I tell you, on the Judgement Day it will be better for Sodom than for you."

John the Baptist had the same question about Jesus – how could he know if what Jesus was doing and saying was right?

Jesus' answer was pretty straight: the things he was doing and saying were making a real difference.

Think

Chances are, you're going to see people come along with new ideas about church and God. How will you know if they're right or not? How does this passage help you?

Pray

... for help from God in figuring out whether new ideas are right or wrong.

Scales of justice

If someone asked whether you were a good person how would you answer? Would you be able to give a list of good things you had done? Would this list be longer than a list of bad things you had done?

 Matthew 11:25–12:21

Jesus Offers Rest to People

25At that time Jesus said, "I praise you, Father, Lord of heaven and earth, because you have hidden these things from the people who are wise and clever. But you have shown them to those who are like little children. 26Yes, Father, this is what you really wanted.

27"My Father has given me all things. No one knows the Son, except the Father. And no one knows the Father, except the Son and those whom the Son chooses to tell.

28"Come to me, all of you who are tired and have heavy loads, and I will give you rest. 29Accept my teachings and learn from me, because I am gentle and humble in spirit, and you will find rest for your lives. 30The teaching that I ask you to accept is easy; the load I give you to carry is light."

Jesus is Lord of the Sabbath

12 At that time Jesus was walking through some fields of grain on a Sabbath day. His followers were hungry, so they began to pick the grain and eat it. 2When the Pharisees saw this, they said to Jesus, "Look! Your followers are doing what is unlawful to do on the Sabbath day."

3Jesus answered, "Have you not read what David did when he and the people with him were hungry? 4He went into God's house, and he and those with him ate the holy bread, which was lawful only for priests to eat. 5And have you not read in the law of Moses that on every Sabbath day the priests in the Temple break this law about the Sabbath day? But the priests are not wrong for doing that. 6I tell you that there is something here that is greater than the Temple. 7The Scripture says, 'I want kindness more than I want animal sacrifices.' You don't really know what those words mean. If you understood them, you would not judge those who have done nothing wrong.

8"So the Son of Man is Lord of the Sabbath day."

Jesus Heals a Man's Hand

9Jesus left there and went into their synagogue, 10where there was a man with a crippled hand. They were looking for a reason to accuse Jesus, so they asked him, "Is it right to heal on the Sabbath day?"

11Jesus answered, "If any of you has a sheep, and it falls into a ditch on the Sabbath day, you will help it out of the ditch. 12Surely a human being is more important than a sheep. So it is lawful to do good things on the Sabbath day."

13Then Jesus said to the man with the crippled hand, "Hold out your hand." The man held out his hand, and it became well again, like the other hand. 14But the Pharisees left and made plans to kill Jesus.

Jesus is God's Chosen Servant

15Jesus knew what the Pharisees were

doing, so he left that place. Many people followed him, and he healed all who were sick. ¹⁶But Jesus warned the people not to tell who he was. ¹⁷He did these things to bring about what Isaiah the prophet had said:

¹⁸"Here is my servant whom I have
    chosen.
    I love him, and I am pleased with him.
    I will put my Spirit upon him,

and he will tell of my justice to all
    people.
¹⁹He will not argue or cry out;
    no one will hear his voice in the streets.
²⁰He will not break a crushed blade of
    grass
    or put out even a weak flame
until he makes justice win the victory.
²¹ In him will the non-Jewish people find
        hope."   *Isaiah 42:1–4*

The Jews believed that by keeping the law and not doing bad things they would be acceptable to God. Jesus cuts right through that. He says that it isn't about doing this, that and the other; it is nothing to do with what we can do, or how good we can be. We are acceptable to God because of his work, not ours.

Think

What two things must we do to find rest in our lives (11:29)?

Does this passage mean that Christians will always have an easy time?

Pray

If there is anything that you are struggling with, ask Jesus to give you rest. Claim the promise for yourself and follow the way of Jesus.

What are you like inside?

Take a look in a mirror and jot down on a piece of paper what you think you are like as a person. Be honest with yourself. Is there a difference between how you act and how you feel?

 Matthew 12:22–45

Jesus' Power is from God

22Then some people brought to Jesus a man who was blind and could not talk, because he had a demon. Jesus healed the man so that he could talk and see. 23All the people were amazed and said, "Perhaps this man is the Son of David!"

24When the Pharisees heard this, they said, "Jesus uses the power of Beelzebul, the ruler of demons, to force demons out of people."

25Jesus knew what the Pharisees were thinking, so he said to them, "Every kingdom that is divided against itself will be destroyed. And any city or family that is divided against itself will not continue. 26And if Satan forces out himself, then Satan is divided against himself, and his kingdom will not continue. 27You say that I use the power of Beelzebul to force out demons. If that is true, then what power do your people use to force out demons? So they will be your judges. 28But if I use the power of God's Spirit to force out demons, then the kingdom of God has come to you.

29"If anyone wants to enter a strong person's house and steal his things, he must first tie up the strong person. Then he can steal the things from the house.

30"Whoever is not with me is against me. Whoever does not work with me is working against me. 31So I tell you, people can be forgiven for every sin and every-

thing they say against God. But whoever speaks against the Holy Spirit will not be forgiven. 32Anyone who speaks against the Son of Man can be forgiven, but anyone who speaks against the Holy Spirit will not be forgiven, now or in the future.

People Know You by Your Words

33"If you want good fruit, you must make the tree good. If your tree is not good, it will have bad fruit. A tree is known by the kind of fruit it produces. 34You snakes! You are evil people, so how can you say anything good? The mouth speaks the things that are in the heart. 35Good people have good things in their hearts, and so they say good things. But evil people have evil in their hearts, so they say evil things. 36And I tell you that on the Judgement Day people will be responsible for every careless thing they have said. 37The words you have said will be used to judge you. Some of your words will prove you right, but some of your words will prove you guilty."

The People Ask for a Miracle

38Then some of the Pharisees and teachers of the law answered Jesus, saying, "Teacher, we want to see you work a miracle as a sign."

39Jesus answered, "Evil and sinful people are the ones who want to see a miracle for a sign. But no sign will be given to them, except the sign of the prophet Jonah. [40]Jonah was in the stomach of the big fish for three days and three nights. In the same way, the Son of Man will be in the grave three days and three nights. [41]On the Judgement Day the people from Nineveh will stand up with you people who live now, and they will show that you are guilty. When Jonah preached to them, they were sorry and changed their lives. And I tell you that someone greater than Jonah is here. [42]On the Judgement Day, the Queen of the South will stand up with you people who live today. She will show that you are guilty, because she came from far away to listen to Solomon's wise teaching. And I tell you that someone greater than Solomon is here.

People Today are Full of Evil

[43]"When an evil spirit comes out of a person, it travels through barren places, looking for a place to rest, but it doesn't find it. [44]So the spirit says, 'I will go back to the house I left.' When the spirit comes back, it finds the house still empty, swept clean and made neat. [45]Then the evil spirit goes out and brings seven other spirits even more evil than it is, and they go in and live there. So the person has even more trouble than before. It is the same way with the evil people who live today."

Do these verses mean that:

- how you look on the outside is most important?

- what's going on inside is *just* as important?

- what you're like on the inside is *more* important than your outside image?

Why do we say wrong and evil things (vs 34,35)?

Think

God hears your unspoken words as well as the ones you say out loud. Does knowing this mean that you want to change?

Pray

Ask God to help you to be the person he wants you to be – inside and outside.

Ask him to forgive you for anything you have thought that you know to be wrong.

How does your garden grow?

You never really know the effect that the things you say and do have on people. People do remember what you say to them – and even if the things you say don't seem to make any difference straight away, you never know when someone will remember something you said days, months or years down the line.

 Matthew 12:46–13:17

Jesus' True Family

46While Jesus was talking to the people, his mother and brothers stood outside, trying to find a way to talk to him. 47Someone told Jesus, "Your mother and brothers are standing outside, and they want to talk to you."

48He answered, "Who is my mother? Who are my brothers?" 49Then he pointed to his followers and said, "Here are my mother and my brothers. 50My true brother and sister and mother and father are those who do what my Father in heaven wants."

A Story About Planting Seed

13 That same day Jesus went out of the house and sat by the lake. 2Large crowds gathered around him, so he got into a boat and sat down, while the people stood on the shore. 3Then Jesus used stories to teach them many things. He said: "A farmer went out to plant his seed. 4While he was planting, some seed fell by the road, and the birds came and ate it all up. 5Some seed fell on rocky ground, where there wasn't much earth. That seed grew very fast, because the ground was not deep. 6But when the sun rose, the plants dried up, because they did not have deep roots. 7Some other seed fell among thorny weeds, which grew and choked the good plants. 8Some other seed fell on good ground where it grew and produced a crop. Some plants made 100 times more, some made 60 times more and some made 30 times more. 9You people who can hear me, listen."

Why Jesus Used Stories to Teach

10The followers came to Jesus and asked, "Why do you use stories to teach the people?"

11Jesus answered, "You have been chosen to know the secrets about the kingdom of heaven, but others cannot know these secrets. 12Those who have understanding will be given more, and they will have all they need. But those who do not have understanding, even what they have will be taken away from them. 13This is why I use stories to teach the people: they see, but they don't really see. They hear, but they don't really hear or understand. 14So they show that the things Isaiah said about them are true:

'You will listen and listen, but you will not understand.
   You will look and look, but you will not learn.

15For the minds of these people have
become stubborn.
They do not hear with their ears,
and they have closed their eyes.
Otherwise they might really understand
what they see with their eyes
and hear with their ears.
They might really understand in their
minds

and come back to me and be healed.'
Isaiah 6:9–10
16But you are blessed, because you see
with your eyes and hear with your ears. 17I
tell you the truth, many prophets and good
people wanted to see the things that you
now see, but they did not see them. And
they wanted to hear the things that you
now hear, but they did not hear them.

Jesus tells the story about the farmer sowing the seed to show us the
different ways people receive what we tell them about God.

- Sometimes it's ignored and nothing happens with it (like the seed that
  falls on the path)

- Sometimes people hear what you've got to say and think it's good to
  begin with – but then they forget all about it (like seed growing on rocky
  soil)

- Sometimes people take on board what you're saying but get distracted
  (like seed choked by brambles)

- Sometimes people will take in what you have to say, and it will grow
  inside them and change them – and maybe one day produce seed of its
  own.

Think

Imagine you're a farmer and the message you've got is like seed
you've got to sow: only you have no idea what kind of ground your
seed's going to end up growing on. What do you do with the seed?

Pray

Ask God to give you the right seeds to plant.

Watch out for weeds!

Sometimes you might think it would be great to be permanently on some amazing, fantastic Christian event. Not a "weed" in sight! Take a moment to think about how this would feel.

But life's not like that!

Matthew 13:18–43

Jesus Explains the Seed Story

18"So listen to the meaning of that story about the farmer. 19What is the seed that fell by the road? That seed is like the person who hears the message about the kingdom but does not understand it. The Evil One comes and takes away what was planted in that person's heart. 20And what is the seed that fell on rocky ground? That seed is like the person who hears the teaching and quickly accepts it with joy. 21But he does not let the teaching go deep into his life, so he keeps it only a short time. When trouble or persecution comes because of the teaching he accepted, he quickly gives up. 22And what is the seed that fell among the thorny weeds? That seed is like the person who hears the teaching but lets worries about this life and the temptation of wealth stop that teaching from growing. So the teaching does not produce fruit in that person's life. 23But what is the seed that fell on the good ground? That seed is like the person who hears the teaching and understands it. That person grows and produces fruit, sometimes 100 times more, sometimes 60 times more and sometimes 30 times more."

A Story About Wheat and Weeds

24Then Jesus told them another story: "The kingdom of heaven is like a man who planted good seed in his field. 25That night, when everyone was asleep, his enemy came and planted weeds among the wheat and then left. 26Later, the wheat grew and the heads of grain grew, but the weeds also grew. 27Then the man's servants came to him and said, 'You planted good seed in your field. Where did the weeds come from?' 28The man answered, 'An enemy planted weeds.' The servants asked, 'Do you want us to pull up the weeds?' 29The man answered, 'No, because when you pull up the weeds, you might also pull up the wheat. 30Let the weeds and the wheat grow together until the harvest time. At harvest time I will tell the workers, "First gather the weeds and tie them together to be burnt. Then gather the wheat and bring it to my barn." '"

Stories of Mustard Seed and Yeast

31Then Jesus told another story: "The kingdom of heaven is like a mustard seed that a man planted in his field. 32That seed is the smallest of all seeds, but when it grows, it is one of the largest garden plants. It becomes big enough for the wild birds to come and build nests in its branches."

33Then Jesus told another story: "The kingdom of heaven is like yeast that a woman took and hid in a large bowl of flour until it made all the dough rise."

34Jesus used stories to tell all these things to the people; he always used stories to teach them. 35This is as the prophet said:
"I will speak using stories;

I will tell things that have been secret since the world was made."

Psalm 78:2

Jesus Explains About the Weeds

³⁶Then Jesus left the crowd and went into the house. His followers came to him and said, "Explain to us the meaning of the story about the weeds in the field."

³⁷Jesus answered, "The man who planted the good seed in the field is the Son of Man. ³⁸The field is the world, and the good seeds are all of God's children who belong to the kingdom. The weeds are those people who belong to the Evil One.

³⁹And the enemy who planted the bad seed is the devil. The harvest time is the end of the world, and the workers who gather are God's angels.

⁴⁰"Just as the weeds are pulled up and burnt in the fire, so it will be at the end of the world. ⁴¹The Son of Man will send out his angels, and they will gather out of his kingdom all who cause sin and all who do evil. ⁴²The angels will throw them into the blazing furnace, where the people will cry and grind their teeth with pain. ⁴³Then the good people will shine like the sun in the kingdom of their Father. You people who can hear me, listen.

Christians will always have to be around people who are not for God. And, if we're not careful, we can get caught up in their way of living.

But the "weeds" aren't on the winning side (v 40)! Who is (v 43)?

Think

How can you protect yourself from the negative influence others could have over you?

What encourages you in this story?

Pray

Ask God to help you stick with him when you have to be with people who don't believe the same as you: people who don't believe in God and follow Jesus.

What you're looking for

What's special to you? Is there anything you really desperately want? What would you do to get it? And when you've got it, what would you do to keep it?

 Matthew 13:44–14:12

Stories of a Treasure and a Pearl

44"The kingdom of heaven is like a treasure hidden in a field. One day a man found the treasure, and then he hid it in the field again. He was so happy that he went and sold everything he owned to buy that field.

45"Also, the kingdom of heaven is like a man looking for fine pearls. 46When he found a very valuable pearl, he went and sold everything he had and bought it.

A Story of a Fishing Net

47"Also, the kingdom of heaven is like a net that was put into the lake and caught many different kinds of fish. 48When it was full, the fishermen pulled the net to the shore. They sat down and put all the good fish in baskets and threw away the bad fish. 49It will be this way at the end of the world. The angels will come and separate the evil people from the good people. 50The angels will throw the evil people into the blazing furnace, where people will cry and grind their teeth with pain."

51Jesus asked his followers, "Do you understand all these things?"

They answered, "Yes, we understand."

52Then Jesus said to them, "So every teacher of the law who has been taught about the kingdom of heaven is like the owner of a house. He brings out both new things and old things he has saved."

Jesus Goes to His Home Town

53When Jesus finished teaching with these stories, he left there. 54He went to his home town and taught the people in the synagogue, and they were amazed. They said, "Where did this man get this wisdom and this power to do miracles? 55He is just the son of a carpenter. His mother is Mary, and his brothers are James, Joseph, Simon and Judas. 56And all his sisters are here with us. Where then does this man get all these things?" 57So the people were upset with Jesus.

But Jesus said to them, "A prophet is honoured everywhere except in his home town and in his own home."

58So he did not do many miracles there because they had no faith.

How John the Baptist Was Killed

14 At that time Herod, the ruler of Galilee, heard the reports about Jesus. 2So he said to his servants, "Jesus is John the Baptist, who has risen from the dead. That is why he can work these miracles."

3Some time before this, Herod had arrested John, tied him up, and put him in prison. Herod did this because of Herodias, who had been the wife of Philip, Herod's brother. 4John had been telling Herod, "It is not lawful for you to be married to Herodias." 5Herod wanted to kill John, but he was afraid of the people, because they believed John was a prophet.

⁶On Herod's birthday, the daughter of Herodias danced for Herod and his guests, and she pleased him. ⁷So he promised with an oath to give her anything she wanted. ⁸Herodias told her daughter what to ask for, so she said to Herod, "Give me the head of John the Baptist here on a dish." ⁹Although King Herod was very sad, he had made a promise, and his dinner guests had heard him. So Herod ordered that what she asked for be done. ¹⁰He sent soldiers to the prison to cut off John's head. ¹¹And they brought it on a dish and gave it to the girl, and she took it to her mother. ¹²John's followers came and got his body and buried it. Then they went and told Jesus.

A lot of people in these stories want things: in two of the stories, Jesus talks about two men who sell everything they own to get hold of something really valuable. Meanwhile, Herod wants to please Herodias so badly, he's willing to kill an innocent man for her.

The difference is in what they want and what they're willing to do for it.

Think

If you do something extreme for something you want, you've got to be sure that what you want is the right thing, and that you're doing it the right way. It's just as bad to do the right wrong thing in order to get or achieve something good as it is to do a bad thing to get something bad.

Ask yourself: are you looking for something that matters? Are you following after something worth risking everything for?

Pray

Ask God to help you work out what you should be looking for and how you should go about getting it.

Worth the risk?

What makes you afraid of being a Christian? It could be standing up for what you believe in front of your non-Christian friends, or it could be going to church where there are no young people your age. Or is there something else that makes you afraid?

 Matthew 14:13–36

More than 5,000 Fed

13When Jesus heard what had happened to John, he left in a boat and went to a lonely place by himself. But the crowds heard about it and followed him on foot from the towns. 14When he arrived, he saw a great crowd waiting. He felt sorry for them and healed those who were sick.

15When it was evening, his followers came to him and said, "No one lives in this place, and it is already late. Send the people away so they can go to the towns and buy food for themselves."

16But Jesus answered, "They don't need to go away. You give them something to eat."

17They said to him, "But we have only five loaves of bread and two fish."

18Jesus said, "Bring the bread and the fish to me." 19Then he told the people to sit down on the grass. He took the five loaves and the two fish and, looking up to heaven, he thanked God for the food. Jesus divided the bread and gave it to his followers, who gave it to the people. 20All the people ate and were satisfied. Then the followers filled twelve baskets with the leftover pieces of food. 21There were about 5,000 men there who ate, not counting women and children.

Jesus Walks on the Water

22Immediately Jesus told his followers to get into the boat and go ahead of him across the lake. He stayed there to send the people home. 23After he had sent them away, he went by himself up into the hills to pray. It was late, and Jesus was there alone. 24By this time, the boat was already far away from land. It was being hit by waves, because the wind was blowing against it.

25Between three and six o'clock in the morning, Jesus came to them, walking on the water. 26When his followers saw him walking on the water, they were afraid. They said, "It's a ghost!" and cried out in fear.

27But Jesus quickly spoke to them, "Have courage! It is I. Do not be afraid."

28Peter said, "Lord, if it is really you, then command me to come to you on the water."

29Jesus said, "Come."

And Peter left the boat and walked on the water to Jesus. 30But when Peter saw the wind and the waves, he became afraid and began to sink. He shouted, "Lord, save me!"

31Immediately Jesus reached out his hand and caught Peter. Jesus said, "Your faith is small. Why did you doubt?"

32After they got into the boat, the wind became calm. 33Then those who were in the boat worshipped Jesus and said, "Truly you are the Son of God!"

34When they had crossed the lake, they

came to shore at Gennesaret. ³⁵When the people there recognised Jesus, they told people in the area there that Jesus had come, and they brought all their sick to him. ³⁶They begged Jesus to let them touch just the edge of his coat, and all who touched it were healed.

What were Peter's courage levels like during this episode? Imagine a horizontal line rising up and down, as you go through each verse, representing how Peter's courage went high and low.

What gave Peter courage to want to walk on water (v 27)?

What made his courage disappear (v 30)?

What should Peter have done?

Think

What things make you afraid to do what Jesus wants you to?

Pray

Tell Jesus about them. Ask that he'll help you stay focused on him and not doubt.

39

Inside image

Gossip, lies, swearing, caring, sympathy, thanks – which of these come out of your mouth regularly? In an old fairytale there are two girls. When they spoke, toads came out of the mouth of the plain one, but pearls out of the mouth of the good-looking one. Weird, huh? But guess who got the prince!

 Matthew 15:1–31

Obey God's Law

15 Then some Pharisees and teachers of the law came to Jesus from Jerusalem. They asked him, 2"Why don't your followers obey the unwritten laws which have been handed down to us? They don't wash their hands before they eat."

3Jesus answered, "And why do you refuse to obey God's command so that you can follow your own teachings? 4God said, 'Honour your father and your mother,' and 'Anyone who says cruel things to his father or mother must be put to death.' 5But you say a person can tell his father or mother, 'I have something I could use to help you, but I have given it to God instead.' 6You teach that person not to honour his father or his mother. You rejected what God said for the sake of your own rules. 7You are hypocrites! Isaiah was right when he said about you:

8"These people show honour to me with words,

but their hearts are far from me.

9Their worship of me is worthless.

The things they teach are nothing but human rules.'"   *Isaiah 29:13*

10After Jesus called the crowd to him, he said, "Listen and understand what I am saying. 11It is not what people put into their mouths that makes them unclean. It is what comes out of their mouths that makes them unclean."

12Then his followers came to him and asked, "Do you know that the Pharisees are angry because of what you said?"

13Jesus answered, "Every plant that my Father in heaven has not planted himself will be pulled up by the roots. 14Stay away from the Pharisees; they are blind leaders. And if a blind person leads a blind person, both will fall into a ditch."

15Peter said, "Explain the example to us."

16Jesus said, "Do you still not understand? 17Surely you know that all the food that enters the mouth goes into the stomach and then goes out of the body. 18But what people say with their mouths comes from the way they think; these are the things that make people unclean. 19Out of the mind come evil thoughts, murder, adultery, sexual sins, stealing, lying and speaking evil of others. 20These things make people unclean; eating with unwashed hands does not make them unclean."

Jesus Helps a Non-Jewish Woman

21Jesus left that place and went to the area of Tyre and Sidon. 22A Canaanite woman from that area came to Jesus and cried out, "Lord, Son of David, have mercy on me! My daughter has a demon, and she is suffering very much."

23But Jesus did not answer the woman. So his followers came to Jesus and begged him, "Tell the woman to go away. She is following us and shouting."

24Jesus answered, "God sent me only to the lost sheep, the people of Israel."

25Then the woman came to Jesus again and bowed before him and said, "Lord, help me!"

26Jesus answered, "It is not right to take the children's bread and give it to the dogs."

27The woman said, "Yes, Lord, but even the dogs eat the crumbs that fall from their masters' table."

28Then Jesus answered, "Woman, you have great faith! I will do what you asked." And at that moment the woman's daughter was healed.

Jesus Heals Many People

29After leaving there, Jesus went along the shore of Lake Galilee. He went up on a hill and sat there.

30Great crowds came to Jesus, bringing with them the lame, the blind, the crippled, those who could not speak and many others. They put them at Jesus' feet, and he healed them. 31The crowd was amazed when they saw that people who could not speak before were now able to speak. The crippled were made strong. The lame could walk, and the blind could see. And they praised the God of Israel for this.

Some people spend ages on looking good, but don't have time for anyone else. God says it's the inside that counts (vs 18,19).

Think

What things come out of your mouth that show the sort of person you are?

What do you spend more time on: getting ready to go out with your friends to the cinema or the shopping centre, or getting ready to spend some time with God?

Pray

Father, please clean my heart so I have loving things to say to others.

Being sure

How sure are you that you know who Jesus is? Put a cross on the line.

Very sure _____ Not at all sure

Matthew 15:32–16:20

More than 4,000 Fed

32Jesus called his followers to him and said, "I feel sorry for these people, because they have already been with me three days, and they have nothing to eat. I don't want to send them away hungry. They might faint while going home."

33His followers asked him, "How can we get enough bread to feed all these people? We are far away from any town."

34Jesus asked, "How many loaves of bread do you have?"

They answered, "Seven, and a few small fish."

35Jesus told the people to sit on the ground. 36He took the seven loaves of bread and the fish and gave thanks to God. Then he divided the food and gave it to his followers, and they gave it to the people. 37All the people ate and were satisfied. Then his followers filled seven baskets with the leftover pieces of food. 38There were about 4,000 men there who ate, besides women and children. 39After sending the people home, Jesus got into the boat and went to the area of Magadan.

The Leaders Ask for a Miracle

16 The Pharisees and Sadducees came to Jesus, wanting to trick him. So they asked him to show them a miracle from God.

2Jesus answered, "At sunset you say we will have good weather, because the sky is red. 3And in the morning you say that it will be a rainy day, because the sky is dark and red. You see these signs in the sky and know what they mean. In the same way, you see the things that I am doing now, but you don't know their meaning. 4Evil and sinful people ask for a miracle as a sign, but they will not be given any sign, except the sign of Jonah." Then Jesus left them and went away.

Guard Against Wrong Teachings

5Jesus' followers went across the lake, but they had forgotten to bring bread. 6Jesus said to them, "Be careful! Beware of the yeast of the Pharisees and the Sadducees."

7His followers discussed the meaning of this, saying, "He said this because we forgot to bring bread."

8Knowing what they were talking about, Jesus asked them, "Why are you talking about not having bread? Your faith is small. 9Do you still not understand? Remember the five loaves of bread that fed the 5,000? And remember that you filled many baskets with the leftovers? 10Or the seven loaves of bread that fed the 4,000 and the many baskets you then also filled? 11I was not talking to you about bread. Why don't you understand that? I am telling you to beware of the yeast of the Pharisees and the Sadducees." 12Then the followers understood that Jesus was not telling them to beware of the yeast used in bread but to beware of the teaching of the Pharisees and the Sadducees.

Peter Says Jesus is the Christ

13When Jesus came to the area of

Caesarea Philippi, he asked his followers, "Who do people say the Son of Man is?"

[14]They answered, "Some say you are John the Baptist. Others say you are Elijah, and still others say you are Jeremiah or one of the prophets."

[15]Then Jesus asked them, "And who do you say I am?"

[16]Simon Peter answered, "You are the Christ, the Son of the living God."

[17]Jesus answered, "You are blessed, Simon son of Jonah, because no person taught you that. My Father in heaven showed you who I am. [18]So I tell you, you are Peter. On this rock I will build my church, and the power of death will not be able to defeat it. [19]I will give you the keys of the kingdom of heaven; the things you don't allow on earth will be the things that God does not allow, and the things you allow on earth will be the things that God allows." [20]Then Jesus warned his followers not to tell anyone he was the Christ.

What did Peter believe (16:16)?

How did he know (16:17)?

Jesus had faith in Peter (16:17–19) because Peter had understood what others could not.

Think

What parts of the Christian faith do you find hard to believe? How do you deal with these things?

What parts of the Christian faith do your friends find hard to believe?

Pray

Ask Jesus to help you grow in your faith, reassure you when you doubt and give you the courage to tell your friends about him.

Out of this world

Have you ever had such a great experience of God that you wanted to stay like that for ever?

 Matthew 16:21–17:13

Jesus Says that He Must Die

²¹From that time on Jesus began telling his followers that he must go to Jerusalem, where the older Jewish leaders, the leading priests, and the teachers of the law would make him suffer many things. He told them he must be killed and then be raised from the dead on the third day.

²²Peter took Jesus aside and told him not to talk like that. He said, "God save you from those things, Lord! Those things will never happen to you!"

²³Then Jesus said to Peter, "Go away from me, Satan! You are not helping me! You don't care about the things of God, but only about the things people think are important."

²⁴Then Jesus said to his followers, "If people want to follow me, they must give up the things they want. They must be willing even to give up their lives to follow me. ²⁵Those who want to save their lives will give up true life, and those who give up their lives for me will have true life. ²⁶It is worth nothing for them to have the whole world if they lose their souls. They could never pay enough to buy back their souls. ²⁷The Son of Man will come again with his Father's glory and with his angels. At that time, he will reward them for what they have done. ²⁸I tell you the truth, some people standing here will see the Son of Man coming with his kingdom before they die."

Jesus Talks with Moses and Elijah

17 Six days later, Jesus took Peter, James and John, the brother of James, up on a high mountain by themselves. ²While they watched, Jesus' appearance was changed; his face became bright like the sun, and his clothes became white as light. ³Then Moses and Elijah appeared to them, talking with Jesus.

⁴Peter said to Jesus, "Lord, it is good that we are here. If you want, I will put up three tents here—one for you, one for Moses and one for Elijah."

⁵While Peter was talking, a bright cloud covered them. A voice came from the cloud and said, "This is my Son, whom I love, and I am very pleased with him. Listen to him!"

⁶When his followers heard the voice, they were so frightened they fell to the ground. ⁷But Jesus went to them and touched them and said, "Stand up. Don't be afraid." ⁸When they looked up, they saw Jesus was now alone.

⁹As they were coming down the mountain, Jesus commanded them not to tell anyone about what they had seen until the Son of Man had risen from the dead.

¹⁰Then his followers asked him, "Why do the teachers of the law say that Elijah must come first?"

¹¹Jesus answered, "They are right to say that Elijah is coming and that he will make everything the way it should be. ¹²But I tell

you that Elijah has already come, and they did not recognise him. They did to him whatever they wanted to do. It will be the same with the Son of Man; those same people will make the Son of Man suffer." 13Then the followers understood that Jesus was talking about John the Baptist.

Peter wanted to hold on to what was happening by setting up camp on the mountain top (17:4)! But Jesus needed to get on with what God had called him to do.

What do you think Peter learned from this experience (17:5,12,13)?

Do you know why it was Moses and Elijah who appeared on the mountain with Jesus?

Think

Why don't we have "mountain top" experiences of God all the time?

What is the best experience of God you have ever had? How did you feel?

Pray

Thank God for the special times when you have felt very close to him. Ask him to help you stay close to him now.

Start small

Do you ever feel that you're not going to be able to succeed in what you're doing? When you've got a difficult time ahead of you, sometimes you need a lot of help. Who do you turn to for help? Friends? Family? God?

Matthew 17:14–18:9

Jesus Heals a Sick Boy

¹⁴When Jesus and his followers came back to the crowd, a man came to Jesus and bowed before him. ¹⁵The man said, "Lord, have mercy on my son. He has epilepsy and is suffering very much, because he often falls into the fire or into the water. ¹⁶I brought him to your followers, but they could not cure him."

¹⁷Jesus answered, "You people have no faith, and your lives are all wrong. How long must I put up with you? How long must I continue to be patient with you? Bring the boy here." ¹⁸Jesus gave a strong command to the demon inside the boy. Then the demon came out, and the boy was healed from that time on.

¹⁹The followers came to Jesus when he was alone and asked, "Why couldn't we force the demon out?"

²⁰Jesus answered, "Because your faith is too small. I tell you the truth, if your faith is as big as a mustard seed, you can say to this mountain, 'Move from here to there,' and it will move. All things will be possible for you." ²¹

Jesus Talks About His Death

²²While Jesus' followers were gathering in Galilee, he said to them, "The Son of Man will be handed over to people, ²³and they will kill him. But on the third day he will be raised from the dead." And the followers were filled with sadness.

Jesus Talks About Paying Taxes

²⁴When Jesus and his followers came to Capernaum, the men who collected the Temple tax came to Peter. They asked, "Does your teacher pay the Temple tax?"

²⁵Peter answered, "Yes, Jesus pays the tax."

Peter went into the house, but before he could speak, Jesus said to him, "What do you think? The kings of the earth collect different kinds of taxes. But who pays the taxes—the king's children or others?"

²⁶Peter answered, "Other people pay the taxes."

Jesus said to Peter, "Then the children of the king don't have to pay taxes. ²⁷But we don't want to upset these tax collectors. So go to the lake and fish. After you catch the first fish, open its mouth and you will find a coin. Take that coin and give it to the tax collectors for you and me."

Who is the Greatest?

18 At that time the followers came to Jesus and asked, "Who is greatest in the kingdom of heaven?"

²Jesus called a little child to him and stood the child before his followers. ³Then he said, "I tell you the truth, you must change and become like little children. Otherwise, you will never enter the kingdom of heaven. ⁴The greatest person in the kingdom of heaven is the one who makes himself humble like this child.

⁵"Whoever accepts a child in my name accepts me. ⁶If one of these little children believes in me, and someone causes that child to sin, it would be better for that person to have a large stone tied around the neck and be drowned in the sea. ⁷How terrible for the people of the world because of the things that cause them to sin. Such things will happen, but how terrible for the one who causes them to happen! ⁸If your hand or your foot causes you to sin, cut it off and throw it away. It is better for you to lose part of your body and live for ever than to have two hands and two feet and be thrown into the fire that burns for ever. ⁹If your eye causes you to sin, take it out and throw it away. It is better for you to have only one eye and live for ever than to have two eyes and be thrown into the fire of hell.

In the first story, Jesus tells his followers that if they've got even a tiny bit of faith in God, he will make them able to do amazing things. That's still true today.

Think

Do you think that having faith will help you to do anything at all? Do you think that what you're trying to do matters?

Pray

Ask God to help your faith to grow, and to help you to do amazing things.

Forgive. i.e. forgive – full stop!

Do you like to be forgiven when you've messed up? To have everything sorted out so you can get on with your life?

 Matthew 18:10–35

A Lost Sheep

10"Be careful. Don't think these little children are worth nothing. I tell you that they have angels in heaven who are always with my Father in heaven. 11

12"If a man has 100 sheep but one of the sheep gets lost, he will leave the other 99 on the hill and go to look for the lost sheep. 13I tell you the truth, he is happier about that one sheep than about the 99 that were never lost. 14In the same way, your Father in heaven does not want any of these little children to be lost.

When a Person Sins Against You

15"If your fellow believer sins against you, go and tell him in private what he did wrong. If he listens to you, you have helped that person to be your brother or sister again. 16But if he refuses to listen, go to him again and take one or two other people with you. 'Every case may be proved by two or three witnesses.' 17If he refuses to listen to them, tell the church. If he refuses to listen to the church, then treat him like a person who does not believe in God or like a tax collector.

18"I tell you the truth, the things you don't allow on earth will be the things God does not allow. And the things you allow on earth will be the things that God allows.

19"Also, I tell you that if two of you on earth agree about something and pray for it, it will be done for you by my Father in heaven. 20This is true because if two or three people come together in my name, I am there with them."

An Unforgiving Servant

21Then Peter came to Jesus and asked, "Lord, when my fellow believer sins against me, how many times must I forgive him? Should I forgive him as many as seven times?"

22Jesus answered, "I tell you, you must forgive him more than seven times. You must forgive him even if he does wrong to you 77 times.

23"The kingdom of heaven is like a king who decided to collect the money his servants owed him. 24When the king began to collect his money, a servant who owed him several thousand pounds was brought to him. 25But the servant did not have enough money to pay his master, the king. So the master ordered that everything the servant owned should be sold, even the servant's wife and children. Then the money would be used to pay the king what the servant owed.

26"But the servant fell on his knees and begged, 'Be patient with me, and I will pay you everything I owe.' 27The master felt sorry for his servant and told him he did not have to pay it back. Then he let the servant go free.

28"Later, that same servant found another servant who owed him a few pounds. The servant grabbed him around the neck and said, 'Pay me the money you owe me!'

²⁹"The other servant fell on his knees and begged him, 'Be patient with me, and I will pay you everything I owe.'

³⁰"But the first servant refused to be patient. He threw the other servant into prison until he could pay everything he owed. ³¹When the other servants saw what had happened, they were very sorry. So they went and told their master all that had happened.

³²"Then the master called his servant in and said, 'You evil servant! Because you begged me to forget what you owed, I told you that you did not have to pay anything. ³³You should have shown mercy to that other servant, just as I showed mercy to you.' ³⁴The master was very angry and put the servant in prison to be punished until he could pay everything he owed.

³⁵"This king did what my heavenly Father will do to you if you do not forgive your brother or sister from your heart."

How much was the man in debt let off (v 24)?

How much did he clobber his friend for (v 28)?

What was the result (vs 32–34)?

What do you think Jesus wants you to learn from this story (vs 21,22,35)?

Think

Do you need to forgive someone in your family?

Can you do something today to sort things out?

Pray

Talk to God about anyone who has hurt you. Ask him to help you forgive them, as he is ready to forgive you. Perhaps you could say "the Lord's Prayer" (Matthew 6:9–15), thinking carefully about what each bit means.

God is for all

Do you ever feel that you are not good enough for God? Or do you feel that you can't be of use to him because you are too young or too inexperienced?

 Matthew 19:1–26

Jesus Teaches About Divorce

19 After Jesus said all these things, he left Galilee and went into the area of Judea on the other side of the Jordan River. ²Large crowds followed him, and he healed them there.

³Some Pharisees came to Jesus and tried to trick him. They asked, "Is it right for a man to divorce his wife for any reason he chooses?"

⁴Jesus answered, "Surely you have read in the Scriptures: when God made the world, 'he made them male and female'. ⁵And God said, 'So a man will leave his father and mother and be united with his wife, and the two will become one body.' ⁶So there are not two, but one. God has joined the two together, so no one should separate them."

⁷The Pharisees asked, "Why then did Moses give a command for a man to divorce his wife by giving her divorce papers?"

⁸Jesus answered, "Moses allowed you to divorce your wives because you refused to accept God's teaching, but divorce was not allowed in the beginning. ⁹I tell you that anyone who divorces his wife and marries another woman is guilty of adultery. The only reason for a man to divorce his wife is if his wife has sexual relations with another man."

¹⁰The followers said to him, "If that is the only reason a man can divorce his wife, it is better not to marry."

¹¹Jesus answered, "Not everyone can accept this teaching, but God has made some able to accept it. ¹²There are different reasons why some men cannot marry. Some men were born without the ability to become fathers. Others were made that way later in life by other people. And some men have given up marriage because of the kingdom of heaven. But the person who can marry should accept this teaching about marriage."

Jesus Welcomes Children

¹³Then the people brought their little children to Jesus so he could put his hands on them and pray for them. His followers told them to stop, ¹⁴but Jesus said, "Let the little children come to me. Don't stop them, because the kingdom of heaven belongs to people who are like these children." ¹⁵After Jesus put his hands on the children, he left that place.

A Rich Young Man's Question

¹⁶A man came to Jesus and asked, "Teacher, what good thing must I do to have life for ever?"

¹⁷Jesus answered, "Why do you ask me about what is good? Only God is good. But if you want to have life for ever, obey the commands."

¹⁸The man asked, "Which commands?"

Jesus answered, "You must not murder anyone; you must not be guilty of adultery; you must not steal; you must not tell lies about your neighbour; ¹⁹honour your father and mother; and love your neighbour as you love yourself.'"

20The young man said, "I have obeyed all these things. What else do I need to do?"

21Jesus answered, "If you want to be perfect, then go and sell your possessions and give the money to the poor. If you do this, you will have treasure in heaven. Then come and follow me."

22But when the young man heard this, he left very sad, because he was rich.

23Then Jesus said to his followers, "I tell you the truth, it will be hard for a rich person to enter the kingdom of heaven. 24Yes, I tell you that it is easier for a camel to go through the eye of a needle than for a rich person to enter the kingdom of God."

25When Jesus' followers heard this, they were very surprised and asked, "Then who can be saved?"

26Jesus looked at them and said, "This is something people cannot do, but God can do all things."

The people brought the children to Jesus so that he could bless them, which meant that they were asking God to have favour on their children.

Why do you think the disciples tried to keep the children away from Jesus?

Who does the kingdom of heaven belong to (v 14)?

Jesus doesn't mean that all children will be saved but that if anyone comes to him in a state of complete dependence on him they will be received.

Think

How do you come before God: confident or in a humble attitude?

Pray

Dear Lord, help me to rely on you. Don't let my self-confidence block my complete relationship with you.

Fair's fair?

If you delivered newspapers five mornings a week and your friend did this one morning a week, who should get paid more? Would it be fair if you both got the same payment?

 Matthew 19:27–20:19

27Peter said to Jesus, "Look, we have left everything and followed you. So what will we have?"

28Jesus said to them, "I tell you the truth, when the age to come has arrived, the Son of Man will sit on his great throne. All of you who followed me will also sit on twelve thrones, judging the twelve tribes of Israel. 29And all those who have left houses, brothers, sisters, father, mother, children or farms to follow me will get much more than they left, and they will have life for ever. 30Many who have the highest place now will have the lowest place in the future. And many who have the lowest place now will have the highest place in the future.

A Story About Workers

20 "The kingdom of heaven is like a person who owned some land. One morning, he went out very early to hire some people to work in his vineyard. 2The man agreed to pay the workers a silver coin for working on that day. Then he sent them into the vineyard to work. 3At about nine o'clock the man went to the market-place and saw some other people standing there, doing nothing. 4So he said to them, 'If you go and work in my vineyard, I will pay you what your work is worth.' 5So they went to work in the vineyard. The man went out again at about twelve o'clock and three o'clock and did the same thing. 6At about five o'clock the

man went to the market-place again and saw others standing there. He asked them, 'Why have you stood here all day doing nothing?' 7They answered, 'No one has given us a job.' The man said to them, 'Then you can go and work in my vineyard.'

8"At the end of the day, the owner of the vineyard said to the foreman of all the workers, 'Call the workers and pay them. Start with the last people I hired and end with those I hired first.'

9"When the workers who were hired at five o'clock came to get their pay, each received a silver coin. 10When the workers who were hired first came to get their pay, they thought they would be paid more than the others. But each one of them also received a silver coin. 11When they got their coin, they complained to the man who owned the land. 12They said, 'Those people were hired last and worked only one hour. But you paid them the same as you paid us who worked hard all day in the hot sun.' 13But the man who owned the vineyard said to one of those workers, 'Friend, I am being fair to you. You agreed to work for a silver coin. 14So take your pay and go. I want to give the man who was hired last the same pay that I gave you. 15I can do what I want with my own money. Are you jealous because I am good to those people?'

16"So those who have the last place now will have the first place in the future, and those who have the first place now will have the last place in the future."

Jesus Talks About His Own Death

17While Jesus was going to Jerusalem, he took his twelve followers aside privately and said to them, 18"Look, we are going to Jerusalem. The Son of Man will be turned over to the leading priests and the teachers of the law, and they will say that he must die. 19They will give the Son of Man to the non-Jewish people to laugh at him and beat him with whips and crucify him. But on the third day, he will be raised to life again."

Sometimes Jesus explains a story that he has just told, but here he doesn't. What do you think this story means?

Who's the man with the vineyard?

Who are the workers?

What are the wages?

Think

God's love and his offer of life are for everyone and anyone who will accept them – they don't depend on what you've done.

Pray

Thank God for his goodness and kindness to all who serve him, including you.

Who's in charge?

It must be great to be a leader. Everyone looks up to you. Everyone wants to hear what you've got to say. Everyone does what you tell them to. It must be great. Right?

 Matthew 20:20–21:11

A Mother Asks Jesus a Favour

²⁰Then the wife of Zebedee came to Jesus with her sons. She bowed before him and asked him to do something for her.

²¹Jesus asked, "What do you want?"

She said, "Promise that one of my sons will sit at your right side and the other will sit at your left side in your kingdom."

²²But Jesus said, "You don't understand what you are asking. Can you drink the cup that I am about to drink?"

The sons answered, "Yes, we can."

²³Jesus said to them, "You will drink from my cup. But I cannot choose who will sit at my right or my left; those places belong to those for whom my Father has prepared them."

²⁴When the other ten followers heard this, they were angry with the two brothers.

²⁵Jesus called all the followers together and said, "You know that the rulers of the non-Jewish people love to show their power over the people. And their important leaders love to use all their authority. ²⁶But it should not be that way among you. Whoever wants to become great among you must serve the rest of you like a servant. ²⁷Whoever wants to become first among you must serve the rest of you like a slave. ²⁸In the same way, the Son of Man did not come to be served. He came to serve others and to give his life as a ransom for many people."

Jesus Heals Two Blind Men

²⁹When Jesus and his followers were leaving Jericho, a great many people followed him. ³⁰Two blind men sitting by the road heard that Jesus was going by, so they shouted, "Lord, Son of David, have mercy on us!"

³¹The people warned the blind men to be quiet, but they shouted even more, "Lord, Son of David, have mercy on us!"

³²Jesus stopped and said to the blind men, "What do you want me to do for you?"

³³They answered, "Lord, we want to see."

³⁴Jesus felt sorry for the blind men and touched their eyes, and at once they could see. Then they followed Jesus.

Jesus Enters Jerusalem as a King

21 As Jesus and his followers were coming closer to Jerusalem, they stopped at Bethphage at the hill called the Mount of Olives. From there Jesus sent two of his followers ²and said to them, "Go to the town you can see ahead of you. When you enter it, you will quickly find a donkey tied there with its colt. Untie them and bring them to me. ³If anyone asks you why you are taking the donkeys, say that the Master needs them, and he will send them at once."

⁴This was to bring about what the prophet had said:

⁵"Tell the people of Jerusalem,
  'Your king is coming to you.
He is gentle and riding on a donkey,
  on the colt of a donkey.'" *Zechariah 9:9*
⁶The followers went and did what Jesus

told them to do. ⁷They brought the donkey and the colt to Jesus and laid their coats on them, and Jesus sat on them. ⁸Many people spread their coats on the road. Others cut branches from the trees and spread them on the road. ⁹The people were walking ahead of Jesus and behind him, shouting,

"Praise to the Son of David!

God bless the One who comes in the name of the Lord!

Praise to God in heaven!" *Psalm 118:26*

¹⁰When Jesus entered Jerusalem, all the city was filled with excitement. The people asked, "Who is this man?"

¹¹The crowd answered, "This man is Jesus, the prophet from the town of Nazareth in Galilee."

James and John wanted all the perks of being leaders without really understanding the hard bits. Sure, Jesus got to ride into Jerusalem with all those people cheering – but it wasn't always going to be that easy. Jesus understood that.

Think

Being a leader means you've got power, but it also means responsibility and stress – and it might mean hardship and suffering. Before you volunteer to be in charge of anyone, ask yourself if you're cut out for that.

Pray

Ask God to help you to respect the people who are in charge of you and to help you to handle the responsibilities you have – the big ones and the small ones – in the right way.

What's louder than words?

Have you ever told someone, "I'll do that for you", or, "I'll pray for you" – and then forgotten?

 Matthew 21:12–32

Jesus Goes to the Temple

12Jesus went into the Temple and threw out all the people who were buying and selling there. He turned over the tables of those who were exchanging different kinds of money, and he upset the benches of those who were selling doves. 13Jesus said to all the people there, "It is written in the Scriptures, 'My Temple will be called a house for prayer.' But you are changing it into a 'hideout for robbers'."

14The blind and crippled people came to Jesus in the Temple, and he healed them. 15The leading priests and the teachers of the law saw that Jesus was doing wonderful things and that the children were praising him in the Temple, saying, "Praise to the Son of David." All these things made the priests and the teachers of the law very angry.

16They asked Jesus, "Do you hear the things these children are saying?"

Jesus answered, "Yes. Haven't you read in the Scriptures, 'You have taught children and babies to sing praises'?"

17Then Jesus left and went out of the city to Bethany, where he spent the night.

The Power of Faith

18Early the next morning, as Jesus was going back to the city, he became hungry. 19Seeing a fig tree beside the road, Jesus went to it, but there were no figs on the tree, only leaves. So Jesus said to the tree,

"You will never again have fruit." The tree immediately dried up.

20When his followers saw this, they were amazed. They asked, "How did the fig tree dry up so quickly?"

21Jesus answered, "I tell you the truth, if you have faith and do not doubt, you will be able to do what I did to this tree and even more. You will be able to say to this mountain, 'Go, fall into the sea.' And if you have faith, it will happen. 22If you believe, you will get anything you ask for in prayer."

Leaders Doubt Jesus' Authority

23Jesus went to the Temple, and while he was teaching there, the leading priests and the older leaders of the people came to him. They said, "What authority do you have to do these things? Who gave you this authority?"

24Jesus answered, "I also will ask you a question. If you answer me, then I will tell you what authority I have to do these things. 25Tell me: when John baptised people, did that come from God or just from other people?"

They argued about Jesus' question, saying, "If we answer, 'John's baptism was from God', Jesus will say, 'Then why didn't you believe him?' 26But if we say, 'It was from people', we are afraid of what the crowd will do because they all believe that John was a prophet."

27So they answered Jesus, "We don't know".

Jesus said to them, "Then I won't tell you what authority I have to do these things.

A Story About Two Sons

28"Tell me what you think about this: a man had two sons. He went to the first son and said, 'Son, go and work today in my vineyard'. 29The son answered, 'I will not go'. But later the son changed his mind and went. 30Then the father went to the other son and said, 'Son, go and work today in my vineyard'. The son answered, 'Yes, sir, I will go and work', but he did not go. 31Which of the two sons obeyed his father?"

The priests and leaders answered, "The first son".

Jesus said to them, "I tell you the truth, the tax collectors and the prostitutes will enter the kingdom of God before you do. 32John came to show you the right way to live. You did not believe him, but the tax collectors and prostitutes believed him. Even after seeing this, you still refused to change your ways and believe him.

Which son promised obedience to his father (v 30)?

Which son practised it (v 29)?

The priests and leaders thought that they were good because they said the right things. The problem was that John the Baptist had told them they needed to change but they hadn't. They said the right things but they hadn't changed their ways.

Think

Do you keep your promises to God? Remember, when you tell him (or anyone) you'll do something, he's ready to help you put your promises into practice.

Pray

Ask God to help you demonstrate by your actions what you say you believe.

Attitudes to God

How would you reply if you got an invitation to the birthday party of the most popular person in your class? Or an invitation to the opening of the latest Hollywood blockbuster?

 Matthew 21:33–22:14

A Story About God's Son

33"Listen to this story: there was a man who owned a vineyard. He put a wall around it and dug a hole for a winepress and built a tower. Then he leased the land to some farmers and left for a trip. 34When it was time for the grapes to be picked, he sent his servants to the farmers to get his share of the grapes. 35But the farmers grabbed the servants, beat one, killed another and then killed a third servant with stones. 36So the man sent some other servants to the farmers, even more than he sent the first time. But the farmers did the same thing to the servants that they had done before. 37So the man decided to send his son to the farmers. He said, 'They will respect my son.' 38But when the farmers saw the son, they said to each other, 'This son will inherit the vineyard. If we kill him, it will be ours!' 39Then the farmers grabbed the son, threw him out of the vineyard and killed him. 40So what will the owner of the vineyard do to these farmers when he comes?"

41The priests and leaders said, "He will surely kill those evil men. Then he will lease the vineyard to some other farmers who will give him his share of the crop at harvest time."

42Jesus said to them, "Surely you have read this in the Scriptures:

'The stone that the builders rejected
  became the cornerstone.
The Lord did this,
  and it is wonderful to us.'

Psalm 118:22–23

43"So I tell you that the kingdom of God will be taken away from you and given to people who do the things God wants in his kingdom. 44The person who falls on this stone will be broken, and on whomsoever that stone falls, that person will be crushed."

45When the leading priests and the Pharisees heard these stories, they knew Jesus was talking about them. 46They wanted to arrest him, but they were afraid of the people, because the people believed that Jesus was a prophet.

A Story About a Wedding Feast

22 Jesus again used stories to teach the people. He said, 2"The kingdom of heaven is like a king who prepared a wedding feast for his son. 3The king invited some people to the feast. When the feast was ready, the king sent his servants to tell the people, but they refused to come.

4"Then the king sent other servants, saying, 'Tell those who have been invited that my feast is ready. I have killed my best bulls and calves for the dinner, and everything is ready. Come to the wedding feast.'

5"But the people refused to listen to the servants and left to do other things. One went to work in his field, and another went to his business. 6Some of the other people grabbed the servants, beat them and killed them. 7The king was furious and sent his army to kill the murderers and burn their city.

8"After that, the king said to his

servants, 'The wedding feast is ready. I invited those people, but they were not worthy to come. ⁹So go to the street corners and invite everyone you find to come to my feast.' ¹⁰So the servants went into the streets and gathered all the people they could find, both good and bad. And the wedding hall was filled with guests.

¹¹"When the king came in to see the guests, he saw a man who was not dressed for a wedding. ¹²The king said, 'Friend, how were you allowed to come in here? You are not dressed for a wedding.' But the man said nothing. ¹³So the king told some servants, 'Tie this man's hands and feet. Throw him out into the darkness, where people will cry and grind their teeth with pain.'

¹⁴"Yes, many people are invited, but only a few are chosen."

How did people in this story respond to the king's invitation? Find these:

- rejected it (22:3)

- ignored it (22:5)

- reacted violently (22:6)

- accepted it and came to the party (22:10)

- accepted it, but didn't let it make a difference (22:11)

What happened when the first group of people invited didn't turn up (22:8,9)?

Think

Has God's invitation to you made a difference in your life? How and why?

Pray

Ask God to help you have the right attitude as you live for him, and to help you change if you need to.

Golden rule

If you're going to manage to live alongside people, you've got to have some ground rules. You've got to know that there is a right way and a wrong way to act.

Fair enough. So why is it that so many people seem to want to use the rules to make other people miserable? That's not the way it should be, surely?

 Matthew 22:15–40

Is It Right to Pay Taxes or Not?

¹⁵Then the Pharisees left that place and made plans to trap Jesus into saying something wrong. ¹⁶They sent some of their own followers and some people from the group called Herodians. They said, "Teacher, we know that you are an honest man and that you teach the truth about God's way. You are not afraid of what other people think about you, because you pay no attention to who they are. ¹⁷So tell us what you think. Is it right to pay taxes to Caesar or not?"

¹⁸But knowing that these leaders were trying to trick him, Jesus said, "You hypocrites! Why are you trying to trap me? ¹⁹Show me a coin used for paying the tax." So the men showed him a coin. ²⁰Then Jesus asked, "Whose image and name are on the coin?"

²¹The men answered, "Caesar's."

Then Jesus said to them, "Give to Caesar the things that are Caesar's, and give to God the things that are God's."

²²When the men heard what Jesus said, they were amazed and left him and went away.

Some Sadducees Try to Trick Jesus

²³That same day some Sadducees came to Jesus and asked him a question. (Sadducees believed that people would not rise from the dead.) ²⁴They said, "Teacher, Moses said if a married man dies without having children, his brother must marry the widow and have children for him. ²⁵Once there were seven brothers among us. The first one married and died. Since he had no children, his brother married the widow. ²⁶Then the second brother also died. The same thing happened to the third brother and all the other brothers. ²⁷Finally, the woman died. ²⁸Since all seven men had married her, when people rise from the dead, whose wife will she be?"

²⁹Jesus answered, "You don't understand, because you don't know what the Scriptures say, and you don't know about the power of God. ³⁰When people rise from the dead, they will not marry, nor will they be given to someone to marry. They will be like the angels in heaven. ³¹Surely you have read what God said to you about rising from the dead. ³²God said, 'I am the

God of Abraham, the God of Isaac and the God of Jacob.' God is the God of the living, not the dead."

33When the people heard this, they were amazed at Jesus' teaching.

The Most Important Command

34When the Pharisees learned that the Sadducees could not argue with Jesus' answers to them, the Pharisees met together. 35One Pharisee, who was an expert on the law of Moses, asked Jesus this question to test him: 36"Teacher, which command in the law is the most important?"

37Jesus answered, "Love the Lord your God with all your heart, all your soul and all your mind.' 38This is the first and most important command. 39And the second command is like the first: 'Love your neighbour as you love yourself.' 40All the law and the writings of the prophets depend on these two commands."

Jesus gave people a lot of advice about the rules they should be following, but at the middle of everything he said and did, there was this one basic rule: love other people, and love God.

Think

Why is concentrating on loving other people and loving God more important than all the other rules? What happens if you're doing this properly?

Pray

Ask God to help you to base everything you do on love.

Don't be a hypocrite

Are you a hypocrite? You know ... you make a show of being super-spiritual when you're with Christians, but when you're out with non-Christian mates, it's a different story. On a Sunday you're belting out "Open the eyes of my heart" with great passion but with your friends you're belting out words which aren't quite as spiritual.

   Matthew 22:41–23:22

Jesus Questions the Pharisees

41While the Pharisees were together, Jesus asked them, 42"What do you think about the Christ? Whose son is he?"

They answered, "The Christ is the Son of David."

43Then Jesus said to them, "Then why did David call him 'Lord'? David, speaking by the power of the Holy Spirit, said,

44'The LORD said to my Lord:

Sit by me at my right side,

until I put your enemies under your control.'   *Psalm 110:1*

45David calls the Christ 'Lord', so how can the Christ be his son?"

46None of the Pharisees could answer Jesus' question, and after that day no one was brave enough to ask him any more questions.

Jesus Accuses Some Leaders

23 Then Jesus said to the crowds and to his followers, 2"The teachers of the law and the Pharisees have the authority to tell you what the law of Moses says. 3So you should obey and follow whatever they tell you, but their lives are not good examples for you to follow. They tell you to do things, but they themselves don't do them. 4They make strict rules and try to force people to obey them, but they are unwilling to help those who struggle under the weight of their rules.

5"They do good things so that other people will see them. They make the boxes of Scriptures that they wear bigger, and they make their special prayer clothes very long. 6Those Pharisees and teachers of the law love to have the most important seats at feasts and in the synagogues. 7They love people to greet them with respect in the market places, and they love to have people call them 'Teacher'.

8"But you must not be called 'Teacher', because you have only one Teacher, and you are all brothers and sisters together. 9And don't call any person on earth 'Father', because you have one Father, who is in heaven. 10And you should not be called 'Master', because you have only one Master, the Christ. 11Whoever is your servant is the greatest among you. 12Whoever makes himself great will be made humble. Whoever makes himself humble will be made great.

13"How terrible for you, teachers of the law and Pharisees! You are hypocrites! You close the door for people to enter the kingdom of heaven. You yourselves don't enter, and you stop others who are trying to enter. 14

15"How terrible for you, teachers of the law and Pharisees! You are hypocrites!

You travel across land and sea to find one person who will change to your ways. When you find that person, you make him more fit for hell than you are.

16"How terrible for you! You guide the people, but you are blind. You say, 'If people swear by the Temple when they make a promise, that means nothing. But if they swear by the gold that is in the Temple, they must keep that promise.' 17You are blind fools! Which is greater: the gold or the Temple that makes that gold holy? 18And you say, 'If people swear by the altar when they make a promise, that means nothing. But if they swear by the gift on the altar, they must keep that promise.' 19You are blind! Which is greater: the gift or the altar that makes the gift holy? 20The person who swears by the altar is really using the altar and also everything on the altar. 21And the person who swears by the Temple is really using the Temple and also everything in the Temple. 22The person who swears by heaven is also using God's throne and the One who sits on that throne.

The Pharisees (religious teachers) in Jesus' day were keen to look good (23:5) and to make other people keep the rules (23:4), but not so keen on living God's way themselves (23:3).

What made them such hypocrites (23:5–7)?

Think

Are you most bothered by what others *think* about you, or by what God *knows* about you?

Pray

Ask for God's help to be the "real thing".

Justice, mercy, faithfulness

A lot of the time, people look at church people and can't say that they're different from anybody else. They'll tell you that they're not better people: they're just religious, and they're smug about it. And they look down on people who aren't religious. This is not, of course, the way it's supposed to be.

 Matthew 23:23–24:8

23"How terrible for you, teachers of the law and Pharisees! You are hypocrites! You give to God one-tenth of everything you earn—even your mint, dill and cumin. But you don't obey the really important teachings of the law—justice, mercy and being loyal. These are the things you should do, as well as those other things. 24You guide the people, but you are blind! You are like a person who picks a fly out of a drink and then swallows a camel!

25"How terrible for you, teachers of the law and Pharisees! You are hypocrites! You wash the outside of your cups and dishes, but inside they are full of things you got by cheating others and by pleasing only yourselves. 26Pharisees, you are blind! First make the inside of the cup clean, and then the outside of the cup can be truly clean.

27"How terrible for you, teachers of the law and Pharisees! You are hypocrites! You are like tombs that are painted white. Outside, those tombs look fine, but inside, they are full of the bones of dead people and all kinds of unclean things. 28It is the same with you. People look at you and think you are good, but on the inside you are full of hypocrisy and evil.

29"How terrible for you, teachers of the law and Pharisees! You are hypocrites! You build tombs for the prophets, and you show honour to the graves of those who lived good lives. 30You say, 'If we had lived during the time of our ancestors, we would not have helped them kill the prophets.' 31But you give proof that you are children of those who murdered the prophets. 32And you will complete the sin that your ancestors started.

33"You are snakes! A family of poisonous snakes! How are you going to escape God's judgement? 34So I tell you this: I am sending to you prophets and wise men and teachers. Some of them you will kill and crucify. Some of them you will beat in your synagogues and chase from town to town. 35So you will be guilty for the death of all the good people who have been killed on earth—from the murder of that good man Abel to the murder of Zechariah son of Berakiah, whom you murdered between the Temple and the altar. 36I tell you the truth, all of these things will happen to you people who are living now.

Jesus Feels Sorry for Jerusalem

37"Jerusalem, Jerusalem! You kill the prophets and stone to death those who are sent to you. Many times I wanted to gather your people as a hen gathers her chicks under her wings, but you did not let me. 38Now your house will be left completely empty. 39I tell you, you will not see me again until that time when you will say, 'God bless the One who comes in the name of the Lord.'"

The Temple will Be Destroyed

24 As Jesus left the Temple and was walking away, his followers came up to him to show him the Temple's buildings. 2Jesus asked, "Do you see all these buildings? I tell you the truth, not one stone will be left on another. Every stone will be thrown down to the ground."

3Later, as Jesus was sitting on the Mount of Olives, his followers came to be alone with him. They said, "Tell us, when will these things happen? And what will be the sign that it is time for you to come again and for this age to end?"

4Jesus answered, "Be careful that no one fools you. 5Many will come in my name, saying, 'I am the Christ', and they will fool many people. 6You will hear about wars and stories of wars that are coming, but don't be afraid. These things must happen before the end comes. 7Nations will fight against other nations; kingdoms will fight against other kingdoms. There will be times when there is no food for people to eat, and there will be earthquakes in different places. 8These things are like the first pains when something new is about to be born.

The Pharisees were exactly the kind of church people I was just talking about. They did all the religious stuff, but it didn't change them. They didn't treat other people well and didn't really love God. No wonder Jesus got so angry with them.

Think

Christians are supposed to be different from other people. They're supposed to fight for justice, to show love and mercy to people, and to be faithful to God. It doesn't matter if you're going to church. If you're not showing it in your everyday life, it doesn't mean anything. Is this you?

Pray

Ask God to show you if you're in danger of becoming like the Pharisees, and to help you not to be.

It's the end of the world as we know it (and I feel fine)

Bad stuff happens all the time: wars, famines, plagues, all sorts of stuff. In far-off countries, people are sent to prison, tortured and even killed, just for saying they follow Jesus. A lot of people think that all this means that the world is going to end soon.

 Matthew 24:9–35

9"Then people will arrest you, hand you over to be hurt and kill you. They will hate you because you believe in me. 10At that time, many will lose their faith, and they will turn against each other and hate each other. 11Many false prophets will come and cause many people to believe lies. 12There will be more and more evil in the world, so most people will stop showing their love for each other. 13But those people who keep their faith until the end will be saved. 14The Good News about God's kingdom will be preached in all the world, to every nation. Then the end will come.

15"Daniel the prophet spoke about 'the destroying terror'. You will see this standing in the holy place." (You who read this should understand what it means.) 16"At that time, the people in Judea should run away to the mountains. 17If people are on the roofs of their houses, they must not go down to get anything out of their houses. 18If people are in the fields, they must not go back to get their coats. 19At that time, how terrible it will be for women who are pregnant or have nursing babies! 20Pray that it will not be winter or a Sabbath day

when these things happen and you have to run away, 21because at that time there will be much trouble. There will be more trouble than there has ever been since the beginning of the world until now, and nothing as bad will ever happen again. 22God has decided to make that terrible time short. Otherwise, no one would go on living. But God will make that time short to help the people he has chosen. 23At that time, someone might say to you, 'Look, there is the Christ!' Or another person might say, 'There he is!' But don't believe them. 24False Christs and false prophets will come and perform great wonders and miracles. They will try to fool even the people God has chosen, if that were possible. 25Now I have warned you about this before it happens.

26"If people tell you, 'The Christ is in the desert', don't go there. If they say, 'The Christ is in the inner room', don't believe it. 27When the Son of Man comes, he will be seen by everyone, like lightning flashing from the east to the west. 28Wherever the dead body is, there the vultures will gather.

29"Soon after the trouble of those days, 'the sun will grow dark,

and the moon will not give its light.
The stars will fall from the sky.
And the powers of the heavens will be
    shaken.'   *Isaiah 13:10; 34:4*
³⁰"At that time, the sign of the Son of
Man will appear in the sky. Then all the
peoples of the world will cry. They will see
the Son of Man coming on clouds in the
sky with great power and glory. ³¹He will
use a loud trumpet to send his angels all
around the earth, and they will gather his
chosen people from every part of the
world.

³²"Learn a lesson from the fig tree:
when its branches become green and soft
and new leaves appear, you know summer
is near. ³³In the same way, when you see
all these things happening, you will know
that the time is near, ready to come. ³⁴I tell
you the truth, all these things will happen
while the people of this time are still living.
³⁵Earth and sky will be destroyed, but the
words I have said will never be destroyed.

Jesus is talking here about the way that the world will one day end. If you don't understand the whole thing, don't worry – Christians have been wondering about what Jesus was going on about, and arguing about it, for hundreds of years. The only thing we should be sure about is that Jesus is going to come back. When he does, it doesn't really matter how bad things get, because he'll have it sorted.

Think

If you knew that Jesus was going to come back in the next 10 minutes, how would you feel? What would you do?

Pray

Ask God to help you to stay faithful, and to be ready for when Jesus does come back.

Tough truth

Who do you know who's not yet a Christian?

_____

_____

_____

Matthew 24:36–25:13

When will Jesus Come Again?

36"No one knows when that day or time will be, not the angels in heaven, not even the Son. Only the Father knows. 37When the Son of Man comes, it will be like what happened during Noah's time. 38In those days before the flood, people were eating and drinking, marrying and giving their children to be married, until the day Noah entered the ark. 39They knew nothing about what was happening until the flood came and destroyed them. It will be the same when the Son of Man comes. 40Two men will be in the field. One will be taken, and the other will be left. 41Two women will be grinding grain with a mill. One will be taken, and the other will be left.

42"So always be ready, because you don't know the day your Lord will come. 43Remember this: if the owner of the house knew what time of night a thief was coming, the owner would watch and not let the thief break in. 44So you also must be ready, because the Son of Man will come at a time you don't expect him.

45"Who is the wise and loyal servant that the master trusts to give the other servants their food at the right time? 46When the master comes and finds the servant doing his work, the servant will be blessed. 47I tell you the truth, the master will choose that servant to take care of everything he owns. 48But suppose that servant is evil, and thinks to himself, 'My master will not come back soon,' 49and he

begins to beat the other servants and eat and get drunk with others like him? 50The master will come when that servant is not ready and is not expecting him. 51Then the master will cut him in pieces and send him away to be with the hypocrites, where people will cry and grind their teeth with pain.

A Story About Ten Bridesmaids

25 "At that time the kingdom of heaven will be like ten bridesmaids who took their lamps and went to wait for the bridegroom. 2Five of them were foolish and five were wise. 3The five foolish bridesmaids took their lamps, but they did not take spare oil for the lamps to burn. 4The wise bridesmaids took their lamps and more oil in jars. 5Because the bridegroom was late, they became sleepy and went to sleep.

6"At midnight someone cried out, 'The bridegroom is coming! Come and meet him!' 7Then all the bridesmaids woke up and got their lamps ready. 8But the foolish ones said to the wise, 'Give us some of your oil, because our lamps are going out.' 9The wise bridesmaids answered, 'No, the oil we have might not be enough for all of us. Go to the people who sell oil and buy some for yourselves.'

10"So while the five foolish bridesmaids went to buy oil, the bridegroom came. The bridesmaids who were ready went in with the bridegroom to the wedding feast. Then

the door was closed and locked.
11"Later the others came back and said, 'Sir, sir, open the door to let us in.' 12But the bridegroom answered, 'I tell you the truth, I don't want to know you.'

13"So always be ready, because you don't know the day or the hour the Son of Man will come.

Jesus is pointing out that there will be no big fanfare warning that he is coming back. It will seem like everything is normal, with people living their lives as they always have.

Not everyone will go to be with Jesus (24:40,41). We can't know for sure about someone else's relationship with God, but ...

Think

Think about the people you listed. God loves these guys even more than you do. Maybe God will include you in his plans to help them know him.

Pray

Pray for them. Look out for what God will do (James 5:16 – the last bit!).

Extra

If God gives you the opportunity to say something to your friends use it. At the same time remember that one of the most powerful ways to show Jesus to your friends is in the way you live.

You did it for me

Have you ever given away money, or possessions, so that others could be helped? Do you ever stop and give your time, by saying 'hello', or money to someone begging on the street? What about the other people in your church? Do you know what needs they have?

 Matthew 25:14–46

A Story About Three Servants

14"The kingdom of heaven is like a man who was going to another place for a visit. Before he left, he called for his servants and told them to take care of his things while he was gone. 15He gave one servant five bags of gold, another servant two bags of gold and a third servant one bag of gold, to each one as much as he could manage. Then he left. 16The servant who got five bags went quickly to invest the money and earned five more bags. 17In the same way, the servant who had two bags invested them and earned two more. 18But the servant who got one bag went out and dug a hole in the ground and hid the master's money.

19"After a long time the master came home and asked the servants what they had done with his money. 20The servant who was given five bags of gold brought five more bags to the master and said, 'Master, you trusted me to care for five bags of gold, so I used your five bags to earn five more.' 21The master answered, 'You did well. You are a good and loyal servant. Because you were loyal with small things, I will let you care for much greater things. Come and share my joy with me.'

22"Then the servant who had been given two bags of gold came to the master and said, 'Master, you gave me two bags of gold to care for, so I used your two bags to earn two more.' 23The master answered,

'You did well. You are a good and loyal servant. Because you were loyal with small things, I will let you care for much greater things. Come and share my joy with me.'

24"Then the servant who had been given one bag of gold came to the master and said, 'Master, I knew that you were a hard man. You harvest things you did not plant. You gather crops where you did not sow any seed. 25So I was afraid and went and hid your money in the ground. Here is your bag of gold.' 26The master answered, 'You are a wicked and lazy servant! You say you knew that I harvest things I did not plant and that I gather crops where I did not sow any seed. 27So you should have put my gold in the bank. Then, when I came home, I would have received my gold back with interest.'

28"So the master told his other servants, 'Take the bag of gold from that servant and give it to the servant who has ten bags of gold. 29Those who have much will get more, and they will have much more than they need. But those who do not have much will have everything taken away from them.' 30Then the master said, 'Throw that useless servant outside, into the darkness where people will cry and grind their teeth with pain.'

The King will Judge All People

31"The Son of Man will come again in his great glory, with all his angels. He will be King and sit on his great throne. ³²All the nations of the world will be gathered before him, and he will separate them into two groups as a shepherd separates the sheep from the goats. ³³The Son of Man will put the sheep on his right and the goats on his left.

³⁴"Then the King will say to the people on his right, 'Come, my Father has given you his blessing. Receive the kingdom God has prepared for you since the world was made. ³⁵I was hungry, and you gave me food. I was thirsty, and you gave me something to drink. I was alone and away from home, and you invited me into your house. ³⁶I was without clothes, and you gave me something to wear. I was sick, and you cared for me. I was in prison, and you visited me.'

³⁷"Then the good people will answer, 'Lord, when did we see you hungry and give you food, or thirsty and give you something to drink? ³⁸When did we see you alone and away from home and invite you into our house? When did we see you without clothes and give you something to wear? ³⁹When did we see you sick or in prison and care for you?'

⁴⁰"Then the King will answer, 'I tell you the truth, anything you did for even the least of my people here, you also did for me.'

⁴¹"Then the King will say to those on his left, 'Go away from me. You will be punished. Go into the fire that burns for ever that was prepared for the devil and his angels. ⁴²I was hungry, and you gave me nothing to eat. I was thirsty, and you gave me nothing to drink. ⁴³I was alone and away from home, and you did not invite me into your house. I was without clothes, and you gave me nothing to wear. I was sick and in prison, and you did not care for me.'

⁴⁴"Then those people will answer, 'Lord, when did we see you hungry or thirsty or alone and away from home or without clothes or sick or in prison? When did we see these things and not help you?'

⁴⁵"Then the King will answer, 'I tell you the truth, anything you refused to do for even the least of my people here, you refused to do for me.'

⁴⁶"These people will go off to be punished for ever, but the good people will go to live for ever.''

Jesus' story about sheep and goats (vs 32,33) is really about how people have cared for others.

Think

What do you think Jesus is saying it's like when:

- you help others who are in need (vs 35,36)?
- you refuse to help others who are in need (vs 43,45)?

Pray

Ask Jesus to show you someone with a need that you can do something about. Now ask him to help you do what you can.

Messy love

When you love someone very much, sometimes you do things for them which:

- some people find embarrassing
- are spur of the moment
- cost you

 Matthew 26:1–19

The Plan to Kill Jesus

26 After Jesus finished saying all these things, he told his followers, 2"You know that the day after tomorrow is the day of the Passover Feast. On that day the Son of Man will be given to his enemies to be crucified."

3Then the leading priests and the Jewish elders had a meeting at the palace of the high priest, named Caiaphas. 4At the meeting, they planned to set a trap to arrest Jesus and kill him. 5But they said, "We must not do it during the feast, because the people might cause a riot."

Perfume for Jesus' Burial

6Jesus was in Bethany at the house of Simon, who had a skin disease. 7While Jesus was there, a woman approached him with an alabaster jar filled with expensive perfume. She poured this perfume on Jesus' head while he was eating.

8His followers were upset when they saw the woman do this. They asked, "Why waste that perfume? 9It could have been sold for a great deal of money and the money given to the poor."

10Knowing what had happened, Jesus said, "Why are you troubling this woman? She did an excellent thing for me. 11You will always have the poor with you, but you will not always have me. 12This woman poured perfume on my body to prepare me for burial. 13I tell you the truth, wherever the Good News is preached in all the world, what this woman has done will be told, and people will remember her."

Judas Becomes an Enemy of Jesus

14Then one of the twelve apostles, Judas Iscariot, went to talk to the leading priests. 15He said, "What will you pay me for giving Jesus to you?" And they gave him 30 silver coins. 16After that, Judas watched for the best time to turn Jesus over.

Jesus Eats the Passover Meal

17On the first day of the Feast of Unleavened Bread, the followers came to Jesus. They said, "Where do you want us to prepare for you to eat the Passover meal?"

18Jesus answered, "Go into the city to a certain man and tell him, 'The Teacher says: the chosen time is near. I will have the Passover with my followers at your house.'" 19The followers did what Jesus told them to do, and they prepared the Passover meal.

When the woman in the story poured the oil over Jesus' head, she did it because she loved him. It didn't matter how messy it was, it didn't matter how expensive it was. She did it because she loved Jesus. The bottle of perfume probably cost her everything she had, and she gave it all up for Jesus.

Think

Have you ever done anything really extravagant for someone out of love? Is there anyone for whom you would do something like that? Would you do this for God?

Pray

Ask God to help you love him more, and to show that love in the way you behave towards other people.

Extra

... but whatever you do, don't feel guilty about not doing enough. God doesn't want you to love him just out of a sense of guilt or because you feel you have to. Try it out, but remember, it should be free. No one can force you to do it.

Let down

Everyone gets let down sometimes. Has someone you cared about let you down or betrayed you? How did it feel?

 Matthew 26:20–46

²⁰In the evening Jesus was sitting at the table with his twelve followers. ²¹As they were eating, Jesus said, "I tell you the truth, one of you will turn against me."

²²This made the followers very sad. Each one began to say to Jesus, "Surely, Lord, I am not the one who will turn against you, am I?"

²³Jesus answered, "The man who has dipped his hand with me into the bowl is the one who will turn against me. ²⁴The Son of Man will die, just as the Scriptures say. But how terrible it will be for the person who hands the Son of Man over to be killed. It would be better for him if he had never been born."

²⁵Then Judas, who would give Jesus to his enemies, said to Jesus, "Teacher, surely I am not the one, am I?"

Jesus answered, "Yes, it is you."

The Lord's Supper

²⁶While they were eating, Jesus took some bread and thanked God for it and broke it. Then he gave it to his followers and said, "Take this bread and eat it; this is my body."

²⁷Then Jesus took a cup and thanked God for it and gave it to the followers. He said, "Every one of you drink this. ²⁸This is my blood which is the new agreement that God makes with his people. This blood is poured out for many to forgive their sins. ²⁹I tell you this: I will not drink of this fruit of the vine again until that day when I drink it new with you in my Father's kingdom."

³⁰After singing a hymn, they went out to the Mount of Olives.

Jesus' Followers will Leave Him

³¹Jesus told his followers, "Tonight you will all stumble in your faith on account of me, because it is written in the Scriptures:

'I will kill the shepherd,
    and the sheep will scatter.'

Zechariah 13:7

³²But after I rise from the dead, I will go ahead of you into Galilee."

³³Peter said, "Everyone else may stumble in their faith because of you, but I will not."

³⁴Jesus said, "I tell you the truth, tonight before the cockerel crows you will say three times that you don't know me."

³⁵But Peter said, "I will never say that I don't know you! I will even die with you!" And all the other followers said the same thing.

Jesus Prays Alone

³⁶Then Jesus went with his followers to a place called Gethsemane. He said to them, "Sit here while I go over there and pray." ³⁷He took Peter and the two sons of Zebedee with him, and he began to be very sad and troubled. ³⁸He said to them, "My heart is full of sorrow, to the point of death. Stay here and watch with me."

³⁹After walking a little farther away from them, Jesus fell to the ground and prayed, "My Father, if it is possible, do not give me this cup of suffering. But do what you want, not what I want." ⁴⁰Then Jesus went

back to his followers and found them asleep. He said to Peter, "You men, could you not stay awake with me for one hour? ⁴¹Stay awake and pray for strength against temptation. The spirit wants to do what is right, but the body is weak."

⁴²Then Jesus went away a second time and prayed, "My Father, if it is not possible for this painful thing to be taken from me, and if I must do it, I pray that what you want will be done."

⁴³Then he went back to his followers, and again he found them asleep, because their eyes were heavy. ⁴⁴So Jesus left them and went away and prayed a third time, saying the same thing.

⁴⁵Then Jesus went back to his followers and said, "Are you still sleeping and resting? The time has come for the Son of Man to be handed over to sinful people. ⁴⁶Get up, we must go. Look, here comes the man who has turned against me."

Jesus knew that Judas was going to turn him in, he knew that his friends were going to fall asleep, and he knew that Peter was going to pretend not to know him. But that didn't once stop him loving them.

Think

If you've ever been let down, what did you do? Did you forgive the people who hurt you? How did you take it? How should you take it?

Pray

Ask God to help you to forgive those people who let you down.

Extra

Christians still share bread and wine together in memory of the way Jesus did that night, just as he said. Have you taken part? Next time you see people re-enacting Jesus' last supper, think about what it means and why we do it.

Who's in control?

Strong people oppress weak people all the time. And when you see stronger people harming the weak, it's usually obvious who's in control.

 Matthew 26:47–68

Jesus is Arrested

⁴⁷While Jesus was still speaking, Judas, one of the twelve apostles, came up. With him were many people carrying swords and clubs who had been sent from the leading priests and the Jewish elders of the people. ⁴⁸Judas had planned to give them a signal, saying, "The man I kiss is Jesus. Arrest him." ⁴⁹At once Judas went to Jesus and said, "Greetings, Teacher!" and kissed him.

⁵⁰Jesus answered, "Friend, do what you came to do."

Then the people came and grabbed Jesus and arrested him. ⁵¹When that happened, one of Jesus' followers reached for his sword and pulled it out. He struck the servant of the high priest and cut off his ear.

⁵²Jesus said to the man, "Put your sword back in its place. All who use swords will be killed with swords. ⁵³Surely you know I could ask my Father, and he would give me more than twelve armies of angels. ⁵⁴But it must happen this way to bring about what the Scriptures say."

⁵⁵Then Jesus said to the crowd, "You came to get me with swords and clubs as if I were a criminal. Every day I sat in the Temple teaching, and you did not arrest me there. ⁵⁶But all these things have happened so that it will come about as the prophets wrote." Then all of Jesus' followers left him and ran away.

Jesus Before the Leaders

⁵⁷Those people who arrested Jesus led him to the house of Caiaphas, the high priest, where the teachers of the law and the Jewish elders were gathered. ⁵⁸Peter followed far behind to the courtyard of the high priest's house, and he sat down with the guards to see what would happen to Jesus.

⁵⁹The leading priests and the whole Jewish council tried to find something false against Jesus so they could kill him. ⁶⁰Many people came and told lies about him, but the council could find no real reason to kill him. Then two people came and said, ⁶¹"This man said, 'I can destroy the Temple of God and build it again in three days.'"

⁶²Then the high priest stood up and said to Jesus, "Aren't you going to answer? Don't you have something to say about their charges against you?" ⁶³But Jesus said nothing.

Again the high priest said to Jesus, "I command you by the power of the living God: tell us if you are the Christ, the Son of God."

⁶⁴Jesus answered, "Those are your words. But I tell you, in the future you will see the Son of Man sitting at the right hand of God, the Powerful One, and coming on clouds in the sky."

⁶⁵When the high priest heard this, he tore his clothes and said, "This man has

said things that are against God! We don't need any more witnesses; you all heard him say these things against God. 66What do you think?"

The people answered, "He should die."

67Then the people there spat in Jesus' face and beat him with their fists. Others slapped him. 68They said, "Prove to us that you are a prophet, you Christ! Tell us who hit you!"

Jesus is beaten up and taken away, but the funny thing is, he's totally in control. He could get a horde of avenging angels to come down and take him away. But he doesn't. Everything that happens is Jesus' call.

Think

If you've been bullied, or if you're just generally being given a hard time, remember that God is in control. He knows what you're going through, and he knows how awful it feels.

Pray

Ask God for strength to get through the hard times.

Extra

Of course, just because God's in control, it doesn't mean that you won't need help. If you are being bullied, find someone you trust – a teacher, a youth worker, someone else – and tell them about it. There is no shame in getting help.

Are you a traitor?

Do you remember three young guys, Shadrach, Meshach and Abednego, who stood up for God when things got hot?

God saved them (full story in Daniel 3).

 Matthew 26:69–27:14

Peter Says He Doesn't Know Jesus

69At that time, as Peter was sitting in the courtyard, a servant girl came to him and said, "You also were with Jesus of Galilee."

70But Peter said to all the people there that he was never with Jesus. He said, "I don't know what you are talking about."

71When he left the courtyard and was at the gate, another girl saw him. She said to the people there, "This man was with Jesus of Nazareth."

72Again, Peter said he was never with him, saying, "I swear I don't know this man Jesus!"

73A short time later, some people standing there went to Peter and said, "Surely you are one of those who followed Jesus. The way you talk proves it."

74Then Peter began to place a curse on himself and swear, "I don't know the man." At once, a cockerel crowed. 75And Peter remembered what Jesus had told him: "Before the cockerel crows, you will say three times that you don't know me." Then Peter went outside and cried bitterly.

Jesus is Taken to Pilate

27 Early the next morning, all the leading priests and elders of the people decided that Jesus should die. 2They tied him, led him away, and turned him over to Pilate, the governor.

Judas Kills Himself

3Judas, the one who had given Jesus to his enemies, saw that they had decided to kill Jesus. Then he was very sorry for what he had done. So he took the 30 silver coins back to the priests and the leaders, 4saying, "I sinned; I handed over to you an innocent man."

The leaders answered, "What is that to us? That's your problem, not ours."

5So Judas threw the money into the Temple. Then he went off and hanged himself.

6The leading priests picked up the silver coins in the Temple and said, "Our law does not allow us to keep this money with the Temple money, because it has paid for a man's death." 7So they decided to use the coins to buy Potter's Field as a place to bury strangers who died in Jerusalem. 8That is why that field is still called the Field of Blood. 9So what Jeremiah the prophet had said came true: "They took 30 silver coins. That is how little the Israelites thought he was worth. 10They used those 30 silver coins to buy the potter's field, as the Lord commanded me."

Pilate Questions Jesus

11Jesus stood before Pilate the governor, and Pilate asked him, "Are you the king of the Jews?"

Jesus answered, "Those are your words."

12When the leading priests and the elders accused Jesus, he said nothing.

13So Pilate said to Jesus, "Don't you hear them accusing you of all these things?"

14But Jesus said nothing in answer to Pilate, and Pilate was very surprised at this.

Why do you think Peter betrayed Jesus (26:70)?

How do you think Peter felt when he realised what he had done (26:75)?

Jesus had told Peter that he was going to betray him (Matthew 26:31–35).

How could Peter still go ahead and deny Jesus even though he had been warned?

Think

Have you ever kept quiet about Jesus because you're scared of what others might think, say or do?

Pray

Lord, forgive me when I let you down. Please fill me with your Spirit. Help me to be brave and not afraid of showing that I'm your follower.

The darkest time

Sometimes, it feels like there's no hope. The worst happens. Where is God in all this?

 Matthew 27:15–44

Pilate Tries to Free Jesus

15Every year at the time of Passover the governor would free one prisoner whom the people chose. 16At that time there was a man in prison, named Barabbas, who was known to be very bad. 17When the people gathered at Pilate's house, Pilate said, "Whom do you want me to set free: Barabbas or Jesus who is called the Christ?" 18Pilate knew that the people had turned Jesus over to him because they were jealous.

19While Pilate was sitting there on the judge's seat, his wife sent this message to him: "Don't have anything to do with that man, because he is innocent. Today I had a dream about him, and it troubled me very much."

20But the leading priests and elders convinced the crowd to ask for Barabbas to be freed and for Jesus to be killed.

21Pilate said, "I have Barabbas and Jesus. Which do you want me to set free for you?"

The people answered, "Barabbas."

22Pilate asked, "So what should I do with Jesus, the one called the Christ?"

They all answered, "Crucify him!"

23Pilate asked, "Why? What wrong has he done?"

But they shouted louder, "Crucify him!"

24When Pilate saw that he could do nothing about this and that a riot was starting, he took some water and washed his hands in front of the crowd. Then he said, "I am not guilty of this man's death. You are the ones who are causing it!"

25All the people answered, "We and our children will be responsible for his death."

26Then he set Barabbas free. But Jesus was beaten with whips and handed over to the soldiers to be crucified.

27The governor's soldiers took Jesus into the governor's palace, and they all gathered around him. 28They took off his clothes and put a red robe on him. 29Using thorny branches, they made a crown, put it on his head, and put a stick in his right hand. Then the soldiers bowed before Jesus and made fun of him, saying, "Hail, King of the Jews!" 30They spat on Jesus. Then they took his stick and began to beat him on the head. 31After they finished, the soldiers took off the robe and put his own clothes on him again. Then they led him away to be crucified.

Jesus is Crucified

32As the soldiers were going out of the city with Jesus, they forced a man from Cyrene, named Simon, to carry the cross for Jesus. 33They all came to the place called Golgotha, which means the Place of the Skull. 34The soldiers gave Jesus wine mixed with gall to drink. He tasted the wine but refused to drink it. 35When soldiers had crucified him, they threw lots to decide who would get his clothes. 36The soldiers sat there and continued watching him. 37They put a sign above Jesus' head with a charge against him. It said: THIS IS JESUS, THE KING OF THE JEWS. 38Two robbers were crucified beside Jesus, one on the right and the other on the left. 39People walked by and insulted Jesus and shook their heads, 40saying, "You said you could destroy the Temple and build it again in three days. So save yourself! Come down from that cross if you are really the Son of God!"

41The leading priests, the teachers of the law and the Jewish elders were also making fun of Jesus. 42They said, "He saved others, but he can't save himself! He says he is the king of Israel! If he is the king, let him come down now from the cross. Then we will believe in him. 43He trusts in God, so let God save him now, if God really wants him. He himself said, 'I am the Son of God.'" 44And in the same way, the robbers who were being crucified beside Jesus insulted him.

Jesus was the Son of God. But he still became a human being and still went through terrible suffering. And the story still has a happy ending.

Think

In the very best times and the very worst times, Jesus is with you and knows what it's like.

Pray

Thank God for Jesus. Thank him that Jesus came to earth, that he died, that he rose again. Thank God that Jesus is always with you.

Dead and . . .

What makes you believe in Jesus? Think carefully: is it because of what others have said or done, or is it because of feelings and thoughts you have had?

 Matthew 27:45–28:10

Jesus Dies

45At noon the whole country became dark, and the darkness lasted for three hours. 46At about three o'clock Jesus cried out in a loud voice, "Eli, Eli, lama sabachthani?" This means, "My God, my God, why have you rejected me?"

47Some of the people standing there who heard this said, "He is calling Elijah."

48Quickly one of them ran and got a sponge and filled it with vinegar and tied it to a stick and gave it to Jesus to drink. 49But the others said, "Don't bother him. We want to see if Elijah will come to save him."

50But Jesus cried out again in a loud voice and died.

51Then the curtain in the Temple was torn into two pieces, from the top to the bottom. Also, the earth shook and rocks broke apart. 52The graves opened, and many of God's people who had died were raised from the dead. 53They came out of the graves after Jesus was raised from the dead and went into the holy city, where they appeared to many people.

54When the army officer and the soldiers guarding Jesus saw this earthquake and everything else that happened, they were very frightened and said, "He really was the Son of God!"

55Many women who had followed Jesus from Galilee to help him were standing at a distance from the cross, watching. 56Mary Magdalene, and Mary the mother of James and Joseph, and the mother of James and John were there.

Jesus is Buried

57That evening a rich man named Joseph, a follower of Jesus from the town of Arimathea, came to Jerusalem. 58Joseph went to Pilate and asked to have Jesus' body. So Pilate gave orders for the soldiers to give it to Joseph. 59Then Joseph took the body and wrapped it in a clean linen cloth. 60He put Jesus' body in a new tomb that he had cut out of a wall of rock, and he rolled a very large stone to block the entrance of the tomb. Then Joseph went away. 61Mary Magdalene and the other woman named Mary were sitting near the tomb.

The Tomb of Jesus is Guarded

62The next day, the day after Preparation Day, the leading priests and the Pharisees went to Pilate. 63They said, "Sir, we remember that while that liar was still alive he said, 'After three days I will rise from the dead.' 64So give the order for the tomb to be guarded closely till the third day. Otherwise, his followers might come and steal the body and tell people that he has risen from the dead. That lie would be even worse than the first one."

65Pilate said, "Take some soldiers and go and guard the tomb the best way you know." 66So they all went to the tomb and made it safe from thieves by sealing the stone in the entrance and putting soldiers there to guard it.

Jesus Rises from the Dead

28 The day after the Sabbath day was the first day of the week. At dawn on the first day, Mary Magdalene and another woman named Mary went to look at the tomb.

²At that time there was a strong earthquake. An angel of the Lord came down from heaven, went to the tomb and rolled the stone away from the entrance. Then he sat on the stone. ³He was shining as bright as lightning, and his clothes were white as snow. ⁴The soldiers guarding the tomb shook with fear because of the angel, and they became like dead men.

⁵The angel said to the women, "Don't be afraid. I know that you are looking for Jesus, who has been crucified. ⁶He is not here. He has risen from the dead as he said he would. Come and see the place where his body was. ⁷And then go quickly and tell his followers, 'Jesus has risen from the dead. He is going into Galilee ahead of you, and you will see him there.'" Then the angel said, "Now I have told you."

⁸The women left the tomb quickly. They were afraid, but they were also very happy. They ran to tell Jesus' followers what had happened. ⁹Suddenly, Jesus met them and said, "Greetings." The women came up to him, took hold of his feet, and worshipped him. ¹⁰Then Jesus said to them, "Don't be afraid. Go and tell my followers to go on to Galilee, and they will see me there."

This death wasn't like others the Roman soldiers had seen. What made them realise that the person they'd crucified was different (27:54)?

What's difficult in these verses to understand (e.g. the eclipse, the earthquake)? Find out what others think.

The tearing of the Temple curtain (27:51) was a sign that Jesus' death had broken down the barrier between God and people.

Think

What difference could/does it make in your life that Jesus died for you?

Pray

Thank you, Jesus, for dying for me. Please help me to understand why you did this.

Alive!

Have you ever had a really, really big surprise? What was it? How did you react?

Matthew 28:11 – Mark 1:20

The Soldiers Report to the Leaders

11While the women went to tell Jesus' followers, some of the soldiers who had been guarding the tomb went into the city to tell the leading priests everything that had happened. 12Then the priests met with the Jewish elders and made a plan. They paid the soldiers a large amount of money 13and said to them, "Tell the people that Jesus' followers came during the night and stole the body while you were asleep. 14If the governor hears about this, we will satisfy him and save you from trouble." 15So the soldiers kept the money and did as they were told. And that story is still spread among the Jewish people even today.

Jesus Talks to His Followers

16The eleven followers went to Galilee to the mountain where Jesus had told them to go. 17On the mountain they saw Jesus and worshipped him, but some of them did not believe it was really Jesus. 18Then Jesus came to them and said, "All power in heaven and on earth is given to me. 19So go and make followers of all people in the world. Baptise them in the name of the Father and the Son and the Holy Spirit. 20Teach them to obey everything that I have taught you, and I will be with you always, even until the end of this age."

MARK

John Prepares for Jesus

1 This is the beginning of the Good News about Jesus Christ, the Son of God, 2as the prophet Isaiah wrote:

"I will send my messenger ahead of you,
    who will prepare your way." *Malachi 3:1*
3"This is a voice of one
    who calls out in the desert:
'Prepare the way for the Lord.
    Make the road straight for him.' "
                                    Isaiah 40:3

4John was baptising people in the desert and preaching a baptism of changed hearts and lives for the forgiveness of sins. 5All the people from Judea and Jerusalem were going out to him. They confessed their sins and were baptised by him in the Jordan River. 6John wore clothes made from camel's hair, had a leather belt around his waist and ate locusts and wild honey. 7This is what John preached to the people: "There is one coming after me who is greater than I; I am not good enough even to kneel down and untie his sandals. 8I baptise you with water, but he will baptise you with the Holy Spirit."

Jesus is Baptised

9At that time Jesus came from the town of Nazareth in Galilee and was baptised by John in the Jordan River. 10Immediately, as Jesus was coming up out of the water, he saw heaven open. The Holy Spirit came down on him like a dove, 11and a voice came from heaven: "You are my Son, whom I love, and I am very pleased with you."

12Then the Spirit sent Jesus into the desert. 13He was in the desert for 40 days and was tempted by Satan. He was with the wild animals, and the angels came and took care of him.

Jesus Chooses Some Followers

¹⁴After John was put in prison, Jesus went into Galilee, preaching the Good News from God. ¹⁵He said, "The right time has come. The kingdom of God is near. Change your hearts and lives and believe the Good News!"

¹⁶When Jesus was walking by Lake Galilee, he saw Simon and his brother Andrew throwing a net into the lake because they were fishermen. ¹⁷Jesus said to them, "Come follow me, and I will make you fish for people." ¹⁸So Simon and Andrew immediately left their nets and followed him.

¹⁹Going a little farther, Jesus saw two more brothers, James and John, the sons of Zebedee. They were in a boat, mending their nets. ²⁰Jesus immediately called them, and they left their father in the boat with the hired workers and followed Jesus.

The Roman soldiers had more than a surprise!

What did they see (Matthew 28:2,3, yesterday's reading)?

What was their reaction (Matthew 28:4,11–15)?

The two women had a surprise too (Matthew 28:5,9).

How did they feel (Matthew 28:5,8,10)? Why?

Think

What does Jesus rising from the dead mean for us?

Pray

Praise God for raising Jesus from the dead!

I want to . . .

Who are the "untouchables" in your school or in your street? Are they the ones who dress differently or look strange? Or are they the ones who have less than you do, who don't have the latest clothes and gizmos?

 Mark 1:21–45

Jesus Forces Out an Evil Spirit

21Jesus and his followers went to Capernaum. On the Sabbath day he went to the synagogue and began to teach. 22The people were amazed at his teaching, because he taught like a person who had authority, not like their teachers of the law. 23Just then, a man was there in the synagogue who had an evil spirit in him. He shouted, 24"Jesus of Nazareth! What do you want with us? Did you come to destroy us? I know who you are—God's Holy One!"

25Jesus commanded the evil spirit, "Be quiet! Come out of the man!" 26The evil spirit shook the man violently, gave a loud cry and then came out of him.

27The people were so amazed they asked each other, "What is happening here? This man is teaching something new, and with authority. He even gives commands to evil spirits, and they obey him." 28And the news about Jesus spread quickly everywhere in the area of Galilee.

Jesus Heals Many People

29As soon as Jesus and his followers left the synagogue, they went with James and John to the home of Simon and Andrew. 30Simon's mother-in-law was sick in bed with a fever, and the people told Jesus about her. 31So Jesus went to her bed, took her hand and helped her up. The fever left her, and she began serving them.

32That evening, after the sun went down, the people brought to Jesus all who were sick and had demons in them. 33The whole town gathered at the door. 34Jesus healed many who had different kinds of sicknesses, and he forced many demons to leave people. But he would not allow the demons to speak, because they knew who he was.

35Early the next morning, while it was still dark, Jesus woke and left the house. He went to a lonely place, where he prayed. 36Simon and his friends went to look for Jesus. 37When they found him, they said, "Everyone is looking for you!"

38Jesus answered, "We should go to other towns around here so I can preach there too. That is the reason I came." 39So he went everywhere in Galilee, preaching in the synagogues and forcing out demons.

Jesus Heals a Sick Man

40A man with a skin disease came to Jesus. He fell to his knees and begged Jesus, "You can heal me if you will."

41Jesus felt sorry for the man, so he reached out his hand and touched him and said, "I will. Be healed!" 42Immediately the disease left the man, and he was healed.

43Jesus told the man to go away at once,

but he warned him strongly, [44]"Don't tell anyone about this. But go and show yourself to the priest. And offer the gift Moses commanded for people who are made well. This will show the people what I have done." [45]The man left there, but he began to tell everyone that Jesus had healed him, and so he spread the news about Jesus. As a result, Jesus could not enter a town if people saw him. He stayed in remote places [where nobody lived], but people came to him from everywhere.

Jesus did something amazing when he met the man with skin disease (v 40). What was it (v 41)?

Imagine how this man – who would have been a social outcast – felt because of Jesus' acceptance of him. What reaction would anyone who had seen Jesus touch and heal the man have?

Think

Some people think that Jesus is only interested in the nice people. Do you reach out to the outcasts, like Jesus did?

Pray

Lord Jesus, show me the people I can reach out to with your love.

Spot the difference!

How do you reckon other people feel about you? Do they look at what you wear and how you act and put you into a little box describing you? What about God, how does God feel about you?

Mark 2:1–22

Jesus Heals a Paralysed Man

2 A few days later, when Jesus came back to Capernaum, the news spread that he was at home. ²Many people gathered together so that there was no room in the house, not even outside the door. And Jesus was teaching them God's message. ³Four people came, carrying a paralysed man. ⁴Since they could not get to Jesus because of the crowd, they dug a hole in the roof right above where he was speaking. When they got through, they lowered the mat with the paralysed man on it. ⁵When Jesus saw the faith of these people, he said to the paralysed man, "Young man, your sins are forgiven."

⁶Some of the teachers of the law were sitting there, thinking to themselves, ⁷"Why does this man say things like that? He is speaking as if he were God. Only God can forgive sins."

⁸Jesus knew immediately what these teachers of the law were thinking. So he said to them, "Why are you thinking these things? ⁹Which is easier: to tell this paralysed man, 'Your sins are forgiven,' or to tell him, 'Stand up. Take your mat and walk'? ¹⁰But I will prove to you that the Son of Man has authority on earth to forgive sins." So Jesus said to the paralysed man, ¹¹"I tell you, stand up, take your mat, and go home." ¹²Immediately the paralysed man stood up, took his mat and walked out while everyone was watching him.

The people were amazed and praised God. They said, "We have never seen anything like this!"

¹³Jesus went to the lake again. The whole crowd followed him there, and he taught them. ¹⁴While he was walking along, he saw a man named Levi son of Alphaeus, sitting in the tax collector's booth. Jesus said to him, "Follow me," and he stood up and followed Jesus.

¹⁵Later, as Jesus was having dinner at Levi's house, many tax collectors and "sinners" were eating there with Jesus and his followers. Many people like this followed Jesus. ¹⁶When the teachers of the law who were Pharisees saw Jesus eating with the tax collectors and "sinners", they asked his followers, "Why does he eat with tax collectors and sinners?"

¹⁷Jesus heard this and said to them, "It is not the healthy people who need a doctor, but the sick. I did not come to invite good people but to invite sinners."

Jesus' Followers are Criticised

¹⁸Now the followers of John and the Pharisees often gave up eating for a certain time. Some people came to Jesus and said, "Why do John's followers and the followers of the Pharisees often give up eating, but your followers don't?"

¹⁹Jesus answered, "The friends of the bridegroom do not give up eating while the bridegroom is still with them. As long as the bridegroom is with them, they cannot

give up eating. ²⁰But the time will come when the bridegroom will be taken from them, and then they will give up eating.

²¹"No one sews a patch of unshrunken cloth over a hole in an old coat. Otherwise, the patch will shrink and pull away—the new patch will pull away from the old coat.

Then the hole will be worse. ²²Also, no one ever pours new wine into old leather bags. Otherwise, the new wine will break the bags, and the wine will be ruined along with the bags. But new wine should be put into new leather bags."

Levi was a tax collector and, because of this, the majority of the Jews did not like him. Tax collectors were seen as conspirators with the Romans.

How was Levi treated by:

Jesus (vs 14,15)? _____

the Pharisees (v 16)? _____

Big difference, huh?

Think

Get this: like Levi, you're totally loved and accepted by Jesus. That can't change, even ...

- when you do things which aren't so great
- if other people's opinions of you aren't so high

Pray

Ask Jesus to help you really believe this! God thinks you're great so live knowing it!

Divided we fall

Could you imagine a football match where everyone on the same side went around tackling each other? Or what about a symphony orchestra all playing a different tune and trying to be the loudest?

Mark 2:23–3:30

Jesus is Lord of the Sabbath

23One Sabbath day, as Jesus was walking through some fields of grain, his followers began to pick some grain to eat. 24The Pharisees said to Jesus, "Why are your followers doing what is not lawful on the Sabbath day?"

25Jesus answered, "Have you never read what David did when he and those with him were hungry and needed food? 26During the time of Abiathar the high priest, David went into God's house and ate the holy bread, which is lawful only for priests to eat. And David also gave some of the bread to those who were with him."

27Then Jesus said to the Pharisees, "The Sabbath day was made to help people; they were not made to be ruled by the Sabbath day. 28So then, the Son of Man is Lord even of the Sabbath day."

Jesus Heals a Man's Hand

3 Another time when Jesus went into a synagogue, a man with a crippled hand was there. 2Some people watched Jesus closely to see if he would heal the man on the Sabbath day so they could accuse him.

3Jesus said to the man with the crippled hand, "Stand up here in the middle of everyone."

4Then Jesus asked the people, "Which is lawful on the Sabbath day: to do good or to do evil, to save a life or to kill?" But they said nothing to answer him.

5Jesus was angry as he looked at the people, and he felt very sad because they were stubborn. Then he said to the man, "Hold out your hand." The man held out his hand and it was healed. 6Then the Pharisees left and began making plans with the Herodians about a way to kill Jesus.

Many People Follow Jesus

7Jesus left with his followers for the lake, and a large crowd from Galilee followed him. 8Also many people came from Judea, from Jerusalem, from Idumea, from the lands across the Jordan River and from the area of Tyre and Sidon. When they heard what Jesus was doing, many people came to him. 9When Jesus saw the crowds, he told his followers to get a boat ready for him to keep people from crowding against him. 10He had healed many people, so all the sick were pushing towards him to touch him. 11When evil spirits saw Jesus, they fell down before him and shouted, "You are the Son of God!" 12But Jesus strongly warned them not to tell who he was.

Jesus Chooses His Twelve Apostles

13Then Jesus went up on a mountain and called to him the men he wanted, and they came to him. 14Jesus chose twelve men and called them apostles. He wanted them to be with him, and he wanted to send them out to preach 15and to have the authority to force demons out of people. 16These are the twelve men he chose: Simon (Jesus named him Peter), 17James and John, the sons of Zebedee (Jesus named them Boanerges, which means

"Sons of Thunder"), ¹⁸Andrew, Philip, Bartholomew, Matthew, Thomas, James the son of Alphaeus, Thaddaeus, Simon the Zealot ¹⁹and Judas Iscariot, who later turned against Jesus.

Some People Say Jesus Has a Devil

²⁰Then Jesus went home, but again a crowd gathered. There were so many people that Jesus and his followers could not eat. ²¹When his family heard this, they went to get him because they thought he was out of his mind. ²²But the teachers of the law from Jerusalem were saying, "Beelzebul is living inside him! He uses power from the ruler of demons to force demons out of people."

²³So Jesus called the people together and taught them with stories. He said, "Satan will not force himself out of people. ²⁴A kingdom that is divided cannot continue, ²⁵and a family that is divided cannot continue. ²⁶And if Satan is against himself and fights against his own people, he cannot continue; that is the end of Satan. ²⁷No one can enter a strong person's house and steal his things unless he first ties up the strong person. Then he can steal things from the house.

²⁸I tell you the truth, all sins that people do and all the things people say against God can be forgiven. ²⁹But anyone who speaks against the Holy Spirit will never be forgiven; he is guilty of a sin that continues for ever."

³⁰Jesus said this because the teachers of the law said that he had an evil spirit inside him.

What did Jesus' family think of him (3:21)?

Who did the teachers of the law think Jesus had living inside him (3:22)?

Who does Satan do all his fighting against (3:26)?

What is the one thing that can't be forgiven (3:29,30)?

Think

The big decision is: who was Jesus? Was he the Son of God, full of the Holy Spirit, or was he an ordinary man, possessed by some evil spirit, or just out of his mind?

Pray

Ask Jesus to reveal himself to you as you pray, and then respond in an appropriate way.

Here I am!

I sometimes wonder why God just doesn't show himself. I mean if he wants everyone to know he is there why doesn't he just appear and say, "Here I am!" Then I read the Bible and realise that is exactly what he did do.

 Mark 3:31–4:20

Jesus' True Family

³¹Then Jesus' mother and brothers arrived. Standing outside, they sent someone in to tell him to come out. ³²Many people were sitting around Jesus, and they said to him, "Your mother and brothers are waiting for you outside."

³³Jesus asked, "Who are my mother and my brothers?" ³⁴Then he looked at those sitting around him and said, "Here are my mother and my brothers! ³⁵My true brother and sister and mother and father are those who do what God wants."

A Story About Planting Seed

4 Again Jesus began teaching by the lake. A great crowd gathered around him, so he sat down in a boat near the shore. All the people stayed on the shore close to the water. ²Jesus taught them many things, using stories. He said, ³"Listen! A farmer went out to plant his seed. ⁴While he was planting, some seed fell by the road, and the birds came and ate it up. ⁵Some seed fell on rocky ground where there wasn't much earth. That seed grew very fast, because the ground was not deep. ⁶But when the sun rose, the plants dried up because they did not have deep roots. ⁷Some other seed fell among thorny weeds, which grew and choked the good plants. So those plants did not produce a crop. ⁸Some other seed fell on good ground and began to grow. It got taller and produced a crop. Some plants made 30 times more, some made 60 times more, and some made 100 times more."

⁹Then Jesus said, "You people who can hear me, listen!"

Jesus Tells Why He Used Stories

¹⁰Later, when Jesus was alone, the twelve apostles and others around him asked him about the stories.

¹¹Jesus said, "You can know the secret about the kingdom of God. But to other people I tell everything by using stories ¹²so that:

'They will look and look, but they will
    not learn.
They will listen and listen, but they will
    not understand.
If they did learn and understand,
    they would come back to me and be
    forgiven.'"   *Isaiah 6:9–10*

Jesus Explains the Seed Story

¹³Then Jesus said to his followers, "Don't you understand this story? If you don't, how will you understand any story? ¹⁴The farmer is like a person who plants God's message in people. ¹⁵Sometimes the teaching falls on the road. This is like the people who hear the teaching of God, but Satan quickly comes and takes away the teaching that was planted in them. ¹⁶Others are like the seed planted on rocky ground. They hear the teaching and quickly accept it with joy. ¹⁷But since they don't allow

the teaching to go deep into their lives, they keep it only a short time. When trouble or persecution comes because of the teaching they accepted, they quickly give up. [18]Others are like the seed planted among the thorny weeds. They hear the teaching, [19]but the worries of this life, the temptation of wealth and many other evil desires keep the teaching from growing and producing fruit in their lives. [20]Others are like the seed planted in the good ground. They hear the teaching and accept it. Then they grow and produce fruit—sometimes 30 times more, sometimes 60 times more and sometimes 100 times more."

What is the secret that Jesus is talking about (v 11)?

The words that Jesus uses can be found in the Old Testament book of Isaiah 6:9,10. Like Isaiah's hearers, not everyone accepted what Jesus was saying.

Think

When you read the Bible, or hear the words from it, what do you take away? Do you hear the words and respond to them? Jesus is offering forgiveness from anything that you have done.

Pray

Dear Lord, show yourself to me. I want to know you are there. Speak to me through the Bible; help me to understand what you say.

Extra

What is easier to remember?

- A lecture on what is right and wrong
- A good story

So, was Jesus making it easier to follow him by speaking in story form?

Has he got it in for pigs?!

Think movies ... video games ... books ... TV ... There's some dodgy spiritual stuff around, isn't there? Has any of it affected you? If you feel that you are strong, what about other people you know, have they been affected by what is out there?

 Mark 4:21–5:13

Use What You Have

21Then Jesus said to them, "Do you hide a lamp under a bowl or under a bed? No! You put the lamp on a lampstand. 22Everything that is hidden will be made clear and every secret thing will be made known. 23You people who can hear me, listen!

24"Think carefully about what you hear. The way you give to others is the way God will give to you, but God will give you even more. 25Those who have understanding will be given more. But those who do not have understanding, even what they have will be taken away from them."

Jesus Uses a Story About Seed

26Then Jesus said, "The kingdom of God is like someone who plants seed in the ground. 27Night and day, whether the person is asleep or awake, the seed still grows, but the person does not know how it grows. 28By itself the earth produces grain. First the plant grows, then the ear and then all the grain in the ear. 29When the grain is ready, the farmer cuts it, because the harvest time has come."

A Story About Mustard Seed

30Then Jesus said, "How can I show you what the kingdom of God is like? What story can I use to explain it? 31The kingdom of God is like a mustard seed, the smallest seed you plant in the ground. 32But when planted, this seed grows and becomes the largest of all garden plants. It produces large branches, and the wild birds can make nests in its shade."

33Jesus used many stories like these to teach the crowd God's message—as much as they could understand. 34He always used stories to teach them. But when he and his followers were alone, Jesus explained everything to them.

Jesus Calms a Storm

35That evening, Jesus said to his followers, "Let's go across the lake." 36Leaving the crowd behind, they took him in the boat just as he was. There were also other boats with them. 37A very strong wind came up on the lake. The waves came over the sides and into the boat so that it was already full of water. 38Jesus was at the back of the boat, sleeping with his head on a pillow. His followers woke him and said, "Teacher, don't you care that we are drowning!"

39Jesus stood up and commanded the wind and said to the waves, "Quiet! Be still!" Then the wind stopped, and it became completely calm.

40Jesus said to his followers, "Why are you afraid? Do you still have no faith?"

41The followers were very afraid and asked each other, "Who is this? Even the wind and the waves obey him!"

A Man with Demons Inside Him

5 Jesus and his followers went to the other side of the lake to the area of the Gerasene people. ²When Jesus got out of the boat, instantly a man with an evil spirit came to him from the burial caves. ³This man lived in the caves, and no one could tie him up, not even with a chain. ⁴Many times people had used chains to tie the man's hands and feet, but he always broke them off. No one was strong enough to control him. ⁵Day and night he would wander around the burial caves and on the hills, screaming and cutting himself with stones. ⁶While Jesus was still far away, the man saw him, ran to him and fell down before him.

⁷The man shouted in a loud voice, "What do you want with me, Jesus, Son of the Most High God? I command you in God's name not to torture me!" ⁸He said this because Jesus was saying to him, "You evil spirit, come out of the man."

⁹Then Jesus asked him, "What is your name?"

He answered, "My name is Legion, because we are many spirits." ¹⁰He begged Jesus again and again not to send them out of that area.

¹¹A large herd of pigs was feeding on a hill near there. ¹²The demons begged Jesus, "Send us into the pigs; let us go into them." ¹³So Jesus allowed them to do this. The evil spirits left the man and went into the pigs. Then the herd of pigs—about 2,000 of them—rushed down the hill into the lake and were drowned.

What was causing the problem for the man (5:2)?

Whatever the exact nature of this guy's problems, he was in trouble (5:3–5).

What did the man call Jesus (5:7)?

What did the demons ask Jesus not to do (5:7)?

Think

Scary: there are powerful spirits around which aren't from God (5:8).

Safe: Jesus has power over them. Totally (5:12,13).

Pray

If you've seen, heard or read anything which still makes you shudder, ask Jesus to sort it.

Don't be afraid: just believe

Sometimes, just plucking up the courage to do a small thing can change everything.

 Mark 5:14–36

14The herdsmen ran away and went to the town and to the countryside, telling everyone about this. So people went out to see what had happened. 15They came to Jesus and saw the man who used to have the many evil spirits, sitting, clothed and in his right mind. And they were frightened. 16The people who saw this told the others what had happened to the man who had the demons living in him, and they told about the pigs. 17Then the people began to beg Jesus to leave their area.

18As Jesus was getting back into the boat, the man who was freed from the demons begged to go with him.

19But Jesus would not let him. He said, "Go home to your family and tell them how much the Lord has done for you and how he has had mercy on you." 20So the man left and began to tell the people in the Ten Towns about what Jesus had done for him. And everyone was amazed.

Jesus Gives Life to a Dead Girl and Heals a Sick Woman

21When Jesus went in the boat back to the other side of the lake, a large crowd gathered around him there. 22A leader of the synagogue, named Jairus, came there, saw Jesus and fell at his feet. 23He begged Jesus, saying again and again, "My daughter is dying. Please come and put your hands on her so she will be healed and will live." 24So Jesus went with him.

A large crowd followed Jesus and pushed very close around him. 25Among them was a woman who had been bleeding for twelve years. 26She had suffered very much from many doctors and had spent all the money she had, but instead of improving, she was getting worse. 27When the woman heard about Jesus, she came up behind him in the crowd and touched his coat. 28She thought, "If I can just touch his clothes, I will be healed." 29Instantly her bleeding stopped, and she felt in her body that she was healed from her disease.

30At once Jesus felt power go out from him. So he turned around in the crowd and asked, "Who touched my clothes?"

31His followers said, "Look at how many people are pushing against you! And you ask, 'Who touched me?'"

32But Jesus continued looking around to see who had touched him. 33The woman, knowing that she was healed, came and fell at Jesus' feet. Shaking with fear, she told him the whole truth. 34Jesus said to her, "Dear woman, you are made well because you believed. Go in peace; be healed of your disease."

35While Jesus was still speaking, some people came from the house of the synagogue leader. They said, "Your daughter is dead. There is no need to bother the teacher any more."

36But Jesus paid no attention to what they said. He told the synagogue leader, "Don't be afraid; just believe."

Why do you think the woman Jesus healed didn't come up to him and ask him to heal her?

Why do you think Jesus treated her so well?

If you were in her position, what would you have done?

Think

The woman Jesus healed didn't have to be especially brave. She just had to do one little thing. Is there anything you need to do to allow God to do something important in your life? It might not even be a big thing.

Pray

God, help me to be brave enough to do what you want me to do, so you can work in my life.

Familiarity=contempt

Sometimes, it's hardest to talk to the people who know you the best. They saw you grow up. They know everything about you – even the embarrassing stuff you did when you were a kid. They might even have seen your baby photos!

 Mark 5:37–6:20

³⁷Jesus let only Peter, James and John the brother of James go with him. ³⁸When they came to the house of the synagogue leader, Jesus found many people there making lots of noise and crying loudly. ³⁹Jesus entered the house and said to them, "Why are you crying and making so much noise? The child is not dead, only asleep." ⁴⁰But they laughed at him. So, after throwing them out of the house, Jesus took the child's father and mother and his three followers into the room where the child was. ⁴¹Taking hold of the girl's hand, he said to her, "Talitha, koum!" (This means, "Young girl, I tell you to stand up!") ⁴²At once the girl stood right up and began walking. (She was twelve years old.) Everyone was completely amazed. ⁴³Jesus gave them strict orders not to tell people about this. Then he told them to give the girl something to eat.

Jesus Goes to His Home Town

6 Jesus left there and went to his home town, and his followers went with him. ²On the Sabbath day he taught in the synagogue. Many people heard him and were amazed, saying, "Where did this man get these teachings? What is this wisdom that has been given to him? And where did he get the power to do miracles? ³He is just the carpenter, the son of Mary and the brother of James, Joseph, Judas and Simon. And his sisters are here with us." So the people were upset with Jesus.

⁴Jesus said to them, "A prophet is honoured everywhere except in his home town and with his own people and in his own home." ⁵So Jesus was not able to work any miracles there except to heal a few sick people by putting his hands on them. ⁶He was amazed at how many people had no faith.

Then Jesus went to other villages in that area and taught. ⁷He called his twelve followers together and got ready to send them out two by two and gave them authority over evil spirits. ⁸This is what Jesus commanded them: "Take nothing for your trip except a walking stick. Take no bread, no bag and no money in your pockets. ⁹Wear sandals, but take only the clothes you are wearing. ¹⁰When you enter a house, stay there until you leave that town. ¹¹If the people in a certain place refuse to welcome you or listen to you, leave that place. Shake its dust off your feet as a warning to them."

¹²So the followers went out and preached that people should change their hearts and lives. ¹³They forced many demons out and put olive oil on many sick people and healed them.

How John the Baptist was Killed

¹⁴King Herod heard about Jesus, because he was now well known. Some people said, "He is John the Baptist, who has risen from the dead. That is why he can work these miracles."

15Others said, "He is Elijah."

Other people said, "Jesus is a prophet, like the prophets who lived long ago."

16When Herod heard this, he said, "I killed John by cutting off his head. Now he has risen from the dead!"

17Herod himself had ordered his soldiers to arrest John and put him in prison in order to please his wife, Herodias. She had been the wife of Philip, Herod's brother, but then Herod had married her. 18John had been telling Herod, "It is not lawful for you to be married to your brother's wife." 19So Herodias hated John and wanted to kill him. But she couldn't, 20because Herod was afraid of John and protected him. He knew John was a good and holy man. Also, though John's preaching always bothered him, he enjoyed listening to John.

People might not react well to what you've got to say, just like Jesus' followers and just like John. They all had tough audiences:

- an important man who wasn't going to like what he heard (6:17,18)

- complete strangers (6:11)

- family and childhood friends (6:2,3)

Who was the toughest audience? Which audience would you have wanted to speak to the least? Who had the most success?

Think

If your family don't understand what you believe, it can be really tough. I know – I've had to face it myself. Don't get upset if they don't want to hear what you've got to say. You shouldn't ever give up on them, but you should recognise that there may be other people who they might listen to rather than you.

Pray

Lord, help me to have patience with the people who know me best.

Just you and him

How and when do you spend time alone with Jesus? Do you manage a few moments at the end of the day, or do you rush through a quick prayer as you wake up? Maybe you have a regular time that you spend with him, set aside from the rest of the day.

Mark 6:21–44

21Then the perfect time came for Herodias to cause John's death. On Herod's birthday, he gave a dinner party for the most important government leaders, the commanders of his army and the most important people in Galilee. 22When the daughter of Herodias came in and danced, she pleased Herod and the people eating with him.

So King Herod said to the girl, "Ask me for anything you want, and I will give it to you." 23He promised her, "Anything you ask for I will give to you—up to half of my kingdom."

24The girl went to her mother and asked, "What should I ask for?"

Her mother answered, "Ask for the head of John the Baptist."

25At once the girl went back to the king and said to him, "I want the head of John the Baptist right now on a dish."

26Although the king was very sad, he had made a promise, and his dinner guests had heard it. So he did not want to refuse what she asked. 27Immediately the king sent a soldier to bring John's head. The soldier went and cut off John's head in the prison 28and brought it back on a dish. He gave it to the girl, and the girl gave it to her mother. 29When John's followers heard this, they came and got John's body and put it in a tomb.

More than 5,000 Fed

30The apostles gathered around Jesus and told him about all the things they had done and taught. 31Crowds of people were coming and going so that Jesus and his followers did not even have time to eat. He said to them, "Come away by yourselves, and we will go to a lonely place to get some rest."

32So they went in a boat by themselves to a lonely place. 33But many people saw them leave and recognised them. So from all the towns they ran to the place where Jesus was going, and they got there before him. 34When he arrived, he saw a great crowd waiting. He felt sorry for them, because they were like sheep without a shepherd. So he began to teach them many things.

35When it was late in the day, his followers came to him and said, "No one lives in this place, and it is already very late. 36Send the people away so they can go to the countryside and towns around here to buy themselves something to eat."

37But Jesus answered, "You give them something to eat."

They said to him, "We would all have to work a month to earn enough money to buy that much bread!"

38Jesus asked them, "How many loaves of bread do you have? Go and see."

When they found out, they said, "Five loaves and two fish."

39Then Jesus told his followers to have the people sit in groups on the green grass. 40So they sat in groups of 50 or 100. 41Jesus took the five loaves and two fish and, looking up to heaven, he thanked

God for the food. He divided the bread and gave it to his followers for them to give to the people. Then he divided the two fish among them all. ⁴²All the people ate and were satisfied. ⁴³The followers filled twelve baskets with the leftover pieces of bread and fish. ⁴⁴There were 5,000 men who ate.

Jesus' friends needed to unwind – big time! Did they need to . . . *(circle which you think is right)*

- be quiet *or* talk?

- be alone with Jesus *or* with the crowd?

- chill *or* get busy?

Who noticed that they needed a break (v 31)?

These verses lead into the feeding of the 5,000 (vs 32–43) where Jesus met more than just the disciples' needs.

Think

You're spending time with Jesus now! How else could you have time alone with Jesus? Have you ever stopped doing something because you realised you needed a break and a chat with Jesus?

Pray

Take this kind of a break: find time to be with Jesus – just you and him. Talk with him about your day (v 30).

Duty

If God is more important than anything else, you don't have to bother with other people, right?

Wrong.

 Mark 6:45–7:13

Jesus Walks on the Water

⁴⁵Immediately Jesus told his followers to get into the boat and go ahead of him to Bethsaida across the lake. He stayed behind to send the people home. ⁴⁶After sending them away, he went into the hills to pray.

⁴⁷That night, the boat was in the middle of the lake, and Jesus was alone on the land. ⁴⁸He saw his followers struggling hard to row the boat, because the wind was blowing against them. Between three and six o'clock in the morning, Jesus came to them, walking on the water, and he wanted to walk past the boat. ⁴⁹But when they saw him walking on the water, they thought he was a ghost and cried out. ⁵⁰They all saw him and were afraid. But immediately Jesus spoke to them and said, "Have courage! It is I. Do not be afraid." ⁵¹Then he got into the boat with them, and the wind became calm. The followers were greatly amazed. ⁵²They did not understand about the miracle of the five loaves, because their minds were closed.

⁵³When they had crossed the lake, they came to shore at Gennesaret and tied the boat there. ⁵⁴When they got out of the boat, people immediately recognised Jesus. ⁵⁵They ran everywhere in that area and began to bring sick people on mats wherever they heard he was. ⁵⁶And everywhere he went—into towns, cities or countryside—the people brought the sick to the market-places. They begged him to let them touch just the edge of his coat, and all who touched it were healed.

Obey God's Law

7 When some Pharisees and some teachers of the law came from Jerusalem, they gathered around Jesus. ²They saw some of Jesus' followers eating food with hands that were not clean, that is, they hadn't washed them. ³(The Pharisees and all the Jews never eat before washing their hands in a special way according to their unwritten laws. ⁴And when they buy something in the market, they never eat it until they have washed themselves in a special way. They also follow many other unwritten laws, such as the washing of cups, pitchers and pots.)

⁵The Pharisees and the teachers of the law said to Jesus, "Why don't your followers obey the unwritten laws which have been handed down to us? Why do your followers eat their food with hands that are not clean?"

⁶Jesus answered, "Isaiah was right when he spoke about you hypocrites. He wrote,

'These people show honour to me with words,

but their hearts are far from me.

⁷Their worship of me is worthless.

The things they teach are nothing but human rules.'   *Isaiah 29:13*

8You have stopped following the commands of God, and you follow only human teachings."

9Then Jesus said to them, "You cleverly ignore the commands of God so you can follow your own teachings. 10Moses said, 'Honour your father and your mother,' and 'Anyone who says cruel things to his father or mother must be put to death.'

11But you say a person can tell his father or mother, 'I have something I could use to help you, but it is Corban—a gift to God.' 12You no longer let that person use that money for his father or his mother. 13By your own rules, which you teach people, you are rejecting what God said. And you do many things like that."

The Pharisees were telling their parents they weren't going to bother with them because they said that they should be giving all their help up to God. But Jesus said that if they were really following God as they should be, they'd be looking after mum and dad.

And this was only one of the things they did.

Jesus had healed many, many people and had even walked on water before he said what he had to say to the Pharisees. But they still weren't going to listen. Why didn't the miracles make a difference?

Think

Have you ever used church as an excuse to avoid doing something for someone else?

Pray

Lord, help me to serve you in all parts of my life, and to remember that in serving others, I serve you.

Be bold!

How would you finish this sentence? Use the space to have a go.
Sometimes I hold back from Jesus because _____

_____

_____

 Mark 7:14–37

¹⁴After Jesus called the crowd to him again, he said, "Every person should listen to me and understand what I am saying. ¹⁵There is nothing people put into their bodies that makes them unclean. People are made unclean by the things that come out of them." ¹⁶

¹⁷When Jesus left the people and went into the house, his followers asked him about this story. ¹⁸Jesus said, "Do you still not understand? Surely you know that nothing that enters someone from the outside can make that person unclean. ¹⁹It does not go into the heart, but into the stomach. Then it goes out of the body." (When Jesus said this, he meant that no longer was any food unclean for people to eat.)

²⁰And Jesus said, "The things that come out of people are the things that make them unclean. ²¹All these evil things begin inside people, in the heart: evil thoughts, sexual sins, stealing, murder, adultery, ²²greed, evil actions, lying, doing sinful things, jealousy, speaking evil of others, pride and foolish living. ²³All these evil things come from inside and make people unclean."

Jesus Helps a Non-Jewish Woman

²⁴Jesus left that place and went to the area around Tyre. When he went into a house, he did not want anyone to know he was there, but he could not stay hidden. ²⁵A woman whose daughter had an evil spirit in her heard that he was there. So she quickly came to Jesus and fell at his feet. ²⁶She was Greek, born in Phoenicia, in Syria. She begged Jesus to force the demon out of her daughter.

²⁷Jesus told the woman, "It is not right to take the children's bread and give it to the dogs. First let the children eat all they want."

²⁸But she answered, "Yes, Lord, but even the dogs under the table can eat the children's crumbs."

²⁹Then Jesus said, "Because of your answer, you may go. The demon has left your daughter."

³⁰The woman went home and found her daughter lying in bed; the demon was gone.

Jesus Heals a Deaf Man

³¹Then Jesus left the area around Tyre and went through Sidon to Lake Galilee, to the area of the Ten Towns. ³²While he was there, some people brought a man to him who was deaf and could not talk plainly. The people begged Jesus to put his hand on the man to heal him.

³³Jesus led the man away from the crowd, by himself. He put his fingers in the man's ears and then spat and touched the man's tongue. ³⁴Looking up to heaven, he sighed and said to the man, "Ephphatha!" (This means, "Be opened.") ³⁵Instantly the man was able to hear and to use his tongue so that he spoke clearly.

36Jesus commanded the people not to tell anyone about what happened. But the more he commanded them, the more they told about it. 37They were completely amazed and said, "Jesus does everything well. He makes the deaf hear! And those who can't talk he makes able to speak."

There were different ethnic groups in Israel back then, too (v 26)! This woman saw Jesus was working mainly with Jews and could easily have kept away from him, but she didn't. What did she get right?

She believed Jesus could change her situation (v 25).

She knew his love stretched to everyone (v 26).

She didn't give up (v 28).

Think

How about you? Do you think Jesus can change your situation and love you?

Pray

... about what holds you back from Jesus – and ask God to help you be more like this woman.

Give and take

Before you get into today's Bible bit, choose either a disciple or someone in the crowd. OK? Now picture yourself as that person, as you read:

 Mark 8:1-26

More than 4,000 People Fed

8 Another time there was a great crowd with Jesus that had nothing to eat. So Jesus called his followers and said, ²"I feel sorry for these people, because they have already been with me for three days, and they have nothing to eat. ³If I send them home hungry, they will faint on the way. Some of them live a long way from here."

⁴Jesus' followers answered, "How can we get enough bread to feed all these people? We are far away from any town."

⁵Jesus asked, "How many loaves of bread do you have?"

They answered, "Seven."

⁶Jesus told the people to sit on the ground. Then he took the seven loaves, gave thanks to God, and divided the bread. He gave the pieces to his followers to give to the people, and they did so. ⁷The followers also had a few small fish. After Jesus gave thanks for the fish, he told his followers to give them to the people as well. ⁸All the people ate and were satisfied. Then his followers filled seven baskets with the leftover pieces of food. ⁹There were about 4,000 people who ate. After they had eaten, Jesus sent them home. ¹⁰Then right away he got into a boat with his followers and went to the area of Dalmanutha.

The Leaders Ask for a Miracle

¹¹The Pharisees came to Jesus and began to ask him questions. Hoping to trap him, they asked Jesus for a miracle from God. ¹²Jesus sighed deeply and said,

"Why do you people ask for a miracle as a sign? I tell you the truth, no sign will be given to you." ¹³Then Jesus left the Pharisees and went in the boat to the other side of the lake.

Guard Against Wrong Teachings

¹⁴His followers had only one loaf of bread with them in the boat; they had forgotten to bring more. ¹⁵Jesus warned them, "Be careful! Beware of the yeast of the Pharisees and the yeast of Herod."

¹⁶His followers discussed the meaning of this, saying, "He said this because we have no bread."

¹⁷Knowing what they were talking about, Jesus asked them, "Why are you talking about not having bread? Do you still not see or understand? Are your minds closed? ¹⁸You have eyes, but you don't really see. You have ears, but you don't really listen. Remember when ¹⁹I divided five loaves of bread for the 5,000? How many baskets did you fill with leftover pieces of food?"

They answered, "Twelve."

²⁰"And when I divided seven loaves of bread for the 4,000, how many baskets did you fill with leftover pieces of food?"

They answered, "Seven."

²¹Then Jesus said to them, "Don't you understand yet?"

Jesus Heals a Blind Man

²²Jesus and his followers came to Bethsaida. There some people brought a blind man to Jesus and begged him to touch the

man. ²³So Jesus took the blind man's hand and led him out of the village. Then he spat on the man's eyes and put his hands on the man and asked, "Can you see now?"

²⁴The man looked up and said, "Yes, I see people, but they look like trees walking around."

²⁵Again Jesus put his hands on the man's eyes. Then the man opened his eyes wide and they were healed, and he was able to see everything clearly. ²⁶Jesus told him to go home, saying, "Don't go into the town."

Did you notice the following facts?

The crowd:

... saw Jesus cared about them.

... saw Jesus meet their needs – big time!

The disciples:

... gave Jesus what they had – which didn't seem much!

... saw Jesus make it HUGE!

Jesus still takes what we offer – our time, our abilities, ourselves – and works it into something much bigger!

Think

In what ways could we continue Jesus' work to feed the hungry today?

Pray

Give yourself to Jesus again – ask him to work with you and through you ... and see what happens!

Jesus still wants to provide for us – so what do you need right now?

Ask Jesus for what you need.

Revealed!

Jesus knew he was going to die. But he also knew that it was all part of the plan. As the plan's end grew nearer and nearer, things around Jesus got stranger and stranger.

Mark 8:27–9:13

Peter Says Jesus is the Christ

27Jesus and his followers went to the towns around Caesarea Philippi. While they were travelling, Jesus asked them, "Who do people say I am?"

28They answered, "Some say you are John the Baptist. Others say you are Elijah, and others say you are one of the prophets."

29Then Jesus asked, "But who do you say I am?"

Peter answered, "You are the Christ."

30Jesus warned his followers not to tell anyone who he was.

31Then Jesus began to teach them that the Son of Man must suffer many things and that he would be rejected by the Jewish elders, the leading priests and the teachers of the law. He told them that the Son of Man must be killed and then rise from the dead after three days. 32Jesus told them plainly what would happen. Then Peter took Jesus aside and began to tell him not to talk like that. 33But Jesus turned and looked at his followers. Then he told Peter not to talk in that way. He said, "Go away from me, Satan! You don't care about the things of God, but only about things people think are important."

34Then Jesus called the crowd to him, along with his followers. He said, "If people want to follow me, they must give up the things they want. They must be willing even to give up their lives to follow me. 35Those who want to save their lives will give up true life. But those who give up their lives for me and for the Good News

will have true life. 36It is worth nothing for them to have the whole world if they lose their souls. 37They could never pay enough to buy back their souls. 38The people who live now are living in a sinful and evil time. If people are ashamed of me and my teaching, the Son of Man will be ashamed of them when he comes with his Father's glory and with the holy angels."

9 Then Jesus said to the people, "I tell you the truth, some people standing here will see the kingdom of God come with power before they die."

Jesus Talks with Moses and Elijah

2Six days later, Jesus took Peter, James and John up on a high mountain by themselves. While they watched, Jesus' appearance was changed. 3His clothes became shining white, whiter than any person could make them. 4Then Elijah and Moses appeared to them, talking with Jesus.

5Peter said to Jesus, "Teacher, it is good that we are here. Let us make three tents—one for you, one for Moses and one for Elijah." 6Peter did not know what to say, because he and the others were so frightened.

7Then a cloud came and covered them, and a voice came from the cloud, saying, "This is my Son, whom I love. Listen to him!"

8Suddenly Peter, James and John looked around, but they saw only Jesus there alone with them.

⁹As they were coming down the mountain, Jesus commanded them not to tell anyone about what they had seen until the Son of Man had risen from the dead.

¹⁰So the followers obeyed Jesus, but they discussed what he meant about rising from the dead.

¹¹Then they asked Jesus, "Why do the teachers of the law say that Elijah must come first?"

¹²Jesus answered, "They are right to say that Elijah must come first and make everything the way it should be. But why does the Scripture say that the Son of Man will suffer much and that people will treat him as if he were nothing? ¹³I tell you that Elijah has already come. And people did to him whatever they wanted to do, just as the Scriptures said it would happen."

Peter knew that Jesus was the special one who would save everybody, but he didn't really understand how. So when Jesus talked about dying, Peter took him to one side and told him not to say stuff like that. And when Moses and Elijah came to talk to Jesus, Peter had no idea what was going on.

Moses and Elijah were the two most important prophets in the Old Testament. When they came to see Jesus, it meant that God was saying that Jesus was finishing off the job they began. He was getting ready to die for everyone. Even God speaks – "listen to Jesus". This was one of the things that happened that proved Jesus was the special one.

Think

Why do you think Jesus told the disciples not to tell anyone?

If you were Peter, how would you react to the stuff that happened around Jesus?

Jesus says that Elijah had already come back. Who does he mean?

Pray

Ask God to help you understand more about who Jesus is.

Mind-blowing

Think of something or someone really powerful – OK? With their power, what things can they do which you can't? If you had their power would you do anything differently to what they do? Now ... could you be that powerful?

Mark 9:14–37

Jesus Heals a Sick Boy

14When Jesus, Peter, James and John came back to the other followers, they saw a great crowd around them and the teachers of the law arguing with them. 15But as soon as the crowd saw Jesus, the people were surprised and ran to welcome him.

16Jesus asked, "What are you arguing about?"

17A man answered, "Teacher, I brought my son to you. He has an evil spirit in him that stops him from talking. 18When the spirit attacks him, it throws him on the ground. Then my son foams at the mouth, grinds his teeth and becomes very stiff. I asked your followers to force the evil spirit out, but they couldn't."

19Jesus answered, "You people have no faith. How long must I stay with you? How long must I put up with you? Bring the boy to me."

20So the followers brought him to Jesus. As soon as the evil spirit saw Jesus, it made the boy lose control of himself, and he fell down and rolled on the ground, foaming at the mouth.

21Jesus asked the boy's father, "How long has this been happening?"

The father answered, "Since he was very young. 22The spirit often throws him into a fire or into water to kill him. If you can do anything for him, please have pity on us and help us."

23Jesus said to the father, "You said, 'If you can!' All things are possible for the one who believes."

24Immediately the father cried out, "I do believe! Help me to believe more!"

25When Jesus saw that a crowd was quickly gathering, he ordered the evil spirit, saying, "You spirit that makes people unable to hear or speak, I command you to come out of this boy and never enter him again!"

26The evil spirit screamed and caused the boy to fall on the ground again. Then the spirit came out. The boy looked as if he were dead, and many people said, "He is dead!" 27But Jesus took hold of the boy's hand and helped him to stand up.

28When Jesus went into the house, his followers began asking him privately, "Why couldn't we force that evil spirit out?"

29Jesus answered, "That kind of spirit can only be forced out by prayer."

Jesus Talks About His Death

30Then Jesus and his followers left that place and went through Galilee. He didn't want anyone to know where he was, 31because he was teaching his followers. He said to them, "The Son of Man will be handed over to people, and they will kill him. After three days, he will rise from the dead." 32But the followers did not understand what Jesus meant, and they were afraid to ask him.

Who is the Greatest?

³³Jesus and his followers went to Capernaum. When they went into a house there, he asked them, "What were you arguing about on the road?" ³⁴But the followers did not answer, because their argument on the road was about which one of them was the greatest.

³⁵Jesus sat down and called the twelve apostles to him. He said, "Whoever wants to be the most important must be last of all and servant of all."

³⁶Then Jesus took a small child and had him stand among them. Taking the child in his arms, he said, ³⁷"Whoever accepts a child like this in my name accepts me. And whoever accepts me accepts the One who sent me."

What's the problem here (v 17)?

Who had tried to sort it (v 18)?

A bit arrogant of them, wasn't it? But Jesus had given them that power (6:7). So, why couldn't they deal with the problem (v 19)?

Think

What do you think Jesus meant by "faith" here (v 19)?

Through the Holy Spirit, Jesus gives us power, too – check out John 14:12 (wow!) and Acts 1:8.

Pray

Ask Jesus to fill you with the Holy Spirit, so that you can witness to his life-changing power!

Out of harm's way

What keeps you from following Jesus? What gets in Jesus' way? Do you allow it to get in the way?

 Mark 9:38–10:16

Anyone Not Against Us is For Us

³⁸Then John said, "Teacher, we saw someone using your name to force demons out of a person. We told him to stop, because he does not belong to our group."

³⁹But Jesus said, "Don't stop him, because anyone who uses my name to do powerful things will not easily say evil things about me. ⁴⁰Whoever is not against us is with us. ⁴¹I tell you the truth, whoever gives you a drink of water because you belong to the Christ will truly get his reward.

⁴²"If one of these little children believes in me, and someone causes that child to sin, it would be better for that person to have a large stone tied around his neck and be drowned in the sea. ⁴³If your hand causes you to sin, cut it off. It is better for you to lose part of your body and live for ever than to have two hands and go to hell, where the fire never goes out. ⁴⁴ ⁴⁵If your foot causes you to sin, cut it off. It is better for you to lose part of your body and to live for ever than to have two feet and be thrown into hell. ⁴⁶ ⁴⁷If your eye causes you to sin, take it out. It is better for you to enter the kingdom of God with only one eye than to have two eyes and be thrown into hell. ⁴⁸In hell the worm does not die; the fire is never put out. ⁴⁹Every person will be salted with fire.

⁵⁰"Salt is good, but if the salt loses its salty taste, you cannot make it salty again. So, be full of salt, and have peace with each other."

Jesus Teaches About Divorce

10 Then Jesus left that place and went into the area of Judea and across the Jordan River. Again, crowds came to him, and he taught them as he usually did.

²Some Pharisees came to Jesus and tried to trick him. They asked, "Is it right for a man to divorce his wife?"

³Jesus answered, "What did Moses command you to do?"

⁴They said, "Moses allowed a man to write out divorce papers and send her away."

⁵Jesus said, "Moses wrote that command for you because you were stubborn. ⁶But when God made the world, 'he made them male and female'. ⁷'So a man will leave his father and mother and be united with his wife, ⁸and the two will become one body.' So there are not two, but one. ⁹God has joined the two together, so no one should separate them."

¹⁰Later, in the house, his followers asked Jesus again about the question of divorce. ¹¹He answered, "Anyone who divorces his wife and marries another woman is guilty of adultery against her. ¹²And the woman who divorces her husband and marries another man is also guilty of adultery."

Jesus Accepts Children

¹³Some people brought their little children to Jesus so he could touch them, but his followers told them to stop. ¹⁴When Jesus saw this, he was upset and said to them, "Let the little children come to me.

Don't stop them, because the kingdom of God belongs to people who are like these children. 15I tell you the truth, you must accept the kingdom of God as if you were a little child, or you will never enter it." 16Then Jesus took the children in his arms, put his hands on them and blessed them.

Do you think that Jesus really meant that you should cut your hand off if it makes you do something wrong?

What do you think he meant?

What does salt do? Why is it useful?

How is a Christian like salt?

Think

Is there anything in your life you need to cut off/cut out? Try and do so. You'll feel better about it.

Pray

Lord, help me to know what to give up, so that I can be closer to you.

What's really important?

Friends? Family? Doing well at school? Take a minute to think about everything that you value.

Mark 10:17–41

A Rich Young Man's Question

17As Jesus started to leave, a man ran to him and fell on his knees before Jesus. The man asked, "Good teacher, what must I do to have life for ever?"

18Jesus answered, "Why do you call me good? Only God is good. 19You know the commands: 'You must not murder anyone. You must not be guilty of adultery. You must not steal. You must not tell lies about your neighbour. You must not cheat. Honour your father and mother.'"

20The man said, "Teacher, I have obeyed all these things since I was a boy."

21Jesus, looking at the man, loved him and said, "There is one more thing you need to do. Go and sell everything you have, and give the money to the poor and you will have treasure in heaven. Then come and follow me."

22He was very sad to hear Jesus say this, and he left very sad, because he was rich.

23Then Jesus looked at his followers and said, "How hard it will be for the rich to enter the kingdom of God!"

24The followers were amazed at what Jesus said. But he said again, "My children, it is very hard to enter the kingdom of God! 25It is easier for a camel to go through the eye of a needle than for a rich person to enter the kingdom of God."

26The followers were even more surprised and said to each other, "Then who can be saved?"

27Jesus looked at them and said, "This is something people cannot do, but God can. God can do all things."

28Peter said to Jesus, "Look, we have left everything and followed you."

29Jesus said, "I tell you the truth, all those who have left houses, brothers, sisters, mother, father, children or farms for me and for the Good News 30will get more than they left. Here in this world they will have a hundred times more homes, brothers, sisters, mothers, children and fields. And with those things, they will also suffer for their belief. But in the age that is coming they will have life for ever. 31Many who have the highest place now will have the lowest place in the future. And many who have the lowest place now will have the highest place in the future."

Jesus Talks About His Death

32As Jesus and the people with him were on the road to Jerusalem, he was leading the way. His followers were amazed, but others in the crowd who followed were afraid. Again Jesus took the twelve apostles aside and began to tell them what was about to happen in Jerusalem. 33He said, "Look, we are going to Jerusalem. The Son of Man will be turned over to the leading priests and the teachers of the law. They will say that he must die, and they will turn him over to the non-Jewish people, 34who will laugh at him and spit on him. They will beat him with whips and crucify him. But on the third day, he will rise to life again."

Two Followers Ask Jesus a Favour

35Then James and John, sons of Zebedee, came to Jesus and said, "Teacher, we want to ask you to do something for us."

36Jesus asked, "What do you want me to do for you?"

37They answered, "Let one of us sit at your right side and one of us sit at your left side in your glory in your kingdom."

38Jesus said, "You don't understand what you are asking. Can you drink the cup that I must drink? And can you be baptised with the same kind of baptism that I must go through?"

39They answered, "Yes, we can."

Jesus said to them, "You will drink the same cup that I will drink, and you will be baptised with the same baptism that I must go through. 40But I cannot choose who will sit at my right or my left; those places belong to those for whom they have been prepared."

41When the other ten followers heard this, they began to be angry with James and John.

What did this guy think was important?

_____ (v 17)

_____ (vs 19,20)

_____ (vs 21,22)

Think

Having money wasn't the problem – letting it become too important was (v 22)! This guy had put money up there with God! We can do that, too – with people, stuff we do or dreams we have.

Pray

Thank Jesus for each thing you value – then ask for his help not to let any of them get too important!

Here comes the king

The British monarchy is famous for all the pomp and ceremony that surrounds much of its activities. The State Opening of Parliament is a strictly planned event, with the timings of the Queen's carriage worked out. Jesus' entry was also planned, but it was a bit simpler.

Mark 10:42–11:14

42Jesus called them together and said, "The non-Jewish people have rulers. You know that those rulers love to show their power over the people, and their important leaders love to use all their authority. 43But it should not be that way among you. Whoever wants to become great among you must serve the rest of you like a servant. 44Whoever wants to become the first among you must serve all of you like a slave. 45In the same way, the Son of Man did not come to be served. He came to serve others and to give his life as a ransom for many people."

Jesus Heals a Blind Man

46Then they came to the town of Jericho. As Jesus was leaving there with his followers and a great many people, a blind beggar named Bartimaeus son of Timaeus was sitting by the road. 47When he heard that Jesus from Nazareth was walking by, he began to shout, "Jesus, Son of David, have mercy on me!"

48Many people warned the blind man to be quiet, but he shouted even more, "Son of David, have mercy on me!"

49Jesus stopped and said, "Tell the man to come here."

So they called the blind man, saying, "Cheer up! Get to your feet. Jesus is calling you." 50The blind man jumped up, left his coat there, and went to Jesus.

51Jesus asked him, "What do you want me to do for you?"

The blind man answered, "Teacher, I want to see."

52Jesus said, "Go, you are healed because you believed." At once the man could see, and he followed Jesus on the road.

Jesus Enters Jerusalem as a King

11 As Jesus and his followers were coming closer to Jerusalem, they came to the towns of Bethphage and Bethany near the Mount of Olives. From there Jesus sent two of his followers 2and said to them, "Go to the town you can see there. When you enter it, you will quickly find a colt tied, which no one has ever ridden. Untie it and bring it here to me. 3If anyone asks you why you are doing this, tell him its Master needs the colt, and he will send it at once."

4The followers went into the town, found a colt tied in the street near the door of a house, and untied it. 5Some people were standing there and asked, "What are you doing? Why are you untying that colt?" 6The followers answered the way Jesus told them to answer, and the people let them take the colt.

7They brought the colt to Jesus and put their coats on it, and Jesus sat on it. 8Many people spread their coats on the road.

Others cut branches in the fields and spread them on the road. ⁹The people were walking ahead of Jesus and behind him, shouting,

"Praise God!
God bless the One who comes in the name of the Lord!   *Psalm 118:26*
¹⁰God bless the kingdom of our father David!
  That kingdom is coming!
Praise to God in heaven!"

¹¹Jesus entered Jerusalem and went into the Temple. After he had looked at everything, since it was already late, he went out to Bethany with the twelve apostles.

¹²The next day as Jesus was leaving Bethany, he became hungry. ¹³Seeing a fig tree in leaf from far away, he went to see if it had any figs on it. But he found no figs, only leaves, because it was not the right season for figs. ¹⁴So Jesus said to the tree, "May no one ever eat fruit from you again." And Jesus' followers heard him say this.

What was Jesus' carriage (11:7)?

What was the royal carpet made of (11:8)?

Think

The Jewish people expected a great king as their Messiah (chosen one/leader) but they were disappointed. Who do you expect Jesus to be?

Pray

That you will treat Jesus as he should be treated and expect him to surprise you.

Authority

If you want to get anything done, if you want to be able to lead people, you have to have the authority to do it. Politicians have authority over the country. The police have authority to uphold the law. Teachers have authority to tell kids what to do in school. But who has the most authority?

Mark 11:15–12:12

Jesus Goes to the Temple

15When Jesus returned to Jerusalem, he went into the Temple and began to throw out those who were buying and selling there. He turned over the tables of those who were exchanging different kinds of money, and he upset the benches of those who were selling doves. 16Jesus refused to allow anyone to carry goods through the Temple courts. 17Then he taught the people, saying, "It is written in the Scriptures, 'My Temple will be called a house for prayer for people from all nations.' But you are changing God's house into a 'hideout for robbers.'"

18The leading priests and the teachers of the law heard all this and began trying to find a way to kill Jesus. They were afraid of him, because all the people were amazed at his teaching. 19That evening, Jesus and his followers left the city.

The Power of Faith

20The next morning as Jesus was passing by with his followers, they saw the fig tree dry and dead, even to the roots. 21Peter remembered the tree and said to Jesus, "Teacher, look! The fig tree you cursed is dry and dead!"

22Jesus answered, "Have faith in God. 23I tell you the truth, you can say to this mountain, 'Go, fall into the sea.' And if

you have no doubts in your mind and believe that what you say will happen, God will do it for you. 24So I tell you to believe that you have received the things you ask for in prayer, and God will give them to you. 25When you are praying, if you are angry with someone, forgive him so that your Father in heaven will also forgive your sins." 26

Leaders Doubt Jesus' Authority

27Jesus and his followers went again to Jerusalem. As Jesus was walking in the Temple, the leading priests, the teachers of the law and the elders came to him. 28They said to him, "What authority do you have to do these things? Who gave you this authority?"

29Jesus answered, "I will ask you one question. If you answer me, I will tell you what authority I have to do these things. 30Tell me: when John baptised people, was that authority from God or just from other people?"

31They argued about Jesus' question, saying, "If we answer, 'John's baptism was from God,' Jesus will say, 'Then why didn't you believe him?' 32But if we say, 'It was from other people,' the crowd will be against us." (These leaders were afraid of the people, because all the people believed that John was a prophet.)

33So they answered Jesus, "We don't know."

Jesus said to them, "Then I won't tell you what authority I have to do these things."

A Story About God's Son

12 Jesus began to use stories to teach the people. He said, "A man planted a vineyard. He put a wall around it and dug a hole for a winepress and built a tower. Then he leased the land to some farmers and left for a trip. ²When it was time for the grapes to be picked, he sent a servant to the farmers to get his share of the grapes. ³But the farmers grabbed the servant and beat him and sent him away empty-handed. ⁴Then the man sent another servant. They hit him on the head and showed no respect for him. ⁵So the man sent another servant, whom they killed. The man sent many other servants; the farmers beat some of them and killed others.

⁶"The man had one person left to send, his son whom he loved. He sent him last of all, saying, 'They will respect my son.'

⁷"But the farmers said to each other, 'This son will inherit the vineyard. If we kill him, it will be ours.' ⁸So they took the son, killed him and threw him out of the vineyard.

⁹"So what will the owner of the vineyard do? He will come and kill those farmers and will give the vineyard to other farmers. ¹⁰Surely you have read this Scripture:

'The stone that the builders rejected
    became the cornerstone.
¹¹The Lord did this,
    and it is wonderful to us.'"

Psalm 118:22–23

¹²The Jewish leaders knew that the story was about them. They wanted to find a way to arrest Jesus, but they were afraid of the people. So the leaders left him and went away.

Who was this guy? He walks into the Temple, tells all the people to get out, refuses to tell the most important people in the city what gives him the right to do all this, and then tells a story which winds them up even more.

Jesus had authority in a way that the chief priests really didn't – the kind of authority where he could tell a tree to die and it did.

Think

In Jesus' story, who do the tenant farmers represent? Who are the servants? Who is the vineyard owner's son? Why did the story wind up the Temple leaders?

How will you respond to the story?

Pray

Jesus, help me to hear the words you have to say and follow them.

Trick questions

It's really annoying when you get asked a question that's designed to catch you out. It doesn't really have an answer. How do you respond when someone does this to you?

 Mark 12:13–34

Is It Right to Pay Taxes or Not?

¹³Later, the Jewish leaders sent some Pharisees and Herodians to Jesus to trap him into saying something wrong. ¹⁴They came to him and said, "Teacher, we know that you are an honest man. You are not afraid of what other people think about you, because you pay no attention to who they are. And you teach the truth about God's way. Tell us: is it right to pay taxes to Caesar or not? ¹⁵Should we pay them, or not?"

But knowing what these men were really trying to do, Jesus said to them, "Why are you trying to trap me? Bring me a coin to look at." ¹⁶They gave Jesus a coin, and he asked, "Whose image and name are on the coin?"

They answered, "Caesar's."

¹⁷Then Jesus said to them, "Give to Caesar the things that are Caesar's, and give to God the things that are God's." The men were amazed at what Jesus said.

Some Sadducees Try to Trick Jesus

¹⁸Then some Sadducees came to Jesus and asked him a question. (Sadducees believed that people would not rise from the dead.) ¹⁹They said, "Teacher, Moses wrote that if a man's brother dies, leaving a wife but no children, then that man must marry the widow and have children for his brother. ²⁰Once there were seven brothers. The first brother married and died, leaving no children. ²¹So the second brother married the widow, but he also died and

had no children. The same thing happened with the third brother. ²²All seven brothers married her and died, and none of the brothers had any children. Finally the woman died too. ²³Since all seven brothers had married her, when people rise from the dead, whose wife will she be?"

²⁴Jesus answered, "Why don't you understand? Don't you know what the Scriptures say, and don't you know about the power of God? ²⁵When people rise from the dead, they will not marry, nor will they be given to someone to marry. They will be like the angels in heaven. ²⁶Surely you have read what God said about people rising from the dead. In the book in which Moses wrote about the burning bush, it says that God told Moses, 'I am the God of Abraham, the God of Isaac and the God of Jacob.' ²⁷God is the God of the living, not the dead. You Sadducees are wrong!"

The Most Important Command

²⁸One of the teachers of the law came and heard Jesus arguing with the Sadducees. Seeing that Jesus gave good answers to their questions, he asked Jesus, "Which of the commands is most important?"

²⁹Jesus answered, "The most important command is this: 'Listen, people of Israel! The Lord our God is the only Lord. ³⁰Love the Lord your God with all your heart, all your soul, all your mind and all your strength.' ³¹The second command is this: 'Love your neighbour as you love yourself.' There are no commands more important than these."

32The man answered, "That was a good answer, Teacher. You were right when you said God is the only Lord and there is no other God besides him. 33One must love God with all his heart, all his mind and all his strength. And one must love his neighbour as he loves himself. These commands are more important than all the animals and sacrifices we offer to God."

34When Jesus saw that the man answered him wisely, Jesus said to him, "You are close to the kingdom of God." And after that, no one was brave enough to ask Jesus any more questions.

When Jesus got asked a whole series of trick questions, he didn't lose his cool – he thought outside the box, and every time turned the question back on the questioner.

What was the most important answer Jesus gave?

Why did they stop asking him questions after that?

Think

What does Jesus' last reply tell you about the right way to respond to people – even the ones who keep asking you stupid questions?

Pray

Lord, help me to be quick with my answers and loving in my behaviour.

Give everything

Which of these would be the largest gift?

- 1% of £300
- 100% of £3.00

 Mark 12:35–13:10

35As Jesus was teaching in the Temple, he asked, "Why do the teachers of the law say that the Christ is the son of David? 36David himself, speaking by the Holy Spirit, said:

'The LORD said to my Lord:
Sit by me at my right side,
until I put your enemies under your
control.'   *Psalm 110:1*

37David himself calls the Christ 'Lord', so how can the Christ be his son?" The large crowd listened to Jesus with pleasure.

38Jesus continued teaching and said, "Beware of the teachers of the law. They like to walk around wearing fancy clothes, and they love people to greet them with respect in the market-places. 39They love to have the most important seats in the synagogues and at feasts. 40But they cheat widows and steal their houses and then try to make themselves look good by saying long prayers. They will receive a greater punishment."

True Giving

41Jesus sat near the Temple money box and watched the people put in their money. Many rich people gave large sums of money. 42Then a poor widow came and put in two very small copper coins, which were not even worth a penny. 43Calling his followers to him, Jesus said, "I tell you the truth, this poor widow gave more than all those rich people.

44They gave only what they did not need. This woman is very poor, but she gave all she had; she gave all she had to live on."

The Temple will Be Destroyed

13 As Jesus was leaving the Temple, one of his followers said to him, "Look, Teacher! How beautiful the buildings are! How big the stones are!"

2Jesus said, "Do you see all these great buildings? Not one stone will be left on another. Every stone will be thrown down to the ground."

3Later, as Jesus was sitting on the Mount of Olives, opposite the Temple, he was alone with Peter, James, John and Andrew. They asked Jesus, 4"Tell us, when will these things happen? And what will be the sign that they are going to happen?"

5Jesus began to answer them, "Be careful that no one fools you. 6Many people will come in my name, saying, 'I am the One,' and they will fool many people. 7When you hear about wars and stories of wars that are coming, don't be afraid. These things must happen before the end comes. 8Nations will fight against other nations, and kingdoms against other kingdoms. There will be earthquakes in different places, and there will be times when there is no food for people to eat. These things are like the first pains when something new is about to be born.

9"You must be careful. People will arrest you and take you to court and beat you in their synagogues. You will be forced to stand before kings and governors, to tell them about me. This will happen to you because you follow me. 10But before these things happen, the Good News must be told to all people.

Who did Jesus say had given most, the poor widow or the rich people (12:43)?

Why did Jesus say this (12:44)?

It is easy to think that this passage is about giving money to God, but it is dealing with something much deeper. It is talking about priorities and commitment.

Think

So, are you willing to give 100 per cent to Jesus – or are you really only giving a little bit of yourself (just enough to look OK to others)?

Pray

Lord Jesus, thank you that you love me 100 per cent. Help me to give myself to you – totally.

Be prepared

How will we know when the world is ending?

Mark 13:11–37

11When you are arrested and judged, don't worry ahead of time about what you should say. Say whatever is given you to say at that time, because it will not really be you speaking; it will be the Holy Spirit.

12"Brothers will give their own brothers to be killed, and fathers will give their own children to be killed. Children will fight against their own parents and cause them to be put to death. 13All people will hate you because you follow me, but those people who keep their faith until the end will be saved.

14"You will see 'the destroying terror' standing where it should not be." (You who read this should understand what it means.) "At that time, the people in Judea should run away to the mountains. 15If people are on the roofs of their houses, they must not go down or go inside to get anything out of their houses. 16If people are in the fields, they must not go back to get their coats. 17At that time, how terrible it will be for women who are pregnant or have nursing babies! 18Pray that these things will not happen in winter, 19because those days will be full of trouble. There will be more trouble than there has ever been since the beginning, when God made the world, until now, and nothing as bad will ever happen again. 20God has decided to make that terrible time short. Otherwise, no one would go on living. But God will make that time short to help the people he has chosen. 21At that time, someone might say to you, 'Look, there is the Christ!' Or another person might say, 'There he is!' But don't believe them. 22False Christs

and false prophets will come and perform great wonders and miracles. They will try to fool even the people God has chosen, if that were possible. 23So be careful. I have warned you about all this before it happens.

24"During the days after this trouble comes,

'the sun will grow dark,
    and the moon will not give its light.
25The stars will fall from the sky.
    And the powers of the heavens will be
        shaken.'   Isaiah 13:10; 34:4

26"Then people will see the Son of Man coming in clouds with great power and glory. 27Then he will send his angels all around the earth to gather his chosen people from every part of the earth and from every part of heaven.

28"Learn a lesson from the fig tree: when its branches become green and soft and new leaves appear, you know summer is near. 29In the same way, when you see these things happening, you will know that the time is near, ready to come. 30I tell you the truth, all these things will happen while the people of this time are still living. 31Earth and sky will be destroyed, but the words I have said will never be destroyed.

32"No one knows when that day or time will be, not the angels in heaven, not even the Son. Only the Father knows. 33Be careful! Always be ready, because you don't know when that time will be. 34It is like a man who goes on a trip. He leaves his house and lets his servants take care of it, giving each one a special job to do. The man tells the servant guarding the door always to be watchful. 35So always be ready, because you don't know when the owner of the house will come back. It might be in the evening, or at midnight, or in the morning while it is still dark, or when the sun rises. 36Always be ready. Otherwise he might come back suddenly and find you sleeping. 37I tell you this, and I say this to everyone: 'Be ready!' "

Jesus tells his followers about some of the stuff that's going to happen just before he comes back – and it's all bad. And a lot of it is more than a little confusing. Don't worry – most Christians aren't sure exactly what it means. But then, we're not going to be sure until this stuff happens, and that's the point, really. It could happen tomorrow. It might not happen for a hundred years.

Think

Are you ready for Jesus to come back?

Pray

Lord, help me to be ready for your return.

Sold out

Take a quick look at a newspaper. Are there any articles where people have sold their stories to the press? Why do people do this?

- They want to be famous
- They want to get rich
- Because it's right

 Mark 14:1–26

The Plan to Kill Jesus

14 It was now only two days before the Passover and the Feast of Unleavened Bread. The leading priests and teachers of the law were trying to find a trick to arrest Jesus and kill him. ²But they said, "We must not do it during the feast, because the people might cause a riot."

A Woman with Perfume for Jesus

³Jesus was in Bethany at the house of Simon, who had a skin disease. While Jesus was eating there, a woman approached him with an alabaster jar filled with very expensive perfume, made of pure nard. She opened the jar and poured the perfume on Jesus' head.

⁴Some who were there became upset and said to each other, "Why waste that perfume? ⁵It was worth a full year's work. It could have been sold and the money given to the poor." And they got very angry with the woman.

⁶Jesus said, "Leave her alone. Why are you troubling her? She did an excellent thing for me. ⁷You will always have the poor with you, and you can help them any time you want. But you will not always have me. ⁸This woman did the only thing she could do for me; she poured perfume on my body to prepare me for burial. ⁹I tell you the truth, wherever the Good News is preached in all the world, what this woman has done will be told, and people will remember her."

Judas Becomes an Enemy of Jesus

¹⁰One of the twelve apostles, Judas Iscariot, went to talk to the leading priests to offer to hand Jesus over to them. ¹¹These priests were pleased about this and promised to pay Judas money. So he watched for the best time to turn Jesus over.

Jesus Eats the Passover Meal

¹²It was now the first day of the Feast of Unleavened Bread when the Passover lamb was sacrificed. Jesus' followers said to him, "Where do you want us to go and prepare for you to eat the Passover meal?"

¹³Jesus sent two of his followers and said to them, "Go into the city and a man carrying a jar of water will meet you. Follow him. ¹⁴When he goes into a house, tell the owner of the house, 'The Teacher says: where is my guest room in which I can eat the Passover meal with my followers?' ¹⁵The owner will show you a large room upstairs that is furnished and ready. Prepare the food for us there."

¹⁶So the followers left and went into the city. Everything happened as Jesus had said, so they prepared the Passover meal.

17In the evening, Jesus went to that house with the twelve. 18While they were all eating, Jesus said, "I tell you the truth, one of you will turn against me—one of you eating with me now."

19The followers were very sad to hear this. Each one began to say to Jesus, "I am not the one, am I?"

20Jesus answered, "It is one of the twelve—the one who dips his bread into the bowl with me. 21The Son of Man will die, just as the Scriptures say. But how terrible it will be for the person who hands the Son of Man over to be killed. It would be better for him if he had never been born."

The Lord's Supper

22While they were eating, Jesus took some bread and thanked God for it and broke it. Then he gave it to his followers and said, "Take it; this is my body."

23Then Jesus took a cup and thanked God for it and gave it to the followers, and they all drank from the cup.

24Then Jesus said, "This is my blood which is the new agreement that God makes with his people. This blood is poured out for many. 25I tell you the truth, I will not drink of this fruit of the vine again until that day when I drink it new in the kingdom of God."

26After singing a hymn, they went out to the Mount of Olives.

The Passover lamb was sacrificed to save the Israelites whilst they were in Egypt. To find out more read the account in Exodus 12.

Why do you think Judas agreed to "sell" Jesus (vs 10,11)?

If you had been there, what would you have thought when Jesus said that one of you would betray him (v 18)?

Think

What things might tempt *you* to be disloyal to Jesus? Why?

Pray

Lord Jesus, forgive me when I let you down. Help me to stay true to you – whatever the cost.

When the chips are down

Everybody thinks they know how they're going to act in a crisis, but when the worst happens, hardly anyone ever acts the way they expected to.

 Mark 14:27–52

Jesus' Followers Will Leave Him

27Then Jesus told the followers, "You will all stumble in your faith, because it is written in the Scriptures:
'I will kill the shepherd,
and the sheep will scatter.'
Zechariah 13:7
28But after I rise from the dead, I will go ahead of you into Galilee."

29Peter said, "Everyone else may stumble in their faith, but I will not."

30Jesus answered, "I tell you the truth, tonight before the cockerel crows twice you will say three times you don't know me."

31But Peter insisted, "I will never say that I don't know you! I will even die with you!" And all the other followers said the same thing.

Jesus Prays Alone

32Jesus and his followers went to a place called Gethsemane. He said to them, "Sit here while I pray." 33Jesus took Peter, James and John with him, and he began to be very sad and troubled. 34He said to them, "My heart is full of sorrow, to the point of death. Stay here and watch."

35After walking a little farther away from them, Jesus fell to the ground and prayed that, if possible, he would not have this

time of suffering. 36He prayed, "Abba, Father! You can do all things. Take away this cup of suffering. But do what you want, not what I want."

37Then Jesus went back to his followers and found them asleep. He said to Peter, "Simon, are you sleeping? Couldn't you stay awake with me for one hour? 38Stay awake and pray for strength against temptation. The spirit wants to do what is right, but the body is weak."

39Again Jesus went away and prayed the same thing. 40Then he went back to his followers, and again he found them asleep, because their eyes were very heavy. And they did not know what to say to him.

41After Jesus prayed a third time, he went back to his followers and said to them, "Are you still sleeping and resting? That's enough. The time has come for the Son of Man to be handed over to sinful people. 42Get up, we must go. Look, here comes the man who has turned against me."

Jesus is Arrested

43At once, while Jesus was still speaking, Judas, one of the twelve apostles, came up. With him were many people carrying swords and clubs who had been sent from the leading priests, the teachers of the law and the Jewish elders.

44Judas had planned a signal for them, saying, "The man I kiss is Jesus. Arrest him and guard him while you lead him away." 45So Judas went straight to Jesus and said, "Teacher!" and kissed him. 46Then the people grabbed Jesus and arrested him. 47One of his followers standing nearby pulled out his sword and struck the servant of the high priest and cut off his ear.

48Then Jesus said, "You came to get me with swords and clubs as if I were a criminal. 49Every day I was with you teaching in the Temple, and you did not arrest me there. But all these things have happened to make the Scriptures come true." 50Then all of Jesus' followers left him and ran away.

51A young man, wearing only a linen cloth, was following Jesus, and the people also grabbed him. 52But the cloth he was wearing came off, and he ran away naked.

Jesus' friends certainly didn't behave the way they expected to. They fell asleep, they hurt someone who wasn't even that dangerous, and they ran away rather than face a fight.

Think

Imagine you were the young man in verses 51 and 52. How scared would you have to be to run away like that? How would you feel afterwards?

Pray

Father, help me to be brave and consistent when things get tough.

Extra

If you find yourself in a crisis, and you mess up, don't beat yourself up about it. We all fail once in a while. Jesus always gives people a second chance – his disciples may have deserted him, but it worked out for them. They eventually became heroes.

When you want the ground to swallow you

Have you ever let down really badly someone you cared about? How did it feel when you realised what you'd done? How did it work out afterwards?

 Mark 14:53–15:5

Jesus Before the Leaders

⁵³The people who arrested Jesus led him to the house of the high priest, where all the leading priests, the Jewish elders and the teachers of the law were gathered. ⁵⁴Peter followed far behind and entered the courtyard of the high priest's house. There he sat with the guards, warming himself by the fire.

⁵⁵The leading priests and the whole Jewish council tried to find something that Jesus had done wrong so they could kill him. But the council could find no proof of anything. ⁵⁶Many people came and told false things about him, but all said different things—none of them agreed.

⁵⁷Then some people stood up and lied about Jesus, saying, ⁵⁸"We heard this man say, 'I will destroy this Temple that people made. And three days later, I will build another Temple not made by people.'" ⁵⁹But even the things these people said did not agree.

⁶⁰Then the high priest stood before them and asked Jesus, "Aren't you going to answer? Don't you have something to say about their charges against you?" ⁶¹But Jesus said nothing; he did not answer.

The high priest asked Jesus another question: "Are you the Christ, the Son of the blessed God?"

⁶²Jesus answered, "I am. And in the future you will see the Son of Man sitting at the right hand of God, the Powerful One, and coming on clouds in the sky."

⁶³When the high priest heard this, he tore his clothes and said, "We don't need any more witnesses! ⁶⁴You all heard him say these things against God. What do you think?"

They all said that Jesus was guilty and should die. ⁶⁵Some of the people there began to spit at Jesus. They blindfolded him and beat him with their fists and said, "Prove you are a prophet!" Then the guards led Jesus away and beat him.

Peter Says He Doesn't Know Jesus

⁶⁶While Peter was in the courtyard, a servant girl of the high priest came there. ⁶⁷She saw Peter warming himself at the fire and looked closely at him.

Then she said, "You also were with Jesus, that man from Nazareth."

⁶⁸But Peter said that he was never with Jesus. He said, "I don't know or under-

stand what you are talking about." Then Peter left and went towards the entrance of the courtyard. And the cockerel crowed.

⁶⁹The servant girl saw Peter there, and again she said to the people who were standing nearby, "This man is one of those who followed Jesus." ⁷⁰Again Peter said that it was not true.

A short time later, some people were standing near Peter saying, "Surely you are one of those who followed Jesus, because you are from Galilee, too."

⁷¹Then Peter began to place a curse on himself and swear, "I don't know this man you're talking about!"

⁷²At once, the cockerel crowed the second time. Then Peter remembered what Jesus had told him: "Before the cockerel crows twice, you will say three times that you don't know me." Then Peter lost control of himself and began to cry.

Pilate Questions Jesus

15 Very early in the morning, the leading priests, the older leaders, the teachers of the law and all the Jewish council decided what to do with Jesus. They tied him, led him away and turned him over to Pilate, the governor.

²Pilate asked Jesus, "Are you the king of the Jews?"

Jesus answered, "Those are your words."

³The leading priests accused Jesus of many things. ⁴So Pilate asked Jesus another question, "You can see that they are accusing you of many things. Aren't you going to answer?"

⁵But Jesus still said nothing, so Pilate was very surprised.

Peter knew straight away what he'd done – what he said he'd never do. If you were in Peter's position, what would you have done? What would you have said? Why do you think Peter did what he did?

Think

Peter felt sorry immediately, and when Jesus rose from the dead, he forgave Peter (John 21:15–17). Jesus always forgives when people are genuinely sorry for what they've done. People aren't so perfect, though. If you've let someone down or betrayed them, make sure that they know you're sorry. They may not forgive you – but Jesus will.

Pray

Jesus, thank you that you always give a second chance. Forgive me for those times I've let people down. Help me to be faithful to my friends and family.

131

Empty promises

Politicians make all sorts of promises when they try to get elected. It's a depressing fact, but the truth is that a lot of really bad politicians get elected because they promise to give people what they want – lower taxes, better jobs, a better lifestyle, all sorts of things. The good people, the people who don't try to make extravagant promises, get pushed to one side and ignored by the crowd.

 Mark 15:6–32

Pilate Tries to Free Jesus

6Every year at the time of the Passover the governor would free one prisoner whom the people chose. 7At that time, there was a man named Barabbas in prison who was a rebel and had committed murder during a riot. 8The crowd came to Pilate and began to ask him to free a prisoner as he always did.

9So Pilate asked them, "Do you want me to free the king of the Jews?" 10Pilate knew that the leading priests had turned Jesus over to him because they were jealous. 11But the leading priests had persuaded the people to ask Pilate to free Barabbas, not Jesus.

12Then Pilate asked the crowd again, "So what should I do with this man you call the king of the Jews?"

13They shouted, "Crucify him!"

14Pilate asked, "Why? What wrong has he done?"

But they shouted even louder, "Crucify him!"

15Pilate wanted to please the crowd, so he freed Barabbas for them. After having Jesus beaten with whips, he handed Jesus over to the soldiers to be crucified.

16The soldiers took Jesus into the governor's palace (called the Praetorium) and called all the other soldiers together. 17They put a purple robe on Jesus and used thorny branches to make a crown for his head. 18They began to call out to him, "Hail, King of the Jews!" 19The soldiers beat Jesus on the head many times with a stick. They spat on him and made fun of him by bowing on their knees and worshipping him. 20After they finished, the soldiers took off the purple robe and put his own clothes on him again. Then they led him out of the palace to be crucified.

Jesus is Crucified

21A man named Simon from Cyrene, the father of Alexander and Rufus, was coming from the fields to the city. The soldiers forced Simon to carry the cross for Jesus. 22They led Jesus to the place called Golgotha, which means the Place of the Skull. 23The soldiers tried to give Jesus wine mixed with myrrh to drink, but he refused. 24The soldiers crucified Jesus and divided his clothes among themselves, throwing lots to decide what each soldier would get.

25It was nine o'clock in the morning when they crucified Jesus. 26There was a sign with this charge against Jesus written on it: THE KING OF THE JEWS. 27They also put two robbers on crosses beside Jesus, one on the right, and the other on the left. 28 29People walked by and insulted Jesus and shook their heads, saying, "You said you could destroy the Temple and build it again in three days. 30So save yourself! Come down from that cross!"

31The leading priests and the teachers of the law were also making fun of Jesus. They said to each other, "He saved other people, but he can't save himself. 32If he is really the Christ, the king of Israel, let him come down now from the cross. When we see this, we will believe in him." The robbers who were being crucified beside Jesus also insulted him.

Barabbas was a terrorist. He tried to get an army together and promised people that he would kick the Romans out of Israel. But the only thing he managed to do was get himself arrested. Still, the chief priests didn't find it too hard to get the crowd to ask for him to be released. Jesus did miracles and stuff, but he told people things they didn't want to hear. It wasn't any contest.

But even though Jesus' way was harder, he was the one who really saved people. Not the terrorist.

Think

When you listen to people, who do you listen to? Do you listen to the people who promise you an easy way out – or the people who might have a better way, which might be harder for you?

Pray

Lord, help me to know who I should listen to. Help me to recognise empty promises when I hear them.

The way to God

Death is a natural part of every living being's existence. It is something that will happen to all of us one day, so why is the death of Jesus so important?

 Mark 15:33–16:8

Jesus Dies

³³At noon the whole country became dark, and the darkness lasted for three hours. ³⁴At three o'clock Jesus cried in a loud voice, "Eli, Eli, lama sabachthani." This means, "My God, my God, why have you rejected me?"

³⁵When some of the people standing there heard this, they said, "Listen! He is calling Elijah."

³⁶Someone there ran and got a sponge, filled it with vinegar, tied it to a stick, and gave it to Jesus to drink. He said, "We want to see if Elijah will come to take him down from the cross."

³⁷Then Jesus cried in a loud voice and died.

³⁸The curtain in the Temple was torn into two pieces, from the top to the bottom. ³⁹When the army officer who was standing in front of the cross saw what happened when Jesus died, he said, "This man really was the Son of God!"

⁴⁰Some women were standing at a distance from the cross, watching; among them were Mary Magdalene, Salome and Mary the mother of James and Joseph. (James was her youngest son.) ⁴¹These women had followed Jesus in Galilee and helped him. Many other women were also there who had come with Jesus to Jerusalem.

Jesus is Buried

⁴²This was Preparation Day. (That means the day before the Sabbath day.)

That evening, ⁴³Joseph from Arimathea was brave enough to go to Pilate and ask for Jesus' body. Joseph, an important member of the Jewish council, was one of the people who was waiting for the kingdom of God to come. ⁴⁴Pilate was amazed that Jesus was already dead, so he called the army officer who had guarded Jesus and asked him if Jesus had already died. ⁴⁵The officer told Pilate that he was dead, so Pilate told Joseph he could have the body. ⁴⁶Joseph bought some linen cloth, took the body down from the cross, and wrapped it in the linen. He put the body in a tomb that was cut out of a wall of rock. Then he rolled a very large stone to block the entrance of the tomb. ⁴⁷And Mary Magdalene and Mary the mother of Joseph saw the place where Jesus was laid.

Jesus Rises from the Dead

16 The day after the Sabbath day, Mary Magdalene, Mary the mother of James, and Salome bought some sweet-smelling spices to put on Jesus' body. ²Very early on that day, the first day of the week, soon after sunrise, the women were on their way to the tomb. ³They said to each other, "Who will roll away for us the stone that covers the entrance of the tomb?"

⁴Then the women looked and saw that the stone had already been rolled away, even though it was very large. ⁵The women entered the tomb and saw a young man wearing a white robe and sitting on the right side, and they were afraid.

⁶But the man said, "Don't be afraid. You are looking for Jesus from Nazareth, who has been crucified. He has risen from the dead; he is not here. Look, here is the place where they laid him. ⁷Now go and tell his followers and Peter, 'Jesus is going into Galilee ahead of you, and you will see him there as he told you before.'"

⁸The women were confused and shaking with fear, so they left the tomb and ran away. They did not tell anyone about what happened, because they were afraid.

Why did God leave Jesus alone to be killed on the cross (15:34)?

The curtain in the Temple (15:38) separated the holiest part of the Temple from the rest. Ordinary people couldn't go there. Why do you think it was torn in two (15:38)?

The death of Jesus was no ordinary event. Both the world and people were changed.

Think

If you'd been there, what would your reaction have been as you saw Jesus die (15:39)?

Pray

Lord Jesus, thank you for dying on the cross for me, so that I can know God.

135

Good things come ...

You believe that God's got a promise for you. You're holding out for him to do what he promised. You wait months ... and then you wait years. And then it feels like your chance has gone. How do you feel?

Mark 16:9 – Luke 1:13

Some Followers See Jesus

9After Jesus rose from the dead early on the first day of the week, he showed himself first to Mary Magdalene. Once in the past, he had forced seven demons out of her. 10After Mary saw Jesus, she went and told his followers, who were very sad and were crying. 11But Mary told them that Jesus was alive. She said that she had seen him, but the followers did not believe her.

12Later, Jesus showed himself to two of his followers while they were walking in the country, but he did not look the same as before. 13These followers went back to the others and told them what had happened, but again, the followers did not believe them.

Jesus Talks to the Apostles

14Later Jesus showed himself to the eleven apostles while they were eating, and he criticised them because they had no faith. They were stubborn and refused to believe those who had seen him after he had risen from the dead.

15Jesus said to his followers, "Go everywhere in the world, and tell the Good News to everyone. 16Anyone who believes and is baptised will be saved, but anyone who does not believe will be punished. 17And those who believe will be able to do these things as proof: they will use my name to force out demons. They will speak in new languages. 18They will pick up

snakes and drink poison without being hurt. They will touch the sick, and the sick will be healed."

19After the Lord Jesus said these things to his followers, he was carried up into heaven, and he sat at the right side of God. 20The followers went everywhere in the world and told the Good News to people, and the Lord helped them. The Lord proved that the Good News they told was true by giving them power to work miracles.

[Verses 9–20 are not included in two of the best and oldest Greek copies of Mark.]

LUKE

Luke Writes About Jesus' Life

1 Many have tried to report on the things that happened among us. 2They have written the same things that we learned from others—the people who saw those things from the beginning and served God by telling people his message. 3Since I myself have studied everything carefully from the beginning, most excellent Theophilus, it seemed good for me to write it out for you. I arranged it in order 4to help you know that what you have been taught is true.

Zechariah and Elizabeth

5During the time Herod ruled Judea, there was a priest named Zechariah who belonged to Abijah's group. Zechariah's wife, Elizabeth, came from the family of Aaron. ⁶Zechariah and Elizabeth truly did what God said was good. They did everything the Lord commanded and were without fault in keeping his law. ⁷But they had no children, because Elizabeth could not have a baby, and both of them were very old.

⁸One day Zechariah was serving as a priest before God, because his group was on duty. ⁹According to the custom of the priests, he was chosen by lot to go into the Temple of the Lord and burn incense. ¹⁰There were a great many people outside praying at the time the incense was offered. ¹¹Then an angel of the Lord appeared to Zechariah, standing on the right side of the incense table. ¹²When he saw the angel, Zechariah was startled and frightened. ¹³But the angel said to him, "Zechariah, don't be afraid. God has heard your prayer. Your wife, Elizabeth, will give birth to a son, and you will name him John.

Zechariah and Elizabeth were waiting patiently for the Messiah (the chosen one) to come and save Israel. They also believed that they were never going to have a son – they were too old (if you lived in Israel in the time the Bible was written, not having a son was a Very Bad Thing). And it had taken them so long that they weren't actually expecting it.

Think

God always keeps his promises. Is there something you're waiting for? Hold on for it.

Pray

Ask God to give you patience while you're waiting for him to keep his promises to you.

Extra

From the end of Mark and the beginning of Luke: how do we know that the stories told in the Bible are true?

The ultimate rescue plan

The time has come. It's been planned for ages, but now God sets about his great rescue plan for humanity. It's time for him to give the world its first Christmas present. How does God choose to deliver his special "package"?

Luke 1:14–45

[14]He will bring you joy and gladness, and many people will be happy because of his birth. [15]John will be a great man for the Lord. He will never drink wine or beer, and even from birth, he will be filled with the Holy Spirit. [16]He will help many people of Israel return to the Lord their God. [17]He will go before the Lord in spirit and power like Elijah. He will make peace between parents and their children and will bring those who are not obeying God back to the right way of thinking, to make a people ready for the coming of the Lord."

[18]Zechariah said to the angel, "How can I know that what you say is true? I am an old man, and my wife is old, too."

[19]The angel answered him, "I am Gabriel. I stand before God, who sent me to talk to you and to tell you this good news. [20]Now, listen! You will not be able to speak until the day these things happen, because you did not believe what I told you. But they will really happen."

[21]Outside, the people were still waiting for Zechariah and were surprised that he was staying so long in the Temple. [22]When Zechariah came outside, he could not speak to them, and they knew he had seen a vision in the Temple. He could only make signs to them and remained unable to speak. [23]When his time of service at the Temple was finished, he went home.

[24]Later, Zechariah's wife, Elizabeth, became pregnant and did not go out of her house for five months. Elizabeth said, [25]"Look what the Lord has done for me! My people were ashamed of me, but now the Lord has taken away that shame."

An Angel Appears to Mary

[26]During Elizabeth's sixth month of pregnancy, God sent the angel Gabriel to Nazareth, a town in Galilee, [27]to a virgin. She was engaged to marry a man named Joseph from the family of David. Her name was Mary. [28]The angel came to her and said, "Greetings! The Lord has blessed you and is with you."

[29]But Mary was very startled by what the angel said and wondered what this greeting might mean.

[30]The angel said to her, "Don't be afraid, Mary; God has shown you his grace. [31]Listen! You will become pregnant and give birth to a son, and you will name him Jesus. [32]He will be great and will be called the Son of the Most High. The Lord God will give him the throne of King David, his ancestor. [33]He will rule over the people of Jacob for ever, and his kingdom will never end."

[34]Mary said to the angel, "How will this happen since I am a virgin?"

[35]The angel said to Mary, "The Holy

Spirit will come upon you, and the power of the Most High will cover you. For this reason the baby will be holy and will be called the Son of God. 36Now Elizabeth, your relative, is also pregnant with a son though she is very old. Everyone thought she could not have a baby, but she has been pregnant for six months. 37God can do anything!"

38Mary said, "I am the servant of the Lord. Let this happen to me as you say!" Then the angel went away.

Mary Visits Elizabeth

39Mary got up and went quickly to a town in the hills of Judea. 40She came to Zechariah's house and greeted Elizabeth. 41When Elizabeth heard Mary's greeting, the unborn baby inside her jumped, and Elizabeth was filled with the Holy Spirit. 42She cried out in a loud voice, "God has blessed you more than any other woman, and he has blessed the baby to whom you will give birth. 43Why has this good thing happened to me, that the mother of my Lord comes to me? 44When I heard your voice, the baby inside me jumped with joy. 45You are blessed because you believed that what the Lord said to you would really happen."

God could have brought Jesus into the world in any way he liked, but ...

- he chose Mary. Why?

- he "blessed" her (v 28). Why?

Look for some clues in verse 38. What was Mary saying she was willing to give up for God?

Think

What would you be willing to give up for God? What does God want you to give up for him? Are the two answers different?

Pray

Praise God for Mary's willingness to accept God's way and for all that he has done for you.

Thank you! Thank you!

How do you feel if someone says thank you for something you've done for them? Does it make you feel good? What if they are saying thank you for something that you don't think was a nice thing to do?

 Luke 1:46–77

Mary Praises God

⁴⁶Then Mary said,
"My soul praises the Lord;
⁴⁷ my heart rejoices in God my Saviour,
⁴⁸because he has shown his concern for his humble servant girl.
From now on, all people will say that I am blessed,
⁴⁹ because the Powerful One has done great things for me.
His name is holy.
⁵⁰God will show his mercy for ever and ever
to those who worship and serve him.
⁵¹He has done mighty deeds by his power.
He has scattered the people who are proud
and think great things about themselves.
⁵²He has brought down rulers from their thrones
and raised up the humble.
⁵³He has filled the hungry with good things
and sent the rich away with nothing.
⁵⁴He has helped his servant, the people of Israel,
remembering to show them mercy
⁵⁵as he promised to our ancestors,
to Abraham and to his children for ever."

⁵⁶Mary stayed with Elizabeth for about three months and then returned home.

The Birth of John

⁵⁷When it was time for Elizabeth to give birth, she had a boy. ⁵⁸Her neighbours and relatives heard how good the Lord was to her, and they rejoiced with her.

⁵⁹When the baby was eight days old, they came to circumcise him. They wanted to name him Zechariah because this was his father's name, ⁶⁰but his mother said, "No! He will be named John."

⁶¹The people said to Elizabeth, "But no one in your family has this name." ⁶²Then they made signs to his father to find out what he would like to name him.

⁶³Zechariah asked for a writing tablet and wrote, "His name is John," and everyone was surprised. ⁶⁴Immediately Zechariah could talk again, and he began praising God. ⁶⁵All their neighbours became alarmed, and in all the mountains of Judea people continued talking about all these things. ⁶⁶The people who heard about them wondered, saying, "What will this child be?" because the Lord was with him.

Zechariah Praises God

⁶⁷Then Zechariah, John's father, was filled with the Holy Spirit and prophesied:
⁶⁸"Let us praise the Lord, the God of Israel,
because he has come to help his people
and has given them freedom.
⁶⁹He has given us a powerful Saviour
from the family of God's servant David.
⁷⁰He said that he would do this

through his holy prophets who lived long ago:

71He promised he would save us from our enemies

and from the power of all those who hate us.

72He said he would give mercy to our fathers

and that he would remember his holy promise.

73God promised Abraham, our father,

74 that he would save us from the power of our enemies

so we could serve him without fear,

75being holy and good before God as long as we live.

76"Now you, child, will be called a prophet of the Most High God.

You will go before the Lord to prepare his way.

77You will make his people know that they will be saved

by having their sins forgiven.

What's surprising about Mary's reaction to the angel's news (v 46)?

Why did she take this "news" as "good news" (vs 46–55)?

How were her words true (vs 48,50,54,55)?

What do you think helped her to say "thank you" to God?

Think

When you know God's done something for you (even if it's not easy to accept), do you say thank you? Do you thank him enough?

Pray

Lord ... THANK YOU! (This should be quite a long prayer.)

The peace child

Jesus was born far away from home, and he was born poor – so poor that he had to spend his first night on earth lying in a feeding trough for animals, bedded in with straw. Why should someone so poor matter so much?

Luke 1:78–2:26

⁷⁸With the loving mercy of our God,
    a new day from heaven will dawn upon
    us.
⁷⁹It will shine on those who live in dark-
    ness,
    in the shadow of death.
It will guide us into the path of peace."
    ⁸⁰And so the child grew up and became strong in spirit. John lived in the desert until the time when he came out to preach to Israel.

The Birth of Jesus

2 At that time, Augustus Caesar sent an order that all people in the countries under Roman rule must list their names in a register. ²This was the first registration; it was taken while Quirinius was governor of Syria. ³And all went to their own towns to be registered.

⁴So Joseph left Nazareth, a town in Galilee, and went to the town of Bethlehem in Judea, known as the town of David. Joseph went there because he was from the family of David. ⁵Joseph registered with Mary, to whom he was engaged and who was now pregnant. ⁶While they were in Bethlehem, the time came for Mary to have the baby, ⁷and she gave birth to her first son. Because there were no rooms left in the inn, she wrapped the baby with pieces of cloth and laid him in a box where animals are fed.

Shepherds Hear About Jesus

⁸That night, some shepherds were in the fields nearby watching their sheep. ⁹Then an angel of the Lord stood before them. The glory of the Lord was shining around them, and they became very frightened. ¹⁰The angel said to them, "Do not be afraid. I am bringing you good news that will be a great joy to all the people. ¹¹Today your Saviour was born in the town of David. He is Christ, the Lord. ¹²This is how you will know him: you will find a baby wrapped in pieces of cloth and lying in a feeding box."

¹³Then a very large group of angels from heaven joined the first angel, praising God and saying:

¹⁴"Give glory to God in heaven,
    and on earth let there be peace among
    the people who please God."

¹⁵When the angels left them and went back to heaven, the shepherds said to each other, "Let's go to Bethlehem. Let's see this thing that has happened which the Lord has told us about."

¹⁶So the shepherds went quickly and found Mary and Joseph and the baby, who was lying in a feeding box. ¹⁷When they had seen him, they told what the angels had said about this child. ¹⁸Everyone was amazed at what the shepherds said to them. ¹⁹But Mary treasured these things and continued to think about them.

20Then the shepherds went back to their sheep, praising God and thanking him for everything they had seen and heard. It had been just as the angel had told them.

21When the baby was eight days old, he was circumcised and was named Jesus, the name given by the angel before the baby began to grow in Mary's womb.

Jesus is Presented in the Temple

22When the time came for Mary and Joseph to do what the law of Moses taught about being made pure, they took Jesus to Jerusalem to present him to the Lord. 23(It is written in the law of the Lord: "Every first-born male shall be given to the Lord.") 24Mary and Joseph also went to offer a sacrifice, as the law of the Lord says: "You must sacrifice two doves or two young pigeons."

Simeon Sees Jesus

25In Jerusalem lived a man named Simeon who was a good man and godly. He was waiting for the time when God would take away Israel's sorrow, and the Holy Spirit was in him. 26Simeon had been told by the Holy Spirit that he would not die before he saw the Christ promised by the Lord.

Can you imagine what it was like? The sky itself shone like the day with an army of angels singing in joy. The world had been waiting for the arrival of Jesus since the day Adam ate that apple. He'd been a long time coming.

Think

Why was it that all the people who first found out about the birth of Jesus were so poor? It's because Jesus didn't just come for the rich and the powerful – he came for everybody. It was part of the plan that the first people who should know about him would be a bunch of shepherds sitting on a hill and a little old man who'd spent his entire life waiting. Jesus came for everybody – even you.

Pray

Thank God for giving Jesus to the world. Thank him that Jesus came to earth for you.

How far can you grow?

How old do you think you should be before you're allowed to:

- baby-sit?
- come home late?
- teach in church?

Are the ages you think are right any different to those your parents or other adults think?

Luke 2:27–52

²⁷The Spirit led Simeon to the Temple. When Mary and Joseph brought the baby Jesus to the Temple to do what the law said they must do, ²⁸Simeon took the baby in his arms and thanked God:

²⁹"Now, Lord, you can let me, your servant,

die in peace as you said.

³⁰With my own eyes I have seen your salvation,

³¹ which you prepared before all people.

³²It is a light for the non-Jewish people to see

and an honour for your people, the Israelites."

³³Jesus' father and mother were amazed at what Simeon had said about him. ³⁴Then Simeon blessed them and said to Mary, "God has chosen this child to cause the fall and rise of many in Israel. He will be a sign from God that many people will not accept ³⁵so that the thoughts of many will be made known. And the things that will happen will make your heart sad, too."

Anna Sees Jesus

³⁶There was a prophetess, Anna, from the family of Phanuel in the tribe of Asher. Anna was very old. She had once been married for seven years. ³⁷Then her husband died, and she was a widow for 84 years. Anna never left the Temple but worshipped God, going without food and praying day and night. ³⁸Standing there at that time, she thanked God and spoke about Jesus to all who were waiting for God to free Jerusalem.

Joseph and Mary Return Home

³⁹When Joseph and Mary had done everything the law of the Lord commanded, they went home to Nazareth, their own town in Galilee. ⁴⁰The little child grew and became strong. He was filled with wisdom, and God's goodness was upon him.

Jesus as a Boy

⁴¹Every year Jesus' parents went to Jerusalem for the Passover Feast. ⁴²When he was twelve years old, they went to the feast as they always did. ⁴³After the feast days were over, they started home. The boy Jesus stayed behind in Jerusalem, but his parents did not know it. ⁴⁴Thinking

144

that Jesus was with them in the group, they travelled for a whole day. Then they began to look for him among their family and friends. 45When they did not find him, they went back to Jerusalem to look for him there. 46After three days they found Jesus sitting in the Temple with the teachers, listening to them and asking them questions. 47All who heard him were amazed at his understanding and answers. 48When Jesus' parents saw him, they were astonished. His mother said to him, "Son, why did you do this to us? Your father and I were very worried about you and have been looking for you."

49Jesus said to them, "Why were you looking for me? Didn't you know that I must be in my Father's house?" 50But they did not understand the meaning of what he said.

51Jesus went with them to Nazareth and was obedient to them. But his mother kept in her mind all that had happened. 52Jesus became wiser and grew physically. People liked him, and he pleased God.

Who was amazed by Jesus' wisdom (v 47)?

How did his parents react (v 48)?

How old was he when all this happened (v 42)?

Jesus was asking some pretty intelligent questions. It is OK for you to ask questions about who and what God is. If you have questions, don't be afraid to ask.

Think

Would you do something for God even if no one else understands? Do you think for yourself or just accept what older people say?

Pray

How old will you be before you teach and set an example for others? Ask God to start work in you now!

That's my son!

Have you ever had to wait for anything? The longer the wait the bigger the anticipation. Sometimes waiting for something to happen can make us feel ill or have other physical effects. But when the waiting is over, the joy usually overcomes the anticipation.

 Luke 3:1–22

The Preaching of John

3 It was the fifteenth year of the rule of Tiberius Caesar. These men were under Caesar: Pontius Pilate, the ruler of Judea; Herod, the ruler of Galilee; Philip, Herod's brother, the ruler of Iturea and Trachonitis; and Lysanias, the ruler of Abilene. ²Annas and Caiaphas were the high priests. At this time, the word of God came to John son of Zechariah in the desert. ³He went all over the area around the Jordan River preaching a baptism of changed hearts and lives for the forgiveness of sins. ⁴As it is written in the book of Isaiah the prophet:
This is the voice of one who calls out:
"Prepare in the desert
 the way for the LORD.
Make a straight road in the dry lands
 for our God.
⁵Every valley should be raised up,
 and every mountain and hill should be
 made flat.
The rough ground should be made level,
 and the rugged ground should be made
 smooth.
⁶Then the glory of the LORD will be
 shown,
 and all people together will see it.
The LORD himself said these things."
Isaiah 40:3–5
⁷To the crowds of people who came to be baptised by John, he said, "You are all

snakes! Who warned you to run away from God's coming punishment? ⁸Do the things that show you really have changed your hearts and lives. Don't begin to say to yourselves, 'Abraham is our father.' I tell you that God could make children for Abraham from these rocks. ⁹The axe is now ready to cut down the trees, and every tree that does not produce good fruit will be cut down and thrown into the fire."

¹⁰The people asked John, "Then what should we do?"

¹¹John answered, "If you have two shirts, share with the person who does not have one. If you have food, share that also."

¹²Even tax collectors came to John to be baptised. They said to him, "Teacher, what should we do?"

¹³John said to them, "Don't take more taxes from people than you have been ordered to take."

¹⁴The soldiers asked John, "What about us? What should we do?"

John said to them, "Don't force people to give you money, and don't lie about them. Be satisfied with the pay you get."

¹⁵Since the people were hoping for the Christ to come, they wondered if John might be the one.

¹⁶John answered everyone, "I baptise you with water, but there is one coming who is greater than I am. I am not good enough to untie his sandals. He will

baptise you with the Holy Spirit and fire. [17]He will come ready to clean the grain, separating the good grain from the chaff. He will put the good part of the grain into his barn, but he will burn the chaff with a fire that cannot be put out." [18]And John continued to preach the Good News, saying many other things to encourage the people.

[19]But John spoke against Herod, the governor, because of his sin with Herodias, the wife of Herod's brother, and because of the many other evil things Herod did.

[20]So Herod did something even worse: he put John in prison.

Jesus is Baptised by John

[21]When all the people were being baptised by John, Jesus also was baptised. While Jesus was praying, heaven opened [22]and the Holy Spirit came down on him in the form of a dove. Then a voice came from heaven, saying, "You are my Son, whom I love, and I am very pleased with you."

It was a new beginning. John the Baptist had said Jesus, the long-awaited Messiah (special messenger from God), was coming. Now it was time …

How would you have reacted if you had heard the voice of God (v 22)?

We can't be sure exactly what people watching the baptism heard – but they knew it was a sign that Jesus was special.

How might God's words (v 22) have encouraged Jesus?

Think

Jesus was only starting his ministry and yet God was pleased. Are you being called to do anything for God?

Pray

Lord God, thank you for sending your Son, Jesus, to earth to show us the way to know you.

Where you're coming from

Everybody comes from somewhere. We've all got parents, grandparents, great-grandparents and ancestors who stretch all through history.

Luke 3:23–38

The Family History of Jesus

23When Jesus began his ministry, he was about 30 years old. People thought that Jesus was Joseph's son.

Joseph was the son of Heli.
24Heli was the son of Matthat.
Matthat was the son of Levi.
Levi was the son of Melki.
Jannai was the son of Joseph.
25Joseph was the son of Mattathias.
Mattathias was the son of Amos.
Amos was the son of Nahum.
Nahum was the son of Esli.
Esli was the son of Naggai.
26Naggai was the son of Maath.
Maath was the son of Mattathias.
Mattathias was the son of Semein.
Semein was the son of Josech.
Josech was the son of Joda.
27Joda was the son of Joanan.
Joanan was the son of Rhesa.
Rhesa was the son of Zerubbabel.
Zerubbabel was the grandson of
    Shealtiel.
Shealtiel was the son of Neri.
28Neri was the son of Melki.
Melki was the son of Addi.
Addi was the son of Cosam.
Cosam was the son of Elmadam.
Elmadam was the son of Er.
29Er was the son of Joshua.

Joshua was the son of Eliezer.
Eliezer was the son of Jorim.
Jorim was the son of Matthat.
Matthat was the son of Levi.
30Levi was the son of Simeon.
Simeon was the son of Judah.
Judah was the son of Joseph.
Joseph was the son of Jonam.
Jonam was the son of Eliakim.
31Eliakim was the son of Melea.
Melea was the son of Menna.
Menna was the son of Mattatha.
Mattatha was the son of Nathan.
Nathan was the son of David.
32David was the son of Jesse.
Jesse was the son of Obed.
Obed was the son of Boaz.
Boaz was the son of Salmon.
Salmon was the son of Nahshon.
33Nahshon was the son of Amminadab.
Amminadab was the son of Admin.
Admin was the son of Arni.
Arni was the son of Hezron.
Hezron was the son of Perez.
Perez was the son of Judah.
34Judah was the son of Jacob.
Jacob was the son of Isaac.
Isaac was the son of Abraham.
Abraham was the son of Terah.
Terah was the son of Nahor.
35Nahor was the son of Serug.
Serug was the son of Reu.
Reu was the son of Peleg.

Peleg was the son of Eber.
Eber was the son of Shelah.
³⁶Shelah was the son of Cainan.
Cainan was the son of Arphaxad.
Arphaxad was the son of Shem.
Shem was the son of Noah.
Noah was the son of Lamech.
³⁷Lamech was the son of Methuselah.

Methuselah was the son of Enoch.
Enoch was the son of Jared.
Jared was the son of Mahalalel.
Mahalalel was the son of Kenan.
³⁸Kenan was the son of Enosh.
Enosh was the son of Seth.
Seth was the son of Adam.
Adam was the son of God.

Yes, it's just a list of names. But every one of the people on the list has a story (you can find some of their stories in the Old Testament). Some of them were good, some of them were bad. They're all part of the story of the world.

Think

Every one of the people in the list was important to the story of Israel and the world. They were all part of Jesus' story, too. And God knew them all, and loved them all, good or bad.

You're part of the story, too – and God knows and loves you, just as he loved your parents, and their parents, and their parents, going back to the beginning of time. And way back then, every single person in the world came from the same place. We're all connected, good and bad.

Pray

Thank God for knowing and loving everyone.

If you're God ...

What tempts you: food, clothes, latest CDs, something else? When you are tempted to do something you know is wrong, how do you react? Do you try and justify your actions or do you just say 'no!'? Perhaps you give in to the temptation and then spend ages saying sorry.

Luke 4:1–30

Jesus is Tempted by the Devil

4 Jesus, filled with the Holy Spirit, returned from the Jordan River. The Spirit led Jesus into the desert ²where the devil tempted Jesus for 40 days. Jesus ate nothing during that time, and when those days were ended, he was very hungry.

³The devil said to Jesus, "If you are the Son of God, tell this rock to become bread."

⁴Jesus answered, "It is written in the Scriptures: 'A person does not live by eating only bread.'"

⁵Then the devil took Jesus and showed him all the kingdoms of the world in an instant. ⁶The devil said to Jesus, "I will give you all these kingdoms and all their power and glory. It has all been given to me, and I can give it to anyone I wish. ⁷If you worship me, then it will all be yours."

⁸Jesus answered, "It is written in the Scriptures: 'You must worship the Lord your God and serve only him.'"

⁹Then the devil led Jesus to Jerusalem and put him on a high place of the Temple. He said to Jesus, "If you are the Son of God, jump down. ¹⁰It is written in the Scriptures:

'He has put his angels in charge of you
 to watch over you.'   *Psalm 91:11*

¹¹It is also written:

'They will catch you in their hands
 so that you will not hit your foot on a
 rock.'"   *Psalm 91:12*

¹²Jesus answered, "But it also says in the Scriptures: 'Do not test the Lord your God.'"

¹³After the devil had tempted Jesus in every way, he left him to wait until a better time.

Jesus Teaches the People

¹⁴Jesus returned to Galilee in the power of the Holy Spirit, and stories about him spread throughout all the area. ¹⁵He began to teach in their synagogues, and everyone praised him.

¹⁶Jesus travelled to Nazareth, where he had grown up. On the Sabbath day he went to the synagogue, as he always did, and stood up to read. ¹⁷The book of Isaiah the prophet was given to him. He opened the book and found the place where this is written:

¹⁸"The Lord has put his Spirit in me,
 because he appointed me to tell the
  Good News to the poor.

He has sent me to tell the captives they
  are free
 and to tell the blind that they can see
  again.   *Isaiah 61:1*

God sent me to free those who have been
  treated unfairly   *Isaiah 58:6*

¹⁹ and to announce the time when the
  Lord will show his kindness."
                             Isaiah 61:2

²⁰Jesus closed the book, gave it back to the assistant and sat down. Everyone in the

synagogue was watching Jesus closely. ²¹He began to say to them, "While you heard these words just now, they were coming true!"

²²All the people spoke well of Jesus and were amazed at the words of grace he spoke. They asked, "Isn't this Joseph's son?"

²³Jesus said to them, "I know that you will tell me the old saying: 'Doctor, heal yourself.' You want to say, 'We heard about the things you did in Capernaum. Do those things here in your own town!'" ²⁴Then Jesus said, "I tell you the truth, a prophet is not accepted in his home town. ²⁵But I tell you the truth, there were many widows in Israel during the time of Elijah. It did not rain in Israel for three and a half years, and there was no food anywhere in the whole country. ²⁶But Elijah was sent to none of those widows, only to a widow in Zarephath, a town in Sidon. ²⁷And there were many with skin diseases living in Israel during the time of the prophet Elisha. But none of them were healed, only Naaman, who was from the country of Syria."

²⁸When all the people in the synagogue heard these things, they became very angry. ²⁹They got up, forced Jesus out of town, and took him to the edge of the cliff on which the town was built. They planned to throw him off the edge, ³⁰but Jesus walked through the crowd and went on his way.

Why do you think the devil was bothering to tempt Jesus like this (vs 3,6,7,9)? Jesus knew what was in store for him, so this could all have looked like an easy way out.

Do you think all the temptations were equally as bad as one another? Why?

Think

Why was it important that Jesus didn't get put off going God's way? What helped him stand up to the devil (vs 4,8,12)?

Pray

Lord Jesus, please help me when I'm struggling to do the right thing. Amen.

Extra

Learn by heart a Bible verse that will help you when you're tempted to do the wrong thing.

Is there a catch?

Would you risk telling David Beckham how to take a free kick? What about teaching Stephen Hawking physics? Or perhaps you'd like to show the Queen how to wave at her subjects?

Luke 4:31–5:11

Jesus Forces Out an Evil Spirit

³¹Jesus went to Capernaum, a city in Galilee, and on the Sabbath day, he taught the people. ³²They were amazed at his teaching, because he spoke with authority. ³³In the synagogue a man who had within him an evil spirit shouted in a loud voice, ³⁴"Jesus of Nazareth! What do you want with us? Did you come to destroy us? I know who you are—God's Holy One!"

³⁵Jesus commanded the evil spirit, "Be quiet! Come out of the man!" The evil spirit threw the man down to the ground before all the people and then left the man without hurting him.

³⁶The people were amazed and said to each other, "What does this mean? With authority and power he commands evil spirits, and they come out." ³⁷And so the news about Jesus spread to every place in the whole area.

Jesus Heals Many People

³⁸Jesus left the synagogue and went to the home of Simon. Simon's mother-in-law was sick with a high fever, and they asked Jesus to help her. ³⁹He came to her side and commanded the fever to leave. It left her, and immediately she got up and began serving them.

⁴⁰When the sun went down, the people brought those who were sick to Jesus. Putting his hands on each sick person, he healed every one of them. ⁴¹Demons came out of many people, shouting, "You are the Son of God." But Jesus commanded the demons and would not allow them to speak, because they knew Jesus was the Christ.

⁴²At daybreak, Jesus went to a lonely place, but the people looked for him. When they found him, they tried to keep him from leaving. ⁴³But Jesus said to them, "I must preach about God's kingdom to other towns, too. This is why I was sent." ⁴⁴Then he kept on preaching in the synagogues of Judea.

Jesus' First Followers

5 One day while Jesus was standing beside Lake Galilee, many people were pressing all around him to hear the word of God. ²Jesus saw two boats at the shore of the lake. The fishermen had left them and were washing their nets. ³Jesus got into one of the boats, the one that belonged to Simon, and asked him to push off a little from the land. Then Jesus sat down and continued to teach the people from the boat.

⁴When Jesus had finished speaking, he said to Simon, "Take the boat into deep water, and put your nets in the water to catch some fish."

⁵Simon answered, "Master, we worked hard all night trying to catch fish, and we caught nothing. But you say to put the nets in the water, so I will." ⁶When the fishermen did as Jesus told them, they caught so many fish that the nets began to break. ⁷They called to their partners in the other boat to come and help them. They

came and filled both boats so full that they were almost sinking.

8When Simon Peter saw what had happened, he bowed down before Jesus and said, "Go away from me, Lord. I am a sinful man!" 9He and the other fishermen were amazed at the many fish they caught,

as were 10James and John, the sons of Zebedee, Simon's partners.

Jesus said to Simon, "Don't be afraid. From now on you will fish for people." 11When the men brought their boats to the shore, they left everything and followed Jesus.

Jesus telling Simon Peter about fishing could seem just as stupid! Simon Peter was an expert fisherman and had spent all night in his boat (5:5). So why *did* he do what Jesus said (5:5)?

What sort of expression do you think Simon Peter had when Jesus told him to take the boat out again?

Why do you think the big catch was a turning point in Simon Peter's friendship with Jesus (5:11)?

Think

Think of some times which have been turning points for you in your friendship with Jesus. Jot them down to remind yourself.

Pray

... that you'll have the same response as Simon to whatever Jesus tells you to do.

153

The popular crowd

At school, it's easy to join in with the teasing and ignore this term's unpopular person. In fact, sometimes if you don't join in, you get teased as well. What would Jesus do?

 Luke 5:12–35

Jesus Heals a Sick Man

¹²When Jesus was in one of the towns, there was a man covered with a skin disease. When he saw Jesus, he bowed before him and begged him, "Lord, you can heal me if you will."

¹³Jesus reached out his hand and touched the man and said, "I will. Be healed!" Immediately the disease disappeared. ¹⁴Then Jesus said, "Don't tell anyone about this, but go and show yourself to the priest and offer a gift for your healing, as Moses commanded. This will show the people what I have done."

¹⁵But the news about Jesus spread even more. Many people came to hear Jesus and to be healed of their sicknesses, ¹⁶but Jesus often slipped away to be alone so he could pray.

Jesus Heals a Paralysed Man

¹⁷One day as Jesus was teaching the people, the Pharisees and teachers of the law from every town in Galilee and Judea and from Jerusalem were there. The power of the Lord was present for him to heal the sick. ¹⁸Just then, some men were carrying on a mat a man who was paralysed. They tried to bring him in and put him down before Jesus. ¹⁹But because there were so many people there, they could not find a way in. So they went up on the roof and lowered the man on his mat through the ceiling into the middle of the crowd right before Jesus. ²⁰Seeing their faith, Jesus said, "Friend, your sins are forgiven."

²¹The Jewish teachers of the law and the Pharisees thought to themselves, "Who is this man who is speaking as if he were God? Only God can forgive sins."

²²But Jesus knew what they were thinking and said, "Why are you thinking these things? ²³Which is easier: to say, 'Your sins are forgiven,' or to say, 'Stand up and walk'? ²⁴But I will prove to you that the Son of Man has authority on earth to forgive sins." So Jesus said to the paralysed man, "I tell you, stand up, take your mat, and go home."

²⁵At once the man stood up before them, picked up his mat and went home, praising God. ²⁶All the people were completely amazed and began to praise God. They were filled with much respect and said, "Today we have seen amazing things!"

Levi Follows Jesus

²⁷After this, Jesus went out and saw a tax collector named Levi sitting in the tax collector's booth. Jesus said to him, "Follow me!" ²⁸So Levi got up, left everything and followed him.

²⁹Then Levi gave a big dinner for Jesus at his house. Many tax collectors and other people were eating there, too. ³⁰But the Pharisees and the men who taught the law for the Pharisees began to complain to Jesus' followers, "Why do you eat and drink with tax collectors and sinners?"

³¹Jesus answered them, "It is not the healthy people who need a doctor, but the sick. ³²I have not come to invite good

people but sinners to change their hearts and lives."

Jesus Answers a Question

³³They said to Jesus, "John's followers often give up eating for a certain time and pray, just as the Pharisees do. But your followers eat and drink all the time."

³⁴Jesus said to them, "You cannot make the friends of the bridegroom give up eating while he is still with them. ³⁵But the time will come when the bridegroom will be taken away from them, and then they will give up eating."

Tax collectors, like Levi, weren't popular (v 30)! Yet Jesus went to his house for a meal (v 29). Levi was not the sort of person you invited home to tea! He was a traitor because he worked for the Romans and he cheated people. Worse still he was friendly with the "wrong sort of people".

What did it cost Levi to follow Jesus (v 28)?

Why do you think Levi invited Jesus round (v 29)?

Why didn't the religious people (the Pharisees) like it (v 30)?

What do you think Jesus' reply in verses 31 and 32 meant?

Are you willing to put yourself out and care for the not-so-popular people?

Think

You've got friends? That's great! Thank God for each of them.

What do you like about them?

What do you think needs some work?

Why do you think they like you?

Are there things about you they'd like to change?

Pray

Take some time to pray for a friend each day. If your friends are Christians, could you pray together this week for the people at school who don't have many friends?

Making choices

What would you choose ...

- Big Mac with fries?
- cheeseburger?
- veggie burger?

Some choices you make aren't very important. But how can you make the right choice when it really matters?

 Luke 5:36–6:23

36Jesus told them this story: "No one takes cloth off a new coat to cover a hole in an old coat. Otherwise, he ruins the new coat, and the cloth from the new coat will not be the same as the old cloth. 37Also, no one ever pours new wine into old leather bags. Otherwise, the new wine will break the bags, the wine will spill out and the leather bags will be ruined. 38New wine must be put into new leather bags. 39No one after drinking old wine wants new wine, because he says, 'The old wine is better.'"

Jesus is Lord over the Sabbath

6 One Sabbath day Jesus was walking through some fields of grain. His followers picked the heads of grain, rubbed them in their hands and ate them. 2Some Pharisees said, "Why do you do what is not lawful on the Sabbath day?"

3Jesus answered, "Have you not read what David did when he and those with him were hungry? 4He went into God's house and took and ate the holy bread, which is lawful only for priests to eat. And he gave some to the people who were with him." 5Then Jesus said to the Pharisees, "The Son of Man is Lord of the Sabbath day."

Jesus Heals a Man's Hand

6On another Sabbath day Jesus went into the synagogue and was teaching, and a man with a crippled right hand was there. 7The teachers of the law and the Pharisees were watching closely to see if Jesus would heal on the Sabbath day so they could accuse him. 8But he knew what they were thinking, and he said to the man with the crippled hand, "Stand up here in the middle of everyone." The man got up and stood there. 9Then Jesus said to them, "I ask you, which is lawful on the Sabbath day: to do good or to do evil, to save a life or to destroy it?" 10Jesus looked around at all of them and said to the man, "Hold out your hand." The man held out his hand, and it was healed.

11But the Pharisees and the teachers of the law were very angry and discussed with each other what they could do to Jesus.

Jesus Chooses His Apostles

12At that time Jesus went off to a mountain to pray, and he spent the night praying to God. 13The next morning, Jesus called his followers to him and chose twelve of them, whom he named apostles: 14Simon (Jesus named him Peter), his brother Andrew, James, John, Philip, Bartholomew, [15]Matthew, Thomas, James son of Alphaeus, Simon (called the Zealot), [16]Judas son of James and Judas Iscariot, who later turned Jesus over to his enemies.

Jesus Teaches and Heals

[17]Jesus and the apostles came down from the mountain, and he stood on level ground. A large group of his followers were there, as well as many people from all around Judea, Jerusalem, and the sea coast cities of Tyre and Sidon. [18]They all came to hear Jesus teach and to be healed of their sicknesses, and he healed those who were troubled by evil spirits. [19]All the people were trying to touch Jesus, because power was coming from him and healing them all.

[20]Jesus looked at his followers and said,
"Happy you people who are poor,
because the kingdom of God belongs to you.
[21]Happy you people who are now hungry,
because you will be satisfied.
Happy you people who are now crying,
because you will laugh with joy.
[22]"People will hate you, shut you out, insult you and say you are evil, because you follow the Son of Man. But when they do, you will be happy. [23]Be full of joy at that time, because you have a great reward waiting for you in heaven. Their ancestors did the same things to the prophets.

What did Jesus do here (6:12)?

What did he do next (6:13)?

Now think. Did Jesus talk to God about ...

- cheese toasties?

- his favourite boat?

- who he should choose to be his disciples?

Think

Prayer involves asking God for help, and getting it. It is a conversation which involves two.

Pray

Lord, when I've got things to decide help me to remember to ask your advice. Amen.

True happiness

Have you ever noticed how when people say, "Wicked!" or, "Cool!" they're actually meaning the opposite, or something different from what they're saying?

Luke 6:24–45

24"But how terrible it will be for you who are rich,
because you have had your easy life.
25How terrible it will be for you who are full now,
because you will be hungry.
How terrible it will be for you who are laughing now,
because you will be sad and cry.
26"How terrible when everyone says only good things about you, because their ancestors said the same things about the false prophets.

Love Your Enemies

27"But I say to you who are listening, love your enemies. Do good to those who hate you, 28bless those who curse you, pray for those who are cruel to you. 29If anyone slaps you on one cheek, offer him the other cheek, too. If someone takes your coat, do not stop him from taking your shirt. 30Give to everyone who asks you, and when someone takes something that is yours, don't ask for it back. 31Do to others what you would want them to do to you. 32If you love only the people who love you, what praise should you get? Even sinners love the people who love them. 33If you do good only to those who do good to you, what praise should you get? Even sinners do that! 34If you lend things to people, always hoping to get something back, what praise should you get? Even sinners lend to other sinners so that they can get back the same amount! 35But love your enemies, do good to them, and lend to them without

hoping to get anything back. Then you will have a great reward and you will be children of the Most High God, because he is kind even to people who are ungrateful and full of sin. 36Show mercy, just as your Father shows mercy.

Look at Yourselves

37"Don't judge other people, and you will not be judged. Don't accuse others of being guilty, and you will not be accused of being guilty. Forgive, and you will be forgiven. 38Give, and you will receive. You will be given much. Pressed down, shaken together and running over, it will spill into your lap. The way you give to others is the way God will give to you."
39Jesus told them this story: "Can a blind person lead another blind person? No! Both of them will fall into a ditch. 40A student is not better than the teacher, but the student who has been fully trained will be like the teacher.
41"Why do you notice the little piece of dust in your friend's eye, but you don't notice the big piece of wood in your own eye? 42How can you say to your friend, 'Friend, let me take that little piece of dust out of your eye' when you cannot see that big piece of wood in your own eye! You hypocrite! First, take the wood out of your own eye. Then you will see clearly to take the dust out of your friend's eye.

Two Kinds of Fruit

43"A good tree does not produce bad fruit, nor does a bad tree produce good fruit. 44Each tree is known by its own fruit. People don't gather figs from thorn-bushes, and they don't get grapes from bushes. 45Good people bring good things out of the good stored in their hearts. But evil people bring evil things out of the evil stored in their hearts. People speak the things that are in their hearts.

What did Jesus say you should do to other people (vs 27–31)?

Jesus encourages us to look at ourselves before we criticise and judge others (v 37). He wants us to make sure our own lives are right and we've sorted out all the big faults we have before we even *think* about looking at the small faults in others (vs 41,42).

What does he say will be given to you if you give to others (v 38)?

Think

When people treat you badly, what does Jesus say your attitude towards them should be (v 31)? And that's not just friends and family (vs 32–34). It means anyone.

What kind of stuff (e.g. books and TV programmes) are you putting into your life? Are they the kind of things which will give you a 'store' of good things to share with others?

Pray

Ask Jesus to help you fill your mind with things that will show his life to others through you.

A helping hand

Someone in trouble? It's not your problem, is it?

Luke 6:46–7:23

Two Kinds of People

46"Why do you call me, 'Lord, Lord,' but do not do what I say? 47I will show you what everyone is like who comes to me and hears my words and obeys. 48That person is like a man building a house who dug deep and laid the foundation on rock. When the floods came, the water tried to wash the house away, but it could not shake it, because the house was built well. 49But the one who hears my words and does not obey is like a man who built his house on the ground without a foundation. When the floods came, the house quickly fell and was completely destroyed."

Jesus Heals a Soldier's Servant

7 When Jesus finished saying all these things to the people, he went to Capernaum. 2There was an army officer who had a servant who was very important to him. The servant was so sick he was nearly dead. 3When the officer heard about Jesus, he sent some Jewish elders to him to ask Jesus to come and heal his servant. 4The men went to Jesus and begged him, saying, "This officer is worthy of your help. 5He loves our people, and he built us a synagogue."

6So Jesus went with the men. He was getting near the officer's house when the officer sent friends to say, "Lord, don't trouble yourself, because I am not worthy to have you come into my house. 7That is why I did not come to you myself. But you only need to command it, and my servant will be healed. 8I, too, am a man under the authority of others, and I have soldiers under my command. I tell one soldier, 'Go,' and he goes. I tell another soldier, 'Come,' and he comes. I say to my servant, 'Do this,' and my servant does it."

9When Jesus heard this, he was amazed. Turning to the crowd that was following him, he said, "I tell you, this is the greatest faith I have found anywhere, even in Israel."

10Those who had been sent to Jesus went back to the house where they found the servant in good health.

Jesus Brings a Man Back to Life

11Soon afterwards Jesus went to a town called Nain, and his followers and a large crowd travelled with him. 12When he came near the town gate, he saw a funeral. A mother, who was a widow, had lost her only son. A large crowd from the town was with the mother while her son was being carried out. 13When the Lord saw her, he felt very sorry for her and said, "Don't cry." 14He went up and touched the coffin, and the people who were carrying it stopped. Jesus said, "Young man, I tell you, get up!" 15And the son sat up and began to talk. Then Jesus gave him back to his mother.

16All the people were amazed and began praising God, saying, "A great prophet has come to us! God has come to help his people."

17This news about Jesus spread through all Judea and into all the places around there.

John Asks a Question

18John's followers told him about all these things. He called for two of his followers 19and sent them to the Lord to ask, "Are you the One who is to come, or should we wait for someone else?"

20When the men came to Jesus, they said, "John the Baptist sent us to you with this question: 'Are you the One who is to come, or should we wait for someone else?'"

21At that time, Jesus healed many people of their sicknesses, diseases and evil spirits, and he gave sight to many blind people.

22Then Jesus answered John's followers, "Go and tell John what you saw and heard here. The blind can see, the crippled can walk and people with skin diseases are healed. The deaf can hear, the dead are raised to life and the Good News is preached to the poor. 23Those who do not stumble in their faith because of me are blessed!"

The woman had a grown-up son (7:14) and was a widow (7:12). Her only son's death (7:12) would have been disastrous. He would probably have been her only source of income.

Jesus could have walked on by, but what was his reaction (7:13–15)?

Think

Are you willing to help people who no one else cares about? Think about the different kinds of people that you could help, and the different ways you could help them.

Pray

Ask God to show you someone you could help today, and the way in which you could help them.

You know what *she* is!

Do you think you're better than other people? It could be for a variety of reasons; because of what they look like or how they act or where they come from. In today's reading, why did Simon think he was better than the woman?

Luke 7:24–50

24When John's followers left, Jesus began talking to the people about John: "What did you go out into the desert to see? A reed blown by the wind? 25What did you go out to see? A man dressed in fine clothes? No, people who have fine clothes and much wealth live in kings' palaces. 26But what did you go out to see? A prophet? Yes, and I tell you, John is more than a prophet. 27This was written about him:

'I will send my messenger ahead of you, who will prepare the way for you.'

Malachi 3:1

28I tell you, John is greater than any other person ever born, but even the least important person in the kingdom of God is greater than John."

29(When the people, including the tax collectors, heard this, they all agreed that God's teaching was good, having been baptized by John. 30But the Pharisees and experts on the law refused to accept God's plan for themselves; they did not let John baptise them.)

31Then Jesus said, "What shall I say about the people of this time? What are they like? 32They are like children sitting in the market place, calling to one another and saying,

'We played music for you, but you did not dance;

we sang a sad song, but you did not cry.'

33John the Baptist came and did not eat bread or drink wine, and you say, 'He has a demon in him.' 34The Son of Man came eating and drinking, and you say, 'Look at him! He eats too much and drinks too much wine, and he is a friend of tax collectors and sinners!' 35But wisdom is proved to be right by what it does."

A Woman Washes Jesus' Feet

36One of the Pharisees asked Jesus to eat with him, so Jesus went into the Pharisee's house and sat at the table. 37A sinful woman in the town learnt that Jesus was eating at the Pharisee's house. So she brought an alabaster jar of perfume 38and stood behind Jesus at his feet, crying. She began to wash his feet with her tears, and she dried them with her hair, kissing them many times and rubbing them with the perfume. 39When the Pharisee who asked Jesus to come to his house saw this, he thought to himself, "If Jesus were a prophet, he would know that the woman touching him is a sinner!"

40Jesus said to the Pharisee, "Simon, I have something to say to you."

Simon said, "Teacher, tell me."

41Jesus said, "Two people owed money to the same banker. One owed 500 silver coins and the other owed 50 silver coins. 42They had no money to pay what they owed, but the banker told both of them they did not have to pay him. Which person will love the banker more?"

43Simon, the Pharisee, answered, "I think it would be the one who owed him the most money."

Jesus said to Simon, "You are right." 44Then Jesus turned towards the woman and said to Simon, "Do you see this woman? When I came into your house, you gave me no water for my feet, but she washed my feet with her tears and dried them with her hair. 45You gave me no kiss of greeting, but she has been kissing my feet since I came in. 46You did not put oil on my head, but she poured perfume on my feet. 47I tell you that her many sins are forgiven, so she showed great love. But the person who is forgiven only a little will love only a little."

48Then Jesus said to her, "Your sins are forgiven."

49The people sitting at the table began to say among themselves, "Who is this who even forgives sins?"

50Jesus said to the woman, "Because you believed, you are saved from your sins. Go in peace."

Everyone knew this woman was "a sinner" (vs 37,39) – probably meaning "prostitute". But Jesus wasn't bothered about her reputation. He knew what she was really like (vs 47,48,50). He knew what Simon was like, too (vs 44–47).

Think

When Jesus looks at you, what attitudes does he see in you towards ...

- others?
- God?

Pray

Lord Jesus, forgive me for my wrong attitudes to others. Help me to love others like you love me.

Grow up!

No, Jesus wasn't telling people off for messing about. This story is all about growing in your relationship with God.

Luke 8:1–21

The Group with Jesus

8 After this, while Jesus was travelling through some cities and small towns, he preached and told the Good News about God's kingdom. The twelve apostles were with him, ²and also some women who had been healed of sicknesses and evil spirits: Mary, called Magdalene, from whom seven demons had gone out; ³Joanna, the wife of Chuza (the manager of Herod's house); Susanna; and many others. These women used their own money to help Jesus and his apostles.

A Story About Planting Seed

⁴When a great crowd was gathered, and people were coming to Jesus from every town, he told them this story:

⁵"A farmer went out to plant his seed. While he was planting, some seed fell by the road. People walked on the seed, and the birds ate it up. ⁶Some seed fell on rock, and when it began to grow, it died because it had no water. ⁷Some seed fell among thorny weeds, but the weeds grew up with it and choked the good plants. ⁸And some seed fell on good ground and grew and made 100 times more."

As Jesus finished the story, he called out, "You people who can hear me, listen!"

⁹Jesus' followers asked him what this story meant.

¹⁰Jesus said, "You have been chosen to know the secrets about the kingdom of God. But I use stories to speak to other people so that:

'You will listen and listen, but you will not understand.

You will look and look, but you will not learn.' *Isaiah 6:9*

¹¹"This is what the story means: the seed is God's message. ¹²The seed that fell beside the road is like the people who hear God's teaching, but the devil comes and takes it away from them so they cannot believe it and be saved. ¹³The seed that fell on rock is like those who hear God's teaching and accept it gladly, but they don't allow the teaching to go deep into their lives. They believe for a while, but when trouble comes, they give up. ¹⁴The seed that fell among the thorny weeds is like those who hear God's teaching, but they let the worries, riches and pleasures of this life keep them from growing and producing good fruit. ¹⁵And the seed that fell on the good ground is like those who hear God's teaching with good, honest hearts and obey it and patiently produce good fruit.

Use What You Have

¹⁶"No one after lighting a lamp covers it with a bowl or hides it under a bed. Instead, the person puts it on a lampstand so those who come in will see the light. ¹⁷Everything that is hidden will become clear, and every secret thing will be made known. ¹⁸So be careful how you listen. Those who have understanding will be given more. But from those who do not have understanding, even what they think they have will be taken away."

Jesus' True Family

¹⁹Jesus' mother and brothers came to

see him, but there was such a crowd they could not get to him. ²⁰Someone said to Jesus, "Your mother and your brothers are standing outside, wanting to see you."

²¹Jesus answered them, "My mother and my brothers are those who listen to God's teaching and obey it!"

The farmer (v 5) is like ...

The seed (v 5) is ...

The path and the birds (v 5) are like ...

The rocky ground with no water (v 6) is like ...

The thorny ground (v 7) is like ...

The good ground (v 8) is like ...

Think

What kind of "ground" are you most like?

What stops you growing in your relationship with God?

What could you do to make sure you grow as a Christian?

Pray

Lord Jesus, help me to listen to your words and keep following you every day.

Sleeping through a storm

Would you sleep through a thunderstorm? There aren't many physical details known about Jesus – but he must have been a heavy sleeper.

Luke 8:22–48

Jesus Calms a Storm

22One day Jesus and his followers got into a boat, and he said to them, "Let's go across the lake." And so they started across. 23While they were sailing, Jesus fell asleep. A very strong wind blew up on the lake, causing the boat to fill with water, and they were in danger.

24The followers went to Jesus and woke him, saying, "Master! Master! We will drown!"

Jesus got up and gave a command to the wind and the waves. They stopped, and it became calm. 25Jesus said to his followers, "Where is your faith?"

The followers were afraid and amazed and said to each other, "Who is this that commands even the wind and the water, and they obey him?"

A Man with Demons Inside Him

26Jesus and his followers sailed across the lake from Galilee to the area of the Gerasene people. 27When Jesus got out on the land, a man from the town who had demons inside him came to Jesus. For a long time he had worn no clothes and had lived in the burial caves, not in a house. 28When he saw Jesus, he cried out and fell down before him. He said with a loud voice, "What do you want with me, Jesus, Son of the Most High God? I beg you, don't

torture me!" 29He said this because Jesus was commanding the evil spirit to come out of the man. Many times it had taken hold of him. Though he had been kept under guard and chained hand and foot, he had broken his chains and had been forced by the demon out into a lonely place.

30Jesus asked him, "What is your name?"

He answered, "Legion," because many demons were in him. 31The demons begged Jesus not to send them into eternal darkness. 32A large herd of pigs was feeding on a hill, and the demons begged Jesus to allow them to go into the pigs. So Jesus allowed them to do this. 33When the demons came out of the man, they went into the pigs, and the herd ran down the hill into the lake and was drowned.

34When the herdsmen saw what had happened, they ran away and reported this in the town and the countryside. 35And people went to see what had happened. When they came to Jesus, they found the man sitting at Jesus' feet, clothed and in his right mind, because the demons were gone. But the people were frightened. 36The people who saw this happen told the others how Jesus had made the man well. 37All the people of the Gerasene country asked Jesus to leave, because they were all very afraid. So Jesus got into the boat and went back to Galilee.

38The man whom Jesus had healed begged to go with him, but Jesus sent him away, saying, 39"Go back home and tell people how much God has done for you." So the man went all over town telling how much Jesus had done for him.

Jesus Gives Life to a Dead Girl and Heals a Sick Woman

40When Jesus got back to Galilee, a crowd welcomed him, because everyone was waiting for him. 41A man named Jairus, a leader of the synagogue, came to Jesus and fell at his feet, begging him to come to his house. 42Jairus' only daughter, about twelve years old, was dying.

While Jesus was on his way to Jairus' house, the people were crowding all around him. 43A woman was in the crowd who had been bleeding for twelve years, but no one was able to heal her. 44She came up behind Jesus and touched the edge of his coat, and instantly her bleeding stopped. 45Then Jesus said, "Who touched me?"

When all the people said they had not touched him, Peter said, "Master, the people are all around you and are pushing against you."

46But Jesus said, "Someone did touch me, because I felt power go out from me." 47When the woman saw she could not hide, she came forwards, shaking, and fell down before Jesus. While all the people listened, she told why she had touched him and how she had been instantly healed. 48Jesus said to her, "Dear woman, you are made well because you believed. Go in peace."

How did the disciples feel during the storm (v 24)?

How did the disciples feel after the storm (v 25)? Why?

Who do you think they thought Jesus was?

Think

What "storms" in your life need calming right now? What are you anxious or worried about? Is there anything that you're feeling overwhelmed by?

Pray

Sometimes it might feel as if God is asleep! But you're safe with him. Ask him about anything that's troubling you now ... and trust him for the calm.

Crowd control

When you're out shopping or pushing your way through crowds at school, do you ever stop to think that God knows and loves each one of those people?

Luke 8:49–9:17

⁴⁹While Jesus was still speaking, someone came from the house of the synagogue leader and said to him, "Your daughter is dead. Don't bother the teacher any more."

⁵⁰When Jesus heard this, he said to Jairus, "Don't be afraid. Just believe, and your daughter will be well."

⁵¹When Jesus went to the house, he let only Peter, John, James and the girl's father and mother go inside with him. ⁵²All the people were crying and feeling sad because the girl was dead, but Jesus said, "Stop crying. She is not dead, only asleep."

⁵³The people laughed at Jesus because they knew the girl was dead. ⁵⁴But Jesus took hold of her hand and called to her, "My child, stand up!" ⁵⁵Her spirit came back into her, and she stood up at once. Then Jesus ordered that she be given something to eat. ⁵⁶The girl's parents were amazed, but Jesus told them not to tell anyone what had happened.

Jesus Sends Out the Apostles

9 Jesus called the twelve apostles together and gave them power and authority over all demons and the ability to heal sicknesses. ²He sent the apostles out to tell about God's kingdom and to heal the sick. ³He said to them, "Take nothing for your trip, neither a walking stick, bag, bread, money or extra clothes. ⁴When you enter a house, stay there until it is time to leave. ⁵If people do not welcome you, shake the dust off your feet as you leave the town, as a warning to them."

⁶So the apostles went out and travelled through all the towns, preaching the Good News and healing people everywhere.

Herod is Confused About Jesus

⁷Herod, the governor, heard about all the things that were happening and was confused, because some people said, "John the Baptist has risen from the dead." ⁸Others said, "Elijah has come to us." And still others said, "One of the prophets who lived long ago has risen from the dead." ⁹Herod said, "I cut off John's head, so who is this man I hear such things about?" And Herod kept trying to see Jesus.

More than 5,000 Fed

¹⁰When the apostles returned, they told Jesus everything they had done. Then Jesus took them with him to a town called Bethsaida where they could be alone together. ¹¹But the people learned where Jesus went and followed him. He welcomed them and talked with them about God's kingdom and healed those who needed to be healed.

¹²Late in the afternoon, the twelve apostles came to Jesus and said, "Send the people away. They need to go to the towns and countryside around here and find places to sleep and something to eat, because no one lives in this place."

¹³But Jesus said to them, "You give them something to eat."

They said, "We have only five loaves of bread and two fish, unless we go and buy food for all these people." 14(There were about 5,000 men there.)

Jesus said to his followers, "Tell the people to sit in groups of about 50 people."

15So the followers did this, and all the people sat down. 16Then Jesus took the five loaves of bread and two fish, and, looking up to heaven, he thanked God for the food. Then he divided the food and gave it to the followers to give to the people. 17They all ate and were satisfied, and what was left over was gathered up, filling twelve baskets.

What did Jesus' disciples want to do with this big crowd (9:12)?

What did Jesus want his disciples to do (9:13)?

The result was one of Jesus' great miracles (9:15–17).

Think

Can you think of three special things that Jesus might want you to learn from this?

1 _____

2 _____

3 _____

Pray

Lord Jesus, help me to be ready and willing to do something for others, whoever they are.

You're the Christ

It's time to get personal. It's OK to say all that stuff about Jesus in church, along with loads of others. But now you're on your own. Jesus wants to know what *you* think.

Luke 9:18–43a

Jesus is the Christ

18Once when Jesus was praying alone, his followers were with him, and he asked them, "Who do the people say I am?"

19They answered, "Some say you are John the Baptist. Others say you are Elijah. And others say you are one of the prophets from long ago who has come back to life."

20Then Jesus asked, "But who do you say I am?"

Peter answered, "You are the Christ from God."

21Jesus warned them not to tell anyone, saying, 22"The Son of Man must suffer many things. He will be rejected by the Jewish elders, the leading priests, and the teachers of the law. He will be killed and after three days will be raised from the dead."

23Jesus said to all of them, "If people want to follow me, they must give up the things they want. They must be willing to give up their lives daily to follow me. 24Those who want to save their lives will give up their lives. But those who give up their lives for me will have true life. 25It is worth nothing for them to have the whole world if they themselves are destroyed or lost. 26If people are ashamed of me and my teaching, then the Son of Man will be ashamed of them when he comes in his glory and with the glory of the Father and the holy angels. 27I tell you the truth, some people standing here will see the kingdom of God before they die."

Jesus Talks with Moses and Elijah

28About eight days after Jesus said these things, he took Peter, John and James and went up on a mountain to pray. 29While Jesus was praying, the appearance of his face changed, and his clothes became shining white. 30Then two men, Moses and Elijah, were talking with Jesus. 31They appeared in heavenly glory, talking about his intended departure which he would soon bring about in Jerusalem. 32Peter and the others were very sleepy, but when they awoke fully, they saw the glory of Jesus and the two men standing with him. 33When Moses and Elijah were about to leave, Peter said to Jesus, "Master, it is good that we are here. Let us make three tents—one for you, one for Moses and one for Elijah." (Peter did not know what he was talking about.)

34While he was saying these things, a cloud came and covered them, and they became afraid as the cloud covered them. 35A voice came from the cloud, saying, "This is my Son, whom I have chosen. Listen to him!"

36When the voice finished speaking, only Jesus was there. Peter, John and James said nothing and told no one at that time what they had seen.

Jesus Heals a Sick Boy

37The next day, when they came down from the mountain, a large crowd met Jesus. 38A man in the crowd shouted to him, "Teacher, please come and look at my son, because he is my only child. ³⁹An evil spirit seizes my son, and suddenly he screams. It causes him to lose control of himself and foam at the mouth. The evil spirit keeps on hurting him and almost never leaves him. ⁴⁰I begged your followers to force the evil spirit out, but they could not do it."

⁴¹Jesus answered, "You people have no faith, and your lives are all wrong. How long must I stay with you and put up with you? Bring your son here."

⁴²While the boy was coming, the demon threw him on the ground and made him lose control of himself. But Jesus gave a strong command to the evil spirit and healed the boy and gave him back to his father. ⁴³All the people were amazed at the great power of God.

Just like today, there were many answers to Jesus' question.

Who did the people say Jesus was (v 19)?

Today people think of Jesus as a historical figure, a good man or even a legend. Have you heard people say that Jesus was something else?

The question that Jesus asked (v 20) is one that echoes through time to us today. "Who do you say I am?"

Think

Who do *you* say Jesus is?

Is this the time for you to tell Jesus that *you* believe in him (not your mates or people at church – but YOU) and want to be committed to him? It might help to find a Christian friend to talk to about this.

Pray

Lord Jesus, help me to know for sure who you are. Give me courage to take a stand for you like Peter did.

Excuses, excuses

Here are some excuses which can stop us doing what Jesus wants.
Circle any which apply to you.

Watching TV

Friends might laugh at me

Computer games

Boy/girlfriends

Too much homework

Don't want to be different

It's too hard

Playing sport

Luke 9:43b–62

Jesus Talks About His Death

While everyone was wondering about all that Jesus did, he said to his followers, ⁴⁴"Don't forget what I tell you now: the Son of Man will be handed over to people." ⁴⁵But the followers did not understand what this meant; the meaning was hidden from them so they could not understand. But they were afraid to ask Jesus about it.

Who is the Greatest?

⁴⁶Jesus' followers began to have an argument about which one of them was the greatest. ⁴⁷Jesus knew what they were thinking, so he took a little child and stood the child beside him. ⁴⁸Then Jesus said, "Whoever accepts this little child in my name accepts me. And whoever accepts me accepts the One who sent me, because whoever is least among you all is really the greatest."

Anyone Not Against Us is For Us

⁴⁹John answered, "Master, we saw someone using your name to force demons out of people. We told him to stop, because he does not belong to our group."

⁵⁰But Jesus said to him, "Don't stop him, because whoever is not against you is for you."

A Town Rejects Jesus

⁵¹When the time was coming near for Jesus to depart, he was determined to go to Jerusalem. ⁵²He sent some men ahead of him, who went into a town in Samaria to make everything ready for him. ⁵³But the people there would not welcome him, because he was set on going to Jerusalem. ⁵⁴When James and John, followers of Jesus, saw this, they said, "Lord, do you want us to call fire down from heaven and destroy those people?"

⁵⁵But Jesus turned and scolded them. ⁵⁶Then they went to another town.

Following Jesus

⁵⁷As they were going along the road, someone said to Jesus, "I will follow you anywhere you go."

⁵⁸Jesus said to them, "The foxes have holes to live in, and the birds have nests,

but the Son of Man has no place to rest his head."

⁵⁹Jesus said to another man, "Follow me!"

But he said, "Lord, first let me go and bury my father."

⁶⁰But Jesus said to him, "Let the people who are dead bury their own dead. You must go and tell about the kingdom of God."

⁶¹Another man said, "I will follow you, Lord, but first let me go and say goodbye to my family."

⁶²Jesus said, "Anyone who begins to plough a field but keeps looking back is of no use in the kingdom of God."

All of the people in 9:57–62 *wanted* to follow Jesus, but the cost was too great. Here's what stopped them. Write the verse number alongside each:

- comfort and possessions (v ...)

- responsibilities (v ...)

- family (v ...)

Think

Life stuff can often get in the way. Write a list of what you care for most in your life – things like belongings, family, friends, God. Think about the order you've put things in. Should you have different priorities?

Pray

Ask God to help you live for him and put him first, whatever the cost.

Woe? Whoa!

Just because we're Christians, it doesn't mean we can tell everyone how great we are and how awful they are. It doesn't work like that.

Luke 10:1–24

Jesus Sends Out the Seventy-two

10 After this, the Lord chose 72 others and sent them out in pairs ahead of him into every town and place where he planned to go. ²He said to them, "There are a great many people to harvest, but there are only a few workers. So pray to God, who owns the harvest, that he will send more workers to help gather his harvest. ³Go now, but listen! I am sending you out like sheep among wolves. ⁴Don't carry a purse, a bag or sandals, and don't waste time talking with people on the road. ⁵Before you go into a house, say, 'Peace be with this house.' ⁶If peaceful people live there, your blessing of peace will stay with them, but if not, then your blessing will come back to you. ⁷Stay in the peaceful house, eating and drinking what the people there give you. A worker should be given his pay. Don't move from house to house. ⁸If you go into a town and the people welcome you, eat what they give you. ⁹Heal the sick who live there, and tell them, 'The kingdom of God is near you.' ¹⁰But if you go into a town, and the people don't welcome you, then go into the streets and say, ¹¹'Even the dust from your town that sticks to our feet we wipe off against you. But remember that the kingdom of God is near.' ¹²I tell you, on the Judge-ment Day it will be better for the people of Sodom than for the people of that town.

Jesus Warns Unbelievers

¹³"How terrible for you, Korazin! How terrible for you, Bethsaida! If the miracles I did in you had happened in Tyre and Sidon, those people would have changed their lives long ago. They would have worn rough cloth and put ashes on themselves to show they had changed. ¹⁴But on the Judgement Day it will be better for Tyre and Sidon than for you. ¹⁵And you, Capernaum, will you be lifted up to heaven? No! You will be thrown down to the depths!

¹⁶"Whoever listens to you listens to me, and whoever refuses to accept you refuses to accept me. And whoever refuses to accept me refuses to accept the One who sent me."

Satan Falls

¹⁷When the 72 came back, they were very happy and said, "Lord, even the demons obeyed us when we used your name!"

¹⁸Jesus said, "I saw Satan fall like lightning from heaven. ¹⁹Listen, I have given you power to walk on snakes and scorpions, power that is greater than the

enemy has. So nothing will hurt you. 20But you should not be happy because the spirits obey you but because your names are written in heaven."

Jesus Prays to the Father

21Then Jesus rejoiced in the Holy Spirit and said, "I praise you, Father, Lord of heaven and earth, because you have hidden these things from the people who are wise and clever. But you have shown them to those who are like little children. Yes,

Father, this is what you really wanted.

22"My Father has given me all things. No one knows who the Son is, except the Father. And no one knows who the Father is, except the Son and those whom the Son chooses to tell."

23Then Jesus turned to his followers and said privately, "You are blessed to see what you now see. 24I tell you, many prophets and kings wanted to see what you now see, but they did not, and they wanted to hear what you now hear, but they did not."

Jesus has given his followers great powers and it may go to our heads sometimes (v 17). But we should never be arrogant about being Christians. We should be humble about it, thankful that we have a place in God's plan, just as Jesus says.

Think

Is your relationship with God affected by how old you are? Has it changed as you've grown older?

Pray

Thank God for being real to you.

Care for others

Which one of these would you describe as your "neighbour"?

- People at church
- The person living next door
- Anyone you pass in the street
- Your mates
- The geeky boy/girl at school
- Someone from another faith

Find the answer in today's story.

 Luke 10:25–11:8

The Good Samaritan

25Then an expert on the law stood up to test Jesus, saying, "Teacher, what must I do to get eternal life?"

26Jesus said, "What is written in the law? What do you read there?"

27The man answered, "Love the Lord your God with all your heart, all your soul, all your strength and all your mind." Also, "Love your neighbour as you love yourself."

28Jesus said to him, "Your answer is right. Do this and you will live."

29But the man, wanting to show the importance of his question, said to Jesus, "And who is my neighbour?"

30Jesus answered, "As a man was going down from Jerusalem to Jericho, some robbers attacked him. They tore off his clothes, beat him, and left him lying there, almost dead. 31It happened that a Jewish priest was going down that road. When he saw the man, he walked by on the other side. 32Next, a Levite came there, and after he went over and looked at the man, he walked by on the other side of the road. 33Then a Samaritan travelling down the road came to where the hurt man was. When he saw the man, he felt very sorry for him. 34The Samaritan went to him, poured olive oil and wine on his wounds and bandaged them. Then he put the hurt man on his own donkey and took him to an inn where he cared for him. 35The next day, the Samaritan brought out two silver coins, gave them to the innkeeper, and said, 'Take care of this man. If you spend more money on him, I will pay it back to you when I come again.' "

36Then Jesus said, "Which one of these three men do you think was a neighbour to the man who was attacked by the robbers?"

37The expert on the law answered, "The one who showed him mercy."

Jesus said to him, "Then go and do what he did."

Mary and Martha

38While Jesus and his followers were travelling, Jesus went into a town. A woman named Martha let Jesus stay at her house. 39Martha had a sister named Mary, who was sitting at Jesus' feet and listening to him teach. ⁴⁰But Martha was busy with all the work to be done. She went in and said, "Lord, don't you care that my sister has left me alone to do all the work? Tell her to help me."

⁴¹But the Lord answered her, "Martha, Martha, you are worried and upset about many things. ⁴²Only one thing is important. Mary has chosen the better thing, and it will never be taken away from her."

Jesus Teaches About Prayer

11 Once Jesus was praying in a certain place. When he finished, one of his followers said to him, "Lord, teach us to pray as John taught his followers."

²Jesus said to them, "When you pray, say:

'Father, may your name always be kept holy.

May your kingdom come.

³Give us the food we need for each day.

⁴Forgive us for our sins,

because we forgive everyone who has done wrong to us.

And do not cause us to be tempted.'"

Continue to Ask

⁵Then Jesus said to them, "Suppose one of you went to your friend's house at midnight and said to him, 'Friend, loan me three loaves of bread. ⁶A friend of mine has come into town to visit me, but I have nothing for him to eat.' ⁷Your friend inside the house answers, 'Don't bother me! The door is already locked, and my children and I are in bed. I cannot get up and give you anything.' ⁸I tell you, if friendship is not enough to make him get up to give you the bread, your boldness will make him get up and give you whatever you need.

What are the two things found in the law that are given as a right answer to Jesus (10:27)?

What do you think is the main thing Jesus wants you to learn from this story? Write it in less than ten words below.

_____

_____

Think

How could you be a good "neighbour" to someone today?

Pray

Lord Jesus, help me to see who needs my help and then to do something about it.

United we stand

A team of people working together is always stronger than a bunch of people doing their own thing.

 Luke 11:9–36

9So I tell you, ask, and God will give to you. Search, and you will find. Knock, and the door will open for you. 10Yes, everyone who asks will receive. The one who searches will find. And everyone who knocks will have the door opened. 11If your children ask for a fish, which of you would give them a snake instead? 12Or, if your children ask for an egg, would you give them a scorpion? 13Even though you are bad, you know how to give good things to your children. How much more will your heavenly Father give the Holy Spirit to those who ask him!"

Jesus' Power is from God

14Once Jesus was sending out a demon that could not talk. When the demon came out, the man who had been unable to speak, then spoke. The people were amazed. 15But some of them said, "Jesus uses the power of Beelzebul, the ruler of demons, to force demons out of people."

16Other people, wanting to test Jesus, asked him to give them a sign from heaven. 17But knowing their thoughts, he said to them, "Every kingdom that is divided against itself will be destroyed. And a family that is divided against itself will not continue. 18So if Satan is divided against himself, his kingdom will not continue. You say that I use the power of Beelzebul to force out demons. 19But if I use the power of Beelzebul to force out demons, what power do your people use to force demons out? So they will be your judges. 20But if I use the power of God to force out

demons, then the kingdom of God has come to you.

21"When a strong person with many weapons guards his own house, his possessions are safe. 22But when someone stronger comes and defeats him, the stronger one will take away the weapons the first man trusted and will give away the possessions.

23"Anyone who is not with me is against me, and anyone who does not work with me is working against me.

The Empty Person

24"When an evil spirit comes out of a person, it travels through dry places, looking for a place to rest. But when it finds no place, it says, 'I will go back to the house I left.' 25And when it comes back, it finds that house swept clean and made neat. 26Then the evil spirit goes out and brings seven other spirits more evil than it is, and they go in and live there. So the person has even more trouble than before."

People Who Are Truly Happy

27As Jesus was saying these things, a woman in the crowd called out to Jesus, "Happy is the mother who gave birth to you and nursed you."

28But Jesus said, "No, happy are those who hear the teaching of God and obey it."

The People Want a Miracle

29As the crowd grew larger, Jesus said, "The people who live today are evil. They want to see a miracle for a sign, but no sign will be given them, except the sign of Jonah. ³⁰As Jonah was a sign for those people who lived in Nineveh, the Son of Man will be a sign for the people of this time. ³¹On the Judgement Day the Queen of the South will stand up with the people who live now. She will show they are guilty, because she came from far away to listen to Solomon's wise teaching. And I tell you that someone greater than Solomon is here. ³²On the Judgement Day the people of Nineveh will stand up with the people who live now, and they will show that you are guilty. When Jonah preached to them, they were sorry and changed their lives. And I tell you that someone greater than Jonah is here.

Be a Light for the World

³³"No one lights a lamp and puts it in a secret place or under a bowl, but on a lampstand so the people who come in can see. ³⁴Your eye is a light for the body. When your eyes are good, your whole body will be full of light. But when your eyes are evil, your whole body will be full of darkness. ³⁵So be careful not to let the light in you become darkness. ³⁶If your whole body is full of light, and none of it is dark, then you will shine bright, as when a lamp shines on you."

Why do you think the church leaders were saying that Jesus was throwing out demons in the name of Beelzebul, a powerful demon (v 15)?

Why was this a stupid thing to say?

Think

If a team isn't 100 per cent committed, it can't succeed. It's the same with you: if you're not 100 per cent committed to Jesus, you won't be an effective follower (see vs 33–36).

Pray

Ask God to help you be consistently committed to following Jesus.

Don't be a hypocrite

What are hypocrites?

- Big, grey animals
- People who say one thing but do another
- Religious people

 Luke 11:37–12:7

Jesus Accuses the Pharisees

37After Jesus had finished speaking, a Pharisee asked Jesus to eat with him. So Jesus went in and sat at the table. 38But the Pharisee was surprised when he saw that Jesus did not wash his hands before the meal. 39The Lord said to him, "You Pharisees clean the outside of the cup and the dish, but inside you are full of greed and evil. 40You foolish people! The same one who made what is outside also made what is inside. 41So give what is in your dishes to the poor, and then you will be fully clean. 42How terrible for you Pharisees! You give God one-tenth of even your mint, your rue and every other plant in your garden. But you fail to be fair to others and to love God. These are the things you should do while continuing to do those other things. 43How terrible for you Pharisees, because you love to have the most important seats in the synagogues, and you love to be greeted with respect in the market places. 44How terrible for you, because you are like hidden graves, which people walk on without knowing."

Jesus Talks to Experts on the Law

45One of the experts on the law said to Jesus, "Teacher, when you say these things, you are insulting us, too."

46Jesus answered, "How terrible for you, you experts on the law! You make strict rules that are very hard for people to obey, but you yourselves don't even try to follow those rules. 47How terrible for you, because you build tombs for the prophets whom your ancestors killed! 48And now you show that you approve of what your ancestors did. They killed the prophets, and you build tombs for them! 49This is why in his wisdom God said, 'I will send prophets and apostles to them. They will kill some, and they will treat others cruelly.' 50So you who live now will be punished for the deaths of all the prophets who were killed since the beginning of the world— 51from the killing of Abel to the killing of Zechariah, who died between the altar and the Temple. Yes, I tell you that you who are alive now will be punished for them all.

52"How terrible for you, you experts on the law. You have taken away the key to learning about God. You yourselves would not learn, and you stopped others from learning, too."

53When Jesus left, the teachers of the law and the Pharisees began to give him trouble, asking him questions about many things and 54trying to catch him saying something wrong.

Don't Be like the Pharisees

12 So many thousands of people had gathered that they were stepping on each other. Jesus spoke first to his followers, saying, "Beware of the yeast of

the Pharisees, because they are hypocrites. ²Everything that is hidden will be shown, and everything that is secret will be made known. ³What you have said in the dark will be heard in the light, and what you have whispered in an inner room will be shouted from the housetops.

⁴"I tell you, my friends, don't be afraid of people who can kill the body but after that can do nothing more to hurt you. ⁵I will show you the one to fear. Fear the one who has the power to kill you and also to throw you into hell. Yes, this is the one you should fear.

⁶"Five sparrows are sold for only two pennies, and God does not forget any of them. ⁷But God even knows how many hairs you have on your head. Don't be afraid. You are worth much more than many sparrows.

The Pharisees looked good in public, but God knew the truth about them (12:3).

Why do you think Jesus used the analogy of yeast (12:1)?

Who was Jesus talking about in 12:5?

Think

Are you a hypocrite?

Does what others see of you match with what God knows about you (12:2,3)?

Pray

Lord, help me to live in a way that pleases you wherever I am, whoever I'm with.

Money

Do you get an allowance? What do you do with it? Spend it all?
Save some and spend some?

Luke 12:8–34

Don't Be Ashamed of Jesus

8"I tell you, all those who stand before others and say they believe in me, I, the Son of Man, will say before the angels of God that they belong to me. 9But all who stand before others and say they do not believe in me, I will say before the angels of God that they do not belong to me.

10"Anyone who speaks against the Son of Man can be forgiven, but anyone who speaks against the Holy Spirit will not be forgiven.

11"When you are brought into the synagogues before the leaders and other powerful people, don't worry about how to defend yourselves or what to say. 12At that time the Holy Spirit will teach you what you must say."

Jesus Warns Against Selfishness

13Someone in the crowd said to Jesus, "Teacher, tell my brother to divide with me the property our father left us."

14But Jesus said to him, "Who said I should judge or decide between you?" 15Then Jesus said to them, "Be careful and guard against all kinds of greed. Life is not measured by how much one owns."

16Then Jesus told this story: "There was a rich man who had some land, which grew a good crop. 17He thought to himself, 'What will I do? I have no place to keep all my crops.' 18Then he said, 'This is what I will do: I will tear down my barns and build bigger ones, and there I will store all my grain and other goods. 19Then I can say to myself, "I have enough good things stored to last for many years. Rest, eat,

drink and enjoy life!"'

20"But God said to him, 'Foolish man! Tonight your life will be taken from you. So who will get those things you have prepared for yourself?'

21"This is how it will be for those who store up things for themselves and are not rich towards God."

Don't Worry

22Jesus said to his followers, "So I tell you, don't worry about the food you need to live, or about the clothes you need in order for your body. 23Life is more than food, and the body is more than clothes. 24Look at the birds. They don't plant or harvest, they don't have storerooms or barns, but God feeds them. And you are worth much more than birds. 25You cannot add any time to your life by worrying about it. 26If you cannot do even the little things, then why worry about the big things? 27Consider how the lilies grow; they don't work or make clothes for themselves. But I tell you that even Solomon with his riches was not dressed as beautifully as one of these flowers. 28God clothes the grass in the field, which is alive today but tomorrow is thrown into the fire. So how much more will God clothe you? Don't have so little faith! 29Don't always think about what you will eat or what you will drink, and don't keep worrying. 30All the people in the world are trying to get these things, and your Father knows you need them. 31But seek God's kingdom, and all the other things you need will be given to you.

Don't Trust in Money

32"Don't fear, little flock, because your Father wants to give you the kingdom. 33Sell your possessions and give to the poor. Get for yourselves purses that will not wear out, the treasure in heaven that never runs out, where thieves can't steal and moths can't destroy. 34Your heart will be where your treasure is.

Jesus is challenging his followers' attitude to their money and possessions.

- God gives us lots of good things, but what does Jesus say we need to be careful about (v 15)?

- What's more important than the things we own (v 21)?

- What's more important to you – getting all the stuff you want, or living like Jesus wants (v 33)?

- What kind of things do you think Jesus meant by "treasure in heaven" (v 33)?

- What should our attitude to money be?

Think

What have you set your heart on (v 34)? How much time do you spend on building your relationship with God?

On a sheet of paper, write these headings at the top of two columns: "Essentials" and "Luxuries". Think of everything you have (e.g. clean water, CDs). Write them down in one of the two columns.

How would a young person in Ethiopia, one of the poorest countries in the world, divide up these things? Is it fair to compare your life with theirs?

Pray

Ask God to help you have the right attitude to your money – and to talk to him about what you spend it on.

In waiting

Think of some things which you have to wait for, but which you also have to be ready for (e.g. waiting for a taxi or a train). What happens if you're *not* ready?

Luke 12:35–59

Always Be Ready

35"Be dressed, ready for service, and have your lamps shining. 36Be like servants who are waiting for their master to come home from a wedding party. When he comes and knocks, the servants immediately open the door for him. 37They will be blessed when their master comes home, because he sees that they are watching for him. I tell you the truth, the master will dress himself to serve and tell the servants to sit at the table, and he will serve them. 38Those servants will be happy when he comes in and finds them still waiting, even if it is midnight or later.

39"Remember this: if the owner of the house knew what time a thief was coming, he would not allow the thief to enter his house. 40So you also must be ready, because the Son of Man will come at a time when you don't expect him!"

Who is the Trusted Servant?

41Peter said, "Lord, did you tell this story to us or to all people?"

42The Lord said, "Who is the wise and trusted servant that the master trusts to give the other servants their food at the right time? 43When the master comes and finds the servant doing his work, the servant will be blessed. 44I tell you the truth, the master will choose that servant to take care of everything he owns. 45But suppose the servant thinks to himself, 'My master will not come back soon,' and he begins to beat the other servants, men and women, and to eat and drink and get drunk. 46The master will come when that servant is not ready and is not expecting him. Then the master will cut him in pieces and send him away to be with the others who don't obey.

47"The servant who knows what his master wants but is not ready, or who does not do what the master wants, will be beaten with many blows! 48But the servant who does not know what his master wants and does things that should be punished will be beaten with few blows. From everyone who has been given much, much will be demanded. And from the one trusted with much, much more will be expected.

Jesus Causes Division

49"I came to set fire to the world, and I wish it were already burning! 50I have a baptism to undergo and I feel very troubled until it is over. 51Do you think I came to give peace to the earth? No, I tell you, I came to divide it. 52From now on, a family with five people will be divided, three against two, and two against three. 53They will be divided: father against son and son against father, mother against daughter and daughter against mother, mother-in-law against daughter-in-law and daughter-in-law against mother-in-law."

Understanding the Times

⁵⁴Then Jesus said to the people, "When you see clouds coming up in the west, you say, 'It's going to rain,' and it happens. ⁵⁵When you feel the wind begin to blow from the south, you say, 'It will be a hot day,' and it happens. ⁵⁶Hypocrites! You know how to understand the appearance of the earth and sky. Why don't you understand what is happening now?

Settle Your Problems

⁵⁷"Why can't you decide for yourselves what is right? ⁵⁸If your enemy is taking you to court, try hard to settle it on the way. If you don't, your enemy might take you to the judge, and the judge might turn you over to the officer, and the officer might throw you into jail. ⁵⁹I tell you, you will not get out of there until you have paid everything you owe."

How were the servants, in this story, ready and waiting for the boss' return (vs 35,36)?

What was their reward (v 37)?

What's this story *really* about (v 40)?

Think

How can you make sure you're ready for Jesus' return?

Pray

Lord, thank you that Jesus is coming back. Help me to be ready.

Do you dig it?

Are you taking care of yourself? Do you keep active by exercising? Do you take care not to eat too much sugar or fat in your diet? Do you make sure that the bungee rope is securely attached before jumping off the bridge?

Well it isn't just your physical self that needs to be taken care of.

 Luke 13:1–21

Change Your Hearts

13 At that time some people were there who told Jesus that Pilate had killed some people from Galilee while they were worshipping. He mixed their blood with the blood of the animals they were sacrificing to God. ²Jesus answered, "Do you think this happened to them because they were more sinful than all others from Galilee? ³No, I tell you. But unless you change your hearts and lives, you will be destroyed as they were! ⁴What about those eighteen people who died when the tower of Siloam fell on them? Do you think they were more sinful than all the others who live in Jerusalem? ⁵No, I tell you. But unless you change your hearts and lives, you will all be destroyed too!"

The Useless Tree

⁶Jesus told this story: "A man had a fig tree planted in his vineyard. He came looking for some fruit on the tree, but he found none. ⁷So the man said to his gardener, 'I have been looking for fruit on this tree for three years, but I never find any. Cut it down. Why should it waste the ground?' ⁸But the servant answered, 'Master, let the tree have one more year to produce fruit. Let me dig up the earth around it and put on some manure. ⁹If the tree produces fruit next year, good. But if not, you can cut it down.' "

Jesus Heals on the Sabbath

¹⁰Jesus was teaching in one of the synagogues on the Sabbath day. ¹¹A woman was there who, for eighteen years, had an evil spirit in her that made her crippled. Her back was always bent; she could not stand up straight. ¹²When Jesus saw her, he called her over and said, "Woman, you are free from your sickness." ¹³Jesus put his hands on her, and immediately she was able to stand up straight and began praising God.

¹⁴The synagogue leader was angry because Jesus healed on the Sabbath day. He said to the people, "There are six days when one has to work. So come to be healed on one of those days, and not on the Sabbath day."

¹⁵The Lord answered, "You hypocrites! Doesn't each of you untie your work animals and lead them to drink water every day—even on the Sabbath day? ¹⁶This woman that I healed, a daughter of Abraham, has been held by Satan for eighteen years. Surely it is not wrong for her to be freed from her sickness on a Sabbath day!" ¹⁷When Jesus said this, all

of those who were criticising him were ashamed, but the entire crowd rejoiced at all the wonderful things Jesus was doing.

Stories of Mustard Seed and Yeast

¹⁸Then Jesus said, "What is God's kingdom like? What can I compare it with? ¹⁹It is like a mustard seed that a man plants in his garden. The seed grows and becomes a tree, and the wild birds build nests in its branches."

²⁰Jesus said again, "What can I compare God's kingdom with? ²¹It is like yeast that a woman took and hid in a large bowl of flour until it made all the dough rise."

What did the tree need in order to have any hope of growing some fruit (13:8)?

What do you need to do to make sure you keep growing in your friendship with Jesus?

What kind of "fruit" does Jesus want to see in your life?

Think

Which of these are you doing to help you grow?

- Reading the Bible
- Praying
- Meeting with Christian friends

Could you do more?

Pray

Thank God for his patience with you (13:8). Ask him to help you grow as a Christian.

Extra

Check out the "fruit" Jesus wants to find in your life in Galatians 5:22,23.

In the spirit of things

Which is more important – the rules themselves or the reason why they're there?

How much should we expect to get back for the stuff we do?

 Luke 13:22–14:14

The Narrow Door

22Jesus was teaching in every town and village as he travelled towards Jerusalem. 23Someone said to Jesus, "Lord, will only a few people be saved?"

Jesus said, 24"Try hard to enter through the narrow door, because many people will try to enter there, but they will not be able. 25When the owner of the house gets up and closes the door, you can stand outside and knock on the door and say, 'Sir, open the door for us.' But he will answer, 'I don't know you or where you come from.' 26Then you will say, 'We ate and drank with you, and you taught in the streets of our town.' 27But he will say to you, 'I don't know you or where you come from. Go away from me, all you who do evil!' 28You will cry and grind your teeth with pain when you see Abraham, Isaac, Jacob and all the prophets in God's kingdom, but you yourselves thrown outside. 29People will come from the east, west, north and south and will sit down at the table in the kingdom of God. 30There are those who have the lowest place in life now who will have the highest place in the future. And there are those who have the highest place now who will have the lowest place in the future."

Jesus will Die in Jerusalem

31At that time some Pharisees came to Jesus and said, "Go away from here! Herod wants to kill you!"

32Jesus said to them, "Go and tell that fox Herod, 'Today and tomorrow I am forcing demons out and healing people. Then, on the third day, I will reach my goal.' 33Yet I must be on my way today and tomorrow and the next day. Surely it cannot be right for a prophet to be killed anywhere except in Jerusalem.

34"Jerusalem, Jerusalem! You kill the prophets and stone to death those who are sent to you. Many times I wanted to gather your people as a hen gathers her chicks under her wings, but you would not let me. 35Now your house is left completely empty. I tell you, you will not see me until that time when you will say, 'God bless the One who comes in the name of the Lord.'"

Healing on the Sabbath

14 On a Sabbath day, when Jesus went to eat at the home of a leading Pharisee, the people were watching Jesus very closely. 2And in front of him was a man with dropsy. 3Jesus said to the Pharisees and experts on the law, "Is it right or wrong to heal on the Sabbath day?" 4But they would not answer his question. So Jesus took the man, healed him and sent him away. 5Jesus said to the Pharisees and teachers of the law, "If your child or ox falls into a well on the Sabbath day, will you not pull him out quickly?" 6And they could not answer him.

Don't Make Yourself Important

7When Jesus noticed that some of the guests were choosing the best places to sit, he told this story: 8"When someone invites you to a wedding feast, don't take the most important seat, because someone more important than you may have been invited. 9The host, who invited both of you, will come to you and say, 'Give this person your seat.' Then you will be embarrassed and will have to move to the last place. 10So when you are invited, go and sit in a seat that is not important. When the host comes to you, he may say, 'Friend, move up here to a more important place.' Then all the other guests will respect you. 11All who make themselves great will be made humble, but those who make themselves humble will be made great."

You will Be Rewarded

12Then Jesus said to the man who had invited him, "When you give a lunch or a dinner, don't invite only your friends, your family, your other relatives and your rich neighbours. At another time they will invite you to eat with them, and you will be repaid. 13Instead, when you give a feast, invite the poor, the crippled, the lame and the blind. 14Then you will be blessed, because they have nothing and cannot pay you back. But you will be repaid when the good people rise from the dead."

If you have a choice between doing something to help someone or going to church, which should you do?

Think

If you've got the opportunity to make yourself look good at someone else's expense, should you do it?

If someone doesn't thank you or isn't able to do anything for you back, should you still help them?

Pray

Lord, help me to be humble, generous and honest in everything I do, and to never use being a Christian as an excuse to avoid helping people.

Party time

You've been invited to a party, but really you don't want to go because ...

- none of your close friends are going
- you don't like the person who's invited you
- you've got too much homework to do
- you'll miss your fave TV show
- you're shy

But what excuse would you make to the person who's invited you?

Luke 14:15–15:10

A Story About a Big Banquet

¹⁵One of those at the table with Jesus heard these things and said to him, "Happy are the people who will share in the meal in God's kingdom."

¹⁶Jesus said to him, "A man gave a big banquet and invited many people. ¹⁷When it was time to eat, the man sent his servant to tell the guests, 'Come. Everything is ready.'

¹⁸"But all the guests made excuses. The first one said, 'I have just bought a field, and I must go and look at it. Please excuse me.' ¹⁹Another said, 'I have just bought five pairs of oxen; I must go and try them. Please excuse me.' ²⁰A third person said, 'I just got married; I can't come.' ²¹So the servant returned and told his master what had happened. Then the master became angry and said, 'Go at once into the streets and alleys of the town, and bring in the poor, the crippled, the blind, and the lame.' ²²Later the servant said to him, 'Master, I did what you commanded, but we still have room.' ²³The master said to the servant, 'Go out to the roads and country lanes, and tell the people there to come so my house will be full. ²⁴I tell you, none of those whom I invited first will eat with me.'"

The Cost of Being Jesus' Follower

²⁵Large crowds were travelling with Jesus, and he turned and said to them, ²⁶"If anyone comes to me but loves his father, mother, wife, children, brothers or sisters—or even life—more than me, he cannot be my follower. ²⁷Whoever is not willing to carry the cross and follow me cannot be my follower. ²⁸If you want to build a tower, you first sit down and decide how much it will cost, to see if you have enough money to finish the job. ²⁹If you don't, you might lay the foundation, but you would not be able to finish. Then all who saw it would make fun of you, ³⁰saying, 'This person began to build but was not able to finish.'

³¹"If a king is going to fight another king, first he will sit down and plan. He will decide if he and his 10,000 soldiers can defeat the other king who has 20,000

soldiers. ³²If he can't, then while the other king is still far away, he will send some people to speak to him and ask for peace. ³³In the same way, you must give up everything you have to be my follower.

Don't Lose Your Influence

³⁴"Salt is good, but if it loses its salty taste, you cannot make it salty again. ³⁵It is no good for the soil or for manure; it is thrown away.

"You people who can hear me, listen."

A Lost Sheep, a Lost Coin

15 The tax collectors and sinners all came to listen to Jesus. ²But the Pharisees and the teachers of the law began to complain: "Look, this man welcomes sinners and even eats with them."

³Then Jesus told them this story: ⁴"Suppose one of you has 100 sheep but loses one of them. Then he will leave the other 99 sheep in the open field and go out and look for the lost sheep until he finds it. ⁵And when he finds it, he happily puts it on his shoulders ⁶and goes home. He calls to his friends and neighbours and says, 'Be happy with me because I found my lost sheep.' ⁷In the same way, I tell you there is more joy in heaven over one sinner who changes his heart and life, than over 99 good people who don't need to change.

⁸"Suppose a woman has ten silver coins, but loses one. She will light a lamp, sweep the house and look carefully for the coin until she finds it. ⁹And when she finds it, she will call her friends and neighbours and say, 'Be happy with me because I have found the coin that I lost.' ¹⁰In the same way, there is joy in the presence of the angels of God when one sinner changes his heart and life."

What's the party in the story about (14:15)?

Who is the person sending out the invites?

Who is invited?

Think

What excuses do you make for refusing God's invitation to spend time with him? For example:

- not reading your Bible regularly
- not praying regularly
- not going to church regularly

Pray

Ask God to forgive you for the times when you treat other things as more important than spending time with him.

Broken relationships

The soap operas on TV do their best to make stories interesting. They tell us of love triangles and broken relationships, of long-lost relatives returning to their homes and much, much more.

How about this as a storyline in your favourite soap?

Luke 15:11–16:8

The Son Who Left Home

¹¹Then Jesus said, "A man had two sons. ¹²The younger son said to his father, 'Give me my share of the property.' So the father divided the property between his two sons. ¹³Then the younger son gathered up all that was his and travelled far away to another country. There he wasted his money in foolish living. ¹⁴After he had spent everything, a time came when there was no food anywhere in the country, and the son was poor and hungry. ¹⁵So he got a job with one of the citizens there who sent the son into the fields to feed pigs. ¹⁶The son was so hungry that he wanted to eat the food the pigs were eating, but no one gave him anything. ¹⁷When he realised what he was doing, he thought, 'All my father's servants have plenty of food. But I am here, almost dying with hunger. ¹⁸I will leave and return to my father and say to him, "Father, I have sinned against God and have done wrong to you. ¹⁹I am no longer worthy to be called your son, but let me be like one of your servants." ' ²⁰So the son left and went to his father.

"While the son was still a long way off, his father saw him and felt sorry for his son. So the father ran to him and hugged and kissed him. ²¹The son said, 'Father, I have sinned against God and have done wrong to you. I am no longer worthy to be called your son.' ²²But the father said to his servants, 'Hurry! Bring the best clothes and put them on him. Also, put a ring on his finger and sandals on his feet. ²³And get our fat calf and kill it so we can have a feast and celebrate. ²⁴My son was dead, but now he is alive again! He was lost, but now he is found!' So they began to celebrate.

²⁵"The older son was in the field, and as he came closer to the house, he heard the sound of music and dancing. ²⁶So he called to one of the servants and asked what all this meant. ²⁷The servant said, 'Your brother has come back, and your father killed the fat calf, because your brother came home safely.' ²⁸The older son was angry and would not go in to the feast. So his father went out and begged him to come in. ²⁹But the older son said to his father, 'I have served you like a slave for many years and have always obeyed your commands. But you never gave me even a young goat to have at a feast with my friends. ³⁰But your other son, who wasted all your money on prostitutes, comes home, and you kill the fat calf for him!' ³¹The father said to him, 'Son, you are always with me, and all that I have is yours. ³²We had to celebrate and be happy because your brother was dead, but now he is alive. He was lost, but now he is found.' "

True Wealth

16 Jesus also said to his followers, "Once there was a rich man who had a manager to take care of his business. This manager was accused of cheating him. ²So he called the manager in and said to him, 'What is this I hear about you? Give me an account of what you have done with my money, because you can't be my manager any longer.' ³The manager thought to himself, 'What will I do since my master is taking my job away from me? I am not strong enough to dig ditches, and I am too proud to beg. ⁴I know what I'll do so that when I lose my job people will welcome me into their homes.'

⁵"So the manager called in everyone who owed the master any money. He asked the first one, 'How much do you owe?' ⁶He answered, '3,000 litres of olive oil.' The manager said to him, 'Take your bill, sit down quickly and write 1,500 litres.' ⁷Then the manager asked another one, 'How much do you owe?' He answered, '18 tonnes of wheat.' Then the manager said to him, 'Take your bill and write 14 tonnes.' ⁸So, the master praised the dishonest manager for being clever. Yes, worldly people are more clever with their own kind than spiritual people are.

What did the son do to break the relationship (15:13,14)?

Who did what to mend the relationship (15:17–20)?

It wasn't just his dad that the son had hurt. Who else (15:18,21)?

Think

Do you look forward to the day when you can leave home and make your mark in the world? Is God involved in your plans for that day?

Pray

Ask God to show you anything you need to sort out with your parents. Tell him you're sorry and ask for courage and his help to put things right.

Rich or poor

Having a good time? That's great – but is it stopping you doing stuff that God wants you to do?

 Luke 16:9–17:4

9"I tell you, make friends for yourselves using worldly riches so that when those riches are gone, you will be welcomed in those homes that continue for ever. 10Whoever can be trusted with a little can also be trusted with a lot, and whoever is dishonest with a little is dishonest with a lot. 11If you cannot be trusted with worldly riches, then who will trust you with true riches? 12And if you cannot be trusted with things that belong to someone else, who will give you things of your own?

13"No servant can serve two masters. The servant will hate one master and love the other, or will follow one master and refuse to follow the other. You cannot serve both God and worldly riches."

God's Law Cannot Be Changed

14The Pharisees, who loved money, were listening to all these things and made fun of Jesus. 15He said to them, "You make yourselves look good in front of people, but God knows what is really in your hearts. What is important to people is hateful in God's sight.

16"The law of Moses and the writings of the prophets were preached until John came. Since then the Good News about the kingdom of God has been told, and everyone tries to enter it by force. 17It would be easier for heaven and earth to pass away than for the smallest part of a letter in the law to be changed.

Divorce and Remarriage

18"If a man divorces his wife and marries another woman, he is guilty of adul-tery, and the man who marries a divorced woman is also guilty of adultery."

The Rich Man and Lazarus

19Jesus said, "There was a rich man who always dressed in the finest clothes and lived in luxury every day. 20And a very poor man named Lazarus, whose body was covered with sores, was laid at the rich man's gate. 21He wanted to eat only the small pieces of food that fell from the rich man's table. And the dogs would come and lick his sores. 22Later, Lazarus died, and the angels carried him to the arms of Abraham. The rich man died, too, and was buried. 23In the place of the dead, he was in much pain. The rich man saw Abraham far away with Lazarus at his side. 24He called, 'Father Abraham, have mercy on me! Send Lazarus to dip his finger in water and cool my tongue, because I am suffer-ing in this fire!' 25But Abraham said, 'Child, remember when you were alive you had the good things in life, but bad things happened to Lazarus. Now he is comforted here, and you are suffering. 26Besides, there is a big pit between you and us, so no one can cross over to you, and no one can leave there and come here.' 27The rich man said, 'Father, then please send Lazarus to my father's house. 28I have five brothers, and Lazarus could warn them so that they will not come to this place of pain.' 29But Abraham said, 'They have the law of Moses and the writings of the prophets; let them learn from them.' 30The rich man said, 'No, father Abraham! If someone goes to them from the dead, they would believe and change their hearts and lives.' ³¹But Abraham said to him, 'If they will not listen to Moses and the prophets, they will not listen to someone who comes back from the dead.' "

Sin and Forgiveness

17 Jesus said to his followers, "Things that cause people to sin will happen, but how terrible for the person who causes them to happen! ²It would be better for you to be thrown into the sea with a large stone around your neck than to cause one of these little ones to sin. ³So be careful!

"If another follower sins, warn him, and if he is sorry and stops sinning, forgive him. ⁴If he sins against you seven times in one day and says that he is sorry each time, forgive him."

The rich man had a fantastic life (16:19). But he didn't go to hell because of his wealth and luxurious lifestyle. What does Jesus' story suggest he *hadn't* done (16:28–31)?

Think

Whether you're rich, poor or something in between – how can you make sure you're OK with God (16:29,31)?

Pray

Lord Jesus, thank you that you came back from the dead, so that I could live for ever. Help me to listen to your words (16:31).

With mustard

Is faith . . .

- magic?
- making yourself believe the impossible?
- doing what God wants you to do?
- trusting in God's greatness and power?
- acting on the basis of what you know about God?

 Luke 17:5–37

How Big is Your Faith?

5The apostles said to the Lord, "Give us more faith!"

6The Lord said, "If your faith were the size of a mustard seed, you could say to this mulberry tree, 'Dig yourself up and plant yourself in the sea,' and it would obey you.

Be Good Servants

7"Suppose one of you has a servant who has been ploughing the ground or caring for the sheep. When the servant comes in from working in the field, would you say, 'Come in and sit down to eat'? 8No, you would say to him, 'Prepare something for me to eat. Then get yourself ready and serve me. After I finish eating and drinking, you can eat.' 9The servant does not get any special thanks for doing what his master commanded. 10It is the same with you. When you have done everything you are told to do, you should say, 'We are unworthy servants; we have only done the work we should do.' "

Be Thankful

11While Jesus was on his way to Jerusalem, he was going through the area between Samaria and Galilee. 12As he came into a small town, ten men who had a skin disease met him there. They did not come close to Jesus 13but called to him, "Jesus! Master! Have mercy on us!"

14When Jesus saw the men, he said, "Go and show yourselves to the priests."

As the ten men were going, they were healed. 15When one of them saw that he was healed, he went back to Jesus, praising God in a loud voice. 16Then he bowed down at Jesus' feet and thanked him. (And this man was a Samaritan.) 17Jesus said, "Weren't ten men healed? Where are the other nine? 18Is this Samaritan the only one who came back to thank God?" 19Then Jesus said to him, "Stand up and go on your way. You were healed because you believed."

God's Kingdom is Within You

20Some of the Pharisees asked Jesus, "When will the kingdom of God come?"

Jesus answered, "God's kingdom is coming, but not in a way that you will be able to see with your eyes. 21People will not say, 'Look, here it is!' or, 'There it is!' because God's kingdom is within you."

22Then Jesus said to his followers, "The time will come when you will want very much to see one of the days of the Son of Man. But you will not see it. 23People will say to you, 'Look, there he is!' or, 'Look, here he is!' Stay where you are; don't go away and search.

When Jesus Comes Again

24"When the Son of Man comes again, he will shine like lightning, which flashes across the sky and lights it up from one side to the other. 25But first he must suffer many things and be rejected by the people of this time. 26When the Son of Man comes again, it will be as it was when Noah lived. 27People were eating, drinking, marrying and giving their children to be married until the day Noah entered the boat. Then the flood came and killed them all. 28It will be the same as during the time of Lot. People were eating, drinking, buying, selling, planting and building. 29But the day Lot left Sodom, fire and sulphur rained down from the sky and killed them all. 30This is how it will be when the Son of Man comes again.

31"On that day, a person who is on the roof and whose belongings are in the house should not go inside to get them. A person who is in the field should not go back home. 32Remember Lot's wife. 33Those who try to keep their lives will lose them. But those who give up their lives will save them. 34I tell you, on that night two people will be sleeping in one bed; one will be taken and the other will be left. 35There will be two women grinding grain together; one will be taken, and the other will be left." 36

37The followers asked Jesus, "Where will this be, Lord?"

Jesus answered, "Where there is a dead body, there the vultures will gather."

The mustard seed is a tiny seed and yet Jesus says that faith of that size can do amazing things.

Faith in God works because it's GOD who is amazingly powerful, not our little bit of "faith".

Think

What would you like to ask God for – for yourself or someone else? Ask yourself: "Is this what God wants?"

Pray

If your answer is "Yes", then pray – and have faith in God.

When things get tough

When things get difficult, do you ...

- give up?
- keep going for a bit, then give in?
- keep going, whatever happens?

Luke 18:1–25

God will Answer His People

18 Then Jesus used this story to teach his followers that they should always pray and never lose hope. ²"In a certain town there was a judge who did not respect God or care about people. ³In that same town there was a widow who kept coming to this judge, saying, 'Give me my rights against my enemy.' ⁴For a while the judge refused to help her. But afterwards, he thought to himself, 'Even though I don't respect God or care about people, ⁵I will see that she gets her rights. Otherwise she will continue to bother me until I am worn out.'"

⁶The Lord said, "Listen to what the unfair judge said. ⁷God will always give what is right to his people who cry to him night and day, and he will not be slow to answer them. ⁸I tell you, God will help his people quickly. But when the Son of Man comes again, will he find those on earth who believe in him?"

Being Right with God

⁹Jesus told this story to some people who thought they were very good and looked down on everyone else: ¹⁰"A Pharisee and a tax collector both went to the Temple to pray. ¹¹The Pharisee stood alone and prayed, 'God, I thank you that I am not like other people who steal, cheat or take part in adultery, or even like this tax collector. ¹²I give up eating twice a week, and I give one-tenth of everything I earn!'

¹³"The tax collector, standing at a distance, would not even look up to heaven. But he beat on his chest because he was so sad. He said, 'God, have mercy on me, a sinner.' ¹⁴I tell you, when this man went home, he was right with God, but the Pharisee was not. All who make themselves great will be made humble, but all who make themselves humble will be made great."

Who will Enter God's Kingdom?

¹⁵Some people brought even their babies to Jesus so he could touch them. When the followers saw this, they told them to stop. ¹⁶But Jesus called for the children, saying, "Let the little children come to me. Don't stop them, because the kingdom of God belongs to people who are like these children. ¹⁷I tell you the truth, you must accept the kingdom of God as if you were a child, or you will never enter it."

A Rich Man's Question

¹⁸A certain leader asked Jesus, "Good Teacher, what must I do to have life for ever?"

¹⁹Jesus said to him, "Why do you call

198

me good? Only God is good. 20You know the commands: 'You must not be guilty of adultery. You must not murder anyone. You must not steal. You must not tell lies about your neighbour. Honour your father and mother.'"

21But the leader said, "I have obeyed all these commands since I was a boy."

22When Jesus heard this, he said to him, "There is still one more thing you need to do. Sell everything you have and give it to the poor, and you will have treasure in heaven. Then come and follow me." 23But when the man heard this, he became very sad, because he was very rich.

24Jesus looked at him and said, "It is very hard for rich people to enter the kingdom of God. 25It is easier for a camel to go through the eye of a needle than for a rich person to enter the kingdom of God."

Which of these does Jesus want us to learn through this story?

☐ God will help those who ask him.

☐ God will answer your prayers to make you shut up.

☐ Pester God.

☐ Keep on trusting God.

Think

How do you normally pray to God? Do you ask once for something and then leave it in God's hands or do you keep asking until you get an answer?

Pray

Sometimes, Lord, it's easy to give up. Help me to keep trusting you and talking to you about the difficult things I'm facing.

All change

Sometimes there are good reasons not to like someone. Meet Zacchaeus ...

Luke 18:26–19:10

Who Can Be Saved?

26When the people heard this, they asked, "Then who can be saved?"

27Jesus answered, "God can do things that are not possible for people to do."

28Peter said, "Look, we have left everything and followed you."

29Jesus said, "I tell you the truth, all those who have left houses, wives, brothers, parents or children for the kingdom of God 30will get much more in this life. And in the age that is coming, they will have life for ever."

Jesus will Rise from the Dead

31Then Jesus took the twelve apostles aside and said to them, "We are going to Jerusalem. Everything the prophets wrote about the Son of Man will happen. 32He will be turned over to those who are not Jews. They will laugh at him, insult him, spit on him, 33beat him with whips and kill him. But on the third day, he will rise to life again." 34The apostles did not understand this; the meaning was hidden from them, and they did not realise what was said.

Jesus Heals a Blind Man

35As Jesus came near the city of Jericho, a blind man was sitting beside the road, begging. 36When he heard the people coming down the road, he asked, "What is happening?"

37They told him, "Jesus, from Nazareth, is going by."

38The blind man cried out, "Jesus, Son of David, have mercy on me!"

39The people leading the group warned the blind man to be quiet. But the blind man shouted even more, "Son of David, have mercy on me!"

40Jesus stopped and ordered the blind man to be brought to him. When he came near, Jesus asked him, 41"What do you want me to do for you?"

He said, "Lord, I want to see."

42Jesus said to him, "Then see. You are healed because you believed."

43At once the man was able to see, and he followed Jesus, thanking God. All the people who saw this praised God.

Zacchaeus Meets Jesus

19 Jesus was going through the city of Jericho. 2A man was there named Zacchaeus, who was a very important tax collector, and he was wealthy. 3He wanted to see who Jesus was, but he was not able because he was too short to see above the crowd. 4He ran ahead to a place where Jesus would come, and he climbed a sycamore tree so he could see him. 5When Jesus came to that place, he looked up and said to him, "Zacchaeus, hurry and come down! I must stay at your house today."

6Zacchaeus came down quickly and welcomed him gladly. 7All the people saw this and began to complain, "Jesus is staying with a sinner!"

8But Zacchaeus stood and said to the Lord, "I will give half of my possessions to the poor. And if I have cheated anyone, I will pay back four times more."

9Jesus said to him, "Salvation has come to this house today, because this man also belongs to the family of Abraham. 10The Son of Man came to find lost people and save them."

As a tax collector for the Romans, Zacchaeus was probably seen as a collaborator with the enemy. Tax collectors in those days were also seen as swindlers, because they took more than people owed. People didn't like him (19:7)!

How did meeting Jesus change Zacchaeus (19:8–10)?

Think

Can you imagine Jesus changing someone you don't like?

Are there ways in which you'd like Jesus to change you?

Pray

Pray for someone you don't like very much, asking God to change them. Ask God to help you change, too, so that you're more like Zacchaeus after his meeting with Jesus.

Use what you've got

What are your top three talents?

1 _____

2 _____

3 _____

 Luke 19:11–40

A Story About Three Servants

¹¹As the people were listening to this, Jesus told them a story because he was near Jerusalem and they thought God's kingdom would appear immediately. ¹²He said: "A very important man went to a country far away to be made a king and then to return home. ¹³So he called ten of his servants and gave a gold coin to each servant. He said, 'Do business with this money until I get back.' ¹⁴But the people in the kingdom hated the man. So they sent a group to follow him and say, 'We don't want this man to be our king.'

¹⁵"But the man became king. When he returned home, he said, 'Call those servants who have my money so I can know how much they earned with it.'

¹⁶"The first servant came and said, 'Sir, I earned ten bags of money with the one you gave me.' ¹⁷The king said to the servant, 'Excellent! You are a good servant. Since I can trust you with small things, I will let you rule over ten of my cities.'

¹⁸"The second servant said, 'Sir, I earned five bags of money with your one.' ¹⁹The king said to this servant, 'You can rule over five cities.'

²⁰"Then another servant came in and said to the king, 'Sir, here is your bag of money which I wrapped in a piece of cloth and hid. ²¹I was afraid of you, because you are a hard man. You even take money that

you didn't earn and gather food that you didn't plant.' ²²Then the king said to the servant, 'I will condemn you by your own words, you evil servant. You knew that I am a hard man, taking money that I didn't earn and gathering food that I didn't plant. ²³Why then didn't you put my money in the bank? Then when I came back, my money would have earned some interest.'

²⁴"The king said to the men who were standing by, 'Take the bag of money away from this servant and give it to the servant who earned ten bags of money.' ²⁵They said, 'But sir, that servant already has ten bags of money.' ²⁶The king said, 'Those who have will be given more, but those who do not have anything will have everything taken away from them. ²⁷Now where are my enemies who didn't want me to be king? Bring them here and kill them before me.'"

Jesus Enters Jerusalem as a King

²⁸After Jesus said this, he went on towards Jerusalem. ²⁹As Jesus came near Bethphage and Bethany, towns near the hill called the Mount of Olives, he sent out two of his followers. ³⁰He said, "Go to the town you can see there. When you enter it, you will find a colt tied there, which no one has ever ridden. Untie it and bring it here to me. ³¹If anyone asks you why you are untying it, say that the Master needs it."

³²The two followers went into town and

found the colt just as Jesus had told them. ³³As they were untying it, its owners came out and asked the followers, "Why are you untying our colt?"

³⁴The followers answered, "The Master needs it." ³⁵So they brought it to Jesus, threw their coats on the colt's back, and put Jesus on it. ³⁶As Jesus rode towards Jerusalem, others spread their coats on the road before him.

³⁷As he was coming close to Jerusalem, on the way down the Mount of Olives, the whole crowd of followers began joyfully shouting praise to God for all the miracles they had seen. ³⁸They said,

"God bless the king who comes in the name of the Lord! *Psalm 118:26*
There is peace in heaven and glory to God!"

³⁹Some of the Pharisees in the crowd said to Jesus, "Teacher, tell your followers not to say these things."

⁴⁰But Jesus answered, "I tell you, if my followers didn't say these things, then the stones would cry out."

The servants were each given a gold coin to use for their master. Which of the servants in the story did the best (vs 16,17,24)? Why?

Of the three talents that you listed, which ones are you using for God? How can you do this?

Think

Are you using the talents God has given you to the best of your ability for him?

Pray

Lord Jesus, help me to use what you've given me for you.

Would you welcome Jesus?

What would you do if the Queen just happened to knock on your door? What about the President of the United States? How would you feel if your favourite pop star rang the doorbell? What would your reaction be, would you be pleased to see them?

If Jesus were to turn up at your door now, would you be pleased to see him?

Luke 19:41–20:19

Jesus Cries for Jerusalem

41As Jesus came near Jerusalem, he saw the city and cried for it, 42saying, "I wish you knew today what would bring you peace. But now it is hidden from you. 43The time is coming when your enemies will build a wall around you and will hold you in on all sides. 44They will destroy you and all your people, and not one stone will be left on another. All this will happen because you did not recognise the time when God came to save you."

Jesus Goes to the Temple

45Jesus went into the Temple and began to throw out the people who were selling things there. 46He said, "It is written in the Scriptures, 'My Temple will be a house for prayer.' But you have changed it into a 'hideout for robbers'!"

47Jesus taught in the Temple every day. The leading priests, the experts on the law and some of the leaders of the people wanted to kill Jesus. 48But they did not know how they could do it, because all the people were listening closely to him.

Jewish Leaders Question Jesus

20 One day Jesus was in the Temple, teaching the people and telling them the Good News. The leading priests, teachers of the law and Jewish elders came up to talk with him, 2saying, "Tell us what authority you have to do these things? Who gave you this authority?"

3Jesus answered, "I will also ask you a question. Tell me: 4when John baptised people, was that authority from God or just from other people?"

5They argued about this, saying, "If we answer, 'John's baptism was from God,' Jesus will say, 'Then why did you not believe him?' 6But if we say, 'It was from other people,' all the people will stone us to death, because they believe John was a prophet." 7So they answered that they didn't know where it came from.

8Jesus said to them, "Then I won't tell you what authority I have to do these things."

A Story About God's Son

9Then Jesus told the people this story:

"A man planted a vineyard and leased it to some farmers. Then he went away for a long time. ¹⁰When it was time for the grapes to be picked, he sent a servant to the farmers to get some of the grapes. But they beat the servant and sent him away empty-handed. ¹¹Then he sent another servant. They beat this servant also, and showed no respect for him, and sent him away empty-handed. ¹²So the man sent a third servant. The farmers wounded him and threw him out. ¹³The owner of the vineyard said, 'What will I do now? I will send my son whom I love. Maybe they will respect him.' ¹⁴But when the farmers saw the son, they said to each other, 'This son will inherit the vineyard. If we kill him, it will be ours.' ¹⁵So the farmers threw the son out of the vineyard and killed him.

"What will the owner of this vineyard do to them? ¹⁶He will come and kill those farmers and will give the vineyard to other farmers."

When the people heard this story, they said, "Let this never happen!"

¹⁷But Jesus looked at them and said, "Then what does this verse mean:

'The stone that the builders rejected

became the cornerstone'? *Psalm 118:22*
¹⁸Everyone who falls on that stone will be broken, and the person on whom it falls, that person will be crushed!"

¹⁹The teachers of the law and the leading priests wanted to arrest Jesus at once, because they knew the story was about them. But they were afraid of what the people would do.

The "son" in the story represents Jesus. Who are the people who kill the son (20:14,15,19)?

Why do you think they didn't welcome Jesus? How did Jesus' story come true?

Think

Jesus is the most important one – the "cornerstone" (20:17).

Do you always welcome him in your life? Check out 1 Peter 2:4–8.

Pray

Lord Jesus, help me to welcome you in my life. Forgive me for any times when, or ways in which I have rejected you.

205

Stupid questions

Have you ever been in a situation where people have asked you loads of really stupid questions about God? Often, it's not because they really want to know this stuff – they're just doing it to catch you out or wind you up.

Luke 20:20–47

Is It Right to Pay Taxes or Not?

20So they watched Jesus and sent some spies who acted as if they were sincere. They wanted to trap Jesus into saying something wrong so they could hand him over to the authority and power of the governor. 21So the spies asked Jesus, "Teacher, we know that what you say and teach is true. You pay no attention to who people are, and you always teach the truth about God's way. 22Tell us, is it right for us to pay taxes to Caesar or not?"

23But Jesus, knowing they were trying to trick him, said, 24"Show me a silver coin. Whose image and name are on it?"

They said, "Caesar's."

25Jesus said to them, "Then give to Caesar the things that are Caesar's, and give to God the things that are God's."

26So they were not able to trap Jesus into anything he said in the presence of the people. And being amazed at his answer, they became silent.

Some Sadducees Try to Trick Jesus

27Some Sadducees, who believed people would not rise from the dead, came to Jesus. 28They asked, "Teacher, Moses wrote that if a man's brother dies and leaves a wife but no children, then that man must marry the widow and have children for his brother. 29Once there were seven brothers. The first brother married and died, but had no children. 30Then the second brother married the widow, and he died. 31And the third brother married the widow, and he died. The same thing happened with all seven brothers; they died and had no children. 32Finally, the woman died also. 33Since all seven brothers had married her, whose wife will she be when people rise from the dead?"

34Jesus said to them, "On earth, people marry and are given to someone to marry. 35But those who will be worthy to be raised from the dead and live again will not marry, nor will they be given to someone to marry. 36In that life they are like angels and cannot die. They are children of God, because they have been raised from the dead. 37Even Moses clearly showed that the dead are raised to life. When he wrote about the burning bush, he said that the Lord is 'the God of Abraham, the God of Isaac and the God of Jacob.' 38God is the God of the living, not the dead, because all people are alive to him."

39Some of the teachers of the law said, "Teacher, your answer was good." 40No one was brave enough to ask him another question.

Is the Christ the Son of David?

41Then Jesus said, "Why do people say that the Christ is the Son of David? 42In the book of Psalms, David himself says:
'The LORD said to my Lord:
   Sit by me at my right side,
43   until I put your enemies under your
      control.'
                                    Psalm 110:1

⁴⁴David calls the Christ 'Lord', so how can the Christ be his son?"

Jesus Accuses Some Leaders

⁴⁵While all the people were listening, Jesus said to his followers, ⁴⁶"Beware of the teachers of the law. They like to walk around wearing fancy clothes, and they love people to greet them with respect in the market places. They love to have the most important seats in the synagogues and at feasts. ⁴⁷But they cheat widows and steal their houses and then try to make themselves look good by saying long prayers. They will receive a greater punishment."

Does Jesus answer the questions he's given?

What does he think of the kind of people who try and catch him out like this?

Think

If people try and catch you out with stupid questions, don't let them get to you. Just stick to the facts.

Pray

Lord, help me to be patient and straight with people.

Give everything

You get two letters. One is from your poor-and-ancient Uncle Fred who's sent you a tiny amount of money. The other is from your wealthy Aunt Flash who's sent you the DVD you *really* wanted (and cash for a DVD player, if you haven't already got one!). So which gift are you most happy with?

Luke 21:1–28

True Giving

21 As Jesus looked up, he saw some rich people putting their gifts into the Temple money box. [2]Then he saw a poor widow putting two small copper coins into the box. [3]He said, "I tell you the truth, this poor widow gave more than all those rich people. [4]They gave only what they did not need. This woman is very poor, but she gave all she had to live on."

The Temple will Be Destroyed

[5]Some people were talking about the Temple and how it was decorated with beautiful stones and gifts offered to God. But Jesus said, [6]"As for these things you are looking at, the time will come when not one stone will be left on another. Every stone will be thrown down."

[7]They asked Jesus, "Teacher, when will these things happen? What will be the sign that they are about to take place?"

[8]Jesus said, "Be careful so you are not fooled. Many people will come in my name, saying, 'I am the One' and, 'The time has come!' But don't follow them. [9]When you hear about wars and riots, don't be afraid, because these things must happen first, but the end will come later."

[10]Then he said to them, "Nations will fight against other nations, and kingdoms against other kingdoms. [11]In various places there will be great earthquakes, sicknesses and a lack of food. Fearful events and great signs will come from heaven.

[12]"But before all these things happen, people will arrest you and treat you cruelly. They will judge you in their synagogues and put you in jail and force you to stand before kings and governors, because you follow me. [13]But this will give you an opportunity to tell about me. [14]Make up your minds not to worry ahead of time about what you will say. [15]I will give you the wisdom to say things that none of your enemies will be able to stand against or prove wrong. [16]Even your parents, brothers, relatives and friends will turn against you, and they will kill some of you. [17]All people will hate you because you follow me. [18]But none of these things can really harm you. [19]By continuing to have faith you will save your lives.

Jerusalem will Be Destroyed

[20]"When you see armies all around Jerusalem, you will know it will soon be destroyed. [21]At that time, the people in Judea should run away to the mountains. The people in Jerusalem must get out, and those who are near the city should not go in. [22]These are the days of punishment to bring about all that is written in the Scriptures. [23]How terrible it will be for women who are pregnant or have nursing babies! Great trouble will come upon this land, and God will be angry with these

people. 24They will be killed by the sword and taken as prisoners to all nations. Jerusalem will be crushed by non-Jewish people until their time is over.

Don't Fear

25"There will be signs in the sun, moon and stars. On earth, nations will be afraid and confused because of the roar and fury of the sea. 26People will be so afraid they will faint, wondering what is happening to the world, because the powers of the heavens will be shaken. 27Then people will see the Son of Man coming in a cloud with power and great glory. 28When these things begin to happen, look up and hold your heads high, because the time when God will free you is near!"

Which gift did Jesus say was the most costly and most valuable (vs 1–4)?

Jesus had a habit of turning things upside down. Can you think of any other things Jesus did which the world would see as back to front or upside down?

Think

How much of yourself are you willing to give to God?

Pray

Lord Jesus, show me where I'm holding back from you. Help me to give myself totally to you.

Eating with meaning

Sometimes eating is more than just scoffing down a burger and chips. Meals can have meaning – like the cake you have to celebrate your birthday. And like this one ...

 Luke 21:29–22:20

Jesus' Words will Live for Ever

²⁹Then Jesus told this story: "Look at the fig tree and all the other trees. ³⁰When their leaves appear, you know that summer is near. ³¹In the same way, when you see these things happening, you will know that God's kingdom is near.

³²"I tell you the truth, all these things will happen while the people of this time are still living. ³³Earth and sky will be destroyed, but the words I have spoken will never be destroyed.

Be Ready All the Time

³⁴"Be careful not to spend your time feasting, drinking or worrying about worldly things. If you do, that day might come on you suddenly, ³⁵like a trap on all people on earth. ³⁶So be ready all the time. Pray that you will be strong enough to escape all these things that will happen and that you will be able to stand before the Son of Man."

³⁷During the day, Jesus taught the people in the Temple, and at night he went out of the city and stayed on the Mount of Olives. ³⁸Every morning all the people got up early to go to the Temple to listen to him.

Judas Becomes an Enemy of Jesus

22 It was almost time for the Feast of Unleavened Bread, called the Passover Feast. ²The leading priests and teachers of the law were trying to find a way to kill Jesus, because they were afraid of the people.

³Satan entered Judas Iscariot, one of Jesus' twelve apostles. ⁴Judas went to the leading priests and some of the soldiers who guarded the Temple and talked to them about a way to hand Jesus over to them. ⁵They were pleased and agreed to give Judas money. ⁶He agreed and watched for the best time to hand Jesus over to them when he was away from the crowd.

Jesus Eats the Passover Meal

⁷The Day of Unleavened Bread came when the Passover lambs had to be sacrificed. ⁸Jesus said to Peter and John, "Go and prepare the Passover meal for us to eat."

⁹They asked, "Where do you want us to prepare it?" ¹⁰Jesus said to them, "After you go into the city, a man carrying a jar of water will meet you. Follow him into the house that he enters, ¹¹and tell the owner of the house, 'The Teacher asks where is the guest room in which I may eat the Passover meal with my followers?' ¹²Then he will show you a large, furnished room upstairs. Prepare the Passover meal there."

¹³So Peter and John left and found everything as Jesus had said. And they prepared the Passover meal.

The Lord's Supper

¹⁴When the time came, Jesus and the apostles were sitting at the table. ¹⁵He said

to them, "I wanted very much to eat this Passover meal with you before I suffer. ¹⁶I will not eat another Passover meal until it is given its true meaning in the kingdom of God."

¹⁷Then Jesus took a cup, gave thanks and said, "Take this cup and share it among yourselves. ¹⁸I will not drink again from the fruit of the vine until God's kingdom comes."

¹⁹Then Jesus took some bread, gave thanks, broke it and gave it to the apostles, saying, "This is my body, which I am giving for you. Do this to remember me." ²⁰In the same way, after supper, Jesus took the cup and said, "This cup is the new agreement that God makes with his people. This new agreement begins with my blood which is poured out for you.

The bread represents Jesus' _____ (22:19).

The wine represents his _____ (22:20).

This makes God's new _____ (22:20) with us.

What does Jesus mean about his blood being poured out (22:20)?

What more could Jesus have given for you?

Think

How does food do you good? It's a bit like that with Jesus! Just looking at him won't do much for you! You need to take him into your life. Often.

Pray

Thank you, Lord Jesus, for doing what you did and for being there for me.

211

Scary times

There can't be many things more terrifying than knowing you are going to be killed shortly!

 Luke 22:21–53

Who will Turn Against Jesus?

21"But one of you will turn against me, and his hand is with mine on the table. 22What God has planned for the Son of Man will happen, but how terrible it will be for that one who turns against the Son of Man."

23Then the apostles asked each other which one of them would do that.

Be like a Servant

24The apostles also began to argue about which one of them was the most important. 25But Jesus said to them, "The kings of the non-Jewish people rule over them, and those who have authority over others like to be called 'friends of the people'. 26But you must not be like that. Instead, the greatest among you should be like the youngest, and the leader should be like the servant. 27Who is more important: the one sitting at the table or the one serving? You think the one at the table is more important, but I am like a servant among you.

28"You have stayed with me through my struggles. 29Just as my Father has given me a kingdom, I also give you a kingdom 30so you may eat and drink at my table in my kingdom. And you will sit on thrones, judging the twelve tribes of Israel.

Don't Lose Your Faith!

31"Simon, Simon, Satan has asked to test all of you as a farmer tests his wheat. 32I have prayed that you will not lose your faith! Help your brothers be stronger when you come back to me."

33But Peter said to Jesus, "Lord, I am ready to go with you to prison and even to die with you!"

34But Jesus said, "Peter, before the cockerel crows this day, you will say three times that you don't know me."

Be Ready for Trouble

35Then Jesus said to the apostles, "When I sent you out without a purse, a bag or sandals, did you need anything?"

They said, "No."

36He said to them, "But now if you have a purse or a bag, carry that with you. If you don't have a sword, sell your coat and buy one. 37The Scripture says, 'He was treated like a criminal,' and I tell you this scripture must come true. It was written about me, and it is happening now."

38His followers said, "Look, Lord, here are two swords."

He said to them, "That is enough."

Jesus Prays Alone

39Jesus left the city and went to the Mount of Olives, as he often did, and his followers went with him. 40When he reached the place, he said to them, "Pray for strength against temptation."

41Then Jesus went about a stone's throw away from them. He kneeled down and prayed, 42"Father, if you are willing, take away this cup of suffering. But do what you want, not what I want." 43Then an angel from heaven appeared to him to strengthen him. 44Being full of pain, Jesus prayed even harder. His sweat was like drops of blood falling to the ground. 45When he finished praying, he went to his followers and found them asleep because of their sadness. 46Jesus said to them, "Why are you sleeping? Get up and pray for strength against temptation."

Jesus is Arrested

47While Jesus was speaking, a crowd came up, and Judas, one of the twelve apostles, was leading them. He came close to Jesus so he could kiss him.

48But Jesus said to him, "Judas, are you using a kiss to give the Son of Man to his enemies?"

49When those who were standing around him saw what was happening, they said, "Lord, should we strike them with our swords?" 50And one of them struck the servant of the high priest and cut off his right ear.

51Jesus said, "Stop! No more of this." Then he touched the servant's ear and healed him.

52Those who came to arrest Jesus were the leading priests, the soldiers who guarded the Temple and the older Jewish leaders. Jesus said to them, "You came out here with swords and clubs as though I were a criminal. 53I was with you every day in the Temple, and you didn't arrest me there. But this is your time—the time when darkness rules."

Jesus was human. What did he say to his Father, God? Check out verse 42.

Why was it so important that Jesus went through with God's plan?

What might the temptation for Jesus have been (v 46)?

Think

What do Jesus' words here teach us about *how* we can pray? Are you willing to do what God wants (rather than what you want)?

Pray

Lord Jesus, thank you for being willing to obey your Father, even though it was such a costly commitment. Help me to obey God, too.

213

Let down

Have you ever let Jesus down? Peter was sure he would always stay loyal to Jesus (Luke 22:33), but ...

 Luke 22:54–23:12

Peter Says He Doesn't Know Jesus

54They arrested Jesus, and led him away, and brought him into the house of the high priest. Peter followed far behind them. 55After the soldiers started a fire in the middle of the courtyard and sat together, Peter sat with them. 56A servant girl saw Peter sitting there in the light, and looking closely at him, she said, "This man was also with him."

57But Peter said this was not true; he said, "Woman, I don't know him."

58A short time later, another person saw Peter and said, "You are also one of them."

But Peter said, "Man, I am not!"

59About an hour later, another man insisted, "Certainly this man was with him, because he is from Galilee, too."

60But Peter said, "Man, I don't know what you are talking about!"

At once, while Peter was still speaking, a cockerel crowed. 61Then the Lord turned and looked straight at Peter. And Peter remembered what the Lord had said: "Before the cockerel crows this day, you will say three times that you don't know me." 62Then Peter went outside and cried bitterly.

The People Make Fun of Jesus

63The men who were guarding Jesus began making fun of him and beating him. 64They blindfolded him and said, "Prove that you are a prophet, and tell us who hit you." 65They said many cruel things to Jesus.

Jesus Before the Leaders

66When day came, the council of the elders of the people, both the leading priests and the teachers of the law, came together and led Jesus to their highest court. 67They said, "If you are the Christ, tell us."

Jesus said to them, "If I tell you, you will not believe me. 68And if I ask you, you will not answer. 69But from now on, the Son of Man will sit at the right hand of the powerful God."

70They all said, "Then are you the Son of God?"

Jesus said to them, "You say that I am."

71They said, "Why do we need witnesses now? We ourselves heard him say this."

Pilate Questions Jesus

23 Then the whole group stood up and led Jesus to Pilate. 2They began to accuse Jesus, saying, "We caught this man telling things that mislead our people. He says that we should not pay taxes to Caesar, and he calls himself the Christ, a king."

3Pilate asked Jesus, "Are you the king of the Jews?"

Jesus answered, "Those are your words."

4Pilate said to the leading priests and the people, "I find nothing against this man."

5They were insisting, saying, "But Jesus makes trouble with the people, teaching all around Judea. He began in Galilee, and now he is here."

Pilate Sends Jesus to Herod

⁶Pilate heard this and asked if Jesus was from Galilee. ⁷Since Jesus was under Herod's authority, Pilate sent Jesus to Herod, who was in Jerusalem at that time. ⁸When Herod saw Jesus, he was very glad, because he had heard about Jesus and had wanted to meet him for a long time. He was hoping to see Jesus work a miracle. ⁹Herod asked Jesus many questions, but Jesus said nothing. ¹⁰The leading priests and teachers of the law were standing there, strongly accusing Jesus. ¹¹After Herod and his soldiers had made fun of Jesus, they dressed him in a kingly robe and sent him back to Pilate. ¹²In the past, Pilate and Herod had always been enemies, but on that day they became friends.

Peter lied three times because he didn't want others to think he had anything to do with Jesus (22:57,58,60).

Think

Peter learnt from his failure (22:62). Jesus forgave him (John 21:15–17) and he became the leader of the early church.

What can you learn from Peter's experience?

Pray

Lord Jesus, I'm sorry for the times I've let you down. Help me not to be afraid of standing up for you.

215

Worth dying for?

Could you cope with being on trial for your faith?

Luke 23:13–43

Jesus Must Die

¹³Pilate called the people together with the leading priests and the Jewish leaders. ¹⁴He said to them, "You brought this man to me, saying he makes trouble among the people. But I have questioned him before you all, and I have not found him guilty of what you say. ¹⁵Also, Herod found nothing wrong with him; he sent him back to us. Look, he has done nothing for which he should die. ¹⁶So, after I punish him, I will let him go free." ¹⁷

¹⁸But the people shouted together, "Take this man away! Let Barabbas go free!" ¹⁹(Barabbas was a man who was in prison for his part in a riot in the city and for murder.)

²⁰Pilate wanted to let Jesus go free and told this to the crowd. ²¹But they shouted again, "Crucify him! Crucify him!"

²²A third time Pilate said to them, "Why? What wrong has he done? I can find no reason to kill him. So I will have him punished and set him free."

²³But they continued to shout, demanding that Jesus be crucified. Their yelling became so loud that ²⁴Pilate decided to give them what they wanted. ²⁵He set free the man who was in jail for rioting and murder, and he handed Jesus over to them to do with him as they wished.

Jesus is Crucified

²⁶As they led Jesus away, Simon, a man from Cyrene, was coming in from the fields. They forced him to carry Jesus' cross and to walk behind him.

²⁷A large crowd of people was following Jesus, including some women who were sad and crying for him. ²⁸But Jesus turned and said to them, "Women of Jerusalem, don't cry for me. Cry for yourselves and for your children. ²⁹The time is coming when people will say, 'Happy are the women who cannot have children and who have no babies to nurse.' ³⁰Then people will say to the mountains, 'Fall on us!' And they will say to the hills, 'Cover us!' ³¹If they act like this now when life is good, what will happen when bad times come?"

³²There were also two criminals led out with Jesus to be put to death. ³³When they came to a place called the Skull, the soldiers crucified Jesus and the criminals—one on his right and the other on his left. ³⁴Jesus said, "Father, forgive them, because they don't know what they are doing."

The soldiers threw lots to decide who would get his clothes. ³⁵The people stood there watching. And the leaders made fun of Jesus, saying, "He saved others. Let him save himself if he is God's Chosen One, the Christ."

³⁶The soldiers also made fun of him, coming to Jesus and offering him some vinegar. ³⁷They said, "If you are the king of the Jews, save yourself!" ³⁸At the top of the cross these words were written: THIS IS THE KING OF THE JEWS.

³⁹One of the criminals on a cross began to shout insults at Jesus: "Aren't you the Christ? Then save yourself and us."

⁴⁰But the other criminal stopped him and said, "You should fear God! You are

getting the same punishment as he is. ⁴¹We are punished justly, getting what we deserve for what we did. But this man has done nothing wrong." ⁴²Then he said, "Jesus, remember me when you come into your kingdom."

⁴³Jesus said to him, "I tell you the truth, today you will be with me in paradise."

The religious leaders of Jesus' day wanted to get rid of him. So they "fixed" things ...

- What was Jesus accused of (v 14)?

- What did the judges, Pilate and Herod, conclude (vs 14,15)?

- What did Pilate want to do (v 20)?

- Why didn't he (vs 21,23,24)?

Think

Jesus was innocent – but he went through this for us, knowing it was part of God's plan. Look back at Luke 18:31–34.

Pray

Thank Jesus for going through so much for you.

217

Knowing God

Stuff I take for granted ...

1 The people who love and care for me
2 Being (generally) healthy
3 Having somewhere to live
4 _____

What would be on your list?

There's something massively important in these Bible verses, which could just be number 4 ...

Luke 23:44–24:12

Jesus Dies

⁴⁴It was about noon, and the whole land became dark until three o'clock in the afternoon, ⁴⁵because the sun did not shine. The curtain in the Temple was torn in two. ⁴⁶Jesus cried out in a loud voice, "Father, I give you my life." After Jesus said this, he died.

⁴⁷When the army officer there saw what happened, he praised God, saying, "Surely this was a good man!"

⁴⁸When all the people who had gathered there to watch saw what happened, they returned home, beating their chests because they were so sad. ⁴⁹But those who were close friends of Jesus, including the women who had followed him from Galilee, stood at a distance and watched.

Joseph Takes Jesus' Body

⁵⁰There was a good and religious man named Joseph who was a member of the Jewish council. ⁵¹But he had not agreed to the other leaders' plans and actions against Jesus. He was from the Jewish town of Arimathea and was waiting for the king-dom of God to come. ⁵²Joseph went to Pilate to ask for the body of Jesus. ⁵³He took the body down from the cross, wrapped it in cloth, and put it in a tomb that was cut out of a wall of rock. This tomb had never been used before. ⁵⁴This was late on Preparation Day, and when the sun went down, the Sabbath day would begin.

⁵⁵The women who had come from Galilee with Jesus followed Joseph and saw the tomb and how Jesus' body was laid. ⁵⁶Then the women left to prepare spices and perfumes.

On the Sabbath day they rested, as the law of Moses commanded.

Jesus Rises from the Dead

24 Very early on the first day of the week, at dawn, the women came to the tomb, bringing the spices they had prepared. ²They found the stone rolled away from the entrance of the tomb, ³but when they went in, they did not find the body of the Lord Jesus. ⁴While they were wondering about this, two men in shining

clothes suddenly stood beside them. ⁵The women were very afraid and bowed their heads to the ground. The men said to them, "Why are you looking for a living person in this place for the dead? ⁶He is not here; he has risen from the dead. Do you remember what he told you in Galilee? ⁷He said the Son of Man must be handed over to sinful people, be crucified and rise from the dead on the third day." ⁸Then the women remembered what Jesus had said.

⁹The women left the tomb and told all these things to the eleven apostles and the other followers. ¹⁰It was Mary Magdalene, Joanna, Mary the mother of James, and some other women who told the apostles everything that had happened at the tomb. ¹¹But they did not believe the women, because it sounded like nonsense. ¹²But Peter got up and ran to the tomb. Bending down and looking in, he saw only the cloth that Jesus' body had been wrapped in. Peter went away to his home, wondering about what had happened.

What happened just before Jesus died (23:44,45)?

There. Did you miss it? It wasn't just a rip in a bit of cloth hanging in the Temple. It was God tearing down the barriers between him and us.

Think

Wow! Being able to communicate with God anytime may be something you take for granted. But it all began here. And Jesus was willing to die to make it possible.

Pray

Stop and think about that. And thank him.

Praise God!

What makes you want to praise God? I don't mean being dragged along to church and made to sing some songs. I'm talking about genuine, self-generated praise.

 Luke 24:13–53

Jesus on the Road to Emmaus

¹³That same day two of Jesus' followers were going to a town named Emmaus, about eleven kilometres from Jerusalem. ¹⁴They were talking about everything that had happened. ¹⁵While they were talking and discussing, Jesus himself came near and began walking with them, ¹⁶but they were kept from recognising him. ¹⁷Then he said, "What are these things you are talking about while you walk?"

The two followers stopped, looking very sad. ¹⁸The one named Cleopas answered, "Are you the only visitor in Jerusalem who does not know what just happened there?"

¹⁹Jesus said to them, "What are you talking about?"

They said, "About Jesus of Nazareth. He was a prophet who said and did many powerful things before God and all the people. ²⁰Our leaders and the leading priests handed him over to be sentenced to death, and they crucified him. ²¹But we were hoping that he would free Israel. Besides this, it is now the third day since this happened. ²²And today some women among us amazed us. Early this morning they went to the tomb, ²³but they did not find his body there. They came and told us that they had seen a vision of angels who said that Jesus was alive! ²⁴So some of our group went to the tomb, too. They found it just as the women said, but they did not see Jesus."

²⁵Then Jesus said to them, "You are foolish and slow to believe everything the prophets said. ²⁶They said that the Christ must suffer these things before he enters his glory." ²⁷Then starting with what Moses and all the prophets had said about him, Jesus began to explain everything that had been written about himself in the Scriptures.

²⁸They came near the town of Emmaus, and Jesus acted as if he were going farther. ²⁹But they begged him, "Stay with us, because it is late; it is almost night." So he went in to stay with them.

³⁰When Jesus was at the table with them, he took some bread, gave thanks, divided it and gave it to them. ³¹And then they were allowed to recognise Jesus. But when they saw who he was, he disappeared. ³²They said to each other, "It felt like a fire burning in us when Jesus talked to us on the road and explained the Scriptures to us."

³³So the two followers got up at once and went back to Jerusalem. There they found the eleven apostles and others gathered. ³⁴They were saying, "The Lord really has risen from the dead! He showed himself to Simon."

³⁵Then the two followers told what had happened on the road and how they recognised Jesus when he divided the bread.

Jesus Appears to His Followers

³⁶While the two followers were telling this, Jesus himself stood right in the middle of them and said, "Peace be with you."

³⁷They were fearful and terrified and thought they were seeing a ghost. ³⁸But

Jesus said, "Why are you troubled? Why do you doubt what you see? ³⁹Look at my hands and my feet. It is I myself! Touch me and see, because a ghost does not have a living body as you see I have."

⁴⁰After Jesus said this, he showed them his hands and feet. ⁴¹While they still could not believe it because they were amazed and happy, Jesus said to them, "Do you have any food here?" ⁴²They gave him a piece of grilled fish. ⁴³While the followers watched, Jesus took the fish and ate it.

⁴⁴He said to them, "Remember when I was with you before? I said that everything written about me must happen—everything in the law of Moses, the books of the prophets and the Psalms."

⁴⁵Then Jesus opened their minds so they could understand the Scriptures. ⁴⁶He said to them, "It is written that the Christ would suffer and rise from the dead on the third day ⁴⁷and that a change of hearts and lives and forgiveness of sins would be preached in his name to all nations, starting at Jerusalem. ⁴⁸You are witnesses of these things. ⁴⁹I will send you what my Father has promised, but you must stay in Jerusalem until you have received that power from heaven."

Jesus Goes Back to Heaven

⁵⁰Jesus led his followers as far as Bethany, and he raised his hands and blessed them. ⁵¹While he was blessing them, he was separated from them and carried into heaven. ⁵²They worshipped him and returned to Jerusalem very happy. ⁵³They stayed in the Temple all the time, praising God.

What did Jesus do to the disciples before he left them (v 50)?

Why do you think he did this?

The disciples had recently witnessed the arrest, trial and brutal execution of Jesus. Then there was the mind-boggling resurrection, and now Jesus was leaving them. What was the disciples' surprising reaction to all this (vs 52,53)?

Write down on a piece of paper, all the reasons you can think of for their being so happy!

Think

How much time do you spend praising God? Is it limited to the time you are at church or when you pray? Do you think you spend enough time praising him?

Pray

Use some of the ideas you've written to help you praise God.

Lighten up!

Ever been somewhere when all the lights have unexpectedly gone out? It's really dark ... you knock over your drink ... you stand on something you'd forgotten was on the floor. Light is important. Without it we can't see where we're going.

John's best friend lightened things up for him.

 John 1:1–28

Christ Comes to the World

1 In the beginning there was the Word. The Word was with God, and the Word was God. ²He was with God in the beginning. ³All things were made by him, and nothing was made without him. ⁴In him there was life, and that life was the light of all people. ⁵The Light shines in the darkness, and the darkness has not overpowered it.

⁶There was a man named John who was sent by God. ⁷He came to tell people the truth about the Light so that through him all people could hear about the Light and believe. ⁸John was not the Light, but he came to tell people the truth about the Light. ⁹The true Light that gives light to all was coming into the world!

¹⁰The Word was in the world, and the world was made by him, but the world did not know him. ¹¹He came to the world that was his own, but his own people did not accept him. ¹²But to all who did accept him and believe in him he gave the right to become children of God. ¹³They did not become his children in any human way— by any human parents or human desire. They were born of God.

¹⁴The Word became human and lived among us. We saw his glory—the glory that belongs to the only Son of the Father—and he was full of grace and truth. ¹⁵John tells the truth about him and cries out, saying, "This is the One I told you about: 'The One who comes after me is greater than I am, because he was living before me.'"

¹⁶Because he was full of grace and truth, from him we all received one gift after another. ¹⁷The law was given through Moses, but grace and truth came through Jesus Christ. ¹⁸No one has ever seen God. But God the only Son is very close to the Father, and he has shown us what God is like.

John Tells People About Jesus

¹⁹Here is the truth John told when the Jews in Jerusalem sent priests and Levites to ask him, "Who are you?"

²⁰John spoke freely and did not refuse to answer. He said, "I am not the Christ."

²¹So they asked him, "Then who are you? Are you Elijah?"

He answered, "No, I am not."

"Are you the Prophet?" they asked.

He answered, "No."

²²Then they said, "Who are you? Give us an answer to tell those who sent us. What do you say about yourself?"

²³John told them in the words of the prophet Isaiah:

222

"This is the voice of one who calls out:
'Prepare in the desert
the way for the LORD.'" *Isaiah 40:3*
24Some Pharisees who had been sent asked John: 25"If you are not the Christ or Elijah or the Prophet, why do you baptise people?"

26John answered, "I baptise with water, but there is one here with you that you don't know about. 27He is the One who comes after me. I am not good enough to untie the strings of his sandals."

28This all happened at Bethany on the other side of the Jordan River, where John was baptising people.

God's first recorded words in the Bible are: "Let there be light" (Genesis 1:3). The light that Jesus brings is stronger than any darkness (v 5).

What has the darkness never been able to do (v 5)? What do you think John means when he says "the darkness"?

Think

Read aloud verses 1–5 again, this time putting "Jesus" in place of "the Word".

Pray

Ask Jesus for his light to show you the way. Tell Jesus about the dark things that are bothering you. Ask for his love to fill the dark corners of your life.

Handing over

It can be really hard to hand over the work you've been doing to someone else, and then to watch them change it and get all the credit. But sometimes it's the right thing to do.

 John 1:29–51

29The next day John saw Jesus coming towards him. John said, "Look, the Lamb of God, who takes away the sin of the world! 30This is the One I was talking about when I said, 'A man will come after me, but he is greater than I am, because he was living before me.' 31Even I did not know who he was, although I came baptising with water so that the people of Israel would know who he is."

32-33Then John said, "I saw the Spirit come down from heaven in the form of a dove and rest on him. Until then I did not know who the Christ was. But the God who sent me to baptise with water told me, 'You will see the Spirit come down and rest on a man; he is the One who will baptise with the Holy Spirit.' 34I have seen this happen, and I tell you the truth: this man is the Son of God."

The First Followers of Jesus

35The next day John was there again with two of his followers. 36When he saw Jesus walking by, he said, "Look, the Lamb of God!"

37The two followers heard John say this, so they followed Jesus. 38When Jesus turned and saw them following him, he asked, "What are you looking for?"

They said, "Rabbi, where are you staying?" ("Rabbi" means "Teacher".)

39He answered, "Come and see." So the two men went with Jesus and saw where he was staying and stayed there with him that day. It was about four o'clock in the afternoon.

40One of the two men who followed Jesus after they heard John speak about him was Andrew, Simon Peter's brother. 41The first thing Andrew did was to find his brother Simon and say to him, "We have found the Messiah." ("Messiah" means "Christ".)

42Then Andrew took Simon to Jesus. Jesus looked at him and said, "You are Simon son of John. You will be called Cephas." ("Cephas" means "Peter".)

43The next day Jesus decided to go to Galilee. He found Philip and said to him, "Follow me."

44Philip was from the town of Bethsaida, where Andrew and Peter lived. 45Philip found Nathanael and told him, "We have found the man that Moses wrote about in the law, and the prophets also wrote about him. He is Jesus, the son of Joseph, from Nazareth."

46But Nathanael said to Philip, "Can anything good come from Nazareth?"

Philip answered, "Come and see."

47As Jesus saw Nathanael coming towards him, he said, "Here is truly an Israelite. There is nothing false in him."

48Nathanael asked, "How do you know me?"

Jesus answered, "I saw you when you were under the fig tree, before Philip told you about me."

49Then Nathanael said to Jesus,

"Teacher, you are the Son of God; you are the King of Israel."

⁵⁰Jesus said to Nathanael, "Do you believe simply because I told you I saw you under the fig tree? You will see greater things than that." ⁵¹And Jesus said to them, "I tell you the truth, you will all see heaven open and 'angels of God going up and coming down' on the Son of Man."

When Jesus arrives, John realises that it's time to hand over the work. And his disciples mostly go and follow Jesus. Jesus doesn't keep things going the same way, though: he brings in new people and goes further than John ever went. John wasn't upset in the least. He knew that it was time to hand over.

Think

Speaking of new people, Nathanael takes a bit of convincing before he'll accept Jesus. He's prejudiced because Jesus' home town is a bit of a dump. He's wrong.

Have you ever made a wrong judgement about someone because of some detail that doesn't matter?

Pray

Father, help me to be wise enough to know when to hand things over to other people, and open-minded enough not to make wrong judgements about people before I know them.

Water > wine

You're at a party. The atmosphere is good; the people are friendly. Everyone is having a great time. The music is pumping and the CD player hasn't been commandeered by someone who's into obscure Swiss dance fusion music. Suddenly the sound system fails. Arrgh!

 John 2:1–25

The Wedding at Cana

2 Two days later there was a wedding in the town of Cana in Galilee. Jesus' mother was there, ²and Jesus and his followers were also invited to the wedding. ³When all the wine was gone, Jesus' mother said to him, "They have no more wine."

⁴Jesus answered, "Dear woman, why come to me? My time has not yet come."

⁵His mother said to the servants, "Do whatever he tells you to do."

⁶In that place there were six stone water jars that the Jews used in their washing ceremony. Each jar held about 100 litres. ⁷Jesus said to the servants, "Fill the jars with water." So they filled the jars to the top.

⁸Then he said to them, "Now take some out and give it to the master of the feast."

So they took the water to the master. ⁹When he tasted it, the water had become wine. He did not know where the wine came from, but the servants who had brought the water knew. The master of the wedding called the bridegroom ¹⁰and said to him, "People always serve the best wine first. Later, after the guests have been drinking awhile, they serve the cheaper wine. But you have saved the best wine till now."

¹¹So in Cana of Galilee Jesus did his first miracle. There he showed his glory, and his followers believed in him.

Jesus in the Temple

¹²After this, Jesus went to the town of Capernaum with his mother, brothers and followers. They stayed there for just a few days. ¹³When it was almost time for the Jewish Passover Feast, Jesus went to Jerusalem. ¹⁴In the Temple he found people selling cattle, sheep and doves. He saw others sitting at tables, exchanging different kinds of money. ¹⁵Jesus made a whip out of cords and forced all of them, both the sheep and cattle, to leave the Temple. He turned over the tables and scattered the money of those who were exchanging it. ¹⁶Then he said to those who were selling pigeons, "Take these things out of here! Don't make my Father's house a place for buying and selling!"

¹⁷When this happened, the followers remembered what was written in the Scriptures: "My strong love for your Temple completely controls me."

¹⁸The Jews said to Jesus, "Show us a miracle to prove you have the right to do these things."

¹⁹Jesus answered them, "Destroy this temple, and I will build it again in three days."

20The Jews answered, "It took 46 years to build this Temple! Do you really believe you can build it again in three days?"

21(But the temple Jesus meant was his own body. 22After Jesus was raised from the dead, his followers remembered that Jesus had said this. Then they believed the Scripture and the words Jesus had said.)

23When Jesus was in Jerusalem for the Passover Feast, many people believed in him because they saw the miracles he did. 24But Jesus did not trust himself to them because he knew them all. 25He did not need anyone to tell him about people, because he knew what was in people's minds.

OK, so it wasn't the sound system that failed! But if you had been one of the servants then, how would you have felt?

John says this is the first miracle. What does it tell us about Jesus (v 11)? What was the response from his followers?

Think

Is it OK for us to ask anything of God?

Will God give us everything we ask for?

Pray

Jesus can transform situations, making something a whole lot better. What situation would you like him to transform? Ask him.

How to know God

The way to really get to know someone is to spend time with him or her. One way to learn something about celebrities today is through interviews. Who would you like to interview if you had the chance? Imagine having a one-to-one conversation with Jesus.

 John 3:1–30

Nicodemus Comes to Jesus

3 There was a man named Nicodemus who was one of the Pharisees and an important Jewish leader. ²One night Nicodemus came to Jesus and said, "Teacher, we know you are a teacher sent from God, because no one can do the miracles you do unless God is with him."

³Jesus answered, "I tell you the truth, unless one is born again, he cannot be in God's kingdom."

⁴Nicodemus said, "But if a person is already old, how can he be born again? He cannot enter his mother's body again. So how can a person be born a second time?"

⁵But Jesus answered, "I tell you the truth, unless one is born from water and the Spirit, he cannot enter God's kingdom. ⁶Human life comes from human parents, but spiritual life comes from the Spirit. ⁷Don't be surprised when I tell you, 'You must all be born again.' ⁸The wind blows where it wants to and you hear the sound of it, but you don't know where the wind comes from or where it is going. It is the same with every person who is born from the Spirit."

⁹Nicodemus asked, "How can this happen?"

¹⁰Jesus said, "You are an important teacher in Israel, and you don't understand these things? ¹¹I tell you the truth, we talk about what we know, and we tell about what we have seen, but you don't accept what we tell you. ¹²I have told you about

things here on earth, and you do not believe me. So you will not believe me if I tell you about things of heaven. ¹³The only one who has ever gone up to heaven is the One who came down from heaven—the Son of Man.

¹⁴"Just as Moses lifted up the snake in the desert, the Son of Man must also be lifted up. ¹⁵So that everyone who believes can have eternal life in him.

¹⁶"God loved the world so much that he gave his one and only Son so that whoever believes in him may not be lost, but have eternal life. ¹⁷God did not send his Son into the world to judge the world guilty, but to save the world through him. ¹⁸People who believe in God's Son are not judged guilty. Those who do not believe have already been judged guilty, because they have not believed in God's one and only Son. ¹⁹They are judged by this fact: the Light has come into the world, but they did not want light. They wanted darkness, because they were doing evil things. ²⁰All who do evil hate the light and will not come to the light, because it will show all the evil things they do. ²¹But those who follow the true way come to the light, and it shows that the things they do were done through God."

Jesus and John the Baptist

²²After this, Jesus and his followers went into the area of Judea, where he stayed with his followers and baptised people.

23John was also baptising in Aenon, near Salim, because there was plenty of water there. People were going there to be baptised. 24(This was before John was put into prison.)

25Some of John's followers had an argument with a Jew about religious washing. 26So they came to John and said, "Teacher, remember the man who was with you on the other side of the Jordan River, the one you spoke about so much? He is baptising, and everyone is going to him."

27John answered, "A man can get only what God gives him. 28You yourselves heard me say, 'I am not the Christ, but I am the one sent to prepare the way for him.' 29The bride belongs only to the bridegroom. But the friend who helps the bridegroom stands by and listens to him. He is thrilled that he gets to hear the bridegroom's voice. In the same way, I am really happy. 30He must become greater, and I must become less important.

I bet you thought you had left your childhood behind (vs 3,4)! What did Jesus mean?

Nicodemus was thinking hard about who Jesus was. At the end of their chat he came away knowing that ...

- beginning a relationship with God is like _____ (v 3).

- to start that new relationship with God, you need the help of _____ (v 6).

Think

What would you ask Jesus about all this?

Pray

Thank God for the Holy Spirit who's helping you (now) to grow in your relationship with him.

"Buy two get one free"

Running a supermarket is a big business and they want your money. Often you will be tempted to buy something that you don't really need. There's nearly always a catch with offers that you see. But not with Jesus – and the woman in this story didn't have to buy anything either.

John 3:31–4:26

The One Who Comes from Heaven

31"The One who comes from above is greater than all. The one who is from the earth belongs to the earth and talks about things on the earth. But the One who comes from heaven is greater than all. 32He tells what he has seen and heard, but no one accepts what he says. 33Whoever accepts what he says has proven that God is true. 34The One whom God sent speaks the words of God, because God gives him the Spirit fully. 35The Father loves the Son and has given him power over everything. 36Those who believe in the Son have eternal life, but those who do not obey the Son will never have life. God's anger stays on them."

Jesus and a Samaritan Woman

4 The Pharisees heard that Jesus was making and baptising more followers than John, 2although Jesus himself did not baptise people, but his followers did. 3Jesus knew that the Pharisees had heard about him, so he left Judea and went back to Galilee. 4But on the way he had to go through the country of Samaria.

5In Samaria Jesus came to the town called Sychar, which is near the field Jacob gave to his son Joseph. 6Jacob's well was there. Jesus was tired from his long trip, so he sat down beside the well. It was about twelve o'clock noon. 7When a Samaritan woman came to the well to get some water, Jesus said to her, "Please give me a drink." 8(This happened while Jesus' followers were in town buying some food.)

9The woman said, "I am surprised that you ask me for a drink, since you are a Jewish man and I am a Samaritan woman." (Jewish people are not friends with Samaritans.)

10Jesus said, "If you only knew the free gift of God and who it is that is asking you for water, you would have asked him, and he would have given you living water."

11The woman said, "Sir, where will you get this living water? The well is very deep, and you have nothing to get water with. 12Are you greater than Jacob, our father, who gave us this well and drank from it himself along with his sons and flocks?"

13Jesus answered, "Everyone who drinks this water will be thirsty again, 14but whoever drinks the water I give will never be thirsty. The water I give will become a spring of water flowing up inside that person, giving eternal life."

15The woman said to him, "Sir, give me this water so I will never be thirsty again and will not have to come back here to get more water."

16Jesus told her, "Go and get your husband and come back here."

17The woman answered, "I have no husband."

Jesus said to her, "You are right to say you have no husband. 18Really you have had five husbands, and the man you live with now is not your husband. You told the truth."

19The woman said, "Sir, I can see that you are a prophet. 20Our ancestors worshipped on this mountain, but you Jews say that Jerusalem is the place where people must worship."

21Jesus said, "Believe me, woman. The time is coming when neither in Jerusalem nor on this mountain will you actually worship the Father. 22You Samaritans worship something you don't understand. We understand what we worship, because salvation comes from the Jews. 23The time is coming when the true worshippers will worship the Father in spirit and truth, and that time is here already. You see, the Father too is actively seeking such people to worship him. 24God is spirit, and those who worship him must worship in spirit and truth."

25The woman said, "I know that the Messiah is coming." (Messiah is the One called Christ.) "When the Messiah comes, he will explain everything to us."

26Then Jesus said, "I am he—I, the one talking to you."

Why do you think this woman was ready to listen to Jesus (4:9)?

What did Jesus do to get her interest (4:10–14)?

Why do you think she was ready to "believe" (4:15)?

Think

What did Jesus mean by "the water I give" (4:14)?

Pray

What's your greatest need? Jesus knows – but he wants you to tell him.

Just people

Are there people you won't talk to?

Who do you avoid? Why do you avoid them?

John 4:27–54

27Just then his followers came back from town and were surprised to see him talking with a woman. But none of them asked, "What do you want?" or "Why are you talking with her?"

28Then the woman left her water jar and went back to town. She said to the people, 29"Come and see a man who told me everything I ever did. Do you think he might be the Christ?" 30So the people left the town and went to see Jesus.

31Meanwhile, his followers were begging him, "Teacher, eat something."

32But Jesus answered, "I have food to eat that you know nothing about."

33So the followers asked themselves, "Has somebody already brought him food?"

34Jesus said, "My food is to do what the One who sent me wants me to do and to finish his work. 35You have a saying, 'Four more months till harvest.' But I tell you, open your eyes and look at the fields ready for harvest now. 36Already, the one who harvests is being paid and is gathering crops for eternal life. So the one who plants and the one who harvests celebrate at the same time. 37Here the saying is true, 'One person plants, and another harvests.' 38I sent you to harvest a crop that you did not work for. Others did the work, and you will finish their work."

39Many of the Samaritans in that town believed in Jesus because of what the woman said: "He told me everything I ever did." 40When the Samaritans came to Jesus, they begged him to stay with them,

so he stayed there two more days. 41And many more believed because of the things he said.

42They said to the woman, "First we believed in Jesus because of what you told us, but now we believe because we heard him ourselves. We know that this man really is the Saviour of the world."

Jesus Heals an Officer's Son

43Two days later, Jesus left and went to Galilee. 44(Jesus had said before that a prophet is not respected in his own country.) 45When Jesus arrived in Galilee, the people there welcomed him. They had seen all the things he did at the Passover Feast in Jerusalem, because they had been there, too.

46Jesus went again to visit Cana in Galilee where he had changed the water into wine. One of the king's important officers lived in the city of Capernaum, and his son was sick. 47When he heard that Jesus had come from Judea to Galilee, he went to Jesus and begged him to come to Capernaum and heal his son, because his son was almost dead. 48Jesus said to him, "You people must see signs and miracles before you will believe in me."

49The officer said, "Sir, come before my child dies."

50Jesus answered, "Go. Your son will live."

The man believed what Jesus told him and went home. 51On the way the man's servants came and met him and told him, "Your son is alive."

52The man asked, "What time did my son begin to get well?"

They answered, "Yesterday at one o'clock the fever left him."

53The father knew that one o'clock was the exact time that Jesus had said, "Your son will live." So the man and all the people who lived in his house believed in Jesus.

54That was the second miracle Jesus did after coming from Judea to Galilee.

People from where Jesus came from didn't talk to people like the woman at the well. She was from a part of the country where the people were the enemies of the people of Israel. But Jesus had a message for everyone – and it didn't matter whether he was supposed to be talking to them or not. They had to hear it. Jesus spoke to everyone – women with bad reputations and royal officials were all the same to him.

Think

In the end, there are no rich people or poor people, black people or white people – there are just people. Jesus didn't treat people differently – he loved them all. So should you.

Pray

Father, help me to show your kind of love to everybody, even those people I'd normally never have anything to do with.

Lame man walks

If Jesus walked into your school today, what miracle might he do?
Who would he help? What would others say?

John 5:1–29

Jesus Heals a Man at a Pool

5 Later Jesus went to Jerusalem for a special Jewish feast. ²In Jerusalem there is a pool with five covered porches, which is called Bethesda in the Jewish language. This pool is near the Sheep Gate. ³Many sick people were lying on the porches beside the pool. Some were blind, some were crippled and some were paralysed. ⁴ ⁵A man was lying there who had been sick for 38 years. ⁶When Jesus saw the man and knew that he had been sick for such a long time, Jesus asked him, "Do you want to be well?"

⁷The sick man answered, "Sir, there is no one to help me get into the pool when the water starts moving. While I am coming to the water, someone else always gets in before me."

⁸Then Jesus said, "Stand up. Pick up your mat and walk." ⁹And immediately the man was well; he picked up his mat and began to walk.

The day this happened was a Sabbath day. ¹⁰So the Jews said to the man who had been healed, "Today is the Sabbath. It is against our law for you to carry your mat on the Sabbath day."

¹¹But he answered, "The man who made me well told me, 'Pick up your mat and walk.'"

¹²Then they asked him, "Who is the man who told you to pick up your mat and walk?"

¹³But the man who had been healed did not know who it was, because there were many people in that place, and Jesus had left.

¹⁴Later, Jesus found the man at the Temple and said to him, "See, you are well now. Stop sinning so that something worse does not happen to you."

¹⁵Then the man left and told the Jews that Jesus was the one who had made him well.

¹⁶Because Jesus was doing this on the Sabbath day, the Jews began to persecute him. ¹⁷But Jesus said to them, "My Father never stops working, and so I keep working, too."

¹⁸This made the Jews try still harder to kill him. They said, "First Jesus was breaking the law about the Sabbath day. Now he says that God is his own Father, making himself equal with God!"

Jesus Has God's Authority

¹⁹But Jesus said, "I tell you the truth, the Son can do nothing alone. The Son does only what he sees the Father doing, because the Son does whatever the Father does. ²⁰The Father loves the Son and shows the Son all the things he himself does. But the Father will show the Son even greater things than this so that you can all be amazed. ²¹Just as the Father raises the dead and gives them life, so also the Son gives life to those he wants to. ²²In fact, the Father judges no one, but he has given the Son power to do all the judging ²³so that all people will honour the Son as much as they honour the Father. Anyone who does not honour the Son does not honour the Father who sent him.

²⁴"I tell you the truth, whoever hears what I say and believes in the One who

sent me has eternal life. That person will not be judged guilty but has already left death and entered life. ²⁵I tell you the truth, the time is coming and is already here when the dead will hear the voice of the Son of God, and those who hear will have life. ²⁶Life comes from the Father himself, and he has allowed the Son to have life in himself as well. ²⁷And the Father has given the Son the power to judge, because he is the Son of Man. ²⁸Don't be surprised at this: a time is coming when all who are dead and in their graves will hear his voice. ²⁹Then they will come out of their graves. Those who did good will rise and have life for ever, but those who did evil will rise to be judged guilty.

What does this miracle tell us about Jesus?

Why do you think Jesus asked the man the strange question in verse 6?

What made Jesus' enemies mad? Do you think it was just that Jesus broke their "Sabbath rules" (vs 17,18)?

Think

Is there anyone in your school that you think Jesus wouldn't help?

Pray

Thank Jesus for his power and authority. Is there something in your life that you'd like Jesus to heal (it doesn't have to be illness)?

Evidence

If you want to prove that you're telling the truth about something, how do you go about it?

John 5:30–6:15

Jesus is God's Son

30"I can do nothing alone. I judge only the way I am told, so my judgement is fair. I don't try to please myself, but I try to please the One who sent me.

31"If only I tell people about myself, what I say does not count. 32But there is another who tells about me, and I know that the things he says about me are true.

33"You have sent people to John, and he has told you the truth. 34It is not that I accept such human telling; I tell you this so you can be saved. 35John was like a burning and shining lamp, and you were happy to enjoy his light for a while.

36"But I have a proof about myself that is greater than that of John. The things I do, which are the things my Father gave me to do, prove that the Father sent me. 37And the Father himself who sent me has given proof about me. You have never heard his voice or seen what he looks like. 38His teaching does not live in you, because you don't believe in the One the Father sent. 39You carefully study the Scriptures because you think they give you eternal life. They do in fact tell about me, 40but you refuse to come to me to have that life.

41"I don't need praise from people. 42But I know you—I know that you don't have God's love in you. 43I have come from my Father and speak for him, but you don't accept me. But when another person comes, speaking only for himself, you will accept him. 44You try to get praise from each other, but you do not try to get the praise that comes from the only God. So

how can you believe? 45Don't think that I will stand before the Father and say you are wrong. The one who says you are wrong is Moses, the one you hoped would save you. 46If you really believed Moses, you would believe me, because Moses wrote about me. 47But if you don't believe what Moses wrote, how can you believe what I say?"

More than 5,000 Fed

6 After this, Jesus went across Lake Galilee (or, Lake Tiberias). 2Many people followed him because they saw the miracles he did to heal the sick. 3Jesus went up on a hill and sat down there with his followers. 4It was almost the time for the Jewish Passover Feast.

5When Jesus looked up and saw a large crowd coming towards him, he said to Philip, "Where can we buy enough bread for all these people to eat?" 6(Jesus asked Philip this question to test him, because Jesus already knew what he planned to do.)

7Philip answered, "We would all have to work a month to buy enough bread for each person to have only a little piece."

8Another one of his followers, Andrew, Simon Peter's brother, said, 9"Here is a boy with five loaves of barley bread and two little fish, but that is not enough for so many people."

10Jesus said, "Tell the people to sit down." This was a very grassy place, and about 5,000 men sat down there. 11Then Jesus took the loaves of bread, thanked God for them and gave them to the people who were sitting there. He did the same with the fish, giving as much as the people wanted.

¹²When they had all had enough to eat, Jesus said to his followers, "Gather the leftover pieces of fish and bread so that nothing is wasted." ¹³So they gathered up the pieces and filled twelve baskets with the pieces left from the five barley loaves.

¹⁴When the people saw this miracle that Jesus did, they said, "He must truly be the Prophet who is coming into the world."

¹⁵Jesus knew that the people planned to come and take him by force and make him their king, so he left and went into the hills alone.

> Jesus didn't just say the words, he actually put his money where his mouth was and proved he could really do the things he said he could.

Think

Bearing in mind that you're unlikely to be feeding 5,000 people with a few fish paste sandwiches any time soon, how can you follow Jesus' example?

Pray

Jesus, help me to prove that I'm as good a Christian as I say I am.

Walking on water

Can you water-ski or windsurf? Are you an extreme water sport person riding the rapids? Or, maybe you just like lying on a lilo in a pool on a hot, sunny day ...

 John 6:16–40

Jesus Walks on the Water

16That evening Jesus' followers went down to Lake Galilee. 17It was dark now, and Jesus had not yet come to them. The followers got into a boat and started across the lake to Capernaum. 18By now a strong wind was blowing, and the waves on the lake were getting bigger. 19When they had rowed the boat about five or six kilometres, they saw Jesus walking on the water, coming towards the boat. The followers were afraid, 20but Jesus said to them, "It is I. Do not be afraid." 21Then they were glad to take him into the boat. At once the boat came to land at the place where they wanted to go.

The People Seek Jesus

22The next day the people who had stayed on the other side of the lake knew that Jesus had not gone in the boat with his followers but that they had left without him. And they knew that only one boat had been there. 23But then some boats came from Tiberias and landed near the place where the people had eaten the bread after the Lord had given thanks. 24When the people saw that Jesus and his followers were not there now, they got into boats and went to Capernaum to find Jesus.

Jesus, the Bread of Life

25When the people found Jesus on the other side of the lake, they asked him, "Teacher, when did you come here?"

26Jesus answered, "I tell you the truth, you aren't looking for me because you saw me do miracles. You are looking for me because you ate the bread and were satisfied. 27Don't work for the food that spoils. Work for the food that stays good always and gives eternal life. The Son of Man will give you this food, because on him God the Father has put his power."

28The people asked Jesus, "What are the things God wants us to do?"

29Jesus answered, "The work God wants you to do is this: believe the One he sent."

30So the people asked, "What miracle will you do? If we see a miracle, we will believe you. What will you do? 31Our fathers ate the manna in the desert. This is written in the Scriptures: 'He rained manna down on them to eat.'"

32Jesus said, "I tell you the truth, it was not Moses who gave you bread from heaven; it is my Father who is giving you the true bread from heaven. 33God's bread is the One who comes down from heaven and gives life to the world."

34The people said, "Sir, give us this bread always."

35Then Jesus said, "I am the bread that gives life. Whoever comes to me will never be hungry, and whoever believes in me will never be thirsty. 36But as I told you before, you have seen me and still don't believe. 37The Father gives me my people. Every one of them will come to me, and I will always accept them. 38I came down from heaven to do what God wants me to do, not what I want to do. 39Here is what the

One who sent me wants me to do: I must not lose even one whom God gave me, but I must raise them all on the last day. ⁴⁰Those who see the Son and believe in him have eternal life, and I will raise them on the last day. This is what my Father wants."

Looking at verses 16–21 it doesn't sound like this was the kind of day (or night) for any kind of watery pursuit!

Which do you think Jesus' followers were more frightened of – the storm or the man walking on the water (v 19)?

What stopped them from being afraid (v 20)?

Think

What did Jesus walking on the water show his followers about him?

Pray

What makes you afraid? Invite Jesus to come into your situation and take away your fears.

Flesh and blood

Christians eat bread and drink wine together because Jesus told them to. What do you think it means?

 John 6:41–71

41The Jews began to complain about Jesus because he said, "I am the bread that comes down from heaven." 42They said, "This is Jesus, the son of Joseph. We know his father and mother. How can he say, 'I came down from heaven'?"

43But Jesus answered, "Stop complaining to each other. 44The Father is the One who sent me. No one can come to me unless the Father draws him to me, and I will raise that person up on the last day. 45It is written in the prophets, 'They will all be taught by God.' Everyone who listens to the Father and learns from him comes to me. 46No one has seen the Father except the One who is from God; only he has seen the Father. 47I tell you the truth, whoever believes has eternal life. 48I am the bread that gives life. 49Your ancestors ate the manna in the desert, but still they died. 50Here is the bread that comes down from heaven. Anyone who eats this bread will never die. 51I am the living bread that came down from heaven. Anyone who eats this bread will live for ever. This bread is my flesh, which I will give up so that the world may have life."

52Then the Jews began to argue among themselves, saying, "How can this man give us his flesh to eat?"

53Jesus said, "I tell you the truth, you must eat the flesh of the Son of Man and drink his blood. Otherwise, you won't have real life in you. 54Those who eat my flesh and drink my blood have eternal life, and I will raise them up on the last day. 55My flesh is true food, and my blood is true drink. 56Those who eat my flesh and drink my blood live in me, and I live in them. 57The living Father sent me, and I live because of the Father. So whoever eats me will live because of me. 58I am not like the bread your ancestors ate. They ate that bread and still died. I am the bread that came down from heaven, and whoever eats this bread will live for ever." 59Jesus said all these things while he was teaching in the synagogue in Capernaum.

The Words of Eternal Life

60When the followers of Jesus heard this, many of them said, "This teaching is hard. Who can accept it?"

61Knowing that his followers were complaining about this, Jesus said, "Does this teaching bother you? 62Then will it also bother you to see the Son of Man going back to the place where he came from? 63It is the Spirit that gives life. The flesh doesn't give life. The words I told you are spirit, and they give life. 64But some of you don't believe." (Jesus knew from the beginning who did not believe and who would turn against him.) 65Jesus said, "That is the reason I said, 'If the Father does not bring a person to me, that one cannot come.'"

66After Jesus said this, many of his followers left him and stopped following him.

67Jesus asked the twelve followers, "Do you want to leave, too?"

68Simon Peter answered him, "Lord, where would we go? You have the words that give eternal life. 69We believe and know that you are the Holy One from God."

70Then Jesus answered, "I chose all twelve of you, but one of you is a devil."

71Jesus was talking about Judas, the son of Simon Iscariot. Judas was one of the twelve, but later he was going to turn against Jesus.

Bread has always been a basic, nourishing food. What do you think Jesus means when he says he is the "bread of life"?

Think

Jesus says that believing in him is like eating food – it keeps you healthy and alive, except that if you believe in Jesus, you'll live for ever. Jesus' love keeps you going. He keeps you strong.

Pray

Father, thank you for Jesus' love to us and the gift of living for ever.

Try it and see

What reasons do people give for not believing in Jesus? Write them in the space below.

_____

_____

_____

 John 7:1–31

Jesus' Brothers Don't Believe

7 After this, Jesus travelled around Galilee. He did not want to travel in Judea, because the Jews there wanted to kill him. ²It was time for the Jewish Feast of Shelters. ³So Jesus' brothers said to him, "You should leave here and go to Judea so your followers there can see the miracles you do. ⁴Anyone who wants to be well known does not hide what he does. If you are doing these things, show yourself to the world." ⁵(Even Jesus' brothers did not believe in him.)

⁶Jesus said to his brothers, "The right time for me has not yet come, but any time is right for you. ⁷The world cannot hate you, but it hates me, because I tell it the evil things it does. ⁸So you go to the feast. I will not go yet to this feast, because the right time for me has not yet come." ⁹After saying this, Jesus stayed in Galilee.

¹⁰But after Jesus' brothers had gone to the feast, Jesus went also. But he did not let people see him. ¹¹At the feast the Jews were looking for him and saying, "Where is that man?"

¹²Within the large crowd there, many people were whispering to each other about Jesus. Some said, "He is a good man."

Others said, "No, he fools the people." ¹³But no one was brave enough to talk about Jesus openly, because they were afraid of the Jews.

Jesus Teaches at the Feast

¹⁴When the feast was about half over, Jesus went to the Temple and began to teach. ¹⁵The Jews were amazed and said, "This man has never studied. How did he learn so much?"

¹⁶Jesus answered, "The things I teach are not my own, but they come from him who sent me. ¹⁷If people choose to do what God wants, they will know that my teaching comes from God and not from me. ¹⁸Those who teach their own ideas are trying to get honour for themselves. But those who try to bring honour to the one who sent them speak the truth, and there is nothing false in them. ¹⁹Moses gave you the law, but none of you obeys that law. Why are you trying to kill me?"

²⁰The people answered, "A demon has come into you. We are not trying to kill you."

²¹Jesus said to them, "I did one miracle, and you are all amazed. ²²Moses gave you the law about circumcision. (But really Moses did not give you circumcision; it came from our ancestors.) And yet you circumcise a baby on a Sabbath day. ²³If a baby can be circumcised on a Sabbath day to obey the law of Moses, why are you

angry at me for healing a person's whole body on the Sabbath day? ²⁴Stop judging by the way things look, but judge by what is really right."

Is Jesus the Christ?

²⁵Then some of the people who lived in Jerusalem said, "This is the man they are trying to kill. ²⁶But he is teaching where everyone can see and hear him, and no one is trying to stop him. Maybe the leaders have decided he really is the Christ. ²⁷But we know where this man is from. And when the real Christ comes, no one will know where he comes from."

²⁸Jesus, teaching in the Temple, cried out, "Yes, you know me, and you know where I am from. But I have not come by my own authority. I was sent by the One who is true, whom you don't know. ²⁹But I know him, because I am from him, and he sent me."

³⁰When Jesus said this, the people tried to take him. But no one was able to touch him, because it was not yet the right time. ³¹But many of the people believed in Jesus. They said, "When the Christ comes, will he do more miracles than this man has done?"

Why were the people in these verses rejecting Jesus? For some clues, look at verses 15, 23 and 24.

They were bothered by man-made rules about what not working on the Sabbath meant (v 23), but didn't really care about showing God's love to others.

Think

It's when you start to live God's way that you get to know Jesus (v 17).

Pray

Help me, Lord Jesus, to choose to live God's way today.

I believe in you

Imagine that you are doing something wrong. You're hoping that you're going to get away with it and no one will find out. But then ... someone sees you. So, you've been caught red-handed. You knew it was wrong. Now everyone knows. Eek!

John 7:32–8:11

The Leaders Try to Arrest Jesus

³²The Pharisees heard the crowd whispering these things about Jesus. So the leading priests and the Pharisees sent some Temple guards to arrest him. ³³Jesus said, "I will be with you a little while longer. Then I will go back to the One who sent me. ³⁴You will look for me, but you will not find me. And you cannot come where I am."

³⁵The Jews said to each other, "Where will this man go so we cannot find him? Will he go to the Greek cities where our people live and teach the Greek people there? ³⁶What did he mean when he said, 'You will look for me, but you will not find me,' and 'You cannot come where I am'?"

Jesus Talks About the Spirit

³⁷On the last and most important day of the feast Jesus stood up and said in a loud voice, "Let anyone who is thirsty come to me and drink. ³⁸If anyone believes in me, rivers of living water will flow out from that person's heart, as the Scripture says." ³⁹Jesus was talking about the Holy Spirit. The Spirit had not yet been given, because Jesus had not yet been raised to glory. But later, those who believed in Jesus would receive the Spirit.

The People Argue About Jesus

⁴⁰When the people heard Jesus' words, some of them said, "This man really is the Prophet."

⁴¹Others said, "He is the Christ."

Still others said, "The Christ will not come from Galilee. ⁴²The Scripture says that the Christ will come from David's family and from Bethlehem, the town where David lived." ⁴³So the people did not agree with each other about Jesus. ⁴⁴Some of them wanted to arrest him, but no one was able to touch him.

Some Leaders Won't Believe

⁴⁵The Temple guards went back to the leading priests and the Pharisees, who asked, "Why didn't you bring Jesus?"

⁴⁶The guards answered, "The words he says are greater than the words of any other person who has ever spoken!"

⁴⁷The Pharisees answered, "So Jesus has fooled you also! ⁴⁸Have any of the leaders or the Pharisees believed in him? No! ⁴⁹But these people, who know nothing about the law, are under God's curse."

⁵⁰Nicodemus, who had gone to see Jesus before, was in that group. He said, ⁵¹"Our law does not judge a man without hearing him and knowing what he has done."

⁵²They answered, "Are you from Galilee, too? Study the Scriptures, and you will learn that no prophet comes from Galilee."

⁵³And everyone left and went home.

The Woman Caught in Adultery

8 Jesus went to the Mount of Olives. ²But early in the morning he went back to the Temple, and all the people

came to him, and he sat and taught them. ³The teachers of the law and the Pharisees brought a woman who had been caught in adultery. They forced her to stand before the people. ⁴They said to Jesus, "Teacher, this woman was caught having sexual relations with a man who is not her husband. ⁵The law of Moses commands that we stone to death every woman who does this. What do you say we should do?" ⁶They were asking this to trick Jesus so that they could have some charge against him.

But Jesus bent down and started writing on the ground with his finger. ⁷When they continued to ask Jesus their question, he rose up and said, "Anyone here who has never sinned can throw the first stone at her." ⁸Then Jesus bent over again and wrote on the ground.

⁹Those who heard Jesus began to leave one by one, first the older men and then the others. Jesus was left there alone with the woman standing before him. ¹⁰Jesus rose up again and asked her, "Woman, where are they? Has no one judged you guilty?"

¹¹She answered, "No one, sir."

Then Jesus said, "I also don't judge you guilty. You may go now, but don't sin any more."

───────────────

[Some early Greek manuscripts do not contain 7:53—8:11.]

The Jewish religious leaders were using the woman to show that Jesus didn't keep their laws (8:5,6). But they were the ones who got caught out!

What do you think Jesus might have been writing in the dust (8:6–8)?

Why do you think the leaders all left (8:9,10)?

Think

Is there anything in your life about which Jesus could be saying: 'Go ... but don't sin any more' (8:11)?

Pray

Thank Jesus for his forgiveness. Ask him to help you put things right if you need to.

Afraid of the dark

How do you feel walking along an unlit street at night, when you are alone or with only one other friend?

 John 8:12–47

Jesus is the Light of the World

¹²Later, Jesus talked to the people again, saying, "I am the light of the world. The person who follows me will never live in darkness but will have the light that gives life."

¹³The Pharisees said to Jesus, "When you talk about yourself, you are the only one to say these things are true. We cannot accept what you say."

¹⁴Jesus answered, "Yes, I am saying these things about myself, but they are true. I know where I came from and where I am going. But you don't know where I came from or where I am going. ¹⁵You judge by human standards. I am not judging anyone. ¹⁶But when I do judge, my judgement is true, because I am not alone. The Father who sent me is with me. ¹⁷Your own law says that when two witnesses say the same thing, you must accept what they say. ¹⁸I am one of the witnesses who speaks about myself, and the Father who sent me is the other witness."

¹⁹They asked, "Where is your father?"

Jesus answered, "You don't know me or my Father. If you knew me, you would know my Father, too." ²⁰Jesus said these things while he was teaching in the Temple, near where the money is kept. But no one arrested him, because the right time for him had not yet come.

The People Misunderstand Jesus

²¹Again, Jesus said to the people, "I will leave you, and you will look for me, but you will die in your sins. You cannot come where I am going."

²²So the Jews asked, "Will Jesus kill himself? Is that why he said, 'You cannot come where I am going'?"

²³Jesus said, "You people are from here below, but I am from above. You belong to this world, but I don't belong to this world. ²⁴So I told you that you would die in your sins. Yes, you will die in your sins if you don't believe that I am he."

²⁵They asked, "Then who are you?"

Jesus answered, "I am what I have told you from the beginning. ²⁶I have many things to say and decide about you. But I tell people only the things I have heard from the One who sent me, and he speaks the truth."

²⁷The people did not understand that he was talking to them about the Father. ²⁸So Jesus said to them, "When you lift up the Son of Man, you will know that I am he. You will know that these things I do are not by my own authority but that I say only what the Father has taught me. ²⁹The One who sent me is with me. I always do what is pleasing to him, so he has not left me alone." ³⁰While Jesus was saying these things, many people believed in him.

Freedom from Sin

³¹So Jesus said to the Jews who believed in him, "If you continue to obey my teaching, you are truly my followers. ³²Then you will know the truth, and the truth will make you free."

³³They answered, "We are Abraham's

children, and we have never been anyone's slaves. So why do you say we will be free?"

³⁴Jesus answered, "I tell you the truth, everyone who lives in sin is a slave to sin. ³⁵A slave does not stay with a family for ever, but a son belongs to the family for ever. ³⁶So if the Son makes you free, you will be truly free. ³⁷I know you are Abraham's children, but you want to kill me because you don't accept my teaching. ³⁸I am telling you what my Father has shown me, but you do what your own father has told you."

³⁹They answered, "Our father is Abraham."

Jesus said, "If you were really Abraham's children, you would do the things Abraham did. ⁴⁰I am a man who has told you the truth which I heard from God, but you are trying to kill me. Abraham did nothing like that. ⁴¹So you are doing the things your own father did."

But they said, "We are not like children who never knew who their father was. God is our Father; he is the only Father we have."

⁴²Jesus said to them, "If God were really your Father, you would love me, because I came from God and now I am here. I did not come by my own authority; God sent me. ⁴³You don't understand what I say, because you cannot accept my teaching. ⁴⁴You belong to your father the devil, and you want to do what he wants. He was a murderer from the beginning and was against the truth, because there is no truth in him. When he tells a lie, he shows what he is really like, because he is a liar and the father of lies. ⁴⁵But because I speak the truth, you don't believe me. ⁴⁶Can any of you prove that I am guilty of sin? If I am telling the truth, why don't you believe me? ⁴⁷The person who belongs to God accepts what God says. But you don't accept what God says, because you don't belong to God."

Being on your own out in the dark can be scary, but spiritual darkness is worse!

- Who will never live in this kind of darkness (v 12)?

- How did Jesus describe himself?

- What is living without Jesus like?

Think

- Do you follow Jesus?
- Are there any areas of "darkness" in your life?
- What can you do about them?

Pray

Ask Jesus to help you follow him and fill you with his light and life.

Blind > sight

Can you see? What would it be like to be totally blind and never to have seen? Close your eyes for a while and try to understand what it is like.

What things that you take for granted are now impossible, or very difficult?

Remember you can just open your eyes again and everything will be fine, but for others it is a different story.

 John 8:48–9:12

Jesus is Greater than Abraham

⁴⁸The Jews answered, "We say you are a Samaritan and have a demon in you. Are we not right?"

⁴⁹Jesus answered, "I have no demon in me. I give honour to my Father, but you dishonour me. ⁵⁰I am not trying to get honour for myself. There is One who wants this honour for me, and he is the judge. ⁵¹I tell you the truth, whoever obeys my teaching will never die."

⁵²The Jews said to Jesus, "Now we know that you have a demon in you! Even Abraham and the prophets died. But you say, 'Whoever obeys my teaching will never die.' ⁵³Do you think you are greater than our father Abraham, who died? And the prophets died, too. Who do you think you are?"

⁵⁴Jesus answered, "If I give honour to myself, that honour is worth nothing. The One who gives me honour is my Father, and you say he is your God. ⁵⁵You don't really know him, but I know him. If I said I did not know him, I would be a liar like you. But I do know him, and I obey what he says. ⁵⁶Your father Abraham was very

happy that he would see my day. He saw that day and was glad."

⁵⁷The Jews said to him, "You have never seen Abraham! You are not even 50 years old."

⁵⁸Jesus answered, "I tell you the truth, before Abraham was even born, I am!" ⁵⁹When Jesus said this, the people picked up stones to throw at him. But Jesus hid himself, and then he left the Temple.

Jesus Heals a Man Born Blind

9 As Jesus was walking along, he saw a man who had been born blind. ²His followers asked him, "Teacher, whose sin caused this man to be born blind—his own sin or his parents' sin?"

³Jesus answered, "It is not this man's sin or his parents' sin that made him be blind. This man was born blind so that God's power could be shown in him. ⁴While it is daytime, we must continue doing the work of the One who sent me. Night is coming, when no one can work. ⁵While I am in the world, I am the light of the world."

⁶After Jesus said this, he spat on the

ground and made some mud with it and put the mud on the man's eyes. ⁷Then he told the man, "Go and wash in the Pool of Siloam." (Siloam means Sent.) So the man went, washed and came back seeing.

⁸The neighbours and some people who had earlier seen this man begging said, "Isn't this the same man who used to sit and beg?"

⁹Some said, "He is the one," but others said, "No, he only looks like him."

The man himself said, "I am the man."

¹⁰They asked, "How did you get your sight?"

¹¹He answered, "The man named Jesus made some mud and put it on my eyes. Then he told me to go to Siloam and wash. So I went and washed, and then I could see."

¹²They asked him, "Where is this man?"

"I don't know," he answered.

The followers of Jesus thought that the man was blind because of sin.

What do you think Jesus meant about daytime and night (9:4,5)?

The man born blind isn't the only one who can't see! In what way are the Jews blind?

Think

How did Jesus answer the people who said that suffering happens because a person sinned (9:2,3)?

Pray

Pray for anyone you know who can't see the truth about Jesus. Ask him to open their eyes. And ask him to help you understand him better, too.

Seeing straight

So many people can't see the truth, even when it's staring them in the face. It's like they're blind.

 John 9:13–41

Pharisees Question the Healing

¹³Then the people took to the Pharisees the man who had been blind. ¹⁴The day Jesus had made mud and healed his eyes was a Sabbath day. ¹⁵So now the Pharisees asked the man, "How did you get your sight?"

He answered, "He put mud on my eyes, I washed, and now I see."

¹⁶So some of the Pharisees were saying, "This man does not keep the Sabbath day, so he is not from God."

But others said, "A man who is a sinner can't do miracles like these." So they could not agree with one another.

¹⁷They asked the man again, "What do you say about him since it was your eyes he opened?"

The man answered, "He is a prophet."

¹⁸The Jews did not believe that he had been blind and could now see again. So they sent for the man's parents ¹⁹and asked them, "Is this your son who you say was born blind? Then how does he now see?"

²⁰His parents answered, "We know that this is our son and that he was born blind. ²¹But we don't know how he can now see. We don't know who opened his eyes. Ask him. He is old enough to speak for himself." ²²His parents said this because they were afraid of the Jews, who had already decided that anyone who said Jesus was the Christ would be put out of the synagogue. ²³That is why his parents said, "He is old enough. Ask him."

²⁴So for the second time, they called the man who had been blind. They said, "You should give God the glory by telling the truth. We know that this man is a sinner."

²⁵He answered, "I don't know if he is a sinner. One thing I do know: I was blind, and now I see."

²⁶They asked, "What did he do to you? How did he make you see again?"

²⁷He answered, "I have already told you, and you didn't listen. Why do you want to hear it again? Do you want to become his followers, too?"

²⁸Then they insulted him and said, "You are his follower, but we are followers of Moses. ²⁹We know that God spoke to Moses, but as for this man we don't even know where he comes from."

³⁰The man answered, "This is a very strange thing. You don't know where he comes from, and yet he opened my eyes. ³¹We all know that God does not listen to sinners, but he listens to anyone who worships and obeys him. ³²Nobody has ever heard of anyone giving sight to a man born blind. ³³If this man were not from God, he could do nothing."

³⁴They answered, "You were born full of sin! Are you trying to teach us?" And they threw him out.

Spiritual Blindness

³⁵When Jesus heard that they had thrown him out, Jesus found him and said, "Do you believe in the Son of Man?"

³⁶He asked, "Who is the Son of Man, sir, so that I can believe in him?"

³⁷Jesus said to him, "You have seen him. The Son of Man is the one talking with you."

³⁸He said, "Lord, I believe!" Then the man worshipped Jesus.

³⁹Jesus said, "I came into this world so that the world would be judged. I came so that the blind will see and so that those who see will become blind."

⁴⁰Some of the Pharisees who were nearby heard Jesus say this and asked, "Are you saying we are blind, too?"

⁴¹Jesus said, "If you were blind, you would not be guilty of sin. But since you keep saying you see, your guilt remains."

Blind men being healed wasn't something you saw every day. Jesus was obviously someone special – but the teachers of the law were so busy getting annoyed that he'd broken one of their rules that they missed the obvious point – there was a man standing in front of them who had been blind until today, and now he could see!

Think

Do you ever miss obvious facts about Jesus?

Pray

Jesus, thank you that you healed people – and still do today. Thank you that you are there for anyone who will open their eyes and see you.

Real life!

What is *really* living? What makes it all worthwhile?

Which of these do you think are important?

- Sport
- Music
- Great exam results
- Loads of money
- A boyfriend/girlfriend
- Cool clothes

But is there more to life than these?

John 10:1–33

The Shepherd and His Sheep

10 Jesus said, "I tell you the truth, the person who does not enter the sheepfold by the door, but climbs in by some other way, is a thief and a robber. ²The one who enters by the door is the shepherd of the sheep. ³The one who guards the door opens it for him. And the sheep listen to the voice of the shepherd. He calls his own sheep by name and leads them out. ⁴When he brings all his sheep out, he goes ahead of them, and they follow him because they know his voice. ⁵But they will never follow a stranger. They will run away from him because they don't know his voice." ⁶Jesus told the people this story, but they did not understand what it meant.

Jesus is the Good Shepherd

⁷So Jesus said again, "I tell you the truth, I am the door for the sheep. ⁸All the people who came before me were thieves and robbers. The sheep did not listen to them. ⁹I am the door, and the person who enters through me will be saved and will be able to come in and go out and find pasture. ¹⁰A thief comes to steal and kill and destroy, but I came to give life—life in all its fullness.

¹¹"I am the good shepherd. The good shepherd gives his life for the sheep. ¹²The worker who is paid to keep the sheep is different from the shepherd who owns them. When the worker sees a wolf coming, he runs away and leaves the sheep alone. Then the wolf attacks the sheep and scatters them. ¹³The man runs away because he is only a paid worker and does not really care about the sheep.

¹⁴⁻¹⁵"I am the good shepherd. I know my sheep, as the Father knows me. And my sheep know me, as I know the Father. I give my life for the sheep. ¹⁶I have other sheep that are not in this flock, and I must bring them also. They will listen to my voice, and there will be one flock and one shepherd. ¹⁷The Father loves me because I give my life so that I can take it back again.

18No one takes it away from me; I give my own life freely. I have the right to give my life, and I have the right to take it back. This is what my Father commanded me to do."

19Again the Jews did not agree with each other because of these words of Jesus. 20Many of them said, "A demon has come into him and made him crazy. Why listen to him?"

21But others said, "A man who is crazy with a demon does not say things like this. Can a demon open the eyes of the blind?"

Jesus is Rejected

22The time came for the Feast of Dedication at Jerusalem. It was winter, 23and Jesus was walking in the Temple in Solomon's Porch. 24The Jews gathered around him and said, "How long will you make us wonder about you? If you are the Christ, tell us plainly."

25Jesus answered, "I have already told you, but you did not believe. The miracles I do in my Father's name show who I am. 26But you don't believe, because you are not my sheep. 27My sheep listen to my voice; I know them, and they follow me. 28I give them eternal life, and they will never die, and no one can steal them out of my hand. 29My Father gave my sheep to me. He is greater than all, and no person can steal my sheep out of my Father's hand. 30The Father and I are one."

31Again the Jews picked up stones to kill Jesus. 32But he said to them, "I have done many good works from the Father. Which of these good works are you killing me for?"

33The Jews answered, "We are not killing you because of any good work you have done, but because you speak against God. You are only a human, but you say you are the same as God!"

What do you think is meant here by the words "life in all its fullness" (v 10)?

What clues do Jesus' words in verse 18 give about his identity?

Think

It's Jesus who makes life mean something – whatever you have or don't have.

Pray

Thank you, Jesus, that you love me and gave your life for me so that I can have life in all its fullness.

Death defeated

Jesus heard that his friend Lazarus was ill, but didn't set off to see him until two days later (look at John 11:1–16). Find out what had happened by the time Jesus arrived.

John 10:34–11:27

³⁴Jesus answered, "It is written in your law that God said, 'I said, you are gods.' ³⁵This Scripture called those people gods who received God's message, and Scripture is always true. ³⁶So why do you say that I speak against God because I said, 'I am God's Son'? I am the one God chose and sent into the world. ³⁷If I don't do what my Father does, then don't believe me. ³⁸But if I do what my Father does, even though you don't believe in me, believe what I do. Then you will know and understand that the Father is in me and I am in the Father."

³⁹They tried to take Jesus again, but he escaped from them.

⁴⁰Then he went back across the Jordan River to the place where John had first baptised. Jesus stayed there, ⁴¹and many people came to him and said, "John never did a miracle, but everything John said about this man is true." ⁴²And in that place many believed in Jesus.

The Death of Lazarus

11 A man named Lazarus was sick. He lived in the town of Bethany, where Mary and her sister Martha lived. ²Mary was the woman who later put perfume on the Lord and wiped his feet with her hair. Mary's brother was Lazarus, the man who was now sick. ³So Mary and Martha sent someone to tell Jesus, "Lord, the one you love is sick."

⁴When Jesus heard this, he said, "This sickness will not end in death. It is for the glory of God, to bring glory to the Son of

God." ⁵Jesus loved Martha and her sister and Lazarus. ⁶But when he heard that Lazarus was sick, he stayed where he was for two more days. ⁷Then Jesus said to his followers, "Let's go back to Judea."

⁸The followers said, "But Teacher, the Jews there tried to stone you to death only a short time ago. Now you want to go back there?"

⁹Jesus answered, "Are there not twelve hours in the day? If anyone walks in the daylight, he will not stumble, because he can see by this world's light. ¹⁰But if anyone walks at night, he stumbles because there is no light to help him see."

¹¹After Jesus said this, he added, "Our friend Lazarus has fallen asleep, but I am going there to wake him."

¹²The followers said, "But Lord, if he is only asleep, he will be all right."

¹³Jesus meant that Lazarus was dead, but his followers thought he meant Lazarus was really sleeping. ¹⁴So then Jesus said plainly, "Lazarus is dead. ¹⁵And I am glad for your sakes I was not there so that you may believe. But let's go to him now."

¹⁶Then Thomas (the one called Didymus) said to the other followers, "Let us also go so that we can die with him."

Jesus in Bethany

¹⁷When Jesus arrived, he learned that Lazarus had already been dead and in the tomb for four days. ¹⁸Bethany was about three kilometres from Jerusalem. ¹⁹Many of the Jews had come there to comfort Martha and Mary about their brother.

20When Martha heard that Jesus was coming, she went out to meet him, but Mary stayed at home. 21Martha said to Jesus, "Lord, if you had been here, my brother would not have died. 22But I know that even now God will give you anything you ask."

23Jesus said, "Your brother will rise and live again."

24Martha answered, "I know that he will rise and live again in the resurrection on the last day."

25Jesus said to her, "I am the resurrection and the life. Those who believe in me will have life even if they die. 26And everyone who lives and believes in me will never die. Martha, do you believe this?"

27Martha answered, "Yes, Lord. I believe that you are the Christ, the Son of God, the One who was to come into the world."

How many days had Lazarus been dead? This wasn't a case of Lazarus being asleep for a while, we're talking dead and buried – literally.

How was Martha feeling towards Jesus (11:21,22)?

Martha expected that Lazarus would come back to life at the end of time (11:24), but Jesus changed her expectations (11:25). New life is here and now – in him.

Think

If you know someone who's died, how could Jesus' words here comfort you?

Pray

Give thanks that Jesus has defeated the ultimate enemy and our biggest fear – death.

Back to life

The one thing everyone is most scared of is dying. But Jesus could defeat death with a word.

John 11:28–57

Jesus Cries

28After Martha said this, she went back and talked to her sister Mary alone. Martha said, "The Teacher is here and he is asking for you." 29When Mary heard this, she got up quickly and went to Jesus. 30Jesus had not yet come into the town but was still at the place where Martha had met him. 31The Jews were with Mary in the house, comforting her. When they saw her stand and leave quickly, they followed her, thinking she was going to the tomb to cry there.

32But Mary went to the place where Jesus was. When she saw him, she fell at his feet and said, "Lord, if you had been here, my brother would not have died."

33When Jesus saw Mary crying and the Jews who came with her also crying, he was upset and was deeply troubled. 34He asked, "Where did you bury him?"

"Come and see, Lord," they said.

35Jesus cried.

36So the Jews said, "See how much he loved him."

37But some of them said, "If Jesus opened the eyes of the blind man, why couldn't he keep Lazarus from dying?"

Jesus Raises Lazarus

38Again feeling very upset, Jesus came to the tomb. It was a cave with a large stone covering the entrance. 39Jesus said, "Move the stone away."

Martha, the sister of the dead man, said, "But, Lord, it has been four days since he died. There will be a bad smell."

40Then Jesus said to her, "Didn't I tell you that if you believed you would see the glory of God?"

41So they moved the stone away from the entrance. Then Jesus looked up and said, "Father, I thank you that you heard me. 42I know that you always hear me, but I said these things because of the people here around me. I want them to believe that you sent me." 43After Jesus said this, he cried out in a loud voice, "Lazarus, come out!" 44The dead man came out, his hands and feet wrapped with pieces of cloth, and a cloth around his face.

Jesus said to them, "Take the cloth off him and let him go."

The Plan to Kill Jesus

45Many of the Jews, who had come to visit Mary and saw what Jesus did, believed in him. 46But some of them went to the Pharisees and told them what Jesus had done. 47Then the leading priests and Pharisees called a meeting of the Jewish council. They asked, "What should we do? This man is doing many miracles. 48If we let him continue doing these things, everyone will believe in him. Then the Romans will come and take away our Temple and our nation."

49One of the men there was Caiaphas, the high priest that year. He said, "You people know nothing! 50You don't realise that it is better for one man to die for the people than for the whole nation to be destroyed."

51Caiaphas did not think of this himself. As high priest that year, he was really prophesying that Jesus would die for the

Jewish nation ⁵²and for God's scattered children to bring them all together and make them one.

⁵³That day they started planning to kill Jesus. ⁵⁴So Jesus no longer travelled openly among the Jews. He left there and went to a place near the desert, to a town called Ephraim and stayed there with his followers.

⁵⁵It was almost time for the Jewish Passover Feast. Many from the country went up to Jerusalem before the Passover to do the special things to make themselves pure. ⁵⁶The people looked for Jesus and stood in the Temple asking each other, "Is he coming to the Feast? What do you think?" ⁵⁷But the leading priests and the Pharisees had given orders that if anyone knew where Jesus was, he must tell them. Then they could arrest him.

Jesus has ultimate power over death: some people think that if Jesus hadn't said Lazarus' name, everyone in the graveyard would have come out.

But the Pharisees wanted to kill him even more. Why? Maybe they were scared. Maybe they were blind to the truth and totally missing the point. Either way, they were part of God's plan – Jesus raised Lazarus from the dead, but soon he would himself die and rise again. And this time, it would be for you and me.

Think

Some people will never see the truth, even when the most amazing things happen. It doesn't mean that we should ever stop loving them or telling them about Jesus, though.

Pray

Jesus, thank you for giving me the chance to live for ever after I die.

Give it up for Jesus!

What's the most important thing you own? The one thing that is precious to you? Do you own anything that would take you a year's work to replace?

 John 12:1–26

Jesus with Friends in Bethany

12 Six days before the Passover Feast, Jesus went to Bethany, where Lazarus lived, whom Jesus had raised from the dead. ²There they had a dinner for Jesus. Martha served the food, and Lazarus was one of the people eating with Jesus. ³Mary brought in half a litre of very expensive perfume made from pure nard. She poured the perfume on Jesus' feet, and then she wiped his feet with her hair. And the sweet smell from the perfume filled the whole house.

⁴Judas Iscariot, one of Jesus' followers, who would later turn against him, was there. Judas said, ⁵"This perfume was worth 300 silver coins. Why wasn't it sold and the money given to the poor?" ⁶But Judas did not really care about the poor; he said this because he was a thief. He was the one who kept the money bag, and he often stole from it.

⁷Jesus answered, "Leave her alone. It was right for her to save this perfume for today, the day for me to be prepared for burial. ⁸You will always have the poor with you, but you will not always have me."

The Plot Against Lazarus

⁹A large crowd of Jews heard that Jesus was in Bethany. So they went there to see not only Jesus but Lazarus, whom Jesus raised from the dead. ¹⁰So the leading priests made plans to kill Lazarus, too. ¹¹Because of Lazarus many of the Jews were leaving them and believing in Jesus.

Jesus Enters Jerusalem

¹²The next day a great crowd who had come to Jerusalem for the Passover Feast heard that Jesus was coming there. ¹³So they took branches of palm trees and went out to meet Jesus, shouting,

"Praise God!
God bless the One who comes in the name of the Lord!
God bless the King of Israel!"

Psalm 118:25–26

¹⁴Jesus found a colt and sat on it. This was as the Scripture says,

¹⁵"Don't be afraid, people of Jerusalem!
Your king is coming,
sitting on the colt of a donkey."

Zechariah 9:9

¹⁶The followers of Jesus did not understand this at first. But after Jesus was raised to glory, they remembered that this had been written about him and that they had done these things to him.

People Tell About Jesus

¹⁷There had been many people with Jesus when he raised Lazarus from the dead and told him to come out of the tomb. Now they were telling others about what Jesus did. ¹⁸Many people went out to meet Jesus, because they had heard about this miracle. ¹⁹So the Pharisees said to each other, "You can see that nothing is going right for us. Look! The whole world is following him."

Jesus Talks About His Death

20There were some Greek people, too, who came to Jerusalem to worship at the Passover Feast. 21They went to Philip, who was from Bethsaida in Galilee, and said, "Sir, we would like to see Jesus." 22Philip told Andrew, and then Andrew and Philip told Jesus.

23Jesus said to them, "The time has come for the Son of Man to receive his glory. 24I tell you the truth, a grain of wheat must fall to the ground and die to make many seeds. But if it never dies, it remains only a single seed. 25Those who love their lives will lose them, but those who hate their lives in this world will keep true life for ever. 26Whoever serves me must follow me. Then my servant will be with me everywhere I am. My Father will honour anyone who serves me.

Mary's special perfume was worth nearly a year's wages (v 5). Perhaps she had got it for her brother Lazarus' burial (vs 1,7).

What do you think she was showing Jesus by pouring it over him (v 3)?

Was Judas right to criticise her (vs 4–6)?

Jesus used Mary's action as an opportunity to tell his friends something important about himself (v 7).

Think

What could you do to thank Jesus for all he's done for you? How might that help others to know him better?

Pray

Spend some time talking to God. Don't ask for anything but thank him for all he has done.

In a nutshell

Jesus knew he didn't have very long before he died on the cross, so he summed up everything he had to say, in some of the last things he said – and did.

John 12:27–13:5

27"Now I am very troubled. Should I say, 'Father, save me from this time'? No, I came to this time in order to suffer. 28Father, bring glory to your name!"

Then a voice came from heaven, "I have brought glory to it, and I will do it again."

29The crowd standing there, who heard the voice, said it was thunder.

But others said, "An angel has spoken to him."

30Jesus said, "That voice was for your sake, not mine. 31Now is the time for the world to be judged; now the ruler of this world will be thrown down. 32If I am lifted up from the earth, I will draw all people towards me." 33Jesus said this to show how he would die.

34The crowd said, "We have heard from the law that the Christ will live for ever. So why do you say, 'The Son of Man must be lifted up'? Who is this 'Son of Man'?"

35Then Jesus said, "The light will be with you for a little longer, so walk while you have the light. Then the darkness will not catch you. If you walk in the darkness, you will not know where you are going. 36Believe in the light while you still have it so that you will become children of light." When Jesus had said this, he left and hid himself from them.

Some People Won't Believe in Jesus

37Though Jesus had done many miracles in front of the people, they still did not believe in him. 38This was to bring about what Isaiah the prophet had said:

"Who would have believed what we
  heard?
Who saw the Lord's power in this?"
Isaiah 53:1

39This is why the people could not believe: Isaiah had also said,

40"Make the minds of these people dumb.
  Shut their ears. Cover their eyes.
Otherwise, they might really understand
  what they see with their eyes
  and hear with their ears.
They might really understand in their
  minds
  and come back to me and be healed."
Isaiah 6:10

41Isaiah said this because he saw Jesus' glory and spoke about him.

42But many believed in Jesus, even many of the leaders. But because of the Pharisees, they did not say they believed in him for fear they would be put out of the synagogue. 43They loved praise from people more than praise from God.

44Then Jesus cried out, "Whoever believes in me is really believing in the One who sent me. 45Whoever sees me sees the One who sent me. 46I have come as light into the world so that whoever believes in me would not stay in darkness.

47"Anyone who hears my words and does not obey them, I do not judge, because I did not come to judge the world, but to save the world. 48There is a judge for those who refuse to believe in me and do not accept my words. The word I have taught will be their judge on the last day.

⁴⁹The things I taught were not from myself. The Father who sent me told me what to say and what to teach. ⁵⁰And I know that eternal life comes from what the Father commands. So whatever I say is what the Father told me to say."

Jesus Washes His Followers' Feet

13 It was almost time for the Jewish Passover Feast. Jesus knew that it was time for him to leave this world and go back to the Father. He had always loved those who were his own in the world, and he loved them all the way to the end.

²Jesus and his followers were at the evening meal. The devil had already persuaded Judas Iscariot, the son of Simon, to turn against Jesus. ³Jesus knew that the Father had given him power over everything and that he had come from God and was going back to God. ⁴So during the meal Jesus stood up and took off his outer clothing. Taking a towel, he wrapped it around his waist. ⁵Then he poured water into a bowl and began to wash the followers' feet, drying them with the towel that was wrapped around him.

Jesus wanted people to know:

- that he was the Son of God (12:45)

- that he came to give light to people and save them from God's judgement (12:46–49)

- that people who follow him gain eternal life (12:50)

And then he showed the disciples that he was humble and loved them (13:1–5).

Think

What was the reaction of the people to what Jesus said and did? What's your reaction?

Pray

Father, thank you for sending Jesus to us. Thank you for his message. Thank you that he died and rose from the dead for everybody, including me.

You'll fail

Think of someone you like and respect. How would you feel if they told you that you were going to fail – badly?

 John 13:6–38

⁶Jesus came to Simon Peter, who said to him, "Lord, are you going to wash my feet?"

⁷Jesus answered, "You don't understand now what I am doing, but you will understand later."

⁸Peter said, "No, you will never wash my feet."

Jesus answered, "If I don't wash your feet, you are not one of my people."

⁹Simon Peter answered, "Lord, then wash not only my feet, but wash my hands and my head, too!"

¹⁰Jesus said, "After a person has had a bath, his whole body is clean. He needs only to wash his feet. And you men are clean, but not all of you." ¹¹Jesus knew who would turn against him, and that is why he said, "Not all of you are clean."

¹²When he had finished washing their feet, he put on his clothes and sat down again. He asked, "Do you understand what I have just done for you? ¹³You call me 'Teacher' and 'Lord', and you are right, because that is what I am. ¹⁴If I, your Lord and Teacher, have washed your feet, you also should wash each other's feet. ¹⁵I did this as an example so that you should do as I have done for you. ¹⁶I tell you the truth, a servant is not greater than his master. A messenger is not greater than the one who sent him. ¹⁷If you know these things, you will be happy if you do them.

¹⁸"I am not talking about all of you. I know those I have chosen. But this is to bring about what the Scripture said: 'The man who ate at my table has turned against me.' ¹⁹I am telling you this now before it happens so that when it happens, you will believe that I am he. ²⁰I tell you the truth, whoever accepts anyone I send also accepts me. And whoever accepts me also accepts the One who sent me."

Jesus Talks About His Death

²¹After Jesus said this, he was very troubled. He said openly, "I tell you the truth, one of you will turn against me."

²²The followers all looked at each other, because they did not know whom Jesus was talking about. ²³One of the followers sitting next to Jesus was the follower Jesus loved. ²⁴Simon Peter made signs to him to ask Jesus whom he was talking about.

²⁵That follower leaned closer to Jesus and asked, "Lord, who is it?"

²⁶Jesus answered, "I will dip this bread into the dish. The man I give it to is the man who will turn against me." So Jesus took a piece of bread, dipped it, and gave it to Judas Iscariot, the son of Simon. ²⁷As soon as Judas took the bread, Satan entered him. Jesus said to him, "The thing that you will do—do it quickly." ²⁸No one at the table understood why Jesus said this to Judas. ²⁹Since he was the one who kept the money bag, some of the followers thought Jesus was telling him to buy what was needed for the feast or to give something to the poor.

³⁰Judas took the bread Jesus gave him and immediately went out. It was night.

³¹When Judas was gone, Jesus said, "Now the Son of Man receives his glory,

and God receives glory through him. ³²If God receives glory through him, then God will give glory to the Son through himself. And God will give him glory quickly."

³³Jesus said, "My children, I will be with you only a little longer. You will look for me, and what I told the Jews, I tell you now: where I am going you cannot come.

³⁴"I give you a new command: love each other. You must love each other as I have loved you. ³⁵All people will know that you are my followers if you love each other."

Peter will Say He Doesn't Know Jesus

³⁶Simon Peter asked Jesus, "Lord, where are you going?"

Jesus answered, "Where I am going you cannot follow now, but you will follow later."

³⁷Peter asked, "Lord, why can't I follow you now? I am ready to die for you!"

³⁸Jesus answered, "Are you ready to die for me? I tell you the truth, before the cockerel crows, you will say three times that you don't know me."

How do you think Peter felt when Jesus told him he was going to let him down (v 38)? Circle the words that apply or add your own:

- Angry
- Bored
- Upset
- Happy
- Confused
- Determined to prove him wrong
- Is he talking about me?
- Grateful
- Excited
- Amazed

Jesus knew all about Peter – his good points and his bad points – and he still really loved him (v 34).

Think

Can Jesus depend on you not to be disloyal to him?

Pray

Thank Jesus that he loves you even when you do let him down.

A room of your own

Can you be sure you'll get to heaven?

Imagine a luxury hotel room has been booked for you at a mystery location. The bus arrives to take you there. Do you:

- get on and rush to the back seat?
- refuse to get on until you know the precise destination?
- decide to camp in your garden instead?

John 14:1–26

Jesus Comforts His Followers

14 Jesus said, "Don't let your hearts be troubled. Trust in God, and trust in me. ²There are many rooms in my Father's house; I would not tell you this if it were not true. I am going there to prepare a place for you. ³After I go and prepare a place for you, I will come back and take you to be with me so that you may be where I am. ⁴You know the way to the place where I am going."

⁵Thomas said to Jesus, "Lord, we don't know where you are going. So how can we know the way?"

⁶Jesus answered, "I am the way, and the truth, and the life. The only way to the Father is through me. ⁷If you really knew me, you would know my Father, too. But now you do know him, and you have seen him."

⁸Philip said to him, "Lord, show us the Father. That is all we need."

⁹Jesus answered, "I have been with you a long time now. Do you still not know me, Philip? Whoever has seen me has seen the Father. So why do you say, 'Show us the Father'? ¹⁰Don't you believe that I am in the Father and the Father is in me? The words I say to you don't come from me,

but the Father lives in me and does his own work. ¹¹Believe me when I say that I am in the Father and the Father is in me. Or believe because of the miracles I have done. ¹²I tell you the truth, whoever believes in me will do the same things that I do. Those who believe will do even greater things than these, because I am going to the Father. ¹³And if you ask for anything in my name, I will do it for you so that the Father's glory will be shown through the Son. ¹⁴If you ask me for anything in my name, I will do it.

The Promise of the Holy Spirit

¹⁵"If you love me, you will obey my commands. ¹⁶I will ask the Father, and he will give you another Helper to be with you for ever—¹⁷the Spirit of truth. The world cannot accept him, because it does not see him or know him. But you know him, because he lives with you and he will be in you.

¹⁸"I will not leave you all alone like orphans; I will come back to you. ¹⁹In a little while the world will not see me any more, but you will see me. Because I live, you will live, too. ²⁰On that day you will know that I am in my Father, and that you

are in me and I am in you. ²¹Those who know my commands and obey them are the ones who love me, and my Father will love those who love me. I will love them and will show myself to them."

²²Then Judas (not Judas Iscariot) said, "But, Lord, why do you plan to show yourself to us and not to the rest of the world?"

²³Jesus answered, "If people love me, they will obey my teaching. My Father will love them, and we will come to them and make our home with them. ²⁴Those who do not love me do not obey my teaching. This teaching that you hear is not really mine; it is from my Father, who sent me.

²⁵"I have told you all these things while I am with you. ²⁶But the Helper will teach you everything and will cause you to remember all that I told you. This Helper is the Holy Spirit whom the Father will send in my name.

In verse 6 what do you understand by the three words Jesus uses to describe himself?

- The Way

- The Truth

- The Life

Think

If Jesus has got a place ready for you in heaven, how can you be sure you'll get there when you die (vs 5,6)?

Pray

Dear Jesus, thank you that you have a place ready for me in heaven. Help me to keep going your way, even when I don't understand everything.

Love for friends

What makes someone your friend?

- They go places with you
- They stick up for you
- They're nice to you

John 14:27–15:27

27"I leave you peace; my peace I give you. I do not give it to you as the world does. So don't let your hearts be troubled or afraid. 28You heard me say to you, 'I am going, but I am coming back to you.' If you loved me, you would be happy that I am going back to the Father, because he is greater than I am. 29I have told you this now, before it happens, so that when it happens, you will believe. 30I will not talk with you much longer, because the ruler of this world is coming. He has no power over me, 31but the world must know that I love the Father, so I do exactly what the Father told me to do.

"Come now, let us go.

Jesus is Like a Vine

15 "I am the true vine; my Father is the gardener. 2He cuts off every branch of mine that does not produce fruit. And he trims and cleans every branch that produces fruit so that it will produce even more fruit. 3You are already clean because of the words I have spoken to you. 4Remain in me, and I will remain in you. A branch cannot produce fruit alone but must remain in the vine. In the same way, you cannot produce fruit alone but must remain in me.

5"I am the vine, and you are the branches. If any remain in me and I remain in them, they produce much fruit.

But without me they can do nothing. 6If any do not remain in me, they are like a branch that is thrown away and then dies. People pick up dead branches, throw them into the fire and burn them. 7If you remain in me and follow my teachings, you can ask anything you want, and it will be given to you. 8You should produce much fruit and show that you are my followers, which brings glory to my Father. 9I loved you as the Father loved me. Now remain in my love. 10I have obeyed my Father's commands, and I remain in his love. In the same way, if you obey my commands, you will remain in my love. 11I have told you these things so that you can have the same joy I have and so that your joy will be the fullest possible joy.

12"This is my command: love each other as I have loved you. 13The greatest love a person can show is to die for his friends. 14You are my friends if you do what I command you. 15I no longer call you servants, because a servant does not know what his master is doing. But I call you friends, because I have made known to you everything I heard from my Father. 16You did not choose me; I chose you. And I gave you this work: to go and produce fruit, fruit that will last. Then the Father will give you anything you ask for in my name. 17This is my command: love each other.

Jesus Warns His Followers

18"If the world hates you, remember that it hated me first. 19If you belonged to the world, it would love you as it loves its own. But I have chosen you out of the world, so you don't belong to it. That is why the world hates you. 20Remember what I told you: a servant is not greater than his master. If people did wrong to me, they will do wrong to you, too. And if they obeyed my teaching, they will obey yours, too. 21They will do all this to you on account of me, because they do not know the One who sent me. 22If I had not come and spoken to them, they would not be guilty of sin, but now they have no excuse for their sin. 23Whoever hates me also hates my Father. 24I did works among them that no one else has ever done. If I had not done these works, they would not be guilty of sin. But now they have seen what I have done, and yet they have hated both me and my Father. 25But this happened so that what is written in their law would be true: 'They hated me for no reason.'

26"I will send you the Helper from the Father; he is the Spirit of truth who comes from the Father. When he comes, he will tell about me, 27and you also must tell people about me, because you have been with me from the beginning.

What makes us God's friends? Put it in your own words:

"We are God's friends if _____ "
(15:14).

What *is* Jesus' command (15:12,17)?

Think

Are you doing what Jesus said?

Pray

Lord Jesus, please help me to do what you command: love others.

Extra

Have you done something loving for someone today?

No need to text!

Mobile phone technology is almost everywhere. We speak to our friends via short, fun text messages. We can do this anywhere and at any time, and if our friend has their phone on, they'll get right back to us. Well here's a message from God: whereva u r he can spk 2 u!

 John 16:1–28

16 "I have told you these things to keep you from giving up. ²People will put you out of their synagogues. Yes, the time is coming when those who kill you will think they are offering service to God. ³They will do this because they have not known the Father and they have not known me. ⁴I have told you these things now so that when the time comes you will remember that I warned you.

The Work of the Holy Spirit

"I did not tell you these things at the beginning, because I was with you then. ⁵Now I am going back to the One who sent me. But none of you asks me, 'Where are you going?' ⁶Your hearts are filled with sadness because I have told you these things. ⁷But I tell you the truth, it is better for you that I go away. When I go away, I will send the Helper to you. If I do not go away, the Helper will not come. ⁸When the Helper comes, he will prove to the people of the world the truth about sin, about being right with God and about judgement. ⁹He will prove to them that sin is not believing in me. ¹⁰He will prove to them that being right with God comes through my going to the Father and not being seen by you any more. ¹¹And the Helper will prove to them that judgement happened when the ruler of this world was judged.

¹²"I have many more things to say to you, but they are too much for you now. ¹³But when the Spirit of truth comes, he will lead you into all truth. He will not speak his own words, but he will speak only what he hears, and he will tell you what is to come. ¹⁴The Spirit of truth will bring glory to me, because he will take what I have to say and tell it to you. ¹⁵All that the Father has is mine. That is why I said that the Spirit will take what I have to say and tell it to you.

Sadness will Become Happiness

¹⁶"After a little while you will not see me, and then after a little while you will see me again."

¹⁷Some of the followers said to each other, "What does Jesus mean when he says, 'After a little while you will not see me, and then after a little while you will see me again'? And what does he mean when he says, 'Because I am going to the Father'?" ¹⁸They also asked, "What does he mean by 'a little while'? We don't understand what he is saying."

¹⁹Jesus saw that the followers wanted to ask him about this, so he said to them, "Are you asking each other what I meant when I said, 'After a little while you will not see me, and then after a little while you will see me again'? ²⁰I tell you the truth, you will cry and be sad, but the world will be happy. You will be sad, but your

sadness will become joy. 21When a woman gives birth to a baby, she has pain, because her time has come. But when her baby is born, she forgets the pain, because she is so happy that a child has been born into the world. 22It is the same with you. Now you are sad, but I will see you again and you will be happy, and no one will take away your joy. 23In that day you will not ask me for anything. I tell you the truth, my Father will give you anything you ask for in my name. 24Until now you have not asked for anything in my name. Ask and you will receive, so that your joy will be the fullest possible joy.

Victory over the World

25"I have told you these things, using stories that hide the meaning. But the time will come when I will not use stories like that to tell you things; I will speak to you in plain words about the Father. 26In that day you will ask the Father for things in my name. I mean, I will not need to ask the Father for you. 27The Father himself loves you. He loves you because you have loved me and believed that I am from God. 28I came from the Father into the world. Now I am leaving the world and going back to the Father."

We can't take it all at once (v 12). But little by little, through our lives, the Holy Spirit will help us understand the truth about Jesus (vs 13,14).

Not bad, eh? Jesus will speak to you through his Holy Spirit. He'll speak to you today, even as you read this.

Think

Do you take time to stop and listen to what Jesus is saying to you through his Holy Spirit?

Pray

Ask the Lord Jesus to help you listen to what he is saying to you today.

Image makers

Do any of these influence your personal choice of "image"?

- Magazines
- Your friends
- The Bible
- Your parents
- Actors on TV
- Pop groups

 John 16:29–17:20

29Then the followers of Jesus said, "You are speaking clearly to us now and are not using stories that are hard to understand. 30We can see now that you know all things. You can answer a person's question even before it is asked. This makes us believe you came from God."

31Jesus answered, "So now you believe? 32Listen to me; a time is coming when you will be scattered, each to his own home. That time is now here. You will leave me alone, but I am never really alone, because the Father is with me.

33"I told you these things so that you can have peace in me. In this world you will have trouble, but be brave! I have defeated the world."

Jesus Prays for His Followers

17 After Jesus said these things, he looked towards heaven and prayed, "Father, the time has come. Give glory to your Son so that the Son can give glory to you. 2You gave the Son power over all people so that the Son could give eternal life to all those you gave him. 3And this is eternal life: that people know you, the only true God, and that they know Jesus Christ, the One you sent. 4Having finished the work you gave me to do, I brought you glory on earth. 5And now, Father, give me glory with you; give me the glory I had with you before the world was made.

6"I showed what you are like to those you gave me from the world. They belonged to you, and you gave them to me, and they have obeyed your teaching. 7Now they know that everything you gave me comes from you. 8I gave them the teachings you gave me, and they accepted them. They knew that I truly came from you, and they believed that you sent me. 9I am praying for them. I am not praying for people in the world but for those you gave me, because they are yours. 10All I have is yours, and all you have is mine. And my glory is shown through them. 11I am coming to you; I will not stay in the world any longer. But they are still in the world. Holy Father, keep them safe by the power of your name, the name you gave me, so that they will be one, just as you and I are one. 12While I was with them, I kept them safe by the power of your name, the name you gave me. I protected them, and only one of them, the one worthy of destruction, was lost so that the Scripture would come true.

¹³"I am coming to you now. But I pray these things while I am still in the world so that these followers can have all my joy in them. ¹⁴I have given them your teaching. And the world has hated them, because they don't belong to the world, just as I don't belong to the world. ¹⁵I am not asking you to take them out of the world but to keep them safe from the Evil One. ¹⁶They don't belong to the world, just as I don't belong to the world. ¹⁷Make them ready for your service through your truth; your teaching is truth. ¹⁸I have sent them into the world, just as you sent me into the world. ¹⁹For their sake, I am making myself ready to serve so that they can be ready for their service of the truth.

²⁰"I pray for these followers, but I am also praying for all those who will believe in me because of their teaching.

Jesus said his followers don't belong to this world (17:14). You live here, but you don't have to *do* or *be* like the media says.

Think

In what ways do you copy what's on TV shows or in magazines? Do you copy what Jesus says?

Pray

Father, sometimes I know I'm not so "cool". But I want to belong to you. It's what *you* think that counts the most.

271

You don't understand

It's dark. It's late. You're sleepy. There's noise and people and you just can't get your mind around what's happening ...

John 17:21–18:18

21Father, I pray that they can be one. As you are in me and I am in you, I pray that they can also be one in us. Then the world will believe that you sent me. 22I have given these people the glory that you gave me so that they can be one, just as you and I are one. 23I will be in them and you will be in me so that they will be completely one. Then the world will know that you sent me and that you loved them just as much as you loved me.

24"Father, I want these people that you gave me to be with me where I am. I want them to see my glory, which you gave me because you loved me before the world was made. 25Father, you are the One who is good. The world does not know you, but I know you, and these people know you sent me. 26I showed them what you are like, and I will show them again. Then they will have the same love that you have for me, and I will live in them."

Jesus is Arrested

18 When Jesus finished praying, he went with his followers across the Kidron Valley. On the other side there was a garden, and Jesus and his followers went into it.

2Judas knew where this place was, because Jesus often met his followers there. Judas was the one who turned against Jesus. 3So Judas came there with a group of soldiers and some guards from the leading priests and the Pharisees. They were carrying torches, lanterns and weapons.

4Knowing everything that would hap-

pen to him, Jesus went out and asked, "Who is it you are looking for?"

5They answered, "Jesus from Nazareth."

"I am he," Jesus said. (Judas, the one who turned against Jesus, was standing there with them.) 6When Jesus said, "I am he," they moved back and fell to the ground.

7Jesus asked them again, "Who is it you are looking for?"

They said, "Jesus of Nazareth."

8"I told you that I am he," Jesus said. "So if you are looking for me, let the others go." 9This happened so that the words Jesus said before would come true: "I have not lost any of the ones you gave me."

10Simon Peter, who had a sword, pulled it out and struck the servant of the high priest, cutting off his right ear. (The servant's name was Malchus.) 11Jesus said to Peter, "Put your sword back. Shouldn't I drink the cup the Father gave me?"

Jesus is Brought Before Annas

12Then the soldiers with their commander and the Jewish guards arrested Jesus. They tied him 13and led him first to Annas, the father-in-law of Caiaphas, the high priest that year. 14Caiaphas was the one who had told the Jews that it would be better if one man died for all the people.

Peter Says He Doesn't Know Jesus

15Simon Peter and another one of Jesus' followers went along after Jesus. This follower knew the high priest, so he went with Jesus into the high priest's courtyard. [16]But Peter waited outside near the door. The follower who knew the high priest came back outside, spoke to the girl at the door, and brought Peter inside. [17]The girl at the door said to Peter, "Aren't you also one of that man's followers?"

Peter answered, "No, I am not!"

[18]It was cold, so the servants and guards had built a fire and were standing around it, warming themselves. Peter also was standing with them, warming himself.

It wasn't surprising Peter was confused. What was his mate Judas doing there with soldiers ... arresting Jesus (18:2,3)?

Peter wasn't going to let Jesus down, like Jesus had said he would (Mark 14:27–31)!

How did Peter respond to the situation (18:10)?

How did Jesus respond (18:4,7,8,11)?

Think

Do you try to do things your way, or Jesus' way?

Pray

... that Jesus will help you to do things his way. Pray that you will be able to think before you act and not rush in.

273

Abandoned

Jesus was tortured, humiliated and sentenced to death. And the worst thing was, the people who did it thought that they were right.

 John 18:19–19:3

The High Priest Questions Jesus

19The high priest asked Jesus questions about his followers and his teaching. 20Jesus answered, "I have spoken openly to everyone. I have always taught in synagogues and in the Temple, where all the Jews come together. I never said anything in secret. 21So why do you question me? Ask the people who heard my teaching. They know what I said."

22When Jesus said this, one of the guards standing there hit him. The guard said, "Is that the way you answer the high priest?"

23Jesus answered him, "If I said something wrong, then say what it was. But if what I said is true, why do you hit me?"

24Then Annas sent Jesus, who was still tied, to Caiaphas the high priest.

Peter Says Again He Doesn't Know Jesus

25As Simon Peter was standing and warming himself, they said to him, "Aren't you one of that man's followers?"

Peter said it was not true; he said, "No, I am not."

26One of the servants of the high priest was there. This servant was a relative of the man whose ear Peter had cut off. The servant said, "Didn't I see you with him in the garden?"

27Again Peter said it wasn't true. At once a cockerel crowed.

Jesus is Brought Before Pilate

28Early in the morning they led Jesus from Caiaphas' house to the Roman governor's palace. They would not go inside the palace, because they did not want to make themselves unclean; they wanted to eat the Passover meal. 29So Pilate went outside to them and asked, "What charges do you bring against this man?"

30They answered, "If he were not a criminal, we wouldn't have brought him to you."

31Pilate said to them, "Take him yourselves and judge him by your own law."

"But we are not allowed to put anyone to death," the Jews answered. 32(This happened so that what Jesus said about how he would die would come true.)

33Then Pilate went back inside the palace and called Jesus to him and asked, "Are you the king of the Jews?"

34Jesus said, "Is that your own question, or did others tell you about me?"

35Pilate answered, "I am not Jewish. It was your own people and their leading priests who handed you over to me. What have you done wrong?"

36Jesus answered, "My kingdom does not belong to this world. If it belonged to this world, my servants would fight so that I would not be given over to the Jews. But my kingdom is from another place."

37Pilate said, "So you are a king!"

Jesus answered, "You are the one saying I am a king. This is why I was born and came into the world: to tell people the truth. And everyone who belongs to the truth listens to me."

38Pilate said, "What is truth?" After he said this, he went out to the Jews again and said to them, "I find nothing against this man. 39But it is your custom that I free one prisoner to you at Passover time. Do you want me to free the 'king of the Jews'?"

40They shouted back, "No, not him! Let Barabbas go free!" (Barabbas was a robber.)

19 Then Pilate ordered that Jesus be taken away and whipped. 2The soldiers made a crown from some thorny branches and put it on Jesus' head and put a purple robe around him. 3Then they came to him many times and said, "Hail, King of the Jews!" and hit him in the face.

The Jewish priests made sure that they kept to all their religious rules and stayed within the law when they sent Jesus to die – because they honestly thought they were doing the right thing.

Peter, meanwhile, denies Jesus for the third time. He instantly regrets it.

Which is worse: to do something wrong and then to feel terrible about it straight away, or to never realise you've done anything wrong?

Think

Make sure that you're on the right team. It can be really easy to think you're following God when you're not. Remember: love God, love other people, keep reading your Bible and be open to what God has to say to you.

Pray

Father, thank you for loving everyone enough to send Jesus to die for us.

The King of the Jews

Just imagine. They never realised that when they were taking the mickey out of him and calling him king that he really was the King.

 John 19:4–27

⁴Again Pilate came out and said to them, "Look, I am bringing Jesus out to you. I want you to know that I find nothing against him." ⁵So Jesus came out, wearing the crown of thorns and the purple robe. Pilate said to them, "Here is the man!"

⁶When the leading priests and the guards saw Jesus, they shouted, "Crucify him! Crucify him!"

But Pilate answered, "Crucify him yourselves, because I find nothing against him."

⁷The Jews answered, "We have a law that says he should die, because he said he is the Son of God."

⁸When Pilate heard this, he was even more afraid. ⁹He went back inside the palace and asked Jesus, "Where do you come from?" But Jesus did not answer him. ¹⁰Pilate said, "You refuse to speak to me? Don't you know I have power to set you free and power to have you crucified?"

¹¹Jesus answered, "The only power you have over me is the power given to you by God. The man who betrayed me to you is guilty of a greater sin."

¹²After this, Pilate tried to let Jesus go. But the Jews cried out, "Anyone who makes himself king is against Caesar. If you let this man go, you are no friend of Caesar."

¹³When Pilate heard what they were saying, he brought Jesus out and sat down on the judge's seat at the place called The Stone Pavement. (In the Jewish language the name is Gabbatha.) ¹⁴It was about noon on Preparation Day of Passover week. Pilate said to the Jews, "Here is your king!"

¹⁵They shouted, "Take him away! Take him away! Crucify him!"

Pilate asked them, "Do you want me to crucify your king?"

The leading priests answered, "The only king we have is Caesar."

¹⁶So Pilate handed Jesus over to them to be crucified.

Jesus is Crucified

The soldiers took charge of Jesus. ¹⁷Carrying his own cross, Jesus went out to a place called The Place of the Skull, which in the Jewish language is called Golgotha. ¹⁸There they crucified Jesus. They also crucified two other men, one on each side, with Jesus in the middle. ¹⁹Pilate wrote a sign and put it on the cross. It read: JESUS OF NAZARETH, THE KING OF THE JEWS. ²⁰The sign was written in the Jewish language, in Latin and in Greek. Many of the Jews read the sign, because the place where Jesus was crucified was near the city. ²¹The leading Jewish priests said to Pilate, "Don't write, 'The King of the Jews'. But write, 'This man said, "I am the King of the Jews."'"

²²Pilate answered, "What I have written, I have written."

²³After the soldiers crucified Jesus, they took his clothes and divided them into four parts, with each soldier getting one part. They also took his long shirt, which was all one piece of cloth, woven from top to bottom. ²⁴So the soldiers said to each

other, "We should not tear this into parts. Let's throw lots to see who will get it." This happened so that this Scripture would come true:

"They divided my clothes among them, and they threw lots for my clothing."

Psalm 22:18

So the soldiers did this.

25Standing near his cross were Jesus' mother, his mother's sister, Mary the wife of Clopas, and Mary Magdalene. 26When Jesus saw his mother and the follower he loved standing nearby, he said to his mother, "Dear woman, here is your son." 27Then he said to the follower, "Here is your mother." From that time on, the follower took her to live in his home.

Pontius Pilate – who wasn't a nice man – didn't like being pushed into killing anyone, especially someone who hadn't done anything that he could see was wrong. So he wrote the sign on the cross just to annoy the priests. He didn't mean it any more than the soldiers did. But what he wrote was true.

Jesus was King. Jesus is still King. And no one realised it at the time, but dying in this awful, humiliating way was the most glorious thing he could have done.

Think

It was because Jesus was King that he had to die and rise again. No one else could have done it.

Pray

Spend some time thanking Jesus again for his love for you. Ask him to make it make a difference in your life.

It's finished!

When would you say, "It's finished!" – for example, after:

- a football match?
- a relationship ends?
- homework is done?
- the last mouthful of chocolate?

How would you say it each time? Triumphantly? With relief? With disappointment?

John 19:28–20:9

Jesus Dies

28After this, Jesus knew that everything had been done. So that the Scripture would come true, he said, "I am thirsty." 29There was a jar full of vinegar there, so the soldiers soaked a sponge in it, put the sponge on a branch of a hyssop plant and lifted it to Jesus' mouth. 30When Jesus tasted the vinegar, he said, "It is finished." Then he bowed his head and died.

31This day was Preparation Day, and the next day was a special Sabbath day. Since the Jews did not want the bodies to stay on the cross on the Sabbath day, they asked Pilate to order that the legs of the men be broken and the bodies be taken away. 32So the soldiers came and broke the legs of the first man on the cross beside Jesus. Then they broke the legs of the man on the other cross beside Jesus. 33But when the soldiers came to Jesus and saw that he was already dead, they did not break his legs. 34But one of the soldiers stuck his spear into Jesus' side, and at once blood and water came out. 35(The one who saw this happen is the one who told us this, and whatever he says is true. And he knows that he tells the truth, and he tells it so that you might believe.) 36These things happened to make the Scripture come true: "Not one of his bones will be broken." 37And another Scripture says, "They will look at the one they stabbed."

Jesus is Buried

38Later, Joseph from Arimathea asked Pilate if he could take the body of Jesus. (Joseph was a secret follower of Jesus, because he was afraid of the Jews.) Pilate gave his permission, so Joseph came and took Jesus' body away. 39Nicodemus, who earlier had come to Jesus at night, went with Joseph. He brought about 30 kilogrammes of myrrh and aloes. 40These two men took Jesus' body and wrapped it with the spices in pieces of linen cloth, which is how the Jewish people bury the dead. 41In the place where Jesus was crucified, there was a garden. In the garden was a new tomb that had never been used before. 42The men laid Jesus in that tomb because it was nearby, and the Jews were preparing to start their Sabbath day.

Jesus' Tomb is Empty

20 Early on the first day of the week, Mary Magdalene went to the tomb while it was still dark. When she saw that

the large stone had been moved away from the tomb, ²she ran to Simon Peter and the follower whom Jesus loved. Mary said, "They have taken the Lord out of the tomb, and we don't know where they have put him."

³So Peter and the other follower started for the tomb. ⁴They were both running, but the other follower ran faster than Peter and reached the tomb first. ⁵He bent down and looked in and saw the strips of linen cloth lying there, but he did not go in. ⁶Then, following him, Simon Peter arrived and went into the tomb and saw the strips of linen lying there. ⁷He also saw the cloth that had been around Jesus' head, which was folded up and laid in a different place from the strips of linen. ⁸Then the other follower, who had reached the tomb first, also went in. He saw and believed. ⁹(They did not yet understand from the Scriptures that Jesus must rise from the dead.)

How do you think Jesus said these words (19:30)?

It was the end of terrible physical suffering for Jesus. But also, he knew his work was done.

Think

Read these verses again slowly to yourself. What does Jesus' death mean for you?

Pray

Lord Jesus, thank you for dying for me so that my sin could be forgiven.

Only a woman!

Here's an eyewitness report from Mary of her meeting with the risen Jesus. What do you think?

 John 20:10–21:3

Jesus Appears to Mary Magdalene

¹⁰Then the followers went back home. ¹¹But Mary stood outside the tomb, crying. As she was crying, she bent down and looked inside the tomb. ¹²She saw two angels dressed in white, sitting where Jesus' body had been, one at the head and one at the feet.

¹³They asked her, "Woman, why are you crying?"

She answered, "They have taken away my Lord, and I don't know where they have put him." ¹⁴When Mary said this, she turned around and saw Jesus standing there, but she did not know it was Jesus.

¹⁵Jesus asked her, "Woman, why are you crying? Whom are you looking for?"

Thinking he was the gardener, she said to him, "Did you take him away, sir? Tell me where you put him, and I will get him."

¹⁶Jesus said to her, "Mary."

Mary turned towards Jesus and said in the Jewish language, "Rabboni." (This means Teacher.)

¹⁷Jesus said to her, "Don't hold on to me, because I have not yet gone up to the Father. But go to my brothers and tell them, 'I am going back to my Father and your Father, to my God and your God.'"

¹⁸Mary Magdalene went and said to the followers, "I saw the Lord!" And she told them what Jesus had said to her.

Jesus Appears to His Followers

¹⁹When it was evening on the first day of the week, the followers were together. The doors were locked, because they were afraid of the Jews. Then Jesus came and stood right in the middle of them and said, "Peace be with you." ²⁰After he said this, he showed them his hands and his side. The followers were thrilled when they saw the Lord.

²¹Then Jesus said again, "Peace be with you. As the Father sent me, I now send you." ²²After he said this, he breathed on them and said, "Receive the Holy Spirit. ²³If you forgive anyone his sins, they are forgiven. If you don't forgive them, they are not forgiven."

Jesus Appears to Thomas

²⁴Thomas (called Didymus), who was one of the twelve, was not with them when Jesus came. ²⁵The other followers kept telling Thomas, "We saw the Lord."

But Thomas said, "I will not believe it until I see the nail marks in his hands and put my finger where the nails were and put my hand into his side."

²⁶A week later the followers were in the house again, and Thomas was with them. The doors were locked, but Jesus came in and stood right in the middle of them. He said, "Peace be with you." ²⁷Then he said to Thomas, "Put your finger here, and look at my hands. Put your hand here in my side. Stop being an unbeliever and believe."

²⁸Thomas said to him, "My Lord and my God!"

²⁹Then Jesus told him, "You believe because you see me. Those who believe without seeing me will be truly happy."

Why John Wrote this Book

³⁰Jesus did many other miracles in the

presence of his followers that are not written in this book. ³¹But these are written so that you may believe that Jesus is the Christ, the Son of God. Then, by believing, you may have life through his name.

Jesus Appears to Seven Followers

21 Later, Jesus showed himself to his followers again—this time at Lake Galilee. This is how he showed himself: ²some of the followers were together— Simon Peter, Thomas (called Didymus), Nathanael from Cana in Galilee, the two sons of Zebedee and two other followers. ³Simon Peter said, "I am going out to fish."

The others said, "We will go with you." So they went out and got into the boat. They fished that night but caught nothing.

Read Mary's eyewitness account again (vs 10–18), but this time pretend it is you telling the story. Try replacing Mary's name with your own.

Which moment do you think is the most amazing? Write it down here:

Think

In Jesus' time, women were thought of as unreliable witnesses. Their evidence was not accepted in court. If John was inventing this story, why would he say a woman saw the risen Jesus first?

Pray

Mary's sadness changed to joy when she met Jesus. Pray that meeting the living Jesus will change the dark parts of your life.

281

A new start

How many times have you done something, or said something, and then wished you hadn't? Do you wish there was some way that you could turn back time?

Is there any way to put right something as terrible as denying Jesus?

 John 21:4–25

⁴Early the next morning Jesus stood on the shore, but the followers did not know it was Jesus. ⁵Then he said to them, "Friends, did you catch any fish?"

They answered, "No."

⁶He said, "Throw your net on the right side of the boat, and you will find some." So they did, and they caught so many fish they could not pull the net back into the boat.

⁷The follower whom Jesus loved said to Peter, "It is the Lord!" When Peter heard him say this, he wrapped his coat around himself. (Peter had taken his clothes off.) Then he jumped into the water. ⁸The other followers went ashore in the boat, dragging the net full of fish. They were not very far from shore, only about a hundred yards. ⁹When the followers stepped out of the boat and onto the shore, they saw a fire of hot coals. There were fish on the fire, and there was bread.

¹⁰Then Jesus said, "Bring some of the fish you have just caught."

¹¹Simon Peter went into the boat and pulled the net to the shore. It was full of big fish, 153 in all, but even though there were so many, the net did not tear. ¹²Jesus said to them, "Come and eat." None of the followers dared ask him, "Who are you?" because they knew it was the Lord.

¹³Jesus came and took the bread and gave it to them, along with the fish.

¹⁴This was now the third time Jesus showed himself to his followers after he was raised from the dead.

Jesus Talks to Peter

¹⁵When they finished eating, Jesus said to Simon Peter, "Simon son of John, do you love me more than these?"

He answered, "Yes, Lord, you know that I love you."

Jesus said, "Feed my lambs."

¹⁶Again Jesus said, "Simon son of John, do you love me?"

He answered, "Yes, Lord, you know that I love you."

Jesus said, "Take care of my sheep."

¹⁷A third time he said, "Simon son of John, do you love me?"

Peter was hurt because Jesus asked him the third time, "Do you love me?" Peter said, "Lord, you know everything; you know that I love you!"

He said to him, "Feed my sheep. ¹⁸I tell you the truth, when you were younger, you tied your own belt and went where you wanted. But when you are old, you will put out your hands and someone else will tie you and take you where you don't want to go." ¹⁹(Jesus said this to show how Peter would die to give glory to God.) Then Jesus said to Peter, "Follow me!"

²⁰Peter turned and saw that the follower Jesus loved was walking behind them. (This was the follower who had leaned against Jesus at the supper and had said, "Lord, who will turn against you?") ²¹When Peter saw him behind them, he asked Jesus, "Lord, what about him?"

²²Jesus answered, "If I want him to live until I come back, that is not your business. You follow me."

²³So a story spread among the followers that this one would not die. But Jesus did not say he would not die. He only said, "If I want him to live until I come back, that is not your business."

²⁴That follower is the one who is telling these things and who has now written them down. We know that what he says is true.

²⁵There are many other things Jesus did. If every one of them were written down, I suppose the whole world would not be big enough for all the books that would be written.

How many times had Peter denied Jesus (John 18:15–27)?

How many times did Jesus ask Peter if he loved him?

What's the job Jesus was giving Peter (vs 15,16,17)?

Jesus showed Peter that he was forgiven and had a special part in God's work.

Think

However you think you've failed God, he will forgive you – and has got something special for you to do.

Pray

Feel you've let Jesus down? Ask him to forgive you and give you a fresh start.

Your witness

The Queen drops in at your house for a cup of tea, slice of cake and little chat. At school, everyone wants to know the full story. Soon the local press are there. You are the only one who knows what went on; it is up to you to say what happened. You are a witness.

Acts 1:1–26

Luke Writes Another Book

1 To Theophilus.
The first book I wrote was about everything Jesus began to do and teach ²until the day he was taken up into heaven. Before this, with the help of the Holy Spirit, Jesus told the apostles he had chosen what they should do. ³After his death, he showed himself to them and proved in many ways that he was alive. The apostles saw Jesus during the 40 days after he was raised from the dead, and he spoke to them about the kingdom of God. ⁴Once when he was eating with them, he told them not to leave Jerusalem. He said, "Wait here to receive the promise from the Father which I told you about. ⁵John baptised people with water, but in a few days you will be baptised with the Holy Spirit."

Jesus is Taken Up into Heaven

⁶When the apostles were all together, they asked Jesus, "Lord, are you now going to give the kingdom back to Israel?"

⁷Jesus said to them, "The Father is the only One who has the authority to decide dates and times. These things are not for you to know. ⁸But when the Holy Spirit comes to you, you will receive power. You will be my witnesses—in Jerusalem, in all of Judea, in Samaria and in every part of the world."

⁹After he said this, as they were watching, he was lifted up, and a cloud hid him from their sight. ¹⁰As he was going, they were looking into the sky. Suddenly, two men wearing white clothes stood beside them. ¹¹They said, "Men of Galilee, why are you standing here looking into the sky? Jesus, whom you saw taken up from you into heaven, will come back in the same way you saw him go."

A New Apostle Is Chosen

¹²Then they went back to Jerusalem from the Mount of Olives. (This mountain is about a kilometre from Jerusalem.) ¹³When they entered the city, they went to the upstairs room where they were staying. Peter, John, James, Andrew, Philip, Thomas, Bartholomew, Matthew, James son of Alphaeus, Simon (known as the Zealot) and Judas son of James were there. ¹⁴They all continued praying together with some women, including Mary the mother of Jesus, and Jesus' brothers.

¹⁵During this time there was a meeting of the believers (about 120 of them). Peter stood up and said, "Brothers and sisters, in the Scriptures the Holy Spirit said through David something that must happen involving Judas. He was one of our own group and served together with us. He led those who arrested Jesus." ¹⁸(Judas bought a field with the money he got for his evil act. But he fell to his death, his

body burst open, and all his intestines poured out. ¹⁹Everyone in Jerusalem learned about this so they named this place Akeldama. In their language Akeldama means "Field of Blood".) ²⁰"In the Book of Psalms," Peter said, "this is written:

'May his place be empty;
    leave no one to live in it.'   *Psalm 69:25*
And it is also written:

'Let another man replace him as leader.'
                                    Psalm 109:8
²¹⁻²²"So now a man must become a witness with us of Jesus' being raised from the dead. He must be one of the men who were part of our group during all the time the Lord Jesus was among us—from the time John was baptising people until the day Jesus was taken up from us to heaven."

²³They put the names of two men before the group. One was Joseph Barsabbas, who was also called Justus. The other was Matthias. ²⁴⁻²⁵The apostles prayed, "Lord, you know the thoughts of everyone. Show us which one of these two you have chosen to do this work. Show us who should be an apostle in place of Judas, who turned away and went where he belongs." ²⁶Then they used lots to choose between them, and the lots showed that Matthias was the one. So he became an apostle with the other eleven.

What had the disciples "witnessed" (vs 1–5)?

What did Jesus say would happen to his disciples (v 8)?

How are you the result of the disciples' witness (v 8)?

Think

Who introduced you to Jesus? Who have you told about Jesus? Whose help do you need to keep on witnessing (v 8)?

Pray

Ask God to fill you with his power so that you can share the Good News about Jesus with others.

Everywhere at once

How can God be with all Christians, everywhere in the world?
The disciples had been worried about Jesus leaving them alone
(John 16:17,18) – but he could only be in one place at one time.
Here's God's answer!

Acts 2:1–28

The Coming of the Holy Spirit

2 When the day of Pentecost came, they were all together in one place. ²Suddenly a noise like a strong, blowing wind came from heaven and filled the whole house where they were sitting. ³They saw something like flames of fire that were separated and stood over each person there. ⁴They were all filled with the Holy Spirit, and they began to speak different languages by the power the Holy Spirit was giving them.

⁵There were some religious Jews staying in Jerusalem who were from every country in the world. ⁶When they heard this noise, a crowd came together. They were all surprised, because each one heard them speaking in his own language. ⁷They were completely amazed at this. They said, "Look! Aren't all these people that we hear speaking from Galilee? ⁸Then how is it possible that we each hear them in our own languages? We are from different places: ⁹Parthia, Media, Elam, Mesopotamia, Judea, Cappadocia, Pontus, Asia, ¹⁰Phrygia, Pamphylia, Egypt, the areas of Libya near Cyrene, Rome ¹¹(both Jews and those who had become Jews), Crete and Arabia. But we hear them telling in our own languages about the great things God has done!" ¹²They were all amazed and confused, asking each other, "What does this mean?"

¹³But others were making fun of them, saying, "They have had too much wine."

Peter Speaks to the People

¹⁴But Peter stood up with the eleven apostles, and in a loud voice he spoke to the crowd: "My fellow Jews, and all of you who are in Jerusalem, listen to me. Pay attention to what I have to say. ¹⁵These people are not drunk, as you think; it is only nine o'clock in the morning! ¹⁶But Joel the prophet wrote about what is happening here today:

¹⁷'God says: In the last days
    I will pour out my Spirit on all kinds of
      people.
Your sons and daughters will prophesy.
    Your old men will dream dreams,
    and your young men will see visions.
¹⁸At that time I will pour out my Spirit
    also on my male slaves and female
      slaves.
¹⁹I will show miracles
    in the sky and on the earth:
    blood, fire and thick smoke.
²⁰The sun will become dark,
    the moon red as blood,
    before the overwhelming and terrible
      day of the LORD comes.
²¹Then anyone who calls on the LORD
    will be saved.'   *Joel 2:28–32*

²²"People of Israel, listen to these words: Jesus from Nazareth was a very special man. God clearly showed this to you by the miracles, wonders and signs he did through Jesus. You all know this, because it happened right here among

you. 23Jesus was given to you, and with the help of those who don't know the law, you put him to death by nailing him to a cross. But this was God's plan which he had made long ago; he knew all this would happen. 24God raised Jesus from the dead and set him free from the pain of death, because death could not hold him. 25For David said this about him:

'I keep the LORD before me always.
Because he is close by my side,
I will not be hurt.
26So I rejoice and am glad.
Even my body has hope,
27because you will not leave me in the grave.
You will not let your holy one rot.
28You will teach me how to live a holy life.
Being with you will fill me with joy.'

Psalm 16:8–11

How does the way the Spirit came demonstrate God's commitment to being with people wherever they are in the world (vs 4,5,8–11)?

The Holy Spirit came so that Christians can know God is with them always, everywhere.

Think

When are the times you feel that God is far away? What do you do?

Pray

Thank Jesus for sending his Spirit so we can all know him.

Jesus – he's the one!

Just a few weeks before, Peter had been swearing and then was nowhere in sight when Jesus needed him. Now ...

Acts 2:29–3:10

29"Brothers and sisters, I can tell you truly that David, our ancestor, died and was buried. His grave is still here with us today. 30He was a prophet and knew God had promised him that he would make a person from David's family a king just as he was. 31Knowing this before it happened, David talked about the Christ rising from the dead. He said:

'He was not left in the grave.
His body did not rot.'

32So Jesus is the One whom God raised from the dead. And we are all witnesses to this. 33Jesus was lifted up to heaven and is now at God's right side. The Father has given the Holy Spirit to Jesus as he promised. So Jesus has poured out that Spirit, and this is what you now see and hear. 34David was not the one who was lifted up to heaven, but he said:

'The LORD said to my Lord,
  "Sit by me at my right side,
35   until I put your enemies under your
    control."'   *Psalm 110:1*

36"So, all the people of Israel should know this truly: God has made Jesus—the man you nailed to the cross—both Lord and Christ."

37When the people heard this, they felt guilty and asked Peter and the other apostles, "What shall we do?"

38Peter said to them, "Change your hearts and lives and be baptised, each one of you, in the name of Jesus Christ for the forgiveness of your sins. And you will receive the gift of the Holy Spirit. 39This promise is for you, for your children and for all who are far away. It is for everyone the Lord our God calls to himself."

40Peter warned them with many other words. He begged them, "Save yourselves from the evil of today's people!" 41Then those people who accepted what Peter said were baptised. About 3,000 people were added to the number of believers that day. 42They spent their time learning the apostles' teaching, sharing, breaking bread and praying together.

The Believers Share

43The apostles were doing many miracles and signs, and everyone felt great respect for God. 44All the believers were together and shared everything. 45They would sell their land and the things they owned and then divide the money and give it to anyone who needed it. 46The believers met together in the Temple every day. They ate together in their homes, happy to share their food with joyful hearts. 47They praised God and were liked by all the people. Every day the Lord added those who were being saved to the group of believers.

Peter Heals a Crippled Man

3 One day Peter and John went to the Temple at three o'clock, the time set each day for the afternoon prayer service. 2There, at the Temple gate called Beautiful Gate, was a man who had been crippled all his life. Every day he was carried to this

gate to beg for money from the people going into the Temple. ³The man saw Peter and John going into the Temple and asked them for money. ⁴Peter and John looked straight at him and said, "Look at us!" ⁵The man looked at them, thinking they were going to give him some money. ⁶But Peter said, "I don't have any silver or gold, but I do have something else I can give you. By the power of Jesus Christ from Nazareth, stand up and walk!" ⁷Then Peter took the man's right hand and lifted him up. Immediately the man's feet and ankles became strong. ⁸He jumped up, stood on his feet and began to walk. He went into the Temple with them, walking and jumping and praising God. ⁹⁻¹⁰All the people recognised him as the crippled man who always sat by the Beautiful Gate begging for money. Now they saw this same man walking and praising God, and they were amazed. They wondered how this could happen.

People were gobsmacked by the healing of the cripple – perhaps Peter and John were, too (3:9)!

What would you have done?

- Made sure everyone knew *you* had done it

- Make sure everyone knew it was Jesus who'd healed the man

Think

Peter and John had changed! So, what or who had made the difference?

Pray

Lord Jesus, thank you for all you enable me to do. Help me always to point others to you.

On trial

If you were put on trial for being a Christian, would you be found guilty?

Would you plead guilty?

 Acts 3:11–4:12

Peter Speaks to the People

[11]While the man was holding on to Peter and John, all the people were amazed and ran to them at Solomon's Porch. [12]When Peter saw this, he said to them, "People of Israel, why are you surprised? You are looking at us as if it were our own power or goodness that made this man walk. [13]The God of Abraham, Isaac and Jacob, the God of our ancestors, gave glory to Jesus, his servant. But you handed him over to be killed. Pilate decided to let him go free, but you told Pilate you did not want Jesus. [14]You did not want the One who is holy and good but asked Pilate to give you a murderer instead. [15]And so you killed the One who gives life, but God raised him from the dead. We are witnesses to this. [16]It was faith in Jesus that made this crippled man well. You can see this man, and you know him. He was made completely well because of trust in Jesus, and you all saw it happen!

[17]"Brothers and sisters, I know you did those things to Jesus because neither you nor your leaders understood what you were doing. [18]God said through the prophets that his Christ would suffer and die. And now God has made these things come true in this way. [19]So you must change your hearts and lives! Come back to God, and he will forgive your sins. Then the Lord will give you times of spiritual rest. [20]And he will send Jesus, the One he chose to be the Christ. [21]But Jesus must stay in heaven until the time comes when all things will be made right again. God told about this time long ago when he spoke. through his holy prophets. [22]Moses said, 'The Lord your God will give you a prophet like me, who is one of your own people. You must listen to everything he tells you. [23]Anyone who does not listen to that prophet will die, cut off from God's people.' [24]Samuel, and all the other prophets who spoke for God after Samuel, told about this time now. [25]You are descendants of the prophets. You have received the agreement God made with your ancestors. He said to your father Abraham, 'Through your descendants all the nations on the earth will be blessed.' [26]God has raised up his servant Jesus and sent him to you first to bless you by turning each of you away from doing evil."

Peter and John at the Council

4 While Peter and John were speaking to the people, Jewish priests, the captain of the soldiers that guarded the Temple and Sadducees came up to them. [2]They were upset because the two apostles were teaching the people and were preaching that people will rise from the dead through the power of Jesus. [3]The Jewish leaders grabbed Peter and John and put them in jail. Since it was already night, they kept them in jail until the next day. [4]But many of those who had heard Peter and John preach

believed the things they said. There were now about 5,000 in the group of believers.

⁵The next day the Jewish rulers, the Jewish elders and the teachers of the law met in Jerusalem. ⁶Annas the high priest, Caiaphas, John and Alexander were there, as well as everyone from the high priest's family. ⁷They made Peter and John stand before them and then asked them, "By what power or authority did you do this?"

⁸Then Peter, filled with the Holy Spirit, said to them, "Rulers of the people and you elders, ⁹are you questioning us about a good thing that was done to a crippled man? Are you asking us who made him well? ¹⁰We want all of you and all the Jewish people to know that this man was made well by the power of Jesus Christ from Nazareth. You crucified him, but God raised him from the dead. This man was crippled, but he is now well and able to stand here before you because of the power of Jesus. ¹¹Jesus is

'the stone that you builders rejected,
which has become the cornerstone.'

Psalm 118:22

¹²Jesus is the only One who can save people. His name is the only power in the world that has been given to save people. We must be saved through him."

Peter and John got arrested for saying that Jesus was Lord. And they used it as an opportunity to tell more people about Jesus – including some of the most important people in the country.

What help did they have?

Think

If you're not afraid of telling people you follow Jesus, the Spirit will help you.

Pray

Ask God to give you the courage to stand up for what you believe in.

Look after others

What kind of things do you like sharing with your friends?

- Your lunch
- Your bus fare
- Your new bike
- Your best CD

Anything else?

Acts 4:13–37

¹³The Jewish leaders saw that Peter and John were not afraid to speak, and they understood that these men had no special training or education. So they were amazed. Then they realised that Peter and John had been with Jesus. ¹⁴Because they saw the healed man standing there beside the two apostles, they could say nothing against them. ¹⁵After the Jewish leaders ordered them to leave the meeting, they began to talk to each other. ¹⁶They said, "What shall we do with these men? Everyone in Jerusalem knows they have done a great miracle, and we cannot say it is not true. ¹⁷But to keep it from spreading among the people, we must warn them not to talk to people any more using that name."

¹⁸So they called Peter and John in again and told them not to speak or to teach at all in the name of Jesus. ¹⁹But Peter and John answered them, "You decide what God would want. Should we obey you or God? ²⁰We cannot keep quiet. We must speak about what we have seen and heard." ²¹The Jewish leaders warned the apostles again and let them go free. They could not find a way to punish them, because all the people were praising God

for what had been done. ²²The man who received the miracle of healing was more than 40 years old.

The Believers Pray

²³After Peter and John left the meeting of Jewish leaders, they went to their own group and told them everything the leading priests and the Jewish elders had said to them. ²⁴When the believers heard this, they prayed to God together, "Lord, you are the One who made the sky, the earth, the sea and everything in them. ²⁵By the Holy Spirit, through our father David your servant, you said:

'Why are the nations so angry?
  Why are the people making useless
    plans?
²⁶The kings of the earth prepare to fight,
  and their leaders make plans together
against the LORD
  and his appointed one.'   *Psalm 2:1–2*
²⁷These things really happened when Herod, Pontius Pilate, those who are not Jews and the Jewish people all came together against Jesus here in Jerusalem. Jesus is your holy servant, the One you made to be the Christ. ²⁸These people made your plan happen because of your power and your

will. ²⁹And now, Lord, listen to their threats. Lord, help us, your servants, to speak your word without fear. ³⁰Help us to be brave by showing us your power to heal. Give proofs and make miracles happen by the power of Jesus, your holy servant."

³¹After they had prayed, the place where they were meeting was shaken. They were all filled with the Holy Spirit, and they spoke God's word without fear.

The Believers Share

³²The group of believers were united in their hearts and spirit. All those in the group acted as though their private property belonged to everyone in the group. In fact, they shared everything. ³³With great power the apostles were telling people that the Lord Jesus was truly raised from the dead. And God blessed all the believers very much. ³⁴No one in the group needed anything. From time to time those who owned fields or houses sold them, brought the money, ³⁵and gave it to the apostles. Then the money was given to anyone who needed it.

³⁶One of the believers was named Joseph, a Levite born in Cyprus. The apostles called him Barnabas (which means "one who encourages"). ³⁷Joseph owned a field, sold it, brought the money and gave it to the apostles.

Incredible generosity broke out in the early Christian church. People gave their money to the apostles (the church leaders) who made sure everyone in the church was properly cared for.

Why was this happening (v 32)?

Think

What could you do to help people in your church who haven't got much money? Talk to your youth leader about this.

Pray

Father, help me to notice those in need in my own church. Please show my church leaders how we should help them.

Caught cheating

Have you ever been caught out in a big lie? What did it feel like?
What were the consequences? Bet they weren't as bad as this.

Acts 5:1–26

Ananias and Sapphira Die

5 But a man named Ananias and his wife Sapphira sold some land. ²He kept back part of the money for himself; his wife knew about this and agreed to it. But he brought the rest of the money and gave it to the apostles. ³Peter said, "Ananias, why did you let Satan rule your thoughts to lie to the Holy Spirit and to keep for yourself part of the money you received for the land? ⁴Before you sold the land, it belonged to you. And even after you sold it, you could have used the money in any way you wanted. Why did you think of doing this? You lied to God, not to us!" ⁵⁻⁶When Ananias heard this, he fell down and died. Some young men came in, wrapped up his body, carried it out and buried it. And everyone who heard about this was filled with fear.

⁷About three hours later his wife came in, but she did not know what had happened. ⁸Peter said to her, "Tell me, was the money you got for your field this much?"

Sapphira answered, "Yes, that was the price."

⁹Peter said to her, "Why did you and your husband agree to test the Spirit of the Lord? Look! The men who buried your husband are at the door, and they will carry you out." ¹⁰At that moment Sapphira fell down by his feet and died. When the young men came in and saw that she was dead, they carried her out and buried her

beside her husband. ¹¹The whole church and all the others who heard about these things were filled with fear.

The Apostles Heal Many

¹²The apostles did many signs and miracles among the people. And they would all meet together on Solomon's Porch. ¹³None of the others dared to join them, but all the people respected them. ¹⁴More and more men and women believed in the Lord and were added to the group of believers. ¹⁵The people placed their sick on beds and mats in the streets, hoping that when Peter passed by at least his shadow might fall on them. ¹⁶Crowds came from all the towns around Jerusalem, bringing their sick and those who were bothered by evil spirits, and all of them were healed.

Leaders Try to Stop the Apostles

¹⁷The high priest and all his friends (a group called the Sadducees) became very jealous. ¹⁸They took the apostles and put them in jail. ¹⁹But during the night, an angel of the Lord opened the doors of the jail and led the apostles outside. The angel said, ²⁰"Go and stand in the Temple and tell the people everything about this new life." ²¹When the apostles heard this, they obeyed and went into the Temple early in the morning and continued teaching.

When the high priest and his friends arrived, they called a meeting of the Jewish leaders and all the important Jewish elders. They sent some men to the jail to bring the apostles to them. ²²But, upon arriving, the officers could not find the apostles. So they went back and reported to the Jewish leaders. ²³They said, "The jail was closed and locked, and the guards were standing at the doors. But when we opened the doors, the jail was empty!" ²⁴Hearing this, the captain of the Temple guards and the leading priests were confused and wondered what was happening.

²⁵Then someone came and told them, "Listen! The men you put in jail are standing in the Temple teaching the people." ²⁶Then the captain and his men went out and brought the apostles back. But the soldiers did not use force, because they were afraid the people would stone them to death.

Ananias and Sapphira had given a lot of money to the church – so why did such a terrible thing happen to them?

Think

The problem wasn't that they kept some money back – the problem was that they lied about it, so they'd look good. If they'd admitted that they weren't giving all the money to the church, such a terrible thing would never have happened.

Pray

Father, forgive me for those times I've told lies. Help me to be honest in everything I do.

The importance of the "little" things

How good are you at cleaning up after yourself?

- Your bedroom?
- The dishes after dinner?
- Yesterday's smelly clothes?

Acts 5:27–6:7

27The soldiers brought the apostles to the meeting and made them stand before the Jewish leaders. The high priest questioned them, 28saying, "We gave you strict orders not to continue teaching in that name. But look, you have filled Jerusalem with your teaching and are trying to make us responsible for this man's death."

29Peter and the other apostles answered, "We must obey God, not human authority! 30You killed Jesus by hanging him on a cross. But God, the God of our ancestors, raised Jesus up from the dead! 31Jesus is the One whom God raised to be on his right side, as Leader and Saviour. Through him, all Jewish people can change their hearts and lives and have their sins forgiven. 32We saw all these things happen. The Holy Spirit, whom God has given to all who obey him, also proves these things are true."

33When the Jewish leaders heard this, they became angry and wanted to kill them. 34But a Pharisee named Gamaliel stood up in the meeting. He was a teacher of the law, and all the people respected him. He ordered the apostles to leave the meeting for a little while. 35Then he said, "People of Israel, be careful what you are planning to do to these men. 36Remember

when Theudas appeared? He said he was a great man, and about 400 men joined him. But he was killed, and all his followers were scattered; they were able to do nothing. 37Later, a man named Judas came from Galilee at the time of the registration. He also led a group of followers and was killed, and all his followers were scattered. 38And so now I tell you: stay away from these men, and leave them alone. If their plan comes from human authority, it will fail. 39But if it is from God, you will not be able to stop them. You might even be fighting against God himself!"

The Jewish leaders agreed with what Gamaliel said. 40They called the apostles in, beat them and told them not to speak in the name of Jesus again. Then they let them go free. 41The apostles left the meeting full of joy because they were given the honour of suffering disgrace for Jesus. 42Every day in the Temple and in people's homes they continued teaching the people and telling the Good News—that Jesus is the Christ.

Seven Leaders are Chosen

6 The number of followers was growing. But during this same time, the Greek-

speaking followers had an argument with the other Jewish followers. The Greek-speaking widows were not getting their share of the food that was given out every day. ²The twelve apostles called the whole group of followers together and said, "It is not right for us to stop our work of teaching God's word in order to serve tables. ³So, brothers and sisters, choose seven of your own men who are good, full of the Spirit and full of wisdom. We will put them in charge of this work. ⁴Then we can continue to pray and to teach the word of God."

⁵The whole group liked the idea, so they chose these seven men: Stephen (a man with great faith and full of the Holy Spirit), Philip, Procorus, Nicanor, Timon, Parmenas and Nicolas (a man from Antioch who had become a Jew). ⁶Then they put these men before the apostles, who prayed and laid their hands on them.

⁷The word of God was continuing to spread. The group of followers in Jerusalem increased, and a great number of the Jewish priests believed and obeyed.

What was the problem (6:1)?

What was the solution (6:2,3)?

Before the seven who were chosen went to work, what did the apostles do?

Think

Do you overlook the seemingly "little" things and therefore miss the other jobs that need doing?

Pray

Ask God to show you what needs to be done and then to give you the strength to do it.

297

In your face

When people look at you, what do they see? What does your face show?

Acts 6:8–7:16

Stephen is Accused

⁸Stephen was richly blessed by God who gave him the power to do great miracles and signs among the people. ⁹But some Jewish people were against him. They belonged to the synagogue of Free Men (as it was called), which included Jewish people from Cyrene, Alexandria, Cilicia and Asia. They all came and argued with Stephen.

¹⁰But the Spirit was helping him to speak with wisdom, and his words were so strong that they could not argue with him. ¹¹So they secretly urged some men to say, "We heard Stephen speak against Moses and against God."

¹²This upset the people, the Jewish elders and the teachers of the law. They came and grabbed Stephen and brought him to a meeting of the Jewish leaders. ¹³They brought in some people to tell lies about Stephen, saying, "This man is always speaking against this holy place and the law of Moses. ¹⁴We heard him say that Jesus from Nazareth will destroy this place and that Jesus will change the customs Moses gave us." ¹⁵All the people in the meeting were watching Stephen closely and saw that his face looked like the face of an angel.

Stephen's Speech

7 The high priest said to Stephen, "Are these things true?"

²Stephen answered, "Brothers and fathers, listen to me. Our glorious God appeared to Abraham, our ancestor, in Mesopotamia before he lived in Haran. ³God said to Abraham, 'Leave your country and your relatives, and go to the land I will show you.' ⁴So Abraham left the country of Chaldea and went to live in Haran. After Abraham's father died, God sent him to this place where you now live. ⁵God did not give Abraham any of this land, not even a foot of it. But God promised that he would give this land to him and his descendants, even before Abraham had a child. ⁶This is what God said to him: 'Your descendants will be strangers in a land they don't own. The people there will make them slaves and will mistreat them for 400 years. ⁷But I will punish the nation where they are slaves. Then your descendants will leave that land and will worship me in this place.' ⁸God made an agreement with Abraham, the sign of which was circumcision. And so when Abraham had his son, Isaac, Abraham circumcised him when he was eight days old. Isaac also circumcised his son, Jacob, and Jacob did the same for his sons, the twelve ancestors of our people.

⁹"Jacob's sons became jealous of Joseph and sold him to be a slave in Egypt. But God was with him ¹⁰and saved him from all his troubles. The king of Egypt liked Joseph and respected him because of the wisdom God gave him. The king made him governor of Egypt and put him in charge of all the people in his palace.

¹¹"Then all the land of Egypt and Canaan became so dry that nothing would grow, and the people suffered very much. Jacob's sons, our ancestors, could not find

anything to eat. ¹²But when Jacob heard there was grain in Egypt, he sent his sons there. This was their first trip to Egypt. ¹³When they went there a second time, Joseph told his brothers who he was, and the king learned about Joseph's family. ¹⁴Then Joseph sent messengers to invite Jacob, his father, to come to Egypt along with all his relatives (75 persons altogether). ¹⁵So Jacob went down to Egypt, where he and his sons died. ¹⁶Later their bodies were moved to Shechem and put in a grave there. (It was the same grave Abraham had bought for a sum of money from the sons of Hamor in Shechem.)

Stephen was brave. He knew about the Scriptures and he loved God, and you could see that in his face. Do you think it mattered whether he was good-looking or not? Do we have any idea what he looked like? Should we care?

Think

You could see Stephen's courage and faith in his face. Think about what you say to other people when you look at them. Is the fact that you believe in Jesus obvious?

Pray

Ask God to make himself obvious when people look at you.

History repeating

One of the reasons we learn about history is so we can avoid making the mistakes people made before us. It doesn't stop us messing up anyway, though.

Acts 7:17–42a

17"The promise God made to Abraham was soon to come true, and the number of people in Egypt grew large. 18Then a new king, who did not know who Joseph was, began to rule Egypt. 19This king tricked our people and was cruel to our ancestors, forcing them to leave their babies outside to die. 20At this time Moses was born, and he was very beautiful. For three months Moses was cared for in his father's house. 21When they put Moses outside, the king's daughter adopted him and raised him as if he were her own son. 22The Egyptians taught Moses everything they knew, and he was a powerful man in what he said and did.

23"When Moses was about 40 years old, he thought it would be good to visit his own people, the people of Israel. 24Moses saw an Egyptian mistreating an Israelite, so he defended the Israelite and punished the Egyptian by killing him. 25Moses thought his own people would understand that God was using him to save them, but they did not. 26The next day when Moses saw two men of Israel fighting, he tried to make peace between them. He said, 'Men, you are brothers. Why are you hurting each other?' 27The man who was hurting the other pushed Moses away and said, 'Who made you our ruler and judge? 28Are you going to kill me as you killed the Egyptian yesterday?' 29When Moses heard him say

this, he left Egypt and went to live in the land of Midian where he was a stranger. While Moses lived in Midian, he had two sons.

30"Forty years later an angel appeared to Moses in the flames of a burning bush as he was in the desert near Mount Sinai. 31When Moses saw this, he was amazed and went near to look closer. Moses heard the Lord's voice say, 32'I am the God of your ancestors, the God of Abraham, Isaac and Jacob.' Moses began to shake with fear and was afraid to look. 33The Lord said to him, 'Take off your sandals, because you are standing on holy ground. 34I have seen the troubles my people have suffered in Egypt. I have heard their cries and have come down to save them. And now, Moses, I am sending you back to Egypt.'

35"This Moses was the same man the two men of Israel rejected, saying, 'Who made you a ruler and judge?' Moses is the same man God sent to be a ruler and saviour, with the help of the angel that Moses saw in the burning bush. 36So Moses led the people out of Egypt. He worked miracles and signs in Egypt, at the Red Sea and then in the desert for 40 years. 37This is the same Moses that said to the people of Israel, 'God will give you a prophet like me, who is one of your own people.' 38This is the Moses who was with the gathering of the Israelites in the desert.

He was with the angel that spoke to him at Mount Sinai, and he was with our ancestors. He received commands from God that give life, and he gave those commands to us.

³⁹"But our ancestors did not want to obey Moses. They rejected him and wanted to go back to Egypt. ⁴⁰They said to Aaron, 'Make us gods who will lead us. Moses led us out of Egypt, but we don't know what has happened to him.' ⁴¹So the people made an idol that looked like a calf. Then they brought sacrifices to it and were proud of what they had made with their own hands. ⁴²But God turned against them and did not try to stop them from worshipping the sun, moon and stars.

Things haven't changed.

Stephen tells the people in the court the story of Moses. Moses passed on God's word, but the people ignored him again and again – and it happened again with Jesus.

Think

People still ignore God today. But people like us are still called by God to speak to them. Just because not everyone's going to listen, it doesn't mean that nobody will ever listen. There are always going to be some people who believe, and that's what makes it worth it.

Pray

Father, give me the persistence to keep telling people about Jesus.

Death or life?

Would you give up everything for Jesus?

The Holy Spirit helped Stephen to speak about Jesus (Acts 6:8). The Jewish leaders didn't like it, especially when Stephen told them *they* had killed God's special messenger . . .

Acts 7:42b–8:1a

This is what is written in the book of the prophets: God says,
'People of Israel, you did not bring me
    sacrifices and offerings
while you travelled in the desert for 40
    years.
43You have carried with you
    your king, the god Sakkuth,
    and Kaiwan your idol
    and the star gods you have made.
So I will send you away as captives
    beyond Damascus.'   *Amos 5:25–27*
44"The Holy Tent where God spoke to our ancestors was with them in the desert. God told Moses how to make this Tent, and he made it like the plan God showed him. 45Later, Joshua led our ancestors to capture the lands of the other nations. Our people went in, and God forced the other people out. When our people went into this new land, they took with them this same Tent they had received from their ancestors. They kept it until the time of David, 46who pleased God and asked God to let him build a house for him, the God of Jacob. 47But Solomon was the one who built the Temple.

48"But the Most High does not live in houses that people build with their hands. As the prophet says:
49'Heaven is my throne,
    and the earth is my footstool.

So do you think you can build a house
    for me? says the Lord.
Do I need a place to rest?
50Remember, my hand made all these
    things!' "   *Isaiah 66:1–2*
51Stephen continued speaking: "You stubborn people! You have not given your hearts to God, nor will you listen to him! You are always against what the Holy Spirit is trying to tell you, just as your ancestors were. 52Your ancestors tried to hurt every prophet who ever lived. Those prophets said long ago that the One who is good would come, but your ancestors killed them. And now you have turned against and killed the One who is good. 53You received the law of Moses, which God gave you through his angels, but you haven't obeyed it."

Stephen is Killed

54When the leaders heard this, they became furious. They were so cross they were grinding their teeth at Stephen. 55But Stephen was full of the Holy Spirit. He looked up to heaven and saw the glory of God and Jesus standing at God's right side. 56He said, "Look! I see heaven open and the Son of Man standing at God's right side."

57Then they shouted loudly and covered their ears and all ran at Stephen. 58They took him out of the city and began to throw stones at him to kill him. And those who told lies against Stephen left their coats with a young man named Saul. ⁵⁹While they were throwing stones, Stephen prayed, "Lord Jesus, receive my spirit." ⁶⁰He fell on his knees and cried in a loud voice, "Lord, do not hold this sin against them." After Stephen said this, he died.

8 Saul agreed that the killing of Stephen was good.

How did Stephen react when he was being stoned (7:60)?

What effect did the persecution of the church have on the followers of Jesus (8:1)?

Did the persecution stop people telling others about Jesus (8:4)?

Take note of 7:58; the young man named Saul was about to take a much larger role in the life of the early church.

Think

Does anything mean so much to you that you would die for it? That's what Jesus meant to Stephen.

Pray

Talk to God about how much Jesus means to you.

A kind of magic?

When God does something special, is it really no more than a magic trick?

Acts 8:1b–25

Troubles for the Believers

On that day the church of Jerusalem began to be persecuted, and all the believers, except the apostles, were scattered throughout Judea and Samaria.

²And some religious people buried Stephen and cried loudly for him. ³Saul was also trying to destroy the church, going from house to house, dragging out men and women and putting them in jail. ⁴And wherever they were scattered, they told people the Good News.

Philip Preaches in Samaria

⁵Philip went to the city of Samaria and preached about the Christ. ⁶When the people there heard Philip and saw the miracles he was doing, they all listened carefully to what he said. ⁷Many of these people had evil spirits in them, but Philip made the evil spirits leave. The spirits made a loud noise when they came out. Philip also healed many weak and crippled people there. ⁸So the people in that city were very happy.

⁹But there was a man named Simon in that city. Before Philip came there, Simon had practised magic and amazed all the people of Samaria. He boasted and called himself a great man. ¹⁰All the people—the least important to the most important—paid attention to Simon, saying, "This man has the power of God, called 'the Great Power!'" ¹¹Simon had amazed them with his magic so long that the people became his followers. ¹²But when Philip told them the Good News about the kingdom of God and the power of Jesus Christ, men and women believed Philip and were baptised. ¹³Simon himself believed, and after he was baptised, he stayed very close to Philip. When he saw the miracles and the powerful things Philip did, Simon was amazed.

¹⁴When the apostles who were still in Jerusalem heard that the people of Samaria had accepted the word of God, they sent Peter and John to them. ¹⁵When Peter and John arrived, they prayed that the Samaritan believers might receive the Holy Spirit. ¹⁶These people had been baptised in the name of the Lord Jesus, but the Holy Spirit had not yet come upon any of them. ¹⁷Then, when the two apostles began laying their hands on the people, they received the Holy Spirit.

¹⁸Simon saw that the Spirit was given to people when the apostles laid their hands on them. So he offered the apostles money, ¹⁹saying, "Give me also this power so that anyone on whom I lay my hands will receive the Holy Spirit."

²⁰Peter said to him, "You and your money should both be destroyed, because you thought you could buy God's gift with money. ²¹You cannot share with us in this work since your heart is not right before God. ²²Change your heart! Turn away

from this evil thing you have done, and pray to the Lord. Maybe he will forgive you for thinking this. ²³I see that you are full of bitter jealousy and ruled by sin."

²⁴Simon answered, "Both of you pray for me to the Lord so the things you have said will not happen to me."

²⁵After Peter and John told the people what they had seen Jesus do and after they had spoken the message of the Lord, they went back to Jerusalem. On the way, they went through many Samaritan towns and preached the Good News to the people.

Simon the magician joined with Jesus' followers, but he completely missed the point. He thought that the arrival of the Holy Spirit was just another magic trick that you could pay for with money. Simon didn't realise what he was dealing with, and didn't understand that the Holy Spirit isn't a tool that you use to get what you want – it's God intervening in your life.

Think

You can't buy or sell the Holy Spirit. The only way you can receive him is by following Jesus. And you can't use the Holy Spirit – the Spirit uses you.

Pray

Ask God to help you to be humble – and think about how you can serve God, rather than trying to make God serve you.

Right place, right time

Ever been sitting, minding your own business, when you suddenly think of something you just *must* do – immediately?

Have you ever been prompted to pray for someone – a friend, a relative?

Have you ever been in a conversation with someone and felt the need to tell them something about Jesus?

Acts 8:26–9:9

Philip Teaches an Ethiopian

26An angel of the Lord said to Philip, "Get ready and go south to the road that leads down to Gaza from Jerusalem—the desert road." 27So Philip got ready and went. On the road he saw a man from Ethiopia, a eunuch. He was an important officer in the service of Candace, the queen of the Ethiopians; he was responsible for taking care of all her money. He had gone to Jerusalem to worship. 28Now, as he was on his way home, he was sitting in his chariot reading from the Book of Isaiah, the prophet. 29The Spirit said to Philip, "Go to that chariot and stay near it."

30So when Philip ran towards the chariot, he heard the man reading from Isaiah the prophet. Philip asked, "Do you understand what you are reading?"

31He answered, "How can I understand unless someone explains it to me?" Then he invited Philip to climb in and sit with him. 32The portion of Scripture he was reading was this:

"He was like a sheep being led to be killed.

He was quiet, as a lamb is quiet while its wool is being cut;
he never opened his mouth.
33 He was shamed and was treated unfairly.
He died without children to continue his family.
His life on earth has ended."
Isaiah 53:7–8

34The officer said to Philip, "Please tell me, who is the prophet talking about—himself or someone else?" 35Philip began to speak, and starting with this same Scripture, he told the man the Good News about Jesus.

36While they were travelling down the road, they came to some water. The officer said, "Look, here is water. Why shouldn't I be baptised?" 37 38Then the officer commanded the chariot to stop. Both Philip and the officer went down into the water, and Philip baptised him. 39When they came up out of the water, the Spirit of the Lord took Philip away; the officer never saw him again. And the officer continued on his way home, full of joy. 40But Philip appeared in a city called

Azotus and preached the Good News in all the towns on the way from Azotus to Caesarea.

Saul is Converted

9 In Jerusalem Saul was still threatening the followers of the Lord by saying he would kill them. So he went to the high priest ²and asked him to write letters to the synagogues in the city of Damascus. Then if Saul found any followers of Christ's Way, men or women, he would arrest them and bring them back to Jerusalem.

³So Saul headed towards Damascus. As he came near the city, a bright light from heaven suddenly flashed around him.

⁴Saul fell to the ground and heard a voice saying to him, "Saul, Saul! Why are you persecuting me?"

⁵Saul said, "Who are you, Lord?"

The voice answered, "I am Jesus, whom you are persecuting. ⁶Get up now and go into the city. Someone there will tell you what you must do."

⁷The people travelling with Saul stood there but said nothing. They heard the voice, but they saw no one. ⁸Saul got up from the ground and opened his eyes, but he could not see. So those with Saul took his hand and led him into Damascus. ⁹For three days Saul could not see and did not eat or drink.

How did the Holy Spirit guide and use Philip to help the Ethiopian official?

How do you think the Holy Spirit was at work in the life of the Ethiopian?

Think

How could God use you to help others know more of him?

Pray

Ask the Holy Spirit to bring to your mind now someone for whom you could pray especially. Ask God to use you to help them.

Attention! Attention!

How far would you go to get other people's attention?

- Pierce your nose (twice at least)
- Shave your head (including eyebrows)
- Dress in your mum's clothes (if you are a girl)
- Dress in your mum's clothes (if you are a boy)

OK, so that last one is just too far ...

Acts 9:10–35

10There was a follower of Jesus in Damascus named Ananias. The Lord spoke to Ananias in a vision, "Ananias!"

Ananias answered, "Here I am, Lord."

11The Lord said to him, "Get up and go to Straight Street. Find the house of Judas, and ask for a man named Saul from the city of Tarsus. He is there now, praying. 12Saul has seen a vision in which a man named Ananias comes to him and lays his hands on him. Then he is able to see again."

13But Ananias answered, "Lord, many people have told me about this man and the terrible things he did to your holy people in Jerusalem. 14Now he has come here to Damascus, and the leading priests have given him the power to arrest everyone who worships you."

15But the Lord said to Ananias, "Go! I have chosen Saul for an important work. He must tell me to those who are not Jews, to kings and to the people of Israel. 16I will show him how much he must suffer for my name."

17So Ananias went to the house of Judas. He laid his hands on Saul and said, "Brother Saul, the Lord Jesus sent me. He is the one you saw on the road on your way here. He sent me so that you can see again and be filled with the Holy Spirit."

18Immediately, something that looked like fish scales fell from Saul's eyes, and he was able to see again! Then Saul got up and was baptised. 19After he ate some food, his strength returned.

Saul Preaches in Damascus

Saul stayed with the followers of Jesus in Damascus for a few days. 20Soon he began to preach about Jesus in the synagogues, saying, "Jesus is the Son of God."

21All the people who heard him were amazed. They said, "This is the man who was in Jerusalem trying to destroy those who trust in this name! He came here to arrest the followers of Jesus and take them back to the leading priests."

22But Saul grew more powerful. His proofs that Jesus is the Christ were so strong that the Jewish people in Damascus could not argue with him.

23After many days, some Jewish people made plans to kill Saul. 24They were watching the city gates day and night, but Saul learned about their plan. 25One night some followers of Saul helped him leave the city by lowering him in a basket through an opening in the city wall.

Saul Preaches in Jerusalem

26When Saul went to Jerusalem, he tried

to join the group of followers, but they were all afraid of him. They did not believe he was really a follower. ²⁷But Barnabas accepted Saul and took him to the apostles. Barnabas explained to them that Saul had seen the Lord on the road and the Lord had spoken to Saul. Then he told them how boldly Saul had preached in the name of Jesus in Damascus.

²⁸And so Saul stayed with the followers, going everywhere in Jerusalem, preaching boldly in the name of the Lord. ²⁹He would often talk and argue with the Jewish people who spoke Greek, but they were trying to kill him. ³⁰When the followers learned about this, they took Saul to Caesarea and from there sent him to Tarsus.

³¹The church everywhere in Judea, Galilee and Samaria had a time of peace and became stronger. Respecting the Lord by the way they lived, and being encouraged by the Holy Spirit, the group of believers continued to grow.

Peter Heals Aeneas

³²As Peter was travelling through all the area, he visited God's people who lived in Lydda. ³³There he met a man named Aeneas, who was paralysed and had not been able to leave his bed for the past eight years. ³⁴Peter said to him, "Aeneas, Jesus Christ heals you. Stand up and make your bed." Aeneas stood up immediately. ³⁵All the people living in Lydda and on the Plain of Sharon saw him and turned to the Lord.

What did God do to attract Saul's attention?

Who did God ask to help Saul (v 10)?

How do you think Ananias felt having to help Saul?

Think

Are you listening out for God?

Pray

Lord, help me to keep my eyes open to see what you want me to do.

Ready to learn

Is there anything that you have a particularly strong opinion about? What would it take for you to change your point of view on the subject?

Has God ever changed your mind about something?

 Acts 9:36–10:23a

Peter Heals Tabitha

36In the city of Joppa there was a follower named Tabitha (whose Greek name was Dorcas). She was always doing good deeds and kind acts. 37While Peter was in Lydda, Tabitha became sick and died. Her body was washed and put in a room upstairs. 38Since Lydda is near Joppa and the followers in Joppa heard that Peter was in Lydda, they sent two messengers to Peter. They begged him, "Hurry, please come to us!" 39So Peter got ready and went with them. When he arrived, they took him to the upstairs room where all the widows stood around Peter, crying. They showed him the shirts and coats Tabitha had made when she was still alive. 40Peter sent everyone out of the room and kneeled and prayed. Then he turned to the body and said, "Tabitha, stand up." She opened her eyes, and when she saw Peter, she sat up. 41He gave her his hand and helped her up. Then he called the saints and the widows into the room and showed them that Tabitha was alive. 42People everywhere in Joppa learned about this, and many believed in the Lord. 43Peter stayed in Joppa for many days with a man named Simon who was a leatherworker.

Peter Teaches Cornelius

10 At Caesarea there was a man named Cornelius, an officer in the Italian group of the Roman army. 2Cornelius was a religious man. He and all the other people who lived in his house worshipped the true God. He gave much of his money to the poor and prayed to God often. 3One afternoon about three o'clock, Cornelius clearly saw a vision. An angel of God came to him and said, "Cornelius!"

4Cornelius stared at the angel. He became afraid and said, "What do you want, Lord?"

The angel said, "God has heard your prayers. He has seen that you give to the poor, and he remembers you. 5Send some men now to Joppa to bring back a man named Simon who is also called Peter. 6He is staying with a man, also named Simon, who is a leatherworker and has a house beside the sea." 7When the angel who spoke to Cornelius left, Cornelius called two of his servants and a soldier, a religious man who worked for him. 8Cornelius explained everything to them and sent them to Joppa.

9About noon the next day as they came near Joppa, Peter was going up to the roof to pray. 10He was hungry and wanted to eat, but while the food was being prepared, he had a vision. 11He saw heaven opened and something coming down that looked like a big sheet being lowered to earth by its four corners. 12In it were all kinds of animals, reptiles and birds. 13Then a voice said to Peter, "Get up, Peter; kill and eat."

¹⁴But Peter said, "No, Lord! I have never eaten food that is unholy or unclean."

¹⁵But the voice said to him again, "God has made these things clean so don't call them 'unholy'!" ¹⁶This happened three times, and at once the sheet was taken back to heaven.

¹⁷While Peter was wondering what this vision meant, the men Cornelius sent had found Simon's house and were standing at the gate. ¹⁸They asked, "Is Simon Peter staying here?"

¹⁹While Peter was still thinking about the vision, the Spirit said to him, "Listen, three men are looking for you. ²⁰Get up and go downstairs. Go with them without doubting, because I have sent them to you."

²¹So Peter went down to the men and said, "I am the one you are looking for. Why did you come here?"

²²They said, "A holy angel spoke to Cornelius, an army officer and a good man; he worships God. All the Jewish people respect him. The angel told Cornelius to ask you to come to his house so that he can hear what you have to say." ²³So Peter asked the men to come in and spend the night.

In the Old Testament there were lots of rules about what animals you could or couldn't eat. Peter would have kept these rules all his life. Now, in this dream, God seemed to be saying to him that it was OK to eat anything (10:11–16).

Think

What else do you think God wanted Peter to change his mind about (clue: Acts 10:28)?

Pray

Are there things, or people, that God might want you to change your mind or attitude toward? Ask him to help you do it.

Everybody welcome

The Good News isn't just for one group of people – it's for everyone in the world.

Acts 10:23b–48

The next day Peter got ready and went with them, and some of the followers from Joppa joined him.

24On the following day they came to Caesarea. Cornelius was waiting for them and had called together his relatives and close friends. 25When Peter entered, Cornelius met him, fell at his feet and worshipped him. 26But Peter helped him up, saying, "Stand up. I too am only a human." 27As he talked with Cornelius, Peter went inside where he saw many people gathered. 28He said, "You people understand that it is against our Jewish law for Jewish people to associate with or visit anyone who is not Jewish. But God has shown me that I should not call any person 'unholy' or 'unclean'. 29That is why I did not argue when I was asked to come here. Now, please tell me why you sent for me."

30Cornelius said, "Four days ago, I was praying in my house at this same time—three o'clock in the afternoon. Suddenly, there was a man standing before me wearing shining clothes. 31He said, 'Cornelius, God has heard your prayer and has seen that you give to the poor and remembers you. 32So send some men to Joppa and ask Simon Peter to come. Peter is staying in the house of a man, also named Simon, who is a leatherworker and has a house beside the sea.' 33So I sent for you immediately, and it was very good of you to come. Now we are all here before God to hear everything the Lord has commanded you to tell us."

34Peter began to speak: "I really under-

stand now that to God every person is the same. 35In every country God accepts anyone who worships him and does what is right. 36You know the message that God has sent to the people of Israel is the Good News that peace has come through Jesus Christ. Jesus is the Lord of all people! 37You know what has happened all over Judea, beginning in Galilee after John preached to the people about baptism. 38You know about Jesus from Nazareth, that God gave him the Holy Spirit and power. You know how Jesus went everywhere doing good and healing those who were ruled by the devil, because God was with him. 39We saw what Jesus did in Judea and in Jerusalem, but the Jews in Jerusalem killed him by hanging him on a cross. 40Yet, on the third day, God raised Jesus to life and caused him to be seen, 41not by all the people, but only by the witnesses God had already chosen. And we are those witnesses who ate and drank with him after he was raised from the dead. 42He told us to preach to the people and to tell them that he is the one whom God chose to be the judge of the living and the dead. 43All the prophets say it is true that all who believe in Jesus will be forgiven their sins through Jesus' name."

44While Peter was still saying this, the Holy Spirit came down on all those who were listening. 45The Jewish believers who came with Peter were amazed that the gift of the Holy Spirit had been given even to those who were not Jews. 46These Jewish believers heard them speaking in different languages and praising God. Then Peter said, 47"Can anyone keep these people from being baptised with water? They have received the Holy Spirit just as we did!"

48So Peter ordered that they be baptised in the name of Jesus Christ. Then they asked Peter to stay with them for a few days.

Originally, the Jewish people had rules about what they were supposed to eat – and who they were supposed to be friends with. But God told both Peter and Cornelius that from now on, the message he had to give was for everyone, and that Peter shouldn't be afraid to go and befriend people from every part of the world.

Think

Because Peter wasn't afraid to go out and talk to people he'd never had anything to do with before, God was able to work in the lives of lots of people who would otherwise have not heard the message. Don't be afraid to talk to people you've never communicated with before – the results may surprise you!

Pray

Ask God for the courage to talk to new people and to go to new places.

313

Where do we go from here?

Have you ever felt like you can't go on? Have you ever felt so low that there seems no way ahead?

Stephen's death was a low point.

 Acts 11:1–30

Peter Returns to Jerusalem

11 The apostles and the believers in Judea heard that some who were not Jewish had accepted God's teaching too. ²But when Peter came to Jerusalem, some Jewish believers argued with him. ³They said, "You went into the homes of people who are not circumcised and ate with them!"

⁴So Peter explained the whole story to them. ⁵He said, "I was in the city of Joppa, and while I was praying, I had a vision. I saw something that looked like a big sheet being lowered from heaven by its four corners. It came very close to me. ⁶I looked inside it and saw animals, wild beasts, reptiles and birds. ⁷I heard a voice say to me, 'Get up, Peter; kill and eat.' ⁸But I said, 'No, Lord! I have never eaten anything that is unholy or unclean.' ⁹But the voice from heaven spoke again, 'God has made these things clean, so don't call them unholy.' ¹⁰This happened three times. Then the whole thing was taken back to heaven. ¹¹Just then three men who were sent to me from Caesarea came to the house where I was staying. ¹²The Spirit told me to go with them without doubting. These six believers here also went with me, and we entered the house of Cornelius. ¹³He told us about the angel he saw standing in his house. The angel said to

him, 'Send some men to Joppa and invite Simon Peter to come. ¹⁴By the words he will say to you, you and all your family will be saved.' ¹⁵When I began my speech, the Holy Spirit came up on them just as he came up on us at the beginning. ¹⁶Then I remembered the words of the Lord. He said, 'John baptised with water, but you will be baptised with the Holy Spirit.' ¹⁷Since God gave them the same gift he gave us who believed in the Lord Jesus Christ, how could I stop the work of God?"

¹⁸When the Jewish believers heard this, they stopped arguing. They praised God and said, "So God is allowing even those who are not Jewish to turn to him and live."

The Good News Comes to Antioch

¹⁹Many of the believers were scattered when they were persecuted after Stephen was killed. Some of them went as far as Phoenicia, Cyprus and Antioch telling the message to others, but only to Jews. ²⁰Some of these believers were people from Cyprus and Cyrene. When they came to Antioch, they spoke also to Greeks, telling them the Good News about the Lord Jesus. ²¹The Lord was helping the believers, and a large group of people believed and turned to the Lord.

²²The church in Jerusalem heard about all of this, so they sent Barnabas to Antioch. ²³⁻²⁴Barnabas was a good man, full of the Holy Spirit and full of faith. When he reached Antioch and saw how God had blessed the people, he was glad. He encouraged all the believers in Antioch always to obey the Lord with all their hearts, and many people became followers of the Lord.

²⁵Then Barnabas went to the city of Tarsus to look for Saul, ²⁶and when he found Saul, he brought him to Antioch. For a whole year Saul and Barnabas met with the church and taught many people

there. In Antioch the followers were called Christians for the first time.

²⁷About that time some prophets came from Jerusalem to Antioch. ²⁸One of them, named Agabus, stood up and spoke with the help of the Holy Spirit. He said, "A very hard time is coming to the whole world. There will be no food to eat." (This happened when Claudius ruled.) ²⁹The believers all decided to help the followers who lived in Judea, as much as each one could. ³⁰They gathered the money and gave it to Barnabas and Saul, who brought it to the elders in Judea.

What happened when the believers were persecuted (v 19)?

Where did they go?

Who did Barnabas encourage the believers to obey (vs 23,24)?

Who did Barnabas get to help (v 26)?

Think

... about how God used Saul, who had been involved in the initial persecution, to build up the new church.

Pray

If you are currently having a bad time pray that God will help you get through it all.

Extra

Romans 8:28 is a verse that has been used by many as a source of hope when going through bad times. Why not try to learn it?

Safe with God

Do you sometimes pray for things without really believing God will answer you?

Acts 12:1–25

Herod Agrippa Hurts the Church

12 During that same time King Herod began to mistreat some who belonged to the church. ²He ordered James, the brother of John, to be killed by the sword. ³Herod saw that the Jewish people liked this, so he decided to arrest Peter, too. (This happened during the time of the Feast of Unleavened Bread.)

⁴After Herod arrested Peter, he put him in jail and handed him over to be guarded by sixteen soldiers. Herod planned to bring Peter before the people for trial after the Passover Feast. ⁵So Peter was kept in jail, but the church prayed earnestly to God for him.

Peter Leaves the Jail

⁶The night before Herod was to bring him to trial, Peter was sleeping between two soldiers, bound with two chains. Other soldiers were guarding the door of the jail. ⁷Suddenly, an angel of the Lord stood there, and a light shone in the cell. The angel struck Peter on the side and woke him up. "Hurry! Get up!" the angel said. And the chains fell off Peter's hands. ⁸Then the angel told him, "Get dressed and put on your sandals." And Peter did. Then the angel said, "Put on your coat and follow me." ⁹So Peter followed him out, but he did not know if what the angel was doing was real; he thought he might be seeing a vision. ¹⁰They went past the first and second guards and came to the iron gate that separated them from the city. The gate opened by itself for them, and they went through it. When they had walked down one street, the angel suddenly left him.

¹¹Then Peter realised what had happened. He thought, "Now I know that the Lord really sent his angel to me. He rescued me from Herod and from all the things the Jewish people thought would happen."

¹²When he considered this, he went to the home of Mary, the mother of John Mark. Many people were gathered there, praying. ¹³Peter knocked on the outside door, and a servant girl named Rhoda came to answer it. ¹⁴When she recognised Peter's voice, she was so happy she forgot to open the door. Instead, she ran inside and told the group, "Peter is at the door!"

¹⁵They said to her, "You are mad!" But she kept on saying it was true, so they said, "It must be Peter's angel."

¹⁶Peter continued to knock, and when they opened the door, they saw him and were amazed. ¹⁷Peter made a sign with his hand to tell them to be quiet. He explained how the Lord led him out of the jail, and he said, "Tell James and the other believers what happened." Then he left to go to another place.

¹⁸The next day the soldiers were very upset and wondered what had happened to Peter. ¹⁹Herod looked everywhere for him but could not find him. So he questioned the guards and ordered that they be killed.

The Death of Herod Agrippa

Later Herod moved from Judea and went to the city of Caesarea, where he stayed. ²⁰Herod was very angry with the people of Tyre and Sidon, but the people of those cities all came in a group to him. After convincing Blastus, the king's personal servant, to be on their side, they asked Herod for peace, because their country got its food from his country.

²¹On a chosen day Herod put on his royal robes, sat on his throne and made a speech to the people. ²²They shouted, "This is the voice of a god, not a human!"

²³Because Herod did not give the glory to God, an angel of the Lord immediately caused him to become sick, and he was eaten by worms and died.

²⁴God's message continued to spread and reach people.

²⁵After Barnabas and Saul finished their task in Jerusalem, they returned to Antioch, taking John Mark with them.

Even though his friends had been praying for Peter, they seemed pretty surprised with the way God answered (vs 15,16)!

Peter escaped from Herod, but what happened to James, John's brother (v 2)?

When you pray for things to happen, do you limit what you ask for? If we were praying for Peter would we ask that he was kept safe or would we ask God to set him free?

Think

Being a follower of Jesus doesn't guarantee we won't get hurt. But we can be sure we'll never be separated from him.

Pray

Ask God to help you trust him more. Expect an answer!

317

I deserve ... what?

Think of someone who has achieved a lot in sport, music or the business world. Did they get where they are by just sitting and waiting?

 Acts 13:1–25

Barnabas and Saul are Chosen

13 In the church at Antioch there were these prophets and teachers: Barnabas, Simeon (also called Niger), Lucius (from the city of Cyrene), Manaen (who had grown up with Herod, the ruler) and Saul. ²They were all worshipping the Lord and gave up eating for a certain time. During this time the Holy Spirit said to them, "Set apart for me Barnabas and Saul to do a special work for which I have chosen them."

³So after they had given up eating and prayed, they laid their hands on Barnabas and Saul and sent them out.

Barnabas and Saul in Cyprus

⁴Barnabas and Saul, sent out by the Holy Spirit, went to the city of Seleucia. From there they sailed to the island of Cyprus. ⁵When they came to Salamis, they preached the Good News of God in the Jewish synagogues. John Mark was with them to help.

⁶They went across the whole island to Paphos where they met a Jewish magician named Bar-Jesus. He was a false prophet ⁷who always stayed close to Sergius Paulus, the governor and a clever man. He asked Barnabas and Saul to come to him, because he wanted to hear the message of God. ⁸But Elymas, the magician, was against them. (Elymas is the name for Bar-Jesus in the Greek language.) He tried to stop the governor from believing in Jesus. ⁹But Saul, who was also called Paul,

was filled with the Holy Spirit. He looked straight at Elymas ¹⁰and said, "You son of the devil! You are an enemy of everything that is right! You are full of evil tricks and lies, always trying to change the Lord's truths into lies. ¹¹Now the Lord will touch you, and you will be blind. For a time you will not be able to see anything—not even the light from the sun."

Then everything became dark for Elymas, and he walked around, trying to find someone to lead him by the hand. ¹²When the governor saw this, he believed because he was amazed at the teaching about the Lord.

Paul and Barnabas Leave Cyprus

¹³Paul and those with him sailed from Paphos and came to Perga, in Pamphylia. There John Mark left them to return to Jerusalem. ¹⁴They continued their trip from Perga and went to Antioch, a city in Pisidia. On the Sabbath day they went into the synagogue and sat down. ¹⁵After the law of Moses and the writings of the prophets were read, the leaders of the synagogue sent a message to Paul and Barnabas: "Brothers, if you have any message that will encourage the people, please speak."

¹⁶Paul stood up, raised his hand and said, "You Israelites and you who worship God, please listen! ¹⁷The God of the Israelites chose our ancestors. He made the people great during the time they lived in Egypt, and he brought them out of that country with great power. ¹⁸And he was

patient with them for 40 years in the desert. ¹⁹God destroyed seven nations in the land of Canaan and gave the land to his people. ²⁰All this happened in about 450 years.

"After this, God gave them judges until the time of Samuel the prophet. ²¹Then the people asked for a king, so God gave them Saul son of Kish. Saul was from the tribe of Benjamin and was king for 40 years. ²²After God took him away, God made David their king. God said about him: 'I have found in David son of Jesse the kind of man I want. He will do all I want him to do.' ²³So God has brought Jesus, one of David's descendants, to Israel to be its Saviour, as he promised. ²⁴Before Jesus came, John preached to all the people of Israel about a baptism of changed hearts and lives. ²⁵When he was finishing his work, he said, 'Who do you think I am? I am not the Christ. He is coming later, and I am not worthy to untie his sandals.'

Giving up eating is also called fasting. The church fasted as a discipline to help them listen to what God wanted them to do. What did God tell them to do (v 2)?

Think

How do you prepare yourself to listen to God?

Pray

That God will help you prepare yourself so that you can hear what he wants to say to you.

Extra

Ask your youth leader about fasting or other ways that might help you focus on God.

The right kind of people

Is there anyone who is left out of God's love? Who are the right kind of people for God?

Acts 13:26–52

26"Brothers, sons of the family of Abraham, and those of you who are not Jews who worship God, listen! The news about this salvation has been sent to us. 27Those who live in Jerusalem and their leaders did not realise that Jesus was the Saviour. They did not understand the words that the prophets wrote, which are read every Sabbath day. But they made them come true when they said Jesus was guilty. 28They could not find any real reason for Jesus to be put to death, but they asked Pilate to have him killed. 29When they had done to him all that the Scriptures had said, they took him down from the cross and laid him in a tomb. 30But God raised him up from the dead! 31After this, for many days, those who had gone with Jesus from Galilee to Jerusalem saw him. They are now his witnesses to the people. 32We tell you the Good News about the promise God made to our ancestors. 33God has made this promise come true for us, his children, by raising Jesus from the dead. We read about this also in Psalm 2:

'You are my son.
　Today I have become your father.'
Psalm 2:7
34God raised Jesus from the dead, and he will never go back to the grave and become dust. So God said:

'I will give you the blessings
　I promised to David.'　*Isaiah 55:3*
35But in another place God says:

'You will not let your holy one rot.'
Psalm 16:10
36David did God's will during his lifetime. Then he died and was buried beside his ancestors, and his body did rot in the grave. 37But the One God raised from the dead did not rot in the grave. 38–39Brothers, understand what we are telling you: you can have forgiveness of your sins through Jesus. The law of Moses could not free you from your sins. But through Jesus everyone who believes is free from all sins. 40Be careful! Don't let what the prophets said happen to you:
41'Look at the nations!
　Watch them and be amazed and
　　shocked.
I will do something in your lifetime
　that you won't believe even when you
　　are told about it.'"　*Habakkuk 1:5*
42While Paul and Barnabas were leaving the synagogue, the people asked them to tell them more about these things on the next Sabbath. 43When the meeting was over, many Jews and those who had changed to the Jewish religion and who worshipped God followed Paul and Barnabas from that place. Paul and Barnabas were persuading them to continue trusting in God's grace.

44On the next Sabbath day, almost everyone in the city came to hear the word of the Lord. 45Seeing the crowd, the Jewish people became very jealous and said insulting things and argued against what

Paul said. 46But Paul and Barnabas spoke very boldly, saying, "We must speak the message of God to you first. But you refuse to listen. You are judging yourselves not worthy of having eternal life! So we will now go to the people of other nations. 47This is what the Lord told us to do, saying:

'I have made you a light for the nations;
you will show people all over the world
the way to be saved.' " *Isaiah 49:6*

48When those who were not Jewish heard Paul say this, they were happy and gave honour to the message of the Lord. And the people who were chosen to have life for ever believed the message.

49So the message of the Lord was spreading through the whole country. 50But the Jewish people stirred up some of the important religious women and the leaders of the city. They started trouble against Paul and Barnabas and forced them out of their area. 51So Paul and Barnabas shook the dust off their feet and went to Iconium. 52But the followers were filled with joy and the Holy Spirit.

Paul and Barnabas went to the Jewish people first – but the Jewish people wouldn't listen. So Paul and Barnabas went to everyone else in town, and these people believed.

Think

God's Good News is for everyone, but you have to accept it. God's people are the people who choose to be grateful for what Jesus has done and do something about it for themselves. Are you one of them?

Pray

Thank God that you're the right kind of person for him.

Effective ministry

I have often thought that a miracle would prove beyond doubt that the Christian message was true. If a miracle was performed, for the whole world to see, shown on all the news channels, then everyone would believe.

Acts 14:1–28

Paul and Barnabas in Iconium

14 In Iconium, Paul and Barnabas went as usual to the Jewish synagogue. They spoke so well that a great many Jews and Greeks believed. ²But some of the Jews who did not believe excited the non-Jewish people and turned them against the believers. ³Paul and Barnabas stayed in Iconium a long time and spoke bravely for the Lord. He showed that his message about his grace was true by giving them the power to work miracles and signs. ⁴But the city was divided. Some of the people agreed with the Jews, and others believed the apostles.

⁵Some who were not Jews, some Jews and some of their rulers wanted to mistreat Paul and Barnabas and to stone them to death. ⁶When Paul and Barnabas learned about this, they ran away to Lystra and Derbe, cities in Lycaonia, and to the areas around those cities. ⁷They announced the Good News there, too.

Paul in Lystra and Derbe

⁸In Lystra there sat a man who had been born crippled; he had never walked. ⁹As this man was listening to Paul speak, Paul looked straight at him and saw that he believed God could heal him. ¹⁰So he cried out, "Stand up on your feet!" The man jumped up and began walking around. ¹¹When the crowds saw what Paul did, they shouted in the Lycaonian language, "The gods have become like humans and have come down to us!" ¹²Then the people began to call Barnabas "Zeus" and Paul "Hermes", because he was the main speaker. ¹³The priest in the temple of Zeus, which was near the city, brought some bulls and flowers to the city gates. He and the people wanted to offer a sacrifice to Paul and Barnabas. ¹⁴But when the apostles, Barnabas and Paul, heard about it, they tore their clothes. They ran in among the people, shouting, ¹⁵"Friends, why are you doing these things? We are only human beings like you. We are bringing you the Good News and are telling you to turn away from these worthless things and turn to the living God. He is the One who made the sky, the earth, the sea and everything in them. ¹⁶In the past, God let all the nations do what they wanted. ¹⁷Yet he proved he is real by showing kindness, by giving you rain from heaven and crops at the right times, by giving you food and filling your hearts with joy." ¹⁸Even with these words, they were barely able to keep the crowd from offering sacrifices to them.

¹⁹Then some Jewish people came from Antioch and Iconium and persuaded the people to turn against Paul. So they threw stones at him and dragged him out of town, thinking they had killed him. ²⁰But the followers gathered around him, and he got up and went back into the town. The next day he and Barnabas left and went to the city of Derbe.

The Return to Antioch in Syria

21Paul and Barnabas told the Good News in Derbe, and many became followers. Paul and Barnabas returned to Lystra, Iconium and Antioch, 22making the followers of Jesus stronger and helping them stay in the faith. They said, "We must suffer many things to enter God's kingdom." 23They chose elders for each church, by praying and giving up eating for a certain time. These elders had trusted the Lord, so Paul and Barnabas put them in the Lord's care.

24Then they went through Pisidia and came to Pamphylia. 25When they had preached the message in Perga, they went down to Attalia. 26And from there they sailed away to Antioch where the believers had put them into God's care and had sent them out to do this work. Now they had finished.

27When they arrived in Antioch, Paul and Barnabas gathered the church together. They told the church all about what God had done with them and how God had made it possible for those who were not Jewish to believe. 28And they stayed there a long time with the followers.

Where were Paul and Barnabas (v 1)?

Where were they speaking (v 1)?

What was the sign that their message was true (v 3)?

Did everyone believe (v 4)?

Think

What is the most effective way to tell others about Jesus?

Pray

Ask God to be with you when you share the Good News with others.

Time for a change

Sometimes, things need to change. Sometimes, they don't. How do you know?

Acts 15:1–21

The Meeting at Jerusalem

15 Then some people came to Antioch from Judea and began teaching the non-Jewish believers: "You cannot be saved if you are not circumcised as Moses taught us." ²Paul and Barnabas were against this teaching and argued with them about it. So the church decided to send Paul, Barnabas and some others to Jerusalem where they could talk more about this with the apostles and elders.

³The church helped them leave on the trip, and they went through the countries of Phoenicia and Samaria, telling all about how those who were not Jewish had turned to God. This made all the believers very happy. ⁴When they arrived in Jerusalem, they were welcomed by the apostles, the elders and the church. Paul, Barnabas and the others told about everything God had done with them. ⁵But some of the believers who belonged to the Pharisee group came forwards and said, "The non-Jewish believers must be circumcised. They must be told to obey the law of Moses."

⁶The apostles and the elders gathered to consider this problem. ⁷After a long debate, Peter stood up and said to them, "Brothers, you know that in the early days God chose me from among you to preach the Good News to those who are not Jewish. They heard the Good News from me, and they believed. ⁸God, who knows the thoughts of everyone, accepted them. He showed this to us by giving them the Holy Spirit, just as he did to us. ⁹To God, those people are not different from us. When they believed, he made their hearts pure. ¹⁰So now why are you testing God by putting a heavy load around the necks of the non-Jewish believers? It is a load that neither we nor our ancestors were able to carry. ¹¹But we believe that we and they too will be saved by the grace of the Lord Jesus."

¹²Then the whole group became quiet. They listened to Paul and Barnabas tell about all the miracles and signs that God did through them among the non-Jewish people. ¹³After they finished speaking, James said, "Brothers, listen to me. ¹⁴Simon has told us how God showed his love for the non-Jewish people. For the first time he is accepting from among them a people to be his own. ¹⁵The words of the prophets agree with this too:

¹⁶'After these things I will return.
  The kingdom of David is like a fallen
    tent.
But I will rebuild its ruins,
  and I will set it up.
¹⁷Then those people who are left alive may
    ask the Lord for help,
  and the other nations that belong to
    me,
says the Lord,
  who will make it happen.
¹⁸ And these things have been known for
    a long time.' *Amos 9:11–12*

¹⁹"So I think we should not bother the non-Jewish people who are turning to

God. ²⁰Instead, we should write a letter to them telling them these things: stay away from food that has been offered to idols (which makes it unclean), any kind of sexual sin, eating animals that have been strangled, and blood. ²¹They should do these things, because for a long time in every city the law of Moses has been taught. And it is still read in the synagogue every Sabbath day."

Paul and the others decide that Christians who weren't born Jewish don't have to follow all the Jewish rules if they want to follow Jesus.

How do they know? They look at what the Bible says and they listen to what God has to say to them.

Think

If you want to decide whether something's the right course of action, you could do a lot worse than talking to other Christians, checking out what the Bible has to say, and praying.

Pray

Got a decision you need to make? Ask God to give you a bit of guidance.

A bad start?

"Bet Paul never lost his temper like I do."

You've just lost your bet!

Acts 15:22–16:10

Letter to Non-Jewish Believers

22The apostles, the elders and the whole church decided to send some of their men with Paul and Barnabas to Antioch. They chose Judas Barsabbas and Silas, who were respected by the believers. 23They sent the following letter with them:

From the apostles and elders, your brothers.

To all the non-Jewish believers in Antioch, Syria and Cilicia:

Greetings!

24We have heard that some of our group have come to you and said things that trouble and upset you. But we did not tell them to do this. 25We have all agreed to choose some messengers and send them to you with our dear friends Barnabas and Paul— 26people who have given their lives to serve our Lord Jesus Christ. 27So we are sending Judas and Silas, who will tell you the same things. 28It has pleased the Holy Spirit that you should not have a heavy load to carry, and we agree. You need to do only these things: 29stay away from any food that has been offered to idols, any animals that have been strangled, blood and any kind of sexual sin. If you stay away from these things, you will do well.

Goodbye.

30So they left Jerusalem and went to Antioch where they gathered the church and gave them the letter. 31When they read it, they were very happy because of the encouraging message. 32Judas and Silas, who were also prophets, said many things to encourage the believers and make them stronger. 33After some time Judas and Silas were sent off in peace by the believers, and they went back to those who had sent them. 34

35But Paul and Barnabas stayed in Antioch and, along with many others, preached the Good News and taught the people the message of the Lord.

Paul and Barnabas Separate

36After some time, Paul said to Barnabas, "We should go back to all those towns where we preached the message of the Lord. Let's visit the believers and see how they are doing."

37Barnabas wanted to take John Mark with them, 38but he had left them at Pamphylia; he did not continue with them in the work. So Paul did not think it was a good idea to take him. 39Paul and Barnabas had such a serious argument about this that they separated and went different ways. Barnabas took Mark and sailed to Cyprus, 40but Paul chose Silas and left. The believers in Antioch put Paul into the Lord's care, 41and he went through Syria and Cilicia, giving strength to the churches.

Timothy Goes with Paul

16 Paul came to Derbe and Lystra, where a follower named Timothy lived. Timothy's mother was Jewish and a believer, but his father was a Greek.

[2]The believers in Lystra and Iconium respected Timothy and said good things about him. [3]Paul wanted Timothy to travel with him, but all the Jews living in that area knew that Timothy's father was Greek. So Paul circumcised Timothy to please the Jews. [4]Paul and those with him travelled from town to town and gave the decisions made by the apostles and elders in Jerusalem for the people to obey. [5]So the churches became stronger in the faith and grew larger every day.

Paul is Called Out of Asia

[6]Paul and those with him went through the areas of Phrygia and Galatia since the Holy Spirit did not let them preach the Good News in the country of Asia. [7]When they came near the country of Mysia, they tried to go into Bithynia, but the Spirit of Jesus did not let them. [8]So they passed by Mysia and went to Troas. [9]That night Paul saw in a vision a man from Macedonia. The man stood and begged, "Come over to Macedonia and help us." [10]After Paul had seen the vision, we immediately prepared to leave for Macedonia, understanding that God had called us to tell the Good News to those people.

Mark had let them down once (Acts 13:13). Paul didn't want to take him again. Barnabas did.

If someone let you down would you ...

- never speak to them again?

- give them a second chance?

- be very suspicious and critical?

Good news! The number of missionary teams just doubled (15:39).

Think

Do you see disagreements as a bad thing or good? Are they needed to clear the air?

Pray

Lord, if I have disagreements with other people, please bring something good out of them.

Conversation starter

How easy do you find it to start a conversation with someone you don't know very well?

- Easy

- Not so easy

- Impossible!

 Acts 16:11–34

Lydia Becomes a Christian

¹¹We left Troas and sailed straight to the island of Samothrace. The next day we sailed to Neapolis. ¹²Then we went by land to Philippi, a Roman colony and the leading city in that part of Macedonia. We stayed there for several days.

¹³On the Sabbath day we went outside the city gate to the river where we thought we would find a special place for prayer. Some women had gathered there, so we sat down and talked with them. ¹⁴One of the listeners was a woman named Lydia from the city of Thyatira whose job was selling purple cloth. She worshipped God, and he opened her mind to pay attention to what Paul was saying. ¹⁵She and all the people in her house were baptised. Then she invited us to her home, saying, "If you think I am truly a believer in the Lord, then come and stay in my house." And she persuaded us to stay with her.

Paul and Silas in Jail

¹⁶Once, while we were going to the place for prayer, a servant girl met us. She had a special spirit in her, and she earned a lot of money for her owners by telling fortunes. ¹⁷This girl followed Paul and us, shouting, "These men are servants of the Most High God. They are telling you how you can be saved."

¹⁸She kept this up for many days. This bothered Paul, so he turned and said to the spirit, "By the power of Jesus Christ, I command you to come out of her!" Immediately, the spirit came out.

¹⁹When the owners of the servant girl saw this, they knew that now they could not use her to make money. So they grabbed Paul and Silas and dragged them before the city rulers in the market place. ²⁰They brought Paul and Silas to the Roman rulers and said, "These men are Jews and are making trouble in our city. ²¹They are teaching things that are not right for us as Romans to do."

²²The crowd joined the attack against them. The Roman officers tore the clothes of Paul and Silas and had them beaten with rods. ²³Then Paul and Silas were thrown into jail, and the jailer was ordered to guard them carefully. ²⁴When he heard this order, he put them far inside the jail and pinned their feet down between large blocks of wood.

²⁵About midnight Paul and Silas were praying and singing songs to God as the other prisoners listened. ²⁶Suddenly, there was a strong earthquake that shook the foundation of the jail. Then all the doors of

the jail broke open, and all the prisoners were freed from their chains. 27The jailer woke up and saw that the jail doors were open. Thinking that the prisoners had already escaped, he got his sword and was about to kill himself. 28But Paul shouted, "Don't hurt yourself! We are all here."

29The jailer told someone to bring a light. Then he ran inside and, shaking with fear, fell down before Paul and Silas. 30He brought them outside and said, "Men, what must I do to be saved?"

31They said to him, "Believe in the Lord Jesus and you will be saved—you and all the people in your house." 32So Paul and Silas told the message of the Lord to the jailer and all the people in his house. 33At that hour of the night the jailer took Paul and Silas and washed their wounds. Then he and all his people were baptised immediately. 34After this the jailer took Paul and Silas home and gave them food. He and his family were very happy because they now believed in God.

How did Paul and friends come to meet Lydia (vs 13,14)?

Paul was ready to spend time talking with Lydia, which meant ...

- she heard more about Jesus (v 14)

- she decided to follow Jesus (v 15)

... and the difference was obvious (v 15).

Think

What opportunities do you have to talk to others about Jesus?

What might show others that you are a "believer"?

Pray

Ask God to give you opportunities (and courage) to talk with other people about your faith.

Check it out

Do you just accept what other people tell you, or do you check it out (politely!)?

What about what you see and hear on the television, or in the paper? Are magazines more trustworthy than your teachers? Is a textbook more reliable than the Internet?

 Acts 16:35–17:15

³⁵The next morning, the Roman officers sent the police to tell the jailer, "Let these men go free."

³⁶The jailer said to Paul, "The officers have sent an order to let you go free. You can leave now. Go in peace."

³⁷But Paul said to the police, "They beat us in public without a trial, even though we are Roman citizens. And they threw us in jail. Now they want to make us go away quietly. No! Let them come themselves and bring us out."

³⁸The police told the Roman officers what Paul said. When the officers heard that Paul and Silas were Roman citizens, they were afraid. ³⁹So they came and told Paul and Silas they were sorry and took them out of jail and asked them to leave the city. ⁴⁰So when they came out of the jail, they went to Lydia's house where they saw some of the believers and encouraged them. Then they left.

Paul and Silas in Thessalonica

17 Paul and Silas travelled through Amphipolis and Apollonia and came to Thessalonica where there was a Jewish synagogue. ²Paul went into the synagogue as he always did, and on each Sabbath day for three weeks, he talked with the Jews about the Scriptures. ³He explained and proved that the Christ must die and then rise from the dead. He said,

"This Jesus I am telling you about is the Christ." ⁴Some of the Jews were convinced and joined Paul and Silas, along with many of the Greeks who worshipped God and many of the important women.

⁵But the Jews became jealous. So they got some evil men from the market-place, formed a mob and started a riot. They ran to Jason's house, looking for Paul and Silas, wanting to bring them out to the people. ⁶But when they did not find them, they dragged Jason and some other believers to the leaders of the city. The people were yelling, "These people have made trouble everywhere in the world, and now they have come here too! ⁷Jason is keeping them in his house. All of them do things against the laws of Caesar, saying there is another king, called Jesus."

⁸When the people and the leaders of the city heard these things, they became very upset. ⁹They made Jason and the others put up a sum of money. Then they let the believers go free.

Paul and Silas Go to Berea

¹⁰That same night the believers sent Paul and Silas to Berea where they went to the Jewish synagogue. ¹¹These Jews were more willing to listen than the Jews in Thessalonica. The Jews in Berea were eager to hear what Paul and Silas said and studied the Scriptures every day to

find out if these things were true. ¹²So, many of them believed, as well as many important Greek women and men. ¹³But the Jews in Thessalonica learned that Paul was preaching the word of God in Berea, too. So they came there, upsetting the people and making trouble. ¹⁴The believers quickly sent Paul away to the coast, but Silas and Timothy stayed in Berea. ¹⁵The people leading Paul went with him to Athens. Then they carried a message from Paul back to Silas and Timothy for them to come to him as soon as they could.

The people in Berea checked out what Paul was saying by looking at the Bible for themselves (17:11). It helped them grow in their faith (17:12).

Think

How much of what you hear do you believe without checking out?

Pray

That God will make you hungry for his words in the Bible.

Extra

How about doing some checking yourself on what people who teach you say about the Bible (e.g. your youth leader, *these notes*). Ask questions, dig deeper.

Whatever you do!

When you're backpacking and the money runs out, you've got to find work. If you want to get your hands on the latest mega games console and you don't have an endless pot of gold, you'll need to find some work and put away the pennies from the paper round or the Saturday job. For Paul, it was all part of God's journey plan.

Acts 17:16–18:4

Paul Preaches in Athens

16While Paul was waiting for Silas and Timothy in Athens, he was troubled because he saw that the city was full of idols. 17In the synagogue, he talked with the Jews and the Greeks who worshipped God. He also talked every day with people in the market-place.

18Some of the Epicurean and Stoic philosophers argued with him, saying, "This man doesn't know what he is talking about. What is he trying to say?" Others said, "He seems to be telling us about some other gods," because Paul was telling them about Jesus and his rising from the dead. 19They got Paul and took him to a meeting of the Areopagus, where they said, "Please explain to us this new idea you have been teaching. 20The things you are saying are new to us, and we want to know what this teaching means." 21(All the people of Athens and those from other countries who lived there always used their time to talk about the newest ideas.)

22Then Paul stood before the meeting of the Areopagus and said, "People of Athens, I can see you are very religious in all things. 23As I was going through your city, I saw the objects you worship. I found an altar that had these words written on it: TO A GOD WHO IS NOT KNOWN. You worship a god that you don't know, and this is the God I am telling you about! 24The God

who made the whole world and everything in it is the Lord of the land and the sky. He does not live in temples built by human hands. 25This God is the One who gives life, breath and everything else to people. He does not need any help from them; he has everything he needs. 26God began by making one person, and from him came all the different people who live everywhere in the world. God decided exactly when and where they must live. 27God wanted them to look for him and perhaps search all around for him and find him, though he is not far from any of us: 28'We live in him. We walk in him. We are in him.' Some of your own poets have said: 'For we are his children.' 29Since we are God's children, you must not think that God is like something that people imagine or make from gold, silver or rock. 30In the past, people did not understand God, and he ignored this. But now, God tells all people in the world to change their hearts and lives. 31God has set a day that he will judge all the world with fairness, by the man he chose long ago. And God has proved this to everyone by raising that man from the dead!"

32When the people heard about Jesus being raised from the dead, some of them laughed. But others said, "We will hear more about this from you later." 33So Paul went away from them. 34But some of the people believed Paul and joined him.

Among those who believed was Dionysius, a member of the Areopagus, a woman named Damaris and some others.

Paul in Corinth

18 Later Paul left Athens and went to Corinth. ²Here he met a Jew named Aquila who had been born in the country of Pontus. But Aquila and his wife, Priscilla, had recently moved to Corinth from Italy, because Claudius commanded that all Jews must leave Rome. Paul went to visit Aquila and Priscilla. ³Because they were tentmakers, just as he was, he stayed with them and worked with them. ⁴Every Sabbath day he talked with the Jews and Greeks in the synagogue, trying to persuade them to believe in Jesus.

Paul got a job using his practical skills as a tentmaker (18:3) so he could carry on doing God's work telling the Jews and Greeks about Jesus (18:4).

Why were Priscilla and Aquila in Corinth (18:2)?

Think

Should we expect our current church workers to be paid, or should they support themselves?

Pray

Ask God to help you to work for him in *all* you do.

Giving up

What makes you feel like giving up?

Acts 18:5–28

5Silas and Timothy came from Macedonia and joined Paul in Corinth. After this, Paul spent all his time telling people the Good News, showing the Jews that Jesus is the Christ. 6But they would not accept Paul's teaching and said some evil things. So he shook off the dust from his clothes and said to them, "If you are not saved, it will be your own fault! I have done all I can do! After this, I will go only to those who are not Jewish." 7Paul left the synagogue and moved into the home of Titius Justus, next to the synagogue. This man worshipped God. 8Crispus was the leader of that synagogue, and he and all the people living in his house believed in the Lord. Many others in Corinth also listened to Paul and believed and were baptised.

9During the night, the Lord told Paul in a vision: "Don't be afraid. Continue talking to people and don't be quiet. 10I am with you, and no one will hurt you because many of my people are in this city." 11Paul stayed there for a year and a half, teaching God's word to the people.

Paul is Brought Before Gallio

12When Gallio was the governor of the country of Southern Greece, some of the Jews came together against Paul and took him to the court. 13They said, "This man is teaching people to worship God in a way that is against our law."

14Paul was about to say something, but Gallio spoke to the Jews, saying, "I would listen to you Jews if you were complaining about a crime or some wrong. 15But the things you are saying are only questions about words and names—arguments about your own law. So you must solve this problem yourselves. I don't want to be a judge of these things." 16And Gallio made them leave the court.

17Then they all grabbed Sosthenes, the leader of the synagogue, and beat him there before the court. But this did not bother Gallio.

Paul Returns to Antioch

18Paul stayed with the believers for many more days. Then he left and sailed for Syria, with Priscilla and Aquila. At Cenchrea Paul cut off his hair, because he had made a promise to God. 19Then they went to Ephesus, where Paul left Priscilla and Aquila. While Paul was there, he went into the synagogue and talked with the Jews. 20When they asked him to stay with them longer, he refused. 21But as he left, he said, "I will come back to you again if God wants me to." And so he sailed away from Ephesus.

22When Paul landed at Caesarea, he went and gave greetings to the church in Jerusalem. After that, Paul went to Antioch. 23He stayed there for a while and then left and went through the regions of Galatia and Phrygia. He travelled from town to town in these regions, giving strength to all the followers.

Apollos in Ephesus and Corinth

24A Jew named Apollos came to Ephesus. He was born in the city of Alexandria and was a good speaker who knew the Scriptures well. 25He had been taught about the way of the Lord and was always very excited when he spoke and taught the truth about Jesus. But the only baptism Apollos knew about was the baptism that

John taught. 26Apollos began to speak very boldly in the synagogue, and when Priscilla and Aquila heard him, they took him to their home and helped him better understand the way of God. 27Now Apollos wanted to go to the country of Southern Greece. So the believers helped him and wrote a letter to the followers there, asking them to accept him. These followers had believed in Jesus because of God's grace, and when Apollos arrived, he helped them very much. 28He argued very strongly with the Jews before all the people, clearly proving with the Scriptures that Jesus is the Christ.

What made life difficult for Paul (vs 6,9,10)?

Who and what helped him keep going (vs 5,7)?

What did Paul do whilst he was in Corinth (vs 5,8,11)?

Think

How could you and Christian friends encourage each other to keep living for God when others make life difficult for you?

Pray

Look again at verse 9. What's God saying to you?

Be baptised!

There are hard things in today's reading, so get thinking.

Acts 19:1–22

Paul in Ephesus

19 While Apollos was in Corinth, Paul was visiting some places on the way to Ephesus. There he found some followers ²and asked them, "Did you receive the Holy Spirit when you believed?"

They said, "We have never even heard of a Holy Spirit."

³So he asked, "What kind of baptism did you have?"

They said, "It was the baptism that John taught."

⁴Paul said, "John's baptism was a baptism of changed hearts and lives. He told people to believe in the One who would come after him, and that One is Jesus."

⁵When they heard this, they were baptised in the name of the Lord Jesus. ⁶Then Paul laid his hands on them, and the Holy Spirit came upon them. They began speaking different languages and prophesying. ⁷There were about twelve people in this group.

⁸Paul went into the synagogue and spoke out boldly for three months. He talked with the Jews and persuaded them to accept the things he said about the kingdom of God. ⁹But some of the Jews became stubborn. They refused to believe and said evil things about the Way of Jesus before all the people. So Paul left them, and, taking the followers with him, he went to the school of a man named Tyrannus. There Paul talked with people every day ¹⁰for two years. Because of his work, every Jew and Greek in the country of Asia heard the word of the Lord.

The Sons of Sceva

¹¹God used Paul to do some very special miracles. ¹²Some people took handkerchiefs and clothes that Paul had used and put them on the sick. When they did this, the sick were healed and evil spirits left them.

¹³But some Jews also were travelling around and making evil spirits go out of people. They tried to use the name of the Lord Jesus to force the evil spirits out. They would say, "By the same Jesus that Paul talks about, I order you to come out!" ¹⁴Seven sons of Sceva, a leading Jewish priest, were doing this.

¹⁵But on one occasion an evil spirit said to them, "I know Jesus, and I know about Paul, but who are you?"

¹⁶Then the man who had the evil spirit jumped on them. Because he was so much stronger than all of them, they ran away from the house naked and hurt. ¹⁷All the people in Ephesus—Jews and Greeks—learned about this and were filled with fear and gave great honour to the Lord Jesus. ¹⁸Many of the believers began to confess openly and tell all the evil things they had done. ¹⁹Some of them who had used magic brought their magic books and burned them before everyone. Those books were worth about 50,000 silver coins.

²⁰So in a powerful way the word of the Lord kept spreading and growing.

²¹After these things, Paul decided to go to Jerusalem, planning to go through the countries of Macedonia and Southern Greece and then on to Jerusalem. He said, "After I have been to Jerusalem, I must also visit Rome." ²²Paul sent Timothy and Erastus, two of his helpers, ahead to Macedonia, but he himself stayed in Asia for a while.

John (v 3) baptised people to prepare them for the coming of Jesus. (Look at Matthew 3:1–12.)

Christian baptism (v 5) is for those who have believed in Jesus.

When a person becomes a Christian, the Holy Spirit comes to live in them (v 6). Sometimes special things happen (v 6) but not always. Look back at the people we've already read about who became Christians (e.g. Acts 16:13–15). Did this happen to them?

Think

Have you been baptised? If you haven't, have you thought about it? If you want to be baptised, you could talk to your church leader about it.

Pray

Talk to God about it.

337

Troublemakers

Why do some people make trouble for Christians?

Acts 19:23–20:6

Trouble in Ephesus

23And during that time, there was some serious trouble in Ephesus about the Way of Jesus. 24A man named Demetrius, who worked with silver, made little silver models that looked like the temple of the goddess Artemis. Those who did this work made much money. 25Demetrius had a meeting with them and some others who did the same kind of work. He told them, "Men, you know that we make a lot of money from our business. 26But look at what this man Paul is doing. He has convinced and turned away many people in Ephesus and in almost all of Asia! He says the gods made by human hands are not real. 27There is a danger that our business will lose its good name, but there is also another danger: people will begin to think that the temple of the great goddess Artemis is not important. Her greatness will be destroyed, but Artemis is the goddess that everyone in Asia and the whole world worships."

28When the others heard this, they became very angry and shouted, "Artemis, the goddess of Ephesus, is great!" 29The whole city became confused. The people grabbed Gaius and Aristarchus, who were from Macedonia and were travelling with Paul, and ran to the theatre. 30Paul wanted to go in and talk to the crowd, but the followers did not let him. 31Also, some leaders of Asia who were friends of Paul sent him a message, begging him not to go into the theatre. 32Some people were shouting one thing, and some were shouting another. The meeting was completely confused; most of them did not know why they had come together. 33The Jews put a man named Alexander in front of the people, and some of them told him what to do. Alexander waved his hand so he could explain things to the people. 34But when they saw that Alexander was a Jew, they all shouted the same thing for two hours: "Great is Artemis of Ephesus!"

35Then the city clerk made the crowd be quiet. He said, "People of Ephesus, everyone knows that Ephesus is the city that keeps the temple of the great goddess Artemis and her holy stone that fell from heaven. 36Since no one can say this is not true, you should be quiet. Stop and think before you do anything. 37You brought these men here, but they have not said anything evil against our goddess or stolen anything from her temple. 38If Demetrius and those who work with him have a charge against anyone they should go to the courts and judges where they can argue with each other. 39If there is something else you want to talk about, it can be decided at the legal town meeting of the people. 40I say this because some people might see this trouble today and say that we are rioting. We could not explain this, because there is no real reason for this meeting." 41After the city clerk said these things, he told the people to go home.

Paul in Macedonia and Greece

20 When the trouble stopped, Paul sent for the followers to come to him. After he had encouraged them and said goodbye, he left and went to the country of Macedonia. 2He said many things to strengthen the followers in the different places on his way through Macedonia. Then he went to Greece, 3where

he stayed for three months. He was ready to sail for Syria, but some Jews were planning something against him. So Paul decided to go back through Macedonia to Syria. ⁴The men who went with him were Sopater son of Pyrrhus, from the city of Berea; Aristarchus and Secundus, from the city of Thessalonica; Gaius, from Derbe; Timothy; and Tychicus and Trophimus, two men from the country of Asia. ⁵These men went on ahead and waited for us at Troas. ⁶We sailed from Philippi after the Feast of Unleavened Bread. Five days later we met them in Troas, where we stayed for seven days.

Number the following, 1 to 3, to show how important you think each was as a reason for the opposition Paul experienced in Ephesus:

☐ Paul's message was changing everyone's lives (19:26)

☐ people were turning away from the goddess, Artemis (19:27)

☐ the silversmiths were losing money (19:24,25,27)

Think

Facing the truth about God will mean changing the way you live – it won't be easy. Ready?

Pray

Ask God to help you live for him and tell others about him – whatever trouble that brings.

Too much talk

Have you ever sat through a talk at church and had your mind wander? Sometimes when the talk gets a little long, or perhaps, dare I say, a little boring, it can be hard to concentrate.

You may have thought the sermons at your church were long! Well, get this!

Acts 20:7–38

Paul's Last Visit to Troas

⁷On the first day of the week, we all met together to break bread, and Paul spoke to the group. Because he was planning to leave the next day, he kept on talking until midnight. ⁸We were all together in a room upstairs, and there were many lamps in the room. ⁹A young man named Eutychus was sitting in the window. As Paul continued talking, Eutychus was falling into a deep sleep. Finally, he went sound asleep and fell to the ground from the third floor. When they picked him up, he was dead. ¹⁰Paul went down to Eutychus, knelt down and put his arms around him. He said, "Don't worry. He is alive now." ¹¹Then Paul went upstairs again, broke bread and ate. He spoke to them for a long time, until it was early morning, and then he left. ¹²They took the young man home alive and were greatly comforted.

The Trip from Troas to Miletus

¹³We went on ahead of Paul and sailed for the city of Assos, where he wanted to join us on the ship. Paul had planned this because he wanted to go to Assos by land. ¹⁴When he met us there, we took him aboard and went to Mitylene. ¹⁵We sailed from Mitylene and the next day came to a place near Chios. The following day we sailed to Samos, and the next day we reached Miletus. ¹⁶Paul had already de-cided not to stop at Ephesus, because he did not want to stay too long in the country of Asia. He was hurrying to be in Jerusalem on the day of Pentecost, if that were possible.

The Elders from Ephesus

¹⁷Now from Miletus Paul sent to Ephesus and called for the elders of the church. ¹⁸When they came to him, he said, "You know about my life from the first day I came to Asia. You know the way I lived all the time I was with you. ¹⁹The Jews made plans against me, which troubled me very much. But you know I always served the Lord unselfishly, and I often cried. ²⁰You know I preached to you and did not hold back anything that would help you. You know that I taught you in public and in your homes. ²¹I warned both Jews and Greeks to change their lives and turn to God and believe in our Lord Jesus. ²²But now I must obey the Holy Spirit and go to Jerusalem. I don't know what will happen to me there. ²³I know only that in every city the Holy Spirit tells me that troubles and even jail wait for me. ²⁴I don't care about my own life. The most important thing is that I complete my mission, the work that the Lord Jesus gave me—to tell people the Good News about God's grace.

²⁵"And now, I know that none of you among whom I was preaching the kingdom

of God will ever see me again. 26So today I tell you that if any of you should be lost, I am not responsible, 27because I have told you everything God wants you to know. 28Be careful for yourselves and for all the people the Holy Spirit has given to you to care for. You must be like shepherds to the church of God, which he bought with the death of his own Son. 29I know that after I leave, some people will come like wild wolves and try to destroy the flock. 30Also, some from your own group will rise up and twist the truth and will lead away followers after them. 31So be careful! Always remember that for three years, day and night, I never stopped warning each of you, and I often cried over you.

32"Now I am putting you in the care of God and the message about his grace. It is able to give you strength, and it will give you the blessings God has for all his holy people. 33When I was with you, I never wanted anyone's money or fine clothes. 34You know I always worked to take care of my own needs and the needs of those who were with me. 35I showed you in all things that you should work as I did and help the weak. I taught you to remember the words Jesus said: 'It is more blessed to give than to receive.'"

36When Paul had said this, he knelt down with all of them and prayed. 37–38And they all cried because Paul had said they would never see him again. They put their arms around him and kissed him. Then they went with him to the ship.

One of the youth group, Eutychus, was sitting on a window ledge. When it got to midnight (v 7), Paul was still going – well, he was leaving the next day and had a lot to tell them. Even the accident (v 9) and raising Eutychus from the dead (v 10) only stopped him temporarily.

When did the meeting finally end (v 11)?

Think

Is there anything which would make you stay at a church meeting much longer than you wanted to?

Pray

Ask God to keep you awake and give you a good appetite for his teaching – even when the sermons are long!

All for God

What would you be prepared to do for God?

- Tell the school bully that Jesus loves him?
- Tell your Geography teacher that God is the reason the world is in this form?

Acts 21:1–25

Paul Goes to Jerusalem

21 After we all said goodbye to them, we sailed straight to the island of Cos. The next day we reached Rhodes, and from there we went to Patara. ²There we found a ship going to Phoenicia, so we went aboard and sailed away. ³We sailed near the island of Cyprus, seeing it to the north, but we sailed on to Syria. We stopped at Tyre because the ship needed to unload its cargo there. ⁴We found some followers in Tyre and stayed with them for seven days. Through the Holy Spirit they warned Paul not to go to Jerusalem. ⁵When we finished our visit, we left and continued our trip. All the followers, even the women and children, came outside the city with us. After we all knelt on the beach and prayed, ⁶we said goodbye and got on the ship, and the followers went back home.

⁷We continued our trip from Tyre and arrived at Ptolemais, where we greeted the believers and stayed with them for a day. ⁸The next day we left Ptolemais and went to the city of Caesarea. There we went into the home of Philip the preacher, one of the seven helpers, and stayed with him. ⁹He had four unmarried daughters who had the gift of prophesying. ¹⁰After we had been there for some time, a prophet named Agabus arrived from Judea. ¹¹He came to us and borrowed Paul's belt and used it to tie his own hands and feet. He said, "The

Holy Spirit says, 'This is how the Jews in Jerusalem will tie up the man who wears this belt. Then they will give him to those who are not Jews.'"

¹²When we all heard this, we and the people there begged Paul not to go to Jerusalem. ¹³But he said, "Why are you crying and making me so sad? I am not only ready to be tied up in Jerusalem, I am ready to die for the Lord Jesus!"

¹⁴We could not persuade him to stay away from Jerusalem. So we stopped begging him and said, "We pray that what the Lord wants will be done."

¹⁵After this, we got ready and started on our way to Jerusalem. ¹⁶Some of the followers from Caesarea went with us and took us to the home of Mnason, where we would stay. He was from Cyprus and was one of the first followers.

Paul Visits James

¹⁷In Jerusalem the believers were glad to see us. ¹⁸The next day Paul went with us to visit James, and all the elders were there. ¹⁹Paul greeted them and told them everything God had done among the non-Jewish people through him. ²⁰When they heard this, they praised God. Then they said to Paul, "Brother, you can see that many thousands of Jews have become believers. And they think it is very important to obey the law of Moses. ²¹They have heard about your teaching, that you tell the

Jews who live among those who are not Jews to leave the law of Moses. They have heard that you tell them not to circumcise their children and not to obey Jewish customs. 22What should we do? They will learn that you have come. 23So we will tell you what to do: four of our men have made a promise to God. 24Take these men with you and share in their cleansing ceremony. Pay their expenses so they can shave their heads. Then it will prove to everyone that what they have heard about you is not true and that you follow the law of Moses in your own life. 25We have already sent a letter to the non-Jewish believers. The letter said: 'Do not eat food that has been offered to idols, or blood or animals that have been strangled. Do not take part in sexual sin.' "

Paul's travels have been going for some time. He's travelled all over telling others about Jesus. It seems that he is now having a quiet rest.

Who turns up and what does he have to say (vs 10,11)?

What was the people's reaction (v 12)?

What was Paul's reaction (v 13)?

Think

Back to our opening question! What would you be prepared to do for God?

Pray

That God will give you the strength to do anything that he asks you to do and that you will know that you are not alone.

Taking it on the chin

Have you ever been given a hard time for something you didn't do?

Acts 21:26–22:5

26The next day Paul took the four men and shared in the cleansing ceremony with them. Then he went to the Temple and announced the time when the days of the cleansing ceremony would be finished. On the last day an offering would be given for each of the men.

27When the seven days were almost over, some Jews from Asia saw Paul at the Temple. They upset all the people and grabbed Paul. 28They shouted, "People of Israel, help us! This is the man who goes everywhere teaching against the law of Moses, against our people and against this Temple. Now he has brought some Greeks into the Temple and has made this holy place unclean!" 29(The Jews said this because they had seen Trophimus, a man from Ephesus, with Paul in Jerusalem. The Jews thought that Paul had brought him into the Temple.)

30All the people in Jerusalem became upset. Together they ran, took Paul and dragged him out of the Temple. The Temple doors were closed immediately. 31While they were trying to kill Paul, the commander of the Roman army in Jerusalem learned that there was trouble in the whole city. 32Immediately he took some officers and soldiers and ran to the place where the crowd was gathered. When the people saw them, they stopped beating Paul. 33The commander went to Paul and arrested him. He told his soldiers to tie Paul with two chains. Then he asked who he was and what he had done wrong. 34Some in the crowd were yelling one thing, and some were yelling another.

Because of all this confusion and shouting, the commander could not learn what had happened. So he ordered the soldiers to take Paul to the army building. 35When Paul came to the steps, the soldiers had to carry him because the people were ready to hurt him. 36The whole mob was following them, shouting, "Kill him!"

37As the soldiers were about to take Paul into the army building, he spoke to the commander, "May I say something to you?"

The commander said, "Do you speak Greek? 38I thought you were the Egyptian who started some trouble against the government not long ago and led 4,000 killers out to the desert."

39Paul said, "No, I am a Jew from Tarsus in the country of Cilicia. I am a citizen of that important city. Please, let me speak to the people."

40The commander gave permission, so Paul stood on the steps and waved his hand to quiet the people. When there was silence, he spoke to them in the Jewish language.

Paul Speaks to the People

22 Paul said, "Friends, fellow Jews, listen to my defence to you." 2When the Jews heard him speaking the Jewish language, they became very quiet. Paul said, 3"I am a Jew, born in Tarsus in the country of Cilicia, but I grew up in this city. I was a student of Gamaliel, who carefully taught me everything about the law of our ancestors. I was very serious about serving God, just as are all of you

here today. ⁴I persecuted the people who followed the Way of Jesus, and some of them were even killed. I arrested men and women and put them in jail. ⁵The high priest and the whole council of elders Jewish can tell you this is true. They gave me letters to the Jewish brothers in Damascus. So I was going there to arrest these people and bring them back to Jerusalem to be punished.

Paul gets accused of all sorts of stuff he hasn't done, gets beaten up and gets arrested. Why? Because he's telling the Good News. Sometimes, people aren't going to like the message you've got and they're going to make you suffer for it.

Even though he's been made to suffer, Paul doesn't get angry, and he doesn't try to get even – he simply says who he is and what he really has done.

Think

If you get picked-on for being a Christian, how should you respond?

Pray

Ask God for help to get you through the hard times, and for the patience not to want to get your own back against those who are making you suffer.

Nothing but the truth

What is your response when Jesus, or going to church, come up in a conversation with your friends? Do you...

- quickly change the subject?
- keep quiet?
- give them the whole story?

Acts 22:6–30

6"At about noon when I came near Damascus, a bright light from heaven suddenly flashed all around me. 7I fell to the ground and heard a voice saying, 'Saul, Saul, why are you persecuting me?' 8I asked, 'Who are you, Lord?' The voice said, 'I am Jesus from Nazareth whom you are persecuting.' 9Those who were with me did not hear the voice, but they saw the light. 10I said, 'What shall I do, Lord?' The Lord answered, 'Get up and go to Damascus. There you will be told about all the things I have planned for you to do.' 11I could not see, because the bright light had made me blind. So my companions led me into Damascus.

12"There a man named Ananias came to me. He was a religious man; he obeyed the law of Moses, and all the Jews who lived there respected him. 13He stood by me and said, 'Brother Saul, see again!' Immediately I was able to see him. 14He said, 'The God of our ancestors chose you long ago to know his plan, to see the Righteous One and to hear words from him. 15You will be his witness to all people, telling them about what you have seen and heard. 16Now, why wait any longer? Get up, be baptised and wash your sins away, trusting in him to save you.'

17"Later, when I returned to Jerusalem, I was praying in the Temple, and I saw a vision. 18I saw the Lord saying to me,

'Hurry! Leave Jerusalem now! The people here will not accept the truth about me.' 19But I said, 'Lord, they know that in every synagogue I put the believers in jail and beat them. 20They also know I was there when Stephen, your witness, was killed. I stood there agreeing and holding the coats of those who were killing him!' 21But the Lord said to me, 'Leave now. I will send you far away to the non-Jewish people.'"

22The crowd listened to Paul until he said this. Then they began shouting, "Kill him! Get him out of the world! He should not be allowed to live!" 23They shouted, threw off their coats and threw dust into the air.

24Then the commander ordered the soldiers to take Paul into the army building and beat him. He wanted to make Paul tell why the people were shouting against him like this. 25But as the soldiers were tying him up, preparing to beat him, Paul said to an officer nearby, "Do you have the right to beat a Roman citizen who has not been proven guilty?"

26When the officer heard this, he went to the commander and reported it. The officer said, "Do you know what you are doing? This man is a Roman citizen."

27The commander came to Paul and said, "Tell me, are you really a Roman citizen?"

He answered, "Yes."

28The commander said, "I paid a lot of money to become a Roman citizen."

But Paul said, "I was born a citizen."

29The men who were preparing to question Paul moved away from him immediately. The commander was frightened because he had already tied Paul, and Paul was a Roman citizen.

Paul Speaks to Jewish Leaders

30The next day the commander decided to learn why the Jews were accusing Paul. So he ordered the leading priests and the Jewish council to meet. The commander took Paul's chains off. Then he brought Paul out and stood him before their meeting.

Paul was about to be beaten up by the mob. He manages to get some protection from the Romans, so what does he do: change the subject away from Jesus or keep quiet? No, he goes and tells them everything about his conversion and how he met Jesus.

Think

What was it that made Paul so confident when it came to telling others about Jesus?

Pray

That God will keep you safe but will also give you opportunities to tell your story of how you met Jesus.

Help in strange places

If you're in a bit of a tight spot, where do you turn for help?

- God
- Parents
- Bible

The above are the obvious ones for Christians. However, for Paul it appeared to come from somewhere different.

Acts 23:1–22

23 Paul looked at the Jewish council and said, "Brothers, I have lived my life with a clear conscience before God up to this day." ²Ananias, the high priest, heard this and told the men who were standing near Paul to hit him on the mouth. ³Paul said to Ananias, "God will hit you, too! You are like a wall that has been painted white. You sit there and judge me, using the law of Moses, but you are telling them to hit me, and that is against the law."

⁴The men standing near Paul said to him, "You cannot insult God's high priest like that!"

⁵Paul said, "Brothers, I did not know this man was the high priest. It is written in the Scriptures, 'You must not curse a leader of your people.'"

⁶Some of the men in the meeting were Sadducees, and others were Pharisees. Knowing this, Paul shouted to them, "My brothers, I am a Pharisee, and my father was a Pharisee. I am on trial here because I believe that people will rise from the dead."

⁷When Paul said this, there was an argument between the Pharisees and the Sadducees, and the group was divided. ⁸(The Sadducees do not believe in angels or spirits or that people will rise from the dead. But the Pharisees believe in them all.) ⁹So there was a great uproar. Some of the teachers of the law, who were Pharisees, stood up and argued, "We find nothing wrong with this man. Maybe an angel or a spirit did speak to him."

¹⁰The argument was beginning to turn into such a fight that the commander was afraid the Jews would tear Paul to pieces. So he told the soldiers to go down and take Paul away and put him in the army building.

¹¹The next night the Lord came and stood by Paul. He said, "Be brave! You have told people in Jerusalem about me. You must do the same in Rome."

¹²In the morning some of the Jews made a plan to kill Paul, and they took an oath not to eat or drink anything until they had killed him. ¹³There were more than 40 Jews who made this plan. ¹⁴They went to the leading priests and the elders Jewish and said, "We have taken an oath not to eat or drink until we have killed Paul. ¹⁵So this is what we want you to do: send a

message to the commander to bring Paul out to you as though you want to ask him more questions. We will be waiting to kill him while he is on the way here."

16But Paul's nephew heard about this plan and went to the army building and told Paul. 17Then Paul called one of the officers and said, "Take this young man to the commander. He has a message for him."

18So the officer brought Paul's nephew to the commander and said, "The prisoner, Paul, asked me to bring this young man to you. He wants to tell you something."

19The commander took the young man's hand and led him to a place where they could be alone. He asked, "What do you want to tell me?"

20The young man said, "The Jews have decided to ask you to bring Paul down to their council meeting tomorrow. They want you to think they are going to ask him more questions. 21But don't believe them! More than 40 men are hiding and waiting to kill Paul. They have all taken an oath not to eat or drink until they have killed him. Now they are waiting for you to agree."

22The commander sent the young man away, ordering him, "Don't tell anyone that you have told me about their plan."

Paul had been arrested, and the commander wanted to find out what all the fuss was about. What had the Jews planned (23:20,21)?

The commander sent Paul to the governor. Paul was being kept safe through the process of the legal system.

Think

Where do you turn when you need immediate help? Be honest – how high is God on your list? Should he be higher?

Pray

That God will be with you in any tight spots that you find yourself in.

Extra

When you have time, take the chance to read the whole of Paul's visit to Jerusalem, arrest and the subsequent events in one go (Acts chapters 21–28).

Your honour, the truth?

Are you good at getting Jesus into the conversation?

Do your friends allow you the time to tell them what you believe?

Acts 23:23–24:16

Paul is Sent to Caesarea

²³Then the commander called two officers and said, "I need some men to go to Caesarea. Get 200 soldiers, 70 horsemen and 200 men with spears ready to leave at nine o'clock tonight. ²⁴Get some horses for Paul to ride so he can be taken to Governor Felix safely." ²⁵And he wrote a letter that said:

²⁶From Claudius Lysias.

To the Most Excellent Governor Felix:

Greetings.

²⁷The Jews had taken this man and planned to kill him. But I learned that he is a Roman citizen, so I went with my soldiers and saved him. ²⁸I wanted to know why they were accusing him, so I brought him before their council meeting. ²⁹I learned that the Jews said Paul did some things that were wrong by their own laws, but no charge was worthy of jail or death. ³⁰When I was told that some of the Jews were planning to kill Paul, I sent him to you at once. I also told those Jews to tell you what they have against him.

³¹So the soldiers did what they were told and took Paul and brought him to the city of Antipatris that night. ³²The next day the horsemen went with Paul to Caesarea, but the other soldiers went back to the army building in Jerusalem. ³³When the horsemen came to Caesarea and gave the letter to the governor, they turned Paul over to him. ³⁴The governor read the letter and asked Paul, "What area are you from?" When he learned that Paul was from Cilicia, ³⁵he said, "I will hear your case when those who are against you come here, too." Then the governor gave orders for Paul to be kept under guard in Herod's palace.

Paul is Accused

24 Five days later Ananias, the high priest, went to the city of Caesarea with some of the Jewish elders and a lawyer named Tertullus. They had come to make charges against Paul before the governor. ²Paul was called into the meeting, and Tertullus began to accuse him, saying, "Most Excellent Felix! Our people enjoy much peace because of you, and many wrong things in our country are being made right through your wise help. ³We accept these things always and in every place, and we are thankful for them. ⁴But not wanting to take any more of your time, I beg you to be kind and listen to our few words. ⁵We have found this man to be a troublemaker, stirring up the Jews everywhere in the world. He is a leader of the Nazarene group. ⁶Also, he was trying to make the Temple unclean, but we stopped him. ⁷ ⁸By asking him questions yourself,

you can decide if all these things are true." ⁹The other Jews agreed and said that all of this was true.

¹⁰When the governor made a sign for Paul to speak, Paul said, "Governor Felix, I know you have been a judge over this nation for a long time. So I am happy to defend myself before you. ¹¹You can learn for yourself that I went to worship in Jerusalem only twelve days ago. ¹²Those who are accusing me did not find me arguing with anyone in the Temple or stirring up the people in the synagogues or in the city. ¹³They cannot prove the things they are saying against me now. ¹⁴But I will tell you this: I worship the God of our ancestors as a follower of the Way of Jesus. The Jews say that the Way of Jesus is not the right way. But I believe everything that is taught in the law of Moses and that is written in the books of the Prophets. ¹⁵I have the same hope in God that they have—the hope that all people, good and bad, will surely be raised from the dead. ¹⁶This is why I always try to do what I believe is right before God and people.

Who was Paul talking to (24:10)?

Were the accusations about Paul true (24:12,13)?

What is Paul a follower of (24:14)?

Paul answered the claims of those accusing him with the claim of what he believed.

Think

Is it appropriate to get Jesus into every discussion?

Pray

That God will give you guidance as to what you should say and when you should say it with regard to Jesus.

Think big!

Do you ever wish you could tell more people about Jesus?

Do you ever dream of telling someone really famous about God? Wouldn't it be good if you were evangelist to the rich and famous?

 Acts 24:17–25:12

17"After being away from Jerusalem for several years, I went back to bring money to my people and to offer sacrifices. 18I was doing this when they found me in the Temple. I had finished the cleansing ceremony and had not made any trouble; no people were gathering around me. 19But there were some Jews from the country of Asia who should be here, standing before you. If I have really done anything wrong, they are the ones who should accuse me. 20Or ask these Jews here if they found any wrong in me when I stood before the Jewish council in Jerusalem. 21But I did shout one thing when I stood before them: 'You are judging me today because I believe that people will rise from the dead!'"

22Felix already understood much about the Way of Jesus. He stopped the trial and said, "When commander Lysias comes here, I will decide your case." 23Felix told the officer to keep Paul guarded but to give him some freedom and to let his friends bring what he needed.

Paul Speaks to Felix and His Wife

24After some days Felix came with his wife, Drusilla, who was Jewish, and asked for Paul to be brought to him. He listened to Paul talk about believing in Christ Jesus. 25But Felix became afraid when Paul spoke about living right, self-control and the time when God will judge the world. He said, "Go away now. When I have

more time, I will call for you." 26At the same time Felix hoped that Paul would give him some money, so he often sent for Paul and talked with him.

27But after two years, Felix was replaced by Porcius Festus as governor. But Felix had left Paul in prison to please the Jews.

Paul Asks to See Caesar

25 Three days after Festus became governor, he went from Caesarea to Jerusalem. 2There the leading priests and the important Jewish leaders made charges against Paul before Festus. 3They asked Festus to do them a favour. They wanted him to send Paul back to Jerusalem, because they had a plan to kill him on the way. 4But Festus answered that Paul would be kept in Caesarea and that he himself was returning there soon. 5He said, "Some of your leaders should go with me. They can accuse the man there in Caesarea, if he has really done something wrong."

6Festus stayed in Jerusalem another eight or ten days and then went back to Caesarea. The next day he told the soldiers to bring Paul before him. Festus was seated on the judge's seat 7when Paul came into the room. The Jewish people who had come from Jerusalem stood around him, making serious charges against him, which they could not prove. 8This is what Paul said to defend himself: "I have done nothing wrong against the

Jewish law, against the Temple or against Caesar."

⁹But Festus wanted to please the Jews. So he asked Paul, "Do you want to go to Jerusalem for me to judge you there on these charges?"

¹⁰Paul said, "I am standing at Caesar's judgement seat now, where I should be judged. I have done nothing wrong to the Jews; you know this is true. ¹¹If I have done something wrong and the law says I must die, I do not ask to be saved from death. But if these charges are not true, then no one can give me to them. I want Caesar to hear my case!"

¹²Festus talked about this with his advisors. Then he said, "You have asked to see Caesar, so you will go to Caesar!"

Where did Festus want to send Paul (25:9)?

Why did Festus want to send Paul there (25:9)?

Paul had been witnessing about his belief throughout his imprisonment. He now wanted to be a witness before Caesar – and they didn't come richer or more famous than him!

Think

Which person in the whole world (famous or not) would you most like to tell about God's love?

Pray

For the person you have just thought about in the previous section.

Important people

Who are the most famous and important people you know about?

Acts 25:13–26:8

Paul Before King Agrippa

¹³A few days later King Agrippa and Bernice came to Caesarea to visit Festus. ¹⁴They stayed there for some time, and Festus told the king about Paul's case. Festus said, "There is a man that Felix left in prison. ¹⁵When I went to Jerusalem, the leading priests and the elders Jewish there made charges against him, asking me to sentence him to death. ¹⁶But I answered, 'When a man is accused of a crime, Romans do not hand him over until he has been allowed to face his accusers and defend himself against their charges.' ¹⁷So when these Jews came here to Caesarea for the trial, I did not waste time. The next day I sat on the judge's seat and commanded that the man be brought in. ¹⁸The Jews stood up and accused him, but not of any serious crime as I thought they would. ¹⁹The things they said were about their own religion and about a man named Jesus who died. But Paul said that he is still alive. ²⁰Not knowing how to find out about these questions, I asked Paul, 'Do you want to go to Jerusalem and be judged there?' ²¹But he asked to be kept in Caesarea. He wants a decision from the emperor. So I ordered that he be held until I could send him to Caesar."

²²Agrippa said to Festus, "I would also like to hear this man myself."

Festus said, "Tomorrow you will hear him."

²³The next day Agrippa and Bernice appeared with great show, acting like very important people. They went into the judgement room with the army leaders and the important men of Caesarea. Then Festus ordered the soldiers to bring Paul in. ²⁴Festus said, "King Agrippa and all who are gathered here with us, you see this man. All the Jewish people, here and in Jerusalem, have complained to me about him, shouting that he should not live any longer. ²⁵When I judged him, I found no reason to order his death. But since he asked to be judged by Caesar, I decided to send him. ²⁶But I have nothing definite to write to the emperor about him. So I have brought him before all of you—especially you, King Agrippa. I hope you can question him and give me something to write. ²⁷I think it is foolish to send a prisoner to Caesar without telling what charges are against him."

Paul Defends Himself

26 Agrippa said to Paul, "You may now speak to defend yourself."

Then Paul raised his hand and began to speak. ²He said, "King Agrippa, I am very happy to stand before you and will answer all the charges the Jewish people make against me. ³You know so much about all the Jewish customs and the things the Jews argue about, so please listen to me patiently.

⁴"All the Jewish people know about my whole life, how I lived from the beginning in my own country and later in Jerusalem. ⁵They have known me for a long time. If

354

they want to, they can tell you that I was a good Pharisee. And the Pharisees obey the laws of the Jewish religion more carefully than any other group. ⁶Now I am on trial because I hope for the promise that God made to our ancestors. ⁷This is the promise that the twelve tribes of our people hope to receive as they serve God day and night. My king, the Jews have accused me because I hope for this same promise! ⁸Why do any of you people think it is impossible for God to raise people from the dead?

It doesn't matter how rich, famous or important someone is, they still need to hear about Jesus. Paul used his arrest as an opportunity to tell people.

Think

Don't ever be intimidated by how powerful or important someone is. They're just a person, after all. Be respectful if they're in authority, but don't be afraid to tell them the Good News.

Pray

God, I thank you that everybody's the same to you, and that you love us all equally and want to know you.

Patience is a virtue

Does it frustrate you that some of your friends are still not Christians? You've been telling them what you believe and showing them God's love by the way you act. You've even managed to help them through difficult times – and yet they still don't believe?

Well it may take time!

Acts 26:9–32

⁹"I, too, thought I ought to do many things against Jesus from Nazareth. ¹⁰And that is what I did in Jerusalem. The leading priests gave me the power to put many of God's people in jail, and when they were being killed, I agreed it was a good thing. ¹¹In every synagogue, I often punished them and tried to make them speak against Jesus. I was so angry against them I even went to other cities to find them and punish them.

¹²"On one occasion the leading priests gave me permission and the power to go to Damascus. ¹³On the way there, at noon, I saw a light from heaven. It was brighter than the sun and flashed all around me and those who were travelling with me. ¹⁴We all fell to the ground. Then I heard a voice speaking to me in the Jewish language, saying, 'Saul, Saul, why are you persecuting me? You are only hurting yourself by fighting me.' ¹⁵I said, 'Who are you, Lord?' The Lord said, 'I am Jesus, the one you are persecuting. ¹⁶Stand up! I have chosen you to be my servant and my witness—you will tell people the things that you have seen and the things that I will show you. This is why I have come to you today. ¹⁷I will keep you safe from your own people and also from those who are not Jewish. I am sending you to them ¹⁸to open their eyes so that they may turn away from darkness

to the light, away from the power of Satan and to God. Then their sins can be forgiven, and they can have a place with those people who have been made holy by believing in me.'

¹⁹"King Agrippa, after I had this vision from heaven, I obeyed it. ²⁰I began telling people that they should change their hearts and lives and turn to God and do things to show they really had changed. I told this first to those in Damascus, then in Jerusalem and in every part of Judea, and also to those who are not Jewish. ²¹This is why the Jews took me and were trying to kill me in the Temple. ²²But God has helped me, and so I stand here today, telling all people, small and great, what I have seen. But I am saying only what Moses and the prophets said would happen— ²³that the Christ would die, and as the first to rise from the dead, he would bring light to the Jewish and non-Jewish people."

Paul Tries to Persuade Agrippa

²⁴While Paul was saying these things to defend himself, Festus said loudly, "Paul, you are out of your mind! Too much study has driven you insane!"

²⁵Paul said, "Most excellent Festus, I am not mad. My words are true and sensible. ²⁶King Agrippa knows about these things, and I can speak freely to

him. I know he has heard about all these things, because they did not happen in a corner. 27King Agrippa, do you believe what the prophets wrote? I know you believe."

28King Agrippa said to Paul, "Do you think you can persuade me to become a Christian in such a short time?"

29Paul said, "Whether it is a short or a long time, I pray to God that not only you but every person listening to me today would be saved and be like me—except for these chains I have."

30Then King Agrippa, Governor Festus, Bernice and all the people sitting with them stood up 31and left the room. Talking to each other, they said, "There is no reason why this man should die or be put in jail." 32And Agrippa said to Festus, "We could let this man go free, but he has asked Caesar to hear his case."

What does Festus think has happened to Paul (v 24)?

What has Paul said (v 25)?

What is King Agrippa's response (v 28)?

Paul knew that getting people to believe could take time, yet it didn't discourage him from telling the truth.

Think

What have you seen to be the most effective way of telling or showing people the Good News?

Pray

That you will continue to show God's love to your friends and that his Holy Spirit will be at work in their lives.

God's promises

TV commercials often promise us the world: the latest hair gel that can make us a hit with the opposite sex, the new magazine that will answer all our problems. Unfortunately, they rarely live up to their promises.

Acts 27:1–26

Paul Sails for Rome

27 It was decided that we would sail for Italy. An officer named Julius, who served in the emperor's army, guarded Paul and some other prisoners. ²We got on a ship that was from the city of Adramyttium and was about to sail to different ports in the country of Asia. Aristarchus, a man from the city of Thessalonica in Macedonia, went with us. ³The next day we came to Sidon. Julius was very good to Paul and gave him freedom to go and visit his friends, who took care of his needs. ⁴We left Sidon and sailed close to the island of Cyprus, because the wind was blowing against us. ⁵We went across the sea by Cilicia and Pamphylia and landed at the city of Myra, in Lycia. ⁶There the officer found a ship from Alexandria that was going to Italy, so he put us on it.

⁷We sailed slowly for many days. We had a hard time reaching Cnidus because the wind was blowing against us, and we could not go any further. So we sailed by the south side of the island of Crete near Salmone. ⁸Sailing past it was hard. Then we came to a place called Fair Havens, near the city of Lasea.

⁹We had lost much time, and it was now dangerous to sail, because it was already after the Day of Cleansing. So Paul warned them, ¹⁰"Men, I can see there will be a lot of trouble on this trip. The ship, the cargo and even our lives may be lost." ¹¹But the captain and the owner of the ship did not agree with Paul, and the officer believed what the captain and owner of the ship said. ¹²Since that harbour was not a good place for the ship to stay for the winter, most of the men decided that the ship should leave. They hoped we could go to Phoenix and stay there for the winter. Phoenix, a city on the island of Crete, had a harbour which faced south-west and north-west.

The Storm

¹³When a good wind began to blow from the south, the men on the ship thought, "This is the wind we wanted, and now we have it." So they pulled up the anchor, and we sailed very close to the island of Crete. ¹⁴But then a very strong wind named the "northeaster" came from the island. ¹⁵The ship was caught in it and could not sail against it. So we stopped trying and let the wind carry us. ¹⁶When we went below a small island named Cauda, we were barely able to bring in the lifeboat. ¹⁷After the men took the lifeboat in, they tied ropes around the ship to hold it together. The men were afraid that the ship would hit the sandbanks of Syrtis, so they lowered the sail and let the wind carry the ship. ¹⁸The next day the storm was blowing us so hard that the men threw out some of the cargo. ¹⁹A day later with their own hands they threw out the ship's equipment. ²⁰When we could not see the sun or the stars for many days, and

the storm was very bad, we lost all hope of being saved.

²¹After the men had gone without food for a long time, Paul stood up before them and said, "Men, you should have listened to me. You should not have sailed from Crete. Then you would not have had all this trouble and loss. ²²But now I tell you to cheer up because none of you will die. Only the ship will be lost. ²³Last night an angel came to me from the God I belong to and worship. ²⁴The angel said, 'Paul, do not be afraid. You must stand before Caesar. And God has promised you that he will save the lives of everyone sailing with you.' ²⁵So men, have courage. I trust in God that everything will happen as his angel told me. ²⁶But we will run aground on an island."

Paul was on his way to Rome. He was going to take the Good News to the biggest stage in the world (at that time).

What threatened that promise?

How did God tell Paul that he would get to Rome (v 23)?

Think

Do you actively look for God's promises in your life?

Pray

Dear Lord, show me clearly where you want me to go, which steps to take and in which direction to turn.

Danger is my middle name

Have you ever been in a dangerous situation? Were you afraid?

Acts 27:27–28:11a

²⁷On the fourteenth night we were still being carried around in the Adriatic Sea. About midnight the sailors thought we were close to land, ²⁸so they lowered a rope with a weight on the end of it into the water. They found that the water was 20 fathoms deep. They went a little further and lowered the rope again. It was 15 fathoms deep. ²⁹The sailors were afraid that we would hit the rocks, so they threw four anchors into the water and prayed for daylight to come. ³⁰Some of the sailors wanted to leave the ship, and they lowered the lifeboat, pretending they were throwing more anchors from the front of the ship. ³¹But Paul told the officer and the other soldiers, "If these men do not stay in the ship, your lives cannot be saved." ³²So the soldiers cut the ropes and let the lifeboat fall into the water.

³³Just before dawn Paul began persuading all the people to eat something. He said, "For the past fourteen days you have been waiting and watching and not eating. ³⁴Now I beg you to eat something. You need it to stay alive. None of you will lose even one hair of your heads." ³⁵After he said this, Paul took some bread and thanked God for it before all of them. He broke off a piece and began eating. ³⁶They all felt better and started eating, too. ³⁷There were 276 people on the ship. ³⁸When they had eaten all they wanted, they began making the ship lighter by throwing the grain into the sea.

The Ship is Destroyed

³⁹When daylight came, the sailors saw land. They did not know what land it was, but they saw a bay with a beach and wanted to sail the ship to the beach if they could. ⁴⁰So they cut the ropes to the anchors and left the anchors in the sea. At the same time, they untied the ropes that were holding the rudders. Then they raised the front sail into the wind and sailed towards the beach. ⁴¹But the ship hit a sandbank. The front of the ship stuck there and could not move, but the back of the ship began to break up from the big waves.

⁴²The soldiers decided to kill the prisoners so none of them could swim away and escape. ⁴³But Julius, the officer, wanted to let Paul live and did not allow the soldiers to kill the prisoners. Instead he ordered everyone who could swim to jump into the water first and swim to land. ⁴⁴The rest were to follow using wooden boards or pieces of the ship. And this is how all the people made it safely to land.

Paul on the Island of Malta

28 When we were safe on land, we learned that the island was called Malta. ²The people who lived there were very good to us. Because it was raining and very cold, they made a fire and welcomed all of us. ³Paul gathered a pile of sticks and was putting them on the fire when a poisonous snake came out because of the heat and bit him on the hand. ⁴The people living on the island saw the snake hanging from Paul's hand and said to each other, "This man must be a murderer! He did not die in the sea, but Justice does not want him to live." ⁵But Paul shook the snake off into the fire and was not hurt. ⁶The people thought that Paul would swell up or fall down dead. They waited and watched him for a long time, but nothing bad happened to him. So they changed their minds and said, "He is a god!"

⁷There were some fields around there owned by Publius, an important man on the island. He welcomed us into his home and was very good to us for three days. ⁸Publius' father was sick with a fever and dysentery. Paul went to him, prayed and put his hands on the man and healed him. ⁹After this, all the other sick people on the island came to Paul, and he healed them, too. ¹⁰–¹¹The people on the island gave us many honours. When we were ready to leave, three months later, they gave us the things we needed.

The sailors were old hands and had seen many voyages, and they were terrified. But Paul wasn't scared at all. Why not?

Think

God has you in his hands. He's looking out for you. With him on your side, you need never be afraid.

Pray

Thank God that you're never on your own, and that he holds you securely in his hands. Write out John 10:27–30 and stick it up somewhere you'll see it every day!

Extra

Don't try this at home disclaimer: just because God rescued Paul from all these wild situations, it doesn't mean that he's going to save you if you're reckless. Paul wasn't looking for trouble or danger and neither should you.

No limits?

Who do you think can become a Christian?

Do you put any limits on who God loves e.g. murderers, rapists, thieves?

Acts 28:11b–31

Paul Goes to Rome

We got on a ship from Alexandria that had stayed on the island during the winter. On the front of the ship was the sign of the twin gods. [12]We stopped at Syracuse for three days. [13]From there we sailed to Rhegium. The next day a wind began to blow from the south, and a day later we came to Puteoli. [14]We found some believers there who asked us to stay with them for a week. Finally, we came to Rome. [15]The believers in Rome heard that we were there and came out as far as the Market of Appius and the Three Inns to meet us. When Paul saw them, he was encouraged and thanked God.

Paul in Rome

[16]When we arrived at Rome, Paul was allowed to live alone, with the soldier who guarded him.

[17]Three days later Paul sent for the Jewish leaders there. When they came together, he said, "Brothers, I have done nothing against our people or the customs of our ancestors. But I was arrested in Jerusalem and given to the Romans. [18]After they asked me many questions, they could find no reason why I should be killed. They wanted to let me go free, [19]but the Jewish people there argued against that. So I had to ask to come to Rome to have my trial before Caesar. But I have no charge to bring against my own people. [20]That is why I wanted to see you and talk with you. I am bound with this chain because I believe in the hope of Israel."

[21]They answered Paul, "We have received no letters from Judea about you. None of our Jewish brothers who have come from there brought news or told us anything bad about you. [22]But we want to hear your ideas, because we know that people everywhere are speaking against this religious group."

[23]Paul and the Jewish people chose a day for a meeting and on that day many more of the Jews met with Paul at the place he was staying. He spoke to them all day long. Using the law of Moses and the prophets' writings, he explained the kingdom of God, and he tried to persuade them to believe these things about Jesus. [24]Some believed what Paul said, but others did not. [25]So they argued and began leaving after Paul said one more thing to them: "The Holy Spirit spoke the truth to your ancestors through Isaiah the prophet, saying,

[26]'Go and tell this people:
You will listen and listen, but you will not understand.
You will look and look, but you will not learn.
[27]Make the minds of these people dumb.
Shut their ears. Cover their eyes.
Otherwise, they might really understand what they see with their eyes
and hear with their ears.
They might really understand in their minds

and come back to me and be healed.'
Isaiah 6:9–10

28"I want you to know that God has also sent his salvation to those who are not Jewish, and they will listen!" 29

30Paul stayed two full years in his own rented house and welcomed all people who came to visit him. 31He boldly preached about the kingdom of God and taught about the Lord Jesus Christ, and no one tried to stop him.

What did Paul do (v 23)?

How did Paul do it (v 23)?

What was the result (v 24)?

Who can also receive salvation (v 28)?

Think

Can God save anyone? Are there limits to receiving salvation?

Pray

Dear God, let me speak of your love so that those who want to listen can hear and respond.

363

Good news?

When was the last time you heard some really good news? What made it *good*?

Romans 1:1–27

1 From Paul, a servant of Christ Jesus. God called me to be an apostle and chose me to tell the Good News.

²God promised this Good News long ago through his prophets, as it is written in the Holy Scriptures. ³⁻⁴The Good News is about God's Son, Jesus Christ our Lord. As a man, he was born from the family of David. But through the Spirit of holiness he was appointed to be God's Son with great power by rising from the dead. ⁵Through Christ, God gave me the special work of an apostle, which was to lead people of all nations to believe and obey. I do this work for him. ⁶And you who are in Rome are also called to belong to Jesus Christ.

⁷To all of you in Rome whom God loves and has called to be his holy people:

Grace and peace to you from God our Father and the Lord Jesus Christ.

A Prayer of Thanks

⁸First I want to say that I thank my God through Jesus Christ for all of you, because people everywhere in the world are talking about your faith. ⁹God, whom I serve with my whole heart by telling the Good News about his Son, knows that I always mention you ¹⁰every time I pray. I pray that I will be allowed to come to you, and this will happen if God wants it. ¹¹I want very much to see you, to give you some spiritual gift to make you strong. ¹²I mean that I want us to help each other with the faith we have. Your faith will help me, and my faith will help you. ¹³Brothers and sisters, I want you to know that I planned many

times to come to you, but this has not been possible. I wanted to come so that I could help you grow spiritually as I have helped the other non-Jewish people.

¹⁴I have a duty to all people—Greeks and those who are not Greeks, the wise and the foolish. ¹⁵That is why I want so much to preach the Good News to you in Rome.

¹⁶I am proud of the Good News, because it is the power God uses to save everyone who believes—to save the Jews first, and also to save those who are not Jews. ¹⁷The Good News shows how God makes people right with himself—that it begins and ends with faith. As the Scripture says, "But those who are right with God will live by trusting in him."

All People Have Done Wrong

¹⁸God's anger is shown from heaven against all the evil and wrong things people do. By their own evil lives they hide the truth. ¹⁹God shows his anger because some knowledge of him has been made clear to them. Yes, God has shown himself to them. ²⁰There are things about him that people cannot see—his eternal power and all the things that make him God. But since the beginning of the world those things have been easy to understand by what God has made. So people have no excuse for the bad things they do. ²¹They knew God, but they did not give glory to God or thank him. Their thinking became useless. Their foolish minds were filled with darkness. ²²They said they were wise, but they became fools. ²³They traded the

glory of God who lives for ever for the worship of idols made to look like earthly people, birds, animals and snakes.

24Because they did these things, God left them and let them go their sinful way, wanting only to do evil. As a result, they became full of sexual sin, using their bodies wrongly with each other. 25They traded the truth of God for a lie. They worshipped and served what had been created instead of the God who created those things, who should be praised for ever. Amen.

26Because people did those things, God left them and let them do the shameful things they wanted to do. Women stopped having natural sex and started having sex with other women. 27In the same way, men stopped having natural sex and began wanting each other. Men did shameful things with other men, and in their bodies they received the punishment for those wrongs.

Who is the Good News about (v 3)?

Where else in the Bible can we read about it (v 2)?

Who was Jesus' great-great-great- etc. grandfather (v 3)?

What marked him out as God's Son (v 4)?

What's the result of this Good News (vs 5–7)?

Why is it good news for *you*?

Think

When was the last time you told somebody else the really Good News?

Pray

Thank God that you are loved by him and called to belong to him.

Judging

Do you ever find yourself laughing at someone for doing something silly or stupid?

How often do you find yourself doing the same thing and wishing that people weren't laughing or noticing you?

 Romans 1:28–2:16

28People did not think it was important to have a true knowledge of God. So God left them and allowed them to have their own worthless thinking and to do things they should not do. 29They are filled with every kind of sin, evil, selfishness and hatred. They are full of jealousy, murder, fighting, lying and thinking the worst about each other. They gossip 30and say evil things about each other. They hate God. They are rude and conceited and boast about themselves. They invent ways of doing evil. They do not obey their parents. 31They are foolish, they do not keep their promises, and they show no kindness or mercy to others. 32They know God's law says that those who live like this should die. But they themselves not only continue to do these evil things, they applaud others who do them.

You People Also are Sinful

2 If you think you can judge others, you are wrong. When you judge them, you are really judging yourself guilty, because you do the same things they do. 2God judges those who do wrong things, and we know that his judging is right. 3You judge those who do wrong, but you do wrong yourselves. Do you think you will be able to escape the judgement of God? 4He has been very kind and patient, waiting for you to change, but you think nothing of his kindness. Perhaps you do not understand

that God's kindness is meant to lead you to change your hearts and lives. 5But you are stubborn and refuse to change, so you are making your own punishment even greater on the day he shows his anger. On that day everyone will see God's right judgements. 6God will reward or punish every person for what that person has done. 7Some people, by always continuing to do good, live for God's glory, for honour and for life that has no end. God will give them life for ever. 8But other people are selfish. They refuse to follow truth and, instead, follow evil. God will give them his punishment and anger. 9He will give trouble and suffering to everyone who does evil—to the Jews first and also to those who are not Jews. 10But he will give glory, honour and peace to everyone who does good—to the Jews first and also to those who are not Jews. 11For God judges all people in the same way.

12People who do not have the law and who are sinners will be lost, although they do not have the law. And, in the same way, those who have the law and are sinners will be judged by the law. 13Hearing the law does not make people right with God. It is those who obey the law who will be right with him. 14(Those who are not Jews do not have the law, but when they freely do what the law commands, they are the law for themselves. This is true even though they do not have the law. 15They show that in their hearts they know what is right and wrong, just as the law commands. And they show this by their thoughts. Sometimes their thoughts tell them they did wrong, and sometimes their thoughts tell them they did right.) 16All these things will happen on the day when God, through Christ Jesus, will judge people's secret thoughts. The Good News that I preach says this.

Why does Paul say we shouldn't judge others (2:1)?

Who is the only one who can judge (2:2)?

There is a hint in 2:3 that the church in Rome believed they were not doing anything wrong and therefore had the right to judge others. Unfortunately they *were* doing wrong.

Think

Does this have any impact on how we deal with criminals?

Pray

Ask God to show you where you are going wrong and to help you change.

You're wrong

What are people *really* like? Are most people good? How do people measure whether they are good or not?

Romans 2:17–3:18

The Jews and the Law

17What about you? You call yourself a Jew. You trust in the law of Moses and boast that you are close to God. 18You know what he wants you to do and what is important, because you have learned the law. 19You think you are a guide for the blind and a light for those who are in darkness. 20You think you can show foolish people what is right and teach those who know nothing. You have the law; so you think you know everything and have all truth. 21You teach others, so why don't you teach yourself? You tell others not to steal, but you steal. 22You say that others must not take part in adultery, but you are guilty of that sin. You hate idols, but you steal from temples. 23You boast about having God's law, but you bring shame to God by breaking his law, 24just as the Scriptures say: "Those who are not Jews speak against God's name because of you."

25If you follow the law, your circumcision has meaning. But if you break the law, it is as if you were never circumcised. 26People who are not Jews are not circumcised, but if they do what the law says, it is as if they were circumcised. 27You Jews have the written law and circumcision, but you break the law. So those who are not circumcised in their bodies, but still obey the law, will show that you are guilty. 28They can do this because a person is not a true Jew if he is only a Jew in his physical body; true circumcision is not only on the outside of the body. 29A person is a Jew only if he is a Jew inside; true circumcision is done in the heart by the Spirit, not by the works of the written law. Such a person gets praise from God rather than from people.

3 So, do Jews have anything that other people do not have? Is there anything special about being circumcised? 2Yes, of course, there is in every way. The most important thing is this: God trusted the Jews with his teachings. 3If some Jews were not faithful to him, will that stop God from doing what he promised? 4No! God will continue to be true even when every person is false. As the Scriptures say:

"So you will be shown to be right when you speak,

and you will win your case." *Psalm 51:4*

5When we do wrong, that shows more clearly that God is right. So can we say that God is wrong to punish us? (I am talking as people might talk.) 6No! If God could not punish us, he could not judge the world.

7A person might say, "When I lie, it really gives him glory, because my lie shows God's truth. So why am I judged a sinner?" 8It would be the same to say, "We should do evil so that good will come." Some people find fault with us and say we teach this, but they are wrong and deserve the punishment they will receive.

All People are Guilty

9So are we Jews better than others? No! We have already said that Jews and those who are not Jews are all guilty of sin. 10As the Scriptures say:

"There is no one who always does what
   is right,
not even one.
11   There is no one who understands.
There is no one who looks to God for
   help.
12All have turned away.
Together, everyone has become
   useless.
There is no one who does anything good;
there is not even one."   *Psalm 14:1–3*
13"Their throats are like open graves;

they use their tongues for telling lies."
   Psalm 5:9
"Their words are like snake poison."
   Psalm 140:3
14   "Their mouths are full of cursing and
   hate."   *Psalm 10:7*
15"They are always ready to kill people.
16   Everywhere they go they cause ruin
   and misery.
17They don't know how to live in peace."
   Isaiah 59:7–8
18   "They have no fear of God."
   Psalm 36:1

Make two lists:

• things that are wrong with the world

• things that are wrong with you

"The law" (2:17) means God's commands in the Old Testament. They're
great for helping us *know* what's right. But they don't mean we always *do*
what's right. Can you think of examples from your own life, when you went
against what you knew was right?

Think

Do you have a sliding scale of how bad things are? Is lying as bad
as stealing etc.?

Pray

Read through the list of things wrong with you. Ask God to
forgive you for them. Now tear up the list – because he has!

Future imperfect

Have you been *absolutely*, totally perfect today? Thought not!

Romans 3:19–4:12

¹⁹We know that the law's commands are for those who have the law. This stops all excuses and brings the whole world under God's judgement, ²⁰because no one can be made right with God by following the law. The law only shows us our sin.

How God Makes People Right

²¹But God has a way to make people right with him without the law, and he has now shown us that way which the law and the prophets told us about. ²²God makes people right with himself through their faith in Jesus Christ. This is true for all who believe in Christ, because all people are the same: ²³all have sinned and are not good enough for God's glory, ²⁴and all need to be made right with God by his grace, which is a free gift. They need to be made free from sin through Jesus Christ. ²⁵God gave him as a way to forgive sin through faith in the blood of Jesus' death. This showed that God always does what is right and fair, as in the past when he was patient and did not punish people for their sins. ²⁶And God gave Jesus to show today that he does what is right. God did this so he could judge rightly and so he could make right any person who has faith in Jesus.

²⁷So do we have a reason to boast about ourselves? No! And why not? It is the way of faith that stops all boasting, not the way of trying to obey the law. ²⁸A person is made right with God through faith, not through obeying the law. ²⁹Is God only the God of the Jews? Is he not also the God of those who are not Jews? ³⁰Of course he is,

because there is only one God. He will make Jews right with him by their faith, and he will also make those who are not Jews right with him through their faith. ³¹So do we destroy the law by following the way of faith? No! Faith causes us to be what the law truly wants.

The Example of Abraham

4 So what can we say that Abraham, the father of our people, learned about faith? ²If Abraham was made right by the things he did, he had a reason to boast. But this is not God's view, ³because the Scripture says, "Abraham believed God, and God accepted Abraham's faith, and that faith made him right with God."

⁴When people work, their pay is not given as a gift, but as something earned. ⁵But people cannot do any work that will make them right with God. So they must trust in him, who makes even evil people right in his sight. Then God accepts their faith, and that makes them right with him. ⁶David said the same thing. He said that people are truly blessed when God, without paying attention to good deeds, makes people right with himself.

⁷"Happy are they
    whose sins are forgiven,
    whose wrongs are pardoned.
⁸Happy is the person
    whom the Lord does not consider
      guilty."   *Psalm 32:1–2*
⁹Is this blessing only for those who are circumcised or also for those who are not circumcised? We have already said that God accepted Abraham's faith and that

faith made him right with God. ¹⁰So how did this happen? Did God accept Abraham before or after he was circumcised? It was before his circumcision. ¹¹Abraham was circumcised to show that he was right with God through faith before he was circumcised. So Abraham is the father of all those who believe but are not circumcised; he is the father of all believers who are accepted as being right with God. ¹²And Abraham is also the father of those who have been circumcised and who live following the faith that our father Abraham had before he was circumcised.

Is there *anyone* who does everything right, always (look back at 3:10)?

You might think that really good Christians keep all the rules in the Bible, but what does Paul say about keeping the "law" (the rules in the Old Testament) (3:20)?

Why do you think that trying to keep all the rules will only show how imperfect we are?

Think

If we want to know God, we need to recognise what we're really like.

Pray

Say sorry to God for things you've done wrong, knowing that he will forgive you.

Ready, aim...

How do you set targets for your life? Do you ...

- go for the safe option?
- attempt things just out of your reach?
- try and go for the virtually impossible?

Romans 4:13–5:11

God Keeps His Promise

¹³Abraham and his descendants received the promise that they would get the whole world. He did not receive that promise through the law, but through being right with God by his faith. ¹⁴If people could receive what God promised by following the law, then faith is worthless. And God's promise to Abraham is worthless, ¹⁵because the law can only bring God's anger. But if there is no law, there is nothing to disobey.

¹⁶So people receive God's promise by having faith. This happens so the promise can be a free gift. Then all of Abraham's children can have that promise. It is not only for those who live under the law of Moses but for anyone who lives with faith like that of Abraham, who is the father of us all. ¹⁷As it is written in the Scriptures: "I am making you a father of many nations." This is true before God, the God Abraham believed, the God who gives life to the dead and who creates something out of nothing.

¹⁸There was no hope that Abraham would have children. But Abraham believed God and continued hoping, and so he became the father of many nations. As God told him, "Your descendants also will be too many to count." ¹⁹Abraham was almost 100 years old, much past the age for having children, and Sarah could not have children. Abraham thought about all

this, but his faith in God did not become weak. ²⁰He never doubted that God would keep his promise, and he never stopped believing. He grew stronger in his faith and gave praise to God. ²¹Abraham felt sure that God was able to do what he had promised. ²²So, "God accepted Abraham's faith, and that faith made him right with God." ²³Those words ("God accepted Abraham's faith") were written not only for Abraham ²⁴but also for us. God will accept us also because we believe in the One who raised Jesus our Lord from the dead. ²⁵Jesus was given to die for our sins, and he was raised from the dead to make us right with God.

Right with God

5 Since we have been made right with God by our faith, we have peace with God. This happened through our Lord Jesus Christ, ²who has brought us into that blessing of God's grace that we now enjoy. And we are happy because of the hope we have of sharing God's glory. ³We also have joy with our troubles, because we know that these troubles produce patience. ⁴And patience produces character, and character produces hope. ⁵And this hope will never disappoint us, because God has poured out his love to fill our hearts. He gave us his love through the Holy Spirit, whom God has given to us.

⁶When we were unable to help our-

selves, at the moment of our need, Christ died for us, although we were living against God. ⁷Very few people will die to save the life of someone else although perhaps for a good person someone might possibly die. ⁸But God shows his great love for us in this way: Christ died for us while we were still sinners.

⁹So through Christ we will surely be saved from God's anger, because we have been made right with God by the blood of Christ's death. ¹⁰While we were God's enemies, he made friends with us through the death of his Son. Surely, now that we are his friends, he will save us through his Son's life. ¹¹And not only that, now we are also very happy in God through our Lord Jesus Christ. Through him we are now God's friends again.

Abraham's target had been set for him (4:18). Was this target achievable by human standards (4:19)?

Abraham had faith in what God had promised. That faith brought acceptance with God, and eventually God's promise to Abraham was fulfilled.

Who else can be accepted by God (4:24)?

Think

Do you know what God's target for you is? Have you asked him?

Pray

That God will show you what he wants you to do.

Extra

You can read the whole account of Abraham in Genesis 11:27–25:8.

Alive in Jesus

Why do we die anyway? Why is Jesus' death and resurrection so important?

Romans 5:12–6:14

Adam and Christ Compared

[12]Sin came into the world because of what one man did, and with sin came death. This is why everyone must die— because everyone sinned. [13]Sin was in the world before the law of Moses, but sin is not counted against us as breaking a command when there is no law. [14]But from the time of Adam to the time of Moses, everyone had to die, even those who had not sinned by breaking a command, as Adam had.

Adam was like the One who was coming in the future. [15]But God's free gift is not like Adam's sin. Many people died because of the sin of that one man. But the grace from God was much greater; many people received God's gift of life by the grace of the one man, Jesus Christ. [16]After Adam sinned once, he was judged guilty. But the gift of God is different. God's free gift came after many sins, and it makes people right with God. [17]One man sinned, and so death ruled all people because of that one man. But now those people who accept God's full grace and the great gift of being made right with him will surely have true life and rule through the one man, Jesus Christ.

[18]So as one sin of Adam brought the punishment of death to all people, one good act that Christ did makes all people right with God. And that brings true life for all. [19]One man disobeyed God, and many became sinners. In the same way, one man obeyed God, and many will be made right. [20]The law came to make sin worse. But when sin grew worse, God's grace increased. [21]Sin once used death to rule us, but God gave people more of his grace so that grace could rule by making people right with him. And this brings life for ever through Jesus Christ our Lord.

Dead to Sin but Alive in Christ

6 So do you think we should continue sinning so that God will give us even more grace? [2]No! We died to our old sinful lives, so how can we continue living with sin? [3]Did you forget that all of us became part of Christ when we were baptised? We shared his death in our baptism. [4]When we were baptised, we were buried with Christ and shared his death. So, just as Christ was raised from the dead by the wonderful power of the Father, we also can live a new life.

[5]Christ died, and we have been joined with him by dying too. So we will also be joined with him by rising from the dead as he did. [6]We know that our old life died with Christ on the cross so that our sinful selves would have no power over us and we would not be slaves to sin. [7]Anyone who has died is made free from sin's control.

[8]If we died with Christ, we know we will also live with him. [9]Christ was raised from the dead, and we know that he cannot die again. Death has no power over him now. [10]Yes, when Christ died, he died to defeat the power of sin just once— enough for all time. He now has a new life, and his new life is with God. [11]In the same way, you should see yourselves as being dead to the power of sin and alive with God through Christ Jesus.

12So, do not let sin control your life here on earth so that you do what your sinful self wants to do. 13Do not offer the parts of your body to serve sin, as things to be used in doing evil. Instead, offer yourselves to God as people who have died and now live. Offer the parts of your body to God to be used in doing good. 14Sin will not be your master, because you are not under law but under God's grace.

What does Jesus' death and resurrection mean for you?

Write, in your own words, one thing from each of these verses:

Verse 5: _____

Verse 6: _____

Verse 8: _____

Verse 10: _____

Verse 11: _____

Think

How does Jesus' life show in the way you live every day?

Pray

Thank Jesus for dying for your sin. Ask him to help you live for him and not to keep on sinning (6:1).

Choices

You find some money. Do you . . .

- keep it?
- hand it in?
- give it to charity?

Every day you face choices about right and wrong. This is the ultimate one.

Romans 6:15–7:13

Be Slaves of Righteousness

¹⁵So what should we do? Should we sin because we are under grace and not under law? No! ¹⁶Surely you know that when you give yourselves like slaves to obey someone, then you are really slaves of that person. The person you obey is your master. You can follow sin, which brings spiritual death, or you can obey God, which makes you right with him. ¹⁷In the past you were slaves to sin—sin controlled you. But thank God, you fully obeyed the things that you were taught. ¹⁸You were made free from sin, and now you are slaves to goodness. ¹⁹I use this example because this is hard for you to understand. In the past you offered the parts of your body to be slaves to sin and evil; you lived only for evil. In the same way now you must give yourselves to be slaves of goodness. Then you will live only for God.

²⁰In the past you were slaves to sin, and goodness did not control you. ²¹You did evil things, and now you are ashamed of them. Those things only bring death. ²²But now you are free from sin and have become slaves of God. This brings you a life that is only for God, and this gives you life for ever. ²³When people sin, they earn what sin pays—death. But God gives us a free gift—life for ever in Christ Jesus our Lord.

An Example from Marriage

7 Brothers and sisters, all of you understand the law of Moses. So surely you know that the law rules over people only while they are alive. ²For example, a woman must stay married to her husband as long as he is alive. But if her husband dies, she is free from the law of marriage. ³But if she marries another man while her husband is still alive, the law says she is guilty of adultery. But if her husband dies, she is free from the law of marriage. Then if she marries another man, she is not guilty of adultery.

⁴In the same way, my brothers and sisters, your old selves died, and you became free from the law through the body of Christ. This happened so that you might belong to someone else—the One who was raised from the dead—and so that we might be used in service to God. ⁵In the past, we were ruled by our sinful selves. The law made us want to do sinful things that controlled our bodies, so the things we did were bringing us death. ⁶In the past, the law held us like prisoners, but our old selves died and we were made free from the law. So now we serve God in a new

way with the Spirit, and not in the old way with written rules.

Our Fight Against Sin

7You might think I am saying that sin and the law are the same thing. That is not true. But the law was the only way I could learn what sin meant. I would never have known what it means to want to take something belonging to someone else if the law had not said, "You must not want to take your neighbour's things." 8And sin found a way to use that command and cause me to want all kinds of things I should not want. But without the law, sin has no power. 9I was alive before I knew the law. But when the law's command came to me, then sin began to live, 10and I died. The command was meant to bring life, but for me it brought death. 11Sin found a way to fool me by using the command to make me die.

12So the law is holy, and the command is holy and right and good. 13Does this mean that something that is good brought death to me? No! Sin used something that is good to bring death to me. This happened so that I could see what sin is really like; the command was used to show that sin is very evil.

God has done what's needed to set you free from sin (6:22). Everyone can choose to accept his gift of life (6:23). It's up to you.

Think

If you want to, you can say "no" to God or you can choose to live for God (6:22). This prayer might help...

Pray

Dear God, I'm sorry for the things I've done wrong. Thank you that you sent Jesus to die for my sins. I accept Jesus as my Lord and want to follow you for the rest of my life.

Extra

If someone asked you what a Christian was, write down three things that you would say:

1 _____

2 _____

3 _____

Why can't I be good?

Did you know that 91 per cent of people suffer from a condition called rhinotellixomania?

What is it? Guess...

- The fear of rhinos
- Picking one's nose
- The love of wildlife programmes

Romans 7:14–8:11

The War Within Us

14We know that the law is spiritual, but I am not spiritual since sin rules me as if I were its slave. 15I do not understand the things I do. I do not do what I want to do, and I do the things I hate. 16And if I do not want to do the hated things I do, that means I agree that the law is good. 17But I am not really the one who is doing these hated things; it is sin living in me that does them. 18Yes, I know that nothing good lives in me—I mean nothing good lives in the part of me that is earthly and sinful. I want to do the things that are good, but I do not do them. 19I do not do the good things I want to do, but I do the bad things I do not want to do. 20So if I do things I do not want to do, then I am not the one doing them. It is sin living in me that does those things.

21So I have learned this rule: when I want to do good, evil is there with me. 22In my mind, I am happy with God's law. 23But I see another law working in my body, which makes war against the law that my mind accepts. That other law working in my body is the law of sin, and it makes me its prisoner. 24What a miserable man I am! Who will save me from this body that brings me death? 25I thank God for saving me through Jesus Christ our Lord!

So in my mind I am a slave to God's law, but in my sinful self I am a slave to the law of sin.

Be Ruled by the Spirit

8 So now, those who are in Christ Jesus are not judged guilty. 2Through Christ Jesus the law of the Spirit that brings life made me free from the law that brings sin and death. 3The law was without power, because the law was made weak by our sinful selves. But God did what the law could not do. He sent his own Son to earth with the same human life that others use for sin. By sending his Son to be an offering to pay for sin, God used a human life to destroy sin. 4He did this so that we could be the kind of people the law correctly wants us to be. Now we do not live following our sinful selves, but we live following the Spirit.

5Those who live following their sinful selves think only about things that their sinful selves want. But those who live following the Spirit are thinking about the things the Spirit wants them to do. 6If people's thinking is controlled by the sinful self, there is death. But if their thinking is controlled by the Spirit, there is life and peace. 7When people's thinking is controlled by the sinful self, they are against God, because they refuse to obey God's law and really are not even able to obey God's law. 8Those people who are ruled by their sinful selves cannot please God.

9But you are not ruled by your sinful selves. You are ruled by the Spirit, if that Spirit of God really lives in you. But the person who does not have the Spirit of Christ does not belong to Christ. 10Your body will always be dead because of sin. But if Christ is in you, then the Spirit gives you life, because Christ made you right with God. 11God raised Jesus from the dead, and if God's Spirit is living in you, he will also give life to your bodies that die. God is the One who raised Christ from the dead, and he will give life through his Spirit that lives in you.

What does Paul (the writer of Romans) find frustrating (7:15,19)?

What two things does he blame for his failure (7:20,21)?

How does he describe that feeling when you know what's right, but you do what's wrong (7:23)?

People have got a problem! Who can help (7:25)?

Think

Have you ever tried to kick a (seriously) bad habit?

Pray

Lord Jesus, I'm weak but you are strong. Let your power flow into me so that I can live for you.

Extra

Bad habits! Everyone's got them (more serious ones than rhino... wotsit!), but what can you do about them?

- Decide you want to change
- Understand that change means working at it
- Establish sources of help (e.g. God, parents, friends, church)
- Live with Christ in charge of your life (WWJD?)

You are not alone

Have you ever felt completely alone – as though no one understood you or cared about what you were going through?

Romans 8:12–39

¹²So, my brothers and sisters, we must not be ruled by our sinful selves or live the way our sinful selves want. ¹³If you use your lives to do the wrong things your sinful selves want, you will die spiritually. But if you use the Spirit's help to stop doing the wrong things you do with your body, you will have true life.

¹⁴The true children of God are those who let God's Spirit lead them. ¹⁵The Spirit we received does not make us slaves again to fear: it makes us children of God. With that Spirit we cry out, "Father". ¹⁶And the Spirit himself joins with our spirits to say we are God's children. ¹⁷If we are God's children, we will receive blessings from God together with Christ. But we must suffer as Christ suffered so that we will have glory as Christ has glory.

Our Future Glory

¹⁸The sufferings we have now are nothing compared to the great glory that will be shown to us. ¹⁹Everything God made is waiting with excitement for God to show his children's glory completely. ²⁰Everything God made was changed to become useless, not by its own wish but because God wanted it and because all along there was this hope: ²¹that everything God made would be set free from ruin to have the freedom and glory that belong to God's children.

²²We know that everything God made has been waiting until now in pain, like a woman ready to give birth. ²³Not only the world, but we also have been waiting with pain inside us. We have the Spirit as the first part of God's promise. So we are waiting for God to finish making us his own children, which means our bodies will be made free. ²⁴We were saved, and we have this hope. If we see what we are waiting for, that is not really hope. People do not hope for something they already have. ²⁵But we are hoping for something we do not have yet, and we are waiting for it patiently.

²⁶Also, the Spirit helps us with our weakness. We do not know how to pray as we should. But the Spirit himself speaks to God for us, even begs God for us with deep feelings that words cannot explain. ²⁷God can see what is in people's hearts. And he knows what is in the mind of the Spirit, because the Spirit speaks to God for his people in the way God wants.

²⁸We know that in everything God works for the good of those who love him. They are the people he called, because that was his plan. ²⁹God knew them before he made the world, and he decided that they would be like his Son so that Jesus would be the firstborn of many brothers. ³⁰God planned for them to be like his Son; and those he planned to be like his Son, he also called; and those he called, he also made right with him; and those he made right, he also glorified.

God's Love in Christ Jesus

³¹So what should we say about this? If God is with us, no one can defeat us. ³²He did not spare his own Son but gave him for us all. So with Jesus, God will surely give us all things. ³³Who can accuse the people

God has chosen? No one, because God is the One who makes them right. 34Who can say God's people are guilty? No one, because Christ Jesus died, but he was also raised from the dead, and now he is on God's right side, begging God for us. 35Can anything separate us from the love Christ has for us? Can troubles or problems or sufferings or hunger or nakedness or danger or violent death? 36As it is written in the Scriptures:

"For you we are in danger of death all the time.

People think we are worth no more than sheep to be killed." *Psalm 44:22*

37But in all these things we have full victory through God who showed his love for us. 38Yes, I am sure that neither death, nor life, nor angels, nor ruling spirits, nothing now, nothing in the future, nor powers, 39nothing above us, nothing below us, nor anything else in the whole world will ever be able to separate us from the love of God that is in Christ Jesus our Lord.

Things weren't easy for the early Christians in Rome. Paul wrote this letter to them, around AD 55, to encourage them. These are God's words to encourage us, too.

Can anything, including death, separate us from God's love (v 39)?

Why can we be sure of God's love, even through death (vs 33,34)?

Think

Are you always sure that God loves you? Do you sometimes need a reminder?

Pray

Thank God, that because of Jesus, nothing can separate you from his love.

Extra

Memorise verse 39. Say it to yourself whenever you need to remind yourself that God loves you.

If only they believed

Is there anyone that you really want to become a Christian?

What would you do, or give, for them to know God?

 Romans 9:1–29

God and the Jewish People

9 I am in Christ, and I am telling you the truth; I do not lie. My feelings are ruled by the Holy Spirit, and they tell me I am not lying. ²I have great sorrow and always feel much sadness. ³I wish I could help my Jewish brothers and sisters, my people. I would even wish that I were cursed and cut off from Christ if that would help them. ⁴They are the people of Israel, God's chosen children. They have seen the glory of God, and they have the agreements that God made between himself and his people. God gave them the law of Moses and the right way of worship and his promises. ⁵They are the descendants of our great ancestors, and they are the earthly family into which Christ was born, who is God over all. Praise him for ever! Amen.

⁶It is not that God failed to keep his promise to them. But only some of the people of Israel are truly God's people, ⁷and only some of Abraham's descendants are true children of Abraham. But God said to Abraham: "The descendants I promised you will be from Isaac." ⁸This means that not all of Abraham's descendants are God's true children. Abraham's true children are those who become God's children because of the promise God made to Abraham. ⁹God's promise to Abraham was this: "At the right time I will return, and Sarah will have a son." ¹⁰And that is not all. Rebekah's sons had the same father, our father Isaac. ¹¹⁻¹²But before the two boys were born, God told Rebek-

ah, "The older will serve the younger." This was before the boys had done anything good or bad. God said this so that the one chosen would be chosen because of God's own plan. He was chosen because he was the one God wanted to call, not because of anything he did. ¹³As the Scripture says, "I loved Jacob, but I hated Esau."

¹⁴So what should we say about this? Is God unfair? In no way. ¹⁵God said to Moses, "I will show kindness to anyone to whom I want to show kindness, and I will show mercy to anyone to whom I want to show mercy." ¹⁶So God will choose the one to whom he decides to show mercy; his choice does not depend on what people want or try to do. ¹⁷The Scripture says to the king of Egypt: "I made you king for this reason: to show my power in you so that my name will be talked about in all the earth." ¹⁸So God shows mercy where he wants to show mercy, and he makes stubborn the people he wants to make stubborn.

¹⁹So one of you will ask me: "Then why does God blame us for our sins? Who can fight his will?" ²⁰You are only human, and human beings have no right to question God. An object should not ask the person who made it, "Why did you make me like this?" ²¹The potter can make anything he wants to make. He can use the same clay to make one thing for special use and another thing for daily use.

²²It is the same way with God. He wanted to show his anger and to let people see his power. But he patiently stayed with

those people he was angry with—people who were due to be destroyed. ²³He waited with patience so that he could make known his rich glory to the people who receive his mercy. He has prepared these people to have his glory, ²⁴and we are those people whom God called. He called us not from the Jews only but also from those who are not Jews. ²⁵As the Scripture says in Hosea:

"I will say, 'You are my people'
    to those I had called 'not my people'.
And I will show my love
    to those people I did not love."

Hosea 2:1, 23

²⁶"They were called,
    'You are not my people',

but later they will be called
    'children of the living God'." *Hosea 1:10*
²⁷And Isaiah cries out about Israel:
"Israel, your people are many,
    like the grains of sand by the sea.
But only a few of them will be left alive to
    return to the LORD.
28   God has announced that he will
        destroy the land completely and
        fairly."   *Isaiah 10:22*
²⁹It is as Isaiah said:
"The Lord All-powerful
    allowed a few of our people to live.
Otherwise we would have been com-
        pletely destroyed
    like the cities of Sodom and
        Gomorrah."   *Isaiah 1:9*

Who did Paul want to believe (v 4)?

What would he be willing to give/do (v 3)?

How does Paul describe the people of Israel? Why are they important in God's plan (vs 4,5)?

Think

Who are the people you want to know God? List their names and remember to pray for them.

Pray

For the people on your list. Not just today but every time that you talk to God.

If you don't tell them

Think about this:

Every day you meet loads of people who never go to church and know very little about God. You are possibly the only Christian some people in your class will ever meet.

 Romans 9:30–10:21

³⁰So what does all this mean? Those who are not Jews were not trying to make themselves right with God, but they were made right with God because of their faith. ³¹The people of Israel tried to follow a law to make themselves right with God. But they did not succeed, ³²because they tried to make themselves right by the things they did instead of trusting in God to make them right. They stumbled over the stone that causes people to stumble. ³³As it is written in the Scripture:

"I will put in Jerusalem a stone that
    causes people to stumble,
a rock that makes them fall.
Anyone who trusts in it will never be
    disappointed."   *Isaiah 8:14; 28:16*

10 Brothers and sisters, the thing I want most is for all the Jews to be saved. That is my prayer to God. ²I can say this about them: they really try to follow God, but they do not know the right way. ³Because they did not know the way that God makes people right with him, they tried to make themselves right in their own way. So they did not accept God's way of making people right. ⁴Christ ended the law so that everyone who believes in him may be right with God.

⁵Moses describes how to be made right by following the law. He says, "A person who obeys these things will live because of them." ⁶But this is what the Scripture says about being made right through faith: "Don't say to yourself, 'Who will go up into heaven?'" (That means, "Who will go up to heaven and bring Christ down to earth?") ⁷"And do not say, 'Who will go down into the world below?'" (That means, "Who will go down and bring Christ up from the dead?") ⁸This is what the Scripture says: "The word is near you; it is in your mouth and in your heart." That is the teaching of faith that we are telling. ⁹If you use your mouth to say, "Jesus is Lord," and if you believe in your heart that God raised Jesus from the dead, you will be saved. ¹⁰We believe with our hearts, and so we are made right with God. And we use our mouths to say that we believe, and so we are saved. ¹¹As the Scripture says, "Anyone who trusts in him will never be disappointed." ¹²That Scripture says "anyone" because there is no difference between those who are Jews and those who are not. The same Lord is the Lord of all and gives many blessings to all who trust in him, ¹³as the Scripture says, "Anyone who calls on the Lord will be saved."

¹⁴But before people can ask the Lord for help, they must believe in him; and before they can believe in him, they must hear about him; and for them to hear about the Lord, someone must tell them; ¹⁵and before someone can go and tell them, that person must be sent. It is written,

"How beautiful is the person who comes to bring good news."

¹⁶But not all the Jews accepted the good news. As Isaiah said, "LORD, who believed what we told them?" ¹⁷So faith comes from hearing the Good News, and people hear the Good News when someone tells them about Christ.

¹⁸But I ask: Didn't people hear the Good News? Yes, they heard—as the Scripture says:

"Their message went out through all the world;

their words go everywhere on earth."

Psalm 19:4

¹⁹Again I ask: Didn't the people of Israel understand? Yes, they did understand. First, Moses says:

"So I will use those who are not a nation to make them jealous;

I will use a nation that does not understand to make them angry."

Deuteronomy 32:21

²⁰Then Isaiah is bold enough to say:

"I was found by those who were not asking me for help.

I said, 'Here I am. Here I am,' to a nation that was not praying to me."

Isaiah 65:1

²¹But about Israel God says,

"All day long I stood ready to accept people who turned against me."

Isaiah 65:2

What must we do to be saved (10:9)? (Note there is an outward action and an inner action here.)

Look again at 10:14,15. How can people hear about God, believe in him and come to know him?

Is the only way to tell people about God by saying words? Are actions more or less important?

Think

Think about some of the people you know at school or college. If you don't help them meet Jesus, who will?

Pray

Ask God to give you the courage to tell others about him.

Family tree

Do you see yourself as an individual Christian or as a member of God's people?

You are both and this passage shows how the two go together.

Romans 11:1–21

God Shows Mercy to All People

11 So I ask: Did God throw out his people? No! I myself am an Israelite from the family of Abraham, from the tribe of Benjamin. ²God chose the Israelites to be his people before they were born, and he has not thrown his people out. Surely you know what the Scripture says about Elijah, how he prayed to God against the people of Israel. ³"Lord," he said, "they have killed your prophets, and they have destroyed your altars. I am the only prophet left, and now they are trying to kill me too." ⁴But what answer did God give Elijah? He said, "But I have left 7,000 people in Israel who have never bowed down before Baal." ⁵It is the same now. There are a few people that God has chosen by his grace. ⁶And if he chose them by grace, it is not for the things they have done. If they could be made God's people by what they did, God's gift of grace would not really be a gift.

⁷So this is what has happened: although the Israelites tried to be right with God, they did not succeed, but the ones God chose did become right with him. The others were made stubborn and refused to listen to God. ⁸As it is written in the Scriptures:

"God gave the people a dull mind so
    they could not understand."
                        Isaiah 29:10
"But to this day the LORD has not given
    you a mind that understands;

you don't really understand what you
    see
with your eyes or hear with your ears."
                        Deuteronomy 29:4
⁹And David says:
"Let their own feasts trap them and
    cause their ruin;
    let their feasts cause them to stumble
        and be paid back.
¹⁰Let their eyes be closed so they cannot
    see
    and their backs be for ever weak from
        troubles."   *Psalm 69:22–23*

¹¹So I ask: when the Jews fell, did that fall destroy them? No! But their mistake brought salvation to those who are not Jews, in order to make the Jews jealous. ¹²The Jews' mistake brought rich blessings for the world, and the Jews' loss brought rich blessings for the non-Jewish people. So surely the world will receive much richer blessings when enough Jews become the kind of people God wants.

¹³Now I am speaking to you who are not Jews. I am an apostle to those who are not Jews, and since I have that work, I will make the most of it. ¹⁴I hope I can make my own people jealous and, in that way, help some of them to be saved. ¹⁵When God turned away from the Jews, he became friends with other people in the world. So when God accepts the Jews, surely that will bring them life after death.

¹⁶If the first piece of bread is offered to God, then the whole loaf is made holy. If

the roots of a tree are holy, then the tree's branches are holy too.

¹⁷It is as if some of the branches from an olive tree have been broken off. You non-Jewish people are like the branch of a wild olive tree that has been joined to that first tree. You now share the strength and life of the first tree, the Jews. ¹⁸So do not boast about those branches that were broken off. If you boast, remember that you do not support the root, but the root supports you. ¹⁹You will say, "Branches were broken off so that I could be joined to their tree." ²⁰That is true. But those branches were broken off because they did not believe, and you continue to be part of the tree only because you believe. Do not be proud, but be afraid. ²¹If God did not let the natural branches of that tree stay, then he will not let you stay if you don't believe.

What image does Paul use for God's people (v 17)?

Why were some branches broken off (v 20)?

What does Paul warn the church in Rome about (v 21)?

Think

Do you take your "belief" seriously?

Pray

Dear Lord, I thank you for your people, those who have gone before and those who believe now. I thank you that I am one of them.

Extra

The early church had its own problems. One of the most damaging was the division between Jewish and Gentile (non-Jewish) Christians. People from both groups were arguing over what a Christian should, or should not, do.

Not just a few nice songs...

How much of today are you going to spend worshipping? Show it by marking an "x" on the line below:

None of it ———————————————————— All of it!

Romans 11:22–12:8

²²So you see that God is kind and also very strict. He punishes those who stop following him. But God is kind to you, if you continue following in his kindness. If you do not, you will be cut off from the tree. ²³And if the Jews will believe in God again, he will accept them back. God is able to put them back where they were. ²⁴It is not natural for a wild branch to be part of a good tree. And you who are not Jews are like a branch cut from a wild olive tree and joined to a good olive tree. But since those Jews are like a branch that grew from the good tree, surely they can be joined to their own tree again.

²⁵I want you to understand this secret, brothers and sisters, so you will understand that you do not know everything: part of Israel has been made stubborn, but that will change when many who are not Jews have come to God. ²⁶And that is how all Israel will be saved. It is written in the Scriptures:

"Then a Saviour will come to Jerusalem
   and to the people of Jacob who have
      turned from sin.
²⁷This is how Israel's guilt will be forgiven;
   this is how its sins will be taken away."
                                      Isaiah 59:20–21; 27:9
²⁸The Jews refuse to accept the Good News, so they are God's enemies. This has

happened to help you who are not Jews. But the Jews are still God's chosen people, and he loves them very much because of the promises he made to their ancestors. ²⁹God never changes his mind about the people he calls and the things he gives them. ³⁰At one time you refused to obey God. But now you have received mercy, because those people refused to obey. ³¹And now the Jews refuse to obey, because God showed mercy to you. But this happened so that they also can receive mercy from him. ³²God has given all people over to their stubborn ways so that he can show mercy to all.

Praise to God

³³Yes, God's riches are very great, and his wisdom and knowledge have no end! No one can explain the things God decides or understand his ways. ³⁴As the Scripture says,

"Who has known the mind of the Lord
   or been able to give him advice?"
                                      Isaiah 40:13
³⁵"No one has ever given God anything
   that he must pay back."   *Job 41:11*
³⁶Yes, God made all things, and everything continues through him and for him. To him be the glory for ever! Amen.

Give Your Lives to God

12 So brothers and sisters, since God has shown us great mercy, I beg you to offer your lives as a living sacrifice to him. Your offering must be only for God and pleasing to him, which is the spiritual way for you to worship. ²Do not change yourselves to be like the people of this world, but be changed within by a new way of thinking. Then you will be able to decide what God wants for you; you will know what is good and pleasing to him and what is perfect. ³Because God has given me a special gift, I have something to say to everyone among you. Do not think you are better than you are. You must decide what you really are by the amount of faith God has given you. ⁴Each one of us has a body with many parts, and these parts all have different uses. ⁵In the same way, we are many, but in Christ we are all one body. Each one is a part of that body, and each part belongs to all the other parts. ⁶We all have different gifts, each of which came because of the grace God gave us. The person who has the gift of prophecy should use that gift in agreement with the faith. ⁷Anyone who has the gift of serving should serve. Anyone who has the gift of teaching should teach. ⁸Whoever has the gift of encouraging others should encourage. Whoever has the gift of giving to others should give freely. Anyone who has the gift of being a leader should try hard when he leads. Whoever has the gift of showing mercy to others should do so with joy.

So, real worship is much more than Sunday church stuff! You can worship all day, every day, by:

- giving your whole life to God (v ...)

- letting yourself be changed by him – starting with what goes on in your mind (v ...)

- using your gifts to serve other people (vs ...)

Think

Are you ready for this kind of worship?

Pray

Look carefully and honestly at the three points again – which ones are you up for? Ask God to help you worship him fully, and then start now!

Start loving

Want to be your best for God? Read on...

Romans 12:9–13:14

⁹Your love must be real. Hate what is evil, and hold on to what is good. ¹⁰Love each other like brothers and sisters. Give each other more honour than you want for yourselves. ¹¹Do not be lazy but work hard, serving the Lord with all your heart. ¹²Be joyful because you have hope. Be patient when trouble comes, and pray at all times. ¹³Share with God's people who need help. Bring strangers in need into your homes.

¹⁴Wish good for those who harm you; wish them well and do not curse them. ¹⁵Be happy with those who are happy, and be sad with those who are sad. ¹⁶Live in peace with each other. Do not be proud, but make friends with those who seem unimportant. Do not think how clever you are.

¹⁷If someone does wrong to you, do not pay him back by doing wrong to him. Try to do what everyone thinks is right. ¹⁸Do your best to live in peace with everyone. ¹⁹My friends, do not try to punish others when they wrong you, but wait for God to punish them with his anger. It is written: "I will punish those who do wrong; I will repay them," says the Lord. ²⁰But you should do this:

"If your enemy is hungry, feed him.
If he is thirsty, give him a drink.
Doing this will be like pouring burning coals on his head." *Proverbs 25:21–22*
²¹Do not let evil defeat you, but defeat evil by doing good.

Christians Should Obey the Law

13 All of you must yield to the government rulers. No one rules unless God has given him the power to rule, and no one rules now without that power from God. ²So those who are against the government are really against what God has commanded. And they will bring punishment on themselves. ³Those who do right do not have to fear the rulers; only those who do wrong fear them. Do you want to be unafraid of the rulers? Then do what is right, and they will praise you. ⁴The ruler is God's servant to help you. But if you do wrong, then be afraid. He has the power to punish; he is God's servant to punish those who do wrong. ⁵So you must yield to the government, not only because you might be punished, but because you know it is right.

⁶This is also why you pay taxes. Rulers are working for God and give their time to their work. ⁷Pay everyone, then, what you owe. If you owe any kind of tax, pay it. Show respect and honour to them all.

Loving Others

⁸Do not owe people anything, except always owe love to each other, because the person who loves others has obeyed all the law. ⁹The law says, "You must not be guilty of adultery. You must not murder anyone. You must not steal. You must not want to take your neighbour's things." All these commands and all others are really only one rule: "Love your neighbour as you love yourself." ¹⁰Love never hurts a neighbour, so loving is obeying all the law.

¹¹Do this because we live in an important time. It is now time for you to wake up from your sleep, because our salvation is nearer now than when we first believed. ¹²The "night" is almost finished, and the "day" is almost here. So we should stop

doing things that belong to darkness and take up the weapons used for fighting in the light. ¹³Let us live in a right way, like people who belong to the day. We should not have wild parties or get drunk. There should be no sexual sins of any kind, no fighting or jealousy. ¹⁴But clothe yourselves with the Lord Jesus Christ and forget about satisfying your sinful self.

It's all summed up at the end of 13:9. What could loving your neighbour mean for you today? Add some possible endings to this sentence: If you love someone, you will...

_____

_____

_____

Think

Look at 13:9,13. Maybe you think you could never be guilty of some of these things. Or perhaps you know that you *have* let God down. Talk to God about it.

Pray

Ask God to help you to "love" others and to be your best for him.

It doesn't harm anyone else!

How do you decide what is right and wrong? Do you ...

- ask your parents?
- do what your friends do?
- read the Bible?
- write to a magazine's letters' page?

 Romans 14:1–15:3

Do Not Criticise Other People

14 Accept into your group someone who is weak in faith, and do not argue about opinions. ²One person believes it is right to eat all kinds of food. But another, who is weak, believes it is right to eat only vegetables. ³The one who knows that it is right to eat any kind of food must not reject the one who eats only vegetables. And the person who eats only vegetables must not think that the one who eats all foods is wrong, because God has accepted that person. ⁴You cannot judge another person's servant. The master decides if the servant is doing well or not. And the Lord's servant will do well because the Lord helps him do well.

⁵Some think that one day is more important than another, and others think that every day is the same. Let all be sure in their own mind. ⁶Those who think one day is more important than other days are doing that for the Lord. And those who eat all kinds of food are doing that for the Lord, and they give thanks to God. Others who refuse to eat some foods do that for the Lord, and they give thanks to God. ⁷We do not live or die for ourselves. ⁸If we live, we are living for the Lord, and if we

die, we are dying for the Lord. So living or dying, we belong to the Lord.

⁹The reason Christ died and rose from the dead to live again was so he would be Lord over both the dead and the living. ¹⁰So why do you judge your brothers or sisters in Christ? And why do you think you are better than they are? We will all stand before God to be judged, ¹¹because it is written in the Scriptures:

"'As surely as I live,' says the Lord,
'Everyone will bow before me and will
promise to follow me.'" *Isaiah 45:23*
¹²So each of us will have to answer to God.

Do Not Cause Others to Sin

¹³For that reason we should stop judging each other. We must make up our minds not to do anything that will make another Christian sin. ¹⁴I am in the Lord Jesus, and I know that there is no food that is wrong to eat. But if a person believes something is wrong, that thing is wrong for him. ¹⁵If you hurt your brother's or sister's faith because of something you eat, you are not really following the way of love. Do not destroy someone's faith by eating food he thinks is wrong, because Christ died for him. ¹⁶Do not allow what you think is

good to become what others say is evil. [17]In the kingdom of God, eating and drinking are not important. The important things are living right with God, peace, and joy in the Holy Spirit. [18]Anyone who serves Christ by living this way is pleasing God and will be accepted by other people.

[19]So let us try to do what makes for peace and help one another. [20]Do not let the eating of food destroy the work of God. All foods are all right to eat, but it is wrong to eat food that causes someone else to sin. [21]It is better not to eat meat or drink wine or do anything that will cause your brother or sister to sin.

[22]Your beliefs about these things should be kept secret between you and God. People are happy if they can do what they think is right without feeling guilty. [23]But those who eat something without being sure it is right are wrong because they did not believe it was right. Anything that is done without believing it is right is a sin.

15 We who are strong in faith should help the weak with their weaknesses, and not please only ourselves. [2]Let each of us please our neighbours for their good, to help them be stronger in faith. [3]Even Christ did not live to please himself. It was as the Scriptures said: "When people insult you, it hurts me."

What is the danger in eating certain foods (14:15)?

What are you not doing if you hurt someone's faith (14:15)?

What are the important things (14:17)?

Think

In your life what things could cause other Christians' faith to be harmed?

Pray

That you will focus on God to guide you as to what you should and shouldn't do.

Extra

A big issue for early Christians was what they ate. Much of the food available, primarily meat, had been used in pagan temples as sacrifices. So the big issue was whether a Christian should eat such meat or not.

Help others

What is your motivation?

- How much money I can make
- How many people will like me
- How much I can help others

 Romans 15:4–29

⁴Everything that was written in the past was written to teach us. The Scriptures give us patience and encouragement so that we can have hope. ⁵Patience and encouragement come from God. And I pray that God will help you all agree with each other the way Christ Jesus wants. ⁶Then you will all be joined together, and you will give glory to God the Father of our Lord Jesus Christ. ⁷Christ accepted you, so you should accept each other, which will bring glory to God. ⁸I tell you that Christ became a servant of the Jews to show that God's promises to the Jewish ancestors are true. ⁹And he also did this so that those who are not Jews could give glory to God for the mercy he gives to them. It is written in the Scriptures:

"So I will praise you, LORD, among the nations.
I will sing praises to your name."
Psalm 18:49

¹⁰The Scripture also says,

"Be happy, you who are not Jews,
together with his people."
Deuteronomy 32:43

¹¹Again the Scripture says,

"All you nations, praise the LORD.
All you people, praise him." *Psalm 117:1*

¹²And Isaiah says,

"The new king will come from the family of Jesse
will stand as a banner for all peoples;
the nations will come together around him

and the place where he lives will be filled with glory."
Isaiah 11:10

¹³I pray that the God who gives hope will fill you with much joy and peace while you trust in him. Then your hope will overflow by the power of the Holy Spirit.

Paul Talks About His Work

¹⁴My brothers and sisters, I am sure that you are full of goodness. I know that you have all the knowledge you need and that you are able to teach each other. ¹⁵But I have written to you very openly about some things I wanted you to remember. I did this because God gave me this special gift: ¹⁶to be a minister of Christ Jesus to those who are not Jews. I served God by teaching his Good News, so that the non-Jewish people could be an offering that God would accept—an offering made holy by the Holy Spirit.

¹⁷So I am proud of what I have done for God in Christ Jesus. ¹⁸I will not talk about anything except what Christ has done through me in leading those who are not Jews to obey God. They have obeyed God because of what I have said and done, ¹⁹because of the power of miracles and the great things they saw, and because of the power of the Holy Spirit. I preached the Good News from Jerusalem all the way around to Illyricum, and so I have finished that part of my work. ²⁰I always want to preach the Good News in places where people have never heard of Christ, because

I do not want to build on the work someone else has already started. 21But it is written in the Scriptures:

"Those who were not told about him will see,

and those who have not heard about him will understand." *Isaiah 52:15*

Paul's Plan to Visit Rome

22This is the reason I was stopped many times from coming to you. 23Now I have finished my work here. Since for many years I have wanted to come to you, 24I hope to visit you on my way to Spain. After I enjoy being with you for a while, I hope you can help me on my trip. 25Now I am going to Jerusalem to help God's people. 26The believers in Macedonia and Southern Greece were happy to give their money to help the poor among God's people at Jerusalem. 27They were happy to do this, and really they owe it to them. These who are not Jews have shared in the Jews' spiritual blessings, so they should use their material possessions to help the Jews. 28After I am sure the poor in Jerusalem get the money that has been given for them, I will leave for Spain and visit you on the way. 29I know that when I come to you I will bring Christ's full blessing.

What should the motivation of those strong in faith be?

What is Paul's prayer (v 5)?

Where can the church find help to be joined together (v 4)?

Paul wanted a unified church to praise God. What would Paul say about your church?

Think

Are you someone who is strong or weak in faith?

Pray

That you will either be able to give help to the weak or find help from the strong.

An open secret

Got any secrets? Go on you can tell me, no one will find out, I can be trusted!

How good are you at keeping secrets? Are you the sort of person others confide in? Or are you the sort of person people tell things to when they need to get the news around quickly?

Romans 15:30–16:27

30Brothers and sisters, I beg you to help me in my work by praying to God for me. Do this because of our Lord Jesus and the love that the Holy Spirit gives us. 31Pray that I will be saved from the non-believers in Judea and that this help I bring to Jerusalem will please God's people there. 32Then, if God wants me to, I will come to you with joy, and together you and I will have a time of rest. 33The God who gives peace be with you all. Amen.

Greetings to the Christians

16 I recommend to you our sister Phoebe, who is a helper in the church in Cenchrea. 2I ask you to accept her in the Lord in the way God's people should. Help her with anything she needs, because she has helped me and many other people also.

3Give my greetings to Priscilla and Aquila, who work together with me in Christ Jesus 4and who risked their own lives to save my life. I am thankful to them, and all the non-Jewish churches are thankful as well. 5Also, greet for me the church that meets at their house.

Greetings to my dear friend Epenetus, who was the first person in the country of Asia to follow Christ. 6Greetings to Mary, who worked very hard for you. 7Greetings to Andronicus and Junias, my relatives, who were in prison with me. They are very important apostles. They were believers in Christ before I was. 8Greetings to Ampliatus, my dear friend in the Lord. 9Greetings to Urbanus, a worker together with me for Christ. And greetings to my dear friend Stachys. 10Greetings to Apelles, who was tested and proved that he truly loves Christ. Greetings to all those who are in the family of Aristobulus. 11Greetings to Herodion, my fellow citizen. Greetings to all those in the family of Narcissus who belong to the Lord. 12Greetings to Tryphena and Tryphosa, women who work very hard for the Lord. Greetings to my dear friend Persis, who also has worked very hard for the Lord. 13Greetings to Rufus, who is a special person in the Lord, and to his mother, who has been like a mother to me also. 14Greetings to Asyncritus, Phlegon, Hermes, Patrobas, Hermas and all the brothers who are with them. 15Greetings to Philologus and Julia, Nereus and his sister, and Olympas, and to all God's people with them. 16Greet each other with a holy kiss. All of Christ's churches send greetings to you.

17Brothers and sisters, I ask you to look out for those who cause people to be against each other and who upset other people's faith. They are against the true teaching you learned, so stay away from them. 18Such people are not serving our Lord Christ but are only doing what pleases themselves. They use fancy talk and fine words to fool the minds of those who do not know about evil. ¹⁹All the believers have heard that you obey, so I am very happy because of you. But I want you to be wise in what is good and innocent in what is evil.

²⁰The God who brings peace will soon defeat Satan and give you power over him.

The grace of our Lord Jesus be with you.

²¹Timothy, a worker together with me, sends greetings, as well as Lucius, Jason and Sosipater, my relatives.

²²I am Tertius, and I am writing this letter from Paul. I send greetings to you in the Lord.

²³Gaius is letting me and the whole church here use his home. He also sends greetings to you, as do Erastus, the city treasurer, and our brother Quartus. ²⁴

²⁵Glory to God who can make you strong in faith by the Good News that I tell people and by the message about Jesus Christ. The message about Christ is the secret that was hidden for long ages past but is now made known. ²⁶It has been made clear through the writings of the prophets. And by the command of the eternal God it is made known to all nations that they might believe and obey.

²⁷To the only wise God be glory for ever through Jesus Christ! Amen.

God can't keep a good thing secret! What's the secret he's let out?

How can we find out about it?

What can it do for us?

Think

What would be a sign of strong faith and what would be a sign of weak faith (16:19,25)?

Pray

Look how Paul finishes his letter. Praise God that he is helping you get to know him, because of what Jesus has done for you.

We're all different

Do you know everyone in your church? Find out ...

- who is the oldest/youngest person?
- how many different places people come from?
- what types of music people like?
- what teams people support?

Sometimes it's not easy getting along with people who're different from you ...

1 Corinthians 1:1–25

1 From Paul. God called me to be an apostle of Christ Jesus because that is what God wanted. Also from Sosthenes, our brother in Christ.

²To the church of God in Corinth, to you who have been made holy in Christ Jesus. You were called to be God's holy people with all people everywhere who pray in the name of the Lord Jesus Christ—their Lord and ours:

³Grace and peace to you from God our Father and the Lord Jesus Christ.

Paul Gives Thanks to God

⁴I always thank my God for you because of the grace God has given you in Christ Jesus. ⁵I thank God because in Christ you have been made rich in every way, in all your speaking and in all your knowledge. ⁶Just as our witness about Christ has been proved to you, ⁷so you have every gift from God while you wait for our Lord Jesus Christ to come again. ⁸Jesus will keep you strong until the end so that there will be no wrong in you on the day our Lord Jesus Christ comes again. ⁹God, who has called you to share everything with his Son, Jesus Christ our Lord, is faithful.

Problems in the Church

¹⁰I beg you, brothers and sisters, by the name of our Lord Jesus Christ that all of you agree with each other and not be split into groups. I beg that you be completely joined together by having the same kind of thinking and the same purpose. ¹¹My brothers and sisters, some people from Chloe's family have told me quite plainly that there are quarrels among you. ¹²This is what I mean: one of you says, "I follow Paul"; another says, "I follow Apollos"; another says, "I follow Peter"; and another says, "I follow Christ." ¹³Christ has been divided up into different groups! Did Paul die on the cross for you? No! Were you baptised in the name of Paul? No! ¹⁴I thank God I did not baptise any of you except Crispus and Gaius ¹⁵so that now no one can say you were baptised in my name. ¹⁶(I also baptised the family of Stephanas, but I do not remember that I baptised anyone else.) ¹⁷Christ did not send me to baptise people but to preach the Good News. And he sent me to preach the Good News without using words of human wisdom so that the cross of Christ would not lose its power.

Christ is God's Power and Wisdom

18The teaching about the cross is foolishness to those who are being lost, but to us who are being saved it is the power of God. 19It is written in the Scriptures:

"Their wise men will lose their wisdom;
their wise men will not be able to
understand." *Isaiah 29:14*

20Where is the wise person? Where is the educated person? Where is the skilled talker of this world? God has made the wisdom of the world foolish. 21Because of the wisdom of God the world did not know God through its own wisdom. So God chose to use the message that sounds foolish to save those who believe. 22The Jews ask for miracles, and the Greeks want wisdom. 23But we preach a crucified Christ. This is a big problem to the Jews, and it is foolishness to those who are not Jews. 24But Christ is the power of God and the wisdom of God to those people God has called—Jews and Greeks. 25Even the foolishness of God is wiser than human wisdom, and the weakness of God is stronger than human strength.

What did Paul say the Corinthians should do (v 10)?

Who else wants us to behave like this (v 10)?

Are there any current arguments in your church? Do you see anything in this passage which could help?

Think

Is there a difference between a quarrel and a disagreement? Can we be united and yet still disagree?

Pray

Choose two people in your church and pray for them today.

Favourite teacher

Who's yours? Mine was a Latin teacher who made a dead language interesting and understandable!

Why is your favourite teacher so good?

 1 Corinthians 1:26–2:16

26Brothers and sisters, look at what you were when God called you. Not many of you were wise in the way the world judges wisdom. Not many of you had great influence. Not many of you came from important families. 27But God chose the foolish things of the world to shame the wise, and he chose the weak things of the world to shame the strong. 28He chose what the world thinks is unimportant and what the world looks down on and thinks is nothing in order to destroy what the world thinks is important. 29God did this so that no one can boast in his presence. 30Because of God you are in Christ Jesus, who has become for us wisdom from God. In Christ we are put right with God, and have been made holy, and have been set free from sin. 31So, as the Scripture says, "If someone wants to boast, he should boast only about the Lord."

The Message of Christ's Death

2 Dear brothers and sisters, when I came to you, I did not come preaching God's secret with fancy words or a show of human wisdom. 2I decided that while I was with you I would forget about everything except Jesus Christ and his death on the cross. 3So when I came to you, I was weak and fearful and trembling. 4My teaching and preaching were not with words of human wisdom that persuade people but with proof of the power that the Spirit gives. 5This was so that your faith would be in God's power and not in human wisdom.

God's Wisdom

6However, I speak a wisdom to those who are mature. But this wisdom is not from this world or from the rulers of this world, who are losing their power. 7I speak God's secret wisdom, which he has kept hidden. Before the world began, God planned this wisdom for our glory. 8None of the rulers of this world understood it. If they had, they would not have crucified the Lord of glory. 9But as it is written in the Scriptures:

"From long ago no one
    has ever heard of a God like you.
No one has ever seen
    a God besides you,
    who helps the people who trust you."

Isaiah 64:4

10But God has shown us these things through the Spirit.

The Spirit searches out all things, even the deep secrets of God. 11Who knows the thoughts that another person has? Only a person's spirit that lives within him knows his thoughts. It is the same with God. No one knows the thoughts of God except the Spirit of God. 12Now we did not receive the spirit of the world, but we received the Spirit that is from God so that we can know all that God has given us. 13And we speak about these things, not with words taught us by human wisdom but with words taught us by the Spirit. And so we explain spiritual truths to spiritual people. [14]A person who does not have the Spirit does not accept the truths that come from the Spirit of God. That person thinks they are foolish and cannot understand them, because they can only be judged to be true by the Spirit. [15]The spiritual person is able to judge all things, but no one can judge him. The Scripture says:

[16]"Who has known the mind of the LORD or been able to give him advice?"

Isaiah 40:13

But we have the mind of Christ.

What does the Holy Spirit teach us (2:11,12)?

What does he train us for?

Find these:

- to speak for God

- to make good judgements about things

Think

Do you know how you learn best? Are you a pictures or words person? Visual or audio?

Pray

Ask God to help you learn more about him, as the Holy Spirit teaches you.

In the public eye?

Think of some famous sporting celebrities. They'd probably be nowhere if it wasn't for the rest of their teams, managers, trainers, physios ...

1 Corinthians 3:1–4:5

Following People is Wrong

3 Brothers and sisters, in the past I could not talk to you as I talk to spiritual people. I had to talk to you as I would to people without the Spirit—babies in Christ. 2The teaching I gave you was like milk, not solid food, because you were not able to take solid food. And even now you are not ready. 3You are still not spiritual, because there is jealousy and quarrelling among you, and this shows that you are not spiritual. You are acting like people of the world. 4One of you says, "I belong to Paul," and another says, "I belong to Apollos." When you say things like this, you are acting like people of the world.

5Is Apollos important? No! Is Paul important? No! We are only servants of God who helped you believe. Each one of us did the work God gave us to do. 6I planted the seed, and Apollos watered it. But God is the One who made it grow. 7So the one who plants is not important, and the one who waters is not important. Only God, who makes things grow, is important. 8The one who plants and the one who waters have the same purpose, and each will be rewarded for his own work. 9We are God's workers, working together; you are like God's farm, God's house.

10Using the gift God gave me, I laid the foundation of that house like an expert builder. Others are building on that foundation, but all people should be careful how they build on it. 11The foundation that has already been laid is Jesus Christ, and no one can lay down any other foundation. 12But if people build on that foundation, using gold, silver, jewels, wood, grass or straw, 13their work will be clearly seen, because the Day of Judgement will make it seen. That Day will appear with fire, and the fire will test everyone's work to show what sort of work it was. 14If the building that has been put on the foundation still stands, the builder will get a reward. 15But if the building is burned up, the builder will suffer loss. The builder will be saved, but it will be as one who escaped from a fire.

16Don't you know that you are God's temple and that God's Spirit lives in you? 17If anyone destroys God's temple, God will destroy that person, because God's temple is holy and you are that temple.

18Do not fool yourselves. If you think you are wise in this world, you should become a fool so that you can become truly wise, 19because the wisdom of this world is foolishness with God. It is written in the Scriptures, "He catches those who are wise in their own clever traps." 20It is also written in the Scriptures, "The Lord knows what wise people think. He knows their thoughts are just a puff of wind." 21So you should not boast about human leaders. All things belong to you: 22Paul, Apollos and Peter; the world, life, death, the present and the future—all these belong to you. 23And you belong to Christ, and Christ belongs to God.

Apostles are Servants of Christ

4 People should think of us as servants of Christ, the ones God has trusted with his secrets. [2]Now in this way those who are trusted with something valuable must show they are worthy of that trust. [3]As for myself, I do not care if I am judged by you or by any human court. I do not even judge myself. [4]I know of no wrong I have done, but this does not make me right before the Lord. The Lord is the One who judges me. [5]So do not judge before the right time; wait until the Lord comes. He will bring to light things that are now hidden in darkness, and will make known the secret purposes of people's hearts. Then God will praise each one of them.

In the Christian world, too, there are loads of well-known people – as well as the backroom boys, who work faithfully for God but will probably never be famous in this life.

According to Paul, what should each person avoid doing (4:5)?

Who really matters (3:7)?

How should we think of each other (3:9)?

Think

Do you see yourself as someone "working" in your church or as a spectator? Do you want that to change?

Pray

Ask God to show you what he wants you to do in, and for, his kingdom – and to help you do it.

Are you a "tutter"?

What sort of Christian are you?

- Do you believe you know it all?
- Do you feel better than other Christians?
- Are you good at pointing out other people's wrongs?

1 Corinthians 4:6–5:8

⁶Brothers and sisters, I have used Apollos and myself as examples so you could learn through us the meaning of the saying, "Follow only what is written in the Scriptures." Then you will not be more proud of one person than another. ⁷Who says you are better than others? What do you have that was not given to you? And if it was given to you, why do you boast as if you did not receive it as a gift?

⁸You think you already have everything you need. You think you are rich. You think you have become kings without us. I wish you really were kings so we could be kings together with you. ⁹But it seems to me that God has put us apostles in last place, like those sentenced to die. We are like a show for the whole world to see— angels and people. ¹⁰We are fools for Christ's sake, but you are very wise in Christ. We are weak, but you are strong. You receive honour, but we are shamed. ¹¹Even to this very hour we do not have enough to eat or drink or to wear. We are often beaten, and we have no homes in which to live. ¹²We work hard with our own hands for our food. When people curse us, we bless them. When they hurt us, we put up with it. ¹³When they tell evil lies about us, we speak nice words about them. Even today, we are treated as though we were the rubbish of the world—the scum of the earth.

¹⁴I am not trying to make you feel ashamed. I am writing this to give you a warning as my own dear children. ¹⁵For though you may have 10,000 teachers in Christ, you do not have many fathers. Through the Good News I became your father in Christ Jesus, ¹⁶so I beg you, please follow my example. ¹⁷That is why I am sending to you Timothy, my son in the Lord. I love Timothy, and he is faithful. He will help you remember my way of life in Christ Jesus, just as I teach it in all the churches everywhere.

¹⁸Some of you have become proud, thinking that I will not come to you again. ¹⁹But I will come to you very soon if the Lord wishes. Then I will know what the proud ones do, not what they say, ²⁰because the kingdom of God is present not in talk but in power. ²¹Which do you want: that I come to you with punishment or with love and gentleness?

Wickedness in the Church

5 It is actually being said that there is sexual sin among you. And it is a kind that does not happen even among people who do not know God. A man there has his father's wife. ²And you are proud! You should have been filled with sadness so that the man who did this should be put out of your group. ³I am not there with you in person, but I am with you in spirit. And I have already judged the man who did that sin as if I were really there. ⁴When you

meet together in the name of our Lord Jesus, and I meet with you in spirit with the power of our Lord Jesus, ⁵then hand this man over to Satan. So his sinful self will be destroyed, and his spirit will be saved on the day of the Lord.

⁶Your boasting is not good. You know the saying, "Just a little yeast makes the whole batch of dough rise." ⁷Take out all the old yeast so that you will be a new batch of dough without yeast, which you really are. For Christ, our Passover lamb, has been sacrificed. ⁸So let us celebrate this feast, but not with the bread that has the old yeast—the yeast of sin and wickedness. Let us celebrate this feast with the bread that has no yeast—the bread of goodness and truth.

What is not good in the Corinthian church (5:6)?

What is the problem with the old yeast (5:8)?

Paul likes using metaphors and he goes for it here. Yeast causes the loaf of bread to rise. In the same way a little sin will make the whole life fall.

Think

The Corinthians were boasting despite getting things wrong. Is there anything you need to sort out in your life?

Pray

That God will help you ditch the bad yeast in your life.

What! No sex?

Maybe sex is a million miles from where you're at, right now...
On the other hand, maybe stuff in conversations or on TV is raising
questions for you. It can get confusing...

1 Corinthians 5:9–6:20

⁹I wrote to you in my earlier letter not to associate with those who sin sexually. ¹⁰But I did not mean you should not associate with those of this world who sin sexually, or with the greedy, or robbers, or those who worship idols. To get away from them you would have to leave this world. ¹¹I am writing to tell you that you must not associate with those who call themselves believers in Christ but who sin sexually, or are greedy, or worship idols, or abuse others with words, or get drunk, or cheat people. Do not even eat with people like that.

¹²⁻¹³It is not my business to judge those who are not part of the church. God will judge them. But you must judge the people who are part of the church. The Scripture says, "You must get rid of the evil person among you."

Judging Problems Among Christians

6 When you have something against another Christian, how can you bring yourself to go before judges who are not right with God? Why do you not let God's people decide who is right? ²Surely you know that God's people will judge the world. So if you are to judge the world, are you not able to judge small cases as well? ³You know that in the future we will judge angels, so surely we can judge the ordinary things of this life. ⁴If you have ordinary cases that must be judged, are you going to appoint people as judges who mean nothing to the church? ⁵I say this to shame you. Surely there is someone among you wise enough to judge a complaint between believers. ⁶But now one believer goes to court against another believer—and you do this in front of unbelievers!

⁷The fact that you have lawsuits against each other shows that you are already defeated. Why not let yourselves be wronged? Why not let yourselves be cheated? ⁸But you yourselves do wrong and cheat, and you do this to other believers!

⁹⁻¹⁰Surely you know that the people who do wrong will not inherit God's kingdom. Do not be fooled. Those who sin sexually, worship idols, take part in adultery, those who are male prostitutes or men who have sexual relations with other men, those who steal, are greedy, get drunk, lie about others or rob—these people will not inherit God's kingdom. ¹¹In the past, some of you were like that, but you were washed clean. You were made holy, and you were made right with God in the name of the Lord Jesus Christ and in the Spirit of our God.

Use Your Bodies for God's Glory

¹²"I am allowed to do all things," but all things are not good for me to do. "I am allowed to do all things," but I will not let anything make me its slave. ¹³"Food is for the stomach, and the stomach for food," but God will destroy them both. The body is not for sexual sin but for the Lord, and the Lord is for the body. ¹⁴By his power God has raised the Lord from the dead and will also raise us from the dead. ¹⁵Surely you know that your bodies are

parts of Christ himself. So I must never take the parts of Christ and join them to a prostitute! ¹⁶It is written in the Scriptures, "The two will become one body." So you should know that anyone who joins with a prostitute becomes one body with the prostitute. ¹⁷But the one who joins with the Lord is one spirit with the Lord.

¹⁸So run away from sexual sin. Every other sin people do is outside their bodies, but those who sin sexually sin against their own bodies. ¹⁹You should know that your body is a temple for the Holy Spirit who is in you. You have received the Holy Spirit from God. So you do not belong to yourselves, ²⁰because you were bought by God for a price. So honour God with your bodies.

Paul is talking about "sexual sin" (6:18) – sex outside of marriage.

Who does it hurt (6:18)?

What should you remember if you're tempted to sin "against your body" (6:19)?

What did Jesus do so you could be put right with God (6:20)?

Think

How could realising that the Holy Spirit lives in you make a difference to how you live?

Pray

Clean me up, Lord, so that my life makes a good home for your Spirit. Help me to honour you in all I do.

Your best shot

Do you have any idea how you're going to end up? What you're going to be doing? Who you're going to end up with?

1 Corinthians 7:1–24

About Marriage

7 Now I will discuss the things you wrote to me about. It is good for a man not to have sexual relations with a woman. ²But because sexual sin is a danger, each man should have his own wife, and each woman should have her own husband. ³The husband should give his wife all that he owes her as his wife. And the wife should give her husband all that she owes him as her husband. ⁴The wife does not have full rights over her own body; her husband shares them. And the husband does not have full rights over his own body; his wife shares them. ⁵Do not refuse to give your bodies to each other, unless you both agree to stay away from sexual relations for a time so you can give your time to prayer. Then come together again so Satan cannot tempt you because of a lack of self-control. ⁶I say this to give you permission to stay away from sexual relations for a time. It is not a command to do so. ⁷I wish that everyone were like me, but each person has his own gift from God. One has one gift, another has another gift.

⁸Now for those who are not married and for the widows I say this: it is good for them to stay unmarried as I am. ⁹But if they cannot control themselves, they should marry. It is better to marry than to burn with sexual desire.

¹⁰Now I give this command for the married people. (The command is not from me; it is from the Lord.) A wife should not leave her husband. ¹¹But if she does leave, she must not marry again, or she should make up with her husband. Also the husband should not divorce his wife.

¹²For all the others I say this (I am saying this, not the Lord): if a Christian man has a wife who is not a believer, and she is happy to live with him, he must not divorce her. ¹³And if a Christian woman has a husband who is not a believer, and he is happy to live with her, she must not divorce him. ¹⁴The husband who is not a believer is made holy through his believing wife. And the wife who is not a believer is made holy through her believing husband. If this were not true, your children would not be clean, but now your children are holy.

¹⁵But if those who are not believers decide to leave, let them leave. When this happens, the Christian man or woman is free. But God called us to live in peace. ¹⁶Wife, you don't know; maybe you will save your husband. And husband, you don't know; maybe you will save your wife.

Live as God Called You

¹⁷But in any case each one of you should continue to live the way God has given you to live—the way you were when God called you. This is a rule I make in all the churches. ¹⁸If a man was already circumcised when he was called, he should not undo his circumcision. If a man was without circumcision when he was called, he should not be circumcised. ¹⁹It is not important if a man is circumcised or not. The important thing is obeying God's

commands. ²⁰Each one of you should stay the way you were when God called you. ²¹If you were a slave when God called you, do not let that bother you. But if you can be free, then make good use of your freedom. ²²Those who were slaves when the Lord called them are free persons who belong to the Lord. In the same way, those who were free when they were called are now Christ's slaves. ²³You all were bought at a great price, so do not become slaves of people. ²⁴Brothers and sisters, each of you should stay as you were when you were called, and stay there with God.

However things turn out for you, it's up to you to do the best with what you've got. It doesn't matter who you are, or who you're in a relationship with (although it's for the best if you get together with another Christian), what you have to do is use what you've got for God's glory in whatever way you can.

Think

You've got no idea what you're going to be doing in twenty years or who your life partner might be – if you have one at all. Just remember to live for God, and it'll all work out.

Pray

Lord, I know it's all in your hands. Help me to trust you with my life.

Blind date

Everywhere we look we are bombarded with images that say in order to be happy and complete you need a partner. We're obsessed with looking our best and being attractive to each other. Now this is natural but...

 1 Corinthians 7:25–8:8

Questions About Getting Married

25Now I write about people who are not married. I have no command from the Lord about this; I give my opinion. But I can be trusted, because the Lord has shown me mercy. 26The present time is a time of trouble, so I think it is good for you to stay the way you are. 27If you have a wife, do not try to become free from her. If you are not married, do not try to find a wife. 28But if you decide to marry, you have not sinned. And if a girl who has never married decides to marry, she has not sinned. But those who marry will have trouble in this life, and I want you to be free from trouble.

29Brothers and sisters, this is what I mean: we do not have much time left. So starting now, those who have wives should live as if they had no wives. 30Those who are crying should live as if they were not crying. Those who are happy should live as if they were not happy. Those who buy things should live as if they own nothing. 31Those who use the things of the world should live as if they were not using them, because this world in its present form will soon be gone.

32I want you to be free from worry. A man who is not married is busy with the Lord's work, trying to please the Lord. 33But a man who is married is busy with things of the world, trying to please his wife. 34He must think about two things—pleasing his wife and pleasing the Lord. A woman who is not married or a girl who has never married is busy with the Lord's work. She wants to be holy in body and spirit. But a married woman is busy with things of the world, as to how she can please her husband. 35I am saying this to help you, not to limit you. But I want you to live in the right way, to give yourselves fully to the Lord without concern for other things.

36If a man thinks he is not doing the right thing with the girl he is engaged to, if she is almost past the best age to marry and he feels he should marry her, he should do what he wants. They should get married. It is no sin. 37But if a man is sure in his mind that there is no need for marriage, and has his own desires under control, and has decided not to marry the one to whom he is engaged, he is doing the right thing. 38So the man who marries his girl does right, but the man who does not marry will do better.

39A woman must stay with her husband as long as he lives. But if her husband dies, she is free to marry any man she wants, but she must marry in the Lord. 40The woman is happier if she does not marry again. This is my opinion, but I believe I also have God's Spirit.

About Food Offered to Idols

8 Now I will write about meat that is sacrificed to idols. We know that "we

all have knowledge." Knowledge puffs you up with pride, but love builds up. ²If you think you know something, you do not yet know anything as you should. ³But if any person loves God, that person is known by God.

⁴So this is what I say about eating meat sacrificed to idols: we know that an idol is really nothing in the world, and we know there is only one God. ⁵Even though there are things called gods, in heaven or on earth (and there are many "gods" and "lords"), ⁶for us there is only one God—our Father. All things came from him, and we live for him. And there is only one Lord—Jesus Christ. All things were made through him, and we also were made through him.

⁷But not all people know this. Some people are still so used to idols that when they eat meat, they still think of it as being sacrificed to an idol. Because their conscience is weak, when they eat it, they feel guilty. ⁸But food will not bring us closer to God. Refusing to eat does not make us less pleasing to God, and eating does not make us better in God's sight.

What does Paul want us to be (7:32)?

What does a married person have to be busy with (7:33,34)?

How does Paul want us to live (7:35)?

Think

Where do you see yourself in five or ten years? Married with a family? Is that your only option?

Pray

Ask God to guide you into relationships that are right so that you can give yourself fully to him.

Free to have rules

Why do sports have lots of rules? I mean, does football need the rules saying that you shouldn't trip someone up, or shove them over? If we know what is right, why do we need the rules?

1 Corinthians 8:9–9:18

9But be careful that your freedom does not cause those who are weak in faith to fall into sin. 10You have "knowledge", so you have freedom to eat in an idol's temple. But someone who is weak in faith might see you eating there and be encouraged to eat meat sacrificed to idols while thinking it is wrong to do so. 11This weak believer for whom Christ died is ruined because of your "knowledge". 12When you sin against your brothers and sisters in Christ like this and cause them to do what they feel is wrong, you are also sinning against Christ. 13So if the food I eat causes them to fall into sin, I will never eat meat again so that I will not cause any of them to sin.

Paul is like the Other Apostles

9 I am a free man. I am an apostle. I have seen Jesus our Lord. You people are all an example of my work in the Lord. 2If others do not accept me as an apostle, surely you do, because you are proof that I am an apostle in the Lord.

3This is the answer I give people who want to judge me: 4do we not have the right to eat and drink? 5Do we not have the right to bring a believing wife with us when we travel as do the other apostles and the Lord's brothers and Peter? 6Are Barnabas and I the only ones who must work to earn our living? 7No soldier ever serves in the army and pays his own salary. No one ever plants a vineyard without eating some of the grapes. No person takes care of a flock without drinking some of the milk.

8I do not say this by human authority; God's law also says the same thing. 9It is written in the law of Moses: "When an ox is working in the grain, do not cover its mouth to keep it from eating." When God said this, was he thinking only about oxen? No. 10He was really talking about us. Yes, that Scripture was written for us, because it goes on to say: "The one who ploughs and the one who works in the grain should hope to get some of the grain for their work." 11Since we planted spiritual seed among you, is it too much if we should harvest from you some things for this life? 12If others have the right to get something from you, surely we have this right, too. But we do not use it. No, we put up with everything ourselves so that we will not keep anyone from believing the Good News of Christ. 13Surely you know that those who work at the Temple get their food from the Temple, and those who serve at the altar get part of what is offered at the altar. 14In the same way, the Lord has commanded that those who tell the Good News should get their living from this work.

15But I have not used any of these rights. And I am not writing this now to get anything from you. I would rather die than have my reason for boasting taken away. 16Telling the Good News does not give me any reason for boasting. Telling the Good

News is my duty—something I must do. And how terrible it will be for me if I do not tell the Good News. [17]If I preach because it is my own choice, I have a reward. But if I preach and it is not my choice to do so, I am only doing the duty that was given to me. [18]So what reward do I get? This is my reward: that when I tell the Good News I can offer it freely. I do not use my full rights in my work of preaching the Good News.

What can freedom cause us to do (8:9)?

If a "weak" believer copies you what might happen (8:11)?

Who do we sin against (8:12)?

Think

Is there anything in your life which could cause someone else to sin or break the rules?

Pray

Ask God to show you the importance of showing others what is right and wrong through the way you act.

Get in training!

If you want to take a pastime activity seriously you need to work at it. If you want to win a race you need to train. If you want to be a grand master at chess you need to work at it.

Want to win a race?

What have you got to do?

1 Corinthians 9:19–10:22

¹⁹I am free and belong to no one. But I make myself a slave to all people to win as many as I can. ²⁰To the Jews I became like a Jew to win the Jews. I myself am not ruled by the law. But to those who are ruled by the law I became like a person who is ruled by the law. I did this to win those who are ruled by the law. ²¹To those who are without the law I became like a person who is without the law. I did this to win those people who are without the law. (But really, I am not without God's law—I am ruled by Christ's law.) ²²To those who are weak, I became weak so I could win the weak. I have become all things to all people so I could save some of them in any way possible. ²³I do all this because of the Good News and so I can share in its blessings.

²⁴You know that in a race all the runners run, but only one gets the prize. So run to win! ²⁵All those who compete in the games use self-control so they can win a crown. That crown is an earthly thing that lasts only a short time, but our crown will never be destroyed. ²⁶So I do not run without a goal. I fight like a boxer who is hitting something—not just the air. ²⁷I treat my body hard and make it my slave so that I myself will not be rejected after I have preached to others.

Warnings from Israel's Past

10 Brothers and sisters, I want you to know what happened to our ancestors who followed Moses. They were all under the cloud and all went through the sea. ²They were all baptised as followers of Moses in the cloud and in the sea. ³They all ate the same spiritual food, ⁴and all drank the same spiritual drink. They drank from that spiritual rock that followed them, and that rock was Christ. ⁵But God was not pleased with most of them, so they died in the desert.

⁶And these things happened as examples for us, to stop us from wanting evil things as those people did. ⁷Do not worship idols, as some of them did. Just as it is written in the Scriptures: "They sat down to eat and drink, and then they got up and sinned sexually." ⁸We must not take part in sexual sins, as some of them did. In one day 23,000 of them died because of their sins. ⁹We must not test Christ as some of them did; they were killed by snakes. ¹⁰Do not complain as some of them did; they were killed by the angel that destroys.

¹¹The things that happened to those people are examples. They were written down to teach us, because we live in a time when all these things of the past have

reached their goal. ¹²If you think you are strong, you should be careful not to fall. ¹³The only temptation that has come to you is that which everyone has. But you can trust God, who will not let you be tempted more than you can stand. But when you are tempted, he will also give you a way to escape so that you will be able to stand it.

¹⁴So, my dear friends, run away from the worship of idols. ¹⁵I am speaking to you as to intelligent people; judge for yourselves what I say. ¹⁶We give thanks for the cup of blessing, which is a sharing in the blood of Christ. And the bread that we break is a sharing in the body of Christ. ¹⁷Because there is one loaf of bread, we who are many are one body, because we all share that one loaf.

¹⁸Think about the Israelites: do not those who eat the sacrifices share in the altar? ¹⁹I do not mean that the food sacrificed to an idol is important. I do not mean that an idol is anything at all. ²⁰But I say that what is sacrificed to idols is offered to demons, not to God. And I do not want you to share anything with demons. ²¹You cannot drink the cup of the Lord and the cup of demons also. You cannot share in the Lord's table and the table of demons. ²²Are we trying to make the Lord jealous? We are not stronger than he is, are we?

Serious about living for God? Then you've got to get training.

The good news: training can be fun. Worship, praying, reading the Bible, helping others, telling people about Jesus – they're all things you can do with others.

The bad news: training is hard work (9:27).

Think

What's your main need for "training"? What could you do about it?

Pray

Ask God to help you with your training programme, both in motivation and application.

I don't need no rules

When we follow Jesus, it's not what we do that saves us, it's our faith in him. That means we can do whatever we like, right? It means we can eat or drink whatever we want to, doesn't it? It means we can watch whatever films or TV takes our fancy... right?

Nope.

1 Corinthians 10:23–11:16

How to Use Christian Freedom

[23]"We are allowed to do all things," but all things are not good for us to do. "We are allowed to do all things," but not all things help others grow stronger. [24]Do not look out only for yourselves. Look out for the good of others also.

[25]Eat any meat that is sold in the meat market. Do not ask questions to see if it is meat you think is wrong to eat. [26]You may eat it, "because the earth belongs to the Lord, and everything in it."

[27]Those who are not believers may invite you to eat with them. If you want to go, eat anything that is put before you. Do not ask questions to see if you think it might be wrong to eat. [28]But if anyone says to you, "That food was offered to idols," do not eat it. Do not eat it because of that person who told you and because eating it might be thought to be wrong. [29]I don't mean you think it is wrong, but the other person might. But why, you ask, should my freedom be judged by someone else's conscience? [30]If I eat the meal with thankfulness, why am I criticised because of something for which I thank God?

[31]The answer is, if you eat or drink, or if you do anything, do it all for the glory of God. [32]Never do anything that might hurt others—Jews, Greeks or God's church—[33]just as I, also, try to please everybody in every way. I am not trying to do what is good for me but what is good for most people so they can be saved.

11 Follow my example, as I follow the example of Christ.

Being Under Authority

[2]I praise you because you remember me in everything, and you follow closely the teachings just as I gave them to you. [3]But I want you to understand this: the head of every man is Christ, the head of a woman is the man and the head of Christ is God. [4]Every man who prays or prophesies with his head covered brings shame to his head. [5]But every woman who prays or prophesies with her head uncovered brings shame to her head. She is the same as a woman who has her head shaved. [6]If a woman does not cover her head, she should have her hair cut off. But since it is shameful for a woman to cut off her hair or to shave her head, she should cover her head. [7]But a man should not cover his head, because he is the likeness and glory of God. But woman is man's glory. [8]Man did not come from woman, but woman came from man. [9]And man was not made

416

for woman, but woman was made for man. [10]So that is why a woman should have a symbol of authority on her head, because of the angels.

[11]But in the Lord women are not independent of men, and men are not independent of women. [12]This is true because woman came from man, but also man is born from woman. But everything comes from God. [13]Decide this for yourselves: is it right for a woman to pray to God with her head uncovered? [14]Even nature itself teaches you that wearing long hair is shameful for a man. [15]But long hair is a woman's glory. Long hair is given to her as a covering. [16]Some people may still want to argue about this, but I would add that neither we nor the churches of God have any other practice.

You don't have to do anything. You don't HAVE to avoid some stuff. But some things just aren't helpful. If you're living for God, you have to keep focused on him. And some stuff probably isn't going to help you concentrate on God.

Think

Think about what you watch on TV, the magazines you read, the music you listen to. Is it all good for you? And if it isn't distracting you from your faith, is it a good example to others who might see you watching/reading/listening to this stuff?

Pray

God, give me wisdom to know what keeps me from dedicating my life to you.

Remember Jesus

Holy Communion, or the Lord's Supper, is a ritual that most churches have on a regular basis. But what is it all about? Why breaking bread and drinking wine?

1 Corinthians 11:17–12:11

The Lord's Supper

17In the things I tell you now I do not praise you, because when you come together you do more harm than good. 18First, I hear that when you meet together as a church you are divided, and I believe some of this. 19(It is necessary to have differences among you so that it may be clear which of you really have God's approval.) 20When you come together, you are not really eating the Lord's Supper. 21This is because when you eat, each person eats without waiting for the others. Some people do not get enough to eat, while others have too much to drink. 22You can eat and drink in your own homes! You seem to think God's church is not important, and you embarrass those who are poor. What should I tell you? Should I praise you? I do not praise you for doing this.

23The teaching I gave you is the same teaching I received from the Lord: on the night when the Lord Jesus was handed over to be killed, he took bread 24and gave thanks for it. Then he broke the bread and said, "This is my body; it is for you. Do this to remember me." 25In the same way, after they ate, Jesus took the cup. He said, "This cup is the new agreement that is sealed with the blood of my death. When you drink this, do it to remember me." 26Every time you eat this bread and drink this cup you are telling others about the Lord's death until he comes.

27So a person who eats the bread or drinks the cup of the Lord in a way that is not worthy of it will be guilty of sinning against the body and the blood of the Lord. 28Look into your own hearts before you eat the bread and drink the cup, 29because all who eat the bread and drink the cup without recognising the body eat and drink judgement against themselves. 30That is why many in your group are sick and weak, and many have died. 31But if we judged ourselves in the right way, God would not judge us. 32But when the Lord judges us, he punishes us so that we will not be destroyed along with the world.

33So my brothers and sisters, when you come together to eat, wait for each other. 34Anyone who is too hungry should eat at home so that in meeting together you will not bring God's judgement on yourselves. I will tell you what to do about the other things when I come.

Gifts from the Holy Spirit

12 Now, brothers and sisters, I want you to understand about spiritual gifts. 2You know the way you lived before

you were believers. You let yourselves be influenced and led away to worship idols—things that could not speak. ³So I want you to understand that no one who is speaking with the help of God's Spirit says, "Jesus be cursed." And no one can say, "Jesus is Lord," without the help of the Holy Spirit.

⁴There are different kinds of gifts, but they are all from the same Spirit. ⁵There are different ways to serve but the same Lord to serve. ⁶And there are different ways that God works through people but the same God. God works in all of us in everything we do. ⁷Something from the Spirit can be seen in each person, for the common good. ⁸The Spirit gives one person the ability to speak with wisdom, and the same Spirit gives another the ability to speak with knowledge. ⁹The same Spirit gives faith to one person. And, to another, that one Spirit gives gifts of healing. ¹⁰The Spirit gives to another person the power to do miracles, to another the ability to prophesy. And he gives to another the ability to know the difference between good and evil spirits. The Spirit gives one person the ability to speak in different kinds of languages and to another the ability to interpret those languages. ¹¹One Spirit, the same Spirit, does all these things, and the Spirit decides what to give each person.

Why the bread (11:24)?

Why the wine (11:25)?

Why the whole thing (11:26)?

Think

How do you view Communion? Do you see it as special or just another tradition in the church?

Pray

Thank Jesus by telling him what it means to you that he died.

How important is your thumb?

Hit it and you'll find out!

1 Corinthians 12:12–13:13

The Body of Christ Works Together

¹²A person's body is only one thing, but it has many parts. Though there are many parts to a body, all those parts make only one body. Christ is like that also. ¹³Some of us are Jews, and some are Greeks. Some of us are slaves, and some are free. But we were all baptised into one body through one Spirit. And we were all made to share in the one Spirit.

¹⁴The human body has many parts. ¹⁵The foot might say, "Because I am not a hand, I am not part of the body." But saying this would not stop the foot from being a part of the body. ¹⁶The ear might say, "Because I am not an eye, I am not part of the body." But saying this would not stop the ear from being a part of the body. ¹⁷If the whole body were an eye, it would not be able to hear. If the whole body were an ear, it would not be able to smell. ¹⁸⁻¹⁹If each part of the body were the same part, there would be no body. But truly God put all the parts, each one of them, in the body as he wanted them. ²⁰So then there are many parts, but only one body.

²¹The eye cannot say to the hand, "I don't need you!" And the head cannot say to the foot, "I don't need you!" ²²No! Those parts of the body that seem to be the weaker are really necessary. ²³And the parts of the body we think are less are the parts to which we give the most honour. We give special respect to the parts we want to hide. ²⁴The more beautiful parts of our body need no special care. But God put the body together and gave more honour to the parts that need it ²⁵so our body would not be divided. God wanted the different parts to care the same for each other. ²⁶If one part of the body suffers, all the other parts suffer with it. Or if one part of our body is honoured, all the other parts share its honour.

²⁷Together you are the body of Christ, and each one of you is a part of that body. ²⁸In the church God has given a place first to apostles, second to prophets and third to teachers. Then God has given a place to those who do miracles, those who have gifts of healing, those who can help others, those who are able to govern, and those who can speak in different languages. ²⁹Not all are apostles. Not all are prophets. Not all are teachers. Not all do miracles. ³⁰Not all have gifts of healing. Not all speak in different languages. Not all interpret those languages. ³¹But you should truly want to have the greater gifts.

Love is the Greatest Gift

And now I will show you the best way of all.

13 I may speak in different languages of people or even angels. But if I do not have love, I am only a noisy bell or a crashing cymbal. ²I may have the gift of prophecy. I may understand all the secret things of God and have all knowledge, and I may have faith so great I can move mountains. But even with all these things,

if I do not have love, then I am nothing. ³I may give away everything I have, and I may even give my body as an offering to be burnt. But I gain nothing if I do not have love.

⁴Love is patient and kind. Love is not jealous, it does not boast, and it is not proud. ⁵Love is not rude, is not selfish, and does not get upset with others. Love does not count up wrongs that have been done. ⁶Love is not happy with evil but is happy with the truth. ⁷Love patiently accepts all things. It always trusts, always hopes, and always remains strong.

⁸Love never ends. There are gifts of prophecy, but they will be ended. There are gifts of speaking in different languages, but those gifts will stop. There is the gift of knowledge, but it will come to an end. ⁹The reason is that our knowledge and our ability to prophesy are not perfect. ¹⁰But when perfection comes, the things that are not perfect will end. ¹¹When I was a child, I talked like a child, I thought like a child, I reasoned like a child. When I became a man, I stopped those childish ways. ¹²It is the same with us. Now we see a dim reflection, as if we were looking into a mirror, but then we shall see clearly. Now I know only a part, but then I will know fully, as God has known me. ¹³So these three things continue for ever: faith, hope and love. And the greatest of these is love.

> We need every part of our body. We need every member of the church. (Yes, even them!) And we need them all to work together (12:18–20).

Think

Do you think that there is enough diversity in the church? What people groups are not represented in your church?

Pray

Who are the people who don't "fit in" easily in your church? Pray that they will be accepted and be able to play their essential part in the body.

Extra

Can you write with your toes?

With some friends, try ...

- picking things up without using your hands
- writing with a pen held by your toes
- crossing a room without using your feet
- finding your way with your eyes shut

Now read 1 Corinthians 12:12–20 again.

Gifts

Some Christians find themselves doing amazing things in church. Some don't. Who's a better Christian?

1 Corinthians 14:1–25

Desire Spiritual Gifts

14 You should seek after love, and you should truly want to have the spiritual gifts, especially the gift of prophecy. ²I will explain why. Those who have the gift of speaking in different languages are not speaking to people; they are speaking to God. No one understands them; they are speaking secret things through the Spirit. ³But those who prophesy are speaking to people to give them strength, encouragement and comfort. ⁴The ones who speak in different languages are helping only themselves, but those who prophesy are helping the whole church. ⁵I wish all of you had the gift of speaking in different kinds of languages, but more, I wish you would prophesy. Those who prophesy are greater than those who can only speak in different languages—unless someone is there who can explain what is said so that the whole church can be helped.

⁶Brothers and sisters, will it help you if I come to you speaking in different languages? No! It will help you only if I bring you a new truth or some new knowledge, or prophecy, or teaching. ⁷It is the same as with lifeless things that make sounds—like a flute or a harp. If they do not make clear musical notes, you will not know what is being played. ⁸And in a war, if the trumpet does not give a clear sound, who will prepare for battle? ⁹It is the same with you. Unless you speak clearly with your tongue, no one can understand what you are saying. You will be talking into the air! ¹⁰It may be true that there are all kinds of sounds in the world, and none is without meaning. ¹¹But unless I understand the meaning of what someone says to me, I will be a foreigner to him, and he will be a foreigner to me. ¹²It is the same with you. Since you want spiritual gifts very much, seek most of all to have the gifts that help the church grow stronger.

¹³The one who has the gift of speaking in a different language should pray for the gift to interpret what is spoken. ¹⁴If I pray in a different language, my spirit is praying, but my mind does nothing. ¹⁵So what should I do? I will pray with my spirit, but I will also pray with my mind. I will sing with my spirit, but I will also sing with my mind. ¹⁶If you praise God with your spirit, those persons there without understanding cannot say amen to your prayer of thanks, because they do not know what you are saying. ¹⁷You may be thanking God in a good way, but the other person is not helped.

¹⁸I thank God that I speak in different kinds of languages more than all of you. ¹⁹But in the church meetings I would rather speak five words I understand in order to teach others than thousands of words in a different language.

²⁰Brothers and sisters, do not think like children. In evil things be like babies, but in your thinking you should be like adults. ²¹It is written in the Scriptures:

"With people who use strange words and foreign languages
The LORD will speak to these people.
But people would not listen to me,"

Isaiah 28:11–12

says the Lord.

²²So the gift of speaking in different kinds of languages is a proof for those who do not believe, not for those who do believe. And prophecy is for people who believe, not for those who do not believe. ²³Suppose the whole church meets together and everyone speaks in different languages. If some people come in who do not understand or do not believe, they will say you are mad. ²⁴But suppose everyone is prophesying and some people come in who do not believe or do not understand. If everyone is prophesying, their sin will be shown to them, and they will be judged by all that they hear. ²⁵The secret things in their hearts will be made known. So they will bow down and worship God saying, "Truly, God is with you."

The answer is, of course, that no one's better. We've all got gifts. Some may be more impressive than others but, in the end, we've all got the Holy Spirit and we're all equal in God's eyes.

Think

The important thing to remember is that if you can do something impressive, like speak in other languages or hear what God is saying, you have to do it at the right time and place, and in the right way. You don't just stand up in the middle of Communion and talk in a language no one else understands – otherwise worship would turn into a free-for-all. That doesn't honour God at all.

Pray

God, thank you for sending the Holy Spirit. Show me my gifts, and show me how to use them.

Happy Easter...

Did you know that *every* Sunday is an Easter celebration? Without the resurrection there'd be no Christianity. That's why Christians come together on Sundays – resurrection day.

Some of the Christians at Corinth weren't convinced...

 1 Corinthians 14:26–15:11

Meetings Should Help the Church

26So, brothers and sisters, what should you do? When you meet together, one person has a song, and another has a teaching. Another has a new truth from God. Another speaks in a different language, and another person interprets that language. The purpose of all these things should be to help the church grow strong. 27When you meet together, if anyone speaks in a different language, it should be only two, or not more than three, who speak. They should speak one after the other, and someone else should interpret. 28But if there is no interpreter, then those who speak in a different language should be quiet in the church meeting. They should speak only to themselves and to God.

29Only two or three prophets should speak, and the others should judge what they say. 30If a message from God comes to another person who is sitting, the first speaker should stop. 31You can all prophesy one after the other. In this way all the people can be taught and encouraged. 32The spirits of prophets are under the control of the prophets themselves. 33God is not a God of confusion but a God of peace.

As is true in all the churches of God's people, 34women should keep quiet in the church meetings. They are not allowed to speak, but they must yield to this rule as the law says. 35If they want to learn something, they should ask their own husbands at home. It is shameful for a woman to speak in the church meeting. 36Did God's teaching come from you? Or are you the only ones to whom it has come?

37Those who think they are prophets or spiritual persons should understand that what I am writing to you is the Lord's command. 38Those who ignore this will be ignored by God.

39So my brothers and sisters, you should truly want to prophesy. But do not stop people from using the gift of speaking in different kinds of languages. 40But let everything be done in a right and orderly way.

The Good News About Christ

15 Now, brothers and sisters, I want you to remember the Good News I brought to you. You received this Good News and continue strong in it. 2And you are being saved by it if you continue believing what I told you. If you do not, then you believed for nothing.

3I passed on to you what I received, of which this was most important: that Christ died for our sins, as the Scriptures say; 4that he was buried and was raised to life on the third day as the Scriptures say; 5and that he was seen by Peter and then by the twelve apostles. 6After that, Jesus was seen by more than 500 of the believers at the same time. Most of them are still living today, but some have died. [7]Then he was seen by James and later by all the apostles. [8]Last of all he was seen by me—as by a person not born at the normal time. [9]All the other apostles are greater than I am. I am not even good enough to be called an apostle, because I persecuted the church of God. [10]But God's grace has made me what I am, and his grace to me was not wasted. I worked harder than all the other apostles. (But it was not I really; it was God's grace that was with me.) [11]So if I preached to you or the other apostles preached to you, we all preach the same thing, and this is what you believed.

What does it take to make you believe something? How many witnesses to the resurrection of Jesus does Paul mention (15:5–8)?

Think

Could you add your name to the list – not because you've *seen* Jesus, but because you've *met* him (like millions of others since Paul wrote this)?

Pray

Lord Jesus, thank you that you're alive!

425

Matters of life and death

Find another reason in today's verses why Easter is *such* great news.

1 Corinthians 15:12–44a

We will be Raised from the Dead

[12]Now since we preached that Christ was raised from the dead, why do some of you say that people will not be raised from the dead? [13]If no one is ever raised from the dead, then Christ has not been raised. [14]And if Christ has not been raised, then our preaching is worth nothing, and your faith is worth nothing. [15]And also, we are guilty of lying about God, because we testified of him that he raised Christ from the dead. But if people are not raised from the dead, then God never raised Christ. [16]If the dead are not raised, Christ has not been raised either. [17]And if Christ has not been raised, then your faith has nothing to it; you are still guilty of your sins. [18]And those in Christ who have already died are lost. [19]If our hope in Christ is for this life only, we should be pitied more than anyone else in the world.

[20]But Christ has truly been raised from the dead—the first one, and proof that those who sleep in death will also be raised. [21]Death has come because of what one man did, but the rising from death also comes because of one man. [22]In Adam all of us die. In the same way, in Christ all of us will be made alive again. [23]But everyone will be raised to life in the right order. Christ was first to be raised. When Christ comes again, those who belong to him will be raised to life, [24]and then the end will come. At that time Christ will destroy all

rulers, authorities and powers, and he will hand over the kingdom to God the Father. [25]Christ must rule until he puts all enemies under his control. [26]The last enemy to be destroyed will be death. [27]The Scripture says that God put all things under his control. When it says "all things" are under him, it is clear this does not include God himself. God is the One who put everything under his control. [28]After everything has been put under the Son, then he will put himself under God, who had put all things under him. Then God will be the complete ruler over everything.

[29]If the dead are never raised, what will people do who are being baptised for the dead? If the dead are not raised at all, why are people being baptised for them?

[30]And what about us? Why do we put ourselves in danger every hour? [31]I die every day. That is true, brothers and sisters, just as it is true that I boast about you in Christ Jesus our Lord. [32]If I fought wild animals in Ephesus only with human hopes, I have gained nothing. If the dead are not raised, "Let us eat and drink, because tomorrow we will die."

[33]Do not be fooled: "Bad friends will ruin good habits." [34]Come back to your right way of thinking and stop sinning. Some of you do not know God—I say this to shame you.

What Kind of Body will We Have?

[35]But someone may ask, "How are the

dead raised? What kind of body will they have?" 36Foolish person! When you sow a seed, it must die in the ground before it can live and grow. 37And when you sow it, it does not have the same "body" it will have later. What you sow is only a bare seed, maybe wheat or something else. 38But God gives it a body that he has planned for it, and God gives each kind of seed its own body. 39All things made of flesh are not the same: people have one kind of flesh, animals have another, birds have another and fish have another. 40Also there are heavenly bodies and earthly bodies. But the beauty of the heavenly bodies is one kind, and the beauty of the earthly bodies is another. 41The sun has one kind of beauty, the moon has another beauty and the stars have another. And each star is different in its beauty.

42It is the same with the dead who are raised to life. The body that is "planted" will ruin and decay, but it is raised to a life that cannot be destroyed. 43When the body is "planted", it is without honour, but it is raised in glory. When the body is "planted", it is weak, but when it is raised, it is powerful. 44The body that is "planted" is a physical body. When it is raised, it is a spiritual body.

Did you get that? This isn't a shrug-your-shoulders, "Yeah, I already knew that" thing. Having life for ever because of what Jesus did that first Easter should hit you every time you think about it!

Back at the beginning of human history, Adam's disobedience brought *death* (v 22). Take a quick look through Genesis 3. The Good News is Jesus' obedience to God in dying on the cross brought *life* (vs 20–22).

Jesus' victory over death changed everything. Paul described death simply as "sleep" (v 20). And one day Christians will wake up and live for ever (v 23).

Think

Did you really get it? Read it again! What are your thoughts and feelings about death now?

Pray

Ask the Holy Spirit to help you see what Jesus did for you when he died and rose again. What do you want to say to Jesus now?

Give it away!

Look out in today's Bible verses for two ways of giving your money away.

1 Corinthians 15:44b–16:24

There is a physical body, and there is also a spiritual body. [45]It is written in the Scriptures: "The first man, Adam, became a living person." But the last Adam became a spirit that gives life. [46]The spiritual did not come first, but the physical and then the spiritual. [47]The first man came from the dust of the earth. The second man came from heaven. [48]People who belong to the earth are like the first man of earth. But those people who belong to heaven are like the man of heaven. [49]Just as we were made like the man of earth, so we will also be made like the man of heaven.

[50]I tell you this, brothers and sisters: flesh and blood cannot have a part in the kingdom of God. Something that will ruin cannot have a part in something that never ruins. [51]But look! I tell you this secret: we will not all sleep in death, but we will all be changed. [52]It will take only a second—as quickly as an eye blinks—when the last trumpet sounds. The trumpet will sound, and those who have died will be raised to live for ever, and we will all be changed. [53]This body that can be destroyed must clothe itself with something that can never be destroyed. And this body that dies must clothe itself with something that can never die. [54]So this body that can be destroyed will clothe itself with that which can never be destroyed, and this body that dies must clothe itself with that which can never die. When this happens, this Scripture will be made true:

"Death is destroyed for ever." *Isaiah 25:8*

[55]"Death, where is your victory? Where is your pain, place of death?"

Hosea 13:14

[56]Death's power to hurt is sin, and the power of sin is the law. [57]But we thank God! He gives us the victory through our Lord Jesus Christ.

[58]So my dear brothers and sisters, stand strong. Do not let anything change you. Always give yourselves fully to the work of the Lord, because you know that your work in the Lord is never wasted.

The Gift for Other Believers

16 Now I will write about the collection of money for God's people. Do the same thing I told the Galatian churches to do: [2]on the first day of every week, each one of you should put aside money as you have been blessed. Save it up so you will not have to collect money after I come. [3]When I arrive, I will send whomever you approve to take your gift to Jerusalem. I will send them with letters of introduction, [4]and if it seems good for me to go also, they will go along with me.

Paul's Plans

[5]I plan to go through Macedonia, so I will come to you after I go through there. [6]Perhaps I will stay with you for a time or even all winter. Then you can help me on my trip, wherever I go. [7]I do not want to see you now just in passing. I hope to stay a longer time with you if the Lord allows it. [8]But I will stay at Ephesus until Pentecost, [9]because a good opportunity for a great and growing work has been given to me now. And there are many people working against me.

[10]If Timothy comes to you, see to it that he has nothing to fear with you, because he is working for the Lord just as I am. [11]So none of you should treat Timothy as unimportant, but help him on his way in peace so that he can come back to me. I am expecting him to come with the brothers.

[12]Now about our brother Apollos: I strongly encouraged him to visit you with the other brothers. He did not at all want to come now; he will come when he has the opportunity.

Paul Ends His Letter

[13]Be careful. Continue strong in the faith. Have courage, and be strong. [14]Do everything in love.

[15]You know that the family of Stephanas were the first believers in Southern Greece and that they have given themselves to the service of God's people. I ask you, brothers and sisters, [16]to follow the leading of people like these and anyone else who works and serves with them.

[17]I am happy that Stephanas, Fortunatus and Achaicus have come. You are not here, but they have filled your place. [18]They have refreshed my spirit and yours. You should recognise the value of people like these.

[19]The churches in the country of Asia send greetings to you. Aquila and Priscilla greet you in the Lord, as does the church that meets in their house. [20]All the brothers and sisters here send greetings. Give each other a holy kiss when you meet.

[21]I, Paul, am writing this greeting with my own hand.

[22]If anyone does not love the Lord, let him be separated from God—lost for ever!

Come, O Lord!

[23]The grace of the Lord Jesus be with you.

[24]My love be with all of you in Christ Jesus.

Did you spot what Paul said about money? He said we should:

- give regularly (e.g. in your church collection each week)

- give in proportion to what you have. Some Christians aim to give a tenth of their income as a "thank you" to God for all he's given them

If you have no income what do you have? What about your time? What about the gifts that you have – what are you good at?

Think

What is one tenth of your "weekly income"? Could you start saving that regularly to support God's work?

Pray

Father, thank you for all the good things you send my way. Help me to give you a regular "thank you" gift back.

Thank God!

When things go wrong, what's your most likely response?

- Arrgh!
- Help!
- Thank you.

2 Corinthians 1:1–24

1 From Paul, an apostle of Christ Jesus. I am an apostle because that is what God wanted. Also from Timothy our brother in Christ.

To the church of God in Corinth, and to all of God's people everywhere in Southern Greece:

²Grace and peace to you from God our Father and the Lord Jesus Christ.

Paul Gives Thanks to God

³Praise be to the God and Father of our Lord Jesus Christ. God is the Father who is full of mercy and all comfort. ⁴He comforts us every time we have trouble, so when others have trouble, we can comfort them with the same comfort God gives us. ⁵We share in the many sufferings of Christ. In the same way, much comfort comes to us through Christ. ⁶If we have troubles, it is for your comfort and salvation, and if we have comfort, you also have comfort. This helps you to accept patiently the same sufferings we have. ⁷Our hope for you is strong, knowing that you share in our sufferings and also in the comfort we receive.

⁸Brothers and sisters, we want you to know about the trouble we suffered in Asia. We had great burdens there that were beyond our own strength. We even gave up hope of living. ⁹Truly, in our own hearts we believed we would die. But this happened so we would not trust in ourselves but in God, who raises people from the dead. ¹⁰God saved us from these great dangers of death, and he will continue to save us. We have put our hope in him, and he will save us again. ¹¹And you can help us with your prayers. Then many people will give thanks for us—that God blessed us because of their many prayers.

The Change in Paul's Plans

¹²This is what we are proud of, and I can say it with a clear heart: in everything we have done in the world, and especially with you, we have had an honest and sincere heart from God. We did this by God's grace, not by the kind of wisdom the world has. ¹³⁻¹⁴We write to you only what you can read and understand. And I hope that as you have understood some things about us, you may come to know everything about us. Then you can be proud of us, as we will be proud of you on the day our Lord Jesus Christ comes again.

¹⁵I was so sure of all this that I made plans to visit you first so you could be blessed twice. ¹⁶I planned to visit you on my way to Macedonia and again on my way back. I wanted to get help from you

for my trip to Judea. 17Do you think that I made these plans without really meaning it? Or maybe you think I make plans as the world does, so that I say "yes, yes" and at the same time "no, no."

18But if you can believe God, you can believe that what we tell you is never both "yes" and "no". 19The Son of God, Jesus Christ, that Silas and Timothy and I preached to you, was not "yes" and "no". In Christ it has always been "yes". 20The "yes" to all of God's promises is in Christ, and through Christ we say "yes" to the glory of God. 21Remember, God is the One who makes you and us strong in Christ. God made us his chosen people. 22He put his mark on us to show that we are his, and he put his Spirit in our hearts to be a guarantee for all he has promised.

23I tell you this, and I ask God to be my witness that this is true: the reason I did not come back to Corinth was to keep you from being punished or hurt. 24We are not trying to control your faith. You are strong in faith. But we are workers with you for your own joy.

OK, so "Thank you" wouldn't be my first words either! But can you find two reasons in these verses why Paul says we *can* thank God, even when things aren't going well?

Verse 3: _____

Verses 4,6: _____

Think

How could difficult times you've been through help you to help others?

Pray

Lord, thank you for your encouragement to me. Help me encourage others who are finding life difficult.

Revenge or forgiveness?

When people hurt me I want to ...

- hit them – hard!
- see them punished
- forgive them

2 Corinthians 2:1–3:6

2 So I decided that my next visit to you would not be another one to make you sad. ²If I make you sad, who will make me glad? Only you can make me glad—particularly the person whom I made sad. ³I wrote you a letter for this reason: that when I came to you I would not be made sad by the people who should make me happy. I felt sure of all of you, that you would share my joy. ⁴When I wrote to you before, I was very troubled and unhappy in my heart, and I wrote with many tears. I did not write to make you sad, but to let you know how much I love you.

Forgive the Sinner

⁵Someone there among you has caused sadness, not to me, but to all of you. I mean he caused sadness to all in some way. (I do not want to make it sound worse than it really is.) ⁶The punishment that most of you gave him is enough for him. ⁷But now you should forgive him and comfort him to keep him from having too much sadness and giving up completely. ⁸So I beg you to show that you love him. ⁹I wrote to you to test you and to see if you obey in everything. ¹⁰If you forgive someone, I also

forgive him. And what I have forgiven—if I had anything to forgive—I forgave it for you, as if Christ were with me. ¹¹I did this so that Satan would not win anything from us, because we know very well what Satan's plans are.

Paul's Concern in Troas

¹²When I came to Troas to preach the Good News of Christ, the Lord gave me a good opportunity there. ¹³But I had no peace, because I did not find my brother Titus. So I said goodbye to them at Troas and went to Macedonia.

Victory Through Christ

¹⁴But thanks be to God, who always leads us in victory through Christ. God uses us to spread his knowledge everywhere like a sweet-smelling perfume. ¹⁵Our offering to God is this: we are the sweet smell of Christ among those who are being saved and among those who are being lost. ¹⁶To those who are lost, we are the smell of death that brings death, but to those who are being saved, we are the smell of life that brings life. So who is able to do this work? ¹⁷We do not sell the word

of God for a profit as many other people do. But in Christ we speak the truth before God, as messengers of God.

Servants of the New Agreement

3 Are we starting to boast about ourselves again? Do we need letters of introduction to you or from you, like some other people? ²You yourselves are our letter, written on our hearts, known and read by everyone. ³You show that you are a letter from Christ sent through us. This letter is not written with ink but with the Spirit of the living God. It is not written on stone tablets but on human hearts.

⁴We can say this, because through Christ we feel certain before God. ⁵We are not saying that we can do this work ourselves. It is God who makes us able to do all that we do. ⁶He made us able to be servants of a new agreement from himself to his people. This new agreement is not a written law, but it is of the Spirit. The written law brings death, but the Spirit gives life.

It's not easy to forgive. Sounds as though the Corinthians had given someone a really hard time (2:6,7).

Paul told them to forgive because:

- if they carried on making the guy feel bad, he might give up his faith (v...)

- Satan is always looking for ways of making trouble between Christians (v...)

Think

Is there someone you need to forgive?

Pray

Ask God to help you with your feelings about anyone who has hurt you – and to forgive them.

I'm so in awe of you!

Have you ever felt nervous? I mean really nervous about something, or about meeting someone? Being presented to a member of the royal family, or another VIP, could make you feel quite nervous.

One day we will be present before the biggest VIP ever, God the Father.

2 Corinthians 3:7–4:15

⁷The law that brought death was written in words on stone. It came with God's glory, which made Moses' face so bright that the Israelites could not continue to look at it. But that glory later disappeared. ⁸So surely the new way that brings the Spirit has even more glory. ⁹If the law that judged people guilty of sin had glory, surely the new way that makes people right with God has much greater glory. ¹⁰That old law had glory, but it really loses its glory when it is compared to the much greater glory of this new way. ¹¹If that law which disappeared came with glory, then this new way which continues for ever has much greater glory.

¹²We have this hope, so we are very bold. ¹³We are not like Moses, who put a covering over his face so the Israelites would not see it. The glory was disappearing, and Moses did not want them to see it fade. ¹⁴But their minds were closed, and even today that same covering hides the meaning when they read the old agreement. That covering is taken away only through Christ. ¹⁵Even today, when they read the law of Moses, there is a covering over their minds. ¹⁶But when a person changes and follows the Lord, that covering is taken away. ¹⁷The Lord is the Spirit, and where the Spirit of the Lord is, there is freedom. ¹⁸Our faces, then, are not covered. We all show the Lord's glory, and we are being changed to be like him. This change in us brings ever greater glory, which comes from the Lord, who is the Spirit.

Preaching the Good News

4 God, with his mercy, gave us this work to do, so we don't give up. ²But we have turned away from secret and shameful ways. We use no trickery, and we do not change the teaching of God. We teach the truth plainly, showing everyone who we are. Then they can know in their hearts what kind of people we are in God's sight. ³If the Good News that we preach is hidden, it is hidden only to those who are lost. ⁴The devil who rules this world has blinded the minds of those who do not believe. They cannot see the light of the Good News—the Good News about the glory of Christ, who is exactly like God. ⁵We do not preach about ourselves, but we preach that Jesus Christ is Lord and that we are your servants for Jesus. ⁶God once said, "Let the light shine out of the darkness!" This is the same God who made his light shine in our hearts by letting

us know the glory of God that is in the face of Christ.

Spiritual Treasure in Clay Jars

7We have this treasure from God, but we are like clay jars that hold the treasure. This shows that the great power is from God, not from us. 8We have troubles all around us, but we are not defeated. We do not know what to do, but we do not give up the hope of living. 9We are persecuted, but God does not leave us. We are hurt sometimes, but we are not destroyed. 10We carry the death of Jesus in our own bodies so that the life of Jesus can also be seen in our bodies. 11We are alive, but for Jesus we are always in danger of death so that the life of Jesus can be seen in our bodies that die. 12So death is working in us, but life is working in you.

13It is written in the Scriptures, "I believed, so I spoke." Our faith is like this too. We believe, and so we speak. 14God raised the Lord Jesus from the dead, and we know that God will also raise us with Jesus. God will bring us together with you, and we will stand before him. 15All these things are for you. And so the grace of God that is being given to more and more people will bring increasing thanks to God for his glory.

Paul knows that he, and others, need not feel nervous or afraid when they stand before God. This is because of the work and love of Christ.

What does the written law refer to?

Think

Paul describes us as servants. Who do you serve and how?

Pray

That the Spirit will bring life in all its fullness to you.

Get right with God

Do other people sometimes misunderstand you?   Yes/No

Do you sometimes misunderstand other people?   Yes/No

 2 Corinthians 4:16–6:2

Living by Faith

16So we do not give up. Our physical body is becoming older and weaker, but our spirit inside us is made new every day. 17We have small troubles for a while now, but they are helping us gain an eternal glory that is much greater than the troubles. 18We set our eyes not on what we see but on what we cannot see. What we see will last only a short time, but what we cannot see will last for ever.

5 We know that our body—the tent we live in here on earth—will be destroyed. But when that happens, God will have a house for us. It will not be a house made by human hands; instead, it will be a home in heaven that will last for ever. 2But now we groan in this tent. We want God to give us our heavenly home, 3because it will clothe us so we will not be naked. 4While we live in this body, we have burdens, and we groan. We do not want to be naked, but we want to be clothed with our heavenly home. Then this body that dies will be fully covered with life. 5This is what God made us for, and he has given us the Spirit to be a guarantee for this new life. 6So we always have courage. We know that while we live in this body, we are away from the Lord. 7We live by what we believe, not by what we can see. 8So I say that we have courage. We really want to be away from this body and be at home with the Lord. 9Our only goal is to please God whether we live here or there, 10because we must all stand before Christ to be judged. Each of us will receive what we should get—good or bad—for the things we did in the earthly body.

Becoming Friends with God

11Since we know what it means to fear the Lord, we try to help people accept the truth about us. God knows what we really are, and I hope that in your hearts you know too. 12We are not trying to prove ourselves to you again, but we are telling you about ourselves so you will be proud of us. Then you will have an answer for those who are proud about things that can be seen rather than what is in the heart. 13If we are out of our minds, it is for God. If we have our right minds, it is for you. 14The love of Christ controls us, because we know that One died for all, so all have died. 15Christ died for all so that those who live would not continue to live for themselves. He died for them and was raised from the dead so that they would live for him.

16From this time on we do not think of anyone as the world does. In the past we thought of Christ as the world thinks, but we no longer think of him in that way. 17If anyone belongs to Christ, there begins a new creation. The old things have gone: everything is made new! 18All this is from God. Through Christ, God made peace between us and himself, and God gave us the work of telling everyone about the peace we can have with him. ¹⁹God was in Christ, making peace between the world and himself. In Christ, God did not hold the world guilty of its sins. And he gave us this message of peace. ²⁰So we have been sent to speak for Christ. It is as if God is calling to you through us. We speak for Christ when we beg you to be at peace with God. ²¹Christ had no sin, but God made him become sin so that in Christ we could become right with God.

6 We are workers together with God, so we beg you: do not let the grace that you received from God be for nothing. ²God says,

"At the right time I will hear your prayers.

On the day of salvation I will help you."   *Isaiah 49:8*

I tell you that the "right time" is now, and the "day of salvation" is now.

The Corinthians seemed to have misunderstood Paul (5:13). He took them back to basics:

- think differently about others, because you know Jesus (5:16,17)

- remember what Jesus has done for you (5:19)

- Jesus forgave – so should we (5:19)

- being right with God means being at peace with others (5:20,21)

Think

Are you right with other people – and God?

Pray

Thank God for what he's done for you through Jesus. Ask him to help you put your relationship with him – and others – right.

Not just soap

Being clean is more than just washing behind the ears. Paul is talking about a complete spiritual exfoliation. And it is not because of a desire to look good but out of a deep respect for God.

2 Corinthians 6:3–7:7

³We do not want anyone to find fault with our work, so nothing we do will be a problem for anyone. ⁴But in every way we show we are servants of God: in accepting many hard things, in troubles, in difficulties and in great problems. ⁵We are beaten and thrown into prison. We meet those who become upset with us and start riots. We work hard, and sometimes we get no sleep or food. ⁶We show we are servants of God by our pure lives, our understanding, patience and kindness, by the Holy Spirit, by true love, ⁷by speaking the truth and by God's power. We use our right living to defend ourselves against everything. ⁸Some people honour us, but others blame us. Some people say evil things about us, but others say good things. Some people say we are liars, but we speak the truth. ⁹We are not known, yet we are well known. We seem to be dying, but we continue to live. We are punished, but we are not killed. ¹⁰We have much sadness, but we are always rejoicing. We are poor, but we are making many people rich in faith. We have nothing, but really we have everything.

¹¹We have spoken freely to you in Corinth and have opened our hearts to you. ¹²Our feelings of love for you have not stopped, but you have stopped your feelings of love for us. ¹³I speak to you as if you were my children. Do to us as we have done—open your hearts to us.

Warning About Those Who Do Not Believe

¹⁴You are not the same as those who do not believe. So do not join yourselves to them. Good and bad do not belong together. Light and darkness cannot share together. ¹⁵How can Christ and Belial, the devil, have any agreement? What can a believer have together with a non-believer? ¹⁶The temple of God cannot have any agreement with idols, and we are the temple of the living God. As God said: "I will live with them and walk with them. And I will be their God, and they will be my people."

¹⁷"You people, leave, leave,
    get out of Babylon!
Touch nothing that is unclean."

Isaiah 52:11; Ezekiel 20:34,41

¹⁸"I will be your father,
    and you will be my sons and daughters,
    says the Lord Almighty."

2 Samuel 7:14; 7:8

7 Dear friends, we have these promises from God, so we should make ourselves pure—free from anything that makes body or soul unclean. We should try to become holy in the way we live, because we respect God.

Paul's Joy

²Open your hearts to us. We have not done wrong to anyone, we have not ruined the faith of anyone, and we have not cheated anyone. ³I do not say this to blame you. I told you before that we love you so much we would live or die with you. ⁴I feel very sure of you and am very proud of you. You give me much comfort, and in all of our troubles I have great joy.

⁵When we came into Macedonia, we had no rest. We found trouble all around us. We had fighting on the outside and fear on the inside. ⁶But God, who comforts those who are troubled, comforted us when Titus came. ⁷We were comforted, not only by his coming but also by the comfort you gave him. Titus told us about your wish to see me and that you are very sorry for what you did. He also told me about your great care for me, and when I heard this, I was much happier.

Use the space below to list anything in your life that you feel makes you unclean.

_____

_____

_____

_____

Think

What is our motivation for being pure? Do we do it out of a fear of God or because of our love for God?

Pray

Talk to God about your list. Say you're sorry and ask for help in order to remain pure in the future.

Think of others

Do you sometimes see someone in distress, or struggling with something, and yet offer no help despite the fact that you know you should?

You know you *should* give to others – but somehow you never quite get round to it.

 2 Corinthians 7:8–8:15

8Even if my letter made you sad, I am not sorry I wrote it. At first I was sorry, because it made you sad, but you were sad only for a short time. 9Now I am happy, not because you were made sad, but because your sorrow made you change your lives. You became sad in the way God wanted you to, so you were not hurt by us in any way. 10The kind of sorrow God wants makes people change their hearts and lives. This leads to salvation, and you cannot be sorry for that. But the kind of sorrow the world has brings death. 11See what this sorrow—the sorrow God wanted you to have—has done to you: it has made you very serious. It made you want to prove you were not wrong. It made you angry and afraid. It made you want to see me. It made you care. It made you want the right thing to be done. You proved you were innocent in the problem. 12I wrote that letter, not because of the one who did the wrong or because of the person who was hurt. I wrote the letter so you could see, before God, the great care you have for us. 13That is why we were comforted.

Not only were we very comforted, we were even happier to see that Titus was so happy. All of you made him feel much better. 14I boasted to Titus about you, and you showed that I was right. Everything we said to you was true, and you have proved that what we boasted about to Titus is

true. 15And his love for you is stronger when he remembers that you were all ready to obey. You welcomed him with respect and fear. 16I am very happy that I can trust you fully.

Christian Giving

8 And now, brothers and sisters, we want you to know about the grace God gave the churches in Macedonia. 2They have been tested by great troubles, and they are very poor. But they gave much because of their great joy. 3I can tell you that they gave as much as they were able and even more than they could afford. No one told them to do it. 4But they begged and pleaded with us to let them share in this service for God's people. 5And they gave in a way we did not expect: they first gave themselves to the Lord and to us. This is what God wants. 6So we asked Titus to help you finish this special work of grace since he is the one who started it. 7You are rich in everything—in faith, in speaking, in knowledge, in truly wanting to help, and in the love you learned from us. In the same way, be strong also in the grace of giving.

8I am not commanding you to give. But I want to see if your love is true by comparing you with others that really want to help. 9You know the grace of our Lord Jesus Christ. You know that Christ was rich, but for you he became poor so that by his becoming poor you might become rich. ¹⁰This is what I think you should do: last year you were the first to want to give, and you were the first who gave. ¹¹So now finish the work you started. Then your "doing" will be equal to your "wanting to do". Give from what you have. ¹²If you want to give, your gift will be accepted. It will be judged by what you have, not by what you do not have. ¹³We do not want you to have troubles while other people are at ease, but we want everything to be equal. ¹⁴At this time you have plenty. What you have can help others who are in need. Then later, when they have plenty, they can help you when you are in need, and all will be equal. ¹⁵As it is written in the Scriptures, "The person who gathered more did not have too much, nor did the person who gathered less have too little."

The Corinthians were great on faith, speaking, knowledge and love. But they had given up on something important:

_____ (8:7).

The poor Christians in Macedonia (Northern Greece) had started and finished collecting, and sent the money (got the T-shirt!). What was their secret (8:5)?

Think

How do you give yourself to God? What difference would it make to your giving to others?

Pray

Talk this through with God.

Give

How could you get rich?

- Win the lottery
- Win the next "Be a pop star" TV show
- Get a highly paid job

2 Corinthians 8:16–9:15

Titus and His Companions Help

¹⁶I thank God because he gave Titus the same love for you that I have. ¹⁷Titus accepted what we asked him to do. He wanted very much to go to you, and this was his own idea. ¹⁸We are sending with him the brother who is praised by all the churches because of his service in preaching the Good News. ¹⁹Also, this brother was chosen by the churches to go with us when we deliver this gift of money. We are doing this service to bring glory to the Lord and to show that we really want to help.

²⁰We are being careful so that no one will criticise us for the way we are handling this large gift. ²¹We are trying hard to do what the Lord accepts as right and also what people think is right.

²²Also, we are sending with them our brother, who is always ready to help. He has proved this to us in many ways, and he wants to help even more now, because he has much faith in you.

²³Now about Titus—he is my partner who is working with me to help you. And about the other brothers—they are sent from the churches, and they bring glory to Christ. ²⁴So show these men the proof of your love and the reason we are proud of you. Then all the churches can see it.

Help for Fellow Christians

9 I really do not need to write to you about this help for God's people. ²I know you want to help. I have been boasting about this to the people in Macedonia, telling them that you in Southern Greece have been ready to give since last year. And your desire to give has made most of them ready to give also. ³But I am sending the brothers to you so that our boasting about you in this will not be empty words. I want you to be ready, as I said you would be. ⁴If any of the people from Macedonia come with me and find that you are not ready, we will be ashamed that we were so sure of you. (And you will be ashamed too!) ⁵So I thought I should ask these brothers to go to you before we do. They will finish getting in order the generous gift you promised so it will be ready when we come. And it will be a generous gift—not one that you did not want to give.

⁶Remember this: the person who plants a little will have a small harvest, but the person who plants a lot will have a big harvest. ⁷Each one should give as he has decided in his heart to give. You should not be sad when you give, and you should not give because you feel forced to give.

God loves the person who gives happily. ⁸And God can give you more blessings than you need. Then you will always have plenty of everything—enough to give to every good work. ⁹It is written in the Scriptures:

"He gives freely to the poor.
The things he does are right and will
continue for ever."   *Psalm 112:9*

¹⁰God is the One who gives seed to the farmer and bread for food. He will give you all the seed you need and make it grow so there will be a great harvest from your goodness. ¹¹He will make you rich in every way so that you can always give freely. And your giving through us will cause many to give thanks to God. ¹²This service you do not only helps the needs of God's people, it also brings much more thanks to God. ¹³It is a proof of your faith. Many people will praise God because you obey the Good News of Christ—the gospel you say you believe—and because you freely share with them and with all others. ¹⁴And when they pray, they will wish they could be with you because of the great grace that God has given you. ¹⁵Thanks be to God for his gift that is too wonderful for words.

How did Jesus make us rich (9:8,9)?

No get-rich-quick schemes for everyday life, but Paul did suggest how the Corinthians could always have enough (9:10,11):

- give what you can (9:11)

- give it willingly (9:13)

Think

What could you give?

Pray

Talk to God about how you could help someone in need.

Don't boast

"I look great! I sound great! I've done great things! In fact I am just totally great: just stand there a moment and bask in my glory! Not too close now, you don't want to tarnish my greatness."

Would you follow someone who spoke like this? Sure?

 2 Corinthians 10:1–11:4

Paul Defends His Ministry

10 I, Paul, am begging you with the gentleness and the kindness of Christ. Some people say that I am easy on you when I am with you and bold when I am away. ²They think we live in a worldly way, and I plan to be very bold with them when I come. I beg you that when I come I will not need to use that same boldness with you. ³We do live in the world, but we do not fight in the same way the world fights. ⁴We fight with weapons that are different from those the world uses. Our weapons have power from God that can destroy the enemy's strong places. We destroy people's arguments ⁵and every proud thing that raises itself against the knowledge of God. We capture every thought and make it give up and obey Christ. ⁶We are ready to punish anyone there who does not obey, but first we want you to obey fully.

⁷You must look at the facts before you. If you feel sure that you belong to Christ, you must remember that we belong to Christ just as you do. ⁸It is true that we boast freely about the authority the Lord gave us. But this authority is to build you up, not to tear you down. So I will not be ashamed. ⁹I do not want you to think I am trying to scare you with my letters. ¹⁰Some

people say, "Paul's letters are powerful and sound important, but when he is with us, he is weak. And his speaking is nothing." ¹¹They should know this: we are not there with you now, so we say these things in letters. But when we are there with you, we will show the same authority that we show in our letters.

¹²We do not dare to compare ourselves with those who think they are very important. They use themselves to measure themselves, and they judge themselves by what they themselves are. This shows that they know nothing. ¹³But we will not boast about things outside the work that was given us to do. We will limit our boasting to the work that God gave us, and this includes our work with you. ¹⁴We are not boasting too much, as we would be if we had not already come to you. But we have come to you with the Good News of Christ. ¹⁵We limit our boasting to the work that is ours, not what others have done. We hope that as your faith continues to grow, you will help our work to grow much larger. ¹⁶We want to tell the Good News in the areas beyond your city. We do not want to boast about work that has already been done in another person's area. ¹⁷But, "If someone wants to boast, he should boast only about the Lord." ¹⁸It is not those who say they are good who are

accepted but those who the Lord thinks are good.

Paul and the False Apostles

11 I wish you would be patient with me even when I am a little foolish, but you are already doing that. ²I am jealous over you with a jealousy that comes from God. I promised to give you to Christ, as your only husband. I want to give you as his pure bride. ³But I am afraid that your minds will be led away from your true and pure following of Christ just as Eve was tricked by the snake with his evil ways. ⁴You are very patient with anyone who comes to you and preaches a different Jesus from the one we preached. You are very willing to accept a spirit or good news that is different from the Spirit and Good News you received from us.

Someone had been stirring up trouble for Paul with the Corinthian Christians (10:10).

How should we make up our minds about people?

- Don't measure people just by what they say about themselves (10:12)

- Look at the effect they have on the lives of others (10:15)

Think
Who is it OK to talk about (10:17)?

Pray
Lord, help me to care more than anything about what you think of me (10:18).

Chuffed

What are you good at? Who are your friends? Where did you come from? Are you proud of it?

2 Corinthians 11:5–33

⁵I do not think that those "great apostles" are any better than I am. ⁶I may not be a trained speaker, but I do have knowledge. We have shown this to you clearly in every way.

⁷I preached God's Good News to you without pay. I made myself unimportant to make you important. Do you think that was wrong? ⁸I accepted pay from other churches, taking their money so I could serve you. ⁹If I needed something when I was with you, I did not trouble any of you. The brothers who came from Macedonia gave me all that I needed. I did not allow myself to depend on you in any way, and I will never depend on you. ¹⁰No one in Southern Greece will stop me from boasting about that. I say this with the truth of Christ in me. ¹¹And why do I not depend on you? Do you think it is because I do not love you? God knows that I love you.

¹²And I will continue doing what I am doing now, because I want to stop those people from having a reason to boast. They would like to say that the work they boast about is the same as ours. ¹³Such men are not true apostles but are workers who lie. They change themselves to look like apostles of Christ. ¹⁴This does not surprise us. Even Satan changes himself to look like an angel of light. ¹⁵So it does not surprise us if Satan's servants also make themselves look like servants who work for what is right. But in the end they will be punished for what they do.

Paul Tells About His Sufferings

¹⁶I tell you again: no one should think I am a fool. But if you think so, accept me as you would accept a fool. Then I can boast a little, too. ¹⁷When I boast because I feel sure of myself, I am not talking as the Lord would talk but as a fool. ¹⁸Many people are boasting about their lives in the world. So I will boast too. ¹⁹You are wise, so you will gladly be patient with fools! ²⁰You are even patient with those who order you around, or use you, or trick you, or think they are better than you, or hit you in the face. ²¹It is shameful to me to say this, but we were too "weak" to do those things to you!

But if anyone else is brave enough to boast, then I also will be brave and boast. (I am talking as a fool.) ²²Are they Hebrews? So am I. Are they Israelites? So am I. Are they from Abraham's family? So am I. ²³Are they serving Christ? I am serving him more. (I am mad to talk like this.) I have worked much harder than they. I have been in prison more often. I have been hurt more in beatings. I have been near death many times. ²⁴Five times the Jews have given me their punishment of 39 lashes with a whip. ²⁵Three different times I was beaten with rods. One time I was almost stoned to death. Three times I was in ships that were wrecked, and one of those times I spent a night and a day in the sea. ²⁶I have gone on many travels and have been in danger from rivers, thieves, my own people, the Jews and those who are not Jews. I have been in danger in cities, in places where no one lives and on the sea. And I have been in danger with false Christians. ²⁷I have done hard and tiring work, and many times I did not sleep. I have been hungry and thirsty, and many times I have been without food. I have been cold and without clothes. ²⁸Besides all this, there is on me every day the load of my concern for all the churches. ²⁹I feel weak every time someone is weak, and I feel upset every time someone is led into sin.

³⁰If I must boast, I will boast about the things that show I am weak. ³¹God knows I am not lying. He is the God and Father of the Lord Jesus Christ, and he is to be praised for ever. ³²When I was in Damascus, the governor under King Aretas wanted to arrest me, so he put guards around the city. ³³But my friends lowered me in a basket through a hole in the city wall. So I escaped from the governor.

> Paul has a lot to be proud about. But he isn't arrogant. The only thing he's going to boast about is Jesus.

Think

How proud are you to be a Christian?

Pray

Spend a bit of time thanking God for giving you something to really be proud of.

447

The weak are strong

One of the eternal themes found in Hollywood films is when the weak hero digs deep and finds amazing strength to defeat the evil villain.

2 Corinthians 12:1–13:4

A Special Blessing in Paul's Life

12 I must continue to boast. It will do no good, but I will talk now about visions and revelations from the Lord. ²I know a man in Christ who was taken up to the third heaven fourteen years ago. I do not know whether the man was in his body or out of his body, but God knows. ³⁻⁴And I know that this man was taken up to paradise. I don't know if he was in his body or away from his body, but God knows. He heard things he is not able to explain, things that no human is allowed to tell. ⁵I will boast about a man like that, but I will not boast about myself, except about my weaknesses. ⁶But if I wanted to boast about myself, I would not be a fool, because I would be telling the truth. But I will not boast about myself. I do not want people to think more of me than what they see me do or hear me say.

⁷So that I would not become too proud of the wonderful things that were shown to me, a painful problem was given to me. This problem was a messenger from Satan, sent to beat me and keep me from being too proud. ⁸I begged the Lord three times to take this problem away from me. ⁹But he said to me, "My grace is enough for you. When you are weak, my power is made perfect in you." So I am very happy to boast about my weaknesses. Then Christ's power can live in me. ¹⁰For this reason I am happy when I have weaknesses, insults, hard times, sufferings and all kinds of troubles for Christ. Because when I am weak, then I am truly strong.

Paul's Love for the Christians

¹¹I have been talking like a fool, but you made me do it. You are the ones who should say good things about me. I am worth nothing, but those "great apostles" are not worth any more than I am! ¹²When I was with you, I patiently did the things that prove I am an apostle—signs, wonders and miracles. ¹³So you received everything that the other churches have received. Only one thing was different: I was not a burden to you. Forgive me for this!

¹⁴I am now ready to visit you the third time, and I will not be a burden to you. I want nothing from you, except you. Children should not have to save up to give to their parents. Parents should save to give to their children. ¹⁵So I am happy to give everything I have for you, even myself. If I love you more, will you love me less?

¹⁶It is clear I was not a burden to you, but you think I was sly and lied to catch you. ¹⁷Did I cheat you by using any of the messengers I sent to you? No, you know I did not. ¹⁸I asked Titus to go to you, and I sent our brother with him. Titus did not cheat you, did he? No, you know that Titus and I did the same thing and with the same spirit.

¹⁹Do you think we have been defending ourselves to you all this time? We have been speaking in Christ and before God. You are our dear friends, and everything we do is to make you stronger. ²⁰I am afraid that when I come, you will not be what I want you to be, and I will not be what you want me to be. I am afraid that

among you there may be arguing, jealousy, anger, selfish fighting, evil talk, gossip, pride and confusion. ²¹I am afraid that when I come to you again, my God will make me ashamed before you. I may be saddened by many of those who have sinned because they have not changed their hearts or turned from their sexual sins and the shameful things they have done.

Final Warnings and Greetings

13 I will come to you for the third time. "Every case must be proved by two or three witnesses." ²When I was with you the second time, I gave a warning to those who had sinned. Now I am away from you, and I give a warning to all the others. When I come to you again, I will not be easy with them. ³You want proof that Christ is speaking through me. My proof is that he is not weak among you, but he is powerful. ⁴It is true that he was weak when he was killed on the cross, but he lives now by God's power. It is true that we are weak in Christ, but for you we will be alive in Christ by God's power.

Paul says that true strength comes when he is weak.

What is he happy to boast about (12:9)?

What things make Paul happy (12:10)?

1 _____

2 _____

3 _____

4 _____

5 _____

Think

According to Acts 20:7–12, Paul was able to heal (in a big way). So why couldn't he take his own pain away (12:8)?

Pray

That God will use your weaknesses to make you strong, to serve him well.

What does God think?

In the end, you can't *make* other people understand you, or think you're wonderful. What's more important than all that?

2 Corinthians 13:5 – Galatians 1:24

⁵Look closely at yourselves. Test yourselves to see if you are living in the faith. You know that Jesus Christ is in you—unless you fail the test. ⁶But I hope you will see that we ourselves have not failed the test. ⁷We pray to God that you will not do anything wrong. It is not important to see that we have passed the test, but it is important that you do what is right, even if it seems we have failed. ⁸We cannot do anything against the truth, but only for the truth. ⁹We are happy to be weak, if you are strong, and we pray that you will become complete. ¹⁰I am writing this while I am away from you so that when I come I will not have to be harsh in my use of authority. The Lord gave me this authority to build you up, not to tear you down.

¹¹Now, brothers and sisters, I say good-bye. Try to be perfect. Do what I have asked you to do. Agree with each other, and live in peace. Then the God of love and peace will be with you.

¹²Greet each other with a holy kiss. ¹³All of God's holy people send greetings to you.

¹⁴The grace of the Lord Jesus Christ, the love of God, and the fellowship of the Holy Spirit be with you all.

GALATIANS

1 From Paul, an apostle. I was not chosen to be an apostle by human beings, nor was I sent from human beings. I was made an apostle through Jesus Christ and God the Father who raised Jesus from the dead. ²This letter is also from all those of God's family who are with me.

To the churches in Galatia:

³Grace and peace to you from God our Father and the Lord Jesus Christ. ⁴Jesus gave himself for our sins to free us from this evil world we live in, as God the Father planned. ⁵The glory belongs to God for ever and ever. Amen.

The Only Good News

⁶God, by his grace through Christ, called you to become his people. So I am amazed that you are turning away so quickly and believing something different from the Good News. ⁷Really, there is no other Good News. But some people are confusing you; they want to change the Good News of Christ. ⁸We preached to you the Good News. So if we ourselves, or even an angel from heaven, should preach to you something different, we should be judged guilty! ⁹I said this before, and now I say it again: you have already accepted the Good News. If anyone is preaching something different to you, he should be judged guilty!

¹⁰Do you think I am trying to make people accept me? No, God is the One I am trying to please. Am I trying to please people? If I still wanted to please people, I would not be a servant of Christ.

Paul's Authority is from God

¹¹Brothers and sisters, I want you to know that the Good News I preached to you was not made up by human beings. ¹²I did not get it from humans, nor did anyone teach it to me, but Jesus Christ showed it to me.

¹³You have heard about my past life in the Jewish religion. I attacked the church

of God and tried to destroy it. [14]I was becoming a leader in the Jewish religion, doing better than most other Jews of my age. I tried harder than anyone else to follow the teachings handed down by our ancestors.

[15]But God had special plans for me and set me apart for his work even before I was born. He called me through his grace [16]and showed his Son to me so that I might tell the Good News about him to those who are not Jewish. When God called me, I did not get advice or help from any person. [17]I did not go to Jerusalem to see those who were apostles before I was.

But, without waiting, I went away to Arabia and later went back to Damascus.

[18]After three years I went to Jerusalem to meet Peter and stayed with him for fifteen days. [19]I met no other apostles, except James, the brother of the Lord. [20]God knows that these things I write are not lies. [21]Later, I went to the areas of Syria and Cilicia.

[22]In Judea the churches in Christ had never met me. [23]They had only heard it said, "This man who was attacking us is now preaching the same faith that he once tried to destroy." [24]And these believers praised God because of me.

> Paul knew the Corinthians might not think he was perfect (13:7). But what mattered most was not whether *they* thought he had failed, but what *God* thought of him and of them (13:5,9).

Think

What matters is how we respond to God, not whether other people have failed us (13:7).

Pray

Think of the people who you feel have let you down. Pray the words of 13:14 for them and for yourself.

What makes a good Christian?

Which of the following make someone a good Christian?

- Going to church
- Not swearing
- Being good

 Galatians 2:1–21

Other Apostles Accepted Paul

2 After fourteen years I went to Jerusalem again, this time with Barnabas. I also took Titus with me. [2]I went because God showed me I should go. I met with the believers there, and in private I told their leaders the Good News that I preach to the non-Jewish people. I did not want my past work and the work I am now doing to be wasted. [3]Titus was with me, but he was not forced to be circumcised, even though he was a Greek. [4]We talked about this problem because some false believers had come into our group secretly. They came in like spies to overturn the freedom we have in Christ Jesus. They wanted to make us slaves. [5]But we did not give in to those false believers for a minute. We wanted the truth of the Good News to continue for you.

[6]Those leaders who seemed to be important did not change the Good News that I preach. (It doesn't matter to me if they were "important" or not. To God everyone is the same.) [7]But these leaders saw that I had been given the work of telling the Good News to those who are not Jewish, just as Peter had the work of telling the Jews. [8]God gave Peter the power to work as an apostle for the Jewish people. But he also gave me the power to work as an apostle for those who are not Jews. [9]James, Peter and John, who seemed to be the leaders, understood that God had given me this special grace, so they accepted Barnabas and me. They agreed that they would go to the Jewish people and that we should go to those who are not Jewish. [10]The only thing they asked us was to remember to help the poor—something I really wanted to do.

Paul Shows that Peter was Wrong

[11]When Peter came to Antioch, I challenged him to his face, because he was wrong. [12]Peter ate with the non-Jewish people until some Jewish people sent from James came to Antioch. When they arrived, Peter stopped eating with those who weren't Jewish, and he separated himself from them. He was afraid of the Jews. [13]So Peter was a hypocrite, as were the other Jewish believers who joined with him. Even Barnabas was influenced by what these Jewish believers did. [14]When I saw they were not following the truth of the Good News, I spoke to Peter in front of them all. I said, "Peter, you are a Jew, but you are not living like a Jew. You are living

452

like those who are not Jewish. So why do you now try to force those who are not Jewish to live like Jews?"

15We were not born as non-Jewish "sinners", but as Jews. 16Yet we know that a person is made right with God not by following the law, but by trusting in Jesus Christ. So we, too, have put our faith in Christ Jesus, that we might be made right with God because we trusted in Christ. It is not because we followed the law, because no one can be made right with God by following the law.

17We Jews came to Christ, trying to be made right with God, and it became clear that we are sinners too. Does this mean that Christ encourages sin? No! 18But I would really be wrong to begin teaching again those things that I gave up. 19It was the law that put me to death, and I died to the law so that I can now live for God. 20I was put to death on the cross with Christ, and I do not live any more—it is Christ who lives in me. I still live in my body, but I live by faith in the Son of God who loved me and gave himself to save me. 21By saying these things I am not going against God's grace. Just the opposite, if the law could make us right with God, then Christ's death would be useless.

How is a person made right with God (2:16)?

What doesn't make a person right with God (2:16)?

Paul is saying that to be a Christian, and therefore right with God, is more than merely doing what is right and keeping the law.

Think

Does this mean that the law (e.g. the Ten Commandments in Exodus 20) is not relevant to us?

Pray

That your relationship with God is not based on keeping religious rules but on faith in Christ.

The rulebook

What are rules for?

Galatians 3:1–20

Blessing Comes Through Faith

3 You people in Galatia were told very clearly about the death of Jesus Christ on the cross. But you were foolish; you let someone trick you. ²Tell me this one thing: how did you receive the Holy Spirit? Did you receive the Spirit by following the law? No, you received the Spirit because you heard the Good News and believed it. ³You began your life in Christ by the Spirit. Now are you trying to make it complete by your own power? That is foolish. ⁴Were all your experiences wasted? I hope not! ⁵Does God give you the Spirit and work miracles among you because you follow the law? No, he does these things because you heard the Good News and believed it.

⁶The Scriptures say the same thing about Abraham: "Abraham believed God, and God accepted Abraham's faith, and that faith made him right with God." ⁷So you should know that the true children of Abraham are those who have faith. ⁸The Scriptures, telling what would happen in the future, said that God would make the non-Jewish people right through their faith. This Good News was told to Abraham beforehand, as the Scripture says: "All nations will be blessed through you." ⁹So all who believe as Abraham believed are blessed just as Abraham was. ¹⁰But those who depend on following the law to make them right are under a curse, because the Scriptures say, "Anyone will be cursed who does not always obey what is written in the Book of the Law." ¹¹Now

it is clear that no one can be made right with God by the law, because the Scriptures say, "Those who are right with God will live by trusting in him." ¹²The law is not based on faith. It says, "A person who obeys these things will live because of them." ¹³Christ took away the curse the law put on us. He changed places with us and put himself under that curse. It is written in the Scriptures, "Anyone whose body is displayed on a tree is cursed." ¹⁴Christ did this so that God's blessing promised to Abraham might come through Jesus Christ to those who are not Jews. Jesus died so that by our believing we could receive the Spirit that God promised.

The Law and the Promise

¹⁵Brothers and sisters, let us think in human terms: even an agreement made between two persons is firm. After that agreement is accepted by both people, no one can stop it or add anything to it. ¹⁶God made promises both to Abraham and to his descendant. God did not say, "and to your descendants". That would mean many people. But God said, "and to your descendant". That means only one person; that person is Christ. ¹⁷This is what I mean: God had an agreement with Abraham and promised to keep it. The law, which came 430 years later, cannot change that agreement and so destroy God's promise to Abraham. ¹⁸If the law could give us Abraham's blessing, then the promise would not be necessary. But that is not possible, because God freely gave his

blessings to Abraham through the promise he had made.

19So what was the law for? It was given to show that the wrong things people do are against God's will. And it continued until the special descendant, who had been promised, came. The law was given through angels who used Moses for a mediator to give the law to people. 20But a mediator is not needed when there is only one side, and God is only one.

The rules in the Old Testament are really there to show you that you can't live up to the rules and be perfect. But you don't have to be: it's faith in Jesus that gets you through.

Think

Do you spend so much time sweating about the rules that it gets you down? That's not how it should be. A wise man once said: "Love, and then do whatever you want." What he meant was, if you really love God and each other, then you'll probably follow the rules without really trying.

Pray

Thank you, Father, that I don't have to be perfect.

Free to live

OK, you see a sign against a wall or on a bench which says "Do not touch – wet paint". What do you (want to) do? If you're anything like me you'll be dying to stick your finger on it. It's probably just the same as "Keep off the grass" or any other sign.

 Galatians 3:21–4:20

The Purpose of the Law of Moses

²¹Does this mean that the law is against God's promises? Never! That would be true only if the law could make us right. But God did not give a law that can bring life. ²²Instead, the Scriptures showed that the whole world is bound by sin. This was so the promise would be given through faith to people who believe in Jesus Christ.

²³Before this faith came, we were all held prisoners by the law. We had no freedom until God showed us the way of faith that was coming. ²⁴In other words, the law was our guardian leading us to Christ so that we could be made right with God through faith. ²⁵Now the way of faith has come, and we no longer live under a guardian.

²⁶⁻²⁷You were all baptised into Christ, and so you were all clothed with Christ. This means that you are all children of God through faith in Christ Jesus. ²⁸In Christ, there is no difference between Jew and Greek, slave and free person, male and female. You are all the same in Christ Jesus. ²⁹You belong to Christ, so you are Abraham's descendants. You will inherit all of God's blessings because of the promise God made to Abraham.

4 I want to tell you this: while those who will inherit their fathers' property are still children, they are no different from slaves. It does not matter that the children

own everything. ²While they are children, they must obey those who are chosen to care for them. But when the children reach the age set by their fathers, they are free. ³It is the same for us. We were once like children, slaves to the useless rules of this world. ⁴But when the right time came, God sent his Son who was born of a woman and lived under the law. ⁵God did this so he could buy freedom for those who were under the law and so we could become his children.

⁶Since you are God's children, God sent the Spirit of his Son into your hearts, and the Spirit cries out, "Father". ⁷So now you are not a slave; you are God's child, and God will give you the blessing he promised, because you are his child.

Paul's Love for the Christians

⁸In the past you did not know God. You were slaves to gods that were not real. ⁹But now you know the true God. Really, it is God who knows you. So why do you turn back to those weak and useless rules you followed before? Do you want to be slaves to those things again? ¹⁰You still follow teachings about special days, months, seasons and years. ¹¹I am afraid for you, that my work for you has been wasted.

¹²Brothers and sisters, I became like you, so I beg you to become like me. You were very good to me before. ¹³You remember that it was because of sickness

that I came to you the first time, preaching the Good News. ¹⁴Though my sickness was a trouble for you, you did not hate me or make me leave. But you welcomed me as an angel from God, as if I were Jesus Christ himself! ¹⁵You were very happy then, but where is that joy now? I am ready to testify that you would have taken out your eyes and given them to me if that were possible. ¹⁶Now am I your enemy because I tell you the truth?

¹⁷Those people are working hard to persuade you, but this is not good for you. They want to persuade you to turn against us and follow only them. ¹⁸It is good for people to show interest in you, but only if their purpose is good. This is always true, not just when I am with you. ¹⁹My little children, again I feel the pain of childbirth for you until you truly become like Christ. ²⁰I wish I could be with you now and could change the way I am talking to you, because I do not know what to think about you.

God gave us the law to show us how to live. It also shows us how much we need Jesus.

Can you think how?

Check your answer with 3:22–25.

Think

When we are told not to do something, why is it that we just want to go out and do it?

Pray

Free from sin and free from the law. Thank Jesus for the freedom that he brings.

457

Ouch!

When Jewish and Muslim boys are born, they get circumcised. This involves cutting off the bit of skin at the end of the penis when the boy is a few days old. This is partly a hygiene thing and partly because it's a sign of dedication to God.

Galatians 4:21–5:15

The Example of Hagar and Sarah

²¹Some of you still want to be under the law. Tell me, do you know what the law says? ²²The Scriptures say that Abraham had two sons. The mother of one son was a slave woman, and the mother of the other son was a free woman. ²³Abraham's son from the slave woman was born in the normal human way. But the son from the free woman was born because of the promise God made to Abraham.

²⁴This story teaches something else: the two women are like the two agreements between God and his people. One agreement is the law that God made on Mount Sinai, and the people who are under this agreement are like slaves. The mother named Hagar is like that agreement. ²⁵She is like Mount Sinai in Arabia and is a picture of the earthly Jewish city of Jerusalem. This city and its people, the Jews, are slaves to the law. ²⁶But the heavenly Jerusalem, which is above, is like the free woman. She is our mother. ²⁷It is written in the Scriptures:

"Be happy, Jerusalem.
    You are like a woman who never gave
        birth to children.
Start singing and shout for joy.
    You never felt the pain of giving birth,
but you will have more children
    than the woman who has a husband."

Isaiah 54:1

²⁸My brothers and sisters, you are God's children because of his promise, as Isaac was then. ²⁹The son who was born in the normal way treated the other son badly. It is the same today. ³⁰But what does the Scripture say? "Throw out the slave woman and her son. The son of the slave woman should not inherit anything. The son of the free woman should receive it all." ³¹So, my brothers and sisters, we are not children of the slave woman, but of the free woman.

Keep Your Freedom

5 We have freedom now, because Christ made us free. So stand strong. Do not change and go back into the slavery of the law. ²Listen, I, Paul, tell you that if you go back to the law by being circumcised, Christ does you no good. ³Again, I warn every man: if you allow yourselves to be circumcised, you must follow all the law. ⁴If you try to be made right with God through the law, your life with Christ is over—you have left God's grace. ⁵But we have the true hope that comes from being made right with God, and by the Spirit we wait eagerly for this hope. ⁶When we are in Christ Jesus, it is not important if we are circumcised or not. The important thing is faith—the kind of faith that works through love.

⁷You were running a good race. Who stopped you from following the true way? ⁸This change did not come from the One who chose you. ⁹Be careful! "Just a little

458

yeast makes the whole batch of dough rise." ¹⁰But I trust in the Lord that you will not believe those different ideas. Whoever is confusing you with such ideas will be punished.

¹¹My brothers and sisters, I do not teach that a man must be circumcised. If I teach circumcision, why am I still being attacked? If I still taught circumcision, my preaching about the cross would not be a problem. ¹²I wish the people who are bothering you would castrate themselves!

¹³My brothers and sisters, God called you to be free, but do not use your freedom as an excuse to do what pleases your sinful self. Serve each other with love. ¹⁴The whole law is made complete in this one command: "Love your neighbour as you love yourself." ¹⁵If you go on hurting each other and tearing each other apart, be careful, or you will completely destroy each other.

Paul's become really angry because he's heard that some people are telling the Christians in Galatia that if they want to be proper Christians, they have to be circumcised and become Jewish. Of course, they don't.

Now that Jesus died and rose again for us, all we need is faith. Which, if you're a guy, is a relief.

Think

Just because a rule isn't in effect any more, it doesn't mean that it was always stupid. But it doesn't apply now. We're free to love God and love one another, knowing that through Jesus, our place in heaven is safe.

Pray

Thank God that the only thing we need to follow Jesus is faith.

Free to serve

God says that there is a wrong and a right way to live our lives. If we follow the Spirit then we should be doing it the right way. God has set us free from the law for a reason . . .

 Galatians 5:16–6:18

The Spirit and Human Nature

¹⁶So I tell you: live by following the Spirit. Then you will not do what your sinful selves want. ¹⁷Our sinful selves want what is against the Spirit, and the Spirit wants what is against our sinful selves. The two are against each other, so you cannot do just what you please. ¹⁸But if the Spirit is leading you, you are not under the law.

¹⁹The wrong things the sinful self does are clear: being sexually unfaithful, not being pure, taking part in sexual sins, ²⁰worshipping gods, doing witchcraft, hating, making trouble, being jealous, being angry, being selfish, making people angry with each other, causing divisions among people, ²¹feeling envy, being drunk, having wild and wasteful parties, and doing other things like these. I warn you now as I warned you before: those who do these things will not inherit God's kingdom. ²²But the Spirit produces the fruit of love, joy, peace, patience, kindness, goodness, faithfulness, ²³gentleness, self-control. There is no law that says these things are wrong. ²⁴Those who belong to Christ Jesus have crucified their own sinful selves. They have given up their old selfish feelings and the evil things they wanted to do. ²⁵We get our new life from the Spirit, so we should follow the Spirit. ²⁶We must not be proud or make trouble with each other or be jealous of each other.

Help Each Other

6 Brothers and sisters, if someone in your group does something wrong, you who are spiritual should go to that person and gently help make him right again. But be careful, because you might be tempted to sin too. ²By helping each other with your troubles, you truly obey the law of Christ. ³If anyone thinks he is important when he really is not, he is only fooling himself. ⁴Each person should judge his own actions and not compare himself with others. Then he can be proud for what he himself has done. ⁵Each person must be responsible for himself.

⁶Anyone who is learning the teaching of God should share all the good things he has with his teacher.

Life is like Planting a Field

⁷Do not be fooled: you cannot cheat God. People harvest only what they plant. ⁸If they plant to satisfy their sinful selves, their sinful selves will bring them ruin. But if they plant to please the Spirit, they will receive eternal life from the Spirit. ⁹We must not become tired of doing good. We will receive our harvest of eternal life at the right time if we do not give up. ¹⁰When we have the opportunity to help anyone, we should do it. But we should give special attention to those who are in the family of believers.

Paul Ends His Letter

¹¹See what large letters I use to write this myself. ¹²Some people are trying to force you to be circumcised so the Jews will accept them. They are afraid they will be attacked if they follow only the cross of

Christ. ¹³Those who are circumcised do not obey the law themselves, but they want you to be circumcised so they can boast about what they forced you to do. ¹⁴I hope I will never boast about things like that. The cross of our Lord Jesus Christ is my only reason for boasting. Through the cross of Jesus my world was crucified, and I died to the world. ¹⁵It is not important if a man is circumcised or uncircumcised. The important thing is being the new people God has made. ¹⁶Peace and mercy to those who follow this rule—and to all of God's people.

¹⁷So do not give me any more trouble. I have scars on my body that show I belong to Christ Jesus.

¹⁸My brothers and sisters, the grace of our Lord Jesus Christ be with your spirit. Amen.

What are the nine characteristics God wants to see in your life (5:22,23)? Write them in the space below.

Think

How have you used your freedom in Christ to serve others?

Consider using some of your "free time" to serve other people.

Pray

Ask God to grow his fruit in you – and let it show to others.

God chose you

What are some of the biggest choices you've had to make in your life? What subjects to take at school, what outfit to wear if you want to impress or any other big choices?

Now, think about your friends. Who chose who?

 Ephesians 1:1–23

1 From Paul, an apostle of Christ Jesus. I am an apostle because that is what God wanted.

To God's holy people living in Ephesus, believers in Christ Jesus:

²Grace and peace to you from God our Father and the Lord Jesus Christ.

Spiritual Blessings in Christ

³Praise be to the God and Father of our Lord Jesus Christ. In Christ, God has given us every spiritual blessing in the heavenly world. ⁴That is, in Christ, he chose us before the world was made so that we would be his holy people—people without blame before him. ⁵Because of his love, God had already decided to make us his own children through Jesus Christ. That was what he wanted and what pleased him, ⁶and it brings praise to God because of his wonderful grace. God gave that grace to us freely, in Christ, the One he loves. ⁷In Christ we are set free by the blood of his death, and so we have forgiveness of sins. How rich is God's grace, ⁸which he has given to us so fully and freely. God, with full wisdom and understanding, ⁹let us know his secret purpose. This was what God wanted, and he planned to do it through Christ. ¹⁰His goal was to carry out his plan, when the right time came, that all things in heaven and on earth would be joined together in Christ as the head. ¹¹In Christ we were chosen to be God's

people, because from the very beginning God had decided this in keeping with his plan. And he is the One who makes everything agree with what he decides and wants. ¹²We are the first people who hoped in Christ, and we were chosen so that we would bring praise to God's glory. ¹³So it is with you. When you heard the true teaching—the Good News about your salvation—you believed in Christ. And in Christ, God put his special mark of ownership on you by giving you the Holy Spirit that he had promised. ¹⁴That Holy Spirit is the guarantee that we will receive what God promised for his people until God gives full freedom to those who are his—to bring praise to God's glory.

Paul's Prayer

¹⁵That is why since I heard about your faith in the Lord Jesus and your love for all God's people, ¹⁶I have not stopped giving thanks to God for you. I always remember you in my prayers, ¹⁷asking the God of our Lord Jesus Christ, the glorious Father, to give you a spirit of wisdom and revelation so that you will know him better. ¹⁸I pray also that you will have greater understanding in your heart so you will know the hope to which he has called us and that you will know how rich and glorious are the blessings God has promised his holy people. ¹⁹And you will know that God's power is very great for us who believe. That power is the same as the great strength ²⁰God

used to raise Christ from the dead and put him at his right side in the heavenly world. [21]God has put Christ over all rulers, authorities, powers and kings, not only in this world but also in the next. [22]God put everything under his power and made him the head over everything for the church, [23]which is Christ's body. The church is filled with Christ, and Christ fills everything in every way.

Try to find answers to these questions in the verses. Put them in your own words.

Who did God choose (v 4)? _____

_____

What had God decided (v 5)? _____

_____

Who did God tell his plans to (v 9)? _____

_____

What is God's plan (v 10)? _____

_____

Think

How does being "adopted" by God (v 5) make a difference to your life?

Pray

Thank you, Lord, for making me part of your family.

From death to life

Have you heard any of those stories about someone who "died" during a heart attack or an operation and then was brought back to life? Here's another way people come back to life.

Ephesians 2:1–3:6

We Now Have Life

2 In the past you were spiritually dead because of your sins and the things you did against God. ²Yes, in the past you lived the way the world lives, following the ruler of the evil powers that are above the earth. That same spirit is now working in those who refuse to obey God. ³In the past all of us lived like them, trying to please our sinful selves and doing all the things our bodies and minds wanted. We should have suffered God's anger because of the way we were. We were the same as all other people.

⁴But God's mercy is great, and he loved us very much. ⁵Though we were spiritually dead because of the things we did against God, he gave us new life with Christ. You have been saved by God's grace. ⁶And he raised us up with Christ and gave us a seat with him in the heavens. He did this for those in Christ Jesus ⁷so that for all future time he could show the very great riches of his grace by being kind to us in Christ Jesus. ⁸I mean that you have been saved by grace through believing. You did not save yourselves: it was a gift from God. ⁹It was not the result of your own work, so you cannot boast about it. ¹⁰God has made us what we are. In Christ Jesus, God made us to do good works, which God planned in advance for us to live our lives doing.

One in Christ

¹¹You were not born Jewish. You are the people the Jews call "uncircumcised". Those who call you "uncircumcised" call themselves "circumcised". (Their circumcision is only something they themselves do on their bodies.) ¹²Remember that in the past you were without Christ. You were not citizens of Israel, and you had no part in the agreements with the promise that God made to his people. You had no hope, and you did not know God. ¹³But now in Christ Jesus, you who were far away from God are brought near through the blood of Christ's death. ¹⁴Christ himself is our peace. He made both Jewish people and those who are not Jews one people. They were separated as if there were a wall between them, but Christ broke down that wall of hate by giving his own body. ¹⁵The Jewish law had many commands and rules, but Christ ended that law. His purpose was to make the two groups of people become one new people in him and in this way make peace. ¹⁶It was also Christ's purpose to end the hatred between the two groups, to make them into one body, and to bring them back to God. Christ did all this with his death on the cross. ¹⁷Christ came and preached peace to you who were far away from God, and to those who were near to God. ¹⁸Yes, it is through Christ we all have the right to come to the Father in one Spirit.

¹⁹Now you who are not Jewish are not foreigners or strangers any longer, but are citizens together with God's holy people. You belong to God's family. ²⁰You are like a building that was built on the foundation of the apostles and prophets. Christ Jesus himself is the most important stone in that building, ²¹and that whole building is

joined together in Christ. He makes it grow and become a holy temple in the Lord. ²²And in Christ you, too, are being built together with the Jews into a place where God lives through the Spirit.

Paul's Work in Telling the Good News

3 So I, Paul, am a prisoner of Christ Jesus for you who are not Jews. ²Surely you have heard that God gave me this work through his grace to help you. ³He let me know his secret by showing it to me. I have already written a little about this. ⁴If you read what I wrote then, you can see that I truly understand the secret about the Christ. ⁵People who lived in other times were not told that secret. But now, through the Spirit, God has shown that secret to his holy apostles and prophets. ⁶This is that secret: that through the Good News those who are not Jews will share with the Jews in God's blessing. They belong to the same body, and they share together in the promise that God made in Christ Jesus.

What were you? _____ (2:1)

Why? _____ (2:1)

What did God do? _____ (2:4,5)

Why? _____ (2:4)

Think

Have you received God's gift of life for yourself (2:8)? You can *now*. Talk to God about it.

What's God's big plan for your life (2:10)?

Pray

Thank God for Jesus and all that his life and death mean for you.

One in Jesus

Do some Christians get up your nose? Perhaps you know one or two very close to you in your own church? You're probably not alone and that's probably one reason why Paul wrote to the Christians at Ephesus...

 Ephesians 3:7–4:16

⁷By God's special gift of grace given to me through his power, I became a servant to tell that Good News. ⁸I am the least important of all God's people, but God gave me this gift—to tell those who are not Jews the Good News about the riches of Christ, which are too great to understand fully. ⁹And God gave me the work of telling all people about the plan for his secret, which has been hidden in him since the beginning of time. He is the One who created everything. ¹⁰His purpose was that through the church all the rulers and powers in the heavenly world will now know God's wisdom, which has so many forms. ¹¹This agrees with the purpose God had since the beginning of time, and he carried out his plan through Christ Jesus our Lord. ¹²In Christ we can come before God with freedom and without fear. We can do this through faith in Christ. ¹³So I ask you not to become discouraged because of the sufferings I am having for you. My sufferings are for your glory.

The Love of Christ

¹⁴So I bow in prayer before the Father ¹⁵from whom every family in heaven and on earth gets its true name. ¹⁶I ask the Father in his great glory to give you the power to be strong inwardly through his Spirit. ¹⁷I pray that Christ will live in your hearts by faith and that your lives will be strong in love and be built on love. ¹⁸And I pray that you and all God's holy people

will have the power to understand the greatness of Christ's love—how wide and how long and how high and how deep that love is. ¹⁹Christ's love is greater than anyone can ever know, but I pray that you will be able to know that love. Then you can be filled with the fullness of God.

²⁰With God's power working in us, God can do much, much more than anything we can ask or imagine. ²¹To him be glory in the church and in Christ Jesus for all time, for ever and ever. Amen.

The Unity of the Body

4 I am in prison because I belong to the Lord. God chose you to be his people, so I tell you now to live the life to which God called you. ²Always be humble, gentle and patient, accepting each other in love. ³You are joined together with peace through the Spirit, so do all you can to continue together in this way. ⁴There is one body and one Spirit, and God called you to have one hope. ⁵There is one Lord, one faith and one baptism. ⁶There is one God and Father of everything. He rules everything and is everywhere and is in everything.

⁷Christ gave each one of us the special gift of grace, showing how generous he is. ⁸That is why it says in the Scriptures,

"When he went up to the heights,
he led a parade of captives,
and he gave gifts to all peoples."

Psalm 68:18

9When it says, "He went up," what does it mean? It means that he first came down to the earth. 10So Jesus came down, and he is the same One who went up above all the sky. Christ did that to fill everything with his presence. 11And Christ gave gifts to people—he made some to be apostles, some to be prophets, some to go and tell the Good News, and some to have the work of caring for and teaching God's people. 12Christ gave those gifts to prepare God's holy people for the work of serving, to make the body of Christ stronger. 13This work must continue until we are all joined together in the same faith and in the same knowledge of the Son of God. We must become like a mature person, growing until we become like Christ and have his perfection.

14Then we will no longer be babies. We will not be tossed about like a ship that the waves carry one way and then another. We will not be influenced by every new teaching we hear from people who are trying to fool us. They make plans and try any kind of trick to fool people into following the wrong path. 15No! Speaking the truth with love, we will grow up in every way into Christ, who is the head. 16The whole body depends on Christ, and all the parts of the body are joined and held together. Each part does its own work to make the whole body grow and be strong with love.

Life in God's family isn't always peace, love and perfect harmony. Next time you're about to blow a fuse or walk out in a huff, remember...

Be _____ accepting _____ (4:2).

Make _____ (4:3).

Think

The church needs all sorts of people (1 Corinthians 12:12–31), even those who get up your nose. Love them as God loves them.

Pray

Pray for the person who really "gets up your nose". Ask God to help you and Christians you know to work at being "one" in Jesus.

Out with the old

Knowing Jesus means things are going to be different. What's got to change?

Ephesians 4:17–5:14

The Way You Should Live

¹⁷In the Lord's name, I tell you this. Do not continue living like those who do not believe. Their thoughts are worth nothing. ¹⁸They do not understand, and they know nothing, because they refuse to listen. So they cannot have the life that God gives. ¹⁹They have lost all feeling of shame, and they use their lives for doing evil. They continually want to do all kinds of evil. ²⁰But what you learned in Christ was not like this. ²¹I know that you heard about him, and you are in him, so you were taught the truth that is in Jesus. ²²You were taught to leave your old self—to stop living the evil way you lived before. That old self becomes worse, because people are fooled by the evil things they want to do. ²³But you were taught to be made new in your hearts, ²⁴to become a new person. That new person is made to be like God—made to be truly good and holy.

²⁵So you must stop telling lies. "Tell each other the truth," because we all belong to each other in the same body. ²⁶When you are angry, do not sin, and be sure to stop being angry before the end of the day. ²⁷Do not give the devil a way to defeat you. ²⁸Those who are stealing must stop stealing and start working. They should earn an honest living for themselves. Then they will have something to share with those who are poor.

²⁹When you talk, do not say harmful things, but say what people need—words that will help others become stronger. Then what you say will do good to those who listen to you. ³⁰And do not make the Holy Spirit sad. The Spirit is God's proof that you belong to him. God gave you the Spirit to show that God will make you free when the final day comes. ³¹Do not be bitter or angry or cross. Never shout angrily or say things to hurt others. Never do anything evil. ³²Be kind and loving to each other, and forgive each other just as God forgave you in Christ.

Living in the Light

5 You are God's children whom he loves, so try to be like him. ²Live a life of love just as Christ loved us and gave himself for us as a sweet-smelling offering and sacrifice to God.

³But there must be no sexual sin among you, or any kind of evil or greed. Those things are not right for God's holy people. ⁴Also, there must be no evil talk among you, and you must not speak foolishly or tell evil jokes. These things are not right for you. Instead, you should be giving thanks to God. ⁵You can be sure of this: no one will have a place in the kingdom of Christ and of God who sins sexually, or does evil things, or is greedy. Anyone who is greedy is serving a false god.

⁶Do not let anyone fool you by telling you things that are not true, because these things will bring God's anger on those who do not obey him. ⁷So have nothing to do with them. ⁸In the past you were full of darkness, but now you are full of light in the Lord. So live like children who belong to the light. ⁹Light brings every kind of goodness, right living and truth. ¹⁰Try to learn what pleases the Lord. ¹¹Have noth-

ing to do with the things done in darkness, which are not worth anything. But show that they are wrong. [12]It is shameful even to talk about what those people do in secret. [13]But the light makes all things easy to see, [14]and everything that is made easy to see can become light. This is why it is said:

"Wake up, sleeper!
  Rise from death,
and Christ will shine on you."

OK. All that stuff in 4:17–19 sounds bad. Maybe you feel, "I've never been that awful!" But how about compared to God's standard?

Is God happy with *all* your thoughts (4:17)?

Are your thoughts sometimes about wrong things you'd like to do or say (4:19)?

No one can live God's way without a new life (4:23,24). You need God's help in chucking out the old ways.

Think

What things in your life need looking at and then chucking out?

Pray

Anything you need to throw out? Our thoughts can be hard to control. Ask God to help you.

A good time?

The issue of alcohol is something we all have to face. Have you got mates who make jokes about drinking too much? Or friends who even go out and drink and beg you to join in? What does the Bible say?

Ephesians 5:15–6:9

¹⁵So be very careful how you live. Do not live like those who are not wise, but live wisely. ¹⁶Use every chance you have for doing good, because these are evil times. ¹⁷So do not be foolish but learn what the Lord wants you to do. ¹⁸Do not be drunk with wine, which will ruin you, but be filled with the Spirit. ¹⁹Speak to each other with psalms, hymns and spiritual songs, singing and making music in your hearts to the Lord. ²⁰Always give thanks to God the Father for everything, in the name of our Lord Jesus Christ.

Wives and Husbands

²¹Yield to obey each other because you respect Christ.

²²Wives, yield to your husbands, as you do to the Lord, ²³because the husband is the head of the wife, as Christ is the head of the church. And he is the Saviour of the body, which is the church. ²⁴As the church yields to Christ, so you wives should yield to your husbands in everything.

²⁵Husbands, love your wives as Christ loved the church and gave himself for it ²⁶to make it belong to God. Christ used the word to make the church clean by washing it with water. ²⁷He died so that he could give the church to himself like a bride in all her beauty. He died so that the church could be pure and without fault, with no evil or sin or any other wrong thing in it. ²⁸In the same way, husbands should love their wives as they love their own bodies. The man who loves his wife loves himself. ²⁹No one ever hates his own body, but feeds and takes care of it. And that is what Christ does for the church, ³⁰because we are parts of his body. ³¹The Scripture says, "So a man will leave his father and mother and be united with his wife, and the two will become one body." ³²That secret is very important—I am talking about Christ and the church. ³³But each one of you must love his wife as he loves himself, and a wife must respect her husband.

Children and Parents

6 Children, obey your parents as the Lord wants, because this is the right thing to do. ²The command says, "Honour your father and mother." This is the first command that has a promise with it— ³"Then everything will be well with you, and you will have a long life on the earth."

470

[4]Fathers, do not make your children angry, but raise them with the training and teaching of the Lord.

Slaves and Masters

[5]Slaves, obey your masters here on earth with fear and respect and from a sincere heart, just as you obey Christ. [6]You must do this not only while they are watching you, to please them. With all your heart you must do what God wants as people who are obeying Christ. [7]Do your work with enthusiasm. Work as if you were serving the Lord, not as if you were serving only men and women. [8]Remember that the Lord will give a reward to everyone, slave or free, for doing good.

[9]Masters, in the same way, be good to your slaves. Do not threaten them. Remember that the One who is your Master and their Master is in heaven, and he treats everyone alike.

Is getting drunk wise or foolish (5:17,18)?

What's the wise way to live (5:18)?

Who does worship (5:19,20) keep at the centre of our lives?

Think

There are loads of issues in life where you have to make a choice. A question 5:18 makes us ask is "Who's in control in your life?"

Pray

Lord Jesus, fill me with your Spirit so that I can have the strength to make wise choices.

Ready for a fight

Hundreds of years ago, when soldiers went out to fight, they'd strap on armour made of metal, chain and leather, which would protect them in the battle ahead.

 Ephesians 6:10 – Philippians 1:11

Wear the Full Armour of God

¹⁰Finally, be strong in the Lord and in his great power. ¹¹Put on the full armour of God so that you can fight against the devil's evil tricks. ¹²Our fight is not against people on earth but against the rulers and authorities and the powers of this world's darkness, against the spiritual powers of evil in the heavenly world. ¹³That is why you need to put on God's full armour. Then on the day of evil you will be able to stand strong. And when you have finished the whole fight, you will still be standing. ¹⁴So stand strong, with the belt of truth tied around your waist and the protection of right living on your chest. ¹⁵On your feet wear the Good News of peace to help you stand strong. ¹⁶And also use the shield of faith with which you can stop all the burning arrows of the Evil One. ¹⁷Accept God's salvation as your helmet, and take the sword of the Spirit, which is the word of God. ¹⁸Pray in the Spirit at all times with all kinds of prayers, asking for everything you need. To do this you must always be ready and never give up. Always pray for all God's people.

¹⁹Also pray for me that when I speak, God will give me words so that I can tell the secret of the Good News without fear. ²⁰I have been sent to preach this Good News, and I am doing that now, here in prison. Pray that when I preach the Good

News I will speak without fear, as I should.

Final Greetings

²¹I am sending to you Tychicus, our brother whom we love and a faithful servant of the Lord's work. He will tell you everything that is happening with me. Then you will know how I am and what I am doing. ²²I am sending him to you for this reason—so that you will know how we are, and he can encourage you.

²³Peace and love with faith to you from God the Father and the Lord Jesus Christ. ²⁴Grace to all of you who love our Lord Jesus Christ with love that never ends.

PHILIPPIANS

1 From Paul and Timothy, servants of Christ Jesus.

To all of God's holy people in Christ Jesus who live in Philippi, including your elders and deacons:

²Grace and peace to you from God our Father and the Lord Jesus Christ.

Paul's Prayer

³I thank my God every time I remember you, ⁴always praying with joy for all of you. ⁵I thank God for the help you gave me while I preached the Good News—help you gave from the first day you believed until now. ⁶God began doing a good work in you, and I am sure he will continue it until it is finished when Jesus Christ comes again.

7And I know that I am right to think like this about all of you, because I have you in my heart. All of you share in God's grace with me while I am in prison and while I am defending and proving the truth of the Good News. 8God knows that I want to see you very much, because I love all of you with the love of Christ Jesus.

9This is my prayer for you: that your love will grow more and more; that you will have knowledge and understanding with your love; 10that you will see the difference between good and bad and will choose the good; that you will be pure and without wrong for the coming of Christ; 11that you will do many good things with the help of Christ to bring glory and praise to God.

Living as a Christian is like being in a battle. But we have many different things to protect us.

Think

Why is:

- truth like a belt?
- righteousness like a breastplate?
- readiness like a pair of army boots?
- faith like a shield?
- salvation like a helmet?
- the Bible (also known as the Word of God) like a sword?

Pray

Thank God for giving you so many things to protect you as you live your Christian life and fight the good fight.

Facing death

Imagine you were diagnosed with a fatal illness and given only a year to live. How would it affect the way you lived your last year? What would you do with the rest of your life?

Philippians 1:12–2:4

Paul's Troubles Help the Work

¹²I want you brothers and sisters to know that what has happened to me has helped to spread the Good News. ¹³All the palace guards and everyone else knows that I am in prison because I am a believer in Christ. ¹⁴Because I am in prison, most of the believers have become more bold in Christ and are not afraid to speak the word of God.

¹⁵It is true that some preach about Christ because they are jealous and ambitious, but others preach about Christ because they want to help. ¹⁶They preach because they have love, and they know that God gave me the work of defending the Good News. ¹⁷But the others preach about Christ for selfish and wrong reasons, wanting to make trouble for me in prison.

¹⁸But it doesn't matter. The important thing is that in every way, whether for right or wrong reasons, they are preaching about Christ. So I am happy, and I will continue to be happy. ¹⁹Because you are praying for me and the Spirit of Jesus Christ is helping me, I know this trouble will bring my freedom. ²⁰I expect and hope that I will not fail Christ in anything but that I will have the courage now, as always, to show the greatness of Christ in my life here on earth, whether I live or die. ²¹To me the only important thing about living is Christ, and dying would be profit for me. ²²If I continue living in my body, I will be able to work for the Lord. I do not know what to choose—living or dying. ²³It is hard to choose between the two. I want to leave this life and be with Christ, which is much better, ²⁴but you need me here in my body. ²⁵Since I am sure of this, I know I will stay with you to help you grow and have joy in your faith. ²⁶You will be very happy in Christ Jesus when I am with you again.

²⁷Only one thing concerns me: be sure that you live in a way that brings honour to the Good News of Christ. Then whether I come and visit you or am away from you, I will hear that you are standing strong with one purpose, that you work together as one for the faith of the Good News, ²⁸and that you are not afraid of those who are against you. All of this is proof that your enemies will be destroyed but that you will be saved by God. ²⁹God gave you the honour not only of believing in Christ but also of suffering for him, both of which bring glory to Christ. ³⁰When I was with you, you saw the struggles I had, and you hear about the struggles I am having now. You yourselves

are having the same kind of struggles.

2 Does your life in Christ give you strength? Does his love comfort you? Do we share together in the Spirit? Do you have mercy and kindness? ²If so, make me very happy by having the same thoughts, sharing the same love, and having one mind and purpose. ³When you do things, do not let selfishness or pride be your guide. Instead, be humble and give more honour to others than to yourselves. ⁴Do not be interested only in your own life, but be interested in the lives of others.

Paul faced death often.

What did he believe was the benefit of him living (v 21,22)?

What would be the benefit if he died (v 23)?

What was his main hope in life and death (v 20)?

Think

What is your main reason for living? Try focussing more of your time and energy on that.

Pray

Talk to God about your feelings on death and dying. Ask him how your priorities look from a heavenly perspective.

Let your light shine

How can the way we act show people who we follow?

Philippians 2:5–30

Be Unselfish like Christ

⁵In your lives you must think and act like Christ Jesus.
⁶Christ himself was like God in every-thing.
But he did not think that being equal with God was something to be used for his own benefit.
⁷But he gave up his place with God and made himself nothing.
He was born to be a man and became like a servant.
⁸And when he was living as a man, he humbled himself and was fully obedient to God,
even when that caused his death— death on a cross.
⁹So God raised him to the highest place. God made his name greater than every other name
¹⁰so that every knee will bow to the name of Jesus—
everyone in heaven, on earth and under the earth.
¹¹And everyone will confess that Jesus Christ is Lord
and bring glory to God the Father.

Be the People God Wants You to Be

¹²My dear friends, you have always obeyed God when I was with you. It is even more important that you obey now while I am away from you. Keep on working to complete your salvation with fear and trembling, ¹³because God is working in you to help you want to do and be able to do what pleases him.

¹⁴Do everything without complaining or arguing. ¹⁵Then you will be innocent and without any wrong. You will be God's children without fault. But you are living with crooked and evil people all around you, among whom you shine like stars in the dark world. ¹⁶You offer the teaching that gives life. So when Christ comes again, I can be happy because my work was not wasted. I ran the race and won. ¹⁷Your faith makes you offer your lives as a sacrifice in serving God. If I have to offer my own blood with your sacrifice, I will be happy and full of joy with all of you. ¹⁸You also should be happy and full of joy with me.

Timothy and Epaphroditus

¹⁹I hope in the Lord Jesus to send Timothy to you soon. I will be happy to learn how you are. ²⁰I have no one else like Timothy, who truly cares for you. ²¹Other people are interested only in their own lives, not in the work of Jesus Christ. ²²You know the kind of person Timothy is. You know he has served with me in telling the Good News, as a son serves his father. ²³I plan to send him to you quickly when I know what will happen to me. ²⁴I am sure that the Lord will help me to come to you soon.

²⁵Epaphroditus, my brother in Christ, works and serves with me in the army of Christ. When I needed help, you sent him to me. I think now that I must send him back to you, ²⁶because he wants very much to see all of you. He is worried because you

476

heard that he was sick. 27Yes, he was sick, and nearly died, but God had mercy on him and me too so that I would not have more sadness. 28I want very much to send him to you so that when you see him you can be happy, and I can stop worrying about you. 29Welcome him in the Lord with much joy. Give honour to people like him, 30because he almost died for the work of Christ. He risked his life to give me the help you could not give in your service to me.

How can we follow Jesus' example? What makes us shine like stars?

Think

Most people, if they really think about it, have to admit that the way that Jesus, the ruler of everything, humbled himself enough to die in such a terrible, humiliating way is completely crazy. And yet, that's the way it was. And the hope we have because of what Jesus did for us through his supreme love is what keeps us going. It's what reminds us that living for him won't be for nothing.

Pray

Thank Jesus for loving us enough to humble himself and die.

Destination: heaven

When you lose at something, do you normally:

- give up?
- complain about the rules?
- have another go?

Philippians 3:1–21

The Importance of Christ

3 My brothers and sisters, be full of joy in the Lord. It is no trouble for me to write the same things to you again, and it will help you to be more ready. [2]Watch out for those who do evil, who are like dogs, who insist on cutting the body. [3]We are the ones who are truly circumcised. We worship God through his Spirit, and our pride is in Christ Jesus. We do not put trust in ourselves or anything we can do, [4]although I might be able to put trust in myself. If anyone thinks he has a reason to trust in himself, he should know that I have greater reason for trusting in myself. [5]I was circumcised eight days after my birth. I am from the people of Israel and the tribe of Benjamin. I am a Hebrew, and my parents were Hebrews. I had a strict view of the law, which is why I became a Pharisee. [6]I was so enthusiastic I tried to hurt the church. No one could find fault with the way I obeyed the law of Moses. [7]Those things were important to me, but now I think they are worth nothing because of Christ. [8]Not only those things, but I think that all things are worth nothing compared with the greatness of knowing Christ Jesus my Lord. Because of him, I have lost all those things, and now I know they are worthless rubbish. This allows me to have Christ [9]and to belong to him. Now I am right with God, not because I followed the law, but because I believed in Christ. God uses my faith to make me right with him. [10]I want to know Christ and the power that raised him from the dead. I want to share in his sufferings and become like him in his death. [11]Then I have hope that I myself will be raised from the dead.

Continuing Towards Our Goal

[12]I do not mean that I am already as God wants me to be. I have not yet reached that goal, but I continue trying to reach it and to make it mine. Christ wants me to do that, which is the reason he made me his. [13]Brothers and sisters, I know that I have not yet reached that goal, but there is one thing I always do. Forgetting the past and straining towards what is ahead, [14]I keep trying to reach the goal and get the prize for which God called me through Christ to the life above.

[15]All of us who are spiritually mature should think this way too. And if there are things you do not agree with, God will make them clear to you. [16]But we should continue following the truth we already have.

[17]Brothers and sisters, all of you should

try to follow my example and to copy those who live the way we showed you. ¹⁸Many people live like enemies of the cross of Christ. I have often told you about them, and it makes me cry to tell you about them now. ¹⁹In the end, they will be destroyed. They do whatever their bodies want, they are proud of their shameful acts, and they think only about earthly things. ²⁰But our homeland is in heaven, and we are waiting for our Saviour, the Lord Jesus Christ, to come from heaven. ²¹By his power to rule all things, he will change our simple bodies and make them like his own glorious body.

What's Paul's attitude to the past (v 13)?

Who does he belong to (v 12)?

Where did God call him to (v 14)?

Think

If you're a Christian, God has started a work in you which he intends to finish in heaven!

Pray

Thank God that the past is forgotten and the future couldn't be better!

Think before you think

Top sports people have fairly equal skills. But the winners are those with the right mental attitude. Being strong is more about how you think than having muscles in the right places.

Philippians 4:1–23

What the Christians are to Do

4 My dear brothers and sisters, I love you and want to see you. You bring me joy and make me proud of you, so stand strong in the Lord as I have told you. 2I ask Euodia and Syntyche to agree in the Lord. 3And I ask you, my faithful friend, to help these women. They served with me in telling the Good News, together with Clement and others who worked with me, whose names are written in the book of life.

4Be full of joy in the Lord always. I will say again, be full of joy.

5Let everyone see that you are gentle and kind. The Lord is coming soon. 6Do not worry about anything, but pray and ask God for everything you need, always giving thanks. 7And God's peace, which is so great we cannot understand it, will keep your hearts and minds in Christ Jesus.

8Brothers and sisters, think about the things that are good and worthy of praise. Think about the things that are true and honourable and right and pure and beautiful and respected. 9Do what you learned and received from me, what I told you, and what you saw me do. And the God who gives peace will be with you.

Paul Thanks the Christians

10I am very happy in the Lord that you have shown your care for me again. You continued to care about me, but there was no way for you to show it. 11I am not telling you this because I need anything. I have learned to be satisfied with the things I have and with everything that happens. 12I know how to live when I am poor, and I know how to live when I have plenty. I have learned the secret of being happy at any time in everything that happens, when I have enough to eat and when I go hungry, when I have more than I need and when I do not have enough. 13I can do all things through Christ, because he gives me strength.

14But it was good that you helped me when I needed it. 15You Philippians remember when I first preached the Good News there. When I left Macedonia, you were the only church that gave me help. 16Several times you sent me things I needed when I was in Thessalonica. 17Really, it is not that I want to receive gifts from you, but I want you to have the good that comes from giving. 18And now I have everything, and more. I have all I need, because Epaphroditus brought your gift to me. It is like a sweet-smelling sacrifice offered to God, who accepts that sacrifice and is pleased with it. ¹⁹My God will use his wonderful riches in Christ Jesus to give you everything you need. ²⁰Glory to our God and Father for ever and ever! Amen.

²¹Greet each of God's people in Christ. Those who are with me send greetings to you. ²²All of God's people greet you, particularly those from the palace of Caesar.

²³The grace of the Lord Jesus Christ be with you all.

Christians need to get their thinking right and then _____

_____ (v 9).

Paul said:

• don't _____

_____ (v 6)

• do think about things that are _____

_____ (v 8)

What sort of thoughts might this mean *not* thinking?

Think

Memorise the words in verse 8 and let them help you when you're tempted to think wrong things.

Pray

Use verse 6 from today's reading to help you talk to God.

481

The truth is good news

You get straight As in your exams. Would you:

(a) ignore them?
(b) pretend you didn't?
(c) tell anyone who'll listen?
(d) faint?

If you are anything like me, you would do (d), then (c)!

 Colossians 1:1–23

1 From Paul, an apostle of Christ Jesus. I am an apostle because that is what God wanted. Also from Timothy, our brother.

²To the holy and faithful brothers and sisters in Christ that live in Colosse:

Grace and peace to you from God our Father.

³In our prayers for you we always thank God, the Father of our Lord Jesus Christ, ⁴because we have heard about the faith you have in Christ Jesus and the love you have for all of God's people. ⁵You have this faith and love because of your hope, and what you hope for is kept safe for you in heaven. You learned about this hope when you heard the message about the truth, the Good News ⁶that was told to you. Everywhere in the world that Good News is bringing blessings and is growing. This has happened with you too, since you heard the Good News and understood the truth about the grace of God. ⁷You learned about God's grace from Epaphras, whom we love. He works together with us and is a faithful servant of Christ for us. ⁸He also told us about the love you have from the Holy Spirit.

⁹Because of this, since the day we heard about you, we have continued praying for you, asking God that you will know fully what he wants. We pray that you will also have great wisdom and understanding in spiritual things ¹⁰so that you will live the kind of life that honours and pleases the Lord in every way. You will produce fruit in every good work and grow in the knowledge of God. ¹¹God will strengthen you with his own great power so that you will not give up when troubles come, but you will be patient. ¹²And you will joyfully give thanks to the Father who has made you able to have a share in all that he has prepared for his people in the kingdom of light. ¹³God has freed us from the power of darkness and brought us into the kingdom of his dear Son. ¹⁴The Son paid for our sins, and in him we have forgiveness.

The Importance of Christ

¹⁵No one can see God, but Jesus Christ is exactly like him. He ranks higher than everything that has been made. ¹⁶Through his power all things were made—things in

heaven and on earth, things seen and unseen, all powers, authorities, lords and rulers. All things were made through Christ and for Christ. 17He was there before anything was made, and all things continue because of him. 18He is the head of the body, which is the church. Everything comes from him. He is the first one who was raised from the dead. So in all things Jesus has first place. 19God was pleased for all of himself to live in Christ. 20And through Christ, God has brought all things back to himself again—things on earth and things in heaven. God made peace through the blood of Christ's death on the cross.

21At one time you were separated from God. You were his enemies in your minds, and the evil things you did were against God. 22But now God has made you his friends again. He did this through Christ's death in the body so that he might bring you into God's presence as people who are holy, with no wrong, and with nothing of which God can judge you guilty. 23This will happen if you continue strong and sure in your faith. You must not be moved away from the hope brought to you by the Good News that you heard. That same Good News has been told to everyone in the world, and I, Paul, help in preaching that Good News.

How many times are the words "Good News" or "gospel" (which means good news) mentioned in these verses?

Which bits tell you that this "Good News" is true?

Good news spreads fast. Paul thanked God because the Good News about Jesus was spreading all over the Roman Empire (v 6).

Think

How do you feel about telling the "Good News" to others?

Pray

Lord Jesus, help me to tell someone else about you.

Don't be fooled!

"Buy a lottery ticket and become a millionaire!"
"Aliens will be landing on earth near you tonight."
"It doesn't matter what you believe as long as you're doing good."

Which would you be most likely to believe?

Colossians 1:24–2:15

Paul's Work for the Church

24I am happy in my sufferings for you. There are things that Christ must still suffer through his body, the church. I am accepting, in my body, my part of these things that must be suffered. 25I became a servant of the church because God gave me a special work to do that helps you, and that work is to tell fully the message of God. 26This message is the secret that was hidden from everyone since the beginning of time, but now it is made known to God's holy people. 27God decided to let his people know this rich and glorious secret which he has for all people. This secret is Christ himself, who is in you. He is our only hope for glory. 28So we continue to preach Christ to each person, using all wisdom to warn and to teach everyone, in order to bring each one into God's presence as a mature person in Christ. 29To do this, I work and struggle, using Christ's great strength that works so powerfully in me.

2 I want you to know how hard I work for you, those in Laodicea, and others who have never seen me. 2I want them to be strengthened and joined together with love so that they may be rich in their understanding. This leads to their knowing fully God's secret, that is, Christ himself. 3In him all the treasures of wisdom and knowledge are safely kept.

4I say this so that no one can fool you by arguments that seem good, but are false. 5Though I am absent from you in my body, my heart is with you, and I am happy to see your good lives and your strong faith in Christ.

Continue to Live in Christ

6As you received Christ Jesus the Lord, so continue to live in him. 7Keep your roots deep in him and have your lives built on him. Be strong in the faith, just as you were taught, and always be thankful.

8Be sure that no one leads you away with false and empty teaching that is only human, which comes from the ruling spirits of this world, and not from Christ. 9All of God lives in Christ fully (even when Christ was on earth), 10and you have a full and true life in Christ, who is ruler over all rulers and powers.

11Also in Christ you had a different kind of circumcision, a circumcision not done by hands. It was through Christ's circumcision, that is, his death, that you were made free from the power of your sinful self. 12When you were baptised, you were buried with Christ, and you were raised up with him through your faith in God's power that was shown when he raised Christ from the dead. ¹³When you were spiritually dead because of your sins and because you were not free from the power of your sinful self, God made you alive with Christ, and he forgave all our sins. ¹⁴He cancelled the debt, which listed all the rules we failed to follow. He took away that record with its rules and nailed it to the cross. ¹⁵God stripped the spiritual rulers and powers of their authority. With the cross, he won the victory and showed the world that they were powerless.

Some people in Colosse were being misled by wrong ideas (2:4). They worked because they didn't sound *too* far from the truth about Jesus.

Think

How can you guard against false ideas and teaching? Look at the end of 2:5.

Pray

Lord, help me not to be taken in by things which sound great, but which will lead me away from the truth about Jesus.

New look

What's most important to you about the way you look?

- Hair
- Clothes
- Body shape
- Your skin

In our world having the "right look" is important – but it'll be different next year! What's the "look" God wants us to have, which doesn't change?

 Colossians 2:16–3:17

Don't Follow People's Rules

¹⁶So do not let anyone make rules for you about eating and drinking or about a religious feast, a New Moon Festival or a Sabbath day. ¹⁷These things were like a shadow of what was to come. But what is true and real has come and is found in Christ. ¹⁸Do not let anyone disqualify you by making you humiliate yourself and worship angels. Such people enter into visions, which fill them with foolish pride because of their human way of thinking. ¹⁹They do not hold tightly to Christ, the head. It is from him that all the parts of the body are cared for and held together. So it grows in the way God wants it to grow.

²⁰Since you died with Christ and were made free from the ruling spirits of the world, why do you act as if you still belong to this world by following rules like these: ²¹"Don't eat this", "Don't taste that", "Don't even touch that thing"? ²²These rules refer to earthly things that are gone as soon as they are used. They are only man-made commands and teachings. ²³They seem to be wise, but they are only part of a man-made religion. They make people

pretend not to be proud and make them punish their bodies, but they do not really control the evil desires of the sinful self.

Your New Life in Christ

3 Since you were raised from the dead with Christ, aim at what is in heaven, where Christ is sitting at the right hand of God. ²Think only about the things in heaven, not the things on earth. ³Your old sinful self has died, and your new life is kept with Christ in God. ⁴Christ is our life, and when he comes again, you will share in his glory.

⁵So put all evil things out of your life: sexual sinning, doing evil, letting evil thoughts control you, wanting things that are evil and greed. This is really serving a false god. ⁶These things make God angry. ⁷In your past, evil life you also did these things.

⁸But now also put these things out of your life: anger, bad temper, doing or saying things to hurt others and using evil words when you talk. ⁹Do not lie to each other. You have left your old sinful life and the things you did before. ¹⁰You have

begun to live the new life, in which you are being made new and are becoming like the One who made you. This new life brings you the true knowledge of God. ¹¹In the new life there is no difference between Greeks and Jews, those who are circumcised and those who are not circumcised, or people who are foreigners, or Scythians. There is no difference between slaves and free people. But Christ is in all believers, and Christ is all that is important.

¹²God has chosen you and made you his holy people. He loves you. So always do these things: show mercy to others, be kind, humble, gentle and patient. ¹³Get along with each other, and forgive each other. If someone does wrong to you, forgive that person because the Lord forgave you. ¹⁴Do all these things; but most important, love each other. Love is what holds you all together in perfect unity. ¹⁵Let the peace that Christ gives control your thinking, because you were all called together in one body to have peace. Always be thankful. ¹⁶Let the teaching of Christ live in you richly. Use all wisdom to teach and instruct each other by singing psalms, hymns and spiritual songs with thankfulness in your hearts to God. ¹⁷Everything you do or say should be done to obey Jesus your Lord. And in all you do, give thanks to God the Father through Jesus.

Take a look at 3:5,8,9. How well are you doing at putting these things out of your life?

Think

What's different about you now that "Christ is all that is important" (3:11)?

Pray

Lord Jesus, help me to be more like you.

No talking!

Is talking the only way you can tell others about Jesus?

Colossians 3:18–4:18

Your New Life with Other People

18Wives, yield to the authority of your husbands, because this is the right thing to do in the Lord.

19Husbands, love your wives and be gentle with them.

20Children, obey your parents in all things, because this pleases the Lord.

21Fathers, do not nag your children. If you are too hard to please, they may want to stop trying.

22Slaves, obey your masters in all things. Do not obey just when they are watching you, to gain their favour, but serve them honestly, because you respect the Lord. 23In all the work you are doing, work the best you can. Work as if you were doing it for the Lord, not for people. 24Remember that you will receive your reward from the Lord, which he promised to his people. You are serving the Lord Christ. 25But remember that anyone who does wrong will be punished for that wrong, and the Lord treats everyone the same.

4 Masters, give what is good and fair to your slaves. Remember that you have a Master in heaven.

What the Christians are to Do

2Continue praying, keeping alert and always thanking God. 3Also pray for us that God will give us an opportunity to tell people his message. Pray that we can preach the secret that God has made known about Christ. This is why I am in prison. 4Pray that I can speak in a way that will make it clear, as I should.

5Be wise in the way you act with people who are not believers, making the most of every opportunity. 6When you talk, you should always be kind and pleasant so you will be able to answer everyone in the way you should.

News About the People with Paul

7Tychicus is my dear brother in Christ and a faithful minister and servant with me in the Lord. He will tell you all the things that are happening to me. 8This is why I am sending him: so you may know how we are and he may encourage you. 9I send him with Onesimus, a faithful and dear brother in Christ, and one of your group. They will tell you all that has happened here.

10Aristarchus, a prisoner with me, and Mark, the cousin of Barnabas, greet you. (I have already told you what to do about Mark. If he comes, welcome him.) 11Jesus, who is called Justus, also greets you. These are the only Jewish believers who work with me for the kingdom of God, and they have been a comfort to me.

12Epaphras, a servant of Jesus Christ, from your group, also greets you. He always prays for you that you will grow to be spiritually mature and have everything God wants for you. 13I know he has worked hard for you and the people in Laodicea and in Hierapolis. 14Demas and our dear friend Luke, the doctor, greet you.

15Greet the brothers in Laodicea. And

greet Nympha and the church that meets in her house. ¹⁶After this letter is read to you, be sure it is also read to the church in Laodicea. And you read the letter that I wrote to Laodicea. ¹⁷Tell Archippus, "Be sure to finish the work the Lord gave you."

¹⁸I, Paul, greet you and write this with my own hand. Remember me in prison. Grace be with you.

Where was Paul when he wrote these words (4:3)? What was he praying for?

What's 4:6 about?

- The answers to your geography homework

- What you say to the PE teacher after a muddy cross-country run

- Talking about Jesus

Could the first two options be part of telling others about Jesus as well? Think about it!

Think

Wherever we are, God wants us to take opportunities that come up to tell others about Jesus (4:5).

Pray

Ask God to help you have the right words to say about him, at the right time.

The real thing

So how do you think you're doing as a Christian?

- Fab!
- OK, I guess...
- I feel like the spiritual equivalent of a slug...

 1 Thessalonians 1:1–2:16

1 From Paul, Silas and Timothy.
To the church in Thessalonica, the church in God the Father and the Lord Jesus Christ:
Grace and peace to you.

The Faith of the Thessalonians

²We always thank God for all of you and mention you when we pray. ³We continually recall before God our Father the things you have done because of your faith and the work you have done because of your love. And we thank him that you continue to be strong because of your hope in our Lord Jesus Christ.

⁴Brothers and sisters, God loves you, and we know he has chosen you, ⁵because the Good News we brought to you came not only with words, but with power, with the Holy Spirit and with sure knowledge that it is true. Also you know how we lived when we were with you in order to help you. ⁶And you became like us and like the Lord. You suffered much, but still you accepted the teaching with the joy that comes from the Holy Spirit. ⁷So you became an example to all the believers in Macedonia and Southern Greece. ⁸And the Lord's teaching spread from you not only into Macedonia and Southern Greece, but now your faith in God has become known everywhere. So we do not need to say anything about it. ⁹People everywhere are telling about the way you

accepted us when we were there with you. They tell how you stopped worshipping idols and began serving the living and true God. ¹⁰And you wait for God's Son, whom God raised from the dead, to come from heaven. He is Jesus, who saves us from God's angry judgement that is sure to come.

Paul's Work in Thessalonica

2 Brothers and sisters, you know our visit to you was not a failure. ²Before we came to you, we suffered in Philippi. People there insulted us, as you know, and many people were against us. But our God helped us to be brave and to tell you his Good News. ³Our appeal does not come from lies or wrong reasons, nor were we trying to trick you. ⁴But we speak the Good News because God tested us and trusted us to do it. When we speak, we are not trying to please people, but God, who tests our hearts. ⁵You know that we never tried to influence you by saying nice things about you. We were not trying to get your money; we had no selfishness to hide from you. God knows that this is true. ⁶We were not looking for human praise, from you or anyone else, ⁷even though as apostles of Christ we could have used our authority over you.

But we were very gentle with you, like a mother caring for her little children. ⁸Because we loved you, we were happy to share not only God's Good News with you, but even our own lives. You had become so dear to us! ⁹Brothers and sisters, I know you remember our hard work and difficulties. We worked night and day so we would not burden any of you while we preached God's Good News to you.

¹⁰When we were with you, we lived in a holy and honest way, without fault. You know this is true, and so does God. ¹¹You know that we treated each of you as a father treats his own children. ¹²We encouraged you, we told you and we insisted that you live good lives for God, who calls you to his glorious kingdom.

¹³Also, we always thank God because when you heard his message from us, you accepted it as the word of God, not the words of humans. And it really is God's message which works in you who believe. ¹⁴Brothers and sisters, your experiences have been like those of God's churches in Christ that are in Judea. You suffered from the people of your own country, as they suffered from the Jews, ¹⁵who killed both the Lord Jesus and the prophets and forced us to leave that country. They do not please God and are against all people. ¹⁶They try to stop us from teaching those who are not Jews so they may be saved. By doing this, they are increasing their sins to the limit. The anger of God has come to them at last.

How does God want you to live? Write the relevant verse number from the Bible bit you've just read that corresponds with the following statements:

Worship God – not other people or things (v . . .)

Be a positive influence (v . . .)

Learn from others' good example (v . . .)

Be joyful – even in tough times (v . . .)

Be strong in Jesus (v . . .)

Do things out of love and faith (v . . .)

Think

Are you getting it right? Look through that list again and remember times when each thing has been true of YOU! And be encouraged!

Pray

Thank God for what he is doing in your life.

Make someone happy

What is the best gift you have ever had?

What is the best thing a friend has done for you?

What is the best thing you have done for a friend?

What is the best gift you have ever given?

Which questions were easier to answer?

1 Thessalonians 2:17–4:12

Paul Wants to Visit Them Again

¹⁷Brothers and sisters, though we were separated from you for a short time, our thoughts were still with you. We wanted very much to see you and tried hard to do so. ¹⁸We wanted to come to you. I, Paul, tried to come more than once, but Satan stopped us. ¹⁹You are our hope, our joy and the crown we will take pride in when our Lord Jesus Christ comes. ²⁰Truly you are our glory and our joy.

3 When we could not wait any longer, we decided it was best to stay in Athens alone ²and send Timothy to you. Timothy, our brother, works with us for God and helps us tell people the Good News about Christ. We sent him to strengthen and encourage you in your faith ³so none of you would be upset by these troubles. You yourselves know that we must face these troubles. ⁴Even when we were with you, we told you we all would have to suffer, and you know it has happened. ⁵Because of this, when I could wait no longer, I sent Timothy to you so I could learn about your faith. I was afraid the devil had tempted you, and then our hard work would have been wasted.

⁶But Timothy now has come back to us from you and has brought us good news about your faith and love. He told us that you always remember us in a good way and that you want to see us just as much as we want to see you. ⁷So, brothers and sisters, while we have much trouble and suffering, we are encouraged about you because of your faith. ⁸Our life is really full if you stand strong in the Lord. ⁹We have so much joy before our God because of you. We cannot thank him enough for all the joy we feel. ¹⁰Night and day we continue praying with all our heart that we can see you again and give you all the things you need to make your faith strong.

¹¹Now may our God and Father himself and our Lord Jesus prepare the way for us to come to you. ¹²May the Lord make your love grow more and multiply for each other and for all people so that you will love others as we love you. ¹³May your hearts be made strong so that you will be holy and without fault before our God and Father when our Lord Jesus comes with all his holy ones.

A Life that Pleases God

4 Brothers and sisters, we taught you how to live in a way that will please

God, and you are living that way. Now we ask and encourage you in the Lord Jesus to live that way even more. ²You know what we told you to do by the authority of the Lord Jesus. ³God wants you to be holy and to stay away from sexual sins. ⁴He wants each of you to learn to control your own body in a way that is holy and honourable. ⁵Don't use your body for sexual sin like the people who do not know God. ⁶Also, do not wrong or cheat another Christian in this way. The Lord will punish people who do those things as we have already told you and warned you. ⁷God called us to be holy and does not want us to live in sin. ⁸So the person who refuses to obey this teaching is disobeying God, not simply a human teaching. And God is the One who gives us his Holy Spirit.

⁹We do not need to write to you about having love for your Christian family, because God has already taught you to love each other. ¹⁰And truly you do love the Christians in all of Macedonia. Brothers and sisters, now we encourage you to love them even more.

¹¹Do all you can to live a peaceful life. Take care of your own business, and do your own work as we have already told you. ¹²If you do, then people who are not believers will respect you, and you will not have to depend on others for what you need.

Relationships are two-way things!

What did Paul and Timothy get out of the relationship (3:7–9)?

What did the guys@thessalonica.greece get (3:10)?

Think

What are people most bothered about: getting from their friends or giving to their friends? Why?

Today, focus on being a giver – not a getter!

Pray

Pray the prayer in 3:12,13 for your friends.

493

Top tips

Think of a group of Christians you belong to (e.g. youth group, cell, local church). Which of the following is it most like?

- A football team: everybody plays to their strengths, but we know how to work together.
- A circus: some people perform, the rest sit back and watch!
- A cyber café: we might meet together, but really everyone's doing their own thing.

 1 Thessalonians 4:13–5:28

The Lord's Coming

13Brothers and sisters, we want you to know about those Christians who have died so you will not be sad, as others who have no hope. 14We believe that Jesus died and that he rose again. So, because of him, God will raise with Jesus those who have died. 15What we tell you now is the Lord's own message. We who are living when the Lord comes again will not go before those who have already died. 16The Lord himself will come down from heaven with a loud command, with the voice of the archangel and with the trumpet call of God. And those who have died believing in Christ will rise first. 17After that, we who are still alive will be gathered up with them in the clouds to meet the Lord in the air. And we will be with the Lord for ever. 18So encourage each other with these words.

Be Ready for the Lord's Coming

5 Now, brothers and sisters, we do not need to write to you about times and dates. 2You know very well that the day the Lord comes again will be a surprise, like a thief that comes in the night. 3While people are saying, "We have peace and we are safe," they will be destroyed quickly. It is like pains that come quickly to a woman having a baby. Those people will not escape. 4But you, brothers and sisters, are not living in darkness, and so that day will not surprise you like a thief. 5You are all people who belong to the light and to the day. We do not belong to the night or to darkness. 6So we should not be like other people who are sleeping, but we should be awake and have self-control. 7Those who sleep, sleep at night. Those who get drunk, get drunk at night. 8But we belong to the day, so we should control ourselves. We should wear faith and love to protect us, and the hope of salvation should be our helmet. 9God did not choose us to suffer his anger but to have salvation through our Lord Jesus Christ. 10Jesus died for us so that we can live together with him, whether we are alive or dead when he comes. 11So encourage each other and give each other strength, just as you are doing now.

Final Instructions and Greetings

12Now, brothers and sisters, we ask you to appreciate those who work hard among you, who lead you in the Lord and teach you. 13Respect them with a very special love because of the work they do.

Live in peace with each other. ¹⁴We ask you, brothers and sisters, to warn those who do not work. Encourage the people who are afraid. Help those who are weak. Be patient with everyone. ¹⁵Be sure that no one pays back wrong for wrong, but always try to do what is good for each other and for all people.

¹⁶Always be joyful. ¹⁷Pray continually, ¹⁸and give thanks whatever happens. That is what God wants for you in Christ Jesus.

¹⁹Do not hold back the work of the Holy Spirit. ²⁰Do not treat prophecy as if it were unimportant. ²¹But test everything. Keep what is good, ²²and stay away from everything that is evil.

²³Now may God himself, the God of peace, make you pure, belonging only to him. May your whole self—spirit, soul and body—be kept safe and without fault when our Lord Jesus Christ comes. ²⁴You can trust the One who calls you to do that for you.

²⁵Brothers and sisters, pray for us.

²⁶Give each other a holy kiss when you meet. ²⁷I tell you by the authority of the Lord to read this letter to all the believers.

²⁸The grace of our Lord Jesus Christ be with you.

There's loads of great advice here about how to get on together. But which three bits does *your* group need to hear right now?

1 _____ (v . . .)

2 _____ (v . . .)

3 _____ (v . . .)

Think

How can you put into practice the three bits your group needs to act on?

Pray

Ask God to help you build these things into your group.

Enemies?

Who makes your life a misery sometimes? Is the urge to get your own back, either verbally or physically, strong?

2 Thessalonians 1:1–2:12

1 From Paul, Silas and Timothy.
To the church in Thessalonica in God our Father and the Lord Jesus Christ:

²Grace and peace to you from God the Father and the Lord Jesus Christ.

Paul Talks About God's Judgement

³We must always thank God for you, brothers and sisters. This is only right, because your faith is growing more and more, and the love that every one of you has for each other is increasing. ⁴So we boast about you to the other churches of God. We tell them about the way you continue to be strong and have faith even though you are being treated badly and are suffering many troubles.

⁵This is proof that God is right in his judgement. He wants you to be counted worthy of his kingdom for which you are suffering. ⁶God will do what is right. He will give trouble to those who trouble you. ⁷And he will give rest to you who are troubled and to us also when the Lord Jesus appears with burning fire from heaven with his powerful angels. ⁸Then he will punish those who do not know God and who do not obey the Good News about our Lord Jesus Christ. ⁹Those people will be punished with a destruction that continues for ever. They will be kept away from the Lord and from his great power. ¹⁰This will happen on the day when the Lord Jesus comes to receive glory because of his holy people. And all the people who have believed will be amazed at Jesus. You will be in that group, because you believed what we told you.

¹¹That is why we always pray for you, asking our God to help you live the kind of life he called you to live. We pray that with his power God will help you do the good things you want and perform the works that come from your faith. ¹²We pray all this so that the name of our Lord Jesus Christ will have glory in you, and you will have glory in him. That glory comes from the grace of our God and the Lord Jesus Christ.

Evil Things will Happen

2 Brothers and sisters, we have something to say about the coming of our Lord Jesus Christ and the time when we will meet together with him. ²Do not become easily upset in your thinking or afraid if you hear that the day of the Lord has already come. Someone may say this in a prophecy or in a message or in a letter as if it came from us. ³Do not let anyone fool you in any way. That day of the Lord will not come until the turning away from God happens and the Man of Evil, who is on his way to hell, appears. ⁴He will be against and put himself above anything called God or anything that people worship. And that Man of Evil will even go into God's Temple and sit there and say that he is God.

⁵I told you when I was with you that all this would happen. Do you not remember? ⁶And now you know what is stopping that Man of Evil so he will appear at the right time. ⁷The secret power of evil is already

working in the world, but there is one who is stopping that power. And he will continue to stop it until he is taken out of the way. [8]Then that Man of Evil will appear, and the Lord Jesus will kill him with the breath that comes from his mouth and will destroy him with the glory of his coming. [9]The Man of Evil will come by the power of Satan. He will have great power, and he will do many different false miracles, signs and wonders. [10]He will use every kind of evil to trick those who are lost. They will die, because they refused to love the truth. (If they loved the truth, they would be saved.) [11]For this reason God sends them something powerful that leads them away from the truth so they will believe a lie. [12]So all those will be judged guilty who did not believe the truth, but enjoyed doing evil.

Who will deal with these people (1:6)?

Who will help you (1:7)?

Strong stuff, eh!

Getting your own back – however you do it – takes a massive amount of negative thought and energy! How were the guys@thessalonica.greece coping? What were they concentrating on instead (1:4,5)?

Think

How do you deal with those who make your life a misery?

Pray

Talk with God about the bullies in your life. Ask for his help.

Life and death!

Have you ever seen a rescue – either on TV or in real life? Keep that in mind as you read.

2 Thessalonians 2:13–3:18

You are Chosen for Salvation

¹³Brothers and sisters, whom the Lord loves, God chose you from the beginning to be saved. So we must always thank God for you. You are saved by the Spirit that makes you holy and by your faith in the truth. ¹⁴God used the Good News that we preached to call you to be saved so you can share in the glory of our Lord Jesus Christ. ¹⁵So, brothers and sisters, stand strong and continue to believe the teachings we gave you in our speaking and in our letter.

¹⁶⁻¹⁷May our Lord Jesus Christ himself and God our Father encourage you and strengthen you in every good thing you do and say. God loved us, and through his grace he gave us a good hope and encouragement that continues for ever.

Pray for Us

3 And now, brothers and sisters, pray for us that the Lord's teaching will continue to spread quickly and that people will give honour to that teaching, just as you did. ²And pray that we will be protected from stubborn and evil people, because not all people believe.

³But the Lord is faithful and will give you strength and will protect you from the Evil One. ⁴The Lord makes us feel sure that you are doing and will continue to do the things we told you. ⁵May the Lord lead your hearts into God's love and Christ's patience.

The Duty to Work

⁶Brothers and sisters, by the authority of our Lord Jesus Christ we command you to stay away from any believer who refuses to work and does not follow the teaching we gave you. ⁷You yourselves know that you should live as we live. We were not lazy when we were with you. ⁸And when we ate another person's food, we always paid for it. We worked very hard night and day so we would not be an expense to any of you. ⁹We had the right to ask you to help us, but we worked to take care of ourselves so we would be an example for you to follow. ¹⁰When we were with you, we gave you this rule: "Anyone who refuses to work should not eat."

¹¹We hear that some people in your group refuse to work. They do nothing but busy themselves in other people's lives. ¹²We command those people and beg them in the Lord Jesus Christ to work quietly and earn their own food. ¹³But you, brothers and sisters, never become tired of doing good.

¹⁴If some people do not obey what we tell you in this letter, then take note of them. Have nothing to do with them so they will feel ashamed. ¹⁵But do not treat them as enemies. Warn them as fellow believers.

Final Words

¹⁶Now may the Lord of peace give you

peace at all times and in every way. The Lord be with all of you.

¹⁷I, Paul, end this letter now in my own handwriting. All my letters have this to show they are from me. This is the way I write.

¹⁸The grace of our Lord Jesus Christ be with you all.

Being a Christian isn't a hobby or a lifestyle choice – it's much more serious than that. Which phrase gives it away (2:13)?

Two people are involved in this rescue – you and God (but mainly God!). Look through the text again and note down who does what!

God

2:13 _____

2:13 _____

2:14 _____

You

2:13 _____

Think

About the TWO things we need to keep on doing from 2:15 – how would you say them in your own words?

Pray

Thank God for rescuing you!

Stupid arguments!

Christians sometimes argue – and hurt each other – over stupid things (maybe you can think of some that have happened to you recently). What's the answer?

1 Timothy 1:1–20

1 From Paul, an apostle of Christ Jesus, by the command of God our Saviour and Christ Jesus our hope.

²To Timothy, a true child to me because you believe:

Grace, mercy and peace from God the Father and Christ Jesus our Lord.

Warning Against False Teaching

³I asked you to stay longer in Ephesus when I went into Macedonia so you could command some people there to stop teaching false things. ⁴Tell them not to spend their time on stories that are not true and on long lists of names in family histories. These things only bring arguments; they do not help God's work, which is done in faith. ⁵The purpose of this command is for people to have love, a love that comes from a pure heart and a good conscience and a true faith. ⁶Some people have missed these things and turned to useless talk. ⁷They want to be teachers of the law, but they do not understand either what they are talking about or what they are sure about.

⁸But we know that the law is good if someone uses it correctly. ⁹We also know that the law is not made for good people but for those who are against the law and for those who refuse to follow it. It is for people who are against God and are sinful, who are not holy and have no religion, who

kill their fathers and mothers, who murder, ¹⁰who take part in sexual sins, who have sexual relations with people of the same sex, who sell slaves, who tell lies, who speak falsely and who do anything against the true teaching of God. ¹¹That teaching is part of the Good News of the blessed God that he gave me to tell.

Thanks for God's Mercy

¹²I thank Christ Jesus our Lord, who gave me strength, because he trusted me and gave me this work of serving him. ¹³In the past I spoke against Christ and persecuted him and did all kinds of things to hurt him. But God showed me mercy, because I did not know what I was doing. I did not believe. ¹⁴But the grace of our Lord was fully given to me, and with that grace came the faith and love that are in Christ Jesus.

¹⁵What I say is true, and you should fully accept it: Christ Jesus came into the world to save sinners, of whom I am the worst. ¹⁶But I was given mercy so that in me, the worst of all sinners, Christ Jesus could show that he has patience without limit. His patience with me made me an example for those who would believe in him and have life for ever. ¹⁷To the King that rules for ever, who will never die, who cannot be seen, the only God, be honour and glory for ever and ever. Amen.

¹⁸Timothy, my child, I am giving you a command that agrees with the prophecies that were given about you in the past. I tell you this so you can follow them and fight the good fight. ¹⁹Continue to have faith and do what you know is right. Some people have rejected this, and their faith has been shipwrecked. ²⁰Hymenaeus and Alexander have done that, and I have given them to Satan so they will learn not to speak against God.

There had been a lot of strange ideas and stories going around Christians in Ephesus. What's Paul's advice to Timothy (vs 3,4)? Why (v 5)?

Think

Are there things that God commands us *not* to do because he loves us?

Pray

Are there people or situations in your life where there are arguments? Pray for these situations. Ask God to help people to have love.

Why pray, when you can worry?

What's happening in the world? Is there stuff that's worrying you? Difficult times can make a difference to the freedom Christians have.

What problems do you hear about on the news, or maybe through your church (social problems, famine, war, injustice, Christians who are persecuted for their faith)?

Could you do anything about them?

1 Timothy 2:1–3:7

Some Rules for Men and Women

2 First, I tell you to pray for all people, asking God for what they need and being thankful to him. ²Pray for rulers and for all who have authority so that we can have quiet and peaceful lives full of worship and respect for God. ³This is good, and it pleases God our Saviour, ⁴who wants all people to be saved and to know the truth. ⁵There is one God and one way human beings can reach God. That way is through Christ Jesus, who is himself human. ⁶He gave himself as a payment to free all people. He is proof that came at the right time. ⁷That is why I was chosen to tell the Good News and to be an apostle. (I am telling the truth; I am not lying.) I was chosen to teach those who are not Jews to believe and to know the truth.

⁸So, I want men everywhere to pray, lifting up their hands in a holy manner,

without anger and arguments.

⁹Also, women should wear proper clothes that show respect and self-control, not using plaited hair or gold or pearls or expensive clothes. ¹⁰Instead, they should do good deeds, which is right for women who say they worship God.

¹¹Let a woman learn by listening quietly and being ready to co-operate in everything. ¹²But I do not allow a woman to teach or to have authority over a man, but to listen quietly, ¹³because Adam was formed first and then Eve. ¹⁴And Adam was not tricked, but the woman was tricked and became a sinner. ¹⁵But she will be saved through having children if they continue in faith, love and holiness, with self-control.

Elders in the Church

3 What I say is true: anyone wanting to become an elder desires a good work.

2An elder must not give people a reason to criticise him, and he must have only one wife. He must be self-controlled, wise, respected by others, ready to welcome guests and able to teach. 3He must not drink too much wine or like to fight, but rather be gentle and peaceful, not loving money. 4He must be a good family leader, having children who co-operate with full respect. 5(If someone does not know how to lead the family, how can that person take care of God's church?) 6But an elder must not be a new believer, or he might be too proud of himself and be judged guilty just as the devil was. 7An elder must also have the respect of people who are not in the church so he will not be criticised by others and caught in the devil's trap.

Paul had got some suggestions!

- Who to pray for (2:1,2)

- What to pray (2:1–3)

- Why to pray (2:1–4)

Think

Do you keep a diary of things you pray for? Why not start now and look back regularly to see how God answers.

Pray

Read a newspaper, looking out for the problems people are having. Talk to God as you read, asking him to help those in power to make things better for people who're suffering.

Be an example

Are you a good example to others? For some people, you might be the only Christian they ever meet. How might your life help them to see Jesus?

1 Timothy 3:8–4:16

Deacons in the Church

8In the same way, deacons must be respected by others, not saying things they do not mean. They must not drink too much wine or try to get rich by cheating others. 9With a clear conscience they must follow the secret of the faith that God made known to us. 10Test them first. Then let them serve as deacons if you find nothing wrong in them. 11In the same way, women must be respected by others. They must not speak evil of others. They must be self-controlled and trustworthy in everything. 12Deacons must have only one wife and be good leaders of their children and their own families. 13Those who serve well as deacons are making an honourable place for themselves, and they will be very bold in their faith in Christ Jesus.

The Secret of Our Life

14Although I hope I can come to you soon, I am writing these things to you now. 15Then, even if I am delayed, you will know how to live in the family of God. That family is the church of the living God, the support and foundation of the truth. 16Without doubt, the secret of our life of worship is great:

He was shown to us in a human body,
    proved right in spirit,
and seen by angels.

He was preached to those who are not Jews,

believed in by the world,
    and taken up in glory.

A Warning About False Teachers

4 Now the Holy Spirit clearly says that in the later times some people will stop believing the faith. They will follow spirits that lie and teachings of demons. 2Such teachings come from the false words of liars whose understanding is destroyed as if by a hot iron. 3They forbid people to marry and tell them not to eat certain foods which God created to be eaten with thanks by people who believe and know the truth. 4Everything God made is good, and nothing should be refused if it is accepted with thanks, 5because it is made holy by what God has said and by prayer.

Be a Good Servant of Christ

6By telling these things to the brothers and sisters, you will be a good servant of Christ Jesus. You will be made strong by the words of the faith and the good teaching which you have been following. 7But do not follow foolish stories that disagree with God's truth, but train yourself to serve God. 8Training your body helps you in some ways, but serving God helps you in every way by bringing you blessings in this life and in the future life too. 9What I say is true, and you should fully accept it. 10This is why we work and struggle: we hope in the living God who is the Saviour of all people, especially of those who believe.

¹¹Command and teach these things. ¹²Do not let anyone treat you as if you are unimportant because you are young. Instead, be an example to the believers with your words, your actions, your love, your faith, and your pure life. ¹³Until I come, continue to read the Scriptures to the people, strengthen them, and teach them. ¹⁴Use the gift you have, which was given to you through prophecy when the group of elders laid their hands on you. ¹⁵Continue to do those things; give your life to doing them so your progress may be seen by everyone. ¹⁶Be careful in your life and in your teaching. If you continue to live and teach rightly, you will save both yourself and those who listen to you.

It's not easy being a good example! Here are some ways you can be. Find the verses which say...

Teach the Bible (v...)

Live right (v...)

Be an example (v...)

Grow in faith (v...)

Encourage others (v...)

Don't be put down (v...)

Speak the truth (v...)

Think

Circle one that you especially need to work on. Underline one that you can do something about today.

Pray

Ask God to help you do it.

We are family

Despite many problems that may occur within families, including break-up and abuse, they are still, in general, a safe environment for many. The ties that bind a family together are stronger than ordinary friendships. Perhaps that is why, when things go wrong, it can hurt so much.

1 Timothy 5:1–25

Rules for Living with Others

5 Do not speak angrily to an older man, but plead with him as if he were your father. Treat younger men like brothers, ²older women like mothers and younger women like sisters. Always treat them in a pure way.

³Take care of widows who are truly widows. ⁴But if a widow has children or grandchildren, let them first learn to do their duty to their own family and to repay their parents or grandparents. That pleases God. ⁵The true widow, who is all alone, puts her hope in God and continues to pray night and day for God's help. ⁶But the widow who uses her life to please herself is really dead while she is alive. ⁷Tell the believers to do these things so that no one can criticise them. ⁸Whoever does not care for his own relatives, especially his own family members, has turned against the faith and is worse than someone who does not believe in God.

⁹To be on the list of widows, a woman must be at least 60 years old. She must have been faithful to her husband. ¹⁰She must be known for her good works—works such as raising her children, accepting strangers, washing the feet of God's people, helping those in trouble and giving her life to do all kinds of good deeds. ¹¹But do not put younger widows on that list. After they give themselves to Christ, they may be pulled away from him by their physical needs, and then they will want to marry again. ¹²They will be judged for not doing what they first promised to do. ¹³Besides that, they would learn to waste their time, going from house to house. And they not only waste their time but also may begin to gossip and busy themselves with other people's lives, saying things they should not say. ¹⁴So I want the younger widows to marry, have children and take care of their homes. Then no enemy will have any reason to criticise them. ¹⁵But some have already turned away to follow Satan.

¹⁶If any woman who is a believer has widows in her family, she should care for them herself. The church should not have to care for them. Then it will be able to take care of those who are truly widows.

¹⁷The elders who lead the church well should receive double honour, especially those who work hard by speaking and teaching, ¹⁸because the Scripture says: "When an ox is working in the grain, do not cover its mouth to keep it from eating," and "A worker should be given his pay."

¹⁹Do not listen to someone who accuses an elder, without two or three witnesses. ²⁰Tell those who continue sinning that they are wrong. Do this in front of the whole church so that the others will have a warning.

21Before God and Christ Jesus and the chosen angels, I command you to do these things without showing favour of any kind to anyone.

22Think carefully before you lay your hands on anyone, and don't share in the sins of others. Keep yourself pure.

23Stop drinking only water, but drink a little wine to help your stomach and your frequent sicknesses.

24The sins of some people are easy to see even before they are judged, but the sins of others are seen only later. 25So also good deeds are easy to see, but even those that are not easily seen cannot stay hidden.

Paul is telling Timothy (who was a young leader) to treat others like family.

How should he treat...

- older men? _____

- younger men? _____

- older women? _____

- younger women? _____

Think

How do you treat other people in your Christian community?

Pray

That your relationships with others in your church will be deep like a family, that your friends will be like brothers and sisters.

Live for King Jesus

...means...

- looking holy?
- being a vicar?
- becoming a monk?
- being BORING!?

Does living for God mean any of these?

 1 Timothy 6:1–21

6 All who are slaves under a yoke should show full respect to their masters so no one will speak against God's name and our teaching. ²The slaves whose masters are believers should not show their masters any less respect because they are believers. They should serve their masters even better, because they are helping believers they love.

You must teach and preach these things.

False Teaching and True Riches

³Anyone who has a different teaching does not agree with the true teaching of our Lord Jesus Christ and the teaching that shows the true way to serve God. ⁴This person is full of pride and understands nothing, but is sick with a love for arguing and fighting about words. This brings jealousy, fighting, speaking against others, evil mistrust ⁵and constant quarrels from those who have evil minds and have lost the truth. They think that serving God is a way to get rich.

⁶Serving God does make us very rich, if we are satisfied with what we have. ⁷We brought nothing into the world, so we can take nothing out. ⁸But, if we have food and clothes, we will be satisfied with that. ⁹Those who want to become rich bring temptation to themselves and are caught in a trap. They want many foolish and harmful things that ruin and destroy people. ¹⁰The love of money causes all kinds of evil. Some people have left the faith, because they wanted to get more money, but they have caused themselves much sorrow.

Some Things to Remember

¹¹But you, man of God, run away from all those things. Instead, live in the right way, serve God, have faith, love, patience and gentleness. ¹²Fight the good fight of faith, grabbing hold of the life that continues for ever. You were called to have that life when you confessed the good confession before many witnesses. ¹³In the sight of God, who gives life to everything, and of Christ Jesus, I give you a command. Christ Jesus made the good confession when he stood before Pontius Pilate. ¹⁴Do what you were commanded to do without wrong or blame until our Lord Jesus Christ comes again. ¹⁵God will make that happen at the right time. He is the blessed and only Ruler, the King of all kings and the Lord of all lords. ¹⁶He is the only One who never dies. He lives in light so bright no one can go near it. No one has ever seen God, or

can see him. May honour and power belong to God for ever. Amen.

17Command those who are rich with things of this world not to be proud. Tell them to hope in God, not in their uncertain riches. God richly gives us everything to enjoy. 18Tell the rich people to do good, to be rich in doing good deeds, to be generous and ready to share. 19By doing that, they will be saving a treasure for themselves as a strong foundation for the future. Then they will be able to have the life that is true life.

20Timothy, guard what God has trusted to you. Stay away from foolish, useless talk and from the arguments of what is falsely called "knowledge". 21By saying they have that "knowledge", some have missed the true faith.

Grace be with you.

No (although, someone living for God might also be any of these!). Paul told Timothy to …

Run away – from what (vs 9–11)?

Live right, like this: _____ (vs 11,12)

Grab hold of: _____ (v 12)

Be like Jesus by: _____ (v 13)

Think

What are the things people live for instead of for God?

Pray

Praise God for what he has done through Jesus for you and for being your King (vs 15,16).

Extra

Look again at verse 15: When this letter was written, if you said, 'Jesus is King', you could be punished by death. The Emperor thought he should be worshipped as a god. As a result, many Christians died for their faith.

You can do better

Take a moment to look back at your life so far. Have you been encouraged as you have grown? Do the compliments towards your work outweigh the criticisms?

 2 Timothy 1:1–2:13

1 From Paul, an apostle of Christ Jesus by the will of God. God sent me to tell about the promise of life that is in Christ Jesus.

²To Timothy, a dear child to me:

Grace, mercy and peace to you from God the Father and Christ Jesus our Lord.

Encouragement for Timothy

³I thank God as I always mention you in my prayers, day and night. I serve him, doing what I know is right as my ancestors did. ⁴Remembering that you cried for me, I want very much to see you so I can be filled with joy. ⁵I remember your true faith. That faith first lived in your grandmother Lois and in your mother Eunice, and I know you now have that same faith. ⁶This is why I remind you to keep using the gift God gave you when I laid my hands on you. Now let it grow, as a small flame grows into a fire. ⁷God did not give us a spirit that makes us afraid but a spirit of power and love and self-control.

⁸So do not be ashamed to tell people about our Lord Jesus, and do not be ashamed of me, in prison for the Lord. But suffer with me for the Good News. God, who gives us the strength to do that, ⁹saved us and made us his holy people. That was not because of anything we did ourselves but because of God's purpose and grace. That grace was given to us through Christ Jesus before time began, ¹⁰but it is now shown to us by the coming of our Saviour Christ Jesus. He destroyed death, and through the Good News he showed us

the way to have life that cannot be destroyed. ¹¹I was chosen to tell that Good News and to be an apostle and a teacher. ¹²I am suffering now because I tell the Good News, but I am not ashamed, because I know Jesus, the One in whom I have believed. And I am sure he is able to protect what he has trusted me with until that day. ¹³Follow the pattern of true teachings that you heard from me in faith and love, which are in Christ Jesus. ¹⁴Protect the truth that you were given; protect it with the help of the Holy Spirit who lives in us.

¹⁵You know that everyone in the country of Asia has left me, even Phygelus and Hermogenes. ¹⁶May the Lord show mercy to the family of Onesiphorus, who has often helped me and was not ashamed that I was in prison. ¹⁷When he came to Rome, he looked eagerly for me until he found me. ¹⁸May the Lord allow him to find mercy from the Lord on that day. You know how many ways he helped me in Ephesus.

A Loyal Soldier of Christ Jesus

2 You then, Timothy, my child, be strong in the grace we have in Christ Jesus. ²You should teach people whom you can trust the things you and many others have heard me say. Then they will be able to teach others. ³Share in the troubles we have like a good soldier of Christ Jesus. ⁴A soldier wants to please the enlisting officer, so no one serving in the army wastes time with everyday matters.

5Also an athlete who takes part in a contest must obey all the rules in order to win. 6The farmer who works hard should be the first person to get some of the food that was grown. 7Think about what I am saying, because the Lord will give you the ability to understand everything.

8Remember Jesus Christ, who was raised from the dead, who is from the family of David. This is the Good News I preach, 9and I am suffering because of it to the point of being bound with chains like a criminal. But God's teaching is not in chains. 10So I patiently accept all these troubles so that those whom God has chosen can have the salvation that is in Christ Jesus. With that salvation comes glory that never ends.

11This teaching is true:

If we died with him, we will also live with him.

12 If we accept suffering, we will also rule with him.

If we refuse to accept him, he will refuse to accept us.

13 If we are not faithful, he will still be faithful,

because he cannot be false to himself.

What does Paul do day and night (1:3)?

Where had the faith first lived (1:5)?

What does Paul want Timothy's gift to do (1:6)?

Think
Do you hand out enough encouragement to your friends?

Pray
For families, that they can pass on the Good News of Jesus to their children, just like Lois and Eunice did.

Extra
Try to learn 1:7 so that you can say it to yourself as an encouragement from God.

Belonging

Who do you belong to?

☐ Parents
☐ No one
☐ God
☐ Yourself

 2 Timothy 2:14–3:11

A Worker Pleasing to God

¹⁴Continue teaching these things, warning people in God's presence not to argue about words. It does not help anyone, and it ruins those who listen. ¹⁵Do the best you can to give yourself to God as the kind of person he will accept. Be a worker who is not ashamed and who uses the true teaching in the right way. ¹⁶Stay away from foolish, useless talk, because that will lead people further away from God. ¹⁷Their evil teaching will spread like a sickness inside the body. Hymenaeus and Philetus are like that. ¹⁸They have left the true teaching, saying that the rising from the dead has already taken place, and so they are destroying the faith of some people. ¹⁹But God's strong foundation continues to stand. These words are written on the seal: "The Lord knows those who belong to him," and "Everyone who wants to belong to the Lord must stop doing wrong."

²⁰In a large house there are not only things made of gold and silver, but also things made of wood and clay. Some things are used for special purposes, and others are made for ordinary jobs. ²¹All who make themselves clean from evil will be used for special purposes. They will be made holy, useful to the Master, ready to do any good work.

²²But run away from the evil young people like to do. Try hard to live right and to have faith, love and peace, together with those who trust in the Lord from pure hearts. ²³Stay away from foolish and stupid arguments, because you know they grow into quarrels. ²⁴And a servant of the Lord must not quarrel but must be kind to everyone, a good teacher and patient. ²⁵The Lord's servant must gently teach those who disagree. Then maybe God will let them change their minds so they can accept the truth. ²⁶And they may wake up and escape from the trap of the devil, who catches them to do what he wants.

The Last Days

3 Remember this! In the last days there will be many troubles, ²because people will love themselves, love money, boast and be proud. They will say evil things against others and will not obey their parents or be thankful or be the kind of people God wants. ³They will not love others, will refuse to forgive, will gossip and will not control themselves. They will be cruel, will hate what is good, ⁴will turn against their friends and will do foolish things without thinking. They will be conceited, will love pleasure instead of God, ⁵and will act as if they serve God but will not have his power. Stay away from

those people. ⁶Some of them go into homes and get control of weak women who are full of sin and are led by many evil desires. ⁷These women are always learning new teachings, but they are never able to understand the truth fully. ⁸Just as Jannes and Jambres were against Moses, these people are against the truth. Their thinking has been ruined, and they have failed in trying to follow the faith. ⁹But they will not be successful in what they do, because as with Jannes and Jambres, everyone will see that they are foolish.

Obey the Teachings

¹⁰But you have followed what I teach, the way I live, my goal, faith, patience and love. You know I never give up. ¹¹You know how I have been hurt and have suffered, as in Antioch, Iconium and Lystra. I have suffered, but the Lord saved me from all those troubles.

Read 2:15 again. What does God want you to do?

It won't always be easy (2:16). But we just need to keep on trusting in God (2:19). You don't even have to be perfect – just do your best.

Think

Have you given yourself to God?

Pray

Turn 2:15 into a prayer, asking God to accept you and make you the person he wants you to be.

The amazing book

This book ...

- tells you how to live
- tells you how to be rich
- gives answers to life's big questions
- tells you about your future
- helps you hear God speaking to you

Amazing, huh?

2 Timothy 3:12–4:22

¹²Everyone who wants to live as God desires, in Christ Jesus, will be hurt. ¹³But people who are evil and cheat others will go from bad to worse. They will fool others, but they will also be fooling themselves.

¹⁴But you should continue following the teachings you learned. You know they are true, because you trust those who taught you. ¹⁵Since you were a child you have known the Holy Scriptures which are able to make you wise. And that wisdom leads to salvation through faith in Christ Jesus. ¹⁶All Scripture is given by God and is useful for teaching, for showing people what is wrong in their lives, for correcting faults and for teaching how to live right. ¹⁷Using the Scriptures, the person who serves God will be capable, having all that is needed to do every good work.

4 I give you a command in the presence of God and Christ Jesus, the One who will judge the living and the dead, and by his coming and his kingdom: ²preach the Good News. Be ready at all times, and tell people what they need to do. Tell them when they are wrong. Encourage them with great patience and careful teaching,

³because the time will come when people will not listen to the true teaching but will find many more teachers who please them by saying the things they want to hear. ⁴They will stop listening to the truth and will begin to follow false stories. ⁵But you should control yourself at all times, accept troubles, do the work of telling the Good News and complete all the duties of a servant of God.

⁶My life is being given as an offering to God, and the time has come for me to leave this life. ⁷I have fought the good fight, I have finished the race, I have kept the faith. ⁸Now, a crown is being held for me—a crown for being right with God. The Lord, the judge who judges rightly, will give the crown to me on that day—not only to me but to all those who have waited with love for him to come again.

Personal Words

⁹Do your best to come to me as soon as you can, ¹⁰because Demas, who loved this world, left me and went to Thessalonica. Crescens went to Galatia, and Titus went to Dalmatia. ¹¹Luke is the only one still with me. Get Mark and bring him with you when you come, because he can help me in

my work here. 12I sent Tychicus to Ephesus. 13When I was in Troas, I left my coat there with Carpus. So when you come, bring it to me, along with my books, particularly the ones written on parchment.

14Alexander the metalworker did many harmful things against me. The Lord will punish him for what he did. 15You also should be careful that he does not hurt you, because he fought strongly against our teaching.

16The first time I defended myself, no one helped me; everyone left me. May they be forgiven. 17But the Lord stayed with me and gave me strength so I could fully tell the Good News to all those who are not Jews. So I was saved from the lion's mouth. 18The Lord will save me when anyone tries to hurt me, and he will bring me safely to his heavenly kingdom. Glory for ever and ever be the Lord's. Amen.

Final Greetings

19Greet Priscilla and Aquila and the family of Onesiphorus. 20Erastus stayed in Corinth, and I left Trophimus sick in Miletus. 21Try as hard as you can to come to me before winter.

Eubulus sends greetings to you. Also Pudens, Linus, Claudia and all the brothers and sisters in Christ greet you.

22The Lord be with your spirit. Grace be with you.

If you're serious about living for God, then doing what you're doing now is a good way to start! Find these things in the verses:

The Bible ...

• teaches right living (v...)

• makes you wise (v...)

• teaches the truth (v...)

• leads to being put right with God (v...)

• is given by God (v...)

• corrects wrong living (v...)

Think

Do you spend enough time with the Bible? How else might you engage with the Bible, especially if you don't like reading?

Pray

Ask God to help you understand and obey his Word.

Say if it's wrong

If you knew a Christian friend was doing or saying something wrong, why might you *not* say anything?

- It's too embarrassing
- I don't want to offend them
- I feel too unimportant
- I'm afraid others might laugh at me

Titus 1:1–2:8

1 From Paul, a servant of God and an apostle of Jesus Christ. I was sent to help the faith of God's chosen people and to help them know the truth that shows people how to serve God. ²That faith and that knowledge come from the hope of life for ever, which God promised to us before time began. And God cannot lie. ³At the right time God let the world know about that life through preaching. He trusted me with that work, and I preached by the command of God our Saviour.

⁴To Titus, my true child in the faith which we share:

Grace and peace from God the Father and Christ Jesus our Saviour.

Titus' Work in Crete

⁵I left you in Crete so you could finish doing the things that still needed to be done and so you could appoint elders in every town, as I directed you. ⁶An elder must not be guilty of doing wrong, must have only one wife, and must have believing children. They must not be known as children who are wild and do not obey. ⁷As a manager of God's work, an elder must not be guilty of doing wrong, being selfish or becoming angry quickly. He must not drink too much wine, like to fight or try to

get rich by cheating others. ⁸An elder must be ready to welcome guests, love what is good, be wise, live right and be holy and self-controlled. ⁹By holding on to the trustworthy word just as we teach it, an elder can help people by using true teaching, and he can show those who are against the true teaching that they are wrong.

¹⁰There are many people who refuse to obey, who talk about worthless things and lead others into the wrong way—mainly those who say all who are not Jews must be circumcised. ¹¹These people must be stopped, because they are upsetting whole families by teaching things they should not teach, which they do to get rich by cheating people. ¹²Even one of their own prophets said, "Cretan people are always liars, evil animals and lazy people who do nothing but eat." ¹³The words that prophet said are true. So firmly tell those people they are wrong so they may become strong in the faith, ¹⁴not accepting Jewish false stories and the commands of people who reject the truth. ¹⁵To those who are pure, all things are pure, but to those who are full of sin and do not believe, nothing is pure. Both their minds and their thinking have been ruined. ¹⁶They say they know God, but their actions show they do not

accept him. They are hateful people, they refuse to obey and they are useless for doing anything good.

Following the True Teaching

2 But you must tell everyone what to do to follow the true teaching. ²Teach older men to be self-controlled, serious, wise, strong in faith, in love and in patience.

³In the same way, teach older women to be holy in their behaviour, not speaking against others or having the habit of too much wine, but teaching what is good.

⁴Then they can teach the young women to love their husbands, to love their children, ⁵to be wise and pure, to be good workers at home, to be kind and to yield to their husbands. Then no one will be able to criticise the teaching God gave us.

⁶In the same way, encourage young men to be wise. ⁷In every way be an example of doing good deeds. When you teach, do it with honesty and seriousness. ⁸Speak the truth so that you cannot be criticised. Then those who are against you will be ashamed because there is nothing bad to say about us.

Paul encouraged Titus to say when he knew something was wrong with what people were teaching about Jesus. Why (1:11,13)?

Think

If you heard someone claiming to give a new teaching about following Jesus, how would you decide if it was true or false?

Pray

Father God, help me to stay true to what I know about Jesus from your Word.

517

Encourage others

"I can live how I like, so long as I believe the right things."

Do you agree?

Or what about ...

"I can live how I like as long as I don't hurt anyone else."

 Titus 2:9–3:15

⁹Slaves should yield to their own masters at all times, trying to please them and not arguing with them. ¹⁰They should not steal from them but should show their masters they can be fully trusted so that in everything they do they will make the teaching of God our Saviour attractive. ¹¹That is the way we should live, because God's grace that can save everyone has come. ¹²It teaches us not to live against God nor to do the evil things the world wants to do. Instead, that grace teaches us to live now in a wise and right way and in a way that shows we serve God. ¹³We should live like that while we wait for our great hope and the coming of the glory of our great God and Saviour Jesus Christ. ¹⁴He gave himself for us so he might pay the price to free us from all evil and to make us pure people who belong only to him—people who are always wanting to do good deeds.

¹⁵Say these things and encourage the people and tell them what is wrong in their lives, with all authority. Do not let anyone treat you as if you were unimportant.

The Right Way to Live

3 Remind the believers to yield to the authority of rulers and government leaders, to obey them, to be ready to do good, ²to speak no evil about anyone, to live in peace and to be gentle and polite to all people.

³In the past we also were foolish. We did not obey, we were wrong, and we were slaves to many things our bodies wanted and enjoyed. We spent our lives doing evil and being jealous. People hated us, and we hated each other. ⁴But when the kindness and love of God our Saviour was shown, ⁵he saved us because of his mercy. It was not because of good deeds we did to be right with him. He saved us through the washing that made us new people through the Holy Spirit. ⁶God poured out richly upon us that Holy Spirit through Jesus Christ our Saviour. ⁷Being made right with God by his grace, we could have the hope of receiving the life that never ends.

⁸This teaching is true, and I want you to be sure the people understand these things. Then those who believe in God will be careful to use their lives for doing good. These things are good and will help everyone.

⁹But stay away from those who have foolish arguments and talk about useless family histories and argue and quarrel about the law. Those things are worth nothing and will not help anyone. ¹⁰After a first and second warning, avoid someone who causes arguments. ¹¹You can know that such people are evil and sinful; their own sins prove them wrong.

Some Things to Remember

¹²When I send Artemas or Tychicus to you, try hard to come to me at Nicopolis, because I have decided to stay there this winter. ¹³Do all you can to help Zenas the lawyer and Apollos on their journey so that they have everything they need. ¹⁴Our people must learn to use their lives for doing good deeds to provide what is necessary so that their lives will not be useless.

¹⁵All who are with me greet you. Greet those who love us in the faith.

Grace be with you all.

> Why should we want to live "in a way that shows we serve God" (2:12)?
>
> What do you think "grace" means (2:11,14)?

Think

How could you encourage others to *live* for God, as well as *say* they believe the right things (2:15)?

Pray

Lord, help me not just to believe in you, but also to live for you.

Extra

GRACE: God's Riches At Christ's Expense

Jesus means change

How do you reckon you've changed as you've got to know Jesus better?

Knowing Jesus means doing things differently – and it's not always easy.

 Philemon 1–25

¹From Paul, a prisoner of Christ Jesus, and from Timothy, our brother.

To Philemon, our dear friend and worker with us; ²to Apphia, our sister; to Archippus, a worker with us; and to the church that meets in your home:

³Grace and peace to you from God our Father and the Lord Jesus Christ.

Philemon's Love and Faith

⁴I always thank my God when I mention you in my prayers, ⁵because I hear about the love you have for all God's holy people and the faith you have in the Lord Jesus. ⁶I pray that the faith you share may make you understand every blessing we have in Christ. ⁷I have great joy and comfort, my brother, because the love you have shown to God's people has refreshed them.

Accept Onesimus as a Brother

⁸So, in Christ, I could be bold and order you to do what is right. ⁹But because I love you, I am pleading with you instead. I, Paul, an old man now and also a prisoner for Christ Jesus, ¹⁰am pleading with you for my child Onesimus, who became my child while I was in prison. ¹¹In the past he was useless to you, but now he has become useful for both you and me.

¹²I am sending him back to you, and with him I am sending my own heart. ¹³I wanted to keep him with me so that in your place he might help me while I am in prison for the Good News. ¹⁴But I did not want to do anything without asking you first so that any good you do for me will be because you want to do it, not because I forced you. ¹⁵Maybe Onesimus was separated from you for a short time so you could have him back for ever— ¹⁶no longer as a slave, but better than a slave, as a loved brother. I love him very much, but you will love him even more, both as a person and as a believer in the Lord.

¹⁷So if you consider me your partner, welcome Onesimus as you would welcome me. ¹⁸If he has done anything wrong to you or if he owes you anything, charge that to me. ¹⁹I, Paul, am writing this with my own hand. I will pay it back, and I will say nothing about what you owe me for your own life. ²⁰So, my brother, I ask that you do this for me in the Lord: refresh my heart in Christ. ²¹I write this letter, knowing that you will do what I ask you and even more.

²²One more thing—prepare a room for me in which to stay, because I hope God will answer your prayers and I will be able to come to you.

Final Greetings

23Epaphras, a prisoner with me for Christ Jesus, sends greetings to you. 24And also Mark, Aristarchus, Demas and Luke, workers together with me, send greetings.

25The grace of our Lord Jesus Christ be with your spirit.

What did Onesimus have to do that wasn't easy (v 12)?

What did Philemon have to do (vs 15–17)?

Think

Is there something you need to do differently because you're a Christian?

Pray

Lord Jesus, change me to be the person you want me to be.

Who can you trust?

Your parents? Your best friend?

More than anyone else, you can trust God... and his Son, Jesus, because...

Hebrews 1:1–2:4

God Spoke Through His Son

1 In the past God spoke to our ancestors through the prophets many times and in many different ways. ²But now in these last days God has spoken to us through his Son. God has chosen his Son to own all things, and through him he made the world. ³The Son reflects the glory of God and shows exactly what God is like. He holds everything together with his powerful word. When the Son made people clean from their sins, he sat down at the right side of God, the Great One in heaven. ⁴The Son became much greater than the angels, and God gave him a name that is much greater than theirs.

⁵This is because God never said to any of the angels,
"You are my Son.
Today I have become your Father."
Psalm 2:7

Nor did God say of any angel,
"I will be his father,
and he will be my son." *2 Samuel 7:14*
⁶And when God brings his firstborn Son into the world, he says,
"All the gods should worship him."
Psalm 97:7
⁷This is what God said about the angels:
"God makes his angels become like winds.
He makes his servants become like flames of fire." *Psalm 104:4*

⁸But God said this about his Son:
"God, your throne will last for ever and ever.
You will rule your kingdom with fairness.
⁹You love right and hate evil,
so God has chosen you from among your friends;
he has set you apart with much joy."
Psalm 45:6–7
¹⁰God also says,
"In the beginning you made the earth,
and your hands made the skies.
¹¹They will be destroyed, but you will remain.
They will all wear out like clothes.
¹²And, like clothes, you will change them
and throw them away.
But you never change,
and your life will never end."
Psalm 102:25–27
¹³And God never said this to an angel:
"Sit by me at my right side
until I put your enemies under your control." *Psalm 110:1*
¹⁴All the angels are spirits who serve God and are sent to help those who will receive salvation.

Our Salvation is Great

2 So we must be more careful to follow what we were taught. Then we will not stray away from the truth. ²The

522

teaching God spoke through angels was shown to be true, and anyone who did not follow it or obey it received the punishment that was earned. ³So surely we also will be punished if we ignore this great salvation. The Lord himself first told about this salvation, and it was proven true to us by those who heard him. ⁴God also proved it by using wonders, great signs, many kinds of miracles and by giving people gifts through the Holy Spirit, just as he wanted.

What has God done through Jesus (1:2)?

Who is Jesus (1:3)?

What has Jesus done (1:3)?

Think

So – Christians have someone FANTASTIC to put their trust in. How does your faith in Jesus show to others?

Pray

Look in a mirror. See how accurately it reflects your image. Pray that Jesus will be reflected to others in you.

Someone who understands

A philosopher once said that to understand a man you have to walk a mile in his shoes. That's (a bit like) what Jesus did by becoming a human, one of us!

 Hebrews 2:5–3:6

Christ Became like Humans

⁵God did not choose angels to be the rulers of the new world that was coming, which is what we have been talking about. ⁶It is written in the Scriptures,

> "But why are people important to you?
> Why do you take care of human beings?
> ⁷You made them a little lower than the angels
> and crowned them with glory and honour. You put them in charge of everything you made.
> 8   You put all things under their control."
>
> *Psalm 8:4-6*

When God put everything under their control, there was nothing left that they did not rule. Still, we do not yet see them ruling over everything. ⁹But we see Jesus, who for a short time was made lower than the angels. And now he is wearing a crown of glory and honour because he suffered and died. And by God's grace, he died for everyone.

¹⁰God is the One who made all things, and all things are for his glory. He wanted to have many children share his glory, so he made the One who leads people to salvation perfect through suffering.

¹¹Jesus, who makes people holy, and those who are made holy are from the same family. So he is not ashamed to call them his brothers and sisters. ¹²He says,

> "Then, I will tell my fellow Israelites about you;
> I will praise you in the public meeting."
>
> *Psalm 22:22*

¹³He also says,

> "I will trust in God."   *Isaiah 8:17*

And he also says,

> "I am here, and with me are the children God has given me."   *Isaiah 8:18*

¹⁴Since these children are people with physical bodies, Jesus himself became like them. He did this so that, by dying, he could destroy the one who has the power of death—the devil— ¹⁵and free those who were like slaves all their lives because of their fear of death. ¹⁶Clearly, it is not angels that Jesus helps, but the people who are from Abraham. ¹⁷For this reason Jesus had to be made like his brothers in every way so he could be their merciful and faithful high priest in service to God. Then Jesus could bring forgiveness for their sins. ¹⁸And now he can help those who are tempted, because he himself suffered and was tempted.

Jesus is Greater than Moses

3 So all of you holy brothers and sisters, who were called by God, think about Jesus, who was sent to us and is the high priest of our faith. ²Jesus was faithful to God as Moses was in God's family. ³Jesus has more honour than Moses, just as the

builder of a house has more honour than the house itself. ⁴Every house is built by someone, but the builder of everything is God himself. ⁵Moses was faithful in God's family as a servant, and he told what God would say in the future. ⁶But Christ is faithful as a Son over God's house. And we are God's house if we keep on being very sure about our great hope.

Why did Jesus have to have a physical body (2:14)?

How does the writer to the Hebrews describe us (2:17)?

... and Jesus (2:17)?

What does that mean for us (2:18)?

Think

Think about your life. What are you tempted to buy? To be like? To watch? To do? Are those things helpful to you?

Pray

Thank Jesus that he understands what you're tempted by, and that he can help you.

525

Straight to the point

Have you ever had an operation to sort out a medical problem? (No... *don't* tell me!)

Hebrews 3:7–4:13

We Must Continue to Follow God

⁷So it is as the Holy Spirit says:
"Today listen to what he says.
⁸Do not be stubborn as in the past
    when you turned against God,
when you tested God in the desert.
⁹There your ancestors tried me and tested
        me
    and saw the things I did for 40 years.
¹⁰I was angry with them.
    I said, 'They are not loyal to me
    and have not understood my ways.'
¹¹I was angry and made a promise,
    'They will never enter my rest.'"
                          Psalm 95:7–11

¹²So brothers and sisters, be careful that none of you has an evil, unbelieving heart that will turn you away from the living God. ¹³But encourage each other every day while it is "today". Help each other so none of you will become hardened because sin has tricked you. ¹⁴We all share in Christ if we keep till the end the sure faith we had in the beginning. ¹⁵This is what the Scripture says:

"Today listen to what he says.
    Do not be stubborn as in the past
    when you turned against God."
                          Psalm 95:7–8

¹⁶Who heard God's voice and was against him? It was all those people Moses led out of Egypt. ¹⁷And with whom was God angry for 40 years? He was angry with those who sinned, who died in the desert. ¹⁸And to whom was God talking when he promised that they would never enter his rest? He was talking to those who did not

obey him. ¹⁹So we see they were not allowed to enter and have God's rest, because they did not believe.

4 Now, since God has left us the promise that we may enter his rest, let us be very careful so none of you will fail to enter. ²The Good News was preached to us just as it was to them. But the teaching they heard did not help them, because they heard it but did not accept it with faith. ³We who have believed are able to enter and have God's rest. As God has said,

"I was angry and made a promise,
    'They will never enter my rest.'"
                          Psalm 95:11

But God's work was finished from the time he made the world. ⁴In the Scriptures he talked about the seventh day of the week: "And on the seventh day God rested from all his works." ⁵And again in the Scripture God said, "They will never enter my rest." ⁶It is still true that some people will enter God's rest, but those who first heard the way to be saved did not enter, because they did not obey. ⁷So God planned another day, called "today". He spoke about that day through David a long time later in the same Scripture used before:

"Today listen to what he says.
    Do not be stubborn."   *Psalm 95:7–8*

⁸We know that Joshua did not lead the people into that rest, because God spoke later about another day. ⁹This shows that the rest for God's people is still coming. ¹⁰Anyone who enters God's rest will rest from his work as God did. ¹¹Let us try as

hard as we can to enter God's rest so that no one will fail by following the example of those who refused to obey.

¹²God's word is alive and working and is sharper than a double-edged sword. It cuts all the way into us, where the soul and the spirit are joined, to the centre of our joints and bones. And it judges the thoughts and feelings in our hearts. ¹³Nothing in all the world can be hidden from God. Everything is clear and lies open before him, and to him we must explain the way we have lived.

God's Word is a bit like the surgeon's knife! He uses it to cut out the bad stuff and put things right. His Word can change our lives for the better.

In what three ways does the writer describe God's Word (4:12)?

1 _____

2 _____

3 _____

What can't we do (4:13)?

Think

How does the Bible show you things that are wrong in your life?

Pray

Be quiet with God for a few minutes and ask him to show you anything that's wrong in your life. What can you do about it?

Jesus – he's the one

What would you say to anyone who asked you why Christians believe Jesus is so important?

Hebrews 4:14–6:8

Jesus is Our High Priest

14Since we have a great high priest, Jesus the Son of God, who has gone into heaven, let us hold on to the faith we have. 15For our high priest is able to understand our weaknesses. When he lived on earth, he was tempted in every way that we are, but he did not sin. 16Let us, then, feel very sure that we can come before God's throne where there is grace. There we can receive mercy and grace to help us when we need it.

5 Every high priest is chosen from among other people. He is given the work of going before God for them to offer gifts and sacrifices for sins. 2Since he himself is weak, he is able to be gentle with those who do not understand and who are doing wrong things. 3Because he is weak, the high priest must offer sacrifices for his own sins and also for the sins of the people.

4To be a high priest is an honour, but no one chooses himself for this work. He must be called by God as Aaron was. 5So also Christ did not choose himself to have the honour of being a high priest, but God chose him. God said to him,

"You are my Son.
Today I have become your Father."
Psalm 2:7

6And in another Scripture God says,
"You are a priest for ever,
a priest like Melchizedek." *Psalm 110:4*

7While Jesus lived on earth, he prayed to God and asked God for help. He prayed with loud cries and tears to the One who could save him from death, and his prayer was heard because he trusted God. 8Even though Jesus was the Son of God, he learned obedience by what he suffered. 9And because his obedience was perfect, he was able to give eternal salvation to all who obey him. 10In this way God made Jesus a high priest, a priest like Melchizedek.

Warning Against Falling Away

11We have much to say about this, but it is hard to explain because you are so slow to understand. 12By now you should be teachers, but you need someone to teach you again the first lessons of God's message. You still need the teaching that is like milk. You are not ready for solid food. 13Anyone who lives on milk is still a baby and knows nothing about right teaching. 14But solid food is for those who are grown up. They have practised in order to know the difference between good and evil.

6 So let us go on to grown-up teaching. Let us not go back over the beginning lessons we learned about Christ. We should not again start teaching about faith in God and about turning away from those acts that lead to death. 2We should not return to the teaching about baptisms, about laying on of hands, about the raising of the dead and eternal judgement. 3And we will go on to grown-up teaching if God allows.

4Some people cannot be brought back again to a changed life. They were once in

God's light, and enjoyed heaven's gift, and shared in the Holy Spirit. ⁵They found out how good God's word is, and they received the powers of his new world. ⁶But they fell away from Christ. It is impossible to bring them back to a changed life again, because they are nailing the Son of God to a cross again and are shaming him in front of others.

⁷Some people are like land that gets plenty of rain. The land produces a good crop for those who work it, and it receives God's blessings. ⁸Other people are like land that grows thorns and weeds and is worthless. It is in danger of being cursed by God and will be destroyed by fire.

See if you can find three things which tell you why Jesus is so important from these verses:

1 _____ (v . . .)

2 _____ (v . . .)

3 _____ (v . . .)

How can you have life for ever with God (5:9)?

Think

How do these verses relate to the beliefs of other faiths?

Pray

Thank Jesus that because he obeyed his Father, God, you can have life for ever.

Extra

You can read about Melchizedek in Genesis 14:17–24. Like Jesus, he was both a priest and king.

"It's * *#!#*!!# true"

Many people use expletives, or swear, when they want to make a point. They believe that this adds weight to their argument. It seems that something similar was common when this passage was written (6:16).

Hebrews 6:9–7:10

⁹Dear friends, we are saying this to you, but we really expect better things from you that will lead to your salvation. ¹⁰God is fair; he will not forget the work you did and the love you showed for him by helping his people. And he will remember that you are still helping them. ¹¹We want each of you to go on with the same hard work all your lives so you will surely get what you hope for. ¹²We do not want you to become lazy. Be like those who through faith and patience will receive what God has promised.

¹³God made a promise to Abraham. And as there is no one greater than God, he used himself when he swore to Abraham, ¹⁴saying, "I will surely bless you and give you many descendants." ¹⁵Abraham waited patiently for this to happen, and he received what God promised.

¹⁶People always use the name of someone greater than themselves when they swear. The oath proves that what they say is true, and this ends all arguing. ¹⁷God wanted to prove that his promise was true to those who would get what he promised. And he wanted them to understand clearly that his purposes never change, so he made an oath. ¹⁸These two things cannot change: God cannot lie when he makes a promise, and he cannot lie when he makes an oath. These things encourage us who came to God for safety. They give us strength to hold on to the hope we have been given. ¹⁹We have this hope as an anchor for the soul, sure and strong. It enters behind the curtain in the Most Holy Place in heaven, ²⁰where Jesus has gone ahead of us and for us. He has become the high priest for ever, a priest like Melchizedek.

The Priest Melchizedek

7 Melchizedek was the king of Salem and a priest for God Most High. He met Abraham when Abraham was coming back after defeating the kings. When they met, Melchizedek blessed Abraham, ²and Abraham gave him a tenth of everything he had brought back from the battle. First, Melchizedek's name means "king of goodness", and he is king of Salem, which means "king of peace". ³No one knows who Melchizedek's father or mother was, where he came from, when he was born, or when he died. Melchizedek is like the Son of God; he continues being a priest for ever.

⁴You can see how great Melchizedek was. Abraham, the great father, gave him a tenth of everything that he won in battle. ⁵Now the law says that those in the tribe of Levi who become priests must collect a tenth from the people—their own people—even though the priests and the people are from the family of Abraham. ⁶Melchizedek was not from the tribe of Levi, but he collected a tenth from Abraham. And he blessed Abraham, the man who had God's promises. ⁷Now everyone knows that the

more important person blesses the less important person. ⁸Priests receive a tenth, even though they are only men who live and then die. But Melchizedek, who received a tenth from Abraham, continues living, as the Scripture says. ⁹We might even say that Levi, who receives a tenth, also paid it when Abraham paid Melchizedek a tenth. ¹⁰Levi was not yet born, but he was in the body of his ancestor when Melchizedek met Abraham.

What two things cannot change (6:18)?

What is the outcome of these two things (6:18)?

The image of an anchor helps us to realise that even when everything around us is being turned upside down, we are firmly attached to God.

Think

When you have doubts and fears you are not alone – many Christians before have felt the same.

Pray

That you will live with the surety of God's promises to you.

There for you

What do you expect of your best mates?

- There for you always
- Let you down sometimes
- Will give up stuff for you
- You'll be friends for ever

Hebrews 7:11–8:6

¹¹The people were given the law based on a system of priests from the tribe of Levi, but they could not be made perfect through that system. So there was a need for another priest to come, a priest like Melchizedek, not Aaron. ¹²And when a different kind of priest comes, the law must be changed, too. ¹³We are saying these things about Christ, who belonged to a different tribe. No one from that tribe ever served as a priest at the altar. ¹⁴It is clear that our Lord came from the tribe of Judah, and Moses said nothing about priests belonging to that tribe.

Jesus is like Melchizedek

¹⁵And this becomes even more clear when we see that another priest comes who is like Melchizedek. ¹⁶He was not made a priest by human rules and laws but through the power of his life, which continues for ever. ¹⁷It is said about him,

"You are a priest for ever,
    a priest like Melchizedek."   *Psalm 110:4*
¹⁸The old rule is now set aside, because it was weak and useless. ¹⁹The law of Moses could not make anything perfect. But now a better hope has been given to us, and with this hope we can come near to God. ²⁰It is important that God did this with an oath. Others became priests without an oath, ²¹but Christ became a priest with God's oath. God said:

"The Lord has made a promise
    and will not change his mind.
'You are a priest for ever.'"   *Psalm 110:4*
²²This means that Jesus is the guarantee of a better agreement from God to his people.

²³When one of the other priests died, he could not continue being a priest. So there were many priests. ²⁴But because Jesus lives for ever, he will never stop serving as priest. ²⁵So he is able always to save those who come to God through him because he always lives, asking God to help them.

²⁶Jesus is the kind of high priest we need. He is holy, sinless, pure, not influenced by sinners and he is raised above the heavens. ²⁷He is not like the other priests who had to offer sacrifices every day, first for their own sins, and then for the sins of the people. Christ offered his sacrifice only once and for all time when he offered himself. ²⁸The law chooses high priests who are people with weaknesses, but the word of God's oath came later than the law. It made God's Son to be the high priest, and that Son has been made perfect for ever.

Jesus is Our High Priest

8 Here is the point of what we are saying: we have a high priest who sits on the right side of God's throne in heaven. ²Our high priest serves in the Most Holy Place, the true place of worship that was made by God, not by humans.

³Every high priest has the work of offering gifts and sacrifices to God. So our high priest must also offer something to God. ⁴If our high priest were now living on earth, he would not be a priest, because there are already priests here who follow the law by offering gifts to God. ⁵The work they do as priests is only a copy and a shadow of what is in heaven. This is why God warned Moses when he was ready to build the Holy Tent: "Be very careful to make everything by the plan I showed you on the mountain." ⁶But the priestly work that has been given to Jesus is much greater than the work that was given to the other priests. In the same way, the new agreement that Jesus brought from God to his people is much greater than the old one. And the new agreement is based on promises of better things.

Jesus is much, much more than a good friend.

What's he done for you (7:27)?

Why can you be sure he'll be there for you always (7:28)?

Think

Do you ever worry that there's something you've done that God won't forgive? Take it to Jesus, your "priest". He's there for you, always (7:27).

Pray

Lord Jesus, thank you that you died to pay the price of my sin.

New deal

A lot of the rules they had in the Old Testament were right for the time they were written. But they'd had their day. A new deal was needed.

Hebrews 8:7–9:12

⁷If there had been nothing wrong with the first agreement, there would have been no need for a second agreement. ⁸But God found something wrong with his people. He says:

"Look, the time is coming, says the
LORD,
when I will make a new agreement
with the people of Israel
and the people of Judah.
⁹It will not be like the agreement
I made with their ancestors
when I took them by the hand
to bring them out of Egypt.
But they broke that agreement,
and I turned away from them, says the
LORD.
¹⁰This is the agreement I will make
with the people of Israel at that time,
says the LORD.
I will put my Teachings in their minds
and write them on their hearts.
I will be their God,
and they will be my people.
¹¹People will no longer have to teach their
neighbours and relatives
to know the LORD,
because all people will know me,
from the least to the most important.
¹²I will forgive them for the wicked things
they did,
and I will not remember their sins any
more."   *Jeremiah 31:31–34*

¹³God called this a new agreement, and so he has made the first agreement old. And anything that is old and worn out is ready to disappear.

The Old Agreement

9 The first agreement had rules for worship and a man-made place for worship. ²The Holy Tent was set up for this. The first area in the Tent was called the Holy Place. In it were the lamp and the table with the bread that was made holy for God. ³Behind the second curtain was a room called the Most Holy Place. ⁴In it was a golden altar for burning incense and the Ark covered with gold that held the old agreement. Inside this Ark was a golden jar of manna, Aaron's rod that once grew leaves, and the stone tablets of the old agreement. ⁵Above the Ark were the creatures that showed God's glory, whose wings reached over the lid. But we cannot tell everything about these things now.

⁶When everything in the Tent was made ready in this way, the priests went into the first room every day to worship. ⁷But only the high priest could go into the second room, and he did that only once a year. He could never enter the inner room without taking blood with him, which he offered to God for himself and for sins the people did without knowing they did them. ⁸The Holy Spirit uses this to show that the

way into the Most Holy Place was not open while the system of the old Holy Tent was still being used. ⁹This is an example for the present time. It shows that the gifts and sacrifices offered cannot make the conscience of the worshipper perfect. ¹⁰These gifts and sacrifices were only about food and drink and special washings. They were rules for the body, to be followed until the time of God's new way.

The New Agreement

¹¹But when Christ came as the high priest of the good things we now have, he entered the greater and more perfect tent. It is not made by humans and does not belong to this world. ¹²Christ entered the Most Holy Place only once—and for all time. He did not take with him the blood of goats and calves. His sacrifice was his own blood, and by it he set us free from sin for ever.

> The old deal God had with people is finished with: Jesus gives us a new, better deal. He brought us together with God. Now it's us, him and God. And that's it.

Think

If God wrote the first deal, what was wrong with it (8:7,8)? It can't have been God's fault, right?

Pray

Thank God for the new deal that Jesus gives.

In a nutshell

Do you try to overcomplicate the Christian message?

Do you get bogged down trying to describe it to others who want to know?

Hebrews 9:13–10:10

¹³The blood of goats and bulls and the ashes of a cow are sprinkled on the people who are unclean, and this makes their bodies clean again. ¹⁴How much more is done by the blood of Christ! He offered himself through the eternal Spirit as a perfect sacrifice to God. His blood will make our consciences pure from useless acts so we may serve the living God.

¹⁵For this reason Christ brings a new agreement from God to his people. Those who are called by God can now receive the blessings he has promised, blessings that will last for ever. They can have those things because Christ died so that the people who lived under the first agreement could be set free from sin.

¹⁶When there is a will, it must be proven that the one who wrote that will is dead. ¹⁷A will means nothing while the person is alive; it can be used only after the person dies. ¹⁸This is why even the first agreement could not begin without blood to show death. ¹⁹First, Moses told all the people every command in the law. Next he took the blood of calves and mixed it with water. Then he used red wool and a branch of the hyssop plant to sprinkle it on the Book of the law and on all the people. ²⁰He said, "This is the blood that begins the Agreement that God commanded you to obey." ²¹In the same way, Moses sprinkled the blood on the Holy Tent and over all the things used in worship. ²²The law says that almost everything must be made clean by blood, and sins cannot be forgiven without blood to show death.

Christ's Death Takes Away Sins

²³So the copies of the real things in heaven had to be made clean by animal sacrifices. But the real things in heaven need much better sacrifices. ²⁴Christ did not go into the Most Holy Place made by humans, which is only a copy of the real one. He went into heaven itself and is there now before God to help us. ²⁵The high priest enters the Most Holy Place once every year with blood that is not his own. But Christ did not offer himself many times. ²⁶Then he would have had to suffer many times since the world was made. But Christ came only once and for all time at just the right time to take away all sin by sacrificing himself. ²⁷Just as everyone must die once and be judged, ²⁸so Christ was offered as a sacrifice once to take away the sins of many people. And he will come a second time, not to offer himself for sin, but to bring salvation to those who are waiting for him.

10 The law is only an unclear picture of the good things coming in the future; it is not the real thing. The people under the law offer the same sacrifices every year, but these sacrifices can never make perfect those who come near to worship God. ²If the law could make them perfect, the sacrifices would have already stopped. The worshippers would be made clean, and they would no longer have a

536

sense of sin. ³But these sacrifices remind them of their sins every year, ⁴because it is impossible for the blood of bulls and goats to take away sins.

⁵So when Christ came into the world, he said:

"You do not want sacrifices and offerings,
but you have prepared a body for me.
⁶You do not ask for burnt offerings
and sacrifices to take away sins.
⁷Then I said, 'Look, I have come.
It is written about me in the book.

My God, I want to do what you want.'"

Psalm 40:6–8

⁸In this Scripture he first said, "You do not want sacrifices and offerings. You do not ask for burnt offerings and offerings to take away sins." (These are all sacrifices that the law commands.) ⁹Then he said, "Look, I have come to do what you want." God ends the first system of sacrifices so he can set up the new system. ¹⁰And because of this, we are made holy through the sacrifice Christ made in his body once and for all time.

The writer is describing the work of Jesus as simply as possible.

• Jesus took away the sins of many people (9:28)

• He will bring salvation

Think

How could you explain the Good News simply to one of your friends?

Pray

That you will understand the simplicity of the Christian message, the implications of what that means, and to live accordingly.

Get close to God

How do you get close to God?

- By wearing really cool clothes
- By telling stupidly funny jokes
- By singing songs in church

Er, no. None of these. The way to get close to God is...

 Hebrews 10:11–39

11Every day the priests stand and do their religious service, often offering the same sacrifices. Those sacrifices can never take away sins. 12But after Christ offered one sacrifice for sins, for ever, he sat down at the right side of God. 13And now Christ waits there for his enemies to be put under his power. 14With one sacrifice he made perfect for ever those who are being made holy.

15The Holy Spirit also tells us about this. First he says:

16"This is the agreement I will make
   with them at that time, says the LORD.
I will put my teachings in their minds
   and write them on their hearts."

Jeremiah 31:33

17Then he says:

"Their sins and the evil things they do—
   I will not remember any more."

Jeremiah 31:34

18Now when these have been forgiven, there is no more need for a sacrifice for sins.

Continue to Trust God

19So, brothers and sisters, we are completely free to enter the Most Holy Place without fear because of the blood of Jesus' death. 20We can enter through a new and living way that Jesus opened for us. It leads us through the curtain—Christ's body.

21And since we have a great priest over God's house, 22let us come near to God with a sincere heart and a sure faith, because we have been made free from a guilty conscience, and our bodies have been washed with pure water. 23Let us hold firmly to the hope that we have confessed, because we can trust God to do what he promised.

24Let us think about each other and help each other to show love and do good deeds. 25You should not stay away from the church meetings, as some are doing, but you should meet together and encourage each other. Do this even more as you see the day coming.

26If we decide to go on sinning after we have learnt the truth, there is no longer any sacrifice for sins. 27There is nothing but fear in waiting for the judgement and the terrible fire that will destroy all those who live against God. 28Anyone who refused to obey the law of Moses was found guilty from the proof given by two or three witnesses. He was put to death without mercy. 29So what do you think should be done to those who do not respect the Son of God, who look at the blood of the agreement that made them holy as no different from others' blood, who insult the Spirit of God's grace? Surely they should have a much worse punishment. 30We

538

know that God said, "I will punish those who do wrong; I will repay them." And he also said, "The Lord will judge his people." ³¹It is a terrible thing to fall into the hands of the living God.

³²Remember those days in the past when you first learnt the truth. You had a hard struggle with many sufferings, but you continued strong. ³³Sometimes you were hurt and attacked before crowds of people, and sometimes you shared with those who were being treated that way. ³⁴You helped the prisoners. You even had joy when all that you owned was taken from you, because you knew you had something better and more lasting.

³⁵So do not lose the courage you had in the past, which has a great reward. ³⁶You must hold on, so you can do what God wants and receive what he has promised. ³⁷For in a very short time,

"The One who is coming will come
    and will not be delayed.
³⁸The person who is right with me
    will live by trusting in me.
But if he turns back with fear,
    I will not be pleased with him."

Habakkuk 2:3–4

³⁹But we are not those who turn back and are lost. We are people who have faith and are saved.

Don't worry about the difficult bits in these verses. See if you can work out the answers to these questions from what you've just read:

What has made it possible for you to come close to God (v 19)?

What has Jesus' death done for you (v 22)?

Think

What are the things that keep you from being close to God? Who does the moving, you or God?

Pray

Lord, I want to feel really close to you. Thank you that I can. Help me get rid of all the things that sometimes keep us apart.

By faith

If God isn't visible, how do you know where he is?

If you weren't there when Jesus rose from the dead, how do you know he really did?

How do you know it's true?

 Hebrews 11:1–22

What is Faith?

11 Faith means being sure of the things we hope for and knowing that something is real even if we do not see it. ²Faith is the reason we remember great people who lived in the past.

³It is by faith we understand that the whole world was made by God's command so what we see was made by something that cannot be seen.

⁴It was by faith that Abel offered God a better sacrifice than Cain did. God said he was pleased with the gifts Abel offered and called Abel a good man because of his faith. Abel died, but through his faith he is still speaking.

⁵It was by faith that Enoch was taken to heaven so he would not die. He could not be found, because God had taken him away. Before he was taken, the Scripture says that he was a man who truly pleased God. ⁶Without faith no one can please God. Anyone who comes to God must believe that he is real and that he rewards those who truly want to find him.

⁷It was by faith that Noah heard God's warnings about things he could not yet see. He obeyed God and built a large boat to save his family. By his faith, Noah showed that the world was wrong, and he became one of those who are made right with God through faith.

⁸It was by faith Abraham obeyed God's call to go to another place God promised to give him. He left his own country, not knowing where he was to go. ⁹It was by faith that he lived like a foreigner in the country God promised to give him. He lived in tents with Isaac and Jacob, who had received that same promise from God. ¹⁰Abraham was waiting for the city that has real foundations—the city planned and built by God.

¹¹He was too old to have children, and Sarah could not have children. It was by faith that Abraham was made able to become a father, because he trusted God to do what he had promised. ¹²This man was so old he was almost dead, but from him came as many descendants as there are stars in the sky. Like the sand on the seashore, they could not be counted.

¹³All these great people died in faith. They did not get the things that God promised his people, but they saw them coming far in the future and were glad. They said they were like visitors and strangers on earth. ¹⁴When people say such things, they show they are looking for a country that will be their own. ¹⁵If they had been thinking about the country they had left, they could have gone back. ¹⁶But they were waiting for a better country—a heavenly country. So God is not ashamed to be called their God, because he has prepared a city for them.

17It was by faith that Abraham, when God tested him, offered his son Isaac as a sacrifice. God made the promises to Abraham, but Abraham was ready to offer his own son as a sacrifice. 18God had said, "The descendants I promised you will be from Isaac." 19Abraham believed that God could raise the dead, and really, it was as if Abraham got Isaac back from death.

20It was by faith that Isaac blessed the future of Jacob and Esau. 21It was by faith that Jacob, as he was dying, blessed each one of Joseph's sons. Then he worshipped as he leaned on the top of his walking stick.

22It was by faith that Joseph, while he was dying, spoke about the Israelites leaving Egypt and told about what to do with his body.

Faith: it's all these Bible heroes had to keep them going. They often had no idea why they were doing what they did, but they did it because they had faith. They were certain that God was leading them, because they had faith.

And it worked out for them in the end, because they had faith.

Think

How much faith do you have in God's plan for you? Do you trust that it's all going to work out?

Pray

Ask God to lead you, and ask for him to help your faith grow.

Faith not fear

Peer pressure is something that we all suffer from, and I mean all of us! Have you ever done what others wanted because you were afraid of what they'd think of you if you didn't?

 Hebrews 11:23–12:6

23It was by faith that Moses' parents hid him for three months after he was born. They saw that Moses was a beautiful baby, and they were not afraid to disobey the king's order.

24It was by faith that Moses, when he grew up, refused to be called the son of the king of Egypt's daughter. 25He chose to suffer with God's people instead of enjoying sin for a short time. 26He thought it was better to suffer for the Christ than to have all the treasures of Egypt, because he was looking for God's reward. 27It was by faith that Moses left Egypt and was not afraid of the king's anger. Moses continued strong as if he could see the God that no one can see. 28It was by faith that Moses prepared the Passover and spread the blood on the doors so the one who brings death would not kill the first-born sons of Israel.

29It was by faith that the people crossed the Red Sea as if it were dry land. But when the Egyptians tried it, they were drowned.

30It was by faith that the walls of Jericho fell after the people had marched around them for seven days.

31It was by faith that Rahab, the prostitute, welcomed the spies and was not killed with those who refused to obey God.

32Do I need to give more examples? I do not have time to tell you about Gideon, Barak, Samson, Jephthah, David, Samuel and the prophets. 33Through their faith they defeated kingdoms. They did what was right, received God's promises and

shut the mouths of lions. 34They stopped great fires and were saved from being killed with swords. They were weak, and yet were made strong. They were powerful in battle and defeated other armies. 35Women received their dead relatives raised back to life. Others were tortured and refused to accept their freedom so they could be raised from the dead to a better life. 36Some were laughed at and beaten. Others were put in chains and thrown into prison. 37They were stoned to death, they were cut in half and they were killed with swords. Some wore the skins of sheep and goats. They were poor, abused and treated badly. 38The world was not good enough for them! They wandered in deserts and mountains, living in caves and holes in the earth.

39All these people are known for their faith, but none of them received what God had promised. 40God planned to give us something better so that they would be made perfect, along with us.

Follow Jesus' Example

12 We have around us many people whose lives tell us what faith means. So let us run the race that is before us and never give up. We should remove from our lives anything that would get in the way and the sin that so easily holds us back. 2Let us look only to Jesus, the One who began our faith and who makes it perfect. He suffered death on the cross. But he accepted the shame as if it were nothing because of the joy that God put

542

before him. And now he is sitting at the right side of God's throne. ³Think about Jesus' example. He held on while wicked people were doing evil things to him. So do not get tired and stop trying.

God is Like a Father

⁴You are struggling against sin, but your struggles have not yet caused you to be killed. ⁵You have forgotten the encouraging words that call you his children:

"My child, don't think the Lord's discipline is worth nothing,
and don't get angry when he corrects you.

⁶The Lord corrects those he loves,
and he punishes everyone he accepts as his child." *Proverbs 3:11–12*

Find all the ways in these verses where faith in God meant Moses and his parents weren't afraid to do right.

Think

Think of some times when you might need to trust in God to help you do what's right, instead of going with the crowd.

Pray

Ask God to help you stand up for what's right, especially when it's not easy.

Learn from hard times

When things go wrong, what's your most likely reaction?

- I'm giving up on God!
- What does God want me to learn from this?

Hebrews 12:7–29

⁷So hold on through your sufferings, because they are like a father's discipline. God is treating you as children. All children are disciplined by their fathers. ⁸If you are never disciplined (and every child must be disciplined), you are not true children. ⁹We have all had fathers here on earth who disciplined us, and we respected them. So it is even more important that we accept discipline from the Father of our spirits so we will have life. ¹⁰Our fathers on earth disciplined us for a short time in the way they thought was best. But God disciplines us to help us, so we can become holy as he is. ¹¹We do not enjoy being disciplined. It is painful, but later, after we have learned from it, we have peace, because we start living in the right way.

Be Careful How You Live

¹²You have become weak, so make yourselves strong again. ¹³Live in the right way so that you will be saved and your weakness will not cause you to be lost.

¹⁴Try to live in peace with all people, and try to live free from sin. Anyone whose life is not holy will never see the Lord. ¹⁵Be careful that no one fails to receive God's grace and begins to cause trouble among you. A person like that can ruin many of you. ¹⁶Be careful that no one takes part in sexual sin or is like Esau and never thinks about God. As the elder son, Esau would have received everything from his father, but he sold all that for a single meal. ¹⁷You remember that after Esau did this, he wanted to get his father's blessing, but his father refused. Esau could find no way to change what he had done, even though he wanted the blessing so much that he cried.

¹⁸You have not come to a mountain that can be touched and that is burning with fire. You have not come to darkness, sadness and storms. ¹⁹You have not come to the noise of a trumpet or to the sound of a voice like the one the people of Israel heard and begged not to hear another word. ²⁰They did not want to hear the command: "If anything, even an animal, touches the mountain, it must be put to death with stones." ²¹What they saw was so terrible that Moses said, "I am shaking with fear."

²²But you have come to Mount Zion, to the city of the living God, the heavenly Jerusalem. You have come to thousands of angels gathered together with joy. ²³You have come to the meeting of God's first-born children whose names are written in heaven. You have come to God, the judge of all people, and to the spirits of good people who have been made perfect. ²⁴You have come to Jesus, the One who brought the new agreement from God to his people, and you have come to the sprinkled blood that has a better message than the blood of Abel.

²⁵So be careful and do not refuse to listen when God speaks. Others refused to listen to him when he warned them on earth, and they did not escape. So it will be worse for us if we refuse to listen to God

who warns us from heaven. 26When he spoke before, his voice shook the earth, but now he has promised, "Once again I will shake not only the earth but also the heavens." 27The words "once again" clearly show us that everything that was made—things that can be shaken—will be destroyed. Only the things that cannot be shaken will remain.

28So let us be thankful, because we have a kingdom that cannot be shaken. We should worship God in a way that pleases him with respect and fear, 29because our God is like a fire that burns things up.

It's not easy living God's way. Just like running a marathon, it takes hard work and discipline. Sometimes we get things wrong. Sometimes life is hard (v 7).

What clues are there in these verses about why difficult things happen (vs 7–9)?

What's the point of God's "discipline" (vs 9–11)?

Think

Do you see discipline, or being told not to do something, as a negative or a positive?

Pray

Ask God to help you learn the lessons he's teaching you now.

Live it out

It's 7.30 a.m. Yesterday's weather forecast said it would be hot and sunny today. So you put on shorts and a T-shirt. Your faith (in the weather forecast) resulted in action (how you dressed).

Hebrews 13:1–25

13 Keep on loving each other as brothers and sisters. ²Remember to welcome strangers, because some who have done this have welcomed angels without knowing it. ³Remember those who are in prison as if you were in prison with them. Remember those who are suffering as if you were suffering with them.

⁴Marriage should be honoured by everyone, and husband and wife should keep their marriage pure. God will judge as guilty those who take part in sexual sins. ⁵Keep your lives free from the love of money, and be satisfied with what you have. God has said,

"I will never leave you;
I will never forget you."
Deuteronomy 31:6

⁶So we can be sure when we say,

"I will not be afraid, because the Lord is my helper.
People can't do anything to me."
Psalm 118:6

⁷Remember your leaders who taught God's message to you. Remember how they lived and died, and copy their faith. ⁸Jesus Christ is the same yesterday, today and for ever.

⁹Do not let all kinds of strange teachings lead you into the wrong way. Your hearts should be strengthened by God's grace, not by obeying rules about foods, which do not help those who obey them.

¹⁰We have a sacrifice, but the priests who serve in the Holy Tent cannot eat from it. ¹¹The high priest carries the blood of animals into the Most Holy Place where he offers this blood for sins. But the bodies of the animals are burnt outside the camp. ¹²So Jesus also suffered outside the city to make his people holy with his own blood. ¹³So let us go to Jesus outside the camp, holding on as he did when he bore our disgrace.

¹⁴Here on earth we do not have a city that lasts for ever, but we are looking for the city that we will have in the future. ¹⁵So through Jesus let us always offer to God our sacrifice of praise, coming from lips that speak his name. ¹⁶Do not forget to do good to others, and share with them, because such sacrifices please God.

¹⁷Obey your leaders and act under their authority. They are watching over you, because they are responsible for your souls. Obey them so that they will do this work with joy, not sadness. It will not help you to make their work hard.

¹⁸Pray for us. We are sure that we have a clear conscience, because we always want to do the right thing. ¹⁹I especially beg you to pray so that God will send me back to you soon.

^{20–21}I pray that the God of peace will give you every good thing you need so you can do what he wants. God raised from the dead our Lord Jesus, the Great Shepherd of the sheep, because of the blood of his death. His blood began the eternal agreement that God made with his people. I pray that God will do in us what pleases him, through Jesus Christ, and to him be glory for ever and ever. Amen.

22My brothers and sisters, I beg you to listen patiently to this message I have written to encourage you, because it is not very long. 23I want you to know that our brother Timothy has been let out of prison. If he arrives soon, we will both come to see you.

24Greet all your leaders and all of God's people. Those from Italy send greetings to you.

25Grace be with you all.

Think about what's happening in your life at the moment. Now look again at the verses. How can your faith be put into action?

Do...

1 _____ (v...)

2 _____ (v...)

Don't do...

1 _____ (v...)

2 _____ (v...)

Think

What could you do to demonstrate your faith in Jesus – at home, with friends, at school?

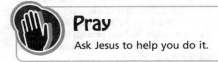

Pray

Ask Jesus to help you do it.

Hear it! Do it!

Hooked on PlayStation 2? What kind of player are you?
Do you...

- read the handbook and tell everyone the theory?
- PLAY?
- play and look back to the instructions for help?
- say you can't do it – it's too hard?

James 1:1–27

1 From James, a servant of God and of the Lord Jesus Christ.

To all of God's people who are scattered everywhere in the world:
Greetings.

Faith and Wisdom

.2My brothers and sisters, when you have many kinds of troubles, you should be full of joy, 3because you know that these troubles test your faith, and this will give you patience. 4Let your patience show itself perfectly in what you do. Then you will be perfect and complete and will have everything you need. 5But if any of you needs wisdom, you should ask God for it. He is generous and enjoys giving to all people, so he will give you wisdom. 6But when you ask God, you must believe and not doubt. Anyone who doubts is like a wave in the sea, blown up and down by the wind. 7–8Such who doubt are thinking two different things at the same time, and they cannot decide about anything they do. They should not think they will receive anything from the Lord.

True Riches

9Believers who are poor should be proud, because God has made them spiritually rich. 10Those who are rich should be proud, because God has helped them to see that they are spiritually poor. The rich will die like a wild flower in the grass. 11The sun rises with burning heat and dries up the plants. The flower falls off, and its beauty is gone. In the same way the rich will die while they are still taking care of business.

Temptation is Not from God

12When people are tempted and still continue strong, they should be happy. After they have proved their faith, God will reward them with life for ever. God promised this to all those who love him. 13When people are tempted, they should not say, "God is tempting me." Evil cannot tempt God, and God himself does not tempt anyone. 14But people are tempted when their own evil desire leads them away and traps them. 15This desire leads to sin, and then the sin grows and brings death.

16My dear brothers and sisters, do not be fooled about this. 17Every good action and every perfect gift is from God. These good gifts come down from the Creator of the sun, moon and stars, who does not change like their shifting shadows. 18God decided to give us life through the word of truth so we might be the most important of all the things he made.

Listening and Obeying

19My dear brothers and sisters, always be willing to listen and slow to speak. Do not become angry easily, 20because anger will not help you live the right kind of life God wants. 21So put out of your life every evil thing and every kind of wrong. Then in gentleness accept God's teaching that is planted in your hearts, which can save you.

22Do what God's teaching says; when you only listen and do nothing, you are fooling yourselves. 23Those who hear God's teaching and do nothing are like people who look at themselves in a mirror. 24They see their faces and then go away and quickly forget what they looked like. 25But the truly happy people are those who carefully study God's perfect law that makes people free, and they continue to study it. They do not forget what they heard, but they obey what God's teaching says. Those who do this will be made happy.

The True Way to Worship God

26People who think they are religious but say things they should not say are just fooling themselves. Their "religion" is worth nothing. 27Religion that God accepts as pure and without fault is this: caring for orphans or widows who need help, and keeping yourself free from the world's evil influence.

"Slow to speak", "Slow to become angry" (v 19) – WHAT?!? Can't do that? What could you do (v 25)?

Try it and see what happens!

Think

Do you find it difficult to put what you read in the Bible into action? Why?

Pray

Ask God to help you do what he says.

It's not what you wear...

Who's the ideal friend?

- Has two season tickets for Man Utd (or other favourite team or event)
- Wears Nike everything
- Gets clothes from a charity shop

 James 2:1–26

Love All People

2 My dear brothers and sisters, as believers in our glorious Lord Jesus Christ, never think some people are more important than others. ²Suppose someone comes into your church meeting wearing nice clothes and a gold ring. At the same time a poor person comes in wearing old, dirty clothes. ³You show special attention to the one wearing nice clothes and say, "Please, sit here in this good seat." But you say to the poor person, "Stand over there," or, "Sit on the floor by my feet." ⁴What are you doing? You are making some people more important than others, and with evil thoughts you are deciding that one person is better.

⁵Listen, my dear brothers and sisters! God chose the poor in the world to be rich with faith and to receive the kingdom God promised to those who love him. ⁶But you show no respect to the poor. The rich are always trying to control your lives. They are the ones who take you to court. ⁷And they are the ones who speak against Jesus, who owns you.

⁸This royal law is found in the Scriptures: "Love your neighbour as you love yourself." If you obey this law, you are doing right. ⁹But if you treat one person as being more important than another, you are sinning. You are guilty of breaking God's law. ¹⁰A person who follows all of God's law but fails to obey even one command is guilty of breaking all the commands in that law. ¹¹The same God who said, "You must not be guilty of adultery," also said, "You must not murder anyone." So if you do not take part in adultery but you murder someone, you are guilty of breaking all of God's law. ¹²In everything you say and do, remember that you will be judged by the law that makes people free. ¹³So you must show mercy to others, or God will not show mercy to you when he judges you. But the person who shows mercy can stand without fear at the judgement.

Faith and Good Works

¹⁴My brothers and sisters, if people say they have faith, but do nothing, their faith is worth nothing. Can faith like that save them? ¹⁵A brother or sister in Christ might need clothes or food. ¹⁶If you say to that person, "God be with you! I hope you stay warm and get plenty to eat," but you do not give what that person needs, your

words are worth nothing. [17]In the same way, faith that is alone—that does nothing—is dead.

[18]Someone might say, "You have faith, but I have deeds." Show me your faith without doing anything, and I will show you my faith by what I do. [19]You believe there is one God. Good! But the demons believe that too, and they tremble with fear.

[20]You foolish person! Must you be shown that faith that does nothing is worth nothing? [21]Abraham, our ancestor, was made right with God by what he did when he offered his son Isaac on the altar. [22]So you see that Abraham's faith and the things he did worked together. His faith was made perfect by what he did. [23]This shows the full meaning of the Scripture that says: "Abraham believed God, and God accepted Abraham's faith, and that faith made him right with God." And Abraham was called God's friend. [24]So you see that people are made right with God by what they do, not by faith only.

[25]Another example is Rahab, a prostitute, who was made right with God by something she did. She welcomed the spies into her home and helped them escape by a different road.

[26]Just as a person's body that does not have a spirit is dead, so faith that does nothing is dead!

Take a careful look at verses 1 and 8. What will you do differently now?

What should we do to our neighbour (v 8)? This piece of the law is found in Leviticus 19:18. Leviticus is a hard book to understand but don't be put off. Go ahead and look up that verse, it's a good place to start.

Think

Remember what Jesus said when the man asked him who his neighbour was (Luke 10:29–37).

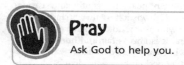

Pray

Ask God to help you.

Put a sock in it!

What do all these have in common?

- The rudder of a boat
- A flame in a forest fire
- The bit of a horse's harness
- A fig tree growing olives
- A wild animal

Give up? To find out read on ...

James 3:1–4:10

Controlling the Things We Say

3 My brothers and sisters, not many of you should become teachers, because you know that we who teach will be judged more strictly. ²We all make many mistakes. If people never said anything wrong, they would be perfect and able to control their entire selves too. ³When we put bits into the mouths of horses to make them obey us, we can control their whole bodies. ⁴Also a ship is very big, and it is pushed by strong winds. But a very small rudder controls that big ship, making it go wherever the person wants. ⁵It is the same with the tongue. It is a small part of the body, but it boasts about great things.

A big forest fire can be started with only a little flame. ⁶And the tongue is like a fire. It is a whole world of evil among the parts of our bodies. The tongue spreads its evil through the whole body. The tongue is set on fire by hell, and it starts a fire that influences all of life. ⁷People can tame every kind of wild animal, bird, reptile and fish, and they have tamed them, ⁸but no one can tame the tongue. It is wild and evil and full of deadly poison. ⁹We use our tongues to praise our Lord and Father, but then we curse people, whom God made like himself. ¹⁰Praises and curses come from the same mouth! My brothers and sisters, this should not happen. ¹¹Do good and bad water flow from the same spring? ¹²My brothers and sisters, can a fig tree make olives, or can a grapevine make figs? No! And a well full of salty water cannot give good water.

True Wisdom

¹³Are there those among you who are truly wise and understanding? Then they should show it by living right and doing good things with a gentleness that comes from wisdom. ¹⁴But if you are selfish and have bitter jealousy in your hearts, do not boast. Your boasting is a lie that hides the truth. ¹⁵That kind of "wisdom" does not come from God but from the world. It is not spiritual; it is from the devil. ¹⁶Where jealousy and selfishness are, there will be confusion and every kind of evil. ¹⁷But the wisdom that comes from God is first of all pure, then peaceful, gentle and easy to please. This wisdom is always ready to help those who are troubled and to do good for others. It is always fair and honest. ¹⁸People who work for peace in a peaceful way plant a good crop of good living.

Give Yourselves to God

4 Do you know where your fights and arguments come from? They come from the selfish desires that war within you. ²You want things, but you do not have them. So you are ready to kill and are jealous of other people, but you still cannot get what you want. So you argue and fight. You do not get what you want, because you do not ask God. ³Or when you ask, you do not receive because the reason you ask is wrong. You want things so you can use them for your own pleasures.

⁴So, you are not loyal to God! You should know that loving the world is the same as hating God. Anyone who wants to be a friend of the world becomes God's enemy. ⁵Do you think the Scripture means nothing that says, "The Spirit that God made to live in us wants us for himself alone." ⁶But God gives us even more grace, as the Scripture says,

"God is against the proud,
but he gives grace to the humble."

Proverbs 3:34

⁷So give yourselves completely to God. Stand against the devil, and the devil will run from you. ⁸Come near to God, and God will come near to you. You sinners, clean sin out of your lives. You who are trying to follow God and the world at the same time, make your thinking pure. ⁹Be sad, cry and weep! Change your laughter into crying and your joy into sadness. ¹⁰Don't be too proud in the Lord's presence, and he will make you great.

They are descriptions of your _____

Which one of the above best describes yours sometimes?

Think

What "sin" do you think does more damage to a community of believers: adultery or gossip?

Pray

Dear Lord, please help me to know when to keep quiet. Forgive me when I say wrong things. Please help me control my tongue and glorify you in *all* I say.

Extra

Can you tick any of these? Have you ever...
- told someone else's secret?
- shared a prayer point about someone without permission?
- passed on gossip?
- sworn at someone?

Is your tongue a little flame that makes a lot of trouble?

Believe it or not

"I scored a hat-trick in the last game!"

"I'm going to the movies with the hottest guy/girl in school!"

"I got the highest marks in the maths test!"

What do these sentences start with?

James 4:11–5:20

You Are Not the Judge

11Brothers and sisters, do not tell evil lies about each other. If you speak against your fellow believers or judge them, you are judging and speaking against the law they follow. And when you are judging the law, you are no longer a follower of the law. You have become a judge. 12God is the only Lawmaker and Judge. He is the only One who can save and destroy. So it is not right for you to judge your neighbour.

Let God Plan Your Life

13Some of you say, "Today or tomorrow we will go to some city. We will stay there a year, do business and make money." 14But you do not know what will happen tomorrow! Your life is like a mist. You can see it for a short time, but then it goes away. 15So you should say, "If the Lord wants, we will live and do this or that." 16But now you are proud and you boast. All of this boasting is wrong. 17Anyone who knows the right thing to do, but does not do it, is sinning.

A Warning to the Rich

5 You rich people, listen! Cry and be very sad because of the troubles that are coming to you. 2Your riches have rotted, and your clothes have been eaten by moths. 3Your gold and silver have rusted, and that rust will be a proof that you were wrong. It will eat your bodies like fire. You saved your treasure for the last days. 4The pay you did not give the workers who harvested your fields cries out against you, and the cries of the workers have been heard by the Lord All-powerful. 5Your life on earth was full of rich living and pleasing yourselves with everything you wanted. You made yourselves fat, like an animal ready to be killed. 6You have judged guilty and then murdered innocent people, who were not against you.

Be Patient

7Brothers and sisters, be patient until the Lord comes again. A farmer patiently waits for his valuable crop to grow from the earth and for it to receive the autumn and spring rains. 8You, too, must be patient. Do not give up hope, because the Lord is coming soon. 9Brothers and sisters, do not complain against each other or you will be judged guilty. And the Judge is ready to come! 10Brothers and sisters, follow the example of the prophets who spoke for the Lord. They suffered many hard things, but they were patient. 11We say they are happy because they did not give up. You have heard about Job's patience, and you know the Lord's purpose for him in the end. You know the Lord is full of mercy and is kind.

Be Careful What You Say

12My brothers and sisters, above all, do not use an oath when you make a promise. Don't use the name of heaven, earth or anything else to prove what you say. When you mean yes, say only "yes", and when you mean no, say only "no" so you will not be judged guilty.

The Power of Prayer

13Anyone who is having troubles should pray. Anyone who is happy should sing praises. 14Anyone who is sick should call the church's elders. They should pray for and pour oil on the person in the name of the Lord. 15And the prayer that is said with faith will make the sick person well; the Lord will heal that person. And if the person has sinned, the sins will be forgiven. 16Confess your sins to each other and pray for each other so God can heal you. When a believing person prays, great things happen. 17Elijah was a human being just like us. He prayed that it would not rain, and it did not rain on the land for three and a half years! 18Then Elijah prayed again, and the rain came down from the sky, and the land produced crops again.

Saving a Soul

19My brothers and sisters, if one of you wanders away from the truth, and someone helps that person come back, 20remember this: anyone who brings a sinner back from the wrong way will save that sinner's soul from death and will cause many sins to be forgiven.

Is it necessary to say half the stuff that we do?

The Bible says boasting is a sign of pride (4:16).

It also says boasting is a lie that hides the truth (James 3:14).

Think

Do you see your gifts as something you use for yourself or for others?

Pray

Thank God for the gifts you have, and seek to use them for others. Ask God to show you when you are bragging and to talk about him instead.

God thinks you're special

Do you have special things at home that you take great care of because they are very important to you?

God thinks *you* are special.

1 Peter 1:1–21

1 From Peter, an apostle of Jesus Christ.

To God's chosen people who are away from their homes and are scattered all around the countries of Pontus, Galatia, Cappadocia, Asia and Bithynia. ²God planned long ago to choose you by making you his holy people, which is the Spirit's work. God wanted you to obey him and to be made clean by the blood of the death of Jesus Christ.

Grace and peace be yours more and more.

We Have a Living Hope

³Praise be to the God and Father of our Lord Jesus Christ. In God's great mercy he has caused us to be born again into a living hope, because Jesus Christ rose from the dead. ⁴Now we hope for the blessings God has for his children. These blessings, which cannot be destroyed or be spoiled or lose their beauty, are kept in heaven for you. ⁵God's power protects you through your faith until salvation is shown to you at the end of time. ⁶This makes you very happy, even though now for a short time different kinds of troubles may make you sad. ⁷These troubles come to prove that your faith is pure. This purity of faith is worth more than gold, which can be proved to be pure by fire but will ruin. But the purity of

your faith will bring you praise and glory and honour when Jesus Christ is shown to you. ⁸You have not seen Christ, but still you love him. You cannot see him now, but you believe in him. So you are filled with a joy that cannot be explained, a joy full of glory. ⁹And you are receiving the goal of your faith—the salvation of your souls.

¹⁰The prophets searched carefully and tried to learn about this salvation. They prophesied about the grace that was coming to you. ¹¹The Spirit of Christ was in the prophets, telling in advance about the sufferings of Christ and about the glory that would follow those sufferings. The prophets tried to learn about what the Spirit was showing them, when those things would happen, and what the world would be like at that time. ¹²It was shown them that their service was not for themselves but for you, when they told about the truths you have now heard. Those who preached the Good News to you told you those things with the help of the Holy Spirit who was sent from heaven—things into which angels desire to look.

A Call to Holy Living

¹³So prepare your minds for service and have self-control. All your hope should be for the gift of grace that will be yours when

Jesus Christ is shown to you. ¹⁴Now that you are obedient children of God do not live as you did in the past. You did not understand, so you did the evil things you wanted. ¹⁵But be holy in all you do, just as God, the One who called you, is holy. ¹⁶It is written in the Scriptures: "You must be holy, because I am holy."

¹⁷You pray to God and call him Father, and he judges each person's work equally. So while you are here on earth, you should live with respect for God. ¹⁸You know that in the past you were living in a worthless way, a way passed down from the people who lived before you. But you were saved from that useless life. You were bought, not with something that ruins like gold or silver, ¹⁹but with the precious blood of Christ, who was like a pure and perfect lamb. ²⁰Christ was chosen before the world was made, but he was shown to the world in these last times for your sake. ²¹Through Christ you believe in God, who raised Christ from the dead and gave him glory. So your faith and your hope are in God.

How does God show that he thinks we're special (vs 18,19)?

How did Peter say we should respond to God's love for us (v 15)?

Think

What might it mean to live in a "holy" way (e.g. at home, at school)?

Pray

Thank God for the fact that he thinks you are special. Ask him to help you to live as he wants.

Basic requirements

Milk is the first thing you live on when you're a baby. It's kind of bland, but it contains all the proteins and stuff you need to grow. When you get a bit older, you get to eat other stuff that's got a bit more substance, and which tastes of something more interesting.

1 Peter 1:22–2:17

22Now that you have made your souls pure by obeying the truth, you can have true love for your Christian brothers and sisters. So love each other deeply with all your heart. 23You have been born again, and this new life did not come from something that dies, but from something that cannot die. You were born again through God's living message that continues for ever. 24The Scripture says,

"All people are like the grass,
and all their glory is like the flowers of the field.
The grass dies and the flowers fall,
25 but the word of the Lord will live for ever." *Isaiah 40:6–8*

And this is the word that was preached to you.

Jesus is the Living Stone

2 So then, rid yourselves of all evil, all lying, hypocrisy, jealousy and evil speech. 2As newborn babies want milk, you should want the pure and simple teaching. By it you can grow up and be saved, 3because you have already examined and seen how good the Lord is.

4Come to the Lord Jesus, the "stone" that lives. The people of the world did not want this stone, but he was the stone God chose, and he was precious. 5You also are like living stones, so let yourselves be used to build a spiritual temple—to be holy priests who offer spiritual sacrifices to God. He will accept those sacrifices

through Jesus Christ. 6The Scripture says:
"I will put a stone in the ground in Jerusalem.
Everything will be built on this important and precious rock.
Anyone who trusts in him
will never be disappointed." *Isaiah 28:16*
7This stone is worth much to you who believe. But to the people who do not believe,
"the stone that the builders rejected
has become the cornerstone."
Psalm 118:22
8Also, he is
"a stone that causes people to stumble,
a rock that makes them fall." *Isaiah 8:14*
They stumble because they do not obey what God says, which is what God planned to happen to them.

9But you are a chosen people, royal priests, a holy nation, a people for God's own possession. You were chosen to tell about the wonderful acts of God, who called you out of darkness into his wonderful light. 10At one time you were not a people, but now you are God's people. In the past you had never received mercy, but now you have received God's mercy.

Live for God

11Dear friends, you are like foreigners and strangers in this world. I beg you to avoid the evil things your bodies want to do that fight against your soul. 12People who do not believe are living all around you and might say that you are doing wrong. Live such good lives that they will see the good things you do and will give glory to God on the day when Christ comes again.

Yield to Every Human Authority

13For the Lord's sake, yield to the people who have authority in this world: the king, who is the highest authority, 14and the leaders who are sent by him to punish those who do wrong and to praise those who do right. 15It is God's desire that by doing good you should stop foolish people from saying stupid things about you. 16Live as free people, but do not use your freedom as an excuse to do evil. Live as servants of God. 17Show respect for all people: love the brothers and sisters of God's family, respect God, honour the king.

If you're new to being a Christian, you have to stick to the basics – learn as much as you can about the Bible, pray, and most of all, get on with living like a Christian. There's plenty of time to learn all the more complicated stuff later.

Think

Are you in a church or in a youth group? Are you getting help with living as a Christian? Does it seem a bit basic? Listen to what they've got to say.

Pray

Ask God to help you learn more about what you believe, when you need to learn it.

Follow Jesus

How easy are these?

(1 = really easy; 10 = impossible)

- Always telling the truth   1 2 3 4 5 6 7 8 9 10
- Admitting you go to church   1 2 3 4 5 6 7 8 9 10
- Putting up with insults   1 2 3 4 5 6 7 8 9 10
- Not retaliating when you're picked on   1 2 3 4 5 6 7 8 9 10

 1 Peter 2:18–3:12

Follow Christ's Example

[18]Slaves, yield to the authority of your masters with all respect, not only those who are good and kind, but also those who are dishonest. [19]A person might have to suffer even when it is unfair, but if he thinks of God and stands the pain, God is pleased. [20]If you are beaten for doing wrong, there is no reason to praise you for being patient in your punishment. But if you suffer for doing good, and you are patient, then God is pleased. [21]This is what you were called to do, because Christ suffered for you and gave you an example to follow. So you should do as he did.
[22]"He had never sinned,
and he had never lied."   *Isaiah 53:9*
[23]People insulted Christ, but he did not insult them in return. Christ suffered, but he did not threaten. He let God, the One who judges rightly, take care of him. [24]Christ carried our sins in his body on the cross so we would stop living for sin and start living for what is right. And you are healed because of his wounds. [25]You were like sheep that wandered away, but now you have come back to the Shepherd and Protector of your souls.

Wives and Husbands

3 In the same way, you wives should yield to your husbands. Then, if some husbands do not obey God's teaching, they will be persuaded to believe without anyone saying a word to them. They will be persuaded by the way their wives live. [2]Your husbands will see the pure lives you live with your respect for God. [3]It is not fancy hair, gold jewellery or fine clothes that should make you beautiful. [4]No, your beauty should come from within you—the beauty of a gentle and quiet spirit that will never be destroyed and is very precious to God. [5]In this same way the holy women who lived long ago and followed God made themselves beautiful, yielding to their own husbands. [6]Sarah obeyed Abraham, her husband, and called him her master. And you women are true children of Sarah if you always do what is right and are not afraid.

[7]In the same way, you husbands should live with your wives in an understanding way, since being answered they are weaker than you. But show them respect, because God gives them the same blessing he gives to you—the grace that

gives true life. Do this so that nothing will stop your prayer.

Suffering for Doing Right

8Finally, all of you should be in agreement, understanding each other, loving each other as family, being kind and humble. 9Do not do wrong to repay a wrong, and do not insult to repay an insult. But repay with a blessing, because you yourselves were called to do this so that you might receive a blessing. 10The Scripture says,

"You must do these things
  to enjoy life and have many happy
    days.
You must not say evil things,
  and you must not tell lies.
11Stop doing evil and do good.
  Look for peace and work for it.
12The Lord sees the good people
  and listens to their prayers.
But the Lord is against
  those who do evil."   *Psalm 34:12–16*

Hard times are part of the deal for Christians (2:20,21).

Whose example are we following when we suffer for doing right (2:21–24)?

Think

What difference could 2:24 mean in the way you live today?

Pray

Ask God to help you do the right thing, no matter what the cost.

Live God's way

Are there some activities that are wrong for Christians to take part in?

1 Peter 3:13–4:11

13If you are trying hard to do good, no one can really hurt you. 14But even if you suffer for doing right, you are blessed.

"Don't be afraid of what they fear;
do not dread those things."

Isaiah 8:12–13

15But respect Christ as the holy Lord in your hearts. Always be ready to answer everyone who asks you to explain about the hope you have, 16but answer in a gentle way and with respect. Keep a clear conscience so that those who speak evil of your good life in Christ will be made ashamed. 17It is better to suffer for doing good than for doing wrong if that is what God wants. 18Christ himself suffered for sins once. He was not guilty, but he suffered for those who are guilty to bring you to God. His body was killed, but he was made alive in the spirit. 19And in the spirit he went and preached to the spirits in prison 20who refused to obey God long ago in the time of Noah. God was waiting patiently for them while Noah was building the boat. Only a few people—eight in all—were saved by water. 21And that water is like baptism that now saves you—not the washing of dirt from the body, but the promise made to God from a good conscience. And this is because Jesus Christ was raised from the dead. 22Now Jesus has gone into heaven and is at God's right side ruling over angels, authorities and powers.

Change Your Lives

4 Since Christ suffered while he was in his body, strengthen yourselves with the same way of thinking Christ had. The person who has suffered in the body is finished with sin. 2Strengthen yourselves so that you will live here on earth doing what God wants, not the evil things people want. 3In the past you wasted too much time doing what non-believers enjoy. You were guilty of sexual sins, evil desires, getting drunk, wild and drunken parties, and hateful idol worship. 4Non-believers think it is strange that you do not do the many wild and wasteful things they do, so they insult you. 5But they will have to explain this to God, who is ready to judge the living and the dead. 6For this reason the Good News was preached to those who are now dead. Even though they were judged like all people, the Good News was preached to them so they could live in the spirit as God lives.

Use God's Gifts Wisely

7The time is near when all things will end. So think clearly and control yourselves so that you will be able to pray. 8Most importantly, love each other deeply, because love will cause many sins to be forgiven. 9Open your homes to each other, without complaining. 10Each of you has received a gift to use to serve others. Be good servants of God's various gifts of grace. ¹¹Anyone who speaks should speak words from God. Anyone who serves should serve with the strength God gives so that in everything God will be praised through Jesus Christ. Power and glory belong to him for ever and ever. Amen.

What are the five things Peter mentions that people who weren't living for God did?

1 _____

2 _____

3 _____

4 _____

5 _____

The activities for you might be different, but what's the really important thing to remember (4:2)?

Think

What will everyone who ignores God have to do one day (4:5)?

Pray

Thank God that he has given you new life. Ask him for strength to live his way.

Don't worry!

What's worrying you at the moment?

1 Peter 4:12–5:14

Suffering as a Christian

¹²My friends, do not be surprised at the terrible trouble which now comes to test you. Do not think that something strange is happening to you. ¹³But be happy that you are sharing in Christ's sufferings so that you will be happy and full of joy when Christ comes again in glory. ¹⁴When people insult you because you follow Christ, you are blessed, because the glorious Spirit, the Spirit of God, is with you. ¹⁵Do not suffer for murder, theft or any other crime, nor because you trouble other people. ¹⁶But if you suffer because you are a Christian, do not be ashamed. Praise God because you wear that name. ¹⁷It is time for judgement to begin with God's family. And if that judging begins with us, what will happen to those people who do not obey the Good News of God?
¹⁸"If it is very hard for a good person to be saved,
the wicked person and the sinner will surely be lost!"

¹⁹So those who suffer as God wants should trust their souls to the faithful Creator as they continue to do what is right.

The Flock of God

5 Now I have something to say to the elders in your group. I also am an elder. I have seen Christ's sufferings, and I will share in the glory that will be shown to us. I beg you to ²shepherd God's flock, for whom you are responsible. Watch over them because you want to, not because you are forced. That is how God wants it. Do it because you are happy to serve, not because you want money. ³Do not be like a ruler over people you are responsible for, but be good examples to them. ⁴Then when Christ, the Chief Shepherd, comes, you will get a glorious crown that will never lose its beauty.

⁵In the same way, younger people should be willing to be under older people. And all of you should be very humble with each other.

"God is against the proud,
but he gives grace to the humble."

Proverbs 3:34

⁶Be humble under God's powerful hand so he will lift you up when the right time comes. ⁷Give all your worries to him, because he cares about you.

⁸Control yourselves and be careful! The devil, your enemy, goes around like a roaring lion looking for someone to eat. ⁹Refuse to give in to him, by standing strong in your faith. You know that your Christian family all over the world is having the same kinds of suffering.

¹⁰And after you suffer for a short time, God, who gives all grace, will make everything right. He will make you strong and support you and keep you from falling. He called you to share in his glory in Christ, a glory that will continue for ever. ¹¹All power is his for ever and ever. Amen.

Final Greetings

¹²I wrote this short letter with the help of Silas, who I know is a faithful brother in

Christ. I wrote to encourage you and to tell you that this is the true grace of God. Stand strong in that grace.

¹³The church in Babylon, chosen like you, sends you greetings. Mark, my son in Christ, also greets you. ¹⁴Give each other a kiss of Christian love when you meet.

Peace to all of you who are in Christ.

Being anxious about stuff can lead you into making mistakes, and then things can get even more difficult. Find the advice Peter gave to some seriously worried Christians in these verses.

Be humble (v...)

Trust God (v...)

Be self-controlled (v...)

Be careful (v...)

Say no to evil (v...)

Think

How many of the things you worry about can be influenced by your actions? A lot of the time we worry about things that we have no control over... but God does!

Pray

Talk to God about the things that are worrying you.

How can I be sure?

How can you be sure that what Christians believe *is* true?

2 Peter 1:1–21

1 From Simon Peter, a servant and apostle of Jesus Christ.

To you who have received a faith as valuable as ours, because our God and Saviour Jesus Christ does what is right.

²Grace and peace be given to you more and more, because you truly know God and Jesus our Lord.

God Has Given Us Blessings

³Jesus has the power of God, by which he has given us everything we need to live and to serve God. We have these things because we know him. Jesus called us by his glory and goodness. ⁴Through these he gave us the very great and precious promises. With these gifts you can share in being like God, and the world will not ruin you with its evil desires.

⁵Because you have these blessings, do your best to add these things to your lives: to your faith, add goodness; and to your goodness, add knowledge; ⁶and to your knowledge, add self-control; and to your self-control, add patience; and to your patience, add service for God; ⁷and to your service for God, add kindness for your brothers and sisters in Christ; and to this kindness, add love. ⁸If all these things are in you and are growing, they will help you to be useful and productive in your knowledge of our Lord Jesus Christ. ⁹But anyone who does not have these things cannot see clearly. He is blind and

has forgotten that he was made clean from his past sins.

¹⁰My brothers and sisters, try hard to be certain that you really are called and chosen by God. If you do all these things, you will never fall. ¹¹And you will be given a very great welcome into the eternal kingdom of our Lord and Saviour Jesus Christ.

¹²You know these things, and you are very strong in the truth, but I will always help you remember them. ¹³I think it is right for me to help you remember as long as I am in this body. ¹⁴I know I must soon leave this body, as our Lord Jesus Christ has shown me. ¹⁵I will try my best so that you may be able to remember these things even after I am gone.

We Saw Christ's Glory

¹⁶When we told you about the powerful coming of our Lord Jesus Christ, we were not telling just clever stories that someone invented. But we saw the greatness of Jesus with our own eyes. ¹⁷Jesus heard the voice of God, the Greatest Glory, when he received honour and glory from God the Father. The voice said, "This is my Son, whom I love, and I am very pleased with him." ¹⁸We heard that voice from heaven while we were with Jesus on the holy mountain.

¹⁹This makes us more sure about the message the prophets gave. It is good for

you to follow closely what they said as you would follow a light shining in a dark place, until the day begins and the morning star rises in your hearts. ²⁰Most of all, you must understand this: no prophecy in the Scriptures ever comes from the prophet's own interpretation. ²¹No prophecy ever comes from what a person wanted to say, but people led by the Holy Spirit spoke words from God.

Here, Peter used his own personal experience of Jesus (vs 16–18) to assure his readers that what he was saying was true.

What were the two pieces of evidence?

Verse 16: _____

Verse 18: _____

You can read the story he mentions in Mark 9:2–13.

Think

What makes *you* sure of God? What do you see in other Christians' lives which helps you to believe in Jesus?

Pray

Thank God for the way he's working in your life.

Pride before a fall

How do you know if you are being taught the truth?

- A leader looks sincere
- All the books agree
- It is hard to understand so it must be true

 2 Peter 2:1–19a

False Teachers

2 There used to be false prophets among God's people, just as you will have some false teachers in your group. They will secretly teach things that are wrong—teachings that will cause people to be lost. They will even refuse to accept the Master, Jesus, who bought their freedom. So they will bring quick ruin on themselves. ²Many will follow their evil ways and say evil things about the way of truth. ³Those false teachers only want your money, so they will use you by telling you lies. Their judgement spoken against them long ago is still coming, and their ruin is certain.

⁴When angels sinned, God did not let them go free without punishment. He sent them to hell and put them in caves of darkness where they are being held for judgement. ⁵And God punished the world long ago when he brought a flood to the world that was full of people who were against him. But God saved Noah, who preached about being right with God, and seven other people with him. ⁶And God also destroyed the evil cities of Sodom and Gomorrah by burning them until they were ashes. He made those cities an example of what will happen to those who are against God. ⁷But he saved Lot from those cities. Lot, a good man, was

troubled because of the dirty lives of evil people. ⁸(Lot was a good man, but because he lived with evil people every day, his good heart was hurt by the evil things he saw and heard.) ⁹So the Lord knows how to save those who serve him when troubles come. He will hold evil people and punish them, while waiting for the Judgement Day. ¹⁰That punishment is especially for those who live by doing the evil things their sinful selves want and who hate authority.

These false teachers are bold and do anything they want. They are not afraid to speak against the angels. ¹¹But even the angels, who are much stronger and more powerful than false teachers, do not accuse them with insults before the Lord. ¹²But these people speak against things they do not understand. They are like animals that act without thinking, animals born to be caught and killed. And, like animals, these false teachers will be destroyed. ¹³They have caused many people to suffer, so they themselves will suffer. That is their pay for what they have done. They take pleasure in openly doing evil, so they are like dirty spots and stains among you. They delight in trickery while eating meals with you. ¹⁴Every time they look at a woman they want her, and their desire for sin is never satisfied. They lead weak people into the trap of sin, and they have taught their hearts to be greedy. God will punish them! ¹⁵These false teachers left the right road and lost their way, following the way Balaam went. Balaam was the son of Beor, who loved being paid for doing wrong. ¹⁶But a donkey, which cannot talk, told Balaam he was sinning. It spoke with a man's voice and stopped the prophet's mad thinking.

¹⁷Those false teachers are like springs without water and clouds blown by a storm. A place in the blackest darkness has been kept for them. ¹⁸They boast with words that mean nothing. By their evil desires they lead people into the trap of sin—people who are just beginning to escape from others who live in error. ¹⁹They promise them freedom, but they themselves are not free. They are slaves of things that will be destroyed.

Peter is concerned that there are people teaching things that are wrong.

What do the false teachers want (v 3)?

What do they refuse (v 1)?

What will happen to them (v 3)?

Think

How can you protect yourself from being taught something that is wrong?

Pray

That God will guide you into his truth and not that which has been created by humanity.

Extra

To know how God has dealt with rebellion against him, read the whole of chapter 2.

Keep going

What might get in the way of you keeping going as a Christian?

 2 Peter 2:19b–3:18

For people are slaves of anything that controls them. 20They were made free from the evil in the world by knowing our Lord and Saviour Jesus Christ. But if they return to evil things and those things control them, then it is worse for them than it was before. 21Yes, it would be better for them to have never known the right way than to know it and to turn away from the holy teaching that was given to them. 22What they did is like this true saying: "A dog goes back to what it has thrown up," and, "After a pig is washed, it goes back and rolls in the mud."

Jesus will Come Again

3 My friends, this is the second letter I have written you to help your honest minds remember. 2I want you to think about the words the holy prophets spoke in the past, and remember the command our Lord and Saviour gave us through your apostles. 3It is most important for you to understand what will happen in the last days. People will laugh at you. They will live doing the evil things they want to do. 4They will say, "Jesus promised to come again. Where is he? Our fathers have died, but the world continues the way it has been since it was made." 5But they do not want to remember what happened long ago. By the word of God heaven was made, and the earth was made from water and with water. 6Then the world was flooded and destroyed with water. 7And that same word of God is keeping heaven and earth that we now have in order to be destroyed by fire. They are being kept for the Judgement Day and the destruction of all who are against God.

8But do not forget this one thing, dear friends: to the Lord one day is as a thousand years, and a thousand years is as one day. 9The Lord is not slow in doing what he promised—the way some people understand slowness. But God is being patient with you. He does not want anyone to be lost, but he wants all people to change their hearts and lives.

10But the day of the Lord will come like a thief. The skies will disappear with a loud noise. Everything in them will be destroyed by fire, and the earth and everything in it will be burnt up. 11In that way everything will be destroyed. So what kind of people should you be? You should live holy lives and serve God, 12as you wait for and look forward to the coming of the day of God. When that day comes, the skies will be destroyed with fire, and everything in them will melt with heat. 13But God made a promise to us, and we are waiting for a new heaven and a new earth where goodness lives.

14Dear friends, since you are waiting for this to happen, do your best to be without sin and without fault. Try to be at peace with God. 15Remember that we are saved because our Lord is patient. Our dear brother Paul told you the same thing when he wrote to you with the wisdom that God gave him. 16He writes about this in all his letters. Some things in Paul's letters are hard to understand, and people who are ignorant and weak in faith explain these things falsely. They also falsely explain the other Scriptures, but they are destroying themselves by doing this.

17Dear friends, since you already know about this, be careful. Do not let those evil people lead you away by the wrong they do. Be careful so you will not fall from your strong faith. 18But grow in the grace and knowledge of our Lord and Saviour Jesus Christ. Glory be to him now and for ever! Amen.

How could you keep growing in God (3:18)? Look in the verses for these ideas:

Be at peace (v . . .)

Be without sin (v . . .)

Be careful (v . . .)

Grow in grace (v . . .)

What do you think Peter meant by each of these?

Think of situations where each of these might mean you doing something differently today.

Think

What's stopping you growing in Jesus?

- Friends who don't follow Jesus
- Listening to wrong ideas about God
- Doing things your way, rather than God's

Pray

Ask God to help you stay close to him and keep growing in your faith.

Eyewitness account

Who would you go to for coaching in your favourite sport? Someone who had just read a book about it, or someone who had represented your country at the Olympics?

 1 John 1:1–2:14

1 We write to you now about what has always existed, which we have heard, we have seen with our own eyes, we have looked at, and we have touched with our hands. We write to you about the Word that gives life. ²He who gives life was shown to us. We saw him and can give proof about it. And now we announce to you that he has life that continues for ever. He was with God the Father and was shown to us. ³We announce to you what we have seen and heard, because we want you also to have fellowship with us. Our fellowship is with God the Father and with his Son, Jesus Christ. ⁴We write this to you so you can be full of joy with us.

God Forgives our Sins

⁵Here is the message we have heard from Christ and now announce to you: God is light, and in him there is no darkness at all. ⁶So if we say we have fellowship with God, but we continue living in darkness, we are liars and do not follow the truth. ⁷But if we live in the light, as God is in the light, we can share fellowship with each other. Then the blood of Jesus, God's Son, cleanses us from every sin.

⁸If we say we have no sin, we are fooling ourselves, and the truth is not in us. ⁹But if we confess our sins, he will forgive our sins, because we can trust God to do what is right. He will cleanse us from all the wrongs we have done. ¹⁰If we say we have not sinned, we make God a liar, and we do not accept God's teaching.

Jesus is our Helper

2 My dear children, I write this letter to you so you will not sin. But if anyone does sin, we have a helper in the presence of the Father—Jesus Christ, the One who does what is right. ²He is the way our sins are taken away, and not only our sins but the sins of all people.

³We can be sure that we know God if we obey his commands. ⁴Anyone who says, "I know God," but does not obey God's commands is a liar, and the truth is not in that person. ⁵But if someone obeys God's teaching, then in that person God's love has truly reached its goal. This is how we can be sure we are living in God: ⁶whoever says that he lives in God must live as Jesus lived.

The Command to Love Others

⁷My dear friends, I am not writing a new command to you but an old command you have had from the beginning. It is the teaching you have already heard. ⁸But also I am writing a new command to you, and you can see its truth in Jesus and in you, because the darkness is passing away, and the true light is already shining.

⁹Anyone who says, "I am in the light," but hates a brother or sister, is still in the darkness. ¹⁰Whoever loves a brother or sister lives in the light and will not cause anyone to stumble in their faith. ¹¹But whoever hates a brother or sister is in darkness, lives in darkness and does not know where to go, because the darkness has made that person blind.

¹²I write to you, dear children,
    because your sins are forgiven through
        Christ.
¹³I write to you, parents,
    because you know the One who existed
        from the beginning.
  I write to you, young people,
    because you have defeated the Evil
        One.

¹⁴I write to you, children,
    because you know the Father.
  I write to you, parents,
    because you know the One who existed
        from the beginning.
  I write to you, young people,
    because you are strong;
    the teaching of God lives in you,
    and you have defeated the Evil One.

John is writing from his own experience. He hasn't just *heard* about Jesus –
he has *lived* with him and written a gospel about him! You can trust what
you read here – because John knows what he is talking about.

Why is John writing this letter?

Reason 1: _____ (1:3)

Reason 2: _____ (1:4)

Think

When you have doubts do you keep quiet or ask someone to
help? Older Christians can really help as they have experienced the
ups as well as the downs.

Pray

Ask God to make you full of joy as you read this week about how
to be sure that you are OK with God.

Don't be deceived

How do you know if you're being told the truth? How do you know if the people leading you are good people who love God?

 1 John 2:15–3:10

¹⁵Do not love the world or the things in the world. If you love the world, the love of the Father is not in you. ¹⁶These are the ways of the world: wanting to please our sinful selves, wanting the sinful things we see and being too proud of what we have. None of these come from the Father, but all of them come from the world. ¹⁷The world and everything that people want in it are passing away, but the person who does what God wants lives for ever.

Reject the Enemies of Christ

¹⁸My dear children, these are the last days. You have heard that the enemy of Christ is coming, and now many enemies of Christ are already here. This is how we know that these are the last days. ¹⁹These enemies of Christ were in our fellowship, but they left us. They never really belonged to us; if they had been a part of us, they would have stayed with us. But they left, and this shows that none of them really belonged to us.

²⁰You have the gift that the Holy One gave you, so you all know the truth. ²¹I do not write to you because you do not know the truth but because you do know the truth. And you know that no lie comes from the truth.

²²Who is the liar? It is the person who does not accept Jesus as the Christ. This is the enemy of Christ: the person who does not accept the Father and his Son. ²³Whoever does not accept the Son does not have the Father. But whoever confesses the Son has the Father, too.

²⁴Be sure you continue to follow the teaching you heard from the beginning. If you continue to follow what you heard from the beginning, you will stay in the Son and in the Father. ²⁵And this is what the Son promised to us—life for ever.

²⁶I am writing this letter about those people who are trying to lead you the wrong way. ²⁷Christ gave you a special gift that is still in you, so you do not need any other teacher. His gift teaches you about everything, and it is true, not false. So continue to live in Christ, as his gift taught you.

²⁸Yes, my dear children, live in him so that when Christ comes back, we can be without fear and not be ashamed in his presence. ²⁹If you know that Christ is all that is right, you know that all who do right are God's children.

We are God's Children

3 The Father has loved us so much that we are called children of God. And we really are his children. The reason the people in the world do not know us is that they have not known him. ²Dear friends, now we are children of God, and we have not yet been shown what we will be in the future. But we know that when Christ comes again, we will be like him, because we will see him as he really is. ³Christ is pure, and all who have this hope in Christ keep themselves pure like Christ.

⁴The person who sins breaks God's law. Yes, sin is living against God's law. ⁵You know that Christ came to take away sins and that there is no sin in Christ. ⁶So anyone who lives in Christ does not go on

sinning. Anyone who goes on sinning has never really understood Christ and has never known him.

7Dear children, do not let anyone lead you the wrong way. Christ is all that is right. So to be like Christ a person must do what is right. 8The devil has been sinning since the beginning, so anyone who continues to sin belongs to the devil. The Son of God came for this purpose: to destroy the devil's work.

9Those who are God's children do not continue sinning, because the new life from God remains in them. They are not able to go on sinning, because they have become children of God. 10So we can see who God's children are and who the devil's children are: those who do not do what is right are not God's children, and those who do not love their brothers and sisters are not God's children.

How can you spot someone who's lying?

- They don't accept that Jesus is King

- They do evil

- They love the things of this world rather than God

Think

Stay alert. Keep reading your Bible and keep praying. Most importantly, stay close to God.

Pray

Ask God to help you know who's who and what's what.

Love other people

What would people think if you had a green face and purple hair? Would they laugh at you? Hassle you? Or, maybe, think you're cool!

1 John 3:11–4:12

We Must Love Each Other

11This is the teaching you have heard from the beginning: we must love each other. 12Do not be like Cain who belonged to the Evil One and killed his brother. And why did he kill him? Because the things Cain did were evil, and the things his brother did were good.

13Brothers and sisters, do not be surprised when the people of the world hate you. 14We know we have left death and have come into life because we love each other. Whoever does not love is still dead. 15Everyone who hates a brother or sister is a murderer, and you know that no murderers have eternal life in them. 16This is how we know what real love is: Jesus gave his life for us. So we should give our lives for our brothers and sisters. 17Suppose someone has enough to live on and sees a brother or sister in need, but does not help. Then God's love is not living in that person. 18My children, we should love people not only with words and talk, but by our actions and true caring.

19–20This is the way we know that we belong to the way of truth. When our hearts make us feel guilty, we can still have peace before God. God is greater than our hearts, and he knows everything. 21My dear friends, if our hearts do not make us feel guilty, we can come without fear into God's presence. 22And God gives us what we ask for because we obey God's commands and do what pleases him. 23This is what God commands: that we believe in

his Son, Jesus Christ, and that we love each other, just as he commanded. 24The people who obey God's commands live in God, and God lives in them. We know that God lives in us because of the Spirit God gave us.

Warning Against False Teachers

4 My dear friends, many false prophets have gone out into the world. So do not believe every spirit, but test the spirits to see if they are from God. 2This is how you can know God's Spirit: every spirit who confesses that Jesus Christ came to earth as a human is from God. 3And every spirit who refuses to say this about Jesus is not from God. It is the spirit of the enemy of Christ, which you have heard is coming, and now he is already in the world.

4My dear children, you belong to God and have defeated them, because God's Spirit, who is in you, is greater than the devil, who is in the world. 5And they belong to the world, so what they say is from the world, and the world listens to them. 6But we belong to God, and those who know God listen to us. But those who are not from God do not listen to us. That is how we know the Spirit that is true and the spirit that is false.

Love Comes from God

7Dear friends, we should love each other, because love comes from God. Everyone who loves has become God's child and knows God. 8Whoever does not love does not know God, because God is

576

love. ⁹This is how God showed his love to us: he sent his one and only Son into the world so that we could have life through him. ¹⁰This is what real love is: it is not our love for God; it is God's love for us in sending his Son to be the way to take away our sins.

¹¹Dear friends, if God loved us that much we also should love each other. ¹²No one has ever seen God, but if we love each other, God lives in us, and his love is made perfect in us.

You're different. You're a follower of Jesus. And that's not always easy (3:13).

Whatever happens, how should we treat others (3:14)?

- Love them

- Laugh at them

- Kick them

It *will* be tough sometimes – you're different. And sometimes that will mean taking action (3:18).

What could you do to show your love for others? Give money? Help out a neighbour? Anything else?

Think

Who might the "others" be?

Pray

... for them. Perhaps write their names here _____

_____

Be confident

Think of three facts that you are certain of, and I mean absolutely certain of; without a doubt these three facts are absolutely true.

1 John 4:13–5:17

¹³We know that we live in God and he lives in us, because he gave us his Spirit. ¹⁴We have seen and can testify that the Father sent his Son to be the Saviour of the world. ¹⁵Whoever confesses that Jesus is the Son of God has God living inside, and that person lives in God. ¹⁶And so we know the love that God has for us, and we trust that love.

God is love. Those who live in love live in God, and God lives in them. ¹⁷This is how love is made perfect in us: that we can be without fear on the day God judges us, because in this world we are like him. ¹⁸Where God's love is, there is no fear, because God's perfect love drives out fear. It is punishment that makes a person fear, so love is not made perfect in the person who fears.

¹⁹We love because God first loved us. ²⁰If people say, "I love God," but hate their brothers or sisters, they are liars. Those who do not love their brothers and sisters, whom they have seen, cannot love God, whom they have never seen. ²¹And God gave us this command: those who love God must also love their brothers and sisters.

Faith in the Son of God

5 Everyone who believes that Jesus is the Christ is God's child, and whoever loves the Father also loves the Father's children. ²This is how we know we love God's children: when we love God and obey his commands. ³Loving God means obeying his commands. And God's commands are not too hard for us, ⁴because everyone who is a child of God conquers the world. And this is the victory that conquers the world—our faith. ⁵So the one who wins against the world is the person who believes that Jesus is the Son of God.

⁶Jesus Christ is the One who came by water and blood. He did not come by water only, but by water and blood. And the Spirit says that this is true, because the Spirit is the truth. ⁷So there are three witnesses that tell us about Jesus: ⁸the Spirit, the water and the blood; and these three witnesses agree. ⁹We believe people when they say something is true. But what God says is more important, and he has told us the truth about his own Son. ¹⁰Anyone who believes in the Son of God has the truth that God told us. Anyone who does not believe makes God a liar, because that person does not believe what God told us about his Son. ¹¹This is what God told us: God has given us eternal life, and this life is in his Son. ¹²Whoever has the Son has life, but whoever does not have the Son of God does not have life.

We Have Eternal Life Now

¹³I write this letter to you who believe in the Son of God so you will know you have eternal life. ¹⁴And this is the boldness we have in God's presence: that if we ask God for anything that agrees with what he wants, he hears us. ¹⁵If we know he hears us every time we ask him, we know we have what we ask from him.

¹⁶If anyone sees a brother or sister sinning (sin that does not lead to eternal death), that person should pray, and God will give the sinner life. I am talking about people whose sin does not lead to eternal death. There is sin that leads to death. I do not mean that a person should pray about that sin. ¹⁷Doing wrong is always sin, but there is sin that does not lead to eternal death.

What three things does John say his readers can know?

1 _____ (4:13)

2 _____ (4:15)

3 _____ (4:15) .

Think

How sure are you that you have eternal life (4:13)?

If you're not sure, talk to an older Christian about it.

Pray

Thank God that you can be sure that he hears you.

A life of love

Who do you find really hard to love? Think about those people as you read these verses.

 1 John 5:18 – 3 John 10

18We know that those who are God's children do not continue to sin. The Son of God keeps them safe, and the Evil One cannot touch them. 19We know that we belong to God, but the Evil One controls the whole world. 20We also know that the Son of God has come and has given us understanding so that we can know the True One. And our lives are in the True One and in his Son, Jesus Christ. He is the true God and the eternal life.

21So, dear children, keep yourselves away from gods.

2 JOHN

1From the Elder.

To the chosen lady and her children:

I love all of you in the truth, and all those who know the truth love you. 2We love you because of the truth that lives in us and will be with us for ever.

3Grace, mercy and peace from God the Father and his Son, Jesus Christ, will be with us in truth and love.

4I was very happy to learn that some of your children are following the way of truth, as the Father commanded us. 5And now, dear lady, this is not a new command but is the same command we have had from the beginning. I ask you that we all love each other. 6And love means living the way God commanded us to live. As you have heard from the beginning, his command is this: live a life of love.

7Many false teachers are in the world now who do not confess that Jesus Christ came to earth as a human. Anyone who does not confess this is a false teacher and

an enemy of Christ. 8Be careful yourselves that you do not lose everything you have worked for, but that you receive your full reward.

9Anyone who goes beyond Christ's teaching and does not continue to follow only his teaching does not have God. But whoever continues to follow the teaching of Christ has both the Father and the Son. 10If someone comes to you and does not bring this teaching, do not welcome or accept that person into your house. 11If you welcome such a person, you share in the evil work.

12I have many things to write to you, but I do not want to use paper and ink. Instead, I hope to come to you and talk face to face so we can be full of joy.

13The children of your chosen sister greet you.

3 JOHN

1From the Elder.

To my dear friend Gaius, whom I love in the truth:

2My dear friend, I know your soul is doing fine, and I pray that you are doing well in every way and that your health is good. 3I was very happy when some brothers and sisters came and told me about the truth in your life and how you are following the way of truth. 4Nothing gives me greater joy than to hear that my children are following the way of truth.

5My dear friend, it is good that you help the brothers and sisters, even those you do not know. 6They told the church about your love. Please help them to continue their trip in a way worthy of God. ⁷They started out in service to Christ, and they have been accepting nothing from non-believers. ⁸So we should help such people; when we do, we share in their work for the truth.

⁹I wrote something to the church, but Diotrephes, who loves to be their leader, will not listen to us. ¹⁰So if I come, I will talk about what Diotrephes is doing, about how he lies and says evil things about us. But more than that, he refuses to accept the other brothers and sisters; he even stops those who do want to accept them and puts them out of the church.

John's letter may have been written to a Christian lady and the "church" that met in her home – or "chosen lady" (2 John 1) might just be another way of saying "church".

What does John say is the command from God (2 John 5)?

What does real love mean (2 John 6)?

Think

What might "living the way God commanded" (2 John 6) mean for you today?

Pray

Lord, sometimes I find it hard to love others. Please fill me with your love today.

Wolf in sheep's clothing

Who's worse? Someone who's bad and who doesn't pretend to be otherwise, or someone who uses good ideas and good teachings to bad ends?

3 John 11 – Jude 11a

11My dear friend, do not follow what is bad; follow what is good. The one who does good belongs to God. But the one who does evil has never known God.

12Everyone says good things about Demetrius, and the truth agrees with what they say. We also speak well of him, and you know what we say is true.

13I have many things I want to write you, but I do not want to use pen and ink. 14I hope to see you soon and talk face to face.

15Peace to you. The friends here greet you. Please greet each friend there by name.

JUDE

1From Jude, a servant of Jesus Christ and a brother of James.

To all who have been called by God. God the Father loves you, and you have been kept safe in Jesus Christ:

2Mercy, peace and love be yours richly.

God will Punish Sinners

3Dear friends, I wanted very much to write to you about the salvation we all share. But I felt the need to write to you about something else: I want to encourage you to fight hard for the faith that was given the holy people of God once and for all time. 4Some people have secretly entered your group. Long ago the prophets wrote about these people who will be judged guilty. They are against God and have changed the grace of our God into a reason for sexual sin. They also refuse to accept Jesus Christ, our only Master and Lord.

5I want to remind you of some things you already know: remember that the Lord saved his people by bringing them out of the land of Egypt. But later he destroyed all those who did not believe. 6And remember the angels who did not keep their place of power but left their proper home. The Lord has kept these angels in darkness, bound with everlasting chains, to be judged on the great day. 7Also remember the cities of Sodom and Gomorrah and the other towns around them. In the same way they were full of sexual sin and people who desired sexual relations that God does not allow. They suffer the punishment of eternal fire, as an example for all to see.

8It is the same with these people who have entered your group. They are guided by dreams and make themselves dirty with sin. They reject God's authority and speak against the angels. [9]Not even the archangel Michael, when he argued with the devil about who would have the body of Moses, dared to judge the devil guilty. Instead, he said, "The Lord punish you." [10]But these people speak against things they do not understand. And what they do know, by feeling, as dumb animals know things, are the very things that destroy them. [11]It will be terrible for them.

People have a real tendency to take the best and brightest things and to make them small and petty. God's not happy with that, obviously.

Think

Are you using your faith as an excuse to do bad things? Think about it. Is this honest? Is this really what you should be doing?

Pray

Lord, help me to be honest with my faith. Help me to serve you and love you, and keep me from twisting what I believe to my own ends.

Same as it ever was?

What do your friends think about you being a Christian?

- You're a bit of a freak
- It's OK, as long as you don't preach to them
- They don't know you're a Christian

 Jude 11b–25

They have followed the way of Cain, and for money they have given themselves to doing the wrong that Balaam did. They have fought against God as Korah did, and like Korah, they surely will be destroyed. 12They are like dirty spots in your special Christian meals you share. They eat with you and have no fear, caring only for themselves. They are clouds without rain, which the wind blows around. They are autumn trees without fruit that are pulled out of the ground. So they are twice dead. 13They are like wild waves of the sea, tossing up their own shameful actions like foam. They are like stars that wander in the sky. A place in the blackest darkness has been kept for them for ever.

14Enoch, the seventh descendant from Adam, said about these people: "Look, the Lord is coming with many thousands of his holy angels to 15judge every person. He is coming to punish all who are against God for all the evil they have done against him. And he will punish the sinners who are against God for all the evil they have said against him."

16These people complain and blame others, doing the evil things they want to do. They boast about themselves, and they flatter others to get what they want.

A Warning and Things to Do

17Dear friends, remember what the apostles of our Lord Jesus Christ said before. 18They said to you, "In the last times there will be people who laugh about God, following their own evil desires which are against God." 19These are the people who divide you, people whose thoughts are only of this world, who do not have the Spirit.

20But dear friends, use your most holy faith to build yourselves up, praying in the Holy Spirit. 21Keep yourselves in God's love as you wait for the Lord Jesus Christ with his mercy to give you life for ever.

22Show mercy to people who have doubts. 23Take others out of the fire, and save them. Show mercy mixed with fear to others, hating even their clothes which are dirty from sin.

Praise God

24God is strong and can keep you from falling. He can bring you before his glory without any wrong in you and can give you great joy. ²⁵He is the only God, the One who saves us. To him be glory, greatness, power and authority through Jesus Christ our Lord for all time past, now and for ever. Amen.

What will people do toward God (v 18)?

What should Christians use to build themselves up (v 20)?

If you stay in God's love, what will you get (v 21)?

What should you do to those who have doubts (v 22)?

Think

Do you need to build yourself up?

Pray

Ask God to build you up, so that you can become effective in telling others about Jesus.

More than a dream

Have you ever had a vivid dream that feels like it is real?

Often when we wake up the dream is clear in our minds but it quickly fades away; what seemed real rapidly seems unreal.

Welcome to Revelation, John's full-blown, Technicolor vision. This is much more than a product of rapid eye movement.

 Revelation 1:1–20

John Tells About this Book

1 This is the revelation of Jesus Christ, which God gave to him, to show his servants what must soon happen. And Jesus sent his angel to show it to his servant John, ²who has told everything he has seen. It is the word of God; it is the message from Jesus Christ. ³Happy is the one who reads the words of God's message, and happy are the people who hear this message and do what is written in it. The time is near when all of this will happen.

Jesus' Message to the Churches

⁴From John.

To the seven churches in the country of Asia:

Grace and peace to you from the One who is and was and is coming, and from the seven spirits before his throne, ⁵and from Jesus Christ. Jesus is the faithful witness, the first among those raised from the dead. He is the ruler of the kings of the earth.

He is the One who loves us, who made us free from our sins with the blood of his death. ⁶He made us to be a kingdom of priests who serve God his Father. To Jesus Christ be glory and power for ever and ever! Amen.

⁷Look, Jesus is coming with the clouds, and everyone will see him, even those who stabbed him. And all peoples of the earth will cry loudly because of him. Yes, this will happen! Amen.

⁸The Lord God says, "I am the Alpha and the Omega. I am the One who is and was and is coming. I am the Almighty."

⁹I, John, am your brother. All of us share with Christ in suffering, in the kingdom and in patience to continue. I was on the island of Patmos, because I had preached the word of God and the message about Jesus. ¹⁰On the Lord's day I was in the Spirit, and I heard a loud voice behind me that sounded like a trumpet. ¹¹The voice said, "Write what you see in a book and send it to the seven churches: to Ephesus, Smyrna, Pergamum, Thyatira, Sardis, Philadelphia and Laodicea."

¹²I turned to see who was talking to me. When I turned, I saw seven golden lampstands ¹³and someone among the lampstands who was "like a Son of Man". He was dressed in a long robe and had a gold band around his chest. ¹⁴His head and hair were white like wool, as white as snow, and his eyes were like flames of fire. ¹⁵His feet were like bronze that glows hot in a furnace, and his voice was like the noise of flooding water. ¹⁶He held seven stars in his right hand, and a sharp two-edged

sword came out of his mouth. He looked like the sun shining at its brightest time.

17When I saw him, I fell down at his feet like a dead man. He put his right hand on me and said, "Do not be afraid. I am the First and the Last. 18I am the One who lives; I was dead, but look, I am alive for ever and ever! And I hold the keys to death and to the place of the dead. 19So write the things you see, what is now and what will happen later. 20Here is the secret of the seven stars that you saw in my right hand and the seven golden lampstands: the seven lampstands are the seven churches, and the seven stars are the angels of the seven churches.

John makes it clear from the beginning that hearing the message isn't enough.

What is it that makes a person happy (v 3)?

What else is required (v 3)?

Think

How easy do you find putting into practice what you hear from God?

Pray

That the Holy Spirit will give you the strength to do what God tells you through his Word.

My first love

The first time you do something often seems special. The first steps you take, the first concert you go to, the first crush you have . . .

Revelation 2:1–17

To the Church in Ephesus

2 "Write this to the angel of the church in Ephesus:

"The One who holds the seven stars in his right hand and walks among the seven golden lampstands says this: ²I know what you do, how you work hard and never give up. I know you do not put up with the false teachings of evil people. You have tested those who say they are apostles but really are not, and you found they are liars. ³You have patience and have suffered troubles for my name and have not given up.

⁴"But I have this against you: you have left the love you had in the beginning. ⁵So remember where you were before you fell. Change your hearts and do what you did at first. If you do not change, I will come to you and will take away your lampstand from its place. ⁶But there is something you do that is right: you hate what the Nicolaitans do, as much as I.

⁷"Every person who has ears should listen to what the Spirit says to the churches. To those who win the victory I will give the right to eat the fruit from the tree of life, which is in the garden of God.

To the Church in Smyrna

⁸"Write this to the angel of the church in Smyrna:

"The One who is the First and the Last, who died and came to life again, says this:

⁹I know your troubles and that you are poor, but really you are rich! I know the bad things some people say about you. They say they are Jews, but they are not true Jews. They are a synagogue that belongs to Satan. ¹⁰Do not be afraid of what you are about to suffer. I tell you, the devil will put some of you in prison to test you, and you will suffer for ten days. But be faithful, even if you have to die, and I will give you the crown of life.

¹¹"Everyone who has ears should listen to what the Spirit says to the churches. Those who win the victory will not be hurt by the second death.

To the Church in Pergamum

¹²"Write this to the angel of the church in Pergamum:

"The One who has the sharp, two-edged sword says this: ¹³I know where you live. It is where Satan has his throne. But you are true to me. You did not refuse to tell about your faith in me even during the time of Antipas, my faithful witness who was killed in your city, where Satan lives.

¹⁴"But I have a few things against you: you have some there who follow the teaching of Balaam. He taught Balak how to cause the people of Israel to sin by eating food offered to idols and by taking part in sexual sins. ¹⁵You also have some who follow the teaching of the Nicolaitans.

16So change your hearts and lives. If you do not, I will come to you quickly and fight against them with the sword that comes out of my mouth.

17"Everyone who has ears should listen to what the Spirit says to the churches.

"I will give some of the hidden manna to everyone who wins the victory. I will also give to each one who wins the victory a white stone with a new name written on it. No one knows this new name except the one who receives it.

In chapters 2 and 3 of Revelation, there are seven letters to seven churches. The first is to the church at Ephesus. The church is doing fairly well, however...

What have they done (v 4)?

What do you think the love they had in the beginning is?

Verse 7 is a recurring theme and phrase and something we should all act upon.

Think

Have you moved forward since becoming a Christian or are you still at the same place spiritually? You may even have lost some of the enthusiasm you had in the beginning

Pray

That God will lead you forward, that you will grow closer to him and that you will listen to the Spirit.

Like a thief

You don't know when Jesus is coming back. If Jesus came back right now, how would you shape up?

 Revelation 2:18–3:13

To the Church in Thyatira

18"Write this to the angel of the church in Thyatira:

"The Son of God, who has eyes that blaze like fire and feet like shining bronze, says this: 19I know what you do. I know about your love, your faith, your service and your patience. I know that you are doing more now than you did at first.

20"But I have this against you: you let that woman Jezebel spread false teachings. She says she is a prophetess, but by her teaching she leads my people to take part in sexual sins and to eat food that is offered to idols. 21I have given her time to change her heart and turn away from her sin, but she does not want to change. 22So I will throw her on a bed of suffering. And all those who take part in adultery with her will suffer greatly if they do not turn away from the wrongs she does. 23I will also kill her followers. Then all the churches will know I am the One who searches hearts and minds, and I will repay each of you for what you have done.

24"But others of you in Thyatira have not followed her teaching and have not learned what some call Satan's deep secrets. I say to you that I will not put any other load on you. 25Only continue in your loyalty until I come.

26"I will give power over the nations to everyone who wins the victory and continues to be obedient to me until the end.

27'You will rule over them with an iron rod,
    as when pottery is broken into pieces.'
Psalm 2:9
28This is the same power I received from my Father. I will also give him the morning star. 29Everyone who has ears should listen to what the Spirit says to the churches.

To the Church in Sardis

3 "Write this to the angel of the church in Sardis:

"The One who has the seven spirits and the seven stars says this: I know what you do. People say that you are alive, but really you are dead. 2Wake up! Make yourselves stronger before what you have left dies completely. I have found that what you are doing is less than what my God wants. 3So do not forget what you have received and heard. Obey it, and change your hearts and lives. So you must wake up, or I will come like a thief, and you will not know when I will come to you. 4But you have a few there in Sardis who have kept their clothes clean, so they will walk with me and will wear white clothes, because they are worthy. 5Those who win the victory will be dressed in white clothes like them. And I will not erase their names from the book of life, but I will say they belong to me before my Father and before his angels. 6Everyone who has ears should listen to what the Spirit says to the churches.

To the Church in Philadelphia

7"Write this to the angel of the church in Philadelphia:

"This is what the One who is holy and true, who holds the key of David, says. When he opens a door, no one can close it. And when he closes it, no one can open it. 8I know what you do. I have put an open door before you, which no one can close. I know you have a little strength, but you have obeyed my teaching and were not afraid to speak my name. 9Those in the synagogue that belongs to Satan say they are Jews, but they are not true Jews; they are liars. I will make them come before you and bow at your feet, and they will know that I have loved you. 10You have obeyed my teaching about not giving up your faith. So I will keep you from the time of trouble that will come to the whole world to test those who live on earth.

11"I am coming soon. Continue strong in your faith so no one will take away your crown. 12I will make those who win the victory to become pillars in the temple of my God, and they will never have to leave it. I will write on them the name of my God and the name of the city of my God, the new Jerusalem, that comes down out of heaven from my God. I will also write on them my new name. 13Everyone who has ears should listen to what the Spirit says to the churches.

The churches in Thyahira and Sardis have both done good stuff in the past, but they've got serious issues they need to sort out. The church in Philadelphia, however, has been faithful to God.

Think

Is there anything in your life that needs to be sorted out? You never know what'll happen tomorrow, so it's best that you sort out what you need to fix straight away.

Pray

God, show me what I need to change about myself and what I do. Give me the strength to change it.

Go for it!

If you're expecting a nice hot cup of tea or a nice glass of chilled juice and what you get is something tepid it is enough to make you sick.

Ever heard of the church that made God sick?

Revelation 3:14–4:11

To the Church in Laodicea

¹⁴"Write this to the angel of the church in Laodicea:

"The Amen, the faithful and true witness, the beginning of all God has made, says this: ¹⁵I know what you do, that you are neither hot nor cold. I wish that you were either hot or cold! ¹⁶But because you are warm—neither hot, nor cold—I am ready to spit you out of my mouth. ¹⁷You say, 'I am rich, and I have become wealthy and do not need anything.' But you do not know that you are really miserable, pitiful, poor, blind and naked. ¹⁸I advise you to buy from me gold made pure in fire so you can be truly rich. Buy from me white clothes so you can be clothed and so you can cover your shameful nakedness. Buy from me medicine to put on your eyes so you can truly see.

¹⁹"I correct and punish those whom I love. So be eager to do right, and change your hearts and lives. ²⁰Here I am! I stand at the door and knock. If you hear my voice and open the door, I will come in and eat with you, and you will eat with me.

²¹"Those who win the victory will sit with me on my throne in the same way that I won the victory and sat down with my Father on his throne. ²²Everyone who has ears should listen to what the Spirit says to the churches."

John Sees Heaven

4 After the vision of these things I looked, and there before me was an open door in heaven. And the same voice that spoke to me before, that sounded like a trumpet, said, "Come up here, and I will show you what must happen after this." ²Immediately I was in the Spirit, and before me was a throne in heaven, and someone was sitting on it. ³The One who sat on the throne looked like precious stones, like jasper and carnelian. All around the throne was a rainbow the colour of an emerald. ⁴Around the throne there were 24 other thrones with 24 elders sitting on them. They were dressed in white and had golden crowns on their heads. ⁵Lightning flashes and noises and thundering came from the throne. Before the throne seven lamps were burning, which are the seven spirits of God.

⁶Also before the throne there was something that looked like a sea of glass, clear like crystal.

In the centre and around the throne were four living creatures with eyes all over them, in front and behind. ⁷The first living creature was like a lion. The second was like a calf. The third had a face like a man.

The fourth was like a flying eagle. 8Each of these four living creatures had six wings and was covered all over with eyes, inside and out. Day and night they never stop saying:

"Holy, holy, holy is the Lord God
Almighty.

He was, he is, and he is coming."

9These living creatures give glory, honour and thanks to the One who sits on the throne, who lives for ever and ever.

10Then the 24 elders bow down before the One who sits on the throne, and they worship him who lives for ever and ever. They put their crowns down before the throne and say:

11"You are worthy, our Lord and God,
to receive glory and honour and power,
because you made all things.

Everything existed and was made,
because you wanted it."

The church in Laodicea did the right things, but they didn't mean them.

They looked OK, but inside it had all gone wrong (3:17).

How could things be put right (look again at 3:19–22)?

Think

Do I just...

- say prayers, or really pray?
- skim through my Bible, or really listen to God?
- go to church, or really worship God?
- doss through life, or really try to live for God?

Pray

Lord Jesus, forgive me for being "lukewarm". Please come in and change me!

Heaven

What will heaven be like?

- Harps and clouds
- Pink and fluffy
- Like earth, but better

Or _____

Revelation 5:1–6:2

5 Then I saw a scroll in the right hand of the One sitting on the throne. The scroll had writing on both sides and was kept closed with seven seals. ²And I saw a powerful angel calling in a loud voice, "Who is worthy to break the seals and open the scroll?" ³But there was no one in heaven or on earth or under the earth who could open the scroll or look inside it. ⁴I cried hard because there was no one who was worthy to open the scroll or look inside. ⁵But one of the elders said to me, "Do not cry! The Lion from the tribe of Judah, David's descendant, has won the victory so that he is able to open the scroll and its seven seals."

⁶Then I saw a Lamb standing in the centre of the throne and in the middle of the four living creatures and the elders. The Lamb looked as if he had been killed. He had seven horns and seven eyes, which are the seven spirits of God that were sent into all the world. ⁷The Lamb came and took the scroll from the right hand of the One sitting on the throne. ⁸When he took the scroll, the four living creatures and the 24 elders bowed

down before the Lamb. Each one of them had a harp and golden bowls full of incense, which are the prayers of God's holy people. ⁹And they all sang a new song to the Lamb:

"You are worthy to take the scroll
and to open its seals,
because you were killed,
and with the blood of your death you
bought people for God
from every tribe, language, people and
nation.
¹⁰You made them to be a kingdom of
priests for our God,
and they will rule on the earth."

¹¹Then I looked, and I heard the voices of many angels around the throne, and the four living creatures, and the elders. There were thousands and thousands of angels, ¹²saying in a loud voice:

"The Lamb who was killed is worthy
to receive power, wealth, wisdom and
strength,
honour, glory and praise!"

¹³Then I heard all creatures in heaven and on earth and under the earth and in the sea saying:

"To the One who sits on the throne
and to the Lamb
be praise and honour and glory and
power
for ever and ever."
¹⁴The four living creatures said,
"Amen," and the elders bowed down
and worshipped.

6 Then I watched while the Lamb
opened the first of the seven seals. I
heard one of the four living creatures say
with a voice like thunder, "Come!" ²I
looked, and there before me was a white
horse. The rider on the horse held a bow,
and he was given a crown, and he rode out,
determined to win the victory.

Read it several times. It's not easy. John was trying to put in words
something beyond our imagination.

Find these two very important things about God and heaven:

• God is holy – special and different (v...)

• Heaven is where everyone worships God (v...)

Think

Do you focus on your future life in heaven? Is that where you are
trying to get to? However difficult the journey, are you facing that
way?

Pray

Use the words in 5:13 to praise God now.

Nowhere to hide

Celebrity status, depending on what "list" you belong to (a, b or c), can get you into any number of special events, film premieres, parties or jungles. It can also mean that you can't hide from the paparazzi etc.

Revelation 6:3–7:8

³When the Lamb opened the second seal, I heard the second living creature say, "Come!" ⁴Then another horse came out, a red one. Its rider was given power to take away peace from the earth and to make people kill each other, and he was given a big sword.

⁵When the Lamb opened the third seal, I heard the third living creature say, "Come!" I looked, and there before me was a black horse, and its rider held a pair of scales in his hand. ⁶Then I heard something that sounded like a voice coming from the middle of the four living creatures. The voice said, "A litre of wheat for a day's pay, and 3 litres of barley for a day's pay, and do not damage the olive oil and wine!"

⁷When the Lamb opened the fourth seal, I heard the voice of the fourth living creature say, "Come!" ⁸I looked, and there before me was a pale horse. Its rider was named death, and Hades was following close behind him. They were given power over a quarter of the earth to kill people by war, by starvation, by disease and by the wild animals of the earth.

⁹When the Lamb opened the fifth seal, I saw under the altar the souls of those who had been killed because they were faithful to the word of God and to the message they had received. ¹⁰These souls shouted in a loud voice, "Holy and true Lord, how long until you judge the people of the earth and punish them for killing us?" ¹¹Then

each one of them was given a white robe and was told to wait a short time longer. There were still some of their fellow servants and brothers and sisters in the service of Christ who must be killed as they were. They had to wait until all of this was finished.

¹²Then I watched while the Lamb opened the sixth seal, and there was a great earthquake. The sun became black like rough black cloth, and the whole moon became red like blood. ¹³And the stars in the sky fell to the earth like figs falling from a fig tree when the wind blows. ¹⁴The sky disappeared as a scroll when it is rolled up, and every mountain and island was moved from its place.

¹⁵Then the kings of the earth, the rulers, the generals, the rich people, the powerful people, the slaves and the free people hid themselves in caves and in the rocks on the mountains. ¹⁶They called to the mountains and the rocks, "Fall on us. Hide us from the face of the One who sits on the throne and from the anger of the Lamb! ¹⁷The great day for their anger has come, and who can stand against it?"

The 144,000 People of Israel

7 After the vision of these things I saw four angels standing at the four corners of the earth. The angels were holding the four winds of the earth to keep them from blowing on the land or on the sea or on any tree. ²Then I saw another angel

coming up from the east who had the seal of the living God. And he called out in a loud voice to the four angels to whom God had given power to harm the earth and the sea. ³He said to them, "Do not harm the land or the sea or the trees until we mark with a sign the foreheads of the people who serve our God." ⁴Then I heard how many people were marked with the sign. There were 144,000 from every tribe of the people of Israel.

⁵From the tribe of Judah 12,000 were marked with the sign,

from the tribe of Reuben 12,000,
from the tribe of Gad 12,000,
⁶from the tribe of Asher 12,000,
from the tribe of Naphtali 12,000,
from the tribe of Manasseh 12,000,
⁷from the tribe of Simeon 12,000,
from the tribe of Levi 12,000,
from the tribe of Issachar 12,000,
⁸from the tribe of Zebulun 12,000,
from the tribe of Joseph 12,000,
and from the tribe of Benjamin 12,000
were marked with the sign.

Who is included in this list (6:15)?

What do they want to be hidden from (6:16)?

Eventually everyone will have to face God!

Think

How do you feel about the use of the word "anger" in this passage?

Pray

Ask God to give you opportunities to tell others about his love – God cannot be ignored forever.

Don't stop – ever!

Do you know what we'll be doing in 1,000 years' time? I do!

 Revelation 7:9–8:13

The Great Crowd Worships God

⁹After the vision of these things I looked, and there was a great number of people, so many that no one could count them. They were from every nation, tribe, people and language of the earth. They were all standing before the throne and before the Lamb, wearing white robes and holding palm branches in their hands. ¹⁰They were shouting in a loud voice, "Salvation belongs to our God, who sits on the throne, and to the Lamb." ¹¹All the angels were standing around the throne and the elders and the four living creatures. They all bowed down on their faces before the throne and worshipped God, ¹²saying, "Amen! Praise, glory, wisdom, thanks, honour, power and strength belong to our God for ever and ever. Amen!"

¹³Then one of the elders asked me, "Who are these people dressed in white robes? Where did they come from?"

¹⁴I answered, "You know who they are, sir."

And the elder said to me, "These are the people who have come out of the great distress. They have washed their robes and made them white in the blood of the Lamb. ¹⁵Because of this, they are before the throne of God. They worship him day and night in his temple. And the One who sits on the throne will be present with them. ¹⁶Those people will never be hungry again, and they will never be thirsty again. The sun will not hurt them, and no heat will burn them, ¹⁷because the Lamb at the

centre of the throne will be their shepherd. He will lead them to springs of water that give life. And God will wipe away every tear from their eyes."

The Seventh Seal

8 When the Lamb opened the seventh seal, there was silence in heaven for about half an hour. ²And I saw the seven angels who stand before God and to whom were given seven trumpets.

³Another angel came and stood at the altar, holding a golden pan for incense. He was given much incense to offer with the prayers of all God's holy people. The angel put this offering on the golden altar before the throne. ⁴The smoke from the incense went up from the angel's hand to God with the prayers of God's people. ⁵Then the angel filled the incense pan with fire from the altar and threw it on the earth, and there were flashes of lightning, thunder and loud noises, and an earthquake.

The Seven Angels and Trumpets

⁶Then the seven angels who had the seven trumpets prepared to blow them.

⁷The first angel blew his trumpet, and hail and fire mixed with blood were poured down on the earth. And a third of the earth, and all the green grass, and a third of the trees were burnt up.

⁸Then the second angel blew his trumpet, and something that looked like a big mountain, burning with fire, was thrown into the sea. And a third of the sea became

blood, ⁹a third of the living things in the sea died, and a third of the ships were destroyed.

¹⁰Then the third angel blew his trumpet, and a large star, burning like a torch, fell from the sky. It fell on a third of the rivers and on the springs of water. ¹¹The name of the star is Wormwood. And a third of all the water became bitter, and many people died from drinking the water that was bitter.

¹²Then the fourth angel blew his trum-pet, and a third of the sun, and a third of the moon, and a third of the stars were struck. So a third of them became dark, and a third of the day was without light, and also the night.

¹³While I watched, I heard an eagle that was flying high in the air cry out in a loud voice, "Trouble! Trouble! Trouble for those who live on the earth because of the remaining sounds of the trumpets that the other three angels are about to blow!"

We'll be worshipping! So why wait?!

There's some really powerful stuff here.

What seven things belong to God, now and always (7:12)?

Think

Choose one of these words and *really* think about it... What does it mean? What ideas, pictures, memories does it spark off for you?

Pray

Link your thoughts to God and worship him!

One last chance

How do you feel about a God of love punishing those who reject him?

- It is bad and shouldn't happen
- It is about time
- How many chances have they had?

Revelation 9:1–10:4

9 Then the fifth angel blew his trumpet, and I saw a star fall from the sky to the earth. The star was given the key to the deep hole that leads to the bottomless pit. ²Then it opened up the hole that leads to the bottomless pit, and smoke came up from the hole like smoke from a big furnace. Then the sun and sky became dark because of the smoke from the hole. ³Then locusts came down to the earth out of the smoke, and they were given the power to sting like scorpions. ⁴They were told not to harm the grass on the earth or any plant or tree. They could harm only the people who did not have the sign of God on their foreheads. ⁵These locusts were not given the power to kill anyone, but to cause pain to the people for five months. And the pain they felt was like the pain a scorpion gives when it stings someone. ⁶During those days people will look for a way to die, but they will not find it. They will want to die, but death will run away from them.

⁷The locusts looked like horses prepared for battle. On their heads they wore what looked like crowns of gold, and their faces looked like human faces. ⁸Their hair was like women's hair, and their teeth were like lions' teeth. ⁹Their chests looked like iron breastplates, and the sound of their wings was like the noise of many horses and chariots hurrying into battle. ¹⁰The locusts had tails with stingers like scorpions, and in their tails was their power to hurt people for five months. ¹¹The locusts had a king who was the angel of the bottomless pit. His name in the Hebrew language is Abaddon and in the Greek language is Apollyon.

¹²The first trouble is past; there are still two other troubles that will come.

¹³Then the sixth angel blew his trumpet, and I heard a voice coming from the horns on the golden altar that is before God. ¹⁴The voice said to the sixth angel who had the trumpet, "Free the four angels who are tied at the great river Euphrates." ¹⁵And they let loose the four angels who had been kept ready for this hour and day and month and year so they could kill a third of all people on the earth. ¹⁶I heard how many troops on horses were in their army—200,000,000.

¹⁷The horses and their riders I saw in the vision looked like this: they had breastplates that were fiery red, dark blue and yellow like sulphur. The heads of the horses looked like heads of lions, with fire, smoke and sulphur coming out of their mouths. ¹⁸A third of all the people on earth were killed by these three terrible

disasters coming out of the horses' mouths: the fire, the smoke and the sulphur. ¹⁹The horses' power was in their mouths and in their tails; their tails were like snakes with heads, and with them they hurt people.

²⁰The other people who were not killed by these terrible disasters still did not change their hearts and turn away from what they had made with their own hands. They did not stop worshipping demons and idols made of gold, silver, bronze, stone and wood—things that cannot see or hear or walk. ²¹These people did not change their hearts and turn away from murder or evil magic, from their sexual sins or stealing.

The Angel and the Small Scroll

10 Then I saw another powerful angel coming down from heaven dressed in a cloud with a rainbow over his head. His face was like the sun, and his legs were like pillars of fire. ²The angel was holding a small scroll open in his hand. He put his right foot on the sea and his left foot on the land. ³Then he shouted loudly like the roaring of a lion. And when he shouted, the voices of seven thunders spoke. ⁴When the seven thunders spoke, I started to write. But I heard a voice from heaven say, "Keep hidden what the seven thunders said, and do not write them down."

What things were the people doing (9:20)?

What did the people need to turn away from (9:21)?

There is an emphasis in 9:20 that, despite what had happened, the people still did not change. Despite being given the chance to change they did not.

Think

What disasters, which are happening now, could we do something about?

Pray

That many people will realise where they are going wrong and will change their ways.

Sounds like a good idea

There are many things which, on paper, seem like a good idea. However, when they are put into practice we see the drawbacks. Governments have this difficulty with the decisions they need to make. A small rise in taxes may seem like a good idea, to pay for this or that hospital, but can the people afford that?

The Good News is good for those who accept it. However, it is not so appealing to those who reject God. It may also be difficult for us to travel on our journey with God, overcoming our doubts and fear.

Revelation 10:5–11:14

⁵Then the angel I saw standing on the sea and on the land raised his right hand to heaven, ⁶and he made a promise by the power of the One who lives for ever and ever. He is the One who made the skies and all that is in them, the earth and all that is in it, and the sea and all that is in it. The angel promised, "There will be no more waiting! ⁷In the days when the seventh angel is ready to blow his trumpet, God's secret will be finished. This secret is the Good News God told to his servants, the prophets."

⁸Then I heard the same voice from heaven again, saying to me: "Go and take the open scroll that is in the hand of the angel that is standing on the sea and on the land."

⁹So I went to the angel and told him to give me the small scroll. And he said to me, "Take the scroll and eat it. It will be sour in your stomach, but in your mouth it will be sweet as honey." ¹⁰So I took the small scroll from the angel's hand and ate it. In my mouth it tasted sweet as honey, but after I ate it, it was sour in my stomach. ¹¹Then I was told, "You must prophesy again about many peoples, nations, languages and kings."

The Two Witnesses

11 I was given a measuring stick like a rod, and I was told, "Go and measure the temple of God and the altar, and count the people worshipping there. ²But do not measure the yard outside the temple. Leave it alone, because it has been given to those who are not God's people. And they will trample on the holy city for 42 months. ³And I will give power to my two witnesses to prophesy for 1,260 days, and they will be dressed in rough cloth to show their sadness."

⁴These two witnesses are the two olive trees and the two lampstands that stand before the Lord of the earth. ⁵And if

anyone tries to hurt them, fire comes from their mouths and kills their enemies. And if anyone tries to hurt them in whatever way, in that same way that person will die. [6]These witnesses have the power to stop the sky from raining during the time they are prophesying. And they have power to make the waters become blood, and they have power to send every kind of trouble to the earth as many times as they want.

[7]When the two witnesses have finished telling their message, the beast that comes up from the bottomless pit will fight a war against them. He will defeat them and kill them. [8]The bodies of the two witnesses will lie in the street of the great city where the Lord was killed. This city is named Sodom and Egypt, which has a spiritual meaning. [9]Those from every race of people, tribe, language and nation will look at the bodies of the two witnesses for three and a half days, and they will refuse to bury

them. [10]People who live on the earth will rejoice and be happy because these two are dead. They will send each other gifts, because these two prophets brought much suffering to those who live on the earth.

[11]But after three and a half days, God put the breath of life into the two prophets again. They stood on their feet, and everyone who saw them became very afraid. [12]Then the two prophets heard a loud voice from heaven saying, "Come up here!" And they went up into heaven in a cloud as their enemies watched.

[13]In the same hour there was a great earthquake, and a tenth of the city was destroyed. 7,000 people were killed in the earthquake, and those who did not die were very afraid and gave glory to the God of heaven.

[14]The second trouble is finished. Pay attention: the third trouble is coming soon.

The imagery is really moving now, as the impending end-times approach.

What story in the Old Testament involves a rainbow?

Two Old Testament prophets were told to eat God's message, who were they?

The message is sweet because it is good news but sour due to its effects.

Think

Are there any parts of the "Good News" that leave a sour feeling inside of you?

Pray

Dear Lord, help me to understand and trust your plan for everyone. Let the sweetness of your Good News linger on my life.

All tied up

I have always liked films and books that tie up all the loose ends. The more complicated the film or book the better my enjoyment when all the strands meet up and everything is explained and falls into place.

Now things are starting to get sorted out in Revelation, time to tie up the loose ends.

 Revelation 11:15–12:12

The Seventh Trumpet

¹⁵Then the seventh angel blew his trumpet. And there were loud voices in heaven, saying:
"The power to rule the world
　now belongs to our Lord and his Christ,
and he will rule for ever and ever."
¹⁶Then the 24 elders, who sit on their thrones before God, bowed down on their faces and worshipped God. ¹⁷They said:
"We give thanks to you, Lord God Almighty,
　who is and who was,
because you have used your great power
　and have begun to rule!
¹⁸The people of the world were angry,
　but your anger has come.
The time has come to judge the dead
and to reward your servants the prophets
　and your holy people,
all who respect you, great and small.
The time has come to destroy those who
　destroy the earth!"
¹⁹Then God's temple in heaven was opened. The Ark that holds the agreement God gave to his people could be seen in his temple. Then there were flashes of lightning, noises, thunder, an earthquake and a great hailstorm.

The Woman and the Dragon

12 And then a great wonder appeared in heaven: a woman was clothed with the sun, and the moon was under her feet, and a crown of twelve stars was on her head. ²She was pregnant and cried out with pain, because she was about to give birth. ³Then another wonder appeared in heaven: there was a giant red dragon with seven heads and seven crowns on each head. He also had ten horns. ⁴His tail swept a third of the stars out of the sky and threw them down to the earth. He stood in front of the woman who was ready to give birth so he could eat her baby as soon as it was born. ⁵Then the woman gave birth to a son who will rule all the nations with an iron rod. And her child was taken up to God and to his throne. ⁶The woman ran away into the desert to a place God prepared for her where she would be taken care of for 1,260 days.

⁷Then there was a war in heaven. Michael and his angels fought against the dragon, and the dragon and his angels fought back. ⁸But the dragon was not strong enough, and he and his angels lost their place in heaven. ⁹The giant dragon was thrown down out of heaven. (He is that old snake called the devil or Satan,

who tricks the whole world.) The dragon with his angels was thrown down to the earth.

¹⁰Then I heard a loud voice in heaven saying:

"The salvation and the power and the kingdom of our God
and the authority of his Christ have now come.
The accuser of our brothers and sisters,
who accused them day and night before our God,
has been thrown down.

¹¹And our brothers and sisters defeated him
by the blood of the Lamb's death
and by the message they preached.
They did not love their lives so much that they were afraid of death.

¹²So rejoice, you heavens
and all who live there!
But it will be terrible for the earth and the sea,
because the devil has come down to you!
He is filled with anger,
because he knows he does not have much time."

Seven is an important number in Revelation and it signifies completeness.

Who is the ruler of the world (11:15)?

At the time of judgement, what will happen (11:18)?

Think

Have a quick flick through Revelation and see how many times numbers are used, especially the number seven, or multiples of it!

Pray

That your faith remains strong and your love for God grows and grows.

The number of the beast

It is probably the most famous number in the world. It certainly ranks alongside 999, or 911, and has kept people guessing as to its real meaning for millennia.

The number is...

Revelation 12:13–13:18

¹³When the dragon saw he had been thrown down to the earth, he hunted for the woman who had given birth to the son. ¹⁴But the woman was given the two wings of a great eagle so she could fly to the place prepared for her in the desert. There she would be taken care of for three and a half years, away from the snake. ¹⁵Then the snake poured water out of its mouth like a river towards the woman so the flood would carry her away. ¹⁶But the earth helped the woman by opening its mouth and swallowing the river that came from the mouth of the dragon. ¹⁷Then the dragon was very angry at the woman, and he went off to make war against all her other children—those who obey God's commands and who have the message Jesus taught.

¹⁸And the dragon stood on the seashore.

The Two Beasts

13 Then I saw a beast coming up out of the sea. It had ten horns and seven heads, and there was a crown on each horn. A name against God was written on each head. ²This beast looked like a leopard, with feet like a bear's feet and a mouth like a lion's mouth. And the dragon gave the beast all of his power and his throne and great authority. ³One of the

heads of the beast looked as if it had been killed by a wound, but this death wound was healed. Then the whole world was amazed and followed the beast. ⁴People worshipped the dragon because he had given his power to the beast. And they also worshipped the beast, asking, "Who is like the beast? Who can make war against it?"

⁵The beast was allowed to say proud words and words against God, and it was allowed to use its power for 42 months. ⁶It used its mouth to speak against God, against God's name, against the place where God lives, and against all those who live in heaven. ⁷It was given power to make war against God's holy people and to defeat them. It was given power over every tribe, people, language and nation. ⁸And all who live on earth will worship the beast—all the people since the beginning of the world whose names are not written in the Lamb's book of life. The Lamb is the One who was killed.

⁹Anyone who has ears should listen:
¹⁰If you are to be a prisoner,
  then you will be a prisoner.
If you are to be killed with the sword,
  then you will be killed with the sword.
This means that God's holy people must have patience and faith.

¹¹Then I saw another beast coming up

out of the earth. It had two horns like a lamb, but it spoke like a dragon. ¹²This beast stands before the first beast and uses the same power the first beast has. By this power it makes everyone living on earth worship the first beast, who had the death wound that was healed. ¹³And the second beast does great miracles so that it even makes fire come down from heaven to earth while people are watching. ¹⁴It fools those who live on earth by the miracles it has been given the power to do. It does these miracles to serve the first beast. The second beast orders people to make an idol to honour the first beast, the one that was wounded by the deadly sword but sprang

to life again. ¹⁵The second beast was given power to give life to the idol of the first one so that the idol could speak. And the second beast was given power to command all who will not worship the image of the beast to be killed. ¹⁶The second beast also forced all people, small and great, rich and poor, free and slave, to have a mark on their right hand or on their forehead. ¹⁷No one could buy or sell without this mark, which is the name of the beast or the number of its name. ¹⁸This takes wisdom. Let the one who has understanding find the meaning of the number, which is the number of a person. Its number is 666.

What was the beast allowed to do (13:5)?

What did the beast speak against (13:6)?

What did its power allow it to do (13:7)?

Who will and will not worship the beast (13:8)?

Think

Does this mean that God allows all bad things to happen?

Pray

Talk to God about getting your name into the Lamb's book of life.

Repent for the end is nigh

The figure wandering around the streets of London in many a film is often the object of fun. With his dour expression and his sandwich board, on which the end of the world is proclaimed, he often seems irrelevant.

Well not here ...

Revelation 14:1–20

The Song of the Saved

14 Then I looked, and there before me was the Lamb standing on Mount Zion. With him were 144,000 people who had his name and his Father's name written on their foreheads. ²And I heard a sound from heaven like the noise of flooding water and like the sound of loud thunder. The sound I heard was like people playing harps. ³And they sang a new song before the throne and before the four living creatures and the elders. No one could learn the new song except the 144,000 who had been bought from the earth. ⁴These are the ones who did not do sinful things with women, because they kept themselves pure. They follow the Lamb everywhere he goes. These 144,000 were bought from among the people of the earth as people to be offered to God and the Lamb. ⁵They were not guilty of telling lies; they are without fault.

The Three Angels

⁶Then I saw another angel flying high in the air. He had the eternal Good News to preach to those who live on earth—to every nation, tribe, language and people. ⁷He preached in a loud voice, "Fear God

and give him praise, because the time has come for God to judge all people. So worship God who made the heavens, and the earth, and the sea, and the springs of water."

⁸Then the second angel followed the first angel and said, "Ruined, ruined is the great city of Babylon! She made all the nations drink the wine of the anger of her adultery."

⁹Then a third angel followed the first two angels, saying in a loud voice: "If anyone worships the beast and his idol and gets the beast's mark on the forehead or on the hand, ¹⁰that one also will drink the wine of God's anger, which is prepared with all its strength in the cup of his anger. And that person will be put in pain with burning sulphur before the holy angels and the Lamb. ¹¹And the smoke from their burning pain will rise for ever and ever. There will be no rest, day or night, for those who worship the beast and his idol or who get the mark of his name." ¹²This means God's holy people must be patient. They must obey God's commands and keep their faith in Jesus.

¹³Then I heard a voice from heaven saying, "Write this: happy are the dead

who die from now on in the Lord."

The Spirit says, "Yes, they will rest from their hard work, and the reward of all they have done stays with them."

The Earth is Harvested

14Then I looked, and there before me was a white cloud, and sitting on the white cloud was One who looked like a Son of Man. He had a gold crown on his head and a sharp sickle in his hand. 15Then another angel came out of the temple and called out in a loud voice to the One who was sitting on the cloud, "Take your sickle and harvest the earth, because the time to harvest has come, and the fruit of the earth is ripe." 16So the One who was sitting on the cloud swung his sickle over the earth,

and the earth was harvested.

17Then another angel came out of the temple in heaven, and he also had a sharp sickle. 18And then another angel, who has power over the fire, came from the altar. This angel called to the angel with the sharp sickle, saying, "Take your sharp sickle and gather the bunches of grapes from the earth's vine, because its grapes are ripe." 19Then the angel swung his sickle over the earth. He gathered the earth's grapes and threw them into the great winepress of God's anger. 20They were trampled in the winepress outside the city, and blood flowed out of the winepress as high as horses' bridles for a distance of about 300 kilometres.

This passage is hard to completely understand but what is clear is that the end is definitely nigh.

Who is the harvester (v 14)?

Why is it time to harvest (v 15)?

Think

Do we tell people often enough that one day it will all come to an end?

Pray

That you will have the right words to say to people when you tell them about God's love.

No more pain

Toothaches and headaches can be a pain, quite literally. With the wonders of modern medicine all we need to do is pop a pill and most times the pain disappears, all gone.

Our world has a few more serious "aches" than mentioned above: war, famine, disease. However, one day all pain will disappear. As will the disasters that Revelation is now talking about.

Revelation 15:1–16:11

The Last Troubles

15 Then I saw another wonder in heaven that was great and amazing. There were seven angels bringing seven disasters. These are the last disasters, because after them, God's anger is finished.

²I saw what looked like a sea of glass mixed with fire. All of those who had won the victory over the beast and his idol and over the number of his name were standing by the sea of glass. They had harps that God had given them. ³They sang the song of Moses, the servant of God, and the song of the Lamb:

"You do great and wonderful things,
Psalm 111:2
Lord God Almighty. *Amos 3:13*
Everything the LORD does is right and true, *Psalm 145:17*
King of the nations.
⁴Everyone will respect you, Lord,
Jeremiah 10:7
and will honour you.
Only you are holy.
All the nations will come
and worship you, *Psalm 86:9–10*
because the right things you have done
are now made known." *Deuteronomy 32:4*
⁵After this I saw that the temple (the Tent of the Agreement) in heaven was

opened. ⁶And the seven angels bringing the seven disasters came out of the temple. They were dressed in clean, shining linen and wore golden bands tied around their chests. ⁷Then one of the four living creatures gave to the seven angels seven golden bowls filled with the anger of God, who lives for ever and ever. ⁸The temple was filled with smoke from the glory and the power of God, and no one could enter the temple until the seven disasters of the seven angels were finished.

The Bowls of God's Anger

16 Then I heard a loud voice from the temple saying to the seven angels, "Go and pour out the seven bowls of God's anger on the earth."

²The first angel left and poured out his bowl on the land. Then ugly and painful sores came upon all those who had the mark of the beast and who worshipped his idol.

³The second angel poured out his bowl on the sea, and it became blood like that of a dead man, and every living thing in the sea died.

⁴The third angel poured out his bowl on the rivers and the springs of water, and they became blood. ⁵Then I heard the angel of the waters saying:

"Holy One, you are the One who is and who was.

You are right to decide to punish these evil people.

⁶They have poured out the blood of your holy people and your prophets.

So now you have given them blood to drink as they deserve."

⁷And I heard a voice coming from the altar saying:

"Yes, Lord God Almighty,

the way you punish evil people is right and fair."

⁸The fourth angel poured out his bowl on the sun, and he was given power to burn the people with fire. ⁹They were burned by the great heat, and they cursed the name of God, who had control over these disasters. But the people refused to change their hearts and lives and give glory to God.

¹⁰The fifth angel poured out his bowl on the throne of the beast, and darkness covered its kingdom. People bit their tongues because of the pain. ¹¹They also cursed the God of heaven because of their pain and the sores they had, but they refused to change their hearts and turn away from the evil things they did.

How many disasters were there (15:1)?

Why would there be no more disasters (15:1)?

What were the people who had won the victory doing (15:2,3)?

Think

Take a look at the passages in the Old Testament that are mentioned here.

Pray

About any "aches" you have, that God will take them away. If everything is going well for you at the moment why not pray for others who may be going through tough times.

Pop idol

What do you think an idol is?

- A rock, or pop, superstar
- A sporting legend
- A wooden model of a god
- Anything that takes priority in your life over God

Revelation 16:12–17:8

¹²The sixth angel poured out his bowl on the great river Euphrates so that the water in the river was dried up to prepare the way for the kings from the east to come. ¹³Then I saw three evil spirits that looked like frogs coming out of the mouth of the dragon, out of the mouth of the beast and out of the mouth of the false prophet. ¹⁴These evil spirits are the spirits of demons, which have power to do miracles. They go out to the kings of the whole world to gather them together for the battle on the great day of God Almighty.

¹⁵"Listen! I will come as a thief comes! Happy are those who stay awake and keep their clothes on so that they will not walk around naked and have people see their shame."

¹⁶Then the evil spirits gathered the kings together to the place that is called Armageddon in the Hebrew language.

¹⁷The seventh angel poured out his bowl into the air. Then a loud voice came out of the temple from the throne, saying, "It is finished!" ¹⁸Then there were flashes of lightning, noises, thunder, and a big earthquake—the worst earthquake that has ever happened since people have been on earth. ¹⁹The great city split into three parts, and the cities of the nations were destroyed. And God remembered the sins of Babylon

the Great, so he gave that city the cup filled with the wine of his terrible anger. ²⁰Then every island ran away, and mountains disappeared. ²¹Giant hailstones, each weighing up to 50 kilogrammes, fell from the sky upon people. People cursed God for the disaster of the hail, because this disaster was so terrible.

The Woman on the Animal

17 Then one of the seven angels who had the seven bowls came and spoke to me. He said, "Come, and I will show you the punishment that will be given to the great prostitute, the one sitting over many waters. ²The kings of the earth sinned sexually with her, and the people of the earth became drunk from the wine of her sexual sin."

³Then the angel carried me away by the Spirit to the desert. There I saw a woman sitting on a red beast. It was covered with names insulting to God written on it, and it had seven heads and ten horns. ⁴The woman was dressed in purple and red and was shining with the gold, precious jewels and pearls she was wearing. She had a golden cup in her hand, a cup filled with evil things and the uncleanness of her sexual sin. ⁵On her forehead a title was written that was secret. This is what was written:

THE GREAT BABYLON
MOTHER OF PROSTITUTES
AND OF THE EVIL THINGS OF THE EARTH

⁶Then I saw that the woman was drunk with the blood of God's holy people and with the blood of those who were killed because of their faith in Jesus.

When I saw the woman, I was very amazed. ⁷Then the angel said to me, "Why are you amazed? I will tell you the secret of this woman and the beast she rides—the one with seven heads and ten horns. ⁸The beast you saw was once alive but is not alive now. But soon it will come up out of the bottomless pit and go away to be destroyed. There are people who live on earth whose names have not been written in the book of life since the beginning of the world. They will be amazed when they see the beast, because he was once alive, is not alive now, but will come again.

The image of the prostitute is used to show the idolatry of the people. They haven't been faithful to God and have turned away from him.

Who has been unfaithful to God (17:2)?

Think

Do you have anything in your life which could be seen as an idol, or which could become an idol?

Pray

Ask God to show you how to deal with anything that is threatening your relationship with him.

How the mighty fall?

How many great historical empires can you think of?

Have any of them lasted for ever?

What would you say is the most powerful empire, or nation, today?

 Revelation 17:9–18:10

9"You need a wise mind to understand this. The seven heads on the beast are seven mountains where the woman sits. 10And they are seven kings. Five of the kings have already been destroyed, one of the kings lives now, and another has not yet come. When he comes, he must stay a short time. 11The beast that was once alive, but is not alive now, is also an eighth king. He belongs to the first seven kings, and he will go away to be destroyed.

12"The ten horns you saw are ten kings who have not yet begun to rule, but they will receive power to rule with the beast for one hour. 13All ten of these kings have the same purpose, and they will give their power and authority to the beast. 14They will make war against the Lamb, but the Lamb will defeat them, because he is Lord of lords and King of kings. He will defeat them with his called, chosen and faithful followers."

15Then the angel said to me, "The waters that you saw, where the prostitute sits, are peoples, races, nations and languages. 16The ten horns and the beast you saw will hate the prostitute. They will take everything she has and leave her naked. They will eat her body and burn her with fire. 17God made the ten horns want to carry out his purpose by agreeing to give the beast their power to rule, until what

God has said comes about. 18The woman you saw is the great city that rules over the kings of the earth."

Babylon is Destroyed

18 After the vision of these things, I saw another angel coming down from heaven. This angel had great power, and his glory made the earth bright. 2He shouted in a powerful voice:

"Ruined, ruined is the great city of
    Babylon!
 She has become a home for demons
and a prison for every evil spirit,
    and a prison for every unclean bird and
        unclean beast.
3She has been ruined, because all the
    peoples of the earth
 have drunk the wine of the desire of her
    sexual sin.
 She has been ruined also because the
    kings of the earth
 have sinned sexually with her,
and the merchants of the earth
 have grown rich from the great wealth
    of her luxury."

4Then I heard another voice from heaven saying:

"Come out of that city, my people,
 so that you will not share in her sins,
 so that you will not receive the disasters
    that will come to her.

614

5Her sins have piled up as high as the sky,
and God has not forgotten the wrongs she has done.
6Give that city the same as she gave to others.
Pay her back twice as much as she did.
Prepare wine for her that is twice as strong
as the wine she prepared for others.
7She gave herself much glory and rich living.
Give her the same amount of suffering and sadness.
She says to herself, 'I am a queen sitting on my throne.
I am not a widow; I will never be sad.'

8So these disasters will come to her in one day:
death, and crying, and great hunger,
and she will be destroyed by fire,
because the Lord God who judges her is powerful."

9The kings of the earth who sinned sexually with her and shared her wealth will see the smoke from her burning. Then they will cry and be sad because of her death. 10They will be afraid of her suffering and stand far away and say:
"Terrible! How terrible for you, great city,
powerful city of Babylon,
because your punishment has come in one hour!"

The prostitute image has now become the image of a city, or nation. Babylon is the name given to the great nation, which will now be ruined.

What has Babylon become the home of (18:2)?

Who has been involved in Babylon's ruin (18:3)?

Think

How much of our society is in step with what is happening in 18:2,3?

Pray

For your country, that it will stand up for moral values in all things.

Babylon's burning

When John wrote Revelation, Babylon was already long gone, destroyed by the Persians, who were beaten by the Greeks, who were beaten by the Romans. Long gone. But not forgotten.

The idea is that the name "Babylon" means big, rich countries who stomp on smaller countries. The names of the countries may change, but they're always there, in charge. Except one day, they won't be.

 Revelation 18:11–24

¹¹And the merchants of the earth will cry and be sad about her, because now there is no one to buy their cargoes— ¹²cargoes of gold, silver, jewels, pearls; fine linen, purple cloth, silk, red cloth; all kinds of citron wood and all kinds of things made from ivory, expensive wood, bronze, iron and marble; ¹³cinnamon, spice, incense, myrrh, frankincense; wine, olive oil, fine flour, wheat; cattle, sheep, horses, carriages; slaves and human lives.

¹⁴The merchants will say,

"Babylon, the good things you wanted
    are gone from you.
All your rich and fancy things have
    disappeared.
    You will never have them again."

¹⁵The merchants who became rich from selling to her will be afraid of her suffering and will stand far away. They will cry and be sad ¹⁶and say:

"Terrible! How terrible for the great city!
    She was dressed in fine linen, purple
        and red cloth,
    and she was shining with gold, precious
        jewels and pearls!

¹⁷All these riches have been destroyed in
    one hour!"

Every sea captain, all those who travel, the sailors, and all those who earn their living from the sea stood far away from Babylon. ¹⁸As they saw the smoke from her burning, they cried out loudly, "There was never a city like this great city!" ¹⁹And they threw dirt on their heads and cried, weeping and were sad. They said:

"Terrible! How terrible for the great city!
All the people who had ships on the sea
    became rich because of her wealth!
But she has been destroyed in one hour!
²⁰Be happy because of this, heaven!
    Be happy, God's holy people and
        apostles and prophets!
God has punished her because of what
    she did to you."

²¹Then a powerful angel picked up a large stone, like one used for grinding grain, and threw it into the sea. He said:

"In the same way, the great city of
    Babylon will be thrown down,
    and it will never be found again.

²²The music of people playing harps and
other instruments, flutes and
trumpets,
will never be heard in you again.
No workman doing any job
will ever be found in you again.
The sound of grinding grain
will never be heard in you again.
²³The light of a lamp
will never shine in you again,

and the voices of a bridegroom and bride
will never be heard in you again.
Your merchants were the world's great
people,
and all the nations were tricked by your
magic.
²⁴You are guilty of the death of the
prophets and God's holy people
and all who have been killed on earth."

This passage is about how, one day, all the big governments and the powerful men will count for nothing. The only King will be Jesus. And when he rules, all the injustices of the world will be put right, and the rich and strong will never again exploit the poor and weak.

Think

One day, everyone will be made equal under the protection of Jesus' justice. But that doesn't mean that we can't do something right now. Do what you can about fair trade and find out about Christian organisations who work to try and bring Jesus' justice in a small way today, like Christian Aid, for example.

Pray

Jesus, this world we live in is full of all kinds of injustices. Thank you that one day it will all be made right. Help me to do what I can right now.

Happy days are here again

What is the happiest experience you have ever had?

- Getting the biggest and best present at Christmas
- Seeing your favourite pop singer in concert
- Something else

Revelation 19:1–16

People in Heaven Praise God

19 After this vision and announcement I heard what sounded like a great many people in heaven saying:
"Hallelujah!
Salvation, glory and power belong to our God,
2   because his judgements are true and right.
He has punished the prostitute
   who made the earth evil with her sexual sin.
He has paid her back for the death of his servants."
   ³Again they said:
"Hallelujah!
She is burning, and her smoke will rise for ever and ever."
   ⁴Then the 24 elders and the four living creatures bowed down and worshipped God, who sits on the throne. They said:
"Amen, Hallelujah!"
   ⁵Then a voice came from the throne, saying:
"Praise our God, all you who serve him
   and all you who honour him, both small and great!"

   ⁶Then I heard what sounded like a great many people, like the noise of flooding water and like the noise of loud thunder. The people were saying:
"Hallelujah!
Our Lord God, the Almighty, rules.
⁷Let us rejoice and be happy
   and give God glory,
because the wedding of the Lamb has come,
   and the Lamb's bride has made herself ready.
⁸Fine linen, bright and clean, was given to her to wear."
(The fine linen means the good things done by God's holy people.)
   ⁹And the angel said to me, "Write this: happy are those who have been invited to the wedding meal of the Lamb!" And the angel said, "These are the true words of God."
   ¹⁰Then I bowed down at the angel's feet to worship him, but he said to me, "Do not worship me! I am a servant like you and your brothers and sisters who have the message of Jesus. Worship God, because the message about Jesus is the spirit that gives all prophecy."

The Rider on the White Horse

¹¹Then I saw heaven opened, and there before me was a white horse. The rider on the horse is called Faithful and True, and he is right when he judges and makes war. ¹²His eyes are like burning fire, and on his head are many crowns. He has a name written on him, which no one but himself knows. ¹³He is dressed in a robe dipped in blood, and his name is the Word of God.

¹⁴The armies of heaven, dressed in fine linen, white and clean, were following him on white horses. ¹⁵Out of the rider's mouth comes a sharp sword that he will use to defeat the nations, and he will rule them with a rod of iron. He will crush out the wine in the winepress of the terrible anger of God the Almighty. ¹⁶On his robe and on his upper leg was written this name: KING OF KINGS AND LORD OF LORDS.

Who are the happy people in this passage (v 9)?

What did John get wrong (v 10)?

Who should we worship (v 10)?

Think

Do you ever get your worship wrong? Do you spend more time trying to enjoy worship than making sure it is directed to the right person?

Pray

Spend some time worshipping God in prayer – tell God how great he is!

The end?

What do you think happens when we die?

- Nothing, we just stop being
- We all go to heaven with God, who is old and has a nice white beard
- We get reincarnated as someone, or something else

 Revelation 19:17–20:15

¹⁷Then I saw an angel standing in the sun, and he called with a loud voice to all the birds flying in the sky: "Come and gather together for the great feast of God ¹⁸so that you can eat the bodies of kings, generals, mighty people, horses and their riders, and the bodies of all people—free, slave, small and great."

¹⁹Then I saw the beast and the kings of the earth. Their armies were gathered together to make war against the rider on the horse and his army. ²⁰But the beast was captured and with him the false prophet who did the miracles for the beast. The false prophet had used these miracles to trick those who had the mark of the beast and worshipped his idol. The false prophet and the beast were thrown alive into the lake of fire that burns with sulphur. ²¹And their armies were killed with the sword that came out of the mouth of the rider on the horse, and all the birds ate the bodies until they were full.

The 1,000 Years

20 I saw an angel coming down from heaven. He had the key to the bottomless pit and a large chain in his hand. ²The angel grabbed the dragon, that old snake who is the devil and Satan, and tied him up for 1,000 years. ³Then he threw him into the bottomless pit, closed it and locked it over him. The angel did this

so he could not trick the people of the earth any more until the 1,000 years were ended. After 1,000 years he must be set free for a short time.

⁴Then I saw some thrones and people sitting on them who had been given the power to judge. And I saw the souls of those who had been killed because they were faithful to the message of Jesus and the message from God. They had not worshipped the beast or his idol, and they had not received the mark of the beast on their foreheads or on their hands. They came back to life and ruled with Christ for 1,000 years. ⁵(The others that were dead did not live again until the 1,000 years were ended.) This is the first raising of the dead. ⁶Happy and holy are those who share in this first raising of the dead. The second death has no power over them. They will be priests for God and for Christ and will rule with him for 1,000 years.

⁷When the 1,000 years are over, Satan will be set free from his prison. ⁸Then he will go out to trick the nations in all the earth—Gog and Magog—to gather them for battle. There are so many people they will be like sand on the seashore. ⁹And Satan's army marched across the earth and gathered around the camp of God's people and the city God loves. But fire came down from heaven and burnt them up. ¹⁰And Satan, who tricked them, was

thrown into the lake of burning sulphur with the beast and the false prophet. There they will be punished day and night for ever and ever.

People of the World are Judged

[11]Then I saw a great white throne and the One who was sitting on it. Earth and sky ran away from him and disappeared. [12]And I saw the dead, great and small, standing before the throne. Then books were opened, and the book of life was opened. The dead were judged by what they had done, which was written in the books. [13]The sea gave up the dead who were in it, and Death and Hades gave up the dead who were in them. Each person was judged by what he had done. [14]And Death and Hades were thrown into the lake of fire. The lake of fire is the second death. [15]And anyone whose name was not found written in the book of life was thrown into the lake of fire.

Who was sitting on the throne (20:11)?

Who was standing before the throne (20:12)?

Who was judged (20:13)?

Who died a second time (20:14,15)?

Think

Have Christians gone soft on the idea of hell and the lake of fire?

Pray

Thank God that your name is in the book of life because Jesus died for you and you asked for the forgiveness and new life his death and resurrection bring.

No more crying

Imagine... a time when all wrongs are put right, when there's no more sadness, no more injustice. And it's going to happen.

Revelation: 21:1–27

The New Jerusalem

21 Then I saw a new heaven and a new earth. The first heaven and the first earth had disappeared, and there was no sea any more. ²And I saw the holy city, the new Jerusalem, coming down out of heaven from God. It was prepared like a bride dressed for her husband. ³And I heard a loud voice from the throne, saying, "Now God's presence is with people, and he will live with them, and they will be his people. God himself will be with them and will be their God. ⁴He will wipe away every tear from their eyes, and there will be no more death, sadness, crying or pain, because all the old ways are gone."

⁵The One who was sitting on the throne said, "Look! I am making everything new!" Then he said, "Write this, because these words are true and can be trusted."

⁶The One on the throne said to me, "It is finished. I am the Alpha and the Omega, the Beginning and the End. I will give free water from the spring of the water of life to anyone who is thirsty. ⁷Those who win the victory will receive this, and I will be their God, and they will be my children. ⁸But cowards, those who refuse to believe, who do evil things, who kill, who sin sexually, who do evil magic, who worship idols and who tell lies—all these will have a place in the lake of burning sulphur. This is the second death."

⁹Then one of the seven angels who had the seven bowls full of the seven last troubles came to me, saying, "Come with me, and I will show you the bride, the wife of the Lamb." ¹⁰And the angel carried me away by the Spirit to a very large and high mountain. He showed me the holy city, Jerusalem, coming down out of heaven from God. ¹¹It was shining with the glory of God and was bright like a very expensive jewel, like a jasper, clear as crystal. ¹²The city had a great high wall with twelve gates with twelve angels at the gates, and on each gate was written the name of one of the twelve tribes of Israel. ¹³There were three gates on the east, three on the north, three on the south and three on the west. ¹⁴The walls of the city were built on twelve foundation stones, and on the stones were written the names of the twelve apostles of the Lamb.

¹⁵The angel who talked with me had a measuring rod made of gold to measure the city, its gates and its wall. ¹⁶The city was built in a square, and its length was equal to its width. The angel measured the city with the rod. The city was 2,200 kilometres long, 2,200 kilometres wide and 2,200 kilometres high. ¹⁷The angel also measured the wall. It was 80 metres high, by human measurements, which the angel was using. ¹⁸The wall was made of jasper, and the city was made of pure gold, as pure as glass. ¹⁹The foundation stones of the city walls were decorated with every kind of jewel. The first foundation was jasper, the second was sapphire, the third was chalcedony, the fourth was emerald, ²⁰the fifth was onyx, the sixth was carnelian, the seventh was chrysolite, the eighth was beryl, the ninth was topaz, the tenth was

chrysoprase, the eleventh was jacinth, and the twelfth was amethyst. ²¹The twelve gates were twelve pearls, each gate having been made from a single pearl. And the street of the city was made of pure gold as clear as glass.

²²I did not see a temple in the city, because the Lord God Almighty and the Lamb are the city's temple. ²³The city does not need the sun or the moon to shine on it, because the glory of God is its light, and the Lamb is the city's lamp. ²⁴By its light the people of the world will walk, and the kings of the earth will bring their glory into it. ²⁵The city's gates will never be shut on any day, because there is no night there. ²⁶The glory and the honour of the nations will be brought into it. ²⁷Nothing unclean and no one who does shameful things or tells lies will ever go into it. Only those whose names are written in the Lamb's book of life will enter the city.

Look at each bit of verse 4 again.

What does this mean for you?

What might these words mean for a friend going through a hard time?

Think

How does this vision of a future with God fit in with what Jesus read out in the synagogue (Luke 4:18,19).

Pray

Whatever you're going through right now, ask God to help you know that there's hope and that he's with you.

Life for ever

Think of the most amazing dream you've ever had. Was it difficult afterwards to remember how it all fitted together?

If you're finding John's description of his dream hard to get your mind round, try to find time to read it all through again.

 Revelation 22:1–21

22 Then the angel showed me the river of the water of life. It was shining like crystal and was flowing from the throne of God and of the Lamb ²down the middle of the street of the city. The tree of life was on each side of the river. It produces fruit twelve times a year, once each month. The leaves of the tree are for the healing of all the nations. ³Nothing that God judges guilty will be in that city. The throne of God and of the Lamb will be there, and God's servants will worship him. ⁴They will see his face, and his name will be written on their foreheads. ⁵There will never be night again. They will not need the light of a lamp or the light of the sun, because the Lord God will give them light. And they will rule as kings for ever and ever.

⁶The angel said to me, "These words can be trusted and are true." The Lord, the God of the spirits of the prophets, sent his angel to show his servants the things that must happen soon.

⁷"Listen! I am coming soon! Happy is the one who obeys the words of prophecy in this book."

⁸I, John, am the one who heard and saw these things. When I heard and saw them, I bowed down to worship at the feet of the angel who showed these things to me. ⁹But the angel said to me, "Do not worship me! I am a servant like you, your brothers the prophets and all those who obey the words in this book. Worship God!"

¹⁰Then the angel told me, "Do not keep secret the words of prophecy in this book, because the time is near for all this to happen. ¹¹Let whoever is doing evil continue to do evil. Let whoever is unclean continue to be unclean. Let whoever is doing right continue to do right. Let whoever is holy continue to be holy."

¹²"Listen! I am coming soon! I will bring my reward with me, and I will repay each one of you for what you have done. ¹³I am the Alpha and the Omega, the First and the Last, the Beginning and the End.

¹⁴"Happy are those who wash their robes so that they will receive the right to eat the fruit from the tree of life and may go through the gates into the city. ¹⁵Outside the city are the evil people, those who do evil magic, who sin sexually, who murder, who worship idols, and who love lies and tell lies.

¹⁶"I, Jesus, have sent my angel to tell you these things for the churches. I am the descendant from the family of David, and I am the bright morning star."

¹⁷The Spirit and the bride say, "Come!"

Let the one who hears this say, "Come!" Let whoever is thirsty come; whoever wishes may have the water of life as a free gift.

¹⁸I warn everyone who hears the words of the prophecy of this book: if anyone adds anything to these words, God will add to that person the disasters written about in this book. ¹⁹And if anyone takes away from the words of this book of prophecy, God will take away that one's share of the tree of life and of the holy city, which are written about in this book.

²⁰Jesus, the One who says these things are true, says, "Yes, I am coming soon."

Amen. Come, Lord Jesus!

²¹The grace of the Lord Jesus be with all. Amen.

Do you remember the tree of life? (Check out Genesis 3:22.) Adam and Eve missed out on it because of their sin. Now – because of Jesus – it's there for us (v 2).

Think

Can all this be for real? Check out verse 6.

Pray

Lord Jesus, thank you, for your gift of life to me.